CO

GEORGIA I. HESSE, ~~Examiner and Chronicle~~ for ~~20 years~~, articles to almost every major North American newspaper and magazine. She is a contributor to *The Penguin Guide to France* and the editorial consultant for this guidebook.

BARRY ANDERSON, a third-generation Californian, has written about the state for more than 30 years, first as a *Sunset Magazine* editor, then as a free-lance writer of magazine and newspaper articles and guidebooks. He has contributed to many publications, including the *Los Angeles Times* and the World of Travel series, and is a past president of the Society of American Travel Writers.

SHIRLEY MAAS FOCKLER is a member of the Society of American Travel Writers and a contributor to *The Penguin Guide to Australia*. She has written for many magazines and newspapers in North America and Oceania. A resident of the San Francisco Bay Area for 32 years, she now lives in Oregon.

MARK GORDON, author of *Once Upon A City,* a humorous history of San Francisco, has written for nearly all the major San Francisco newspapers and magazines. He also leads specialized tours of the city, including a "Historic Bar Crawl."

TOM HORTON is the author of the *Dolphin Guide to San Francisco* and *Super Span: The Golden Gate Bridge,* and has contributed to *The Penguin Guide to Hawaii.* He is a ten-year resident of San Francisco and owns a restaurant in the Bay Area.

JACQUELINE KILLEEN writes about food and restaurants for *San Francisco Focus* magazine. She is also the author of several books about the inns and restaurants of California and a native San Franciscan.

CAROLE TERWILLIGER MEYERS, author of *Weekend Adventures for City-Weary People: Overnight Trips in Northern California* and *San Francisco Family Fun,* has lived in Berkeley for 18 years. She writes a weekly travel column for the *San Francisco Examiner.*

BEA PIXA is a 27-year resident of San Francisco and has written a column for the *San Francisco Examiner* for many years. She has also contributed articles on a variety of subjects to many national publications.

SHARON SILVA has written several books, including *Best Restaurants of the San Francisco Bay Area* and *Exploring the Best Ethnic Restaurants of the Bay Area*. Silva is a contributing editor at *San Francisco Focus* magazine, for which she writes a bimonthly dining column, and a three-time recipient of the White Award for criticism.

ELOISE SNYDER was a reporter for the *San Francisco Examiner* before becoming a free-lance travel writer. She is based in Jackson, in California's Gold Country, where she has lived for 15 years.

DAVID W. TOLL is the author of *The Compleat Nevada Traveler*. He is a publisher and journalist and lives in Gold Hill, Nevada.

THE PENGUIN TRAVEL GUIDES

THE PENGUIN GUIDE TO SAN FRANCISCO

& NORTHERN CALIFORNIA

1991

ALAN TUCKER

General Editor

PENGUIN BOOKS

PENGUIN BOOKS

Published by the Penguin Group
Viking Penguin, a division of Penguin Books USA Inc.,
375 Hudson Street, New York, New York 10014, U.S.A.
Penguin Books Ltd, 27 Wrights Lane,
London W8 5TZ, England
Penguin Books Australia Ltd, Ringwood,
Victoria, Australia
Penguin Books Canada Ltd, 2801 John Street,
Markham, Ontario, Canada L3R 1B4
Penguin Books (N.Z.) Ltd, 182–190 Wairau Road,
Auckland 10, New Zealand

Penguin Books Ltd, Registered Offices:
Harmondsworth, Middlesex, England

First published in Penguin Books 1991

1   3   5   7   9   10   8   6   4   2

ISBN 0 14 019.930 6
ISSN 1049-1449

Printed in the United States of America

Set in ITC Garamond Light
Designed by Beth Tondreau Design
Maps by Volti Graphics
Illustrations by Bill Russell
Copyedited by Cynthia Sophiea
Fact-checked in California by Stuart Nixon
Edited by Susan Shook

THIS GUIDEBOOK

The Penguin Travel Guides are designed for people who are experienced travellers in search of exceptional information that will help them sharpen and deepen their enjoyment of the trips they take.

Where, for example, are the interesting, isolated, fun, charming, or romantic places to stay that are within your budget? The hotels and bed & breakfasts described by our writers (each of whom is an experienced travel writer who either lives in or regularly tours the city or region of Northern California he or she covers) are some of the special places, in all price ranges except for the lowest—not the run-of-the-mill, heavily marketed places on every travel agent's CRT display and in advertised airline and travel-agency packages. We indicate the approximate price level of each accommodation in our descriptions of it (no indication means it is moderate), and at the end of every chapter we supply contact information so that you can get precise, up-to-the-minute rates and make reservations.

The Penguin Guide to San Francisco & Northern California 1991 highlights the more rewarding parts of the city and the northern half of the state so that you can quickly and efficiently home in on a good itinerary.

Of course, the guides do far more than just help you choose a hotel and plan your trip. *The Penguin Guide to San Francisco & Northern California 1991* is designed for use *in* California. Our Penguin California writers tell you what you really need to know, what you can't find out so easily on your own. They identify and describe the truly out-of-the-ordinary restaurants, shops, activities, and sights, and tell you the best way to "do" your destination.

Our writers are highly selective. They bring out the significance of the places they cover, capturing the personality and the underlying cultural and historical resonances of a city or region—making clear its special appeal. For exhaustive detailed coverage of cultural attractions, we suggest that you also use a supplementary reference-type guide-book—probably a locally produced publication—along with the Penguin Guide.

The Penguin Guide to San Francisco & Northern California 1991 is full of reliable and timely information, revised each year. We would like to know if you think we've left out some very special place.

ALAN TUCKER
General Editor
Penguin Travel Guides

375 Hudson Street
New York, New York 10014
or
27 Wrights Lane
London W8 5TZ

CONTENTS

MAPS

THE
PENGUIN
GUIDE TO
SAN FRANCISCO
& NORTHERN
CALIFORNIA
1991

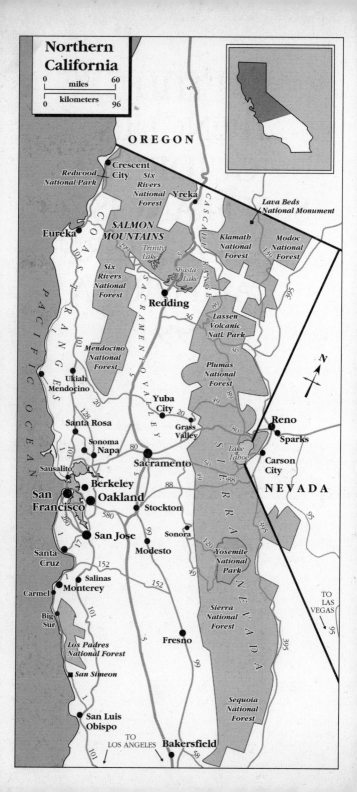

Northern California

0 miles 60

0 kilometers 96

OREGON

Crescent City
Redwood National Park
Six Rivers National Forest
Yreka
Lava Beds National Monument

Eureka
SALMON MOUNTAINS
Trinity Lake
Shasta Lake
Klamath National Forest
Modoc National Forest

Six Rivers National Forest
CASCADE RANGE
Redding
Lassen Volcanic Natl. Park

PACIFIC OCEAN
COAST RANGES
SACRAMENTO VALLEY
Mendocino National Forest

Plumas National Forest

Ukiah
Mendocino

Yuba City
Santa Rosa
Grass Valley
Reno
Sparks
SIERRA
Lake Tahoe
Sonoma
Napa
Sacramento
Carson City
Sausalito
NEVADA

Berkeley
Oakland
San Francisco
Stockton

San Jose
Sonora

Santa Cruz
Modesto

Salinas
Monterey
Carmel
NEVADA
Yosemite National Park

Big Sur

Los Padres National Forest
Fresno

San Simeon

Sierra National Forest

TO LAS VEGAS

Sequoia National Forest

San Luis Obispo

TO LOS ANGELES
Bakersfield

OVERVIEW

By Georgia I. Hesse

Georgia I. Hesse, Travel Editor of the San Francisco Examiner and Chronicle *for 20 years, has contributed travel articles to almost every major North American newspaper and magazine. She is a contributor to* The Penguin Guide to France *and the editorial consultant for this guidebook.*

> "San Francisco's changing, changing,
> But no matter whatever comes,
> There'll still be Grace Cathedral
> And crumpets and tea at Blum's."

That memorable ditty from a forgettable musical expressed the character of the city (and much of Northern California) in the late 1950s: stylish, optimistic, as self-assured as the gloved and behatted ladies who sat in their proper pews on Sundays, carried pink boxes of goodies home from Blum's, and smiled "Good taste costs no more" to each other, with a tip of the flowery hat to Gump's.

But Blum's is gone. Gump's is no longer a family affair. Gays are married in Grace Cathedral. "Nostalgia," as Herb Caen, the city's celebrator, reminds us, "is a thing of the past." What's going on here?

The Age of Aquarius has waxed and waned; the flower children have faded. This is the age of the activist, the coming of the Greens. Battle lines have been drawn between the Earth First! protesters and the lumber companies in the redwood–Douglas fir forests of Humboldt and Del Norte counties. The streets of San Francisco are loud with complaints and cries of the homeless, the underemployed, and the AIDS sufferers.

1

The truth is, the woes of the world have come to Northern California, and the citizens don't like it one bit. After all, this is El Dorado, the earthly Utopia of which even the sophisticated Robert Louis Stevenson, riding the rails over the Sierra Nevada, could write, "All the passengers . . . thronged with shining eyes upon the platform. . . . At every turn we could look further into the land of our happy future. . . . For this indeed was our destination—this was 'the good country' we had been going to so long."

The trouble is, they just keep coming, bringing to the land of the sons of the pioneers diseases of development: overcrowding, erosion of personal safety, pollution, water worries, and the need to pay attention to the Big E's: environment, energy, and ecology.

The typical Northern Californian (a "native" who's been around five years or more) would close the Golden Gates, issue a Redwood Passport (but only to travellers with money and a round-trip ticket home), and buy a doormat reading *Go Away.*

In the mid-1970s Ernest Callenbach, an editor at the University of California press, gave the language a new word, even a new concept, when he wrote a visionary little novel entitled *Ecotopia.* In this book, the year is 1999 and it's been a brave new world since back in the 1980s, when Northern California, Oregon, and Washington seceded from the United States in order to create a more perfect union. In the resulting high-tech, low-energy society, bicycles have replaced BMWs, potholes have become flowerbeds, trees are the Significant Others, and the president is female. (This last may happen some day, if former San Francisco mayor Dianne Feinstein has her way.)

The idea was embraced by Joel Garreau in his 1981 study of new American realities, *The Nine Nations of North America.* He considers San Francisco the capital of Ecotopia, which stretches along the Pacific coast from Point Conception near Santa Barbara north to Anchorage, Alaska. In this compelling civilization, the clean silicon chip is king and sunshine heats the homes of the few poor as well as those with hot tubs, although a smiling Japanese banker in San Francisco says, "We see California already as part of Japan. Oh, yes. California Prefecture."

The name California has an interesting origin, as described by historian George R. Stewart. Its first occurrence seems to have been in a long 16th-century poem, *Las Sergas de Esplandián,* by Garcí Ordóñez de Montalvo. The poem pictures California as an island in the ocean, inhabited by

Amazon-like women, and rich in gold and precious stones. A Spanish exploration party in about 1524 spread rumors of the existence of such an island floating in the Pacific, and when Hernando Cortés came upon what is today the tip of peninsular Mexico, he named it California. Under Spanish-Mexican rule, what is today the American state was called Alta, or upper, California, while the skinny peninsula was, and is, Baja (lower) California in Mexico.

In truth, Northern California lives in a room of its own, with walls near Carmel-Monterey in the south and the Oregon line in the north, windows looking out onto the Pacific, and the back doors of Lake Tahoe and Reno, Nevada, on the east. Even outsiders admit there's something different about it, witness a William Hamilton cartoon in the *New Yorker:* At a perky cocktail party, presumably someplace Back East, the hostess murmurs, "Nan and Gordon are from California, but Northern California."

The compulsive chauvinism of Northern Californians irritates everybody else, even their neighbors. In Oregon, cars wear bumper stickers reading, "Don't Californicate Oregon." John Steinbeck's *Travels with Charley* deals with the subject: "We who were born here [in his case, in Salinas], and our parents also felt a strange superiority over newcomers, barbarians, *forestieri,* and they, the foreigners, resented us and even made a rude poem about us: The miner came in forty-nine, The whores in fifty-one/And when they got together, They made a native son."

No question about it: The people here are different from those elsewhere. "Have a nice day now, honey," croons the waitress in a far north Eureka café; you think to step on her toes, but you don't because she smiles and she means it. (Elsewhere, her tone might imply, "I hope your legs drop off.") "What do *you* think of leveraged buyouts?" asks the parking-garage attendant, handing you a receipt. Or, "Well," the doorman grins as he helps a mink-wrapped dowager into her flashy Alfa-Romeo Spyder, "so much for stereotypes." Then there is the urban Oz of Marin County, where a child sniffles, "Sorry. I always cry at Tchaikovsky."

If Northern Californians are different, it may be because of the land: big, bold, of an immense variety, and sparsely inhabited (even though new census results may show that one in ten Americans lives in California).

In the recent past, travellers believed that San Francisco was all there was in the north. They placed Carmel, Monterey, even Yosemite, and perhaps a drop of Wine Country, within their mental borders of the city, eyes glazing over at talk of Eureka, even of Mendocino, certainly of Sacramento. Foreign visitors unused to the grandeur of American geography still imagine San Francisco to be a rather European suburb of Los Angeles.

Without a doubt, the traveller's Northern California does begin in **San Francisco** (unless you drive south from Washington or Oregon states); it probably always will. The city is the transportation hub, after all, and still the major lure.

Yet the city is only one intriguing element in the composition called the **Bay Area**, with the counterpoints of Marin County to the north; on the east, the cities of Berkeley and Oakland; to the south, Palo Alto and Stanford University, the rugged coast and hills, beaches, and parks of San Mateo County.

Visitors who want to stay in San Francisco can easily acquaint themselves with these stellar surroundings on day trips, which is what we have done in this text. And then there are the delights beyond the immediate Bay Area:

Wine Country is a world of its own. Increasingly, all of California is wine country; one would not be shocked should a sprig of Sirah spring up in Death Valley. In Northern California, however, Wine Country means, in the main, Napa and Sonoma counties, with significant swatches in Mendocino and Lake counties. Wine Country feels, smells, tastes, and even looks like southern France or northern Italy, and its mood is definitely Mediterranean. Days stretch out and slow down near the vineyards, breezes blow more fragrantly, the sun shines more salubriously, city strife slips into *la dolce vita*. It's possible to see a corner of Wine Country in one day: It's more fun if you spend at least three.

If Wine Country evokes the Old Country, the **Redwood Country** speaks of ancient Earth. Long, long thoughts follow you as you stroll in the shadows of giants that were young when Christianity was born, descendants of ancestors around before the glacial ages. Sun, shade, blistered hills and pelting rains, wave-battered shores and craggy cliffs: This is elemental earth. The welcoming inns, warming fireplaces, and well-set tables come as civilizing dividends.

The call of the lonesome wild still echos in the big northeast, in the little-known, often untracked counties of Siskiyou, Modoc, Shasta, and Lassen, called here **Northeastern California**. It remains almost as unfamiliar to most Californians as to people from beyond the state's borders. Here ghost towns fade and crumble; great peaks remain snow-capped right into summer; limestone caverns reveal an underworld of fluted columns, stone draperies, and stalactites and stalagmites studded with crystals; wrinkled lava beds hint at the growing of the globe. For the adventurous wanderer, this is hunting, fishing, hiking, and being-alone country at its most compelling.

"Boys, I believe I have found a gold mine," said James W. Marshall in measured tones, standing near a sluice gate on the south fork of the American River. The date was January 24, 1848, and the West—and the whole world—was listening. The Gold Rush really began that day. **Gold Country** still lives in the little mining towns that sleep along Highway 49; towns with names like Angels Camp, Sutter Creek, Fiddletown, Volcano, and Rough 'N Ready. Gone with the wind are Freeze-Out, Bed Bug, and Mme. Pantaloons. (The latter's spirit lingers in the lobby-bar of the Louisiana House and National Hotel in Jackson, where a piano and gutbucket still beat out the stomping songs of the bawdy old days.)

The Central Valley stretches from old-gold Butte County in the north through the Sacramento and San Joaquin valleys. Stockton, born in 1847, watched as thousands of Argonauts poured through in the early 1850s, bound for the gold fields. The state's capital, **Sacramento**, boasts the Old Sacramento Historical Park, the elaborate State Capitol, and one of America's finest railroad collections.

To roam Gold Country best, follow Highway 49 south along its length from Plumas County, in the north, through Sierra, Yuba, Nevada, Placer, El Dorado, Amador, Tuolumne, Mariposa, and Madera counties. It comes to an end (or beginning) south of **Yosemite National Park**, which is also covered in this chapter.

To Northern Californians, their backyard begins at **Lake Tahoe**, which bathes the California–Nevada state line, and reaches into Nevada at least as far as **Carson City** and **Reno**. Here, the range of the Sierra Nevada holds its spine against the sky, and of the sapphire cup of Lake Tahoe Mark Twain wrote, "The air . . . is very pure and fine, bracing and delicious, and why shouldn't it be? It is the same air the angels breathe."

This is family vacation country par excellence, with summer water sports, dinner cruises on paddle-wheel boats, more than 20 winter ski resorts (Heavenly Valley is the largest in the country), many historical spots, and the gaming-dining-showtime complexes.

"Everyone was delighted with the appearance of things," wrote Richard Henry Dana, Jr., in *Two Years Before the Mast*. It was the 1830s, and he had just arrived off the coast of

Monterey. "[This], as far as my observation goes, is decidedly the pleasantest and most civilized-looking place in California." France celebrates its Grande Corniche, Italy boasts its Amalfi Drive, but Northern California claims to best any oceanside stretch with the Pacific Coast Highway, Highway 1, winding south of San Francisco along the **Central Coast** to Monterey and beyond.

Monterey and **Carmel** are endlessly seductive; sea lions sport and bark off Point Lobos, and anyone with an eye for smashing seascapes should stop to picnic along **Big Sur** of Henry Miller fame. Eventually, you arrive at **Hearst Castle** near Cambria, the house that William Randolph built.

Inland, don't miss a call at **San Juan Bautista**, one of the finest examples of California missions; collectors of such wonders will wander as far as Mission San Antonio at Jolon.

In Northern California, you can have almost any weather you want. The snow stays up in the mountains where it belongs (usually), and in winter the San Franciscan can ski and sail on the same long weekend. If the coastline is too chilly, drive up and over the Coast Range and into a near-permanent summer. When Sacramento scorches, you can answer the fog horns calling from San Francisco.

The search for the essence of Northern California is perhaps a futile one, stretching as it does from the nearly untracked wilderness of the Redwood Country's Lost Coast to the downtown DV8 club in San Francisco's SoMa. Is that essence a European one, born of Spanish political and religious expansion? (Even today, many visitors from overseas describe San Francisco as "the most European city in America.")

Is the essence American, involving the special challenge of the unconquered frontier, the Manifest Destiny to civilize a heathen land, the ineffable attraction of the "west of the West" (in Theodore Roosevelt's felicitous phrase)?

Is Northern California *Ultima Thule,* the final jumping-off place? (The hundreds of people who have leapt from the Golden Gate Bridge may have believed that; interestingly, they tend to jump facing toward the beautiful city by the bay rather than looking west toward nothingness.)

Are Northern Californians the restless heirs of what was called the Great California Lottery, the rush for gold? "Vice seems more alluring here," one William Swain wrote home from the fields in 1850. "Sabbath days here are spent by miners mostly hunting, prospecting for gold, and gambling. Very little attention is paid to morals . . . Say to all my friends:

stay at home. Tell my enemies to come" (from *The World Rushed In,* J.S. Holliday).

The experience of Northern California is all these things, and many more. Travellers come to it expecting sun and find fog; wanting momentary craziness and discovering a very permanent culture; anticipating, perhaps, a rush of the risqué, the kooky, and the hipped-out, only to recognize an old-fashioned, determined, all-American work ethic. All the signs of our times are here, from "Welcome" in 40 languages (some of them misspelled) to "Trespassers will be violated."

The quest remains; one thing Northern California is not is static. With Walt Whitman, it looks west toward the Far East and asks: "But where is what I started for so long ago? And why is it yet unfound?"

USEFUL FACTS

When to Go

Northern California is a complexity of microclimates; in some seasons there can be a difference of 30 degrees Fahrenheit between the coast and 30 miles inland or between San Francisco and the areas north and south of it. Usually, and in most regions, rain falls between December and February, thus making mid-September to mid-November and mid-March through June the most pleasant months to visit San Francisco proper, although fog can creep in at any time. August in the city is cold, clammy, and overcast almost every year.

In the Sierra Nevada temperatures fall below zero in winter and soar to over 100 degrees in midsummer; Gold Country is much the same. In the summertime, Redwood Country coastal temperatures average from 50 to 60 degrees F and 75 to 90 degrees inland, and in winter, around 40 to 50 degrees. Snow is very rare except on the highest inland elevations. In Yosemite National Park winter temperatures range from 25 to 50 degrees F and in summer from 50 to 90 degrees F. Similar conditions pertain throughout the northeast part of the state such as in Lassen National Park. Because of varying altitudes it's always wise to pack a windbreaker or heavy sweater.

Entry Documents

The United States no longer requires visas from citizens of Great Britain, Canada, Japan, most western European countries, Australia, or New Zealand under a 90-day visa waiver plan for pleasure trips only. Citizens of Hong Kong are required to obtain visas from the local American consulate.

Arrival at Major Gateways by Air

San Francisco, Oakland, and San Jose international airports are the major air gateways in the northern part of the state.

Just 16 miles south of the city, **San Francisco International Airport** (SFO) is the sixth-busiest airport in the world, served by more than 30 major scheduled carriers. The complex comprises three buildings: the South, International, and North terminals, each with an upper level for departures and a lower level for arrivals. A complimentary shuttle bus circles the upper roadway every five minutes and stops in front of each terminal.

SFO's widely known medical clinic in the International Terminal offers the services of a doctor or registered nurse and special assistance to the handicapped. From the airport call 70444 from a white courtesy phone; from outside, Tel: (415) 877-0444.

No charge is made for baggage carts in the international arrival area; in the domestic arrival area, the charge is $1, with a 25-cent refund if the cart is returned to a rack. Foreign exchange is available in all three terminals.

SFO was the country's first airport to establish a Bureau of Exhibitions and Cultural Education and is unique in having a curator and museum professionals on the premises. Five gallery areas host 40 exhibitions yearly.

SFO is connected to the eastern, downtown part of San Francisco by Highway 101; visitors to the western half of the city (largely residential) can take 101 north to the Interstate 380 interchange, then west to the interchange with Interstate Highway 280 (marked Daly City). Follow 280 to State Highway 1 and into town via 19th Avenue and Golden Gate Park. This is also the most direct route for visitors headed for Marin County. Watch for Golden Gate Bridge direction signs.

Complimentary shuttle service between the airport and several nearby hotels and motels is available; use the courtesy phone at the hotel/motel board in the baggage claim areas.

Taxi service from the airport to downtown San Francisco costs about $25 and takes 20 to 30 minutes. Ride-sharing for two or more people to a maximum of three destinations is permitted.

SFO Airporter (buses) charges $6 one way, $10 round trip

between the airport and Union Square in the heart of town, stopping at the following central hotels: Le Méridien, Grand Hyatt, Westin St. Francis, Nikko/Hilton, Parc Fifty-Five, and Marriott Moscone. The first departure from SFO is at 6:10 A.M. and the last at 11:10 P.M., with departures every 20 minutes in between; no reservations are required. Pickups are on the lower level at the luggage claim area; Tel: (415) 673-2433.

Airport Express leaves SFO every 20 minutes from 7:00 A.M. to 10:00 P.M. to the following San Francisco hotels: Handlery, Hotel David, Shannon, Four Seasons Clift, Hotel California, and Geary Hotel. The fare is $8; Tel: (415) 775-5121.

Reliable ground transportation is offered 24 hours a day by the vans of Super Shuttle. For rates (about $10 to downtown, credit cards accepted) and reservations to or from SFO, call (415) 558-8500.

Airport Connection serves SFO, San Francisco, East Bay, and the Peninsula; reservations, which should be made at least three hours in advance of pickup, are recommended; Tel: (415) 877-0901. From SFO use the white courtesy telephones and dial 70901. The current fare is approximately $10 to San Francisco; pickup is on the upper level in the red-and-white zones. Good Neighbors Airport Shuttle arranges door-to-door service from any location in San Francisco to SFO, or a return, between 5:00 A.M. and 11:00 P.M.; for pickup at SFO call 875-7552 before claiming your luggage.

Yellow Airport Shuttle offers 24-hour door-to-door service from residences and hotels in San Francisco to either SFO or Oakland International (OAK). Reservations are required and the fare between SFO and downtown is $10; Tel: (415) 282-7433.

Marin Airporter maintains scheduled bus service every half hour between SFO and the Marin County cities of Novato, Ignacio, Terra Linda, Larkspur, Mill Valley, and Sausalito from 6:00 A.M. to midnight; Tel: (415) 461-4222. All suburban boarding is at the center island, lower level.

Bay Area Bus Service Airporter runs between SFO and OAK each hour from 7:00 A.M. to midnight, with stops on call at Treasure Island, Oakland Army Base, and Oakland Hyatt Regency. The fee is $7; Tel: (415) 444-4200 or 632-5506.

The BayPorter Express connects SFO to San Jose International (SJC) for a fee of $16.

For coach transportation to cities in the nearby East Bay, call Concord/Berkeley Airport Connection; Tel: (800) AIRPORT. To Sonoma County, call Sonoma County Airport Express; Tel: (707) 584-4400 or (800) 327-2024. The fare is $20 round trip, $12 one way.

For distant destinations such as Sacramento, call Greyhound Bus Lines; Tel: (415) 558-6680 or 558-6789.

Airport Connection now offers the following door-to-door van services: SFO to and from downtown hotels, $8; SFO–San Mateo County, $13–$17; SFO–Santa Clara County, $13–$17; SFO–Alameda County, $13–$17; SFO–Contra Costa, $13–$17; Tel: (415) 877-0901.

Rental-car companies with desks at SFO include Alamo, Alpine, American International, Apple, AVCar, Avis, Budget, Dollar, General, Hertz, National, Payless RPM, Showcase, Snappy, Thrifty, and Wheels for Rent. Rental car booths are located in the baggage claim areas.

Oakland International Airport (OAK) is 11 miles southeast of Oakland, on Highway 880 (take the Hegenberger exit), and 19 miles southeast across the Bay Bridge from San Francisco. Taxis charge about $18–$19 between downtown Oakland and OAK, $35 and up (plus $1 bridge toll) to locations in San Francisco.

Oakland International is served by more than 30 airlines, including American, Air Canada, Alaska, Alitalia, British Airways, Braniff, Continental, Canadian, Delta, KLM, Mexicana, Northwest, Pan Am, SAS, Singapore, TWA, and United.

The Air-BART shuttle (BART is the Bay Area's subway) departs from the shelter on the center island outside the main airport entrance every five minutes from 6:00 A.M. to midnight Mondays through Saturdays, and from 9:00 A.M. on Sundays. The ride to the Coliseum station of BART is $1. To Oakland City Center take the Richmond train; the fare is 80 cents. To downtown San Francisco (Embarcadero, Montgomery, Powell, or Civic Center stations) take the Daly City train for $1.90.

AC Transit Bus number 61 goes to downtown Oakland every 30 to 60 minutes depending upon the time of day.

For coach service to points east such as Pleasanton and Castro Valley, call San Ramon Valley Airporter Express at (415) 484-4044; to Napa, Vallejo, and nearby towns, call Grapevine Airport Service at (707) 253-9093.

Rental-car companies at OAK are Avis, Budget, Dollar, Hertz, and National.

San Jose International Airport (SJC) is 3 miles northwest of town via Highways 101 and 17/880. In 1990 Terminal A was opened, the airport's first new facility in 25 years. Thirteen commercial airlines now serve SJC, including Alaska, American, Continental, Delta, Mexicana, TWA, United, and USAir.

By taxi from downtown it's only a 10 to 15 minute ride at a cost of about $10. Santa Clara County Transit Bus number 64 departs from the shelter outside baggage claim to downtown every 15 minutes from 6:00 A.M. to 12:07 A.M., for $1.

Rental-car companies at the airport include Avis, Budget, Dollar, Hertz, and National, with desks on the lower level off the lobby.

Arrival by Train

Amtrak trains connect San Francisco with Portland and Seattle to the north and Los Angeles to the south daily via the Coast Starlight. The superliner California Zephyr runs to and from Chicago via Omaha, Denver, and Salt Lake City, providing daily service to Stockton, Merced-Yosemite, Fresno, Bakersfield, and San Joaquin Valley points. The San Joaquin links the Bay Area with Merced (gateway to Yosemite National Park) and Bakersfield.

Shuttle buses meet arrivals at the Oakland depot at 16th and Wood streets and transfer passengers to the Transbay Terminal in San Francisco at First and Mission streets, where you can take a bus or taxi to your destination. For information and rates call (800) 872-7245 in the U.S. and (800) 4-AMTRAK in Canada.

Arrival by Bus

San Francisco and the Bay Area are served by Greyhound Bus Lines (Greyhound Depot, 50 Seventh Street, San Francisco; Tel: 415-558-6680) and Greyhound-Trailways Bus System (Transbay Terminal, First and Mission streets, San Francisco; Tel: 415-558-6789).

Arrival by Cruise Ship

The official passenger terminal is Pier 35, within walking distance of Pier 39, a complex of shops, restaurants, and an entertainment center near the colorful and lively Fisherman's Wharf to the west.

At this writing cruise companies calling regularly in San Francisco include Admiral Cruises, American-Hawaii, Cunard, Hapag Lloyd, Holland America Line, P&O Lines, Princess Cruises, Regency Cruises, Royal Viking Line, Seabourn, and Sitmar.

Passenger facilities are primitive by international standards and a constant source of dispute.

Renting a Car

Visitors from other countries who wish to rent a car in the U.S. must be 25 years or older, present a valid passport and driver's license from the country of residence, and show a return ticket for air or sea travel. In some cases prepayment may be required. Almost all major international credit cards are accepted.

A word to the wise: Don't get a standard shift unless you know how to shift into gear from a stop on a very steep hill, with cars stopped behind you—especially if you're going to drive in San Francisco.

Local Time

All of Northern California is in the Pacific Standard time zone, three hours behind New York and Montreal (Eastern Standard), two hours behind Chicago and Winnipeg (Central Standard), one hour behind Denver and Calgary (Mountain Standard), eight hours behind London, 18 hours behind Sydney, and 20 hours behind Auckland. (If flying west across the Pacific from San Francisco, you lose a day; travelling in the other direction, you gain a day.) During daylight savings time there will be an hour's variance, because countries and cities go on and off daylight savings at different times.

Currency

In San Francisco major foreign exchange brokers are Associated Foreign Exchange, Inc., at 201 Sansome Street, Tel: (415) 781-7683; Foreign Exchange, Ltd., 415 Stockton Street, near Union Square, Tel: (415) 397-4700; and Deak International, 100 Grant Avenue, Tel: (415) 362-3452, or at SFO Airport, Tel: (415) 583-4029. The Bank of America branches also provide exchange services.

The $1 coin, rarely seen in most of the United States, is common in Nevada and in other states where slot gambling machines are legal.

Telephoning

The international country code for the United States is 1. Northern California uses five area codes: 415 for San Francisco and cities in the Northern Peninsula and immediate East Bay areas such as Oakland; 408 for Southern Peninsula cities such as San Jose, Santa Cruz, and Monterey-Carmel; 707 for Napa, Eureka, and general Redwood Country locations north to the Oregon border; 916 for inland and northern towns such as Sacramento, locations in Modoc, Lassen, and Shasta national forests up to the Oregon line, and Lake

Tahoe; and 209 for Gold Country spots. All Nevada employs area code 702.

In September, 1991, the new area code 501 will go into effect for the East Bay counties of Contra Costa and Alameda.

Electrical Current
Current in the U.S. is 110/120 volts. Foreign-made appliances may require adapters and North American flat-blade plugs.

Business Hours and Holidays
Normally, business hours are 9:00 A.M. to 5:00 P.M. Mondays through Fridays; some of the largest banks have extended their hours to conform to these times and are open for certain hours even on Saturdays. Shopping malls, major department stores, supermarkets, and all but the smallest businesses operate seven days a week. In San Francisco several large food markets and some drugstores are open 24 hours a day, 365 days a year.

Government agencies, banks, and post offices close for several national holidays: January 1 (New Year's Day); January 15 (Martin Luther King's birthday); President's Day, honoring George Washington and Abraham Lincoln (observed in mid-February on a Monday between their birthdays); the last Monday in May (Memorial Day); July 4 (Independence Day); the first Monday in September (Labor Day); the second Monday in October (Columbus Day); November 11 (Veterans Day); the fourth Thursday in November (Thanksgiving Day); and December 25 (Christmas).

Credit Cards
Major credit cards from overseas affiliated with Visa or MasterCard are widely accepted, as are foreign-held cards such as American Express, Diner's Club, and the like.

Accommodations
Hotels and motels of most major national chains have members in San Francisco and Northern California. (See details under Accommodations Reference at the end of each chapter.) In addition, several smaller groups operate throughout the region. Prestigious France-based Relais & Châteaux has five members in Northern California: Sherman House in San Francisco, Timberhill Ranch near Cazadero on the Sonoma County coast, Meadowood Resort Hotel in St. Helena in Napa County, Auberge du Soleil in Rutherford in the Napa Valley, and Stonepine in Carmel Valley.

Bed-and-breakfast inns are booming in popularity; several

regional referral services can supply information about them: Bed & Breakfast Innkeepers of Northern California, Tel: (800) 284-4667; Bed & Breakfast Innkeepers of Santa Cruz and Half Moon Bay, Tel: (408) 425-8212; The Inns of Point Reyes, Tel: (415) 663-1420; Bed and Breakfast Innkeepers of the Monterey Peninsula, Tel: (408) 375-5284; Bed & Breakfast Inns of Sonoma Valley, Tel: (707) 996-5339; Wine Country Bed & Breakfast Inns, Tel: (707) 433-INNS; Bed & Breakfast Innkeepers of Napa Valley, Tel: (800) 443-6082; Mendocino Coast Innkeepers Association, Tel: (707) 964-6725; Bed & Breakfast Inns of Humboldt County, Tel: (707) 786-4000; Bed & Breakfast Inns of the Gold Country, Tel: (916) 626-6136; Inns of Grass Valley and Nevada City, Tel: (916) 477-6634; Sacramento Innkeepers' Association, Tel: (916) 441-3214; Yosemite Bed & Breakfast, Tel: (209) 966-2456.

In addition, all-suite hotels are proliferating; among the best of them are the Embassy Suites; in Napa, Tel: (707) 953-9540, and in South San Francisco, Tel: (415) 589-3400 or (800) 362-3779.

For Further Information

The San Francisco Visitor Information Center, in Benjamin Swig Pavilion on the lower level of Hallidie Plaza at Market and Powell streets, answers questions and distributes maps and information brochures weekdays from 9:00 A.M. to 5:00 P.M., Saturdays until 3:00 P.M., and Sundays from 10:00 A.M. to 2:00 P.M.; Tel: (415) 391-2000, twenty-four hours a day.

For travel details and a handbook with maps, listings of accommodations, restaurants, museums, and more, contact the Redwood Empire Association, Humboldt Bank Building, 785 Market Street, 15th Floor, San Francisco, CA 94103-2022; Tel: (415) 543-8334. (If ordered by mail, the Redwood Empire publication costs $1.)

A general source of information is the California Office of Tourism, Department of Commerce, 1121 L Street, Suite 103, Sacramento, CA 95814; Tel: (916) 322-1396.

For weather information call (916) 447-6941 or (415) 364-7974; for road conditions call California Highway Patrol, Tel: (916) 445-7623, or Caltrans, Tel: (415) 557-3755.

For information on camping, weather, and road conditions in the national parks, call (415) 556-0560 or 556-6030; for state park information call (415) 456-1286.

In San Francisco a free (if made within area code 415) Cityline now gives news and information 24 hours a day in more than 150 categories, from national news to weather, sports, finance, and even to historical trivia; Tel: (415) 512-5000.

—*Georgia I. Hesse*

BIBLIOGRAPHY

THOMAS R. AIDALA, *Hearst Castle, San Simeon* (1985). Illustrated. William Randolph Hearst was an insatiable collector of European arts and artifacts and much of what he collected ended up at Hearst Castle, San Simeon, a baronial estate that is now a state park.

HERBERT ASBURY, *The Barbary Coast* (1933). Chinatown slaves, shanghaied sailors, bordellos, and vigilantes come to life in this vivid history of San Francisco's underworld.

RICHARD BATMAN, *The Outer Coast* (1985). The human interest side of history—from Father Serra's feuds with the military commander at Monterey to Richard Henry Dana's nostalgic return to California and San Francisco in 1859—enlivens this study of the first decades of California settlement.

MORTON BEEBE, *San Francisco* (1985). Beebe photographed his hometown from every angle for this popular volume. His photographs are accompanied by words from such local writers as Herb Caen, Tom Cole, Herbert Gold, and Kevin Starr.

GEOFFREY BELL, *The Golden Gate and the Silver Screen* (1984). The San Francisco Bay Area was a movie-producing center early in the century, with such companies as Essanay churning out Westerns at Niles in Alameda County. This volume provides an illustrated history of the action.

PAUL BERTOLLI AND ALICE WATERS, *Chez Panisse Cooking: New Tastes and Techniques* (1988). Exploration of the philosophy behind the cooking at Waters's trend-setting Berkeley restaurant, as well as an account of recipes, special menus, and sources for fresh and pure ingredients.

JOHN BOESSENECKER, *Badge and Buckshot: Lawlessness in Old California* (1988). A San Francisco attorney peers into the past at famous outlaws and the men who tracked them down, from Rattlesnake Dick to John C. Boggs, Sheriff of Calaveras County and nemesis of badmen.

SARA HOLMES BOUTELLE, *Julia Morgan, Architect* (1988). A leading figure in the world of Northern California architecture, Morgan designed some 700 buildings, including William Randolph Hearst's Xanadu, Hearst Castle.

JOSEPH E. BROWN, *Monarchs of the Mist* (1982). A fascinating (and illustrated) collection of information about Redwood National Park and the ever-magnificent Coast Redwoods.

HERB CAEN, *Baghdad-by-the-Bay* (1949). Newspaper columnist Caen has chronicled the San Francisco that is, was, and never-was for more than four decades. This 40-year-old volume is pure nostalgia for those who knew the city "when."

THOMAS W. CHINN, *Bridging the Pacific: San Francisco Chinatown and Its People* (1989). An examination of San Francisco's Chinatown and its people, past and present.

DAVID COHEN AND RICH SMOLAN, *A Day in the Life of California* (1988). On April 1, 1988, a team of 100 people photographed the people and places of California. Images from the day's record clearly define the differences between north and south.

STEVE COUCH, *Steinbeck Country* (1973). A photographic essay on the places and people of Steinbeck's Salinas Valley, Monterey Peninsula, and Big Sur. Excerpts from Steinbeck's books introduce each section.

RICHARD HENRY DANA, JR., *Two Years Before the Mast* (1840). The writer, a seaman on a brig engaged in the California tallow-hide trade, recorded his observations of life in Mexican California of the late 1830s.

NARSAI M. DAVIS AND DORIS MUSCATINE, *Monday Night at Narsai's* (1987). From 1972 to 1984, Narsai's was a Marin County restaurant regarded as being on the cutting edge of California cuisine. This volume reproduces the menus for chef Narsai's famous fixed-menu Monday night dinners.

ROY ANDRES DE GROOT, *The Wines of California, the Pacific Northwest and New York* (1982). The author begins with an introduction to American wines and then turns to the "best wines of the best vineyards and wineries." His choices of the top 200 American vineyards and wineries include fewer than two dozen from outside California, and most of his California choices are in the north. He concludes with profiles of the vineyards, wineries, and leading wine makers.

LINDA WEST ECKHARDT, *The New West Coast Cuisine* (1985). The writer defines the new cuisine with discussion of ingredients and recipes.

CURT GENTRY, *The Last Days of the Late, Great State of California* (1968). Gentry tackles the ultimate disaster scenario: An earthquake lurches out of the sea at Point Arena, California trembles, the earth cracks along fault lines, and everything west of the chasm disappears into the sea. Breathless reading.

ALLEN GINSBERG, *Collected Poems 1947–1980* (1984). Ginsberg was the poet laureate of San Francisco's 1950s Beat Generation; his angry, pungent verse of that era brought him into court on obscenity charges.

HERBERT GOLD, *Dreaming* (1989). Gold, a fixture of San Francisco's contemporary literary scene, writes about a none-too-successful wheeler-dealer who moves across a familiar cityscape, ranging from Enrico's in North Beach to the Marina and the Avenues. In *Travels in San Francisco* (1990), Gold provides a guide to "hanging out" in a city he considers to be the last great metropolitan village.

JOHN GRAVES, T.H. WATKINS, AND ROBERT H. BOYLE, *The Water Hustlers* (1971). A Sierra Club publication examining the machinations of water politics in California, Texas, and New York.

Great Chefs of San Francisco (1983). Thirteen cooking classes presented on public television by San Francisco Bay Area kitchen greats were compiled in this masters' cookbook with recipes and details on the chefs and their workplaces. Includes such chefs as Jeremiah Tower (Santa Fe Bar & Grill), Mark Miller (Fourth Street Grill), and Masataka Kobayashi (Masa's).

Guide to California Wine Country (1979, frequent revisions). Most of this practical guide from Sunset Books focuses on wine in Northern California. Winery descriptions are accompanied by regional maps.

GARY HAMILTON AND NICOLE WOOLSEY BIGGART, *Governor Reagan, Governor Brown* (1984). An examination of the gubernatorial styles and philosophies of two very different men—one an ex-actor, the other, his successor, a young ex-theologian who was nicknamed Governor Moonbeam.

DASHIELL HAMMETT, *The Maltese Falcon* (1929). Detective Sam Spade works the foggy streets of San Francisco in this classic mystery.

JAMES D. HART, *A Companion to California* (1987). Director of the Bancroft Library at the University of California, Berkeley, the late Hart has compiled an encyclopedic guide to people, places, and events in the state.

BRET HARTE, *The Luck of Roaring Camp* (1868), *The Out-casts of Poker Flat* (1869). These classics, written when Harte edited the *Overland Monthly,* present a picturesque, sentimental view of Gold Rush days. (Found today in anthologies.)

J. S. HOLLIDAY, *The World Rushed In* (1981). A masterful account of the 1849 stampede to the California goldfields. At its core are the diary and letters of 49er William Swain, who was lured from Youngstown, New York, by the promise of fortune on the western slope of the Sierra Nevada. Excerpts from an additional 500 diaries and letter collections help make this one of the best late-20th-century volumes on the Gold Rush.

MILDRED BROOKE HOOVER, ED., *Historic Spots in California* (1932). Recently reissued, this book belongs on the shelf of every enthusiast of California, covering as it does pivotal sites from the opening up of the state by the Spanish explor-ers to the development of the 1930s.

JOSEPH HENRY JACKSON, *Anybody's Gold* (1941). An anecdotal history of Mother Lode mining settlements. Half of the book is devoted to the towns as they are in modern (1941) times (illustrated by E. H. Suydam).

ROBINSON JEFFERS, *Roan Stallion* (1925), *The Women at Point Sur* (1927), *Give Your Heart to The Hawks* (1933). Poems by Jeffers can best be described as intense, brooding, and even dour, but he wrote with passion about the Califor-nia landscape, particularly the rugged Big Sur country south of the Monterey Peninsula.

MAXINE HONG KINGSTON, *China Men* (1977). Novelist Kings-ton tells the story of Chinese immigration to America through the experiences of the men of her family. Of particular inter-est are segments dealing with "The Father from China," who entered America via the immigration station at Angel Island, San Francisco Bay, and "The Grandfather of the Sierra Moun-tains," an 1860s laborer on the railroad. *The Woman Warrior* (1976) describes the painful but often hilarious experience of growing up Chinese in Stockton, California.

THEODORA KROEBER, *Ishi In Two Worlds: A Biography of the Last Wild Indian in North America* (1961). A poignant ac-count of the life of the last member of California's Yahi tribe.

ANNE LAMOTT, *Joe Jones* (1985). Lamott, a San Francisco native who lives on a houseboat, writes about people beyond the mainstream. The backgrounds and allusions of her novels ring true to the Bay Area of the 1980s.

NIGEY LENNON, *Mark Twain in California* (1982). Samuel Clemens arrived in San Francisco from Virginia City, Nevada, in May, 1864. Here he fit into the lively and large literary Bohemia, where he produced the work that brought him his first national notice. Lennon brings this period to life.

OSCAR LEWIS, *San Francisco: Mission to Metropolis* (2nd ed., 1980). Lewis, regarded by some as the dean of San Francisco history, published this book in 1960. For this revised edition, he expanded on "The Contemporary Scene."

JACK LONDON, *The Star Rover* (1915). The fictionalized story of out-of-body and past-life experiences of turn-of-the-century California outlaw Ed Morrell. The book is considered London's last great work. *The Valley of the Moon* (1913) focuses on the Sonoma area where London built his last home.

RUTHANNE LUM McCUNN, *Thousand Pieces of Gold* (1981). A biographical novel about Lalu Nathoy (later Polly Bemis), a Chinese woman who was brought to San Francisco to be sold in the 1870s. Although she spent most of her American life in the Northwest, Bemis's story provides background on San Francisco's underground trade in Chinese women.

JOHN MEYERS MEYERS, *San Francisco's Reign of Terror* (1966). A critical look at the vigilantes who took law, order, and punishment into their own hands during the city's turbulent 1850s.

LEONARD MICHAELS, ED., *West of the West: Imagining California* (1989). Fine writers such as Tom Wolfe, Joan Didion, Gore Vidal, Gertrude Stein, M.F.K. Fisher, and Simone de Beauvoir record their experiences in this novelistic journey through the Golden State.

HENRY MILLER, *Big Sur and the Oranges of Hieronymus Bosch* (1958). An insider's account of life in the literary-arts colony on the Big Sur coast in the 1940s and 1950s.

FRANCES MOFFAT, *Dancing on the Brink of the World* (1977). A longtime society editor of the *San Francisco Chronicle,* Moffat records the antics of San Francisco's rich, elite, and sometimes not-too-respectable Golden Circle. The story stretches from the city's birth to contemporary times.

KRISTIN MOORE, *Mother Lode: A Pictorial Guide to California's Gold Rush Country* (1983). Text and photographs begin with Mariposa and cover a 319-mile chain of villages to the northernmost mines.

Jo Mora, *Californios* (1949). Artist-sculptor Mora wrote and illustrated this collector's piece on Old California and the men called *vaqueros,* the first American cowboys. (Readers who visit Carmel Mission will see another example of Mora's talent: He designed the ceremonial sarcophagus of Father Junípero Serra.)

Dale L. Morgan, *Jedediah Smith and the Opening of the West* (1953). Beaver trapper Smith was the first Yankee to reach California by an overland route. He also made the first recorded trip from California to Oregon in 1828 by way of the precipitous mountains of the far North Coast.

John Muir, *My First Summer in the Sierra* (1911). Muir, walker, writer, conservationist, and founder of the Sierra Club, published this account of his 1866 Sierra Nevada summer when he was 73.

Stuart Nixon, *Redwood Empire* (1966). History, geography, personality profiles, and photographs blend in a portrait of Northern California.

Frank Norris, *The Octopus* (1901). This heavy-handed but powerful novel focuses of the greed and ruthlessness of the builders of the Southern Pacific Railroad.

Jean-Nicolas Perlot, trans. by Helen Harding Bretnor, *Goldseeker* (1985). The first English translation of a young Belgian's adventures in Monterey, the Southern Mines, and Yosemite during the Gold Rush.

Charles Perry, *Haight-Ashbury: A History* (1984). Perry's description of the world of Be-Ins, Love-Ins, flamboyance, grass, and LSD was garnered from participants and from the voluminous media coverage of a movement that grew from 1965 to 1966, peaked in the summer of 1967, and died in 1968.

Elizabeth Pomada and Michael Larsen, *The Painted Ladies Revisited* (1989). A district-by-district examination, in text and color photography, of the restoration of San Francisco's 19th-century and turn-of-the-century houses commonly called Victorians. The text sketches histories of individual houses, while Douglas Keister's photographs provide beautiful illustrations.

LAWRENCE CLARK POWELL, *California Classics: The Creative Literature of the Golden State* (1971). A compendium of good or famous efforts in California letters.

HAL ROTH, *Pathways in the Sky, The Story of the John Muir Trail* (1965). A detailed, illustrated description of the Sierra Nevada trail named after California's great conservationist and founder of the Sierra Club.

GALEN ROWELL, *The Yosemite* (1989). One hundred color photographs by a contemporary mountaineer and master photographer celebrate Yosemite National Park's centennial. Each photograph is accompanied by excerpts from *The Yosemite* by conservationist John Muir.

WILLIAM SAROYAN, *The Human Comedy* (1943). Homer Macauly, the fastest telegram bicycle messenger in the San Joaquin Valley, is the key character in Saroyan's first novel, a story about a small-town family during World War II.

VIKRAM SETH, *The Golden Gate* (1986). This novel in verse takes the clichés and characters of contemporary life in San Francisco and the Bay Area and shapes them into a fresh, delightful story of loneliness, loss, and gentle love.

RANDY SHILTS, *The Mayor of Castro Street* (1981). A biography of Harvey Milk, the San Francisco city supervisor and gay community leader assassinated by Dan White. It also provides background on the lifestyles and politics of the nation's largest gay community.

KEVIN STARR, *Material Dreams: California Through the 1920s* (1990). Starr, a Northern California historian, is writing a serial history on what he calls "America and the California Dream"; this is the third volume.

JOHN STEINBECK, *The Grapes of Wrath* (1939). This Pulitzer Prize–winning novel about Dust Bowl migrants—called Oakies and Arkies in California—delivers as strong a human and social message today as it did half a century ago. Steinbeck's *Cannery Row* (1945), published as Monterey's sardine fishing-and-packing industry was on its deathbed, has become California myth, shaping perceptions of Monterey for two generations.

W. A. SWANBERG, *Citizen Hearst* (1961). Biography of William Randolph Hearst, the newspaper publishing tycoon, power manipulator, and builder of Hearst Castle, San Simeon, whose Northern California family roots extended to Gold Rush days.

GORDON THOMAS AND MAX MORGAN WITTS, *The San Francisco Earthquake* (1971). Interviews with 1906 earthquake survivors, other eyewitness accounts, and insurance, Red Cross, and military records sketch a compelling picture of an event that has passed beyond history into folklore.

MARK TWAIN, *Roughing It* (1871). In Twain's own words, this book is a "personal narrative" and a "record of several years of variegated vagabondizing" in Nevada, Northern California, and Hawaii.

JOHN VAN DER ZEE, *The Gate: The True Story of the Design and Construction of the Golden Gate Bridge* (1986). The people, the politics, and the technology that produced San Francisco's great bridge are thoroughly scrutinized in this volume.

STEPHEN VINCENT, ED., *O California!* (1989). California's geography described though beautifully-reproduced landscape paintings by the state's 19th-century and early 20th-century artists and words from their contemporaries.

PAUL WEBSTER, *The Mighty Sierra* (1972). An illustrated, comprehensive view of the mountain range that extends 400 miles from Tehachapi Pass to Lassen Peak.

—*Shirley Maas Fockler*

SAN FRANCISCO

By Georgia I. Hesse

The port of San Francisco ... is a marvel of nature, and might well be called the harbor of harbors, because of its great capacity, and of several small bays which it enfolds in its margins or beach and in its islands. Indeed, although in my travels I saw very good sites and beautiful country, I saw none which pleased me so much as this. And I think that if it could be well settled like Europe there would not be anything more beautiful in all the world, for it has the best advantages for founding in it a most beautiful city, with all the conveniences desired, by land as well as by sea, with that harbor so remarkable and so spacious, in which may be established shipyards, docks, and anything that might be wished. ...

—Pedro Font, *Complete Diary of Anza's California Expeditions,* 1776

San Francisco began by being beautiful. Like Paris, its very name sings a siren song to people around the globe; but Paris owes its distinction to architecture, while San Francisco was blessed by nature.

Even philosopher Josiah Royce, who felt nature to be a poor teacher, fell under the spell of the physical place: "The high dark hills on the western shore of the Bay, the water at their feet, the Golden Gate that breaks through them and opens up to one the view of the sea beyond, the smoke-obscured city at the south of the Gate, and the barren ranges yet farther to the left, these are the permanent background

23

whereon many passing shapes of light and shadow, of cloud and storm, of mist and of sunset glow are projected as I watch all from my station on the hillside." (Royce was born in Grass Valley, California, of all unlikely places, went on to teach at the University of California and, later, at Harvard. His words here are from *Fugitive Essays,* 1879.)

In modern days, novelist John Steinbeck, more used to creating word-paintings of poverty than eloquent eulogies, was moved to write (in *Travels with Charley*), "I saw her across the bay, from the great road that bypasses Sausalito and enters the Golden Gate Bridge. The afternoon sun painted her white and gold—rising on her hills like a noble city in a happy dream . . . this gold-and-white acropolis rising wave on wave against the blue of the Pacific sky was a stunning thing, a painted thing like a picture of a medieval Italian city which can never have existed. . . ."

But she does exist, sometimes in more than three dimensions. Twilight is the finest time, in October, perhaps, when from every hill (about six times as many as in Rome) the bay runs to meet the sea beyond the Gate, framed by the baked golden hills of Marin and the deepening blue of the sky that stretches west of the sunset toward Asia. A skinny finger of fog slips beneath the Golden Gate Bridge, and all around the darkening waters, golden dots of light wink on in salute— and one is glad to live nowhere else.

It is such moments the San Franciscan holds to himself, like inexpressible secrets, when faced with the dreary dramas of city life in the 1990s: the drugs, the homelessness, the pathetic politics. Despite inroads of urban angst, San Francisco remains a retreat for the joyous, the creative, and the civilized.

MAJOR INTEREST

Union Square area
Chinatown
Nob Hill's mansions
North Beach, for Italian atmosphere
Fisherman's Wharf
Golden Gate National Recreation Area (hikes along the bay)
Golden Gate Bridge
The Marina and the Palace of Fine Arts
Cow Hollow, for dining and shopping
Pacific Heights Victorians
Japantown

Ethnic dining on Clement Street
Golden Gate Park (museums and nature)
Civic Center museum and performing arts area
Mission Dolores
SoMa (South of Market) café scene
Ocean Beach and Land's End, especially for the
     Palace of the Legion of Honor
Cable cars

San Francisco (Spanish for Saint Francis, he of Assisi in Italy) derives its name from the Misión San Francisco de Asís, sixth in the series of 21 mission churches built in New Spain as outposts of the empire by the Franciscan order, largely under the direction of Father Junípero Serra. (Born in Majorca, Serra is buried within the walls of Mission San Carlos Borromeo del Río in Carmel and is being considered for sainthood by the Roman Catholic Church.)

The entrance to San Francisco Bay had been missed for more than 200 years by European explorers (perhaps it was hidden in fog) when on November 1, 1769, Sergeant José de Ortega, pathfinder for Gaspar de Portolá's expedition, marched overland in search of the "lost" bay of Monterey. Approaching from the south, he climbed a ridge and spotted the wide bay, the islands, and all the lands around.

(It was a North American, however, who christened the entrance to the great inland waterway. In his *Memoirs,* General John Charles Frémont wrote, "To this gate I gave the name of *Chrysopylae,* or Golden Gate; for the same reason that the harbor of Byzantium was called Chrysoceras, or Golden Horn.")

The site of the Presidio (fort) of San Francisco was selected by Juan Bautista de Anza on March 28, 1776 (three months to the day before Thomas Jefferson presented the Declaration of Independence to the American Congress); one wall of that fort remains as part of the Officers' Club of today's Presidio. That same year, on October 9, San Francisco's mission (missions and forts went hand in gun in early California) was dedicated at a place also picked by Anza, on the bank of a little lake and stream flowing into it (now filled). He called the stream *Arroyo de los Dolores,* having found it on the Friday of Sorrows (*dolores*). Over the years the church came by its present name, Mission Dolores. So San Francisco was born.

Some contemporary statistics: the city's population is only about 732,000, but as a metropolitan *area,* this is the nation's

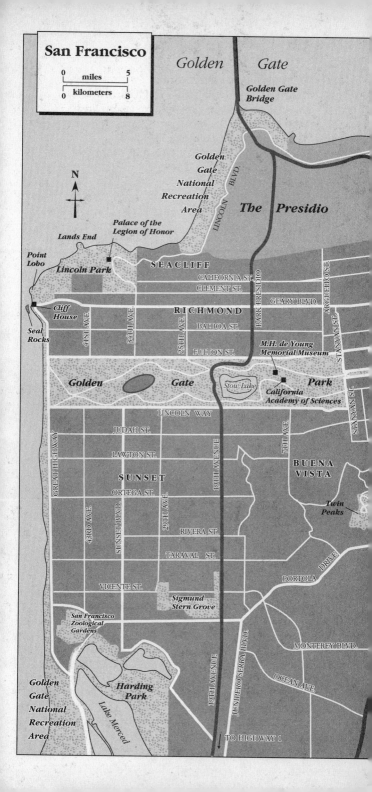

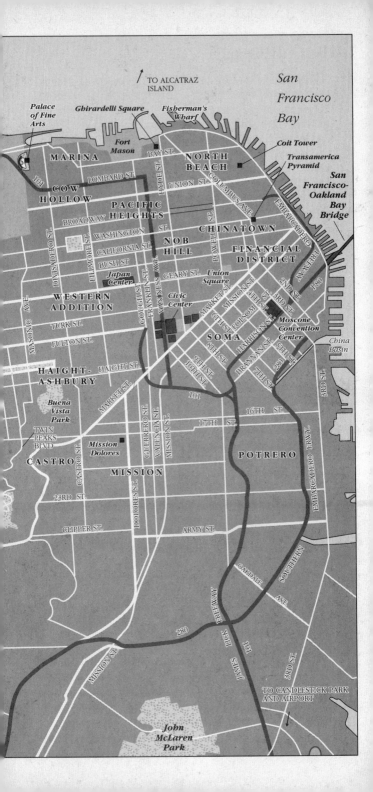

fourth largest; there are 14,000 surviving Victorian dwellings; the city claims the crookedest street in the world, Lombard Street; its narrowest street is DeForest Way (at four and a half feet) and its steepest are Filbert from Leavenworth to Hyde and 22nd between Church and Vicksburg, both boasting a 31.5 degree grade.

In a day of increasing sameness and sterility, San Francisco delights in the diversity of its neighborhoods; sometimes it seems you should have a passport to go from one to another. "Chinoiserie, chiaroscuro, chili sauce" was one writer's description of the city's ethnic mix (forgetting the teriyaki). Even the weather refuses homogeneity: Union Square can be bathed in sunlight while the shoppers on West Portal near the ocean shiver in fog.

Not all the neighborhoods are equally enticing, of course. Here, we describe those of most interest to the traveller. We begin at Union Square, the traditional stepping-off spot for a tour of the town, and proceed roughly north, with detours to the east and west, through the areas that constitute the core of interest for visitors—the Financial District, Chinatown, Nob Hill, and North Beach. All of these areas lie east of Van Ness Avenue, a major north–south artery. After reaching the shores of San Francisco Bay, we ramble west along Fisherman's Wharf to the Golden Gate Bridge, and backtrack east through the Marina, heading roughly south, again with detours to the east and west, particularly to Golden Gate Park, through the neighborhoods west of Van Ness Avenue. South on to Mission Dolores and then two nighttime haunts, the Civic Center and SoMa (South of Market), the first for museums, symphony, and opera, the second for more café-oriented culture, all three south of Union Square. Then it's to Ocean Beach, at ocean's edge far to the west of downtown and west of Golden Gate Park. We end with a few of the city's specialties—cable cars, sports, and a roundup of annual events.

UNION SQUARE

This rectangular crossroads is perhaps the single space uniting the several elements and attitudes of the city. The chic center for the "shop 'til you drop" set, it is also where pigeons and protesters come to see and be part of the scene. This is the stage set for such outrageous characters as Sadie, Sadie the Rabbi Lady and the Sisters of Perpetual Indulgence (look especially for Sister Boom-Boom), as it was for now-beloved characters of the past such as "Emperor" Norton or James King of William, and even the sandal-footed beatniks of 1958 who marched down from North Beach on a "Squaresville Tour," following a bongo drummer and startling the stylish shoppers in Gump's, Shreve's, and I. Magnin's. (These blocks were made for walking; park your car at the underground Union Square Garage, the Downtown Center Garage at Mason and O'Farrell streets, or, less expensively, a block away at the Sutter-Stockton Garage.)

Union Square, bounded by Stockton, Powell, Post, and Geary streets, was originally a mighty sandbank called O'Farrell's Mountain. Presented to the city in 1850 by John W. Geary, first American mayor of San Francisco, it was leveled and turned into a green, flowery two-and-a-half-acre park. When the Civil War threatened, the square saw its first demonstrations as pro-Union rallies were staged here to protest the secession of the southern states, and the name Union Square stuck.

The square has as its center the Dewey Monument, a 90-foot granite shaft that celebrates Commodore George Dewey's triumph over the Spanish navy at Manila Bay in 1898 during the Spanish-American War; should you wish to salute him, you may do so at **Dewey's**, a pub across Powell Street in the St. Francis Hotel. The face of the goddess Victory who crowns the monument is supposed to have been sculpted in the likeness of Alma de Bretteville Spreckels. (The civic benefactress, with her husband Adolph, gave the city its California Palace of the Legion of Honor, as well as that museum's collection of Rodin sculptures.)

Five churches and one synagogue first commanded this square, with private clubs spaced between them. Then, in 1904, Charles T. Crocker (of the banking Crockers) decided his city needed proper accommodations for the growing clutch of bonanza kings, and decreed the building of the **St. Francis Hotel** on the west side of the square. Resulting commerce eased the churches farther west in the direction of Van Ness Avenue, although the Congregational stopped only a block west at the corner of Post and Mason, where it still stands.

Whether events have been fashionable or felonious, the St. Francis has lived on center stage. Until the wane of proper dress in the 1960s, the white-gloved (and behatted) ladies of San Francisco took Monday luncheons in the St. Francis Mural Room, and lest those gloves be allowed to touch filthy lucre, any coins returned to their hands were first carefully washed and dried. (They still are; the man at

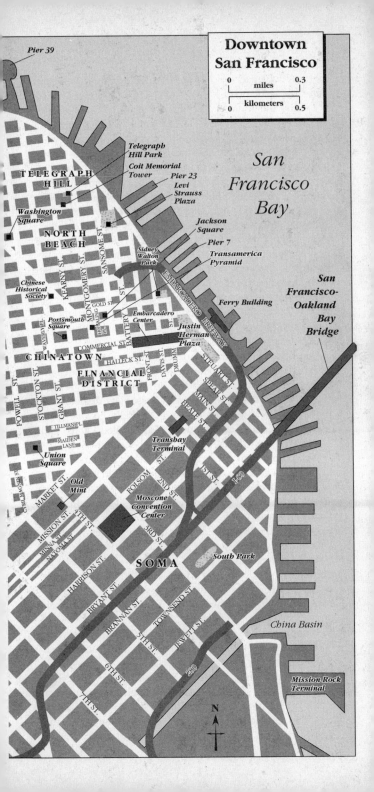

Downtown San Francisco

| 0 | miles | 0.3 |

| 0 | kilometers | 0.5 |

Pier 39

Telegraph Hill Park

Coit Memorial Tower

Pier 23

Levi Strauss Plaza

San Francisco Bay

TELEGRAPH HILL

Washington Square

NORTH BEACH

Jackson Square

Pier 7

Transamerica Pyramid

Sidney Walton Park

Chinese Historical Society

KEARNY ST.

MONTGOMERY ST.

SANSOME ST.

GOLD ST.

Ferry Building

San Francisco-Oakland Bay Bridge

Portsmouth Square

BATTERY ST.

Embarcadero Center

WAVERLY PL.

EMBARCADERO FREEWAY

Justin Herman Plaza

COMMERCIAL ST.

HALLECK ST.

FRONT ST.

DAVIS ST.

DRUMM ST.

STEUART ST.

CHINATOWN

FINANCIAL DISTRICT

POWELL ST.

STOCKTON ST.

GRANT ST.

SPEAR ST.

MAIN ST.

BEALE ST.

TILLMAN PL.

MAIDEN LANE

Union Square

Old Mint

MARKET ST.

Transbay Terminal

1ST ST.

I-80

O'FARRELL ST.

MISSION ST.

MINNA ST.

NATOMA ST.

FOLSOM ST.

2ND ST.

Moscone Convention Center

3RD ST.

SOMA

South Park

HARRISON ST.

BRYANT ST.

BRANNAN ST.

TOWNSEND ST.

China Basin

5TH ST.

JAVETT ST.

6TH ST.

280

Mission Rock Terminal

7TH ST.

N

the washing machine is Arnold Batliner, who boasts the same age as the hotel.)

During the four-day fire that followed the 1906 earthquake, residents of the hotel streamed in shock into the square, including bibulous reveler John Barrymore, who was pressed by the militia into stacking bricks. His uncle, thespian John Drew, was moved to remark, "It took an act of God to get Jack out of bed and the U. S. Government to get him to work." Queen Elizabeth slept here in March of 1983, occupying with her entourage the entire 31st floor of suites; at the other extreme, silent-screen star Fatty Arbuckle killed Virgina Rappe here on Labor Day in 1921. It was also here that President Gerald Ford walked out to be fired upon by Sarah Jane Moore in 1975, and where Al Jolson died while playing a poker hand.

Face outward as you ride the glass elevators of the St. Francis Tower and watch Union Square and its surrounding high-rises swim up into view. It's among the best perspectives in town.

The opposite, southeast corner of the square had been ruled since 1896 by another relic, the City of Paris department store, until it was replaced in 1983 by controversial, almost harlequin-dressed Neiman-Marcus. Its dramatic rotunda, however, was retained, with its Belle Epoque glass dome of a barque afloat under a sky of fleur-de-lis, and bearing the motto of Paris: It Floats and Never Sinks.

Well before high noon, giving the slip to beggars, brown baggers, do-gooders, and sidewalk traders in tawdry, the ladies and gentlemen who frequent Union Square proper are all in their places with dignified faces for luncheon at **Campton Place** (an elegant little retreat with its outstanding restaurant), the **Rotunda** at Neiman-Marcus, **Kuleto's** in the Villa Florence hotel, **Janot's** at 44 Campton Place (an alley between Sutter and Post), or (a few steps up on Bush) **Le Central**, where columnist Herb Caen and/or his buddy Willie Brown, speaker of the State Assembly, and/or Wilkes Bashford (clothier to the upper crust) may be spotted chatting at a windowside table.

Shopping is the sine qua non of the Union Square experience, but even strollers will appreciate the amble down **Maiden Lane**, an elegant pedestrian alley once known as Morton Street, which runs from Stockton for two blocks east to Kearny Street. (Morton Street was notable for a number of ladies of the night; hence, with the smartening-up of the area, the new name Maiden Lane.) The atmosphere is the neat streets of Paris; the one tourist sight is the **Circle**

Gallery building at number 140, designed by Frank Lloyd Wright in 1949.

At 250 Post Street between Stockton and Grant, **Gump's** is not only the oldest but the most prestigious Asian art dealer in the city. Founded in 1865 by the Gump brothers, two German immigrants, it is a veritable museum as well, a destination for anyone interested in Asian arts. The Jade Room is particularly fascinating.

San Francisco boasts dozens of art galleries of all persuasions and in several districts of town; the region around Union Square is particularly proud of its collection. In Maiden Lane, for example, in addition to Circle Gallery, you'll find **Conacher Galleries**, number 134 (contemporary art, rare prints); **Hanson Galleries**, number 153 (contemporary oils, watercolors, sculpture, limited editions); **Maiden Lane Gallery**, number 111 (American masters); **Orientations**, number 34 (18th- and 19th-century Oriental art and antiques); and **Richard Thompson Gallery**, number 80 (oils, limited-edition prints by 20th-century American Impressionists).

Two blocks to the north of Union Square, Sutter Street—and the streets running north and south of it—could be called Gallery Row (see Shopping below).

Always intriguing to visitors, the curbside flower stands around Union Square sell blooms in season for a bit less than florists. Vendors owe their colorful outlets to Michael Harry de Young (of the *Chronicle* newspaper dynasty), who allowed young people to sell flowers in front of the De Young building years ago. The stands were licensed in 1904 and today are a bona fide attraction for residents as well as outsiders.

The district's most endearing artwork is the **Ruth Asawa Fountain**, created by the local sculptor to capture the spirit of the city in bronze. It sits on the Stockton Street steps leading to the entrance of the Grand Hyatt Hotel on the corner of Post and Stockton streets.

Although not of interest to everyone, the **Old Mint** (opened in 1854) is one of the curious attractions in town, housed in one of the finest examples of Federal Classical Revival architecture in the West. Some of its working rooms have been restored, and there's a Western art display and a collection of pioneer gold coins. Most dramatic is the pyramid of gold bars valued at $5 million and shown in a circular vault. The Mint is at Fifth and Mission streets, just a four-block walk south of Union Square, and can be visited on weekdays free of charge; Tel: 974-0788.

Union Square celebrates spring with April's Rhododendron Days, midsummer with the Cable Car Bell-Ringing Contest, and midwinter with the Chinese New Year Pageant.

From Union Square, theaters and several good restaurants are a few steps away to the west; burgeoning SoMa sits to the south; the shops, restaurants, hotels, and green spaces of the Embarcadero wait to the northeast beyond the Financial District; and Nob Hill, Chinatown, Russian Hill, North Beach, Telegraph Hill, and Fisherman's Wharf are to the north, reachable by foot (for the exercise), cable car, or bus.

THE FINANCIAL DISTRICT

The Wall Street of the West, they call it: the stretch of Montgomery Street from Market north to Washington Street. More recently it's been dubbed San Francisco's canyon country. (Walk east from Union Square on Post Street to reach Montgomery.)

The main Financial District stretches from Market Street north to Jackson Street and from Kearny Street and Chinatown on the west to Drumm Street and the Embarcadero Center buildings on the east. (A few square blocks to the south of Market are technically part of the district, but are of less interest to visitors.)

Money and Montgomery Street have always been mated. It was on Montgomery on May 12, 1848, that Sam Brannan, a Mormon settler and publisher of San Francisco's first newspaper, the *California Star,* yelled out the news that initiated one of history's greatest runs for the riches. "Holding high a bottle full of gold dust," writes J. S. Holliday in *The World Rushed In,* "Brannan shouted: 'Gold! Gold! Gold from the American River!' By the middle of June, San Francisco stood half empty, with three-quarters of the men off to the mines, most stores closed, the *alcalde*'s office shut, the newspapers suspended, outbound ships at anchor deserted by their crews. News from San Jose, Benicia, Sonoma, all the same— empty streets, abandoned businesses, fields of grain opened to roaming cattle."

Standing in front of the soaring Bank of America today (perhaps near the abstract black-granite sculpture known locally as "the banker's heart"), watching dapper business-people bound for lunch 55 floors up at the Carnelian Room or the private Banker's Club, it's difficult to think of this as a former morass where mules mired, even drowned, in the ooze. ("This street impassable," read one street-sign of the time, "not even jackassable.")

The shanty town that in 1849 sprang into being in San Francisco (a canvas tent called El Dorado was rented out to gamblers for $40,000 per year) was constructed on the carcasses of ships. All the streets we walk today east of Montgomery between California and Broadway began as wharves. Offshore lay an armada of ghost ships whose crews had careened off for gold; maritime historians estimate that 100 vessels were hauled into the shallows to serve as stores and warehouses, or were sunk for fill and building foundations.

The booming, naughty (some said vice-ridden) Victorian city died on April 18, 1906, when the earthquake shook the city to its shale-and-sandstone foundation. (A Los Angeles newspaper supposedly headlined the story, "San Francisco Punished!") In the following three years the town rushed to rebuild (sidewalk placards pleaded, "Don't talk earthquake, talk business"), especially in this district, with the result that it became what architectural writer Randolph Delehanty called "an up-to-date Edwardian city of remarkable architectural coherence."

The shades of some of San Francisco's illustrious literati haunt these skyscraper-shadowed streets. On the southeast corner of Montgomery and Washington, where the Transamerica Pyramid soars today, the storied Monkey Block (really Montgomery Block) first served financiers and law firms and later was occupied by the offices and/or hangouts of Ambrose Bierce, Bret Harte, William Randolph Hearst, Rudyard Kipling, Jack London, Robert Louis Stevenson, and Mark Twain. At the Washington Street corner, the Bank Exchange Saloon was a favored watering place, much frequented by the eccentric Emperor Norton; crusading newspaper editor James King of William was brought here, bleeding, after being shot by rival editor James Casey.

Around in the Financial District

Walkers probably will approach this trading enclave (Randolph Delehanty has called it "... undoubtedly the most pleasant, and though costly, most efficient office core in the United States") from Union Square, most handily by walking east on Post Street to its meeting with Montgomery.

Here, you are faced with the soaring, rose-granite Pacific Telesis Tower and its adjoining Crocker Galleria, a very handsome shopping arena. If it's lunchtime, consider the pleasant **Circolo Restaurant & Champagneria** on the Sutter Street side of the building, which serves Italian specialties and boasts a wood-burning pizza oven as well as bar murals from the Old Poodle Dog, a San Franciscan institution that came to an end some years ago. On the same block, at number 191, the **Galleria Park** is a splendid place to stay at a most reasonable rate.

If you have strolled down Sutter Street from Union Square, you will have passed (and should stop at) **Lascaux**, where the sizzle of the fast-track set slows down to country-French speed. It's a great cellar-level retreat at 250 Sutter; Tel: 391-1555. On the other hand, should you want to sample Old California atmosphere, plan a long lunch at **Sam's Grill**, 374 Bush Street near Kearny (really in a tiny alley named Belden). One of the city's oldest restaurants (with waiters to match), it has served some of the best petrale sole in town from one decade into the next.

It's unlikely that the traveller with limited time would spend the hours to inspect in detail all of the striking buildings on show in this district. But be sure to note the 47-story **First Interstate Center** at the corner of Sansome and California streets, a complex design that incorporates the shells of four old office buildings, a retail concourse, smart offices, and—of first importance—the elegant **Mandarin Oriental** hotel.

Just down the street at 240 California (between Battery and Front), the **Tadich Grill**, scarcely changed since its birth in 1849, is California's oldest restaurant, one of a distinguished clan created by Yugoslavian immigrants; fresh seafood is their claim to fame, though grilled foods are also good. No reservations are taken and the pre-lunch line stretches down the block, so your best bet is to arrive for a late lunch (2:00 P.M. or after) or an early dinner (6:00 P.M.).

One of the most dominant structures on San Francisco's skyline is the **Bank of America** at 555 California Street, between Kearny and Montgomery. When you stare at its intriguing zigzag façade closely, you will admire it; from a distance it stands out as a black-red slab at odds with the city's general pastel appearance. In any case it's worth the long ride to the top to the **Carnelian Room** for American cuisine or to the **Pacific Room** for cocktails, or simply to admire what their 52nd-floor position offers—the most stunning views in town.

Within the Wells Fargo Bank headquarters at 464 California Street, the **Wells Fargo History Room** (entrance at 420 Montgomery) traces the fascinating story of the Gold Rush and the famous overland stages that helped finance (if not win) the West.

Tradition lives at **Jack's**, 615 Sacramento Street, a shrine in its 1864 premises, where the waiters are definitely in charge, the menu is printed daily, recognized dowagers and men-about-town get the best tables, and the rex sole and sand dabs are worth writing tomes about; Tel: 986-9854.

Another bank with an eye on history is the Bank of Canton at 555 Montgomery, where the **Pacific Heritage Museum** (entrance on 608 Commercial Street) displays rotating exhibits centering on the history of artistic, cultural, and economic interchanges among peoples of the Pacific Rim.

Central, or Long, Wharf, which ran almost 3,000 feet out into the bay from between Sacramento and Clay streets, was the lively landing place for Pacific Mail steamers and, in the 1850s, "became the favorite promenade. Buildings perched on piles sprang up quickly on either side, and commission houses, groceries, saloons, mock auctions, cheap-John shops, and peddlers did a thriving business" (*Historic Spots in California*). The wharf is now landlocked Commercial Street, running between Grant and Embarcadero Center; you can look down upon it from windows in the luxurious **Park Hyatt**.

North of Commercial and Clay, at 600 Montgomery Street, is the **Transamerica Pyramid**, one of the most hotly debated high-rises in history when it topped out at 853 feet in 1972; now most San Franciscans have learned to like it. The observatory on the 27th floor is open to the public at no charge during business hours.

Jackson Square

Cross Washington Street from the Pyramid and enter the one-block alley named Hotaling that leads to Jackson Square. **Hotaling Place**, with its hitching posts and almost Dickensian air, is one of the most charm-filled footpaths in town. Its name recalls Anson Parsons Hotaling, who erected a building near here in 1866 to house his whiskey business as well as a rich collection of books and paintings; its iron shutters helped it survive the earthquake and fire of 1906. According to the chroniclers of the time, when local clergymen interpreted the quake as divine retribution for the city's notorious wickedness, a wit named Charles Field penned the question: "If, as they say, God spanked the town for being over-frisky/Why did He burn His churches down and spare Hotaling's whiskey?"

Jackson Square, which is not really a square but a district, was named a historic area in 1971; it has been much reworked and reawakened, and today lies between Washington and Pacific on the south and north and Sansome and Columbus on the west and east.

This area was the infamous Barbary Coast of the late 19th century, somewhat glorified today but part of a dramatically depraved past. Named after the pirate refuges of the Mediterranean's Barbary Coast (Morocco, Algiers, Tunis, Tripoli), it is said to have given currency to the terms "to shanghai" (to kidnap men to make up a ship's crew, especially with the help of "Mickey Finns," another local creation) and "hoodlum" (the cry of "Huddle 'em!" shouted by bullies pursuing human prey).

Today, following ingenious restoration and refurbishing, the lime-encrusted bricks have been scraped and sandblasted, the wood painted subtle colors, the fine Federal-style façades enhanced with plane trees and shrubs. Decorators (selling mostly to the trade), followed by admen, architects, and attorneys, have moved into the landmark buildings, and refinement has replaced raffishness.

Dining Around the Square

New and lively, **Bix** at 56 Gold Street (between Sansome and Montgomery) is called by its owner an updated supper club; certainly it recalls the era of transatlantic liners, the nights of torch singers and wailing saxophones. The food is oldfashioned and delicious (Tel: 433-6300). A traditional favorite that had fallen on sad times has risen again, newly elegant in decor and innovative in its kitchen: For a smart evening out, try the **Blue Fox** at 659 Merchant Street (off Montgomery); Tel: 981-1177.

A true trattoria, glittery and high tech, **Ciao** attracts young professionals at lunch and dinner and serves drinks to the after-business crowd at 230 Jackson Street. **Ernie's**, in a city of classic restaurants, just keeps getting better. From the linoleum floors of its opening in 1934, it has long metamorphosed into antiques, damask walls, and French crystal—and cuisine to match. It's a power house for dinner (no lunch served), at 847 Montgomery Street; Tel: 397-5969.

Pimm's Cup originally came to the West Coast at **India House**, the city's first Indian restaurant (it opened in 1947) and one of its most atmospheric, at 350 Jackson Street. With its patio and guitarist, **Las Mañanitas** is instant Mexico with a Continental touch. Dance to salsa and jazz on Fridays and Saturdays at 850 Montgomery Street.

Because the greater Financial District and Jackson Square are spread over a rather large area between Union Square, Market Street, and North Beach–Telegraph Hill, you may want to make use of public buses from time to time. Heavy traffic runs south on Columbus Avenue, which turns into Montgomery Street, from North Point Street near Hyde Street Pier to Market Street and beyond; look for the number 15 bus. Along Sansome the best choice is number 42 (the Red Arrow Loop), which runs north from Pine up Sansome to the Embarcadero and beyond. As the Gold Arrow Loop, number 42 operates in the opposite direction from North Point Street and Fisherman's Wharf, returning down Battery Street.

EMBARCADERO CENTER AREA

From Union Square, you can wander your way northeast through the Financial District to Embarcadero Center, or walk east on Geary to its juncture with Market Street, cross Market, and take a streetcar numbered 8, 21, or 31 to the end of the line (signed Ferry Terminal).

You'll notice **Lotta's Fountain** at the meeting of Geary, Market, and Kearny streets. Once a watering trough for horses, then a bronze drinking fountain for human beings, this structure was presented to the city in 1875 by much-loved Lotta Crabtree, "the California Diamond," an actress of Gold Rush days. It was here on Christmas Eve in 1910 that soprano Luisa Tetrazzini sang carols to streets full of en-thralled listeners.

On the next corner, the old Palace Hotel (now the Sheraton-Palace and just reopened following an 18-month renovation) has been a player on the local stage since its opening in 1910 (on the site of an even-older marvel erased by the 1906 earthquake). President Warren G. Harding died in the former in 1923, Hawaii's King Kalakaua in the latter in 1891, and in 1906 Enrico Caruso (appearing locally in *Carmen*) was so shaken by the earthquake that he is said to have run into the street in his nightshirt, swearing never to sing in the city again.

In the alley called Annie Street just to the west of the Sheraton-Palace, the **Maltese Grill** has become one of the city's most popular restaurants for its innovative treatment of the Mediterranean cooking of Italy, France, and Spain; Tel: 777-1955.

Several blocks farther east, the foot of Market Street steps into Justin Herman Plaza.

Embarcadero Center

Justin Herman Plaza, with its controversial, walk-through Vaillancourt Fountain (some think this concrete structure is a hideous modern intrusion, others find it refreshingly unorthodox), is a welcoming oasis of greenery and ease at the end of bustling, trafficky Market Street. Off it, the five-block complex of **Embarcadero Center** (also known as Rockefeller Center West for the developer who cooperated with architect John Portman) is considered by many city planners, and even some San Franciscans, to be the very model of an urban showpiece.

Set on three levels of open-air plazas connected by pedestrian walkways above the streets, the center is a clutch of almost 200 shops, boutiques, restaurants, cafés, galleries, and—at Building Five—the **Hyatt Regency**.

A map and directory of the Center may be picked up at kiosks throughout the complex; don't try to get around without it.

At any season a shopper's fancy lightly turns to thoughts of a *truite meunière,* perhaps, or *tagliarini* with salmon and peas. The perfect dish is at hand somewhere in the Center: at splendid **Splendido's** (Building Four, Podium Level), or **Four Star** (Three, Podium), **La Fuente** (Two, Podium), **Gaylord India** (One, Podium), **Harbor Village Restaurant** (Chinese; Four, Lobby), **New Eagle Bar & Café** (Four, Podium), or the two **Scott's** (seafood; both Three, Podium).

In 1988 two new buildings were added to the Embarcadero group, Embarcadero West and the Park Hyatt Hotel with its handsome **Park Grill**, on either side of the Neoclassical Federal Reserve Bank.

Three attractive, interesting places for lunch and dinner in this district are just south of Market and Embarcadero Center: **Umberto Ristorante Italiano** at 141 Steuart Street (fine Florentine cuisine, handsome cellar rooms; Tel: 543-8021); **Roti** in the Hotel Griffon at 155 Steuart Street (a European-style bistro from the folks who gave you Fog City Diner—more on that later—Tel: 495-6500); and **Orient Express** at One Market Plaza/50 Steuart Street (seafood, Middle Eastern, Mediterranean specialties; Tel: 957-1776).

The Ferry Building

It's difficult to believe today, but the Ferry Building (1896), at harbor's edge at the end of Market Street, was for decades the tallest structure in town. Modeled after the Giralda tower of Seville's cathedral, it stood as the symbol of the city, welcoming millions of rail travellers (who were coming across the bay from the rail terminal in Oakland) and ferry passengers. Alas, its silhouette has long been rendered unimportant by the ugly, mid-air Embarcadero Freeway that speeds by between the tower and the rest of the city, impeding the view. (The freeway has been impassable since the 1989 earthquake, and may be torn down in favor of water-level lanes that would sweep grandly along the bay toward Chinatown and Fisherman's Wharf.)

Today the Ferry Building serves as headquarters for the San Francisco Port Authority and the private World Trade Center club rooms. Golden Gate Transit and the Red & White Fleet now bring more than 40 ferries each weekday to Piers 1 and 1½ at the building, and plans are underway to build five more berths for even more ferries in an attempt to relieve earthquake-worsened auto congestion and to decrease car traffic on the San Francisco–Oakland Bay Bridge.

On the bay side of the Embarcadero (a two-way street that runs beneath the freeway along the waterfront from Berry Street in the south to Fisherman's Wharf in the north), the Ferry Building is the marker from which piers are numbered: odd numbers to the north, even numbers to the south. The wide sidewalk serves as a track for joggers who pound along, seemingly oblivious to the fine harbor view. Several worthwhile restaurants sit at water's edge: **Sinbad's Pier 2** (seafood), the **Waterfront** at Pier 7 (seasonal local and imported seafood), and **Pier 23 Café** (California creative, funky atmosphere).

Dining at Walton Square

Abutting Embarcadero Center on the north, the Alcoa Building (a giant black box with an eerie exoskeleton) and the high-rise apartment complex of Golden Gateway signal the sheltered presence of **Walton Square**, a welcome, small, green space with a fountain bordered north and south by Pacific and Jackson streets, east and west by Front and Davis streets.

In good weather, brown baggers lunch on the grass, usually tidying up after themselves; for the visitor as well, the main interest here is in dining. **Square One** at 190 Pacific Street is one of the most innovative, excitingly eclectic restaurants in the state, with an emphasis on classic Mediterranean cooking, touched by California care for fresh ingredients (there's also a distinguished wine list); Tel: 788-1110.

(At 130 Pacific, just a few doors east of Square One, **TravelMarket** is a good source for travel books, maps, carry-on bags, and more.)

On the square's south side, hidden within the Golden Gateway complex on a wide walkway called Davis Court, **l'Olivier** (465 Davis Court) remains an enclave of excellence in the French style, unknown to many San Franciscans and well worth the search; Tel: 981-7824. At 607 Front Street, **MacArthur Park** serves oak-smoked baby back ribs often voted the best in the Bay Area, as well as salads, fresh fish, and aged meats in a very pretty garden setting.

A block west of the square at 290 Pacific, **Lafayette** adds nouvelle nuances to its French entrées, many of them with a pinch of Provence. It's small, convivial, and especially pleasant at lunch.

Levi Strauss Plaza

Landscape architect Lawrence Halprin has achieved the essence of urban greening in Levi Strauss Plaza, which lies just west of the Embarcadero between Greenwich and Union streets (north and south) and Sansome and Battery streets (east and west). If you're driving, this is a devil of a place to get into because of the one-way streets and the strange angles cut by the Embarcadero. The easiest approach is to go north on Sansome from downtown and into the public parking lot on the corner of Sansome and Greenwich.

The firm that gave its name to this plaza, and now has its headquarters here, was founded in 1853 as a wholesaler of dry goods and clothing, and supplied work pants made of denim material to the miners in Nevada during the Comstock bonanza days of the 1860s. A Reno tailor named Jacob W. Davis, finding he had to make too-frequent repairs to the pants, finally used harness-making tools to rivet the pocket corners and other areas of stress. He and Strauss applied for and received a patent on the process in 1873, and Levis took over the world. The original factory headquarters at 250 Valencia Street in the Mission district are now open for one-and-a-half-hour tours on Wednesdays at 10:30 A.M. (make reservations well in advance; Tel: 565-9153).

The waterfront today is much enhanced by the low-rise headquarters building off Levi Strauss Plaza, which blends so smoothly into the site it seems always to have been here. A dramatic granite fountain makes a stunning centerpiece.

On the north of the square, a branch of the noted Italian bakery-restaurant **Il Fornaio** is a popular stop. **Fog City**

Diner, across from the plaza at 1300 Battery Street, is one of the finest and most delightful dining sites in the city, most fun (and most crowded) at lunch. Here, chef Cindy Pawlcyn created the appetizers called "small plates," inspiring the practice of "grazing" through the menu, tasting several specialties. Don't miss the crab cakes; Tel: 982-2000.

If you do not want to walk the considerable distance from Embarcadero Center to Levi Strauss Plaza, take the number 42 bus north up Sansome Street to stops on the Embarcadero (the line continues along to Bay Street, North Point, and stops just south of The Cannery, Fisherman's Wharf, and Ghirardelli Square). In the opposite direction, number 42 runs south on Battery Street to California Street, where you can pick up the cable-car line.

CHINATOWN

The Chinese capital of the Western world, Chinatown is a 24-block labyrinth of food markets selling every Oriental delicacy you know of (and some you may not wish to encounter), fine restaurants in varying price ranges, temples, clan houses, souvenir stores, art and furniture shops, and banks, newspaper offices, and travel agencies where little English is spoken—all overlooked by a roofscape of arched eaves, carved cornices, and filigreed balconies.

Although it expands and shrinks as buildings rise and fall, Chinatown is generally considered to be bounded by Bush Street on the south, Broadway on the north, and Kearny and Stockton streets on the east and west. It is northeast of Union Square and west of Embarcadero Center.

How and why did the Chinese come to settle in such numbers? James Benét sums it up in *A Guide to San Francisco* (now out of print): "In 1848 three Chinese, probably the first, arrived in the brigantine *Eagle* to become servants for a prominent San Francisco family. Many more came to 'Gum Sahn' (Chinese for 'golden hills'), as they called San Francisco, during the Gold Rush. Though there were reportedly only 789 Chinese men and two Chinese women in the state at the beginning of 1850, there were more than 12,000 by the end of the following year—and yet only seven were women."

During the late 1860s and early 1870s thousands of Chinese laborers were imported to do *ku li* work (Chinese meaning "bitter toil," Anglicized to coolie), especially on the construction of the Central Pacific Railway. When Rudyard

Kipling visited in the 1880s he described the community as "A ward of the city of Canton set down in the most eligible business quarter of the place." In fact, the area that would become Chinatown had been the site of the first real settlement of San Francisco.

While San Francisco was born in 1776 with the dedication of the Presidio and the foundation of Misión San Francisco de Asís, the initial settlement of the city as we know it today did not occur for another 59 years—and then under a different name.

Captain William A. Richardson arrived in San Francisco in 1822, when the Mexican flag was flying over the Presidio, and by 1825 had determined to found a port town at the best anchoring place on San Francisco Bay. He selected Yerba Buena Cove (where much of the Financial District now sits on fill), and pitched a tent for himself and his family where Grant Avenue runs today between Clay and Washington streets. Within three months he had replaced it with a wooden house, the first in the new city of **Yerba Buena** (meaning "good herb," the wild mint). This site is described in Stanford University Press's *Historic Spots in California* as "... the first habitation ever erected in Yerba Buena. At the time, Richardson's only neighbors were bears, coyotes and wolves. The nearest people lived either at the Presidio or at Mission Dolores." Richardson was also the "solitary settler" described in Richard Henry Dana's *Two Years Before the Mast.* Today the name Yerba Buena is attached to the island on which the western span of the San Francisco–Oakland Bay Bridge is anchored.

Portsmouth Square

Originally the central plaza of the small Spanish settlement, this square in the heart of today's Chinatown takes its name from the U.S. sloop of war *Portsmouth,* captained by one John B. Montgomery who came ashore on July 9, 1846, at what is now the corner of Clay and Leidesdorff streets to take possession of Yerba Buena and its northern frontier for the United States, raising the Stars and Stripes on the plaza.

Today, smaller than it was a century and a half ago, Portsmouth is a green park atop the Portsmouth Square Garage, an unattractive but handy place to park your car while walking in the area. (The other choice is St. Mary's Square Garage at the corner of Kearny and California streets.)

Portsmouth is ignored by many visitors to Chinatown,

perhaps because they're intimidated by the happy squeals and squeaks of Asian children at play or the presence of old men bent over chess and checker boards. Thus they miss the Robert Louis Stevenson Monument and another corner of history. ". . . It was here Robert Louis went to observe at close range and to talk to the flotsam and jetsam of humanity drifting in from the mighty Pacific Ocean. Who knows but he found here Long John Silver and Blind Pew?" (from *Historic Spots*).

There are plans to place a cast-bronze replica of the flimsy Goddess of Democracy, created by the students killed in Beijing's Tiananmen Square in 1989, here in the plaza.

The saloons and gambling dens of Portsmouth Plaza in the 1850s have been replaced by a Holiday Inn on the east, across Kearny Street, and to the north at 720 Washington Street by **Buddha's Universal Church**, stark and white on the exterior and handsomely decorated on the interior. Tours for visitors are given on Sundays only between 1:00 and 3:00 P.M.

On the west, the square (much smaller than in its plaza days) is walled off and overlooked by a business building, on the sixth floor of which is the beautiful **Empress of China** restaurant. Although more expensive than most of its neighbors, it's popular with visitors for its setting and because English is well understood by the friendly staff; enter at 838 Grant Avenue.

Grant Avenue

For many travellers, Chinatown begins at the **Gateway to Chinatown** at Grant Avenue and Bush Street, a green-and-ochre doorway adorned with benevolent dragons and stone lions; this southern gateway to Chinatown first opened in 1970. (Should you want to walk here from Union Square, go east on Maiden Lane, then north on Grant past Post and Sutter streets to Bush.) Through the gate, you step onto Grant Avenue, surely the most famous street in Chinatown.

Grant Avenue is San Francisco's oldest artery (though some still claim that distinction for 16th Street along the old road to the bay from Mission Dolores). The muddy, rutted original street was *calle de la Fundación* (Street of the Founding) in the Spanish settlement of Yerba Buena. With Yankee rule, the name was changed to Dupont (to honor naval Captain Samuel F. Du Pont, though misspelled), but by the late 1800s, Du Pon Gai (as the Chinese called it; *gai* means "street") had gained such an unsavory reputation as the sinful site of tong wars, opium dens, and slave sing-song girls that the downtown merchants fostered an upgrading name change to Grant (for Ulysses S., the country's 18th president).

Grant is indisputably (and successfully) commercial and tourist oriented. At the gateway the Chinese-character street signs, dragon-entwined lampposts, and pagoda-topped telephone booths begin. Here the Guang-zhou dialect (Cantonese) is the mother tongue, and the rash of restaurants ranges from the **Imperial Palace** to hole-in-the-wall bakeries selling irresistible moon cakes and sesame cookies. (Imperial Palace is one of the best restaurants, Oriental or Occidental, in the city. In beautiful surroundings, order such specialties as minced squab with plum sauce and Peking duck. It's at 919 Grant Avenue.)

Two blocks north of Bush Street, a most un-Chinese structure dominates the setting: **Old St. Mary's Church** at the Grant–California street corner. This was the first Roman Catholic cathedral on the Pacific Coast (1854); its brick supposedly sailed around Cape Horn, while its granite base is believed to have come from China.

On **St. Mary's Square**, a tiny, tidy park across California Street from Old St. Mary's, a 12-foot rose-granite-and-stainless-steel statue of Sun Yat-sen, founder of the Chinese republic, by the city's beloved sculptor Beniamino Bufano faces a bronze screen commemorating Americans of Chinese ancestry who gave their lives for America in World Wars I and II. Sun Yat-sen founded the city's *Young China* newspaper in the early 1900s.

A longtime favorite restaurant at 717 California Street (a few steps west of Grant) is **Yamato**, not Chinese but Japanese, with imaginative dishes and a choice of Western or Oriental seating (low tables with leg wells). Across the street at number 718, **Cathay House** has been a landmark since 1938. It's quite inexpensive.

If, as tradition says, dragons are benevolent, the Bank of America branch at 701 Grant fairly roars with good will—golden dragons breathe fire from its front columns and doors, and 60 dragon medallions line the façade. The Citibank Savings branch at 845 Grant answers with grimacing temple dogs.

When Johnny Kan opened nearby **Kan's** in 1953 it immediately became one of the country's best-known Chinese restaurants. Today Johnny has gone but his welcoming tradition lingers at 708 Grant.

Around the corner at 743 Washington Street, the **Old Chinese Telephone Exchange** has become the Bank of Canton, but preserves its delightful, slightly giddy Oriental aspect. (Until 1949, when the dial system was installed, this exchange was staffed by operators fluent in English and in five Chinese dialects. Because Chinese ideograms are not arranged in "alphabetical" order, the directory went by streets, the ones with the most subscribers being listed first.)

At 650 Commercial Street (a bit to the east in the Financial District) between Kearny and Montgomery, the important role of Chinese immigrants in the development of the West's mining, rail, and fishing industries is delineated in the **Chinese Historical Society of America**. The collection includes artifacts, photos, and Gold Rush relics, and is open noon to 4:00 P.M. Wednesdays through Sundays.

Farther north on Grant at Jackson Street, veer west into little **Ross Alley**, a hive of jewelry shops where prices are not low but not exorbitant either, and quality is high. You can also visit the **Golden Gate Fortune Cookie Factory**.

Handcarved dragons guard the entrance to **Grand Palace Restaurant**, 950 Grant Avenue, where dim sum snacking is a pleasant pastime. At Broadway, Grant leaps from Chinatown into the pasta-panettone belt of North Beach (see below).

Stockton Street

Grant Avenue is theater; Stockton Street, one block to its west, is workaday life, a hustle and bustle of Asians in a world largely untrammeled by tourism. The feel of it is very foreign to a visitor, even to the San Franciscan who encounters here several civilizations that may be very different from his own.

From Union Square, the way leads north past the handy Sutter-Stockton Garage and into the Stockton Tunnel, which runs under Nob Hill from Sutter to Sacramento Street. Immediately at its north end you plunge into a very different sea, as much today as in the 1870s, when an eastern visitor, Benjamin F. Taylor, wrote, ". . . at the turn of a corner and the breadth of a street, think of dropping with the abruptness of a shifting dream into China, beneath the standard of Hoang-ti who sits upon the dragon throne. . . ."

Immediately upon your exit from the tunnel, nod your respects in a westerly direction toward the **Cameron House** at 920 Sacramento Street, where one Donaldina Cameron of the Presbyterian Church "saved" more than 2,000 slave sing-song girls who, with the connivance of U.S. officials, were imported, bought, and sold to brothels and individual owners.

At 843 Stockton Street, the gaudy headquarters of the

Chinese Six Companies (formally, the Chinese Consolidated Benevolent Association) is a banquet of beasts (guardian lions, dragons, birds, fish) and a tempest of colors (lucky red, glaring yellow, glossy green, brilliant blue). The Six Companies organized in the 1850s to represent the six different districts of the Canton (Guang-zhou) province that operated the U.S. depot of the Chinese labor trade; political and business disputes still tend to be arbitrated here.

The **U.S. Post Office—cum—Kong Chow Temple** at the corner of Stockton and Clay streets represents the oldest family association in the United States. The temple proper, on the top floor, is open to the public daily, and its antique furnishings will remind you of Hong Kong or Singapore. The patron deity is Kuan Ti, god of those undertaking hazardous work (such as the Gold Rush's *ku li*).

On the opposite side of Stockton, the very fine **Celadon** restaurant glows with that distinctive glaze invented during the Tang dynasty. It's quieter than most Chinese restaurants (a blessing), the atmosphere is elegant, and the broiled lobster with ginger sauce may turn you into a ram (a beast of good taste). A few steps east of Stockton off Sacramento, the alley known as Hang Ah stars the **Hang Ah Tea Room**, a great place to go for dim sum.

Farther east of Stockton and of Hang Ah Alley, turn north into the second opening off Sacramento, **Waverly Place**. It's only two blocks long, but it may put you more in mind of China than any other cultural corner in town. A street of brothels before the 1906 earthquake, it's now a collection of architecturally interesting family and benevolent association offices. The one structure worth visiting is **Tien Hou Temple** (often spelled Tin How) at 125 Waverly. Established by one of the first three Chinese to arrive in San Francisco, it features an altar to Tien Hou, Queen of the Heavens and Goddess of the Seven Seas, that had been installed on the ship for daily worship during the long crossing and later was removed to the temple. From the ground floor, climb the stairs to the temple, a fine place for contemplation of the cultures that make up San Francisco; open daily.

The Chinese devotion to dining becomes clear along the Stockton blocks numbered 1000–1200, a cacaphonous conglomeration of ginger roots and bamboo shoots, golden-glazed ducks and whole drawn pigs, lichee nuts, sharks' fins, seahorses, tankfuls of fish, and crates of cackling chickens.

Chinatown officially ends at Broadway, where North Beach begins (see below).

NOB HILL

Originally, historians say, it was Fern Hill, then Hill of Golden Promise, then California Street Hill and/or Nob Hill. Whatever. For more than a century, Nob Hill, just west of Chinatown, has been associated in travellers' imaginations with the upper crust, le beau monde.

There are two explanations for the name Nob. The more prosaic one is that it means merely "knob" or rounded hill, but the one preferred by most San Franciscans makes it a contraction of the Hindu word *nabob* or *nawab:* "a wealthy or powerful person; especially a person who has made a large fortune in India or another country of the East."

San Francisco's nobs made their fortunes in the West in the mid-1800s in gold, silver, and railroading. At the time of the 1848 gold strike, this scrub-covered hill rising 376 feet above the waterfront was virtually inaccessible; its steep grade (24.8 degrees on the south face) made the ascent difficult for even the strongest horses. Then Andrew S. Hallidie invented the cable cars, and the uphill climb became a power trip.

There had been a handful of fine houses on the hill: Senator George Hearst (father of the founder of the newspaper empire and great-grandfather of today's publisher of the *San Francisco Examiner*) is said to have inhabited a Spanish stucco mansion; William T. Coleman seems to have built a Roman villa in a walled garden. With the advent of the cable car, though, the real rush was on.

Among the first to build their fanciful mansions on the rise (in the 1870s) were the railroad barons of the Central (then Southern) Pacific Railroad known as the Big Four: Charles Crocker, Leland Stanford, Mark Hopkins, and Collis Huntington. (At the time, some dubbed them the Four-Armed Cuttlefish. Today they are remembered more politely in the **Big Four** restaurant of California Street's Huntington hotel.) Close on the barons' heels trod the Bonanza Kings of the Comstock Lode: James Flood and James G. Fair. Their creations were flights of flamboyance, outbursts of ornamentation, exuberance carried to excess, and they must have been wonderful to behold; however, all but one burned in 1906.

Stand today near the one survivor, an imposing brownstone erected by Flood (at 1000 California Street at Mason) in 1886. Aloof as ever behind its solid-brass filigree fence, it is now the **Pacific Union Club**, a domain of contemporary magnates currently under attack from women and minorities excluded from membership.

From "the P-U," as it's irreverently known, you can look all around to where the palaces once stood. On the immediate east, the **Fairmont Hotel** occupies the block where James G. Fair ("Bonanza Jim") intended to build his home. His marriage broke up before he could do so, and he left the site to his children. Daughter Theresa Alice (Tessie) had begun work on a grand hotel, but before it opened, while furniture stood crated on its lawns, came the earthquake. Novelist Gertrude Atherton left a memorable description of the fire that swept uphill on April 19, 1906: "I forgot the doomed city as I gazed at the Fairmont, a tremendous volume of white smoke pouring from where its roof had been, every window a shimmer sheet of gold; not a flame, not a spark shot forth. The Fairmont will never be as demonic in its beauty again." One year to the day later, the hotel reopened, a masterwork of the architectural art of Julia Morgan.

Just across California Street to the southeast of the P-U, Mary Hopkins (wife of Mark) brought forth the most ostentatious of all the homes of the Nob-ility. As described by Randolph Delehanty, it was "a phantasmagoria of turrets, gables, pinnacles, and chimneys with a great Gothic-style conservatory." What Mark (who liked to pull weeds in his garden) felt about it is not known. Today's stately **Mark Hopkins Inter-Continental** opened on the site in 1926, and has a history of debuts, dinner dancing, Junior League doings, and Barbara Hutton honeymoons. It set the style in skyrooms when the **Top of the Mark** opened in 1939, just in time for the men of World War II's Pacific forces to flock up to the 537-foot-high bar in order to say good-bye to the city and their sweethearts.

The Hopkins's downhill neighbors on the east were the Stanfords. (Stanford had bought the whole block and sold the uphill portion to his partner.) Like the other barons, the Stanfords were not entirely happy in their house, an Italianate structure of truly imposing demeanor. Their beloved boy, Leland Stanford, Jr., died at age 15 on a family trip to Italy, and the bereaved parents endowed in his memory the prestigious university that bears his name (see Day Trips from San Francisco). Today the massive granite-and-basalt wall that buttresses two sides of the block is the only vestige of the Stanfords's city estate, and the **Stanford Court Hotel** rises here above California and Powell streets where the city's three cable-car lines intersect.

Just down the slope, one of the city's best examples of Neoclassical architecture, a 17-columned building erected in 1909 for Metropolitan Life Insurance, then home to Cogswell College, will in 1991 become **The Ritz-Carlton** hotel. Part of the site was occupied by Grace Episcopal Church, which was destroyed in the 1906 earthquake and succeeded by Grace Cathedral atop Nob Hill. Renowned landscape architect Thomas Church designed the ornamental garden courtyard.

To the southwest of the P-U Club, the stylish **Huntington Hotel** should, historically speaking, be called the Tobin, because the corner it dominates at California and Taylor was first graced by 1849 gold-seeker Richard Tobin's Victorian mansion. A succession of royals has slept at the Huntington (Princesses Margaret and Grace, Prince Charles) as well as a clutch of celebrities—Alistair Cooke, Luciano Pavarotti, Lauren Bacall, and Leontyne Price among them. In a little alcove near the ladies' restroom by the entrance to the Big Four restaurant there's a photographic display of Nob Hill as it looked in 1877, by the renowned Eadweard Muybridge; it's a museum piece worth seeking out.

Across a tiny lane to the west of the Pacific Union Club, lovely little **Huntington Park**, with a copy of Rome's Fountain of the Turtles in the center, is a serene spot where the David Colton abode once stood; it was purchased by Collis P. Huntington in 1892. After the 1906 fire, Huntington's widow gave the site to the city, and now it's a proper setting for perambulators and poodles and historically minded passersby.

To the west of Huntington Park across Taylor Street rises the great, gray pile of **Grace Episcopal Cathedral**, the largest Gothic structure in the West. Two residences of the Charles Crocker family once stood on this block; when both homes were burned in 1906 the land was donated to the church, although construction of the cathedral did not begin until 1927. Today it is much visited by those in search of beauty as well as by believers; the magnificent organ and the excellent boys' choir are attractions in themselves. None of the cathedral's treasures is more arresting than its Lorenzo Ghiberti doors, casts of the gilded-bronze doors created by the 15th-century sculptor for the baptistry in Florence. Their ten rectangular reliefs depict scenes from the Old Testament; they stand at the top of the steps to the cathedral's east entrance.

Directly south of the cathedral, the **Masonic Temple** is of interest for the concerts played in its hall and for its well-located parking garage. (Other parking areas are at the

Crocker Garage between Mason and Taylor, and under the
Fairmont, entry from Powell.)

In addition to the restaurants within Nob Hill's hotels,
several other rooms at the top are worth checking out. When
you arrive at **Le Club**, you know that the demons of bad taste
and incivility will never find you. The expense-account and
anniversary set takes the traditional French cuisine and
cosseting seriously at 1250 Jones Street; Tel: 771-5400.

When **Vanessi's** was down in North Beach, it was spirited,
robust, and the place to go for a good, old-fashioned Italian
time. Now that it's on Nob Hill (at 1177 California Street), it's
spirited, robust, and the place to go for a good, old-
fashioned Italian time; Tel: 771-2422. Just a block down the
Mason Street hill from the Mark Hopkins, at 900 Pine Street,
the small and pretty bistro **Rue Lepic** serves unpretentious
but properly prepared French food. It's a favorite when you
don't want to splurge but want things right.

RUSSIAN HILL

This hill is a fashionable residential district defined by the
Russian Hill Neighbors Association as 34 blocks between
Pacific Avenue on the south and Francisco on the north,
Taylor on the east and Polk on the west. It is just north of
Nob Hill and was named for the graves of several Russian fur
trappers who were interred atop the mount; the precise sites
are no longer known.

According to *Historic Spots in California,* "Gallows for the
first official execution in San Francisco were erected one
hundred feet west of the summit . . . and there a Spaniard
who had committed a murder in Happy Valley—now the
vicinity of Mission Street between First and Third streets—
was hanged."

The one renowned tourist attraction on Russian Hill is the
so-called crookedest street in the world, a section of **Lombard Street** that twists eastward and downhill along the nine
hairpins between Hyde and Leavenworth streets. At this
writing, dwellers along Lombard are petitioning the city to
outlaw traffic except by residents.

If you have a particular interest in San Francisco's residential architecture, take the Hyde Street cable car to its stop at
Hyde and Lombard and walk around the neighborhood, or
take a taxi to the intersection of Russian Hill Place and
Vallejo, considered the hill's summit. Several interesting

houses are in the immediate area, including those on the cul-de-sac of Florence Street.

NORTH BEACH

As an observer of the local scene put it some time ago, "Naples is just across the street from Hong Kong." The split personality once so evident where Chinatown's Grant Avenue runs north into Broadway and Columbus Avenue has become less distinct in recent years, however, since Chinese families have been crowded out of their traditional home and have settled in North Beach with the Italians. Now you're likely to find tea-smoked duck next to *dindo,* lamb Szechwan edging *sacripantina.*

The first Italians arrived during the Gold Rush and were followed by thousands during the next decades, most of them from northern Italy—Genoa, Piedmont, and Tuscany. The first Sicilian fishermen came in the early 1880s, and by 1885 the community had established its own Italian Chamber of Commerce.

Cradled by Telegraph Hill on the east and Russian Hill on the west, North Beach really was a beach in the 1850s, when the shore of the bay extended far inland between the two hills. Today it remains a bohemian bastion, where the action is in cabarets, jazz clubs, galleries, inns, and several caffès and *ristorantes* worth a drive across town.

Washington Square

Nobody knows precisely which street marks the northern boundary of the Beach, but everybody agrees that the heart of the matter is Washington Square, with Filbert Street and the imposing **Church of Saints Peter and Paul** on the north, and by Union, Powell, Stockton, and Columbus forming the other sides of this five-sided square.

If the purpose of a park is public pleasure, Washington Square ranks among the most pleasant little greenswards in the country. Children scamper and giggle, watched by their grandmothers; grandfathers stretch out under the shade trees; young people picnic; and tourists come out of the **Washington Square Inn**, smile, and stroll across the square to see what's happening at Washington Square Bar & Grill. On Sundays pretty young girls and handsome dandies dally in front of Saints Peter and Paul, awaiting the arrival of yet another Italian bride and groom.

The church, beautifully illuminated at night, is a neo-Romanesque classic, designed in 1922 but not completed for 20 years. Known as "the church of the fishermen," it's the departure site for the annual Columbus Day Celebration parade. Inside, the church is as thronged with saints as the square is with squatters; it well repays a short visit.

Washington Square Bar & Grill at 1707 Powell Street is a noisy, happy institution, especially popular with members of the local and national media, who have made of it their hideout. Drinks are pleasantly outsized, the menu features fresh pastas daily, and the kitchen staff has a good hand with fish. This is a fine place to introduce yourself to local petrale sole, which many San Franciscans prefer to the Dover variety.

On the south side of the square, **Fior d'Italia** at 601 Union Street claims to be the oldest Italian restaurant in town; it has been serving veal parmigiana for more than a century, and some of the original waiters seem still to be around; Tel: 986-1886. Also a square institution, **Coit Liquors** at 585 Columbus is a fine place to shop for picnic wines, especially some Italian favorites you can't find everywhere. On the corner at 673 Union Street, **Little City Antipasti Bar** serves drinks and *antipasti* all day long.

Broadway

This strip, which slices east to west from the Embarcadero to Lyon Street and the Presidio, lives several lives. In North Beach from the Embarcadero to the Broadway Tunnel it's gaudy, glittering, raucous, and even rude. (In the 1960s the devil-may-care days of Carol Doda and the Topless Mother of Eight, this stretch of the street was called, with a nod to Italy, the Bay of Nipples.) At the western end of the tunnel, Broadway blossoms with small businesses, crosses Van Ness, and matures into the conservative chic of Pacific Heights' monumental *palazzi,* such as the James Leary Flood mansion at number 2120 that's now the Hamlin School.

In the 1930s and 1940s Broadway was a fairly unsavory haunt of bootleggers and frequenters of brothels and pool halls. The 1950s are now considered the good old days, when Mort Sahl, Lenny Bruce, Barbra Streisand, and other soon-to-be superstars played Enrico Banducci's hungry i, and such clubs as the Purple Onion, Barnaby Conrad's El Matador, and the Jazz Workshop catered to a loud, lively, good-time crowd, watched over by the sidewalk table-sitters at Enrico's.

In the 1960s the scene changed again, with the arrival of more than 20 topless clubs of increasing raunchiness. It's still bawdy, but since the late 1970s it has cleaned up its act somewhat; most travellers, except the youngest and most active, may prefer to visit only during the day.

The newest attempt to bring back the good old spirit on the strip is **Rumors**, at Kearny and Broadway, where pasta is the accompaniment to cappuccino, live music, and poetry readings. Even the prices are a look back at the past. Farther east, those who like it hot and hotter cannot resist **Hunan** at 924 Sansome (at Broadway), where the tough come to cry happily while cooking their tonsils. Moving back to the west: **The Stone** at 412 Broadway offers comedy, light rock, jazz, and even music the middle-aged can dance to. Call to see what's going on; Tel: 391-8282.

A new taste blossoms along Broadway these days at **Helmand**, number 430, where Afghani cuisine is making a hit; the look is civilized and the prices extremely reasonable. A celebrated and rather new Chinese restaurant farther west at 450–52 Broadway, **Brandy Ho's** is theatrical in appearance, rewarding in taste. The cuisine is Hunan, without the use of MSG. Try the sweet-and-sour spareribs. People-watching at outside tables is the sport at the landmark **Enrico's**, 504 Broadway, a great spot for a lazy lunch in the sun.

At 540 Broadway, **Columbus Books** sells both new and used books, with a particularly decent travel section. Here, you can either continue up Columbus or take a sharp right onto upper Grant Avenue (for which see below).

There's nothing smart or stylish about dining à la Basque in San Francisco, but if you're in the mood for old-fashioned, long-table, family-style food, try one of the city's traditional Basque cafés. Two right at hand here are **Basque Hotel and Restaurant** at 15 Romolo Place (an alley north of Broadway between Kearny and Columbus), and **Des Alpes**, 732 Broadway.

At the corner of Columbus and Broadway, look south and back into the 1950s, where two landmarks of the Beat Generation, **Vesuvio's** and the **City Lights Booksellers and Publishers**, face each other along tiny Adler Place. The movement's credo was Jack Kerouac's *On the Road,* published in 1957, and the place you sat to read it was Lawrence Ferlinghetti's City Lights, perhaps in the company of Allen Ginsberg, Gregory Corso, Norman Mailer, and such non-

"beats" as Kenneth Patchen, Alan Watts, and Kenneth Rexroth. It wasn't a Parisian salon, but perhaps as close as San Francisco will get to one.

Just south, Vesuvio's lives under a sign over the entrance that reads, "We are itching to get away from Portland, Oregon." Artists and poets, the nostalgic and the curious, come to see who else is here; the upstairs is quieter and has a booth dedicated to Lady Psychiatrists.

If you walk south two blocks on Columbus to Jackson, you'll find **Thomas Bros. Maps**, with an unequalled selection of maps of every size, shape, and persuasion, as well as atlases, guides, globes, interesting software products for street-finding, and more.

Upper Grant Avenue

To gain a sense of North Beach, to savor it, you should walk both upper Grant and Columbus from Broadway.

Upper Grant—haunted by the ghosts of such well-known Beat Generation hangouts as The Place and the Coexistence Bagel Shop—is now a hodgepodge of garment shops, galleries, cappuccino houses, collectibles stores, and small cafés. The traffic is north, one-way, and tight. The Beatniks' Coffee Gallery at number 1353 is now the **Lost & Found Saloon**, where you may choose to be either. At 601 Vallejo, corner of Grant, the **Caffè Trieste** continues through the century just as it began, serving coffee and meals in the traditional Italian manner; coffee beans are sold, retail and wholesale, at number 609.

Some people like mucking about in boats; others beat it to hardware stores and let their eyes glaze over with joy as they rummage among tools, a few of which have no recognizable use. The place for that pastime is **Figoni** at number 1351, so old-fashioned it still has that Sherwin-Williams Cover the Earth paint sign. Small boxes demanding to be opened and sorted through line the wooden shelves.

Columbus Avenue

The diagonal of Columbus cuts across the grid pattern of North Beach from Washington Street northwest to Beach Street. It's really Little Italy's Main Street. Caffès cluster along Columbus, interspersed with such finds as **Molinari's Delicatessen** at number 373, which has been a local landmark since 1896. The deli makes its own ravioli and *tagliarini* and cures its own dry salami. After café-sitting, amble into **Biordi**

Art Imports at 412 Columbus, where the hand-painted din-
nerware and the gourmet gadgets may prove irresistible
(purchases can be shipped).

The **Caffè Roma** coffeehouse next door is particularly
easygoing, and no one will mind if you while an hour away
with your cappuccino. There's even a curiously country-style
inn here, one of the few recommendable places to stay in
the area, though it can be noisy at night: the **Millefiori Inn**.

At 1435 Stockton Street, corner of Columbus, the Eureka
Federal Savings building houses on its mezzanine the **North
Beach Museum**, where the history of this whole area—
Chinatown, North Beach, and Fisherman's Wharf—is illus-
trated in changing exhibits of photographs and relics.

On the corner where Columbus, Stockton, and Grant
meet, the **North Beach Restaurant** remains a favorite with
local regulars despite occasional swipes by critics (usually
from somewhere else) who complain it's too crowded and
popular. Well? They do a superb job with calamari and other
local compulsions. The zaniest show in town, *Beach Blanket
Babylon,* carries on, apparently in permanence, at **Club
Fugazi** (see Bars and Nightlife section), 678 Green Street, in
a little wedge between Columbus and Powell.

San Francisco's *Epicurean Rendezvous* magazine ranks
Buca Giovanni, 800 Greenwich Street at Columbus, among
the top 100 restaurants in Northern California, no mean
achievement for this brick-walled, semi-cellar that opened in
1983 to serve Tuscan specialties. Don't miss the round ravi-
olini stuffed with eggplant and Gorgonzola in a basil sauce;
Tel: 776-7766. Across the street, North Beach Playground saw
success approach for many budding athletic stars, among
them Joe DiMaggio. Several blocks farther north on Columbus you'll reach Beach Street and Fisherman's Wharf, but
first make a detour to the east along Greenwich Street to
Telegraph Hill.

TELEGRAPH HILL

The first European to see San Francisco Bay, José de Ortega
climbed the 275-foot hill then called La Loma Alta on November 1, 1769—and from there spotted a whole new world. In
the early 1840s, Loma Alta was dubbed Windmill Hill, but in
1849 it began to be used as a station from which to observe
incoming vessels, and was often called Signal Hill. Watchers
within a two-story house would signal by semaphore the
type of ship arriving to people concerned in the city below:

side-wheeler, sailing vessel, etc. On October 29, 1850, the
station signaled the arrival of the steamer *Oregon,* bearing
the news that California had been admitted to the Union.
Stories say that huge hilltop bonfires burned all night. In
1853 Loma Alta became the first western telegraph station,
and the name Telegraph Hill stuck.

The first inhabitants of the hill had been grazing goats,
which were gradually displaced by little homes that rose
atop the hill, populated by Italians, Spaniards, Portuguese, or
French as the hill became the Latin Quarter, and later, in the
1890s, the Artists' Colony. Mark Twain lived on Telegraph
Hill, as did Frank Norris, Joaquin Miller, Ambrose Bierce,
Charles Warren Stoddard, and actor Edwin Booth. Bret Harte
complained that goats browsed on the geraniums in his
second-story windows and clattered over the roof at night
"like heavy hailstones."

Today Telegraph Hill is an apartment- and cottage-covered
rise with North Beach around its feet, the Embarcadero and
waterfront below its steep eastern face (where sailors once
dug out ballast for their ships and which was used as a quarry
after 1906). It looks west toward Russian Hill, once separated
from it by a swamp. Telegraph Hill remains a much-sought-
after address, especially among people in newspapers, broad-
casting, advertising, and the like, who may hope some of the
genius of the past will rub off on them.

Seeing the Hill

The steep, wooden Filbert Street steps at the corner of
Kearny Street lead up the west side of hill, flanked by lovely
gardens. An alternative to climbing the steps is the number
39 Coit bus, which can be boarded at Washington Square or
along Bay Street south of Fisherman's Wharf. The hill traffic
is terrible in summers, curving slowly up Telegraph Hill
Boulevard; it's recommended not to drive but to climb the
steps or take the bus.

Just east of the curve where Lombard becomes Telegraph
Hill Boulevard you'll spot a bench and bas-relief memorial
to Guglielmo Marconi, inventor of wireless telegraph, and
thus right at home on this hill.

On top, the famous monument often likened to a fire-
hose nozzle is **Coit Tower**, a memorial to the volunteer
firemen of early days (who well deserved it), built with a
bequest from Mrs. Lillie Hitchcock Coit, who at age eight in
1851 came to the city with her family and became a fire buff
(and, eventually, an honorary firefighter). The memorial,

which she dedicated to "the purpose of adding beauty to the city I have always loved," was erected in 1933 after her death.

The interior is covered with murals depicting the working life of 1930s California; 20 local artists were employed in a most unusual work-relief project for its time. The works differ markedly in style and substance, but are worth seeing. An elevator in the tower goes up to a platform from which 20-odd steps lead to the open loggia with a panoramic view; carry your wide-angle and telephoto lenses. Also atop the hill, in Pioneer Park, is an unremarkable bronze statue of Columbus.

Two sets of steps lead down the eastern side: the Greenwich Steps and the Filbert Steps. The former, hidden by foliage, begin near the light pole at the corner of the round-about, across from the tower. They lead to Montgomery Street and **Julius Castle** at number 1541. Built in 1921 by an exuberant Italian hand, this restaurant has always been popular with visitors for its views of the bay. It has been revitalized and now presents respectable European cuisine, perhaps a bit elevated in price to match the view. There's valet parking, a necessity (see Bars and Nightlife.)

The Filbert Steps march precariously down from Telegraph Hill Boulevard itself from a point before you reach Coit Tower; they are an extension of the ones coming up from Kearny, and they descend among lovely gardens maintained by residents as a tribute to the late Grace Marchant, the enthusiast of city beautification who was the force behind their creation. Near their intersection with Montgomery, at number 1349, you'll find **The Shadows**, once a rustic German restaurant, now an airy aerie specializing in contemporary French cuisine.

Continuing down Filbert, peek into pretty, flowery Napier Lane. The steps become a concrete stairway, unattractive but more stable, when they cross the former quarry at the bottom of the hill, depositing you near Levi Plaza (see Embarcadero Center Area above).

FISHERMAN'S WHARF AREA

The Fisherman's Wharf of history, of tourism, and of a San Franciscan's imagination are three very different entities. Historically, the waterfront from Taylor to Leavenworth streets was set aside in 1900 by local authorities as the province of commercial fishermen, who had been catching in the bay since 1848. Since then it has stretched west to

Hyde Street and east to Pier 39. To the tourist, it may mean the happy honky-tonk along Jefferson Street, loud with street musicians, clowns, and vendors of (mostly) junky jewelry, or a swirl of shops selling tee-shirts, sandals, and trinkets. There are also many "attractions" and "amusements" of doubtful value.

To the San Franciscan, however (he stays away in summer), the Wharf is a wider term that includes some of the old seafood restaurants, the historic ships, the National Maritime Museum, The Cannery complex off Leavenworth Street, Ghirardelli Square off Beach Street between Larkin and Polk, and the Golden Gate National Recreation Area. It behooves the thoughtful traveller to take the locals' view.

The Wharf area, north of North Beach and northwest of Telegraph Hill, is served by the Powell–Mason cable cars from Powell and Market streets to Taylor and Bay; by the Powell–Hyde line from the Powell/Market turntable to Victorian Park; by MUNI bus number 19 from Civic Center up Polk; and by bus number 30 from Union Square through the heart of North Beach.

In the 1960s the Wharf was transformed for the better by the metamorphosis of the Ghirardelli Chocolate Factory and the rebuilding of the California Fruit Cannery, and in 1978 by the building of Pier 39. We look at the whole district— and its associated attractions, such as ferry excursions—from east to west.

Pier 39

Once an abandoned cargo dock, Pier 39 today is a thronging waterfront marketplace that ranks among the town's top tourism beats. Its two levels of shops and restaurants are connected by a pedestrian bridge to a 1,000-car garage on Beach Street that offers the best and easiest parking along the whole seaside sweep. (There is also a garage at Jefferson and Jones, and one underneath Ghirardelli Square.)

On the east side of Pier 39, small boats bob in a 350-berth marina (at this writing, herds of honking sea lions are calling it home, to the amusement of visitors and the vast irritation of boaters). From the west side, the craft of the Blue & Gold Fleet depart on periodic cruises (frequent daily departures, dependent on season; Tel: 781-7877) and from the entrance of the pier, the motorized cable cars of Pier 39 Cable Car Co. leave frequently for one-hour trips (Tel: 39-CABLE).

Within the complex, the **San Francisco Experience**, a theatrical trip through the city's past and present in light, sound, and special effects, offers shows daily, every half hour; Tel: 982-7550. (During the October, 1989, earthquake, the audience at the Experience confused special effects with reality.)

That the architecture of Pier 39 represents Old San Francisco is a fiction; it more resembles an attempt at New England Quaint. Although this is a fast-food lover's fantasyland, it is possible to step out of the stream and into the comparative quiet of a handful of recommended restaurants, all on the second level. Spacious **Dante's Sea Catch** serves seafood in a casual though proper setting with smashing views at the very end of the pier; the old **Eagle Café**, a waterfront hangout for fishermen and longshoremen since 1928, was moved here from its original site and is as real and innocently raunchy as ever (breakfast and lunch only). **Swiss Louis** calls its cuisine Italian-Continental, while **Old Swiss House** goes for French fare modified by Swiss-style lace curtains and beamed ceilings. **Vannelli's** serves fine seafood, while **Yet Wah** lists 200 dishes from across China; bring your appetite.

Alcatraz

The tomb-like bulk of the bastion of Alcatraz pokes up from the glistening bay in sharp contrast to the bustling, park-like scene at **Pier 41**, where ferry passengers waiting to board photograph the flower gardens, the high-flying balloons, and the passing cable cars and horse-drawn carriages.

Fact and fiction collide in the story of Alcatraz, *La Isla de los Alcatraces* (Isle of Pelicans). "Hellcatraz," it has been called; also, more familiarly, The Rock, a fearsome fortification since 1858 that became a maximum security federal prison in the 1930s. In 1963 the last 27 inmates were transferred to other penal institutions, and in 1971 the Native Americans who had subsequently claimed it were evacuated.

Alcatraz joined the Golden Gate National Recreation Area when that entity was created in 1972 and, under the custody of the National Park Service, is now one of the most popular attractions in California.

It's a ruin now, but the main block with its steel bars, claustrophobic cells, mess hall, library, and "dark holes" stands intact. It is difficult to imagine, but three inmates—Frank Lee Morris and John and Clarence Anglin—tunneled out with sharpened spoons in 1962 after years of struggle. They were never found.

Access to the 12-acre island is free; the ferry fee is minimal. Red & White ferries cast off from Pier 41 at 45-minute intervals (every half hour on weekends). The tour includes a self-guided trail, slide show, audio-cassette tours narrated by former guards and prisoners, and special programs. Wear comfortable shoes and warm clothing whatever the season, and make reservations up to two weeks in advance during summer; the fee can be charged to MasterCard or VISA (Tel: 392-7469; for tour information, Tel: 546-2896).

Also from Pier 41, ferries of the Red & White Fleet (see Getting Around below) depart on excursion sailings to Vallejo and the Marine World Africa USA amusement park (Tel: 546-BOAT); **Pier 43½** is the departure point for Angel Island (see below) and Tiburon (see Day Trips from San Francisco) Tel: 435-2131; as well as for sightseeing boats that do a 45-minute bay circuit.

The **U.S.S. Pampanito**, a World War II submarine built in 1943 at Portsmouth Naval Shipyard, New Hampshire, is open to the public daily at Pier 45. Operated by the National Maritime Museum Association, it offers exhibits and self-guided audio tours.

Angel Island

The largest, least-known island in the bay is Angel, more precisely *Nuestra Señora de los Angeles,* christened on August 13, 1775, by Lieutenant Juan Manuel de Ayala, who probably was the first European to sail into the bay through the Golden Gate. Today it is a California State Park with a resident population of eight caretakers, four park rangers, and 200 or so deer, and serves (to those in on the secret) as a San Francisco escape hatch.

The 740-acre island is reached by Red & White ferries from Fisherman's Wharf (Tel: 546-2896 for seasonal schedules), and is also linked by short trips across Raccoon Strait from Tiburon in Marin County (see Day Trips from San Francisco). Pack a lunch, and from the dock in the island's small cove, climb a grassy rise to the picnic tables. After lunch you can amble the 12 miles of roads and hiking trails. A small museum and partially restored immigration station (almost 200,000 Chinese passed through it from 1910 to 1940) contain relics of the island's past as a military post and quarantine station. Tel: 435-1915 for information on types and locations of campsites; Tel; (800) 444-7275 for reservations only.

Seafood by the Bay

Dining, especially on seafood, is and always has been a major diversion around Fisherman's Wharf. Old Italian names reveal the fishermen's inheritance—**Alioto's No. 8** (the oldest restaurant on the wharf); **Lolli's Castagnola** (one Tomasso Castagnola seems to have invented the walkaway crab cocktail in 1916); **Pompeii's Grotto** (fresh seafood and Italian cuisine for more than 40 years); **A. Sabella's** (more than 65 years old); **Scoma's** (Pier 47, behind the fishing fleet); and **Tarantino's** (little neck clams, fettucine).

Cozy, slightly noisy, family-oriented **Caesar's** has been in business near the water at 2299 Powell Street for 36 years. **Pizzeria Uno**, 2323 Powell Street, is one of the chain that began with Chicago's deep-dish version. Across from Pier 43½, **Franciscan** serves fresh seafood with an unobstructed view of the bay; announcements are made of in- and outbound ships. If seafood palls, try **Little Spain**, 1333 Columbus, for *paella* and *tapas*.

It is a sorry truism that none of San Francisco's best seafood is served at the Wharf, perhaps because the clientele of the cafés tends to be tourists having a great time, who are less demanding than locals. We mention these for travellers who feel they must eat (not dine) at the Wharf.

Along the way, three bakeries are worth a call: **Blue Chip Cookies**, 757 Beach Street, **Boudin Bakery** at 156 Jefferson Street, for the original San Francisco sourdough French bread and sandwiches, and **Le Carrousel Patisserie** in Pier 39, for European-style tortes, croissants, pastries, and sandwiches.

Around in the Wharf Area

Originally the Del Monte Fruit Company's peach-canning plant, **The Cannery** was built in 1909, and for a time was the world's largest produce plant. In 1968 a new concrete building was constructed within the original brick shell, with such success that the new looks amiably old.

At 2801 Leavenworth at the foot of Columbus Avenue, The Cannery today is a spectrum of more than 50 shops, galleries, and restaurants. The most notable feature of the **Chart House** pub is what newspaper publisher William Randolph Hearst brought from Albyns Hall in England, a 17th-century manor house: Jacobean oak paneling, fireplace mantels, and the superbly worked plaster ceiling. **Bombay Palace** specializes in tandoori-grilled dishes.

At 633 Beach Street, between Columbus and Hyde and across from The Cannery, the **American Carousel Museum** shows off the finest examples of antique carousel animals created between 1880 and 1930. America's woodcraft heritage is illuminated by workshop demonstrations in restoration techniques and displays of carousel merriment including historic photos, two authentic band organs, a gift shop, and even docent tours; Tel: 928-0550.

Hyde Street Pier

Travellers accustomed to going down to the sea in comfort aboard today's ocean liners can only wonder at the courage and stamina of those sailors of the past in their cramped quarters: cold, seasick, and sometimes, surely, afraid. Across the street from The Cannery at the Hyde Street Pier (built to serve the ferry traffic that subsequently ceased after the debut of the Golden Gate Bridge), the **San Francisco Maritime National Historical Park** maintains a cache of historical nautical treasures: six old vessels, of which three may be boarded. The graceful, three-masted, deep-waterman *Balclutha* was launched in Scotland in 1886: this steel-hulled survivor of the Cape Horn fleet was a veteran of trade in spirits and salmon, hardware and coal and wheat. It is symbol of San Francisco's seafaring heritage. *Eureka,* last of the side-wheel–powered ferries to operate in the U.S., built in 1890, hauled freight and passengers for the Northern Pacific Railroad. Built in 1895, the *C. A. Thayer* was the Pacific Coast's last commercial schooner, now retired after service in the lumber industry and in two wars. The historic fleet also includes the scow schooner *Alma,* the oceangoing tug *Hercules,* and the side-wheel river tug *Eppleton Hall,* which cannot be boarded. The **Maritime Book Store** at the pier's entrance sells books about ships and sailing as well as valuable regional guides.

A formal little greensward designed by renowned landscape architect Thomas D. Church, **Victorian Park** is a pleasant place to sit next to the Hyde Street Pier while waiting for a cable car of the Powell–Hyde line. On the other hand, you might idle the minutes (or hours) away at the **Buena Vista Café**, 2765 Hyde Street, where Irish coffee is said to have been introduced to the United States from Ireland. No credit cards and no reservations are accepted, and the squeezing for a seat is legendary. Nonetheless, it's one of the must-see cafés in the city, decade in and decade out.

Across Beach Street from Ghirardelli Square (see below) the **National Maritime Museum** at the foot of Polk Street was built in 1939 more or less in the shape of a ship. It houses meticulously executed ship models, large ship relics, and beautifully carved and painted figureheads staring into ocean space with unblinking eyes. On the second floor, a collection of photos, models, paintings, maps, and handicrafts stand witness to the seagoing tradition of the city. The museum is open Wednesdays through Sundays.

Ghirardelli Square

The first and still among the most attractive urban redeveloped landmarks in the country, Ghirardelli Square (pronounced GEAR-ar-deli) today boasts eye-opening views of the bay and more than 70 shops and restaurants (some of them destinations in their own right for San Franciscans). The oldest red-brick building in the complex, the Woolen Mill, dates from 1864 (Civil War uniforms were made here). Domingo Ghirardelli from Rapallo, Italy, began making chocolate here in 1893, and built a factory that produced it until the early 1960s. In 1962, fearing that the decaying Victorian complex might be destroyed, Mrs. William P. Roth and her son William Matson Roth (of the Matson Line) bought it and commissioned its metamorphosis into an environmentally enhancing mall. It occupies the block bounded by North Point, Polk, Beach, and Larkin streets.

Like an old European arcade, Ghirardelli suits amblers and oglers almost as well as shoppers and diners, especially around holiday seasons, when it becomes a fiesta of live music, entertainment, and people-watching.

Soothing to both the eye and the inner self is the **Mandarin**, on the top floor of the Woolen Mill, with its tiled floors, Chinese art, and an opulence appealing to those who associate Chinese food with the plainest and simplest surroundings. For more than 20 years owner Cecilia Chiang has overseen a kitchen capable of serving authentic Mandarin, Hunan, and Szechwan dishes. Because the restaurant is within a major tourist attraction, however, recipes on the regular menu are sometimes altered to suit tastes of beginners as well as experts in Chinese cooking; if you want classical seasoning or special dishes, just ask.

Paprikas Fono, decorated in Hungarian country style, is the province of the friendly Fonos family, who cook their country's specialties with élan, adding fresh fish dishes to the menu as well. Don't miss the *gulyas* (English speakers call it goulash). **Gaylord India** is a comfortable, restful, roomy place with a memorable view of the bay, and though purists sometimes complain, most diners leave not only satisfied but delighted.

Compadres Mexican Bar & Grill serves south-of-the-border specialties in a gleefully tropical setting (Tel: 885-2266); **Dixie's Yacht Club Bar & Café** serves homemade soups and light entrées, with live after-dark entertainment (Tel: 928-4733); **Ghirardelli's** will drive you to delicious caloric excess with Italian gelato, espresso, and cappuccino, along with chocolates and other desserts to mix and match; **Pacific Café** presents fresh seafood and grilled steaks (Tel: 775-1173); and **Vicolo Pizzeria** will delight you with deep-dish pizzas in six daily dramatic versions (Tel: 776-1331).

Among the shops, of particular interest are **Circle Gallery** (contemporary graphics and jewelry), **Carlo Baron Leather**, **Original Furs by Max**, **William Silva** (designer fashions), **Kilkenny Shop** (Irish imports), and **The Nature Company** (books, prints, gifts).

GOLDEN GATE NATIONAL RECREATION AREA

"It's like living in a great, gray pearl," someone once remarked about San Francisco. Indeed, often the air is opalescent, the meeting of sea and sky above the bay a clean, foggy gray sparkling like diffused-light diamonds. A gem of a trek almost any time is one west from Fisherman's Wharf along the bay through the Golden Gate National Recreation Area, established in 1972, and, at 72,815 acres with 28 miles of coastline, the largest urban park in the world.

The walk may be started here and there along the area's length; the most logical starting point (especially if you are coming from Fisherman's Wharf) is to take the **Golden Gate Promenade**, a footpath three and a half miles long from the Hyde Street Pier around curving Aquatic Park, past the historic houses of Fort Mason and Fort Mason Cultural Center, along Marina Green to Old Fort Point and under the south tower of the Golden Gate Bridge. (Dedicated walkers can continue west along seaside trails all the way to Land's End and Cliff House on the open ocean; see the Ocean Beach and Land's End section below.) You could also approach on foot from the northern end of Van Ness Avenue, or by bus from downtown to the GGNRA headquarters via MUNI buses numbers 47 and 49 from Civic Center.

If you arrive at your starting point at Fort Mason by car, do two things: First, drive up Franklin Street off Bay, past several historic Victorian houses (still occupied by officers and enlisted men; the commandant's residence is an Officers' Club), and follow the curve around to **GGNRA Headquarters**, where you may pick up a fine map and ask questions; second, return to Bay and turn right (west), pass Gough and Octavia, and turn right on Laguna Street and into the parking lot for Fort Mason. This is the best starting point for the walk if you have a car to leave.

Fort Mason Cultural Center

The bluff above Fort Mason was the site of a small battery established in 1797 by Spanish soldiers from the Presidio, which, under President Millard Fillmore in the 1850s, became one of three U.S. Army reservations in San Francisco. Through stands of stately trees, the walk winds back through the fort to Aquatic Park.

At Fort Mason's Pier 3 floats the S.S. *Jeremiah O'Brien,* last of the unaltered Liberty ships. (These were slow cargo ships built in large numbers for the U.S. Merchant Marine during World War II; O'Brien himself was the first American captain to capture a British vessel during the Revolution.) The ship is open to the public except on major holidays, and on the third weekend of every month the steam engine is turned over at slow speed at the dock to give visitors a look at one of the last surviving ship's engines of this type in the world. Each May two five-hour cruises are made on the bay; Tel: 441-3101.

Fort Mason itself has become a lively arts-and-recreation community that offers more than 1,000 activities monthly and houses more than 50 resident groups; Tel: 441-5706. **Greens,** in Building A, is San Francisco's—and maybe the country's—most creative vegetarian restaurant, with cooking so good it attracts diners of every stripe. Don't be surprised if dinners are booked a month in advance; Tel: 771-6222. Greens also runs the **Tassajara Bakery** here, which produces some of the finest breads in existence; Tel: 771-6330.

Also in Building A, the **San Francisco Craft and Folk Art Museum** mounts witty and elegant exhibitions of contemporary crafts, American folk arts, and traditional ethnic arts from home and abroad, complemented by an enticing gift shop; Tel: 775-0990. Dedicated to the preservation, collection, and display of Italian-American and Italian art, culture, and history, the **Museo Italiano Americano** includes the works of prominent contemporary artists. In Building C; Tel: 673-2200.

Nationally recognized exhibitions and popular field trips to black historical sites are sponsored by the **African-American Historical and Cultural Society**, a combination museum, art gallery, historical society, and resource library focusing on African-Americans and black Californians. It is also in Building C; Tel: 441-0640.

The **Mexican Museum of San Francisco** is the only one of its kind in the U.S., with works that range from the pre-Hispanic period to contemporary art. On display are many pieces by Chicano artists, folk artists, and those of the Colonial period; **La Tienda**, its shop, sells Mexican arts and crafts. The museum and its shops are in Building D; Tel: 441-0404. The **Magic Theater**, also in Building D, was one of the first companies in the country to devote itself to the production of new American works; its season extends year round, except for September; Tel: 441-8822.

Fort Point National Historical Site

In 1776, on this "extremity of the white cliff at the inner point of the entrance to the port," Colonel Juan Bautista de Anza erected a cross to mark the site of a proposed fort. **Fort Point**, a classic brick fortification completed in 1861, once housed 149 cannons—none of which was ever fired in anger. It's said the fort was copied after the design of Fort Sumter at Charleston, South Carolina. National Park Service guides in Civil War uniforms conduct daily tours of the bastion.

The Presidio and Presidio Heights

The site for the San Francisco Presidio (fort) was selected by Juan Bautista de Anza on March 28, 1776. Today it commands a spacious, spectacular site of 1,540 acres in one of the best settings in the entire city, on the heights just south of the Golden Gate. It's the headquarters of the United States Sixth Army and employs some 6,000 military and civilian personnel.

There are no attractions within the Presidio directed toward visitors as such; if you have an automobile and plenty of time to explore, take a drive around the grounds, entering through the Presidio gates at Lombard and Lyon streets

in the Marina or at Presidio Avenue and Pacific from Presidio
Heights.

Presidio Heights, while not part of the military reservation, edges the Presidio's woody preserve to the south. Here,
as on Russian Hill, the chief interest for the traveller is
walking or driving up and down streets lined by very attractive houses—especially those on Jackson and Washington
streets. Cruise (but quietly) around circular, prestigious
Presidio Terrace, entered off the meeting of Washington and
Arguello streets.

Just south of Presidio Terrace at Arguello and Lake, the
Temple Emanu-El, a superb example of modern Byzantine
architecture, is the city's major center of Reform Judaism.

Arguello Boulevard owes its name to one of the actors in
a historic tragedy, as sketched by James Benét: "It concerns
the wooing of Concepcion Argüello, daughter of the Presidio's commander, by Count N. P. Rezanov, who visited the
Bay in 1805 to seek supplies for the Russian colony at Sitka.

"Rezanov won the lady's love, and with her help and her
father's also won permission to trade; then he sailed for
home. For many years Concepcion faithfully awaited his
return or a message, but finally entered a convent. It was 36
years later that she learned he had died before reaching
Russia."

GOLDEN GATE BRIDGE

On May 24, 1987, more than 200,000 diehard bridge buffs
walked, sang, and danced across the 50-year-old Golden
Gate Bridge, causing the great span, the world's longest such
single-suspension, to sag in the middle by ten feet, terrifying
city authorities.

One of the most durable city symbols on earth, the
Golden Gate Bridge itself is not golden (that name was first
applied to the natural harbor entrance), but a giant, graceful,
red-orange span leaping from San Francisco north to the
shores of Marin County.

It's worth mentioning that at its peak the tidal surge
through the Gate is 3 times the flow of the Amazon and 14
times that of the Mississippi. This is a fierce place, where
currents sweep through the watery slot at up to 60 m.p.h.,
winds whip the headlands, and fog pours over the oceanside
hills like an opaque waterfall.

Engineer Joseph Strauss and his determined assistant Clif-
ford Paine were the dynamic forces behind the dream and

the completion of it: not only a struggle against the elements but also against the politicians and voters who did not understand visionaries.

Finally it stood, and is best appreciated by the free walk across, which is 1.2 miles long and takes about an hour (including time out for photos). There's always wind; wear a sweater. For good views of the span, drivers should stop at the **Toll Plaza and Visitor Center** at the south (city side) and the **Vista Point** turnoff from the north (Marin County) side.

Over the years, hundreds of suicides have been committed in leaps off the bridge; always by jumpers looking toward the great city that somehow failed them—or vice versa.

THE MARINA

Heading back from the Golden Gate Bridge, stop in the Marina district, between Fort Point and Fort Mason. This is San Francisco's Mediterranean, a low-rise, waterside, and wide-sky pastel neighborhood, where strolling is the accepted speed until you slow down and stretch out on Marina Green, and where yachts bob at their moorings on the bay.

Basically, the Marina may be said to idle between Lombard Street on the south (an extension of Van Ness Avenue/ Highway 101, which runs north through the city, then west as Lombard, then north across the Golden Gate Bridge into Marin County) and the bayside greenswards of Fort Mason and Marina Green on the north, and from Van Ness in the east to Richardson and Doyle drives (approaches to the bridge). Up the hills to the south rise the associated worlds of Union Street and Pacific Heights (see below).

Sadly but dramatically, the Marina's most recent role on the national stage was played in October 1989, when the earthquake struck this neighborhood with particular force, the fiery results lighting up the TV sets of a nation. Many blocks are still undergoing restoration.

Palace of Fine Arts

The Marina sits upon land reclaimed from a tidal marsh and lagoon that was filled in as the site for the Panama-Pacific International Exposition of 1915. Officially, the fair saluted the opening of the Panama Canal; in reality, it celebrated the rebuilding of the earthquake-ravaged region as a part of the City Beautiful movement some 75 years ago.

The Exposition was nothing if not elaborate, consisting of

a complex of enormous wood-and-plaster palaces dedicated to the arts, education, machinery, horticulture, transportation, agriculture, and more, all joined by landscaped courts and buttressed by colonnades. The exteriors of these eccentricities were decorated in Neoclassical fashion; on the inside, they were simple sheds.

Of these, only the Palace of the Fine Arts remains (not to be confused with the California Palace of the Legion of Honor museum, as frequently happens in print). Designed by Berkeley architect Bernard Maybeck, whose artistic contributions to American style are often compared to those of Louis Sullivan and Frank Lloyd Wright, it had curving wings, within which lay a three-acre park. Its peristyle of Corinthian columns faced a lagoon, above which rose an octagonal temple of Roman arches and columns surmounted by a 160-foot-high dome. After the fair, it was allowed to fall into disrepair as the city's very own romantic ruin.

By the late 1950s philanthropist Walter S. Johnson, who lived across the street, had become saddened by the sight of it. With his funds and energy, plus a 1959 city bond issue, and matching funds from the state, the building was reconstructed (one might say really built for the first time) with reinforced concrete. Today it stands as an Old World outcrop in a delightful residential setting at Baker and Beach streets, just one and a half blocks from Marina Boulevard and a harbor afloat with colorful yachts. Ducks and swans paddle on the mirror-like pond in front, oblivious that women came here to do their laundry in the 1850s.

The Palace now houses the **Exploratorium**, an internationally acclaimed museum of science, art, and human perception, featuring some 650 exhibits to be manipulated, tinkered with, or activated by push buttons. (It inspired some displays in Paris's La Villette science center.) This is a museum that is particularly attractive to children and families, and, in fact, you may want to visit it even if you decide to skip the rest of the Marina. To reach the Exploratorium by public transportation, take the number 30 or number 30X bus from Caltrain Depot at Fourth and Townsend streets or, more handily, from stops along Kearny in the Financial District or Columbus Avenue in North Beach; Tel: 563-7337 or 561-0360 (taped information).

Ambling the Marina

The Palace and Exploratorium aside, the Marina is a thoroughly residential district sliced by Lombard (the highway,

San Francisco Bay

0   miles   0.5

0   kilometers   0.8

Fort Mason

Golden Gate National Recreation Area

MARINA BLVD.

Palace of Fine Arts

BEACH ST.

BEACH ST.

BAY ST.

MARINA

FRANCISCO ST.

CHESTNUT ST.

LOMBARD ST.

The Presidio

GREENWICH ST.

FILBERT ST.

UNION ST.

Octagon House

COW HOLLOW

N

PACIFIC HEIGHTS

GREEN ST.

VALLEJO ST.

BROADWAY

PACIFIC AVE.

JACKSON ST.

Haas-Lilienthal House

WASHINGTON ST.

Alta Plaza

CLAY ST.

Lafayette Square

SACRAMENTO ST.

CALIFORNIA ST.

PINE ST.

BUSH ST.

SUTTER ST.

POST ST.

EUCLID ST.

Japan Center

GEARY BLVD.

O'FARRELL ST.

WESTERN ADDITION

ELLIS ST.

EDDY ST.

TURK ST.

REDWOOD ST.

GOLDEN GATE AVE.

MC ALLISTER ST.

University of San Francisco

FULTON ST.

Alamo Square

IVY ST.

Opera House

GROVE ST.

HAYES ST.

FELL ST.

OAK ST.

PAGE ST.

HAIGHT-ASHBURY

HAIGHT ST.

WALLER ST.

Buena Vista Park

DUBOCE AVE.

MARKET ST.

BUENA VISTA AVE. W.

CARL ST.

16TH STREET

17TH STREET

MARKET ST.

18TH STREET

Mission Dolores

19TH STREET

MISSION

VAN NESS AVE.

POLK ST.

LAGUNA ST.

OCTAVIA

GOUGH ST.

FRANKLIN ST.

DOLORES ST.

GUERRERO ST.

VALENCIA ST.

MISSION ST.

FILLMORE ST.

STEINER ST.

PIERCE ST.

SCOTT ST.

DIVISADERO ST.

BRODERICK ST.

BAKER ST.

LYON ST.

PRESIDIO AVE.

MASONIC AVE.

SHRADER ST.

COLE ST.

ASHBURY ST.

CASTRO ST.

WEBSTER ST.

lined by restaurants, motels, and small stores, is the main feeder to the Golden Gate Bridge from the southern part of the state) and by Chestnut, the local shopping/supping/sipping street. In recent years restaurants have mushroomed on both streets, some of which lure residents from all over town. (As if that weren't enough, the shops and restaurants of Union Street in the Cow Hollow area—see below—are just a few blocks south of the Marina.)

An inspiration from the fertile imagination of Jeremiah Tower (who no longer owns it), **Balboa Café** at 3199 Fillmore Street at Greenwich is a noisy, happy wateringhole serving unsurpassed and simple things: the Balboa burger, pepper steak, and seafood fettucine among them. No reservations are accepted. The prices are as pleasant as the home-made pastas at **E'Angelo**, 2234 Chestnut Street.

Monroe's at 1968 Lombard Street has maintained its privileged position as a San Francisco classic for almost 40 years, serving generous portions of traditional Continental dishes in the atmosphere of an English club. Here's the local source for beef Wellington; Tel: 567-4550. A lighthearted informality that's not overly friendly relaxes the visitor to **La Pergola**, an oasis of northern Italian cooking at 2060 Chestnut Street.

When haute cuisine has become *de trop* and what you need are hearty food and generous drinks with an overlay of enthusiasm, you can't do better than to join the local gang at its neighborhood hangout, **Liverpool Lil's**, at 2492 Lyon Street, corner of Baker. It feels like a pub and serves meals until midnight. Hamburgers and sandwiches of zany combinations make **Chestnut Street Bar and Grill** at 2231 Chestnut popular all hours of the day. It's particularly pleasant to sit in the garden here when it's warm.

Samui Thai is a newcomer to the Marina, specializing in southern Thai cuisine influenced by Malaysian cooking. The service here, at 2414 Lombard Street at Scott, is impeccable. **Izzy's Steak & Chop House** remembers Izzy Gomez, whose saloon was the toast of the town in the 1920s and 1930s. Try a dry-aged steak or a grappa fizz.

Enthusiasts of Indian cuisine could not do better than to make the pilgrimage to **Peacock**, on the edge of the Marina at 2800 Van Ness Avenue, an elegant escape with individually appointed dining rooms set in a pre-1906 Victorian mansion. Don't miss the tandoori prawns or the Pimm's Cup; Tel: 928-7001.

Reviewers raved when **Rodin** came on the scene, serving French nouvelle cuisine in a small, softly lighted café at 1779

Lombard Street. The service is smooth, the cooking assured; Tel: 563-8566.

Scott's, the seafood house at 2400 Lombard (at Scott Street, hence the name) became a star the night it opened. It's hugely popular, yet the service never seems hurried. It's a good place to order abalone properly done—if you've just come into an inheritance; Tel: 563-8988. (There are two relatives, Scott's Seafood Grill and Scott's Carriage House, both at Three Embarcadero Center.)

One of the Bay Area's best delis is **Lucca Delicatessen**, definitely the best place in the Marina for assembling a picnic. It's at 2120 Chestnut Street, and does not accept credit cards.

Before leaving the Marina, take a drive west along Marina Boulevard from Gas House Cove (next to Fort Mason), past Marina Green to **Baker Street** (last exit before the Golden Gate Bridge). This street is flanked by proud, patrician homes of a Mediterranean persuasion, looking across the bay toward the now-green, now-golden hills of Marin County. You may even be persuaded to join the dog walkers, picnickers, and kite-fliers having a lazy afternoon in the sun on the half-mile **Marina Green**.

To take public transportation to and from the Marina (to Chestnut Street, for example), your best choice is the number 30 Stockton bus, which goes north on Kearny, through the Stockton Tunnel, up Columbus to North Point, then to Van Ness and along Chestnut Street.

COW HOLLOW

The stretch of Union Street running west of Van Ness Avenue between Russian Hill and the Presidio just south of the Marina is known as Cow Hollow to traditionalists, but just **Union Street** to shoppers and diners with no hankering for history. Only four blocks uphill (south) of Chestnut, it's frequently considered part of the Marina, and many of the restaurants mentioned in that section are just a few blocks from here.

In post–Gold Rush days this was a green dale watered by small streams seeking the bay. It attracted farmers, among them one George W. Hatman who established a dairy ranch here in 1861, giving the hollow its countrified name. On the heels of Hatman came 30 or so more farmers, and soon hundreds of cows shared the grasslands with wild ducks, quail, and rabbits.

Besides supplying milk to the city, the hollow served as a communal wash basin. Fresh water was so scarce along the Barbary Coast in the 1850s that rich miners sent their laundry to Honolulu and even to China to be washed. Laguna Pequena, a little lake in the area that would now be bounded by Franklin, Octavia, Filbert, and Lombard streets, was used by the washerwomen who took in laundry from the Presidio's officers and by housewives who congregated there from the city on washdays. This was Washerwoman's Lagoon.

This bucolic era ended in the 1880s as pollution, that old villain, permeated the valley from sausage factories, tanneries, and slaughterhouses. When the aromas wafted uphill to the homes of the Bonanza Kings in adjacent Pacific Heights, it was all over. The cows were banished in 1891, and Washerwoman's Lagoon was filled in.

By the middle of this century Union Street was a nondescript gathering place of hardware stores, garages, mom-and-pop groceries, and five-and-dimes. Then the decorators who had already restored Jackson Square came around for a look at the old clapboard dwellings, the converted carriage houses, and the surviving stables and barns, and began the regeneration of the late 1950s with a few stylish antique shops and home furnishings showrooms; by 1964 Cow Hollow had become a faubourg with flair.

Cow Hollow, like so much of San Francisco, demands to be seen on foot, partly because of its tucked-away corners that the motorist misses, partly because the parking problem will give you ulcers or migraines. There is public parking at Union–Laguna Parking, 1910 Union Street, a handy place to leave your auto while ambling up and down the seven-block stretch of Union Street between Franklin on the east and Steiner on the west.

The best public transportation from downtown is the number 45 bus westbound on Sutter Street. From the Financial District, board number 41 westbound on Sacramento Street, or catch the number 41 along Columbus Avenue in North Beach. Get off the bus at the corner of Union and Franklin streets and walk west, or ride to the Steiner Street intersection and walk east.

Union is a window-shopper's happy hunting ground for home furnishings, antiques, handicrafts, custom-made clothing, art objects and imports, books and gifts and linens, specialty foods and feminine fripperies. Handily interspersed are pubs, delis, cafés, snack spots, and restaurants representing about a dozen cuisines (see below).

The Hollow's handsomest creations are the clusters of old Victorians, artfully refurbished, some metamorphosed into smart shopping compounds. Fine old façades are painted subtle shades with colorful gingerbread trims, wrought-iron fences have been retained, and, in some places, gas lights reinstalled.

At the corner of Gough and Union streets, visit the **Octagon House**. Eight-sided houses were once believed to bring good luck. This one, built in 1861 and purchased in 1952 by the National Society of Colonial Dames, is one of the few remaining local examples of the style. Furnished with colonial and Federal-period antiques, it is open to the public from noon to 3:00 P.M. on the second and fourth Thursdays of the month and on the second Sunday of each month; closed January and holidays (Tel: 441-7512).

After the Octagon House, admire the house at 1851 Union, in 1884 a stable facing Washerwoman's Lagoon, now an atmospheric restaurant, **Pietro's**. Next, amble into Charlton Court, a cul-de-sac off the south side of Union's 1900 block, believed to have been a milk-wagon loading yard. The 1873 and 1896 Victorians at numbers 2 and 4 are today **The Bed and Breakfast Inn**.

Three circa 1870 residences, including a pair of "wedding houses" (identical bungalows with a common center wall) at 1980 Union, encompass several shops and cafés, and the old Laurel Vale Dairy at number 1981 is now the home of **Earthly Goods**, women's apparel.

The three-story mansion at 2040 Union was erected around 1870 by early dairyman James W. Cudworth, with lumber brought around Cape Horn. It houses several boutiques and **L'Entrecôte de Paris**, which has a glass-enclosed sidewalk terrace and cozy interior where steaks and the city's best *pommes frites* are specialties; Tel: 931-5006.

What was a barn at 2044 Union, now occupied by a house, was a hideout for a pair of notorious looters known as the Gas-Pipe Thieves.

One block north, the eccentric **Vedanta Society Temple** at 2963 Webster on the corner of Filbert was built between 1905 and 1908 as a reflection of Hindu religious philosophy; the result was an amalgam of Moorish columns, lobated windows, cusped arches, crenellated towers, and onion domes. The countrified grounds of **St. Mary the Virgin Episcopal Church** at 2325 Union are often used for weddings. The Eternal Fountain here is fed by a spring that once watered the Cow Hollow herds.

Shopping and Dining
on Union Street

In the block between Gough and Octavia, two ethnic art galleries on the north side of the street are **Images of the North**, at number 1782, for Eskimo art, sandstone sculptures, etc.; and **A Touch of Asia** at number 1784, for sculptures, screens, and other wonders from several cultures.

Across the street, **Margaritaville** at number 1787 is a merry Mexican spot for contemporary music, vivid videos, and great margaritas.

Between Octavia and Laguna, **Mai's Vietnamese** at number 1838 has pleasant decor and delightful cooking at reasonable prices. At number 1848, **Oggetti** sells stationery and paper products, beautifully made in Florence.

On the south side in the same block, **L'Escargot** at number 1809 is a formal, candle-lighted rendezvous where many beautiful people enjoy the veal and lamb dishes; Tel: 567-0222. Pretty **Laura Ashley** creations wait for you and your children at number 1827, and the restaurant–jazz club **Pasand** is at number 1875; Tel: 927-4498.

Between Laguna and Buchanan, **Perry's** at number 1944 remains a popular spot for searching singles, but everyone else seems to enjoy it, too, possibly because the American standard hamburgers and fried chicken are much above standard. Everybody in town has visited at least once.

Between Buchanan and Webster, **Prego** at number 2000 is the kind of pasta place you always wanted—except you wish they'd take reservations. It's sophisticated yet hip, chic yet youthful, crowded yet cool. The pasta is homemade, the pizzas from an oak-burning brick oven.

Between Fillmore and Steiner, consider **Doidge's Kitchen** at number 2217, a great place for breakfast (some say this is where the Social Register takes its hangovers).

POLK STREET AND
VAN NESS AVENUE

Polk Street used to be referred to as *Polkstrasse,* and in some circles it still is, a reference to the city's old German population once concentrated here. Unlike some other ethnic groups, they have long since dispersed. Today its two-mile march from the bay and Cow Hollow south to Market Street parallel to Van Ness offers everything from the silly to the serviceable to the sinful (both gay and straight).

In a sense, Polk has always been a commercial street, though around the turn of the century it catered to the carriage trade that rolled down from Nob Hill. Today, despite an occasional aristocratic outcrop (such as **Freed, Teller, and Freed** for tea, coffee, and spices at number 1326 and **Mayes Oyster House** at number 1233), it's a mixed bag of small food stores, health shops, too-trendy outlets, and what-not places selling what you can't imagine anybody's wanting.

Most visitors to the city will be more comfortable on Polk the farther north they are (near the Union Street and Pacific Heights areas, there are several good restaurants; see below). South of California Street the street is known as Polk Gulch, a focus of the gay population.

When you drive along Van Ness today you strain to imagine it as what it was intended to be, and in part was, before the 1906 earthquake and fire: San Francisco's Champs-Elysées. (Of course, Paris's Champs-Elysées isn't the Champs-Elysées anymore, either.) This is the north–south axis of San Francisco, the nervous center of traffic, the throughway you try to avoid and can't. An extension of U.S. Highway 101 up from the south (linked to the Golden Gate Bridge by Lombard, which cuts from east to west at a 90 degree angle), it seems without personality or distinction to the driver speeding along.

It wasn't always this way, and civil authorities are puzzling about how to regain a bit of its erstwhile elegance. Named for then newly elected mayor James Van Ness and laid out in 1854 as a spacious boulevard to be lined by mansions set on large lots, it was described in 1892 as "our one show street, purely a residence section." Gingerbreads by the dozen, gaudy or demure, danced up and down the city's widest street.

Then came 5:13 A.M. on April 18, 1906. The earth shook and the sky burned: Some 514 blocks had gone up in flames when the army engineers decided to dynamite Van Ness as a firebreak. It worked: All the eastern side of the avenue was in ruins, but, with a few exceptions, the west side and the rest of the city were saved. Thus the richest reliquary of Victoriana remains west of Van Ness—Pacific Heights, for example.

Following the fire, commerce came to the formerly stylish street, and then in the 1920s, the heyday of automobiles as luxuries, palatial showrooms arose, many of them now turned to other uses. The northern end of Van Ness, like that of Polk, boasts a great diversity of dining spots. (For the best ones farther south, see Civic Center below.)

Around Polk and Van Ness

Acquerello ("watercolor" in Italian) is an apt name for this pretty, softly lighted room where *nuovo cucina* wonders such as *involtini* of veal with marjoram and prosciutto are created; the wine list is another wonder. The restaurant is at 1722 Sacramento Street between Polk and Van Ness.

The **Café Majestic** in the Majestic Hotel, restored to its stately splendor, is a perfect setting for rediscovered recipes from Old California: grilled chicken Nellie Melba with wild mushrooms, for instance. The address is 1500 Sutter Street, two blocks west of Van Ness.

If France can have haute cuisine, why not her former colony Vietnam? Here it is, served in style in the handsome, roomy **Golden Turtle**, 2211 Van Ness Avenue between Broadway and Vallejo; don't miss the fresh crab in ginger-and-garlic sauce. The prices are as friendly as the staff. **Harris'** (2100 Van Ness at Pacific) specializes in steak, and nobody anywhere does it better. High ceilings, booth seatings, and a man-size arrangement of space suit the prime-cut quality.

On the quieter end of Polk at number 2323 (between Green and Union), **Casablanca** is a meeting of North Africa and France, and a smooth one. The mood is Mediterranean and mellow, the menu entertainingly eclectic.

About as quiet as an air-raid siren, **Hard Rock Café** at 1699 Van Ness near Sacramento is a smash: cars crashing through walls, waitresses dressed like 1950s carhops, eardrum-rending rock, and, as an accent, great burgers and fries. It's not for everybody, but everybody seems to struggle to get in. In distinct contrast, **Matterhorn Swiss Restaurant** at 2323 Van Ness near Green is warm, restrained, and intimate, offering dishes from the Valais region; dinners only. Try the veal bratwurst with *rösti.*

PACIFIC HEIGHTS

You'll be permitted to live in Pacific Heights even if your last name isn't Spreckels or Getty, even if your employer is neither Queen Elizabeth II nor Mikhail Gorbachev. But such connections would help, especially in this most expensive district in one of the most costly cities in the country.

This posh purlieu rises between California and Green streets on the south and north, and Van Ness and Presidio avenues on the east and west. The best way to explore it is to drive out one street and back the next, stopping to ogle at will. If you haven't the time for that, at least browse along Broadway between Webster and Lyon streets, noting particularly **Hamlin School**, 2120 Broadway, and the **Convent of the Sacred Heart**, at number 2222. Both were mansions built at different times for James L. Flood, the son of James C., one of the so-called Bonanza Kings, who rose from saloon-keeper to multimillionaire as a result of speculation in Nevada's Comstock Lode.

Also of unusual historical and architectural interest are the **Spreckels Mansion**, 2080 Washington Street, built in 1912 for Adolph and Alma de Bretteville Spreckels (patrons of the California Palace of the Legion of Honor) and the **Bourn Mansion**, 2550 Webster Street near Broadway, erected for William Bowers Bourn, whose wealth came from gold, gas, and water. The great Georgian Revival estate called Filoli in Woodside (see Day Trips from San Francisco) and Christian Brothers' Greystone Cellars in St. Helena (see Wine Country) were also built for Bourn.

The California Historical Society makes its home in the **Whittier Mansion** at 2090 Jackson Street at Laguna, a massive red-sandstone mansion built between 1894 and 1896 for the director of what has become today's Pacific Gas & Electric Company. Remarkable for the latest in mechanical contrivances at the time, it survived the 1906 earthquake with only a few toppled chimneys. It contains fine 19th-century furniture and fittings in the various period rooms. The fine-arts collection presents a graphic picture of early Californiana and the development of the state from its beginnings through 1906. The mansion is open from 1:00 to 4:30 P.M. Tuesdays through Sundays; Tel: 567-1848.

Victorian and Edwardian houses cluster around California and Franklin streets, and the only fully furnished Victorian in the city open to the public, the **Haas-Lilienthal House**, is nearby at 2007 Franklin Street at Jackson. Built in 1886 in the Queen Anne style, it survived the 1906 earthquake and fire intact, and sheltered successive members of the family until Alice Haas Lilienthal died in 1972. Two years later, her heirs donated the ornate home to the Foundation for San Francisco's Architectural Heritage. It may be visited from noon to 4:00 P.M. on Wednesdays and from 11:00 A.M. to 4:30 P.M. Sundays; Tel: 441-3004.

In the area of Lafayette Park, near Gough Street and Clay, there are several eminent Victorians, and Washington Street between Octavia and Laguna also has a grouping of fine homes.

From Fillmore between Broadway and Vallejo there is a grand view of the Marina district, the bay, the Golden Gate Bridge, and the Marin hills beyond. Where Broderick crosses Broadway the sidewalk is so steep it's been made into a stairway; the view is an excitement in itself.

At least two companies conduct walking tours that emphasize the city's stately homes. **Heritage Walks**, sponsored by the Foundation for San Francisco's Architectural Heritage, headquartered in the Haas-Lilienthal House, explores Pacific Heights and several other districts; Tel: 441-3004. **San Francisco Discovery Walks**, 1200 Taylor Street, Suite 32, leads strolls that show off gardens, Victorian interiors, and much more; reservations are required, Tel: 673-2894.

Some of the most glorious views in town, or anywhere, may be captured on film and in memory from **Sherman House** at 2160 Green Street. **Mansions Hotel** joins the twin-towered Queen Anne built by Utah Senator Richard C. Chambers in 1887 to the Greek Revival house next door (previously the Hermitage) with one address, 2220 Sacramento Street. (For both, see Accommodations.)

Most of the public action in Pacific Heights goes on around Fillmore Street, a once-seedy, even scary thoroughfare that's become safe and diverting. Lunch only is served at the delightful deli called **Vivande Porta Via**, 2125 Fillmore between California and Sacramento. The pastas, cheeses, sandwiches, and salads on the menu (also available for takeout) lure lovers of good food from all over town.

The **Elite Café**'s Cajun cuisine draws crowds to this small, bright, convivial café at 2049 Fillmore at California. You'll probably have to wait for a table; no reservations accepted. **Rasselas** offers an unusual combination: American jazz joined to spicy Ethiopian cooking at 2801 California Street.

Right on the edge of Pacific Heights at 2080 Van Ness Avenue between Laguna and Buchanan, **Tutto Bene** serves small platters of northern Italian dishes, allowing the practice of "grazing" that's a current California craze. The bar is very lively.

Seafood of all sorts (12 to 18 varieties of oysters daily) is served at **Pacific Heights Bar & Grill**, which is really just beyond the border of that regal region at 2001 Fillmore Street. Try the seafood risotto.

JAPANTOWN

Only about four percent of San Francisco's approximately 12,500 citizens of Japanese descent live in Japantown (Nihonmachi), which is in great part a new town within an old city, south of Pacific Heights. It is bounded by Geary Boulevard on the south, California Street on the north, and Octavia and Fillmore streets on the east and west.

The Japanese population of San Francisco has experienced a fragmented history, due to the destruction of their central settlement south of Market by the 1906 earthquake, the Alien Land Law of 1913 (depriving Japanese-Americans of the right to buy farm land), and the dislocations of 1941 when Japanese-Americans, both aliens and citizens, were sent to internment camps as a result of World War II's anti-Japanese hysteria.

As a result of postwar urban-renewal programs, old, Victorian, low-income houses and shops yielded to the relentless parade of "modern," stern, and spare streets and structures that gives Japantown its clean, redeveloped appearance, so surprising when compared with the creaky but amiable appearance of Chinatown.

The easiest way for a motorist to approach Japantown is by driving west on Geary from downtown, then parking at the city garage underneath Japan Center. The number 38 Geary bus from Union Square also brings you directly here.

Unfortunately, various housing projects in the nearby Western Addition area have experienced problems with drug-inspired rip-offs and minor violence—don't wander alone, especially at night. This, however, has little impact on Japan Center, which is what you are really here to see.

Japan Center

For the traveller, this is the heart of the matter, a three-block showcase (bounded by Post and Geary, north and south, and Laguna and Fillmore east and west). It was dedicated in 1968, complete with restaurants, sushi bars, art galleries, bookstores, hotels, theaters, convention facilities, and shops specializing in Asian products and designs. Many Japanese who live elsewhere in the city throng the center for shopping, dining, and such celebrations as the annual Cherry Blossom Festival.

Although architectural writer Randolph Delehanty calls the center itself "... a period piece of sterile 1960s mall design, a monument to the bad city planning and worse architecture of 1960s urban renewal," the decor of the individual shops and the many restaurants has done much to soften and relax the rigidity of the original plan.

American and European visitors who want to savor one of San Francisco's cosmopolitan corners by sleeping there have discovered the **Miyako Hotel** at 1625 Post Street at the eastern end of the Center. Its recent four-year renovation program included the addition of the **Asuka Brasserie** (Continental and Japanese cuisine), which has made it a destination for diners.

On the north side of the Center across Post Street, **Nihonmachi Mall**, in the middle of the block between Laguna and Webster streets, is a handsome mini-Ginza with a gardened pedestrian area, shops, and small restaurants—almost all of them inexpensive. The briny oceanside scent that floats over the area is the result of fresh seafood being prepared: tuna, albacore, salmon roe, yellowtail.

Of the many restaurants at your disposal (in the Center's upper-floor west building, there's a restaurant row that transports you immediately to a tiny passageway in Kyoto), among the best is **Sanppo** at 1702 Post Street at Buchanan (try the one-pot *yosenabe*). Accomplished, cheerful, and spotless, **Isuzu** at 1581 Webster Street may serve the best tempura in town.

At 1640 Post Street, across the street from Japan Center, **Korean House** was one of the city's first Korean restaurants, especially recognized for hearty fish and meat soup-stews. Next door, the **New Korea House** serves a smashing Korean barbecue. **Mifune** at number 1737 is notable among noodle nuts, while **Seoul Garden** at 22 Peace Plaza in the Center grills unusual Korean dishes and has very friendly service.

A three or four-block walk north from Japan Center, depending upon where you are, **Oritalia** joins the Orient to Italy, an inspired idea. Shiitake mushrooms meet sun-dried tomatoes, Chinese noodles are introduced to olive oil. All dishes are dim sum or tapas style (appetizers), leading to a great grazing experience at 1915 Fillmore Street (at Pine).

Japanese Shopping

Eating is not all there is to Japantown. Within the Center, **Kinokuniya Bookstore** is well known for an excellent stock of Japanese- and English-language books about Japan, handsome art books, and some distinctive papers. The **International Art Guild Society**, a shop in a very small space, stocks

19th-century and contemporary prints. Vintage kimonos (some wedding versions, worn once, that originally cost as much as $10,000 may be had for hundreds) and inexpensive *happi* coats are for sale at **Shige Nighiguchi Kimonos. Soko Hardware** at 1698 Post Street brings hardware freaks from around town for beautifully crafted Japanese tools.

If most of Japantown is new, a stony piece of history still sits at the corner of Franklin Street (just east of Japantown) and Starr King Way—a tiny street that runs southeast from Geary and becomes O'Farrell Street. This is the Romanesque-style **First Unitarian Church**, where Thomas Starr King served as pastor from 1860 to 1864. A great apostle of the Union cause, he is said to have inspired California to remain in the Union by his "matchless oratory," and now lies under the white-marble tomb facing Franklin, under the palm tree on the corner.

The glorious **St. Mary's Catholic Cathedral of the Assumption** (1111 Gough Street at Geary) rose in the shape of a Greek cross to replace the old church on Van Ness that burned in 1962. Grand as it is from the outside, its true beauty is appreciated only from the interior, where you'll see its great cupola and stained glass. The organ is a masterpiece; concerts are performed here occasionally throughout the year, and the experience of hearing one in such a setting is unforgettable (Tel: 567-2020).

CLEMENT STREET AND GEARY BOULEVARD

In the **Richmond District**, about 3.5 miles west of downtown (or 1.5 miles west of Japantown), is the restaurant row of Clement Street. One block north of Geary Boulevard, Clement begins at Arguello Boulevard and runs west to Seal Rocks, within the boundaries of Fort Miley at the edge of the Pacific Ocean. Clement and the other streets are nothing if not jumbled and uninteresting architecturally, but they offer some of the best cafés in town for sampling international cuisines (especially Asian ones). California Street, one block north of Clement, has its share of worthwhile cafés, and they are included here. (See Dining for even more choices.)

Within the last six years, there has been an outburst of Thai flavors throughout town, with more and more interest in this complex, spicy cuisine. No newcomer, however, has replaced **Khan Toke Thai House** in popularity and handsome Thai decor. (Seating is on cushions on the floor.) At 5937 Geary Boulevard, it's worth the trip from downtown. Don't miss the seafood with hot peppers and lemon grass. Like the little café around the corner in Paris, **Le St. Tropez** is a cozy bistro with always-reliable cooking (try the wild mushroom ravioli). Its candle-lit tables, a fireplace, and antique copper pots add to the French flavors at 126 Clement at Second Avenue. **Ocean Restaurant** at 726 Clement Street keeps packing them in for seafood with a Chinese flavor; freshness and fine ingredients are the guidelines. The decor is rather ordinary, but you don't eat that.

The latest rage in the Richmond district is **Mandalay**, 4348 California Street, where unusual Burmese cuisine (such as curried beef and potato wontons with chile sauce) is pleasantly served and explained. Classic country-French food is the lure at **Le Cyrano**, 4143 Geary Boulevard. The menu changes only rarely, the fine service never varies.

Dishes unavailable in most regions of the United States are served at **Cambodia House**, 5625 Geary Boulevard, where warm service is a highlight and the food is delicious and inexpensive. From all around the area, diners flock to **Kabuto Sushi**, 5116 Geary Boulevard, to watch the fastest sushi slicer in town. Only the freshest fish is used.

The menu changes often at **l'Avenue**, 3854 Geary at Third Avenue, a comfortably proper American bistro with a huge repertoire of recipes. Hearty, rich dishes alternate with delicate, simple ones. It's very busy, so you may have to lunch or dine early or late.

Narai at 2229 Clement Street is noisy, but that's because people are enjoying the combination of Thai and Chinese cooking (crab rolls, spicy sour seafood soup). If you're homesick for a taste of Singapore, you'll head directly for simple, spare **Straits Café**, 3300 Geary Street, where the tastes are as cosmopolitan as that city itself, a blending of Chinese, Malaysian, Indian, Thai, and Indonesian cooking.

El Sombrero has been at 5800 Geary Street for a very long time, serving Anglo-Mex cooking with no surprises and relatively few spices (unless you ask). The margaritas are huge and delicious, the atmosphere friendly and informal.

Two non-culinary neighborhood landmarks are the Russian Orthodox **Holy Virgin Cathedral** at 6222 Geary Boulevard (glorious choir singing, a tradition for music lovers on Easter), and **Temple Emanu-el** at Arguello Boulevard and Lake Street (one of the most handsome structures in the city).

Geary is a major auto thoroughfare. For public transportation, the number 38 bus runs out all the way from the Transbay Terminal; the Geary Limited (number 38L) makes fewer stops and so is faster. For Clement, the choice is the number 2 bus, which reaches Clement from the Ferry Terminal via Sutter Street.

GOLDEN GATE PARK

Once upon a time, almost a century and a half ago, a barren land- and seaside-scape ran out from settled San Francisco toward the sea: the Outside Lands, they called it then, the domain of sand dunes and the scrubby sand oak. Then came city surveyor William Hammond Hall, who in 1870 began to reclaim San Francisco's Sahara. His successor was a creative, cranky, persevering Scot named John McLaren, who was (according to park historian Raymond Clary) "... either a martinet or a benevolent dictator ... and he loved Scotch." McLaren reigned from 1887 (when the first children's playground in a public park in the U.S. was established) until his death in 1943. When McLaren arrived, the 1,017 acres of today's park were simply "a dreary waste of shifting sand hills where a blade of grass cannot be raised without four posts to support it and keep it from blowing away." Now it is a glory, a national treasure, an unnaturally landscaped (but admirable and successful) bit of rural Victoriana in the city. It is south of Clement Street and the Richmond district, stretching west of Haight-Ashbury, which is itself southwest of Union Square and downtown.

McLaren was well-known then and is remembered now for his loathing of memorial statues: He called them "stookies," and spent his life hiding them in bushes or planting fast-growing shrubs around them when they were donated. A statue (what else?) was donated to his memory upon his death; it's in the Rhododendron Dell near one of Robert Burns by the same sculptor, M. Earl Cummings, and another of San Francisco's Civil War hero-clergyman Thomas Starr King. If you miss all three, the ghost of McLaren will probably smile.

The drives through the park are endlessly confusing, and for successful negotiation a map is required. (The Visitor Information Center on Hallidie Plaza supplies one, as does park headquarters at McLaren Lodge, corner of Fell and Stanyan at the eastern entrance of the park; Tel: 558-3706.) In general, the east–west route in the northern part of the park is the John F. Kennedy Drive; in the southern part, Martin Luther King, Jr., Drive, but there are several others.

Three distinguished museums are at home in the park: the California Academy of Sciences, the Asian Art Museum, and the M. H. de Young Memorial Museum.

Within memory, it was possible for a local newspaper wag to write, "Why not put San Francisco's three museums together and have *one* bad museum?" Time, tides, and talent certainly have changed that picture. Today two of the museums—the M. H. de Young Memorial Museum in Golden Gate Park and the Palace of the Legion of Honor at Land's End—are linked in **San Francisco Fine Arts Museums**; a membership in the Museum Society allows admission to both, as well as to the Asian Art Museum, which occupies a specially constructed wing of the de Young. Each is open Wednesdays through Sundays from 10:00 A.M. to 5:00 P.M.; for membership information, Tel: 750-3636. (Also, one admission charge allows entry to all three on the same day; keep your ticket stub.) A twenty-four-hour hot line provides current information on schedules of special exhibitions for the Fine Arts Museums; Tel: 863-3330 or 750-3659 (recorded information).

Through astute management of funds, intelligent reorganization, wily personnel-drafting worthy of the San Francisco 49ers, and a gift of Croesus-like riches, these three museums now rank with the best in the country. Recognizing an enlivened audience in the Bay Area, other museums of quality have planted solid roots in the city.

Handily for the traveller, both the Asian Art and the de Young museums are located in Golden Gate Park, facing another winner, the California Academy of Sciences, across the Music Concourse. (For more on the Palace of the Legion of Honor, see Ocean Beach and Land's End below.)

California Academy of Sciences

The oldest scientific institution on the West Coast, the California Academy of Sciences was founded in 1853 and occupied several homes before moving to Golden Gate Park (southeast of the Music Concourse) in 1916. Today it comprises the **Natural History Museum**, the Morrison Planetarium with its Laserium light-and-sound show, and the Steinhart Aquarium. (Academy Bay in the Galapagos Islands was named for this museum, which sponsored one of the earliest expeditions there.)

News was made in 1990 with the opening of a new exhibit hall in the Natural History Museum called Life Through Time, the most comprehensive and up-to-date explanation of evolution in the world. Visitors journey through more than three billion years, through geological faults and sea fossils, through the lives of multicellular organisms and early land animals. They meet millipedes, dinosaurs, mammals that coexisted with dinosaurs, birds, and true mammals, rhinos, whales, and—eventually—human beings. An ingenious computer program called LIFEmap allows the visitor to select any life form and trace its genealogy through billions of years.

The Natural History complex also includes Wild California (land and marine animals and plants), Wattis Hall of Human Cultures (from the Arctic to desert Australia), African Safari (dioramas), The Far Side of Science Gallery (159 original cartoons by Gary Larson giving a weird new perspective on science and research), Hohfeld Earth & Space Hall (ride the Safe-Quake that simulates two of the city's famous tremors), and Gem & Mineral Hall (more than 1,000 specimens).

Steinhart Aquarium claims the most diverse fish collection in the world, with more than 1,000 species. The **Fish Roundabout** puts you in the middle of fast-swimming fish of the open ocean; there's also the largest living tropical coral reef in the country.

Morrison Planetarium presents daily sky shows in Northern California's largest inside universe; the **Laserium** presents live laser shows Thursday through Sunday evenings; Tel: 750-7141.

Within the Academy, on the lower floor of Cowell Hall, the **Jungle Café** is open for light meals until one hour before closing. The **Academy Store** offers a wide selection of books, posters, toys, and gifts.

The Academy of Sciences is open every day of the year, with extended evening hours from July 4 through Labor Day until 7:00 P.M.; the first Wednesday of each month there is no admission charge (Tel: 750-7145).

To drive to the Academy from Union Square, take Geary Street west to Masonic, go south on Masonic until you turn right (west) onto Fell Street and continue straight into Golden Gate Park, where you veer left at Middle Drive to the parking area.

Also from Union Square, take the number 38 Geary bus and transfer at Sixth Avenue to the number 44 O'Shaughnessy bus, which runs into the park. The number 44 connects with many bus lines, with the Forest Hill MUNI Metro station, and with the Glen Park BART station; for more information, Tel: 673-MUNI.

Asian Art Museum

San Francisco received the artistic distinction worthy of a Pacific Rim capital when, in the 1960s, Chicago insurance executive, international envoy, and Olympics Committee chairman Avery Brundage bequeathed his enormous collection of Asian treasures to the city. A showcase museum designed especially to house it was constructed next to the De Young Museum (see below); it opened in 1966.

On the main floor, the recent reinstallation of the permanent Chinese galleries has doubled the number of objects on display; many works are now on view for the first time. The Chinese scroll paintings and the objects in the Magnin Jade Room are extraordinary.

The second-floor galleries are devoted to the arts of Iran, Turkey, Syria, Afghanistan, India, Tibet, Nepal, Pakistan, Korea, Japan, and Southeast Asia, in addition to the recently reinstalled Himalayan Gallery; Tel: 668-8921.

M. H. de Young Memorial Museum

The city's oldest, most diversified art museum evolved from vigorous backing and support of the California Midwinter International Exposition of 1894 by Michael Harry de Young who, with his older brother Charles, published the *Daily Morning and Evening Chronicle* (ancestor of today's *Chronicle*). All profits from that fair went to the construction of a major museum around the nucleus of a city collection. It opened in 1919, designed by Louis Christian Mullgardt to echo his Court of the Ages at the 1915 Panama-Pacific International Exposition, of which the Palace of Fine Arts in the Marina is the last remaining structure.

Ignored until fairly recently, the de Young's collection of American paintings is just now being recognized for its excellence, partly because in 1988 American works within the San Francisco Fine Arts Museums grouping (which includes the de Young, the Legion of Honor, and the Asian Art museums) were concentrated at the de Young, while European ones were grouped at the California Palace of the Legion of Honor (see Ocean Beach and Land's End below). Although the American collection can't compete with that of New York's Metropolitan or Boston's Museum of Fine Arts, it ranks as the most comprehensive west of Chicago.

The de Young now has 21 galleries of American art from the 17th century to the 20th. One great strength is a most unusual group of trompe l'oeil and still-life works from the turn of the century. The most important acquisition in recent years was the gift in 1979 by the John D. Rockefeller III family of more than a hundred canvases, including the de Young's best Copley, its only Homer, two George Caleb Binghams, a Thomas Eakins portrait, and more.

Three galleries of British art lead into the primary emphasis on American art. The works date from the reign of George III and into the early 19th century, altogether an era of outstanding Neoclassical and Rococo achievements. Among the major painters represented are Constable, Reynolds, and Gainsborough. Paintings have been integrated with the furniture and decorative arts of their periods.

The museum also boasts an important textile collection as well as powerful exhibitions from Africa, Oceania, and the Americas, and significant holdings of ancient art. The **Archives of American Art**, a branch of the Smithsonian Institution, is housed in the de Young (open only by appointment); Tel: 556-2530.

The museum's bookstore is very well stocked and the **Café de Young** (walk through galleries 21–25 in the east wing to reach it) is a pleasant cafeteria with a tiny garden for outdoor dining; Tel: 750-3600 or 750-3659 (taped information).

Around in the Park

There are, of course, reasons to visit the park other than the museums. From east to west (downtown to the ocean), main attractions include the **Conservatory of Flowers**, the oldest building in the park and modeled after London's Kew Gardens, a glassy Victorian glory with permanent tropical displays and seasonal exhibitions; **Strybing Arboretum and Botanical Gardens**, a 70-acre growing library of 6,000 species of plants, including a Cape Province Garden and a New World Cloud Forest, Queen Wilhelmina Tulip Garden, succulents, and California natives; and the **Music Concourse**, where Sunday concerts are held at 1:00 P.M.

Just west of the Music Concourse, the **Japanese Tea Garden** is a five-acre legacy of contemplation from the 1894 International Exposition. Amble around and under maples, magnolia, wisteria, cherries, pines, cedars, quince, bamboo, ginkgo.

Then, on the shores of Stow Lake, appears **Kinmen Pavilion**, composed of 6,000 wooden pieces shipped from Taipei,

Taiwan, a sister city. North of Stow Lake you'll find (near Rainbow Falls) **Prayerbook Cross**, a 57-foot sandstone memorial (a copy of an ancient Celtic cross) that commemorates the first North American service employing the Anglican Book of Common Prayer. The service was performed by Francis Fletcher, chaplain to Sir Francis Drake, on June 24, 1579, on the shores of Marin County.

The less-frequented west end of the park is home on the range for a herd of bison; where the Pacific breaks there's the Dutch windmill, restored in 1981.

Golden Gate Park is best seen on foot or by bicycle (bicycles can be rented along Stanyan Street) but, failing that, drive in early in the morning and on a weekday, especially in summer. The parking strips around the Music Concourse are best for museum-goers; otherwise, parking all along the drives bordering the meadows is permitted.

To reach the park by public transportation from downtown, take the number 38 bus west on Geary Street out to Sixth Avenue, then transfer to the southbound number 44 O'Shaughnessy, which will let you off right at the Music Concourse, the heart of the cultural matter.

Although there's a cafeteria in the de Young Museum, picnicking is the best solution for easing hunger in the park. Should that prove impractical, drive west on M. L. King, Jr., Drive, turn left on Park Presidio Boulevard/19th Avenue (which cuts right through the middle of the park) and, on the southern edge of the park, you'll spot the informal **19th Avenue Diner**. It's on nobody's list of great places, but it serves good, solid food when and where you need it.

HAIGHT-ASHBURY

Some people call it Holistic Haight, others just The Haight, the former flower-power haven of Haight-Ashbury that ranges irregularly from the panhandle leading into Golden Gate Park south along Clayton, Belvedere, Ashbury, and the streets climbing up the rise of Buena Vista Park. To the east is the Western Addition area and, beyond that, the Civic Center. Today, more than two decades after 1967's Summer of Love, the Haight is a gentrifying street scene mixing what one might call blue-collar yuppie with a dash of punk.

Landscaping and cable car–line construction began in what were called the Outer Lands in the 1870s, and elaborate houses sprang up in the late 1880s and 1890s, most of them Queen Annes. Ashbury Heights was cosmopolitan, and after the earthquake of 1906 the district enjoyed a building boom. In 1924 a San Francisco *Examiner* columnist wrote, "There is a comfortable maturity about the compact little city San Francisco knows as Haight-Ashbury ... a nice uphol-stered, fuchsia garden sort of grownup-ness, just weathered enough to be nice, and new enough to be looking ahead to the future instead of sighing futilely over the past."

Came the Depression, the Bohemianism of the late 1950s, and then, in 1966, Ken Kesey (author of *One Flew Over the Cuckoo's Nest*), who proclaimed a Trips Festival. As Randolph Delehanty puts it: "Thousands attended, dropped acid and spaced-out on rock music. The word 'hippie' was born. Through a new kind of music, psychedelic rock, the pacific hippie message spread around the country and the world ... In the Haight, Victoriana came back ... bands had names like ... Big Brother and the Holding Company ... Jefferson Airplane, and the enduring Grateful Dead."

Victorian houses were painted in psychedelic colors, an avalanche of publicity poured adjectives over the area, and Gray Line even introduced a tour (in sealed buses) called the Hippie Hop. But, sadly and predictably, drug violence followed the flowers and the Haight began its swift spiral downward, to come to a cheap death with the influx of heroin in the early 1970s.

What most San Franciscans remember of the Haight is the skid-row days of the 1970s, with boarded-up storefronts, torched Victorians, the homeless stretched in the streets, and pathetic sanitary conditions. The Summer of Love died an early, ugly death.

What will interest today's traveller are some unusual stores (see Shopping) and nightlife (see that section), as well as the **Spreckels Mansion** bed and breakfast at 737 Buena Vista Avenue West (see Accommodations).

CIVIC CENTER

Architectural critics have called the Civic Center "the grand-est in the country." Basically, it consists of a plaza flanked by eight buildings to the east and west of Van Ness Avenue between Franklin and Leavenworth streets and, north and south, between Golden Gate Avenue and Hayes Street. It is southwest of Union Square and just north of Market Street.

The nucleus of this composition is the French Renais-sance–style **City Hall**, with a dome taller than the U. S. Capi-tol's. Across the street, the **Performing Arts Center**, the second-largest such complex in the United States, after Lincoln Center in New York, comprises the War Memorial Opera House, Louise M. Davies Symphony Hall, Veterans Building (housing the Museum of Modern Art and Herbst Theater), and Harold L. Zellerbach Rehearsal Hall. (Tours of the Performing Arts Center are offered every Monday from 10:00 A.M. to 2:30 P.M. on the hour and the half hour; Tel: 552-8338.)

To the southeast of City Hall, the Civic Auditorium seats more than 7,000 people for conventions and sports or cultural events. Brooks Exhibit Hall, where giant trade shows, computer fairs, and the like are held, was installed in 1958 beneath Civic Center Plaza.

The **Public Library**, east across the plaza from City Hall, is a handsome Beaux Arts building that houses some one-and-a-half million volumes, and is home to several special collections of old maps, newspapers, and material on the 1906 earthquake and fire. (In 1995 the library is slated to move to a newly constructed building nearby, while the Asian Art Museum will be moved into the present library structure.)

San Francisco Museum of Modern Art

Occupying the third and fourth floors of the Veterans Building, the Museum of Modern Art was the first in California devoted to works of the 20th century. Rotating displays show works from the permanent collection by artists such as Kandinsky, Matisse, Picasso, Clyfford Still, Albers, Calder, and Noguchi, as well as contemporary California artists. There's a lively schedule of changing exhibitions (especially creative in the field of photography), and an innovative Department of Architecture and Design. The bookstore is particularly well stocked with works on modern art. The museum is closed only on Mondays; Tel: 863-8800.

The San Francisco Ballet

Founded in 1933, the San Francisco Ballet is America's oldest professional company. In recent years, under artistic director Helgi Tomasson, former choreographer and principal dancer with the New York City Ballet, the S. F. Ballet has attained a firm position among the leading companies of the world. The company launches its season every December with a lavish production of *The Nutcracker,* to which families have been going for generations.

The ballet performs in the War Memorial Opera House in Civic Center at 301 Van Ness Avenue; Tel: 621-3838. In 1983 the Ballet Building was opened at 455 Franklin Street, directly behind the Opera House, to allow the dancers more and better space for practicing *bourrées* and *pas de deux*.

The San Francisco Opera

The true San Franciscan is prouder of the San Francisco Opera and the splendid Beaux Arts **War Memorial Opera House** than any institution in the city—whether or not he ever sets foot inside it. The single biggest social event of the year is September's Opening Night at the Opera, when the smart set still strolls slowly up the steps, gowned, bejeweled, and tuxedoed, and everybody else who can squeeze into the street comes to gape and ogle. It's about the last scene of Old San Francisco on the town.

The opera company itself was founded in 1923 and moved into the Opera House (the first such civic house in the country) on October 15, 1932, with Lily Pons in Puccini's *La Tosca*. The magnificent house seats 3,252 patrons for the fall season from September to December. Until the completion of the Symphony Hall in 1980, the opera season was followed in the Opera House by that of the symphony. Now a short opera season takes place in late-spring/early-summer, and a major extension of the season is being considered.

Tickets may be difficult to obtain, because the season is usually fully subscribed; Tel: 864-3330. A solution is to turn up about an hour before a performance, when unused tickets are hawked on the street.

The Opera House proudly claims to be the birthplace of the United Nations, which was founded here in 1945.

The San Francisco Symphony

Founded in 1911 as the nation's first municipally supported symphony, the San Francisco Symphony played its seasons in the Opera House until 1980, when it moved into the admirable **Louise M. Davies Symphony Hall**, which manages to echo the monumental architecture of the Civic Center complex. The season in the 3,036-seat house (some seats even in a semicircle *behind* the orchestra) runs from October through May under the direction of maestro Herbert Blomstedt.

In addition, the symphony sponsors the annual Merrill Lynch Great Performers Series of soloists and visiting orchestras, the spring Mostly Mozart series, June's Beethoven Festival, and the Summer Pops performances. For the Davies box office, Tel: 431-5400.

A winning bronze sculpture by Henry Moore, *Large Four-Piece Reclining Figure,* sits before the curved glass façade of Davies Hall at Van Ness and Grove streets.

Dining and Shopping Around the Civic Center

Since the opening of Symphony Hall there has been a welcome blossoming of good-to-excellent restaurants in the immediate area. **Stars** is alive with the energy and originality of superchef-owner Jeremiah Tower at 150 Redwood Alley (between McAllister and Golden Gate); Tel: 861-7827. The prices and the noise level are high, but diners are having too much fun to notice; the main room is spacious, and the cocktail area in the middle of it is always packed. It's all dedicated to the excitement of eating well.

Harry's Bar and American Grill has a woody, roomy appeal, and serves hearty Italian fare as befits its spiritual inheritance from Venice and Florence. The service is very willing at 500 Van Ness Avenue.

The bright, simple decor of **Hayes Street Grill** at 320 Hayes near Franklin is seconded by the simple, tasteful treatment of seafood. Several grilled meats are also available. Service, alas, is not a strong suit. The blending of classic cuisines that the Chinese call *nanyang cai* (cuisine of the southern ocean) is the delightful dividend diners discover at a rather new restaurant, **Monsoon**, in Opera Plaza, 601 Van Ness Avenue. It's big, it's beautiful, and sure to be a success.

The Tower touch is evident again (but in a very different sense from that at Stars) in **690**, at 690 Van Ness Avenue. This is no place for quiet conversation; dulcet tones would not be heard. **Act IV** finally has the kitchen its gracious decor and atmosphere have deserved. In the Inn at the Opera, at 333 Fulton Street behind the Opera House, it serves a special after-theater supper as well as lunch and dinner.

The **California Culinary Academy** at 625 Polk Street off Turk shows off the developing techniques and expertise of its student cooks. It's interesting to watch future chefs at work, and the prices are right. Fish grilled over mesquite and several innovative specialties added to an informal, welcoming atmosphere have made **Zuni** one of the best-liked restaurants in town. It's at 1658 Market Street near Franklin. A cozy yet elegant quality in new quarters have

enhanced the fine, often-inspired French cuisine served at
Zola's, 395 Hayes Street at Gough. A loud, lively, restaurant-
cum-jazz club is **Kimball's**, 300 Grove Street.

In addition, three worthwhile "fast-food" cafés in the
neighborhood are **Stars Café**, a tiny adjunct of Stars itself,
555 Golden Gate Avenue at Van Ness; **Spuntino**, for self-
served Italian nibbling, 524 Van Ness Avenue; and **Vicolo
Pizzeria**, 201 Ivy Street near Grove.

A three-hour walking Maltese Falcon Tour through San
Francisco as seen by local detective fiction writer Dashiell
Hammett departs on Sundays at noon from the front of the
Public Library (see above).

Across the street from Davies Hall, the **S.F. Opera Shop** has
an extensive array of books, records, posters, gifts, tee-shirts,
and other souvenirs; **Vorpal Gallery** specializes in fine prints
at 393 Grove Street.

MISSION DOLORES

Simple little Mission Dolores (properly, Mission San Francisco of Assisi) is the most provocative single sight in the city,
yet it is normally ignored by both San Franciscans and
visitors because its neighborhood is otherwise of little interest, except to the people who live here (at Dolores and 16th
streets, three blocks south of busy Market Street and southwest of Civic Center).

Yet the story of this church and its sisters is the story of
the settlement of California by the Spanish, who dominated
Alta (Upper) California (as opposed to Mexican Baja—
Lower—California.)

"Spaced along the California coast a stiff day's march
apart" (to quote from Sunset Books' *The California Missions*) "stand 21 mission churches, simple and massive structures of adobe [mud] and stone ... Some ... are smothered
in the metropolitan embrace, enclosed on all sides by the
structures of a newer day. Others stand free in open valleys,
still retaining some measure of the pastoral charm that was
their original setting. Nearly all of them are merely token
survivals of once-widespreading structures that were miniature cities teeming with activity. Like shells found on the
beach, the missions that stand in varying degrees of restoration seem washed up on the shores of time, the life within
long since departed."

Originally there had been no plans to name a mission
after St. Francis of Assisi, founder of the Franciscan order, a

fact protested by Father Junípero Serra to the inspector-general of Mexico, José de Galvez. "If St. Francis wishes a mission," Galvez responded, "let him show you a good port, and then let it bear his name." So in 1769, when Gaspar de Portolá's explorers discovered San Francisco Bay, the chroniclers of the party declared, "This is the port to which [Galvez] referred and to which the Saint has led us."

San Francisco today is so cosmopolitan, its heritage such a cultural cocktail, that to step into Mission Dolores is to be surprised by a sense of sadness at the lost simplicity, the forgotten lineage from that early settlement. The interior is beautiful in its joining of the rude tile floors and thick adobe walls to the gilded and brightly painted Baroque altar, the *reredos* (altar screens), and the stunning ceiling, covered with earth-toned chevron designs, a pattern supposed to have been adapted from the Costanoan people. (The native tribal groups of the region were grouped together in the Spanish mind as Costanoans, "coastal dwellers.")

Equally interesting is the small, crowded cemetery on the south side of the Mission, where lie the famous, the infamous, and the anonymous. Among the former are Don Luis Antonio Argüello, first governor of Mexican California, and Francisco de Haro and José Noe, Yerba Buena's first and last *alcaldes* (mayors). The infamous include James P. Casey, murderer of crusading newspaper editor James King of William. Most touching is a rock shrine marked "To the neglected and forgotten who rest here"; some 5,515 Native Americans were buried in mass graves, most victims of European diseases.

The squat Mission is dwarfed by its immediate neighbor on the north, the gaudy (by comparison) Mission Dolores Basilica, begun in 1913 and given its soaring towers in 1926. (The term *basilica* denotes a church that is a consecrated place of pilgrimage and of great artistic merit; this was the fourth church in the U.S. to be so honored—status was given in 1952 by Pope Pius XII—and the first west of the Mississippi.)

The services of the Mass are held in the old Mission daily, except Sundays, at 7:30 A.M. Sunday Mass is celebrated in the Basilica; Tel: 621-8203. (The last Mission in the 21-church chain was San Francisco Solano in Sonoma—see Wine Country.)

To reach Mission Dolores, take the J Church streetcar from any subway stop along Market Street to Church and 16th streets, then walk a block east to Dolores. (Confusingly, Church Street is one block west of Dolores Street.) You can also take MUNI Metro/BART, which runs under Market Street, from stations at the Embarcadero, Montgomery, Powell, or Civic Center to the Church Street Station.

SOMA (SOUTH OF MARKET)

Sometime in the late 1980s somebody shook San Francisco and everything loose fell south of Market into what old-timers call "south of the slot" ("slot" refers to the apertures where the cables propelling the streetcars lay) and contemporaries call SoMa (doubtless an echo of New York's SoHo). SoMa constitutes part, but far from all, of the Mission District that, as its name implies, grew up around the mission church of San Francisco de Asís. As such, the district was an early one, and predominantly home to Spanish and Mexican settlers, followed in the 1860s by German and Scandinavian immigrants. Businesses here tended to be small and rents low, and between 1950 and 1970 the Latino community doubled each decade. Today this community also grows as a result of the unrest continuing throughout Central America, and now includes large numbers of Guatemalans, Salvadorians, Costa Ricans, Nicaraguans, and Colombians, with their attendant shops and restaurants.

Randolph Delehanty has called the Mission a revolving door into American society. The casual traveller, however, will find less to interest him in the Hispanic part of this neighborhood than in most other parts of the city, unless he wants to seek out particular Latin dishes, spices, and condiments. Cafés, taquerías, Mexican bakeries, and specialty stores give 24th Street a particularly *simpático* air (see Dining for suggestions on eating out in this neighborhood). We concentrate here on the more café-oriented part of the Mission District that is known as SoMa.

Physically, SoMa is roughly a two-mile-square grid of one-way streets and narrow alleys bounded by Market Street on the north, China Basin and 17th Street on the south, the Embarcadero on the east, and 10th and Division streets on the west. (The whole area is geographically skewed; no streets run in precise directions.)

Essentially, SoMa is an attitude. The South of Market district metamorphosed from a smart residential area in the 1850s and 1860s (Rincon Hill and South Park are examples) to a small business center, followed by a skid-row slum, and now to an avant-garde arts quarter. Higher rents elsewhere, combined with empty buildings and lower rents in SoMa, have attracted small cafés, galleries, experimental theaters, warehouses, studios, factory outlets, a wholesale flower mart, nightclubs of all creative forms, and the dramatic Showplace Square design center.

Maybe it all began in 1981 with the **George R. Moscone Center**, named for the mayor slain with Supervisor Harvey Milk in 1978; the entire project is to be completed in 1992. The convention center, which covers an 11-acre site entered from Howard Street between Third and Fourth streets, is built mostly underground; its six-acre, column-free exhibit hall is one of the largest in the world.

Overlooking Moscone Center and a great swatch of SoMa, the **San Francisco Marriott** at 777 Market Street and Fourth opened in October, 1989, to huzzahs for its convention and conference facilities and hisses for its architecture. Local critics dub it the Giant Jukebox, but everyone seems to enjoy the **View Lounge** on the 39th floor, with dramatic views through a 35-foot fan window over the Financial District to Alcatraz and the Oakland docks beyond the Bay Bridge.

Satellite restaurants have crowded into the area: the loud, cheerful, traditional Mexican **Cadillac Bar and Grill**, 325 Minna, off Fifth Street between Mission and Howard; light, fresh, Mexican **Chevy's**, 150 Fourth Street; and comfortable, old-fashioned, generous **Max's Diner**, 311 Third Street.

South Park

Between Brannan and Bryant streets on the south and north and Third and Second streets on the west and east, the tiny oval of South Park is for some reason difficult to find, even when you know where it is. A few years ago it was a pathetic slum, dangerous and depressing. Yet in the 1850s some of the city's most fashionable residences stood here, enjoying the town's most salubrious weather. James Benét tells the tale (in *A Guide to San Francisco*): "George Gordon, a former neighbor of the Brontë family in Yorkshire, married a barmaid and felt compelled to emigrate to California. He developed the park in 1852 in imitation of a London square and sold its 64 lots to prominent citizens. He is said to have imported English sparrows as well as roses.

"Gordon's personal tragedy, his wife's revenge on him by making their daughter an alcoholic, was the subject of Gertrude Atherton's first novel, *A Daughter of the Vine*."

Thinking of an old romance, an old sadness, take a seat (try to reserve one) at **South Park Café** (108 South Park), a tiny, colorful spot that's very French in feeling; Tel: 495-7275. Right at hand at 462 Bryant, you can purchase French, Californian, and German wines at **Connoisseur Wine Imports**.

Jack London's birthplace is marked with a plaque on the Wells Fargo Bank at Brannan and Third streets.

The new **Friends of Photography** museum is located in the **Ansel Adams Center**, the largest arts facility in SoMa, with five exhibition galleries, a bookstore, and a library. One gallery is devoted exclusively to Adams's photographs. It's open Tuesdays through Sundays at 250 Fourth Street, just a three-block walk south of Market; Tel: 495-7000.

Cafés in SoMa

As happens with any district during revitalization, SoMa greets every new café with joyful welcome, then drops it for the even newer one on the block. Here are some that show signs of lasting. (All are better choices for lunch than for dinner, partially because of the seediness of the surrounding area.)

From 1906 to 1954, the San Francisco power-lunch crowd gathered at a Sutter Street Financial District restaurant called the **Fly Trap** to eat the classic Gold Rush dish, Hangtown Fry. (Ordered by miners who had struck it rich, it involved oysters, eggs, and bacon.) In 1989 the Fly Trap was reborn at 606 Folsom near Third.

It's worth an expedition to **Eddie Jacks** for the fried polenta sticks with Gorgonzola sauce alone. The California grill cooking is called inventive, the scene happening, the crowd compelling. It's at 1151 Folsom Street off Seventh.

At **Eddie Rickenbacker's**, nostalgia for World War I is the theme, people who barely remember World War II are the crowd. The mood is happy, the hamburgers terrific, and the location at 133 Second Street between Mission and Howard is handy.

At Mission and Spear streets, the site of the former Rincon Annex Post Office, a masterwork of civic design, is being reworked as a complex of shops, offices, and apartments called Rincon Center. An ambitious new Italian restaurant, **Etrusca**, opened at the heart of the Center (101 Spear Street), a project of the owner of the Il Fornaio chain. In a stunning setting, especially dramatic in the evening, the main courses match the pastas in excellence, not always the case elsewhere. This is rapidly becoming a new old favorite.

At the southern tip of SoMa, deep in the docklands of China Basin, the **Mission Rock Resort** serves some of the best hamburgers in San Francisco on outside decks that overlook slips and dry docks. It's extremely casual, even slipshod, but a great place for lunch on a sunny day. Take Third Street south, then turn east on Mission Rock Street to China Basin Street, where the restaurant sits waterside at number 817.

The **Dolphin P. Rempp** is an old sailing ship that transported lumber and spices to the South Pacific and South America around the turn of the century. In her long history, as the good ship *Ellen,* she also carried troops, smuggled rum, and starred in *Mutiny on the Bounty.* Now she sits at Pier 42, near the southern end of the Embarcadero, and her galley serves a wide range of seafoods. Squint and you'll think you're back in clipper days. Parking is available alongside the ship.

OCEAN BEACH AND LAND'S END

On the far western rim of San Francisco, where rugged cliffs rise out of the sea, an immigrant once constructed a wooden fairy-tale château, a French confection seven stories high with turrets and towers and spires that perched atop a rocky outcrop at the end of a continent. This was the **Cliff House** that Adolph Sutro built.

Sutro was the kind of man who made San Francisco in the years immediately after the Gold Rush of 1849. Born in Prussia in 1830, he came with his family to the United States after the Revolution of 1848, and in 1859 joined the rush to the Comstock Lode in Nevada. After an 18-year battle against nature, politicians, and the Bank of California, he finally made his fortune—though not from silver. He engineered, financed, and constructed a great tunnel through a mountain that was being mined, making drainage and ventilation possible for the first time. When it was finished, conditions for the miners were much improved, and royalties from use of his tunnel had made Sutro rich.

Retiring to San Francisco, Sutro bought vast chunks of land, including San Miguel Rancho (where Twin Peaks and other central hills rise today); he is said to have owned one-twelfth of all the land in the city. He planted gardens, collected art, gathered a famous library (a part of which is housed near San Francisco State University), built his Cliff House château and the nearby Sutro Baths (the world's largest indoor swimming pools of both fresh- and saltwater), and served as San Francisco's mayor from 1894 to 1896.

The first Cliff House, a restaurant preceding Sutro's version, was built in 1863 and could be reached from down-town San Francisco only by carriages that plied the Point Lobos Toll Road. Sutro bought the operation in 1883, but the house was badly damaged four years later when the schooner *Parallel,* loaded with dynamite, struck and blew up on the rocks below. Then, on Christmas Day, 1894, the Cliff House burned down to its stony foundation.

Two years later, Sutro completed his fanciful château-restaurant, which became enormously fashionable, only to burn down in its turn in 1907. (There's still a brisk trade in postcards featuring that improbable palace.)

Today's Cliff House, the fifth in the series, is a squat, bland building totally unworthy of its splendid setting. It is worth visiting, however, for its site and for other attractions in the immediate area. Within the building at 1090 Point Lobos Avenue is the **Musée Méchanique**, reminiscent of an old penny arcade, that claims to have the world's largest collection of coin-operated, antique musical machines.

San Franciscans showing off their city sometimes repair with their guests to the Cliff House bar, the **Ben Butler Room**, to watch the sun set behind Seal Rocks and perhaps to raise a salute to Adolph Sutro. **Upstairs at the Cliff House** is best for a Sunday brunch or late lunch. There's an unusual menu of 30 omelettes.

The **Camera Obscura** on the seaside shelf below the building is of particular interest to children, who can't imagine a world B.C.—Before Cameras. Entering the large, darkened box-like structure, you see images of external objects received through an aperture, as with a convex lens. At the nearby visitors' center of the Golden Gate National Recreation Area, you may pick up a map of that region, as well as several helpful brochures.

Offshore Sights

About 400 feet offshore, the sea smashes up against **Seal Rocks**, where Stellar sea lions (not seals at all) loll lazily, oblivious to the army of tourists aiming at them with tele-photo lenses. Of the many ships that have wrecked in the roiling waters outside the Golden Gate, one—the freighter *Ohioan*—grounded in 1936 just to the north of Seal Rocks.

On a fogless day, you may be able to spot the **Farallon Islands**, seven giant rocks rising out of the ocean about 30 miles away. They are thought to have been discovered by an expedition from New Spain in 1543. In 1579 Sir Francis Drake landed there to secure a supply of seal meat, birds, and eggs, and named the site the Islands of St. James. In 1775 Lieutenant Juan Francisco de la Bodéga (after whom Bodega Bay to the north in Sonoma County was named) called them *Farallones de los Frailes* (Friars' Cliffs), and that is still the name today.

It's not often realized that the Russians sailed as far south as this: They developed the islands as a fur station between 1809 and 1812 in their quest for sea otter pelts. The Farallons were (and are) a rich rookery, and during the Gold Rush, when a boiled egg in the city cost 75 cents, egg wars broke out among competing hunters. The Farallons today are a bird sanctuary.

Oceanic Society Expeditions, Building E at Fort Mason, operates the naturalist-led **Farallon Islands Excursions**. These isles form the largest seabird rookery along the Pacific Coast south of Alaska. Tours run June–November; Tel: 474-3385.

North of Cliff House

Immediately to the north of Cliff House, the **Sutro Baths** were built in 1896, six indoor, fresh- and saltwater swimming pools that spread over three acres, complete with gardened parterres. They closed after World War II, and the building burned to the ground in 1966. Today they lie in ruins, not romantic but simply ugly.

Rising above the ruins, **Point Lobos** is the westernmost reach of the city, a rough palisade the Spanish called *Punta de los Lobos* (Point of the Sea Wolves, as they called sea lions). It's a dramatic lookout point reached by a little trail that leads from the sidewalk on the north side of Point Lobos Avenue.

Beyond, wild and usually deserted, the promontory of **Land's End** pokes above the Pacific between Seal Rocks Beach (not the same as Seal Rocks) and China Beach. It is accessible by fairly steep trails, some of which wind down to the surf. If you intend to make this hike, inquire about conditions at the aforementioned visitors' center near the Cliff House. Every year several people are swept away at Land's End, and not only during storms.

East of Cliff House, atop the bluff across Point Lobos Avenue, Sutro established his home (now long gone) and gardens on **Sutro Heights**, where he planted fir, Monterey cypress, and Norfolk pine, allowing the public free access to the grounds and gardens. When he died in 1898 his daughter Dr. Emma Sutro Meritt (one of California's pioneer women physicians) inherited his property, which she bequeathed to the city upon her death in 1938.

In recent years sadly neglected, Sutro Heights is a fine place for melancholy walks in early evening. Today a part of the Golden Gate Recreation Area (see the section on the eastern part of it earlier in the chapter), it has been spruced up to include a dramatic overlook and a rock garden. A marked path leads to it from the parking lot on the south side of Point Lobos Avenue, a few yards uphill and around a bend from Cliff House. (For a hike between the Sutro Baths and the Palace of the Legion of Honor, discussed next, see the end of the Palace section.)

California Palace of the Legion of Honor

High on wind-whipped Land's End, 200 feet above the Pacific where the view stretches west toward the Far East, the Legion of Honor commands a natural artwork grander than any man-made masterpiece. The first Europeans to set foot upon this spectacular bluff were Captain Fernando Rivera y Moncada and Father Francisco Palou, who in 1774 set up a crude cross on its summit above ocean and bay (which, at that time, a ship had never entered).

This creamy Neoclassical pile at the city's extreme northwest corner stands as dramatic evidence of the French connections so germane to the early life of San Francisco. Mrs. Adolph B. Spreckels (wife of one of the several sons of German-born sugar baron Claus Spreckels) had been born Alma de Bretteville, one of local society's ladies of French origin. She married Adolph in 1908, when she was 24 and he 50.

An enthusiast and student of art, Mrs. Spreckels was moved by the French pavilion at the Panama-Pacific Exposition, a replica of the Palais de la Légion d'Honneur in Paris, and commissioned the construction of a lasting version as a memorial to Californians killed in World War I. Designed by George A. Applegarth, it was dedicated on Memorial Day, 1924. Another Spreckels gift, one of the five original bronze casts of Rodin's *The Thinker,* welcomes you when you pass through the Court of Honor to the museum's entrance. (The outer entrance is flanked by large equestrian statues of El Cid and Joan of Arc by Anna Hyatt Huntington.)

At the end of 1989 the Legion of Honor unveiled 15 new galleries, including one of the finest collections of Rodin sculpture in the world and significant European art from the 17th century through the 19th, as well as Medieval art galleries, completing the Legion's permanent presentation of eight centuries of European art. The **Achenbach Foundation for the Graphic Arts** here is the largest collection of prints in the West.

The **Café Chantecler** is open during museum hours for lunches and aperitifs, and on Saturdays and Sundays at 4:00 P.M. Ludwig Altman and John Fenstermaker alternately give organ concerts in the Rodin Gallery; Tel: 750-3600 or 750-3659 (taped information).

The Legion of Honor's exhibits are worth seeing even if you do not plan to explore the rest of the Ocean Beach (see below) and Land's End area. Drivers from the Marina district can reach the Legion of Honor through the Presidio on Lincoln Boulevard, which becomes El Camino del Mar; turn left at the museum marker onto Legion of Honor Drive (El Camino comes to an end just after the turn).

From downtown, drive west on Geary Boulevard to 34th Avenue, turn right and cross Clement into Lincoln Park Municipal Golf Course and onto Legion of Honor Drive. (The rolling golf greens lie above cemeteries of Chinese, Italian, Greek, Jewish, and other national groups; when the city bought the land for a park in 1910, it promised never to remove the graves.) The flagpole at the parking lot directly in front of the museum marks the end of the old transcontinental Lincoln Highway.

By public transportation, board bus number 38 at Union Square or at stops farther along Geary Street, ride to 33rd Avenue, and transfer to number 18 for the last short leg to the museum.

For a hike after the museum visit, seek out the **Land's End Trail** near the end of El Camino del Mar. The trail winds around and atop the cliffs through wind-bent cypress trees, passes above crashing surf, and ends at the Cliff House parking lot and the ruins of the Sutro Baths. The path is the former roadbed of the Ferries & Cliff House Railway, a narrow-gauge road along which trains ran from 1888 to 1906.

Another refreshing trip after a morning in the museum is a drive through the maze of mansions known as **Sea Cliff**. (If you are coming from the museum, wind your way east on El Camino del Mar.) Sea Cliff is strictly residential and does not consider itself a thoroughfare; in fact, inhabitants of the area discourage all traffic, as would anyone privileged to live in such a quiet retreat atop such a spectacular site. Sea Cliff Avenue itself is only five or six blocks ("turns" might be a more appropriate word) long, running between the jig-jogs of 25th Avenue, Scenic Way, 26th and 27th avenues, and El Camino. It officially comes to a dead end north of 30th Avenue. Below these curves, where houses turn their windows and greenswards toward the sea, breakers beat on Baker and China beaches and the view stretches west past the Marin hills to Japan.

South of Cliff House

When San Franciscans say they are going to the beach, they usually mean **Ocean Beach**, which stretches from Cliff House south to the Fort Funston part of the Golden Gate Recreation Area and then to the oceanside golf course of the Olympic Country Club, a distance just under five miles. The wide Great Highway runs much of that length, with parking available between the north- and southbound lanes.

Jogging, playing ball, running with dogs, and picnicking are the pleasures at Ocean Beach; swimming is not. The undertow is as mean as a white shark along this strand; even wading is discouraged.

At the western edge of Golden Gate Park between Fulton Street and Lincoln Way there sits a small, white-pillared structure designed by Willis Polk in 1921. It hides within a stunning series of frescoes executed by locally recognized painter Lucien Labaudt in the mid-1930s. In the spirit of the day, they depict the working life of San Francisco; quotes from such writers as Bret Harte and Joaquin Miller complete the decoration. The frescoes have been freshened recently, and plans, albeit shaky, are underway to create a fine restaurant and bar in this curious corner.

Less than 3.5 miles south of Cliff House along the Great Highway you can turn east on Sloat Boulevard to the **San Francisco Zoo**, which occupies 65 acres of a 125-acre site slated to be fully developed by the year 2000. The zoo was born in 1889 with the gift from the *San Francisco Examiner* of a single grizzly bear named Monarch. Much-maligned during the last few years, the zoo has hired a new director with great plans and promises for bringing the institution up to international standards; Tel: 661-4844 or 661-2023.

If you continue east on Sloat Boulevard to 19th Avenue, you will arrive at **Sigmund Stern Grove**, a 33-acre forest of eucalyptus and redwood trees surrounding a grassy hollow, where on summer Sunday afternoons free performances of opera, ballet, symphony, folk music, and jazz are presented. Picnicking is encouraged; Tel: 398-6551.

Drivers can reach Cliff House and Ocean Beach by taking

Geary Boulevard west from downtown and veering right at 40th Avenue onto Point Lobos Avenue. In less than a mile you'll spot the Cliff House parking lot to the south of the avenue; metered parking also is available all along the road at this point, in front of Cliff House and down the hill in the center of the Great Highway.

From the Marina, drive west on the Golden Gate Bridge approach, take the 19th Avenue (Highway 1) exit before the toll booths, proceed south to Geary, then west as above. From Golden Gate Park, drive west to one of the two beach exits and directly onto the Great Highway, then turn north. Geary bus number 38 and Geary Limited number 38L will take you all the way from Union Square to 48th Avenue at Sutro Heights Park, from which it's only a few yards to Cliff House. To avoid even that walk, you can transfer to the number 18 bus at 46th Avenue, which continues to Cliff House, Golden Gate Park/Ocean Beach, and beyond.

SOUTH OF GOLDEN GATE PARK
The Sunset and South

When you come to the Sloat Boulevard–19th Avenue corner of Sigmund Stern Grove, you have arrived at the approximate center of a largely residential area little known to tourists and worth exploring only for those who have time on their hands and a wish to know San Francisco in depth. Frequently, this whole area is lumped under the designation of **The Sunset**, but the situation is more complicated than that. To the north of Sloat and east of 19th Avenue are the home-lined streets of the Sunset and Parkside areas; to the south and east are Lakeside, Stonestown (encompassing San Francisco State University), and Park Merced. North and west of the same corner are West of Twin Peaks, Forest Hill, Miraloma Park, West Portal, St. Francis Wood (which rivals Sea Cliff for fine homes), Westwood Park, and Ingleside.

Within Stonestown, **Stonestown Galleria** is a handsome shopping center, recently renovated, that claims to have been one of the first malls built. S.F. State, adjoining it to the south, is an urban university with little of interest to non-students.

If it's meal-time and something simple will suit, continue south on Sloat to the traffic light where Sloat meets Portola Drive, and take a sharp left onto West Portal Avenue. This short commercial street serves the surrounding neighborhood with banks, small clothing stores and food markets, a post office, a bookstore—most of the essentials of the daily routine. The best restaurant here is **Café for All Seasons** at number 150, where the menu is California nouvelle and reservations are always required; Tel: 665-0900. **Anne's Kitchen**, at number 362, features simple, delicious dishes cooked with a Thai touch; Tel: 665-7920. **Il Giardino** at number 215 offers dinners of familiar, homey Italian cooking, and you'll find Japanese cuisine at **Fuji** at number 301.

The small **Spiazzo** opened at 33 West Portal in 1990 and, for an inexpensive pasta and pizza place, boasts a most innovative menu. Across the street, the little deli/bakery **Café de Leon** is a good place to order picnic lunches or a snack to eat on the premises. Old-fashioned Italian food in great portions is served in dark, masculine, often loud **Gold Mirror** four blocks north of West Portal at 800 Taraval Street. It's probably the most authentic Old-World Italian hangout this side of North Beach.

From West Portal you can take a drive past the handsome homes in **St. Francis Woods**. The easiest way to begin is by taking 14th Avenue south from West Portal, crossing Portola Drive in a southeasterly direction onto San Anselmo, and then wandering along the snaky streets. To return to downtown, take Portola Drive north, which becomes upper Market Street. From the West Portal station, Muni travels to major downtown stops along Market Street.

The Castro

Where Portola Drive becomes Market Street at the corner of Castro and 17th streets, the heart of the Castro beats. (To those who live in the neighborhood and call their home Castro Village, its center is at Castro and 18th, one block south.) Castro Street itself is quite long, running from Waller Street in the north (east of Buena Vista Park) to 30th Street in the south. The Castro proper (also referred to as Noe Valley) extends only between Diamond on the east and Church on the west, 16th Street on the north and 25th on the south.

As the world knows, this is the center of gay life in San Francisco. (Polk Street was once the center, but most of the action moved here in the late 1970s.) Not every traveller will have an interest in investigating this area, but those who do have the best chance of seeing local life on Sundays, when the streets are swarming with shoppers, diners-out, sightseers, and promenaders.

As you walk, or even if you are just driving through, you will notice the shops on the south side of Market between

16th and 17th streets, where men's and women's clothing designed to make statements of all kinds is displayed in shop windows. It is often expensive and extravagant; as Dorothy said to Toto, "We're not in Kansas anymore." Right in the middle of this block, **Café San Marcos**, overlooking the street, caters to a mixture of residents and visitors.

Outsiders frequent the Castro particularly when film retrospectives are being held at the **Castro Theater** (429 Castro between 17th and 18th). Timothy Pflueger, a renowned regional architect of the 1920s, was responsible for this outburst of Spanish Renaissance elaboration—not to say excess.

The best restaurant in the area is really on the edge of the Castro, at 708 14th Street, corner of Market. **Le Piano Zinc** is a stylish French-inspired *boite* where the cuisine is exciting, although service can be uninspired. Reservations are suggested, and are required on weekends; Tel: 431-5266. Also worth noting is **Leticia's**, at 2223 Market between Sanchez and 15th, for Mexican cooking and good Sunday brunch, and **Sushi Gen** at 4248 18th Street at Diamond.

CABLE CARS

The only National Historical Landmarks you can ride are San Francisco's beloved cable cars, an ingenious invention of London-born Andrew S. Hallidie, who began by designing lifting machines for gold mines. The first of "Hallidie's follies" made its maiden run on August 2, 1873, from the top of Clay Street down Nob Hill's precipitous east side. It worked so well that by 1880 there were eight lines operating along 112 miles of cable.

Although there have been repeated attempts to abolish the cable cars in favor of more economical motor coaches (in the interests of efficiency and safety), and despite the ordeal of a two-year "open-heart" surgery of the entire system (1982 to 1984), the only vehicles of their kind in the world are still in service.

Two lines run from the turntable at Powell and Market streets (near below-street-level Hallidie Plaza, where you'll find the Visitor Information Center of the San Francisco Convention & Visitors Bureau); a third line begins at California and Market streets.

There's no more amusing manner of sampling the city's sweeping views than by riding a cable car. The most spectacular ride is on the Powell–Hyde line (cars are clearly marked), with vertical and lateral zigzags from Powell/ Market up over Nob and Russian hills to its turntable in Victorian Park on the northern waterfront. Stop for an Irish coffee at the **Buena Vista Café** here before the run back; nearby are the Ghirardelli Square shops-restaurants complex, the Maritime Museum, historic ships, the Cannery, and Fisherman's Wharf.

The Powell–Mason line runs from Powell/Market over Nob Hill (where there's a stop for Nob Hill hotels) and down to Bay Street and the hubbub of Fisherman's Wharf, three short blocks away.

The California Street line begins at the foot of that street in the Financial District (and near the Embarcadero), cuts through Chinatown's heart at Grant Avenue, crests at Nob Hill, and ends at Van Ness Avenue.

In summer the line of would-be passengers at Powell/ Market is discouraging in the extreme; it may be better to try boarding at a stop farther along the route. Self-service ticket dispensers are located at all terminals and major stops, where a $6 all-day MUNI adult pass is also available.

The **Cable Car Museum, Powerhouse, and Car Barn** is housed in a three-level, red-brick building at Washington and Mason streets. It shows off scale models of cable cars, the original prototype car number 8, and vintage photographs. From a special viewing room visitors can watch the underground wheels playing out the cables. A 16-minute film, *The Cable Car and How It Works,* is shown continually. The Cable Car Museum is open daily; Tel: 474-1887.

SPORTING SAN FRANCISCO

As 1990 began, the Bay Area had gone uncharacteristically gaga about its sports teams, which were (also uncharacteristically) winning every trophy in sight. As a rule, most San Franciscans wax warmly about a winning team and wail waspishly about a losing one, an attitude generally attributed to fair-weather fansmanship—and blamed in large part on the city's generally fair weather, which is enough to distract even the most ardent sports fan.

In 1990, though, the 49ers had won football's Super Bowl for the fourth time in the last eight years, the Giants had won the pennant in the National League, the Oakland Athletics had won the World Series, and the oft-slumping Golden State Warriors basketball team was enjoying its second playoff season in 12 years. (Behind the pros, university players crowded the region's winners' circles: In the last decade, Stanford University, the University of California at Berkeley, San Jose State, University of San Francisco, and Santa Clara University had won 53 national championships— 29 of them by more-brains-than-brawn Stanford.) There's even talk of importing a hockey team in 1991. It's pretty heady stuff.

The **San Francisco 49ers**, the most successful of the local professional teams, play football at windy Candlestick Park, a controversial 60,000-seat stadium eight miles south of town that even faithful fans love to hate. To watch Joe Montana and company, it's wise to bundle up in a ski parka, wear warm socks and gloves, and carry along earmuffs. To drive to Candlestick, take Highway 101 south to the Candlestick Park exit, then follow Giants Drive and Gilman Avenue, following posted directions to the parking lots; Tel: 468-2249 (49ers ticket office) or 392-7469 (Ticketron). It's much easier and less expensive to take the special ballpark transportation services provided on game days. Bus number 9X departs Sutter and Montgomery streets (Financial District), makes a handful of stops, then goes express to Candlestick; bus number 47 runs from Clay and Van Ness with stops on Van Ness and on Mission, then express to the park; Tel: 673-MUNI for information.

The **San Francisco Giants**, coached by "Hum-Baby" Roger Craig, played a humbler game in 1990 than the year before, but diehards still brave the wintry (even in summer) winds of Candlestick to cheer and jeer them on. For details on getting to Candlestick, see 49ers above; Tel: 467-8000 (tickets), 982-9400 (the Giants Dugout store, 170 Grand Avenue), or 392-7469 (Ticketron).

As the baseball world knows, the Giants' lease will be up in 1993; at this writing, the team plans to move to Santa Clara County (south on the Peninsula), where a new stadium will be built for them.

The winning **Oakland A's**, World Series champions in 1989 (when they dueled the Giants in the first-ever Trans-Bay series and the whole area was shaken by the 1989 earthquake), are very popular in most years with San Franciscans as well as East Bay fans. They play baseball in the Oakland–Alameda County Coliseum Complex. Drive across the San Francisco–Oakland Bay Bridge, then take the Nimitz Freeway (Highway 880) south to the Hegenberger Road turnoff and head left (northeast) to the Coliseum. For public transportation, take BART's Fremont–Daly City line from Civic Center, Powell Street, Montgomery Street, or Embarcadero stations to the Coliseum/Oakland Airport station, then follow an aerial walkway into the stadium; Tel: 638-0500 (tickets).

The Bay Area's now up, now down **Golden State Warriors** play basketball at the Oakland–Alameda County Coliseum as well. For information and tickets, Tel: 638-6000.

CITY WIDE CELEBRATIONS

You can tell a city by what it does in its spare time. San Francisco eats, drinks, and makes merry in myriad manners. The silliest of the city's episodic outbreaks is the **Examiner Bay to Breakers** race held in May, when up to 100,000 perfectly mad men, women, and children tear across town along a seven-and-a-half-mile course from near Justin Herman Plaza at the Embarcadero, through Golden Gate Park, and to the oceanside Great Highway.

Seeded runners are allowed to start in front so they don't have to fight the crowds (in 1990 Arturo Barrios set a speed record of 34:31.2), and have sometimes reached the finish line before the last few thousand have started. Some people make a day of it, pushing baby buggies, stopping to dance the boogaloo, careening into other "centipedes." (A centipede is a group of runners racing together in one costume: a giant papier-mâché toothbrush from the School of Dentistry, for example, or doctors joined in a 34-vertebrae spinal column, or a jogging Golden Gate Bridge.) Then there are the individual zanies: the Medflies chasing tomatoes, and the Paleolithic cave people among them. The only elements missing are sanity, sobriety, and any sense of civic disobedience at this 79-year-old celebration of craziness.

Here are some other special events, month by month. If you need more information, contact the San Francisco Convention and Visitors Bureau; Tel: 391-2000.

January: The International Boat Show at Moscone Center (Tel: 521-2558) and the San Francisco Sports and Boat Show at the Cow Palace in suburban Brisbane (Tel: 931-2500) get the sportsmen started for the spring season. The Dr. Martin Luther King, Jr., Birthday Celebration brings thousands of followers and enthusiasts to Civic Auditorium; Tel: 771-6300.

February: The Chinese New Year Celebration, one of the biggest and best in the world, is an eight-day extravaganza of pageants, outdoor competitions, cultural programs, fireworks, and a superb parade led by a deliciously scary dragon; Tel: 391-2000. Also in February, the Golden Gate Kennel

Club sponsors the All-Breed Dog Show at the Cow Palace (Tel: 530-1466), and the Bay Area Women's Philharmonic Orchestra, the only orchestra in the country dedicated to performances of the works of contemporary women composers, plays at the First Congregational Church at Post and Mason streets (Tel: 626-4888).

March: Spring bows with bursts of blooms at Macy's Easter Flower Show, luring horticulturists from all around the West; Tel: 393-3358. San Francisco's St. Patrick's Day Parade is one of the largest, loudest shows of the year, the apex of an observance that includes religious services at St. Patrick's Church, flag-raising ceremonies in Civic Center, festivities at the United Irish Cultural Center, the Grand Marshall's Dinner, and happy hanging-out at several Irish pubs: **Harrington's**, where the brew bunch spills right out in front of 245 Front Street; **Ireland's 32**, 3653 Buchanan Street (young professionals and their parents at play in the Marina; **Pat O'Shea's Mad Hatter**, 3848 Geary Boulevard (the awning reads We Cheat Tourists and Drunks); and the **Plough & Stars**, 116 Clement Street (long, wooden tables and Irish Republic banners).

March is also the month for the Battle of the Harmonicas at Old Fillmore Auditorium (Tel: 567-2060); Tulipmania, guided tours of one of the city's largest tulip beds out of Pier 39 (Tel: 981-8030); and the West Coast Computer Fair in Brooks Hall, Civic Center (Tel: 617-449-6600).

April: On March 31, 1991, hundreds of people will hike up Mount Davidson, west of Twin Peaks, for the annual Easter Sunrise Service at the base of a 103-foot-high cross. More than 2,000 Californians of Japanese descent, performers from Japan, and enthusiasts of things Japanese participate in an elaborate offering of Japanese culture and customs in the annual Cherry Blossom Festival in Japantown. The big parade is always the highlight; Tel: 563-2313. April also brings Opening Day of the Yachting Season on San Francisco Bay (Tel: 391-2000), the San Francisco Landscape and Garden Show at Fort Mason (Tel: 221-1310), and the Grand National Junior Livestock and Horse Show at the Cow Palace (Tel: 469-6065).

May: The two-day Cinco de Mayo Parade and Celebration commemorates the Mexican victory over the French army at Puebla on May 5, 1867; Tel: 826-1401. The San Francisco Historic Trolley Festival begins (throughout the month), putting into commercial use along Market Street vintage streetcars from around the world; Tel: 673-6864. Mardi Gras, San Francisco style, means *Carneval* near the end of May, celebrated in the Mission District since 1979. Like the city itself, this event transcends traditional ethnic borders, cele-brating the passions and pleasures of life in Africa, Polynesia, Asia, Europe, Central America, South America, and the Carib-bean. It's a salsa ball that brings out half a million festive folks; Tel: 826-1401.

June: The Cable Car Bell-Ringing Championships lure hun-dreds of onlookers and listeners to a clanging-good party in Union Square; Tel: 391-2000. The Lesbian and Gay Freedom Day Parade attracts local and national TV attention to goings-on along Market Street; Tel: 864-3733. The Stern Grove Mid-summer Musical Festival begins in June and lasts through August, bringing free outdoor Sunday performances of sym-phonic, operatic, jazz, country, and rock music as well as dance to the remarkable redwood grove in the West Portal/ Sunset District; Tel: 398-6551.

July: San Francisco's maritime heritage is celebrated dur-ing the Festival of the Sea with sea chanteys, dances, art demonstrations, children's programs, and more, at Hyde Street Pier/Aquatic Park; Tel: 556-0560. The Fourth of July Celebration and Fireworks attracts thousands of early-evening picnickers to Crissy Field in the Marina, where the night sky glows, sparkles, and rockets against the Golden Gate Bridge backdrop; Tel: 777-7120.

August: The City Sports Walk Week attempts to bring some fitness to life in San Francisco with a seven-mile hike to the headlands, a three-mile walk up Telegraph Hill to Coit Tower, and a stroller-stride/hill-stride through the city; Tel: 546-6150. The Nihonmachi Street Fair features live entertainment, a children's world, arts-and-crafts shows, and food stalls in Japantown; Tel: 922-8700.

September: Japantown continues buzzing with the Japan-town Summer Festival, with music, food, dancing, and mar-tial arts and flower arranging demonstrations; Tel: 922-9300.

October: The month's action begins with Fleet Week, when naval vessels and support ships are open to the public, and the Blue Angels precision jet-fighter flight team soars and roars in aerial maneuvers over the bay and city; Tel: 395-3922. The Italian community and everybody else commemorate Columbus's arrival in the New World in the annual Columbus Day Celebration on and around the actual holiday, October 12. Queen Isabella is crowned, civic ceremonies are held, Columbus comes ashore at Fisherman's Wharf, and there's a stirring Sunday parade. The procession of the Madonna del Lume and the blessing of the fishing fleet and the animals is a perpetuation of the centuries-old Sicilian folk rite venerating the patroness of fishermen. Religious services are held at the

Church of Saints Peter and Paul in North Beach, followed by a march to the Wharf for the blessings; Tel: 391-2000. Late in October and usually into November, the annual Jazz in the City Festival features the finest in local, national, and international jazz groups; Tel: 864-5449. Also in October and November, the Grand National Livestock Expo Rodeo and Horse Show is staged at the Cow Palace; Tel: 469-6000.

November: Early in the month, the annual KQED-TV Food and Wine Festival takes place in the Concourse Exhibition Center; Tel: 553-2230. The San Francisco Automobile Show is held mid-month at Moscone Convention Center; Tel: 673-2016.

December: The American Conservatory Theater (ACT) gives its annual production of *A Christmas Carol* (usually at the Geary Theater; this year as yet undecided); Tel: 749-2228. Traditional Christmas-season performances of *The Messiah* by the San Francisco Symphony and *The Nutcracker* by the San Francisco Ballet are also presented.

GETTING AROUND

On Foot

An anonymous writer once opined, "When you get tired of walking around San Francisco, you can always lean against it."

The central city, with Union Square as its hub, is admirable for ambling, with enticing shops, cafés and restaurants, small and stylish hotels, theaters, and more near at hand (and foot) in the Financial District, Chinatown, and Embarcadero Center. However, steep hills and long distances to Fisherman's Wharf, Golden Gate Park, the Marina, and other sights make public transportation more practical for longer excursions.

Committed strollers will want to consider one of at least thirteen walking tours spiced with tales of the city, visits to landmarks, peeks into secret gardens and alleys, and stops at neighborhood cafés; ask for a list of them at the visitors' center at Hallidie Plaza (Tel: 391-2000).

By Car

San Francisco's celebrated hills (40 of them, of which the best-known seven are Nob, Russian, Telegraph, Rincon, Twin Peaks, Lone Mountain, and Mount Davidson) can drive an uninitiated motorist crazy. The street you travel along while trying to find a certain address is likely to bump abruptly into a park or a hill, forcing you to go back, forth, and

around until you discover where it begins again. Some hills
(up Divasadero Street, for example) are so steep you have
the sensation of taking off or landing in a small airplane.
Experienced, patient drivers may wish to rent a car; others
might prefer to use public transportation in the city, picking
up a rental car just before trips into the countryside. If you
do plan to drive in the city, rent a car with automatic
transmission unless you can shift gears expertly going up a
steep hill from a stop.

Limousines may be rented from any of several firms for
point-to-point travel or sightseeing; for general information,
call Associated Limousine Operators of San Francisco; Tel:
563-1000 or 824-2660. San Francisco's taxis are often cited as
the most expensive in the country. However, they are very
efficient and easily hailed on downtown streets. In residential areas you'd be wise to telephone about 15 to 20 minutes
beforehand (check the Yellow Pages for phone numbers).

If you are driving, the first route to follow is the celebrated **49-Mile Drive**, an unsurpassed sweep that will give
you an introduction to places you'll want to get to know
better later. Marked by blue-and-white seagull signs bearing
the words Scenic Drive, it begins and ends at Civic Center.
The free San Francisco Visitor Map from the Visitor Center
shows it in detail.

On Land

San Francisco Municipal Railway (MUNI) operates more
than 1,000 vehicles—the fabled cable cars, light-rail vehicles,
electric buses, and motor coaches—to and from all major
areas of the city. At this writing the fare is 85 cents for all but
cable cars, which are $2; exact fare is required. If you intend
to make extensive use of public transport, buy a map of the
MUNI routes (available at the Visitor Center, bookstores, and
newspaper stands for $1.50).

A San Francisco Municipal Railway Passport is sold for
one day ($6) or for three consecutive days ($10) and
provides unlimited rides on public transportation, including the cable cars. With the pass, discounts are also available for several museums and other sights. Passes are sold
at the Hallidie Plaza Visitor Information Center at Powell
and Market streets; the STUBS ticket booths on Union
Square and Ghirardelli Square; the cable-car terminals and
the ticket booth at Pier 39; the City Hall information booth;
and Victorian Park; Tel: 673-6864.

Cable cars run along three routes: the Powell–Hyde line
from Powell and Market streets to Victorian Park, near the

Maritime Museum and Aquatic Park (for the most dramatic views); the Powell–Mason line from Powell and Market to Bay Street, three blocks from Fisherman's Wharf; and the California Street line from the foot of Market Street up and across Nob Hill to Van Ness Avenue. Riders should buy tickets before boarding from the self-service machines at all terminals and major stops; a $6 all-day MUNI adult pass is dispensed from the machines as well.

The 71-mile **Bay Area Rapid Transit** (BART) system links 8 San Francisco stations with Daly City to the southwest and with 25 stations in the East Bay. It's not just a transit system; it can be a road to urban adventure. Detrain at Embarcadero station for a miniworld of 140 shops, restaurants, and bars; at Berkeley in the East Bay for the University of California campus; at Lake Merritt station for the Oakland Museum and Jack London Square (a 15-minute walk). All tickets are dispensed from machines at the stations; for further assistance call 788-BART.

AC Transit operates buses out of San Francisco's Transbay Terminal at First and Mission streets to communities in the East Bay and in Alameda and Contra Costa counties, via the Bay Bridge; Tel: 839-2882.

Golden Gate Transit, also out of the Transbay Terminal, links San Francisco to Marin and Sonoma counties by bus across the Golden Gate Bridge. For information on city routes, schedules, and pickup stops, Tel: 332-6600.

Samtrans, also located in the Transbay Terminal, offers services from San Francisco to SFO and to cities on the Peninsula as far south as Palo Alto; Tel: 761-7000.

See Useful Facts above for details on getting to San Francisco from local airports.

On Sea

There are ferries again on San Francisco Bay. The opening of the Golden Gate Bridge in 1937 washed away the 50 white and orange arks that once cruised the harbor, but contemporary traffic, pollution problems, and the effects of the 1989 earthquake have signaled a sea change in the public's appreciation of water transportation.

Golden Gate Ferries depart from the south end of the Ferry Building on the Embarcadero on frequent sailings to Sausalito and to Larkspur in Marin County. Snacks and beverages of all kinds are sold on the crossings, making them minicruises. At this writing the fare on the sleek M.V. *Golden Gate* for the 30-minute trip to Sausalito is $3.50 one way for adults. Three 725-passenger ferries provide frequent daily service to Larkspur for $2.20 for adults and $1.65 for children (weekdays) or $3 and $2.25 respectively (weekends and holidays). Handicapped people and seniors receive 50 percent discounts everyday; Tel: 332-6600.

Red & White Fleet vessels depart from Pier 43 ½ at Fisherman's Wharf for Sausalito (adults, $4; children, $2), and for Tiburon ($4.50 and $2.25). In summer and on winter weekends, there's also service to Angel Island for picnicking and hiking; Tel: 546-2896.

Excursion cruises run daily from Pier 41 to Marine World Africa USA in Vallejo; Tel: 546-BOAT.

Since the 1989 earthquake, regular Red & White ferry service has been operating between San Francisco's Ferry Building and Oakland's Jack London Square. As of this writing they depart Jack London (at the foot of Broadway) begining at 9:00 A.M. on weekends, with the last departure of the day from San Francisco at 5:00 P.M. Weekday schedules begin at 6:00 A.M. from Jack London, with frequent service until the last run from San Francisco at 7:00 P.M. A.C. Transit and MUNI transfers are included in the ferry ticket price; Tel: 546-BOAT.

A bay cruise of one and one quarter hours under both the Golden Gate and Bay bridges, within yards of Alcatraz, and along the city's scenic and historical waterfront is offered by the big boats of the **Blue & Gold Fleet**, with frequent departures from Pier 39 (adults, $5). Sailings are fully narrated and snacks and drinks are sold; Tel: 781-7877.

You can party on the bay aboard the *City of San Francisco,* the 151-foot vessel of **Hornblower Dining Yachts**. Patterned after the classic steamers of the early 1900s, it has three enclosed decks and formally appointed dining salons. Dinner-dance cruises depart nightly from Pier 33 at the foot of Bay Street, with luncheon sailings on Fridays and brunch cruises on weekends; Tel: 394-8900.

In the Air
The choppers of **San Francisco Helicopter Tours** fly daily from the Hyatt Regency–Oakland for tours of the bay, trips to the Wine Country, and along the coast to Monterey; pickup from San Francisco hotels is available. Most popular is the Vista Flight over the Bay Bridge and Golden Gate Bridge, Alcatraz, and past the city skyline; Tel: 667-3800.

Relive the golden days of DC3s on a one-hour flight with **Sentimental Journeys Sky Tours**, sipping drinks and munching hors d'oeuvres as you gaze down at San Francisco, the bay, and the Marin coastline. Charters are available through-out the region; Tel: 667-3800 or (800) 634-1165.

Sightseeing

At least ten companies operate sightseeing tours by van or coach in San Francisco and the immediate area, from three-and-a-half hour to overnight trips. Check the listings at the San Francisco Visitor Center or ask at your hotel for recom-mendations. The best known is The Gray Line; Tel: 558-9400.

Specialty Touring

Cable Car Charters steers you through San Francisco in style aboard motorized cable cars that depart daily from a spot near Pier 41 on narrated, one-hour tours; Tel: 922-2425.

City's Finest Concierge tailors getaways to the individual, suiting accommodations, transportation, dining, and enter-tainment to moderate or extravagant requirements; Tel: 362-2143 or (800) 877-5777.

The Union Street Association instituted the **DAS (Dining and Shopping) Bus** in 1990. This luxury bus picks up passen-gers from various areas in the city and drops them off at key dining and shopping areas: Union Street, Union Square, Embarcadero Center, Fisherman's Wharf, and North Beach. For a reasonable daily fare, riders can be shoppers begin-ning at 10:00 A.M. and diners until 10:00 P.M. Schedule information is available at local retail outlets and from hotel concierges.

An experienced naturalist leads **A Day in Nature**, half-day nature escapes in the Marin Headlands or Muir Woods that include a gourmet picnic. Reservations are required; Tel: 673-0548.

Free Wheelin' Tours escorts beer enthusiasts to four local breweries with tastings at each; the tours focus on home-brewing techniques. Pizza is included and reservations are required; Tel: 443-ALES.

Wildflowers, wildlife, geology, Native American heritage, redwood forests, even the San Andreas earthquake fault are explored by **Rodeo Beach Center: Nature Walks & Field Trips**, with naturalists as guides. Reservations are required; Tel: 332-8200.

Visits to hotels, churches, theaters, homes, factories, and more are the purlieu of **Ticketeasy**, with lunch or dinner often included; Tel: 956-1765.

At least a dozen other firms have created unusual ways to see the city; pick up a list at the Visitor Center.

—*Georgia I. Hesse*

ACCOMMODATIONS

Considering its small size among the world's star cities, San Francisco can take pride in its complement of fine hotels in all price categories except that of the lowest. For rooms at the top, expect to pay $225 to $350 for doubles, up to and even more than $1,000 for two-room suites. Some in this bracket are the traditional, world-recognized palaces; others are newer, smaller, less famous but equally regal hotels, also charging palatial prices.

An encouraging trend is the burgeoning of new, small, middle-range hotels reflecting what is known locally as European style: well-managed, handsomely outfitted inns with superb service but few frills. Most of these occupy renovated old buildings that had become tired, if not seedy. Rates in these range from about $90 to $150 for doubles; from $125 to $300 for suites.

There are also some inns and bed and breakfasts. The latter is an inexact and misleading term to those who think of it in the British-European sense, where it implies good, clean rooms that are also inexpensive—in San Francisco some of these charge as much or more than the top hotels. A moderate range for doubles is $90 to $180.

A few all-suite hotels are sprouting in the city, though less vigorously than elsewhere in California and the nation. Some are excellent value for money spent, with two-bedroom suites for a reasonable $250 or so, well-suited to families on an extended visit or to business-cum-pleasure travellers. A handful of small, long-established hotels offer doubles as low as $75, but they are real finds.

With all these options available, you are unlikely to choose a motel or motor hotel in San Francisco; the best ones sit along northern Van Ness Avenue and Lombard Street in the Marina, which are segments of U.S. Highway 101 and are handy for drivers hastening through town. They charge between $75 and $150 for doubles.

San Francisco International Airport is unusually well equipped with hotels of a high standard. The best ones are listed here for travellers who, alas, must skip San Francisco proper or catch an early-morning flight.

Traditionally, hotels cluster around such centers as Nob

Hill, Union Square, and the Financial District, but because the city is so compact, location may be less important than other qualities. For that reason, we cover them here by the styles set out above rather than geographically.

All San Francisco is in area code 415; the United States code is 1. A central service number is San Francisco Reservations; Tel: 543-8996 or (800) 333-8996. Our entries give zip codes, but of course they should be preceded by "San Francisco, California."

The Palaces

Fairmont Hotel and Tower. Sophisticated, elegant, with the showiest lobby this side of the Gold Rush, the Fairmont signals the Nob Hill of San Francisco's glory days. It was named for James G. "Bonanza Jim" Fair, one of the fabled silver Bonanza Kings who died while the foundations for his mansion were being laid on this site. Its restaurants and bars are as unrestrained as the Neo-Renaissance pile itself: the **Squire** off the lobby for fine dining; the **Crown Room** for drinking and dining while gazing off toward Japan; and **Bella Voce** (informal Italian cuisine with opera-singing servers in evening, and coffee-shop style from 6:00 A.M. to 3:00 P.M.); **Mason's** for regional American cooking and supper-club piano; the **Art Deco Cirque Lounge** (piano and dancing); the **New Orleans Room** off the lobby (sipping and swing music); the **Sweet Corner** (coffee shop); the **Tonga Room** (Polynesian-campy food and drinks around a giant swimming pool complete with storms). Men's and women's hair stylists here are among the city's most competent and chic; there is also a health spa on the premises.

950 Mason Street, 94106. Tel: 772-5000, 772-5147 (room reservations), 772-5144 (restaurant reservations), (800) 527-4727 (general reservations). The Fairmont is a member of Leading Hotels of the World; in U.S. and Canada, Tel: (800) 223-6800; in United Kingdom, Tel: (800) 181-123; in Australia, Tel: (008) 222-033; Fax: 772-5026.

Four Seasons Clift. Quiet, understated, with impeccable service, the Clift was a San Francisco tradition long before it entered the Four Seasons family (which did nothing, happily, except improve it). The guest rooms are tastefully furnished and unusually large. The handsome old **Redwood Room** is a restful, wood-paneled retreat; the **French Room**'s cuisine is as outstanding, and expensive, as its decor.

495 Geary Street (near Union Square), 94102. Tel: 775-4700 or (800) 332-3442; Fax: 775-4621.

Hyatt Regency. The distinctive John Portman innovations

here—architectural planes, open spaces, and ceiling-soaring lobby—make you feel, entering from the street, as if you are falling up. There's a Regency Club (the Hyatt chain's VIP floor) and an exercise room. The top-floor **Equinox** bar-and-restaurant revolves above a striking lower-city view; there are big-band tea dancing and jazz concerts in the lobby, as well as free airport transportation.

Five Embarcadero Center, 94111. Tel: 788-1234 or (800) 233-1234 (worldwide reservations); Fax: 989-7448.

Mark Hopkins Inter-Continental. There can be no smarter address than 1 Nob Hill, occupied once by the mansion of a member of the Big Four, who built the transcontinental railroad, but who like James G. Fair died before moving in. It's famous for the sky-high **Top of the Mark** cocktail lounge's magnificent views over city and bay (the best corner is supposed to be the northeast). The **Nob Hill Restaurant** serves California-French cuisine in a prosperous, oak-paneled, 19th-century atmosphere; you can take in the pleasant garden air in an off-the-lobby lounge.

1 Nob Hill, 94108. Tel: 392-3434 or (800) 332-4246; Fax: 421-3302.

Park Hyatt. European-style luxury arrived in Embarcadero Center when this 360-room hotel opened in 1989; many suites offer balconies. The **Park Grill** serves international specialties in a club-like setting; there are health-club privileges.

333 Battery Street, 94111. Tel: 392-1234; in U.S. and Canada, Tel: 233-1234; Fax: 421-2433.

The Pan-Pacific. Designed by renowned architect John Portman and once named the Portman, this luxurious 330-room hotel opened in September 1987. In June 1990, it became an elegant member of the Pan-Pacific family, owned by the Tokyu Corporation of Japan. The hotel implements an Asian idea of service, stressing personal valets on each of the 21 floors, private limousine service to and from the airport, health-club facilities, and flexible check-out hours. The third-floor atrium lobby makes spectacular use of marble, sculpture, and a fireplace before which you can cozy up and read for hours. **The Grill** specializes in fragrant Provençal cookery, with some spa menus; the **Club** on the 21st floor offers light refreshments and cocktails with which to salute the view.

500 Post Street (near Union Square), 94102. Tel: 771-8600 or (800) 533-6465; in Canada (except Vancouver), Tel: (800) 663-1515; in Vancouver, Tel: (604) 662-3223; in England, Tel: (07) 491-3812; in Australia, Tel: (02) 264-1122; in New Zealand, Tel: (9) 366-3000; Fax: 398-0267.

The Stanford Court. Just down Nob Hill and east of the Mark Hopkins, toward the Powell Street cable-car line, this prestigious hotel occupies the mansion site of another Big Four member and the founder of Stanford University, Leland Stanford. It's renowned for a striking courtyard entry (for cars) with Tiffany-style glass dome, woody and club-like lobby, and the personal service rarely found in a large city hotel. (San Franciscans hope its new owners, Stouffer Hotels, can keep it up to snuff.) **Fournou's Ovens** features French cuisine in a smart country-kitchen setting; there's a lovely lounge at the entry, one floor above the restaurant.

905 California Street, 94108. Tel: 989-3500 or (800) 468-3471; Fax: 391-0513.

Westin St. Francis. One of the old-time treasures of Union Square, this grande dame with its modern tower now caters (alas) to many tour groups. From **Victor's** on the 32nd floor there's a smashing view of the central city to accompany Continental-California cuisine. The lushly decorated, almost antic **Compass Rose** off the lobby is a bar in the grand manner, while **Dewey's** provides drinks and light meals in pub-like surroundings; also available are the **English Grill** (fine dining in a comfortably old-fashioned setting), the **Dutch Kitchen** (informal), and **Oz** (a fashionable disco).

335 Powell Street, 94102. Tel: 397-7000; Fax: 774-0124.

Petits Palaces

Campton Place. Opened in 1983 in a reworking of two turn-of-the-century buildings half a block north of the northeastern corner of Union Square, Campton quickly took its place at the very pinnacle among small, luxurious hotels in the entire country. Objets d'art, fine furnishings, and professional and caring service are among its hallmarks; many rooms are rather small. The restaurant of the same name in the hotel has become one of the finest in the city.

340 Stockton Street, 94108. Tel: 781-5555; (800) 235-4300 (in California) or (800) 647-4007 (nationwide). Campton Place is a member of Worldwide Preferred Hotels; in U.S., Tel: (800) 323-7500; in England, Tel: (081) 995-8211; in Australia, Tel: (02) 235-1111; in New Zealand, Tel: (09) 396-974. It belongs, as well, to Hotels Concorde; in U.S., Tel: (402) 334-6664; in Canada, Tel: (416) 926-7800; in England, Tel: (071) 937-8033; in Australia, Tel: (02) 267-2144; Fax: 955-8536.

Donatello. The restaurant in this elegant place is so outstanding that it gave its name to the hotel not long after its opening. Italian in design, craftsmanship, cuisine, and warm welcome, the hotel boasts soothing interiors of travertine,

Italian marble, Venetian glass, antiques, and Fortuny fabrics. Even spoiled San Francisco diners acclaim **Donatello** the restaurant for serving the best northern Italian cuisine in town; the tiny bar off the two dining rooms is fittingly quiet, a retreat in itself.

501 Post Street (near Union Square), 94102. Tel: 441-7100; (800) 792-9837 (in California) or (800) 227-3184 (nationwide); Fax: 885-8842.

Huntington. Whatever is smart, restrained, elegant, and quietly luxurious is at home here, where the third among the Big Four (Collis P. Huntington) is remembered on Nob Hill. Rooms and suites are spacious for a small hotel. The **Big Four Restaurant and Bar**, named for the Big Four railroad magnates, is warm, uncrowded, refined, and serves award-winning American dishes in a masculine atmosphere particularly appreciated by women who dislike "lady-finger" rooms.

1075 California Street, 94108. Tel: 474-5400; (800) 652-1539 (in California) or (800) 227-4683 (nationwide). The Huntington is a member of Small Luxury Hotels; Tel: (800) 862-7272 (in California) or (800) 345-3457 (nationwide); Fax: 474-6227.

Mandarin Oriental. Perhaps nowhere else in the world can you sit in your bathtub and overlook an eye-popping view—with no eyes popping back at you unless they come from a helicopter. This superb hotel of the Mandarin Oriental Group occupies the top 11 floors of two 48-story towers connected by sky bridges in the Financial District. The decor of guest rooms is clean, spare, and Oriental, with artistic touches reminiscent of Asian scrollwork. **Silks** is a remarkably beautiful restaurant, with innovative American-California cuisine to match.

222 Sansome Street, 94104. Tel: 885-0999 or (800) 223-6800; in Canada, Tel: (800) 663-0787. Mandarin Oriental belongs to Leading Hotels of the World; in U.S. and Canada, Tel: (800) 223-6800; in United Kingdom, Tel: (800) 181-123; in Australia, Tel: (008) 222-033; Fax: 433-0289.

The Ritz-Carlton. Scheduled to open in March or April 1991, this member of the distinguished chain will have 336 guest rooms within a stately Nob Hill building that once served as Pacific Coast headquarters of the Metropolitan Life Insurance Company and later as the home of Cogswell College. Built in 1909, the massive white structure has been rehabilitated completely; its interior will be decorated with 18th- and 19th-century antiques and art works. In addition to an intimate dining room, the Ritz-Carlton will boast the city's only indoor-and-terraced hotel café, a complete business center, a fitness center with swimming pool, and conference facilities.

600 Stockton Street, 94108. Tel: 296-7465 or (800) 241-3333; in Australia, Tel: 252-888; Fax: 296-8559.

The Sherman House. Its small size (eight rooms, six apartments) should classify it as an inn, but the remarkable building, the exquisite taste of its renovation, its smashing views, and its historic legacy qualify the Sherman as a small palace. Leander S. Sherman arrived in 1861 with music as his passion, and he built his Sherman Clay & Co. into the leading supplier of musical instruments in the West. Luisa Tetrazzini, Madame Ernestine Schumann-Heink, and Enrico Caruso performed in what is today a small but splendid foyer. The cuisine at the Sherman's restaurant is remarkable.

2160 Green Street (Pacific Heights, near the Marina), 94123. Tel: 563-3600. Sherman House is one of only five U.S. members in Northern California of the prestigious French Relais & Châteaux group; in U.S. and Canada, Tel: (713) 783-8033; in Australia, Tel: (02) 957-4511; Fax: 563-1881.

European-style Inns
The Bedford. This 1929 building three blocks west of Union Square has been renovated to the style Lord Wedgwood appreciated when he passed through long ago. Enjoy the **Wedgwood Bar**, the **Café Champagne**, the airy decor, and the personal service.

761 Post Street, 94109. Tel: 673-6040, (800) 652-1889 (in California) or (800) 227-5642 (nationwide); Fax: 563-6739.

Diva. In the heart of the theater district, this is a high-tech, high-profile inn where the decor glitters and the service sparkles; amenities include VCRs and mini-refrigerators.

440 Geary Street, 94102. Tel: 885-0200 or (800) 553-1900 (outside California); Fax: 346-4407.

Inn at Union Square. People who have stayed here once often refuse to stay anywhere else. Most floors offer a sitting area with fireplace; try the penthouse suite with fireplace, bar, whirlpool, and sauna. Antiques abound; afternoon tea is served.

440 Post Street, 94102. Tel: 397-3510 or (800) 288-4346; Fax: 989-0529.

Galleria Park. The Art Nouveau lobby speaks of 1911; the amenities (complete with a rooftop jogging park), of the 1990s. There has been attention to good lighting for business-oriented visitors, and meeting facilities are available. Two restaurants are adjacent: **Bentley's Seafood Grill** and **Brasserie Chambord.**

191 Sutter Street (in the Financial District), 94104. Tel:

781-3060, (800) 792-9855 (in California) or (800) 792-9639 (nationwide); Fax 433-4409.

The Griffon. Up from the 1906 waterfront days comes a hotel with the mood of the moment, the service of yesterday. Guests may use an adjoining athletic club; some penthouse suites have redwood terraces. The **Bistro Rôti** specializes in spit-roasted entrées created by the three restaurateurs who gave Fog City Diner to San Francisco and Mustards and Tra Vigne to the Napa Valley.

155 Steuart Street (near the Embarcadero), 94105. Tel: 495-2100 or (800) 321-2201; Fax 495-2100.

Inn at the Opera. Meticulous care has been taken to transform this 1927 apartment house into an exciting retreat. Located near the Opera House, Symphony Hall, and the Museum of Modern Art in the Civic Center, it is very small and specializes in personal services for the vacationer or business traveller. The **Act IV** lounge and restaurant is like a personal discovery you might make in London or Paris.

333 Fulton Street, 94102. Tel: 863-8400, (800) 423-9610 (in California) or (800) 325-2708 (nationwide); Fax: 861-0821.

Juliana. A historic (1903) inn near Union Square has been reborn. Reflecting the theme of art in San Francisco, the Juliana's guest rooms are decorated with rotating collections of artwork supplied by local galleries for admiration or even purchase. The lobby is intimate, with a wood-burning marble fireplace. The adjacent restaurant has closed; at this writing a new one is in the planning stages.

590 Bush Street, 94108. Tel: 392-2540, (800) 372-8800 (in California) or (800) 382-8800 (nationwide); Fax: 391-8447.

Kensington Park. Sherry before the fireplace and a grand piano in the lobby set the civilized tone for this renovated 1924 hotel, in updated but traditional English dress. Continental breakfast is a part of the soothing package.

450 Post Street (near Union Square), 94102. Tel: 788-6400 or (800) 553-1900; Fax: 885-3268.

The Majestic. Edwardian atmosphere, antiques, and careful attention to detail mark this restored 1902 hotel; many rooms have fireplaces and refrigerators. **Café Majestic** specializes in Old San Francisco recipes and in-house pastries.

1500 Sutter Street (west of Van Ness), 94109. Tel: 441-1100, (800) 252-1155 (in California) or (800) 824-0094 (nationwide); Fax 673-7331.

The Millefiori Inn. Each of the 16 rooms has a different, stylish decor; that and sophisticated service make this a surprise in the heart of North Beach. But don't expect the quiet of a residential side-street inn.

444 Columbus Avenue, 94133. Tel: 433-9111.

Miyako Hotel. Traditional Japan meets California in rooms and restaurants; lovely touches abound in sunken tubs, rice-paper *shoji* screens, and a lobby garden with waterfall. Classically designed Japanese rooms and suites are available, some with redwood saunas. The **Asuka Brasserie** here is excellent.

1625 Post Street (Japantown), 94115. Tel: 922-3200 or (800) 533-4567; Fax: 921-0417.

The Monticello Inn. To step into this colonial-style 1906 lobby, furnished in Federal-period decor with Chippendale reproductions, fireplace, and reading-and-writing parlor is to step back into a more gracious age. Early American in appearance, colors, and details, it's also old-fashioned in its welcome. The **Corona Bar & Grill**, off the lobby, has become the city's standard for judging innovative Mexican-California cuisine.

80 Cyril Magnin Street (three blocks southwest of Union Square), 94102. Tel: 392-8800 or (800) 669-7777; Fax: 391-8447.

The Prescott. Urban elegance, understated *luxe,* living-room lobby, Native American artifacts, suites with VCRs and whirlpools, honor-bar/refrigerators, wines in the library in the evening—such is the gracious air of this upscale inn (near Union Square) with one of the finest, most popular restaurants in the city, **PosTrio**. Room service by Wolfgang Puck? Believe it.

545 Post Street, 94102. Tel: 563-0303 or (800) 283-7322; Fax: 563-6831.

Raphael. This was among the first of the city's European-style inns and has been refurbished recently; its café is open 24 hours.

386 Geary Street (one block west of Union Square), 94102. Tel: 986-2000 or (800) 821-5343; Fax: 397-2447.

The Regis. French and English antiques and art meet harmoniously in this deluxe inn in the heart of the theater district. A complete business center adds to the business traveller's comfort. Smart **Regina's** serves French-Creole cuisine at lunch and dinner.

490 Geary Street, 94102. Tel: 928-7900, (800) 854-0011 (in California) or (800) 345-4443 (nationwide); Fax 441-8788.

Villa Florence. Convenient to both smart shopping and theater-going, this renovated 1908 building celebrates Tuscany, complete with a 16th-century trompe l'oeil lobby mural and a 17th-century velvet tapestry. **Kuleto's** off the lobby has become one of the most popular Italian cafés in town, with

original pastas, fresh fish, on-premises bakery, and a carved
Brunswick bar brought around Cape Horn on a clipper ship.

225 Powell Street (Union Square), 94102. Tel: 397-7700,
(800) 243-5700 (in California) or (800) 553-4411 (nationwide); Fax: 397-7700, ext. 253.

Vintage Court. A day in Wine Country is the mood in this
reworked 1913 house, with guest rooms named for California wineries and a cozy lobby in which to sit and sip before
the fireplace. **Masa's Restaurant** has been acclaimed as one
of the finest French rooms in the country.

650 Bush Street (two blocks north of Union Square),
94108. Tel: 392-4666, (800) 654-7266 (in California) or (800)
654-1100 (nationwide); in Canada, Tel: (800) 843-6076; Fax:
392-4666.

Bed and Breakfasts

Archbishops' Mansion. Built in 1904 to house the archbish-
opric of San Francisco and so occupied until 1945, this Belle
Epoque villa was (and is) one of the city's largest homes,
overlooking a registered Historic District between Civic Center and Golden Gate Park. The world within is an eclectic
mix of European and Asian art and antiques; unusual for a
bed and breakfast, laundry and cleaning are available.

1000 Fulton Street (Alamo Square), 94117. Tel: 563-7872.

The Bed and Breakfast Inn. This is probably the place that
locally fueled the fad for bed and breakfasts. In a mews off
Union Street, two of the ten rooms open to the garden; the
sense is that the country has come to the city.

2–4 Charlton Court (Cow Hollow), 94123. Tel: 921-9784.

Hermitage House. This gracious Greek Revival home, in
Pacific Heights south of Union Street, was built for Judge
Charles Slack in the early 1900s. It's complete with seven
fireplaces, and polished redwood shines everywhere. It's
also handy to the number 1 bus.

2224 Sacramento Street, 94115. Tel: 921-5515.

Mansions Hotel. San Francisco eccentric Robert Pritikin
commands this gorgeous Queen Anne home built (recently
joined to the one next door) in Pacific Heights for Utah
Senator Richard Chambers in 1887. Concerts and magic
shows are staged in the Music Room and sometimes Claudia
(a resident ghost) plays the piano. Dining is excellent; the
garden displays sculptures by late local genius Beniamino
Bufano.

2220 Sacramento Street, 94115. Tel: 929-9444.

The Monte Cristo. Built in 1875, this Victorian once
served as a bordello, and legends linger. Rooms, unusually

spacious for a bed and breakfast, have Early American and English furnishings; great breakfasts are served.

600 Presidio Avenue (Western Addition), 94115. Tel: 931-1875.

Petite Auberge. This is a French country inn right in the city, complete with some fireplaces and a super-competent concierge, sheltered from the downtown traffic. People who've stayed here try to keep it for themselves.

863 Bush Street (three blocks north of Union Square), 94108. Tel: 928-6000; Fax: 775-5717.

Queen Anne. Oak panels, a Spanish cedar staircase, antiques, and fireplaces distinguish this house built by James G. Fair (the Silver King) in 1890 as Miss Mary Lake's School for Girls. It has lived several lives, currently a smart and stylish one with Sherry in the parlor; some rooms have fireplaces and wet bars.

1590 Sutter Street (south Pacific Heights), 94108. Tel: 441-2828, (800) 262-2663 (in California) or (800) 227-3970 (nationwide); Fax: 775-5212.

Spreckels Mansion. Built in 1887 for sugar executive Richard Spreckels, this five-room inn offers great city views, fireplaces, wine in the library, antiques, and spaciousness unmatched by other bed and breakfasts.

737 Buena Vista Avenue West (near Haight-Ashbury), 94117. Tel: 861-3008.

Washington Square Inn. Deliciously decorated with French and English country furnishings, this 15-room inn offers a restful setting in Old San Francisco.

1660 Stockton Street (North Beach), 94133. Tel: 981-4220.

White Swan. A country-English theme is carried out with antiques, fine fabrics, and a common room near a tiny garden, where breakfast and high tea are served. All rooms have baths, fireplaces, and refrigerators. It's a surprising hideaway in the heart of happenings.

845 Bush Street (three blocks north of Union Square), 94108. Tel: 775-1755.

Suites

Ellesmere. All suites here boast kitchens, VCRs, wet bars, phone-answering machines, and oversized desks. There are health-club privileges, a business center, and a no-tipping policy.

655 Powell Street (Nob Hill), 94108. Tel: 477-4600, (800) 334-6966 (in California) or (800) 426-6161 (nationwide).

Hyde Park Suites. Settling down here at the foot of residential Russian Hill, you will feel like a San Franciscan, with a view of Alcatraz and the bay. There are one- and two-bedroom suites with wet bars and kitchens, extensive business facilities, and free limousine service to downtown.

2655 Hyde Street (near Fisherman's Wharf), 94109. Tel: 771-0200 or (800) 227-3608.

Nob Hill Apartments. Individually and smartly decorated, outfitted with designer kitchens and baths, these are fashionable pieds-à-terre for travellers combining business with pleasure; a health club is available.

1234 Jones Street, 94109. Tel: 775-0566.

Nob Hill Lambourne. Executives staying here can be provided with fax machines, computers, and other business essentials *en suite*. Health-club memberships are available; airport limo pickups can be arranged.

725 Pine Street, 94109. Tel: 433-2287.

Trinity Executive Suites. Trinity arranges suites ranging from studios to penthouses in 11 San Francisco locations.

333 Bay Street (near Fisherman's Wharf), 94108. Tel: 433-3330 or 477-0400.

Small Finds

Beresford. With small, tidy rooms and friendly personnel, this is probably the most reasonably priced hotel in town; there are refrigerators and honor bars in each room. The **White Horse** café on the premises serves breakfast and lunch; the bar is a replica of an Edinburgh pub. Sutter Street is tops for art galleries and antiques and specialty shops.

635 Sutter Street (three blocks northwest of Union Square), 94102. Tel: 673-3330 or (800) 533-6533.

Beresford Arms. Under the same management as the above, this is fine for families, with kitchens in about half the rooms, some in-room whirlpools.

701 Post Street (three blocks west of Union Square), 94109. Tel: 673-2600 or (800) 533-6533.

Savoy. Reopened in the spring of 1990 after extensive reworking, this reasonably priced inn offers touches usually associated with more expensive accommodations; there's a restaurant and cocktail lounge.

580 Geary Street (three blocks west of Union Square), 94102. Tel: 441-2700 or (800) 227-4223.

Motor Hotels

Best Western Kyoto Inn. A café, valet service, in-room Japanese-style steam baths, and some balconies make this a popular motor hotel in a quiet location.

1800 Sutter Street (Japantown), 94115. Tel: 921-4000; Fax: 923-1064.

Chelsea Motor Inn. This spot has all the essentials, including covered parking; plenty of cafés are nearby.

2095 Lombard Street (Marina), 94123. Tel: 563-5600.

Cow Hollow Motor Inn. Covered parking and some suites make this a good stopover spot; many cafés are in the immediate vicinity.

2190 Lombard Street (Marina), 94123. Tel: 921-5800.

Vagabond–Midtown. A 24-hour café, a small heated pool, a meeting room, and some refrigerators and balconies make this a handy Highway 101 turnoff right in town.

2550 Van Ness Avenue (near Marina), 94109. Tel: 776-7500.

At the Airport

Amfac. An indoor pool, concierge, shopping arcade, barber-and-beauty salon, health-club privileges, and a luxury level (the Concierge Floor) make this a city hotel come to the airport.

1380 Bayshore Highway, Burlingame, 94010. Tel: 347-5444; Fax: 340-7345.

Best Western Grosvenor Airport Inn. All the amenities you expect are here, as well as in-room steam baths and whirlpools; there are also health-club privileges.

380 South Airport Boulevard, South San Francisco, 94080. Tel: 873-3200 or (800) 528-1234; Fax: 871-4369.

Clarion Hotel. Some private patios and balconies are available at this very pleasant place with heated pool, café and bar, gift shop, and exercise room.

401 East Millbrae Avenue, Millbrae, 94030. Tel: 692-6363 or (800) CLARION; Fax: 697-8735.

Embassy Suites–Burlingame. As is usually the case, you seem to get more than you pay for at Embassy: indoor pool, whirlpool, sauna, steam room, afternoon refreshments, health-club privileges, refrigerators, and lavish landscaping.

150 Anza Boulevard, Burlingame, 94010. Tel: 342-4600 or (800) EMBASSY; Fax: 343-8137.

Embassy Suites–South San Francisco. Just 2 miles north of the airport, this complex offers two-room suites with microkitchens, wet bars, refrigerators, two color TVs, and VCRs, as well as meeting rooms, atrium lobby, indoor pool, and spa. You'll find good food here at Gregory's.

250 Gateway Boulevard, South San Francisco, 94080. Tel: 589-3400 or (800) EMBASSY.

Hilton. Right at the airport grounds, this is a very popular overnight stop with pool, café and bar, concierge, exercise room, and balconies.

Box 8355, San Francisco Airport, San Mateo County, 94128. Tel: 589-0770 or (800) HILTONS; Fax: 589-4696.

Holiday Inn–Crowne Plaza. This is a big, downtown sort of place with suites, indoor pool, café and bar, meeting rooms, covered valet parking, exercise room, sauna, and a luxury floor (the Crowne Level) with concierge, in-room movies, wet bars, and complimentary refreshments.

600 Airport Boulevard, Burlingame, 94010. Tel: 340-8500 or (800) HOLIDAY; Fax: 343-1546.

Hyatt Regency. There are more than 750 rooms in what is nearer a resort than an airport hotel: heated pool, supervised children's activities on Friday and Saturday evenings, 24-hour room service and deli, convention facilities, exercise club, sauna, and wet bars; the luxury level is the Regency Club, with a private lounge and concierge assistance.

1333 Bayshore Highway, Burlingame, 94010. Tel: 347-1234 or (800) 233-1234, Fax: 696-2669.

Marriott Airport. An indoor pool with poolside service is an unusual amenity in this fine stopover spot with entertainment, dancing, concierge, shopping arcade, and exercise room. The luxury floor—the Concierge Level—offers a private lounge, wet bars, and more.

1800 Old Bayshore Highway, Burlingame, 94010. Tel: 692-9100 or (800) 228-9290; Fax: 692-8016.

Radisson Inn. A café, dining room, and bar are on the premises, as well as gift shop, exercise room, whirlpool, sauna, and some in-room refrigerators. There's even a luxury floor, the Personalized Plaza Level, with private lounge and free drinks.

275 South Airport Boulevard, South San Francisco, 94080. Tel: 873-3550 or (800) 333-3333; Fax: 873-4524.

Sofitel. This member of the French chain, 6 miles south of the airport, boasts a lagoon-side setting, well-trained staff, four restaurants, and a spa. There's also fine cooking at the **Baccarat** restaurant.

223 Twin Dolphin Drive, Redwood City, 94061. Tel: 598-9000.

Westin. Such luxuries as an indoor pool with service, large suites, valet parking, concierge, exercise room, sauna, health-club privileges, and some wet bars are available. The luxury level is the Executive Club, with private lounge and free drinks.

1 Old Bayshore Highway, Millbrae, 94030. Tel: 692-3500 or (800) 228-3000; Fax: 872-8111.

Nota bene: A smashing place to dine near the airport is **Jin Jiang-Kee Joon's Penthouse**, where superb Chinese classical cuisine is served in a Sung Dynasty setting, complete with aviary and pond (433 Airport Boulevard in Burlingame; Tel: 348-1122 for reservations and directions).

—*Georgia I. Hesse*

DINING

There are few cities more dedicated to dining out than San Francisco, where immigration and a matchless site between the Pacific and the bountiful San Joaquin Valley have combined to produce a table of astonishing diversity. Stop any two people on the street, according to a recent demographic study, and there's an 84 percent chance that they're from different ethnic groups. San Franciscans hail from every corner of the globe—and take their bread in the styles of Addis Ababa, New Delhi, Beijing, and Paris, to name just a few.

With an Asian community now reckoned at more than a third of the population, San Francisco's strongest culinary suit is the Far East. Its southern Chinese restaurants are surpassed in quality and authenticity only by their rivals in Hong Kong; they are among the more than 1,500 local establishments that represent virtually every food tradition of the Far East. But San Francisco also speaks with a decidedly Italian accent at dinner, and among the city's more notable accomplishments is that creative blending of Mediterranean and New World influences known as California cuisine.

North Beach
For more than a century, this sunny enclave between Russian and Telegraph hills has been San Francisco's Little Italy, populated by generations of *emigrati* from Tuscany, Sicily, and Genoa. In the heart of the old neighborhood at 800 Greenwich Street, two blocks north of Washington Square, stands **Buca Giovanni**. The presiding genius in this cozy cellar trattoria is the Lucca-born Giovanni Leoni, who makes his own pastas, roasts his own coffee, and even raises his own fresh herbs, vegetables, and rabbits on a Northern California farm. The emphasis is on the light sauces and game specialties of Tuscany. Tel: 776-7766.

Many of North Beach's original restaurants were family-style establishments that delivered large portions of hearty

Italian fare at low prices. That tradition continues at the homey **Capp's Corner**, 1600 Powell Street at Vallejo, where a five-course dinner costs less than an entrée at many restaurants. The atmospheric bar, a hangout for longtime residents of the Beach, is a friendly place to pass the time while waiting for a table. Tel: 989-2589.

In recent years thousands of Italian-descended newcomers from South America have emigrated to the Bay Area, introducing their own variations on the basic Italian themes. Among them are Argentines José and Marta Castellucci, who have won an enthusiastic following with grilled, marinated meats and poultry à la Buenos Aires. Indeed, grilled specialties are the whole story at the couple's tiny **Il Pollaio** at 555 Columbus Avenue, near Green Street. Right next door in the bright, tile-lined **Castellucci Ristorante**, however, the grill provides only the centerpiece for a wider menu. The homemade sausage, served on a bed of garlic-infused greens, is sensational, as are the polenta with Gorgonzola sauce and a full array of fresh pastas. Tel: 362-2774.

For decades Basque shepherds from the California and Nevada hills would spend part of each year in a string of North Beach boardinghouses near the lovely Our Lady of Guadalupe church. Echoes of that world live on at 732 Broadway between Stockton and Powell streets in the charming **Des Alpes**, a French-Basque restaurant with a comfortable foyer bar where old gents in their berets still gather to reminisce over a *pastis*. In the adjacent dining room the tables groan under enormous five-course prix-fixe meals that vary daily. Call ahead for the choices, which range from sweetbreads *en croûte* to pan-fried sole and roast lamb. Tel: 391-4249.

Lower Broadway was all honky-tonk bars and strip joints until the mid-1980s, when adult videos consigned live burlesque to the historical ash heap. Since then a restaurant boomlet has been underway, with its unlikely leaders in two Afghan immigrants named Mahmood and Wazhma Karzai. Their **Helmand**, at 430 Broadway near Montgomery Street, offers some of the most exotic fare in town, in surroundings so elegantly appointed with Central Asian carpets and furnishings that the modesty of this restaurant's typical dinner check is remarkable. Tel: 362-0641.

Levi Strauss Plaza, a bit out of the way in the eastern shadow of Telegraph Hill, was uncertain ground for restaurants before the late-1988 opening of **Il Fornaio**. Overnight this classically designed dining room at 1265 Battery Street was among the city's most popular wateringholes, people-watching posts, and northern Italian restaurants. You're likely to see the luminaries of municipal politics and media rubbing shoulders here with visiting actors and corporate tycoons. What draws them is each other, of course—plus an oak-fired brick oven that turns out superb roast meats and pizzas, at surprisingly reasonable prices. There's also a bakery on the premises. Tel: 986-0100.

On the southern slope of Telegraph Hill, at 470 Green, near Grant, the pastel quarters of **Maykadeh** are the setting for one of the West's most ambitious Iranian kitchens. Historically, a *maykadeh* was a mix of club and restaurant where the Persian intelligentsia met to enjoy fine food and wine. The tradition is respected here with exquisite shish kebabs, complex braised meats and vegetables, and sauces bound with homemade yogurt. A large Iranian clientele attests to the authenticity of the recipes. Tel: 362-8286.

In a city where seeking out offbeat regional kitchens is a serious pastime, **Ristorante Albona**, at 545 Francisco, near Mason, was bound to be a hit. It serves the cuisine of the Adriatic region of Istria, where Slavic, Venetian, and Austrian recipes mingled. The name refers to the village of Albona (renamed Labin when it passed from Italian to Yugoslav control after World War II). Plump, delicious *crafi albonesi* (dumplings filled with raisins, nuts, and three cheeses) betray the imprint of both Italian raviolis and Slavic *vareniki*. The grilled cod with polenta and the sausage-and-herb-stuffed roast pork loin are also highly recommended. Tel: 441-1040.

At the easternmost end of old North Beach, at 190 Pacific Street, where Italian fruit wholesalers once plied their trade (since relocated to the suburbs), sits **Square One**, a handsome, upscale dining room overlooking a small greensward. At the helm of this acclaimed establishment is Joyce Goldstein, author of the celebrated *Mediterranean Kitchen* and of a regularly changing menu that tends to favor the robust over the refined. Especially popular are Wednesday evenings, when Square One offers a culinary tour of a single Italian region, including such unusual stops as Basilicata, Calabria, and Sardinia. Tel: 788-1110.

Notwithstanding its name, Italian classics are the mainstay of one of North Beach's most beloved neighborhood institutions, the resolutely old-fashioned U.S. **Restaurant**. The locals flock to this unpretentious establishment at 431 Columbus Avenue, near Vallejo Street, for the hearty dishes—osso buco, *coteghino* sausage with beans, pasta al pesto—that sustained their ancestors in the Old Country. But this is also the best place for an Italo-American breakfast of eggs, potatoes, and Italian sausages. No credit cards.

Nearby, at 1707 Powell Street, close to Union, is the equally popular **Washington Square Bar and Grill**, a favorite elbow-bending stop for local journalists. The always busy bar opens onto a handsome wood-paneled dining room, where the straightforward Italian menu lists an excellent fried calamari, plus simply cooked meats and pastas. Tel: 982-8123.

Chinatown

The 24 blocks that form the commercial heart of Chinatown are home to nearly 150 restaurants, most of them catering to the tastes of the southern Chinese who are the majority of San Francisco's Asian-descended residents. Although Cantonese is the neighborhood's predominant cuisine, it is far from the sole southern idiom. The modest **Fortune Restaurant**, at 675 Broadway near Stockton Street, features Chao Zhou cuisine, a seafood-based fare from the southern coastal city of Shantou that is regarded as a true haute cuisine by the gastronomes of Hong Kong. Three classic Chao Zhou dishes at Fortune will explain why: deep-fried balls of prawn and fish meat wrapped in bean-curd skin; a thin, crisp oyster cake; and *pomfret* showered with garlic and ginger.

Chinatown boasts a vast number of Hong Kong–style barbecue houses; their hallmark is a front window full of roast ducks, poached chickens, and braised squabs. One of the best of the genre, directly across the street from the Fortune at 674 Broadway, is **Hing Lung**, a late-hours, brass-trimmed barbecue-and-noodle house favored by import-export tycoons and kung fu–crazy teens alike. In addition to the duck, they come for roast suckling pig and stir-fried rice noodles.

A clutch of restaurants serving dim sum, the small plates of savories and sweets that the Cantonese take with their midday tea, climbs Pacific Avenue between Grant and Powell. These two blocks boast such respected dim sum palaces as **Hong Kong Teahouse**, **Miriwa**, and **New Asia**, which serve literally hundreds of plates each morning, as well as a tiny old-timer, **Tung Fong**. On weekends the crowds make waiting for a table inevitable.

Many of Chinatown's popular Cantonese dinner houses are small, noisy, and utterly indifferent to questions of decor. **Lichee Garden**, at 1416 Powell near Broadway, counters this "good food in a hole in the wall" syndrome with classic fare served in a comfortable, tableclothed ambience. Some of the kitchen's best dishes appear only on the Chinese-language menu; ask your waiter to decode the specialties. Two dishes on the English menu should not be missed: the duck and jellyfish salad and the shrimp-stuffed bean curd.

In 1988 Shanghai-born Peter Fang decided to buck the southern Chinese tide in Chinatown when he opened the **House of Nanking** at 919 Kearny, near Jackson Street. Within no time this simple diner, featuring the vinegar-spiced dishes of Jiangsu Province and neighboring Shanghai, was a smashing success. Fang turns out his Shanghai fried noodles, pan-fried pork buns, and drunken chicken in a tiny kitchen open to the full view of his admiring diners.

For a reminder of prewar Chinatown, when it was home to a bachelor society of workingmen whose families stayed behind in Asia, stop by **Sun Wah Kue** at 848 Washington, near Stockton Street. The booth-lined dining room with its marble-topped tables and generations of paint is where local Chinese-Americans have traditionally gone for an all-American lunch of rare roast beef, homemade pie, and fresh-baked biscuits at almost prewar prices.

The Union Square Area

The skyline of downtown San Francisco has been reshaped dramatically in recent decades, with new hotel towers defining much of the changing picture. One of those towers is the Nikko Hotel (222 Mason), whose crowning story houses the exquisite **Benkay** restaurant. In an elegant dining room appointed with small Zen gardens and yards of ebony wood, kimono-clad waitresses carry trays of delicacies as refined as those found in a top Kyoto *ryokan*. The *kaiseki* dinners, elaborate set meals that vary with the season, make for a memorable splurge. Tel: 394-1111.

The earnest exploration of Mexico's rich regional culinary nuances was long overdue when chef Reed Hearon undertook the task in the **Corona Bar & Grill** at 88 Cyril Magnin Street, off the lobby of the Monticello Inn. His *paella,* loaded with chicken, spicy chorizo sausages, and seafood, is flavored with a medley of herbs and spices that authoritatively distinguishes it from all Spanish antecedents. Corona's chocolate-lined flan makes a rich finish to your meal. At lunch the tables here hum with conspiratorial conversations between editors and the better-paid reporters from the nearby *San Francisco Chronicle* and *Examiner.* Tel: 392-5500.

There are no secrets at **Faz**, 132 Bush near Sansome Street, a favorite lunch spot with the office-tower crowd: The in-house smoked fish, meats, and game for which Faz is famous are on display right inside the door. The contemporary décor includes an old-fashioned counter with ringside seats for observing the action. A mixed smoked-fish platter changes according to what's available; mahi mahi, eel, tuna, mackerel, and salmon are among the possibilities. Tel: 362-4489.

Near the foot of Market Street, at Four Embarcadero Center, the three-piece-suit set crowds the elegant **Harbor Village** at noon for exceptional dim sum. In the evening the cast broadens to embrace lodgers from nearby hotels and families gathered for a special celebration. The branch of a famous Hong Kong restaurant empire, Harbor Village has secured as its executive chef Hui Pui Wing, one of the Crown Colony's brightest culinary lights, whose reputation rests on mastery of both traditional and nouvelle interpretations of Cantonese cuisine. Tel: 781-8833.

John's Grill (63 Ellis between Stockton and Powell) is San Francisco the way Dashiell Hammett's private eyes knew it. No surprise there as the author of *The Maltese Falcon* was himself a faithful customer of this venerable establishment (founded just two years after the great 1906 quake). The ambience is men's club—white tablecloths, a dark-wood bar, portraits of noted regulars, and waiters in black jackets who remember your name at the second reservation. The grilled petrale sole is deservedly famous, and the mixed drinks speak of honesty as well as sophistication. Tel: 986-0069.

Those longing for an afternoon tea break will be well rewarded by a visit to the **Bread and Honey Tea Room** of the King George Hotel (334 Mason Street, between O'Farrell and Geary), which offers traditional British service in a cozy, classically appointed setting. An array of savories and sweets accompanies an interesting selection of fine teas, brewed to meet the expectations of the fussiest British traveller. The refined, art-lined **Compass Rose** at Union Square's St. Francis Hotel also serves a respectable afternoon tea.

Famed California restaurant interior designer Pat Kuleto gave the foyer of his **Kuleto's** the look of an Old San Francisco bar, albeit with a new line of Italian appetizers to sample over drinks. At the rear of the first dining room, an open kitchen turns out northern Italian pastas and grilled meats; farther into the premises is a second, more formal dining room. Located in the Villa Florence at 221 Powell, this sunny Mediterranean dinner house is a great favorite of regular guests at the many hotels around Union Square. Tel: 397-7720.

Located about midway between Union Square and the heart of the Financial District, **Le Central**, at 453 Bush Street (near Grant Street), presents honest, provincial French fare in a lively bistro setting. The lunchtime crowd usually includes local power brokers deep in conversation over plates of long-simmered *cassoulet,* respectable Alsatian *choucroute garni,* or lightly poached salmon crowned with hollandaise sauce. The dinner hour is less boisterous. Tel: 391-2233.

Although it has been around for nearly a decade, **Masa's** still boasts the most sought-after reservation in San Francisco, with three weeks' advance notice necessary to garner a table. Named for its late founding chef Masataka Kobayashi, Masa's serves sophisticated French cuisine in the formal dining room of the charming Vintage Court hotel, at 648 Bush. The kitchen staff, which carries on the highly refined style of its original master, presents exquisitely prepared portions that are as petite as the dinner checks are monumental. This restaurant is arguably the most expensive in the city—and the most highly regarded. Tel: 989-7154.

Hotel dining rooms, unlike their counterparts elsewhere, are some of San Francisco's premier restaurants. Notable evidence lies in the comfortable yet reserved **Pierre at the Hotel Méridien** (15 Third Street). The original menu concept, which stresses a faithful rendering of the pre-nouvelle Gallic table, was designed by Michelin-starred chef Alain Chapel of Meaunais, who still regularly reviews the offerings. Throughout the year the Pierre invites chefs from France's leading kitchens to prepare special prix-fixe menus from their repertoires. For an informal meal, stop by the Méridien's **Café Justin**, which offers a brasserie menu with a strong Provençal accent. Tel: 974-6400 or 974-1029.

Chef Wolfgang Puck, creator of the now-legendary Spago in Los Angeles and the Chinois in Santa Monica, carried his vision of California cuisine north to the Prescott Hotel in downtown San Francisco in 1989, and the city's makers and shakers immediately began lining up for breakfast, lunch, and dinner at his chic, palm-lined **PosTrio**, 545 Post, near Mason Street. The menu matches the finest local products—Sonoma County lamb, Dungeness crab, Sacramento Delta vegetables—with Mediterranean culinary traditions. Tel: 776-7825.

At the opposite end of the San Francisco restaurant timeline is **Tadich Grill**, the city's oldest, which was started during the Gold Rush by three Yugoslav immigrants as a coffee stand for sailors dropping anchor in Yerba Buena Harbor. In its turn-of-the-century grill room at 240 California Street (near Battery Street), Financial District heavy hitters regularly line up for seats at the long counter or in one of the polished walnut booths. The main attraction is seafood prepared by the Buich family, who have overseen the operation since 1929. In keeping with its old-fashioned ways, Tadich takes no reservations and accepts no credit cards.

Sam's Grill, 374 Bush Street near Kearny, is another of San Francisco's legendary seafood restaurants. Like Tadich, it caters to the bankers and brokers set, who favor its simple preparations of local seafood and air-shipped East Coast shellfish. A no-reservations policy has Sam's loyal patrons lining up a full 30 minutes before the noon whistle to nab a table in the comfortably clubby dining room, complete with curtained booths. Open weekdays only, the restaurant closes in the early evening.

In 1988 the owners of Wu Kong, one of the most successful restaurants in restaurant-crazy Hong Kong, opened a San Francisco branch of their **Wu Kong** in the Rincon Center (101 Spear Street near Mission Street), a beautifully renovated historical site famed for its extraordinary Art Deco murals. The menu features the regional specialties of Shanghai, the lower Yangtze Valley, and the North China plain, all served in a spacious, chandeliered dining room. Among the marvelous dishes of its Hong Kong-and-Shanghai-trained chefs are a vegetarian "goose" composed of bean-curd sheets and mushrooms, velvety braised pork shoulder atop a bed of spinach, and the juicy pork-filled steamed buns called *xiao long bao* (little dragon packets). Tel: 957-9300.

Civic Center and the Van Ness Corridor

Brazil fever hit the Bay Area in the late 1980s in a wave of dance fads, *Carneval* celebrations, and restaurants. At its crest was **Bahía**, ensconced in two Franklin Street buildings not far from the staid corridors of City Hall. One serves as a nightclub (Franklin at Market), the other as a dinner house (41 Franklin), and both draw large numbers of the under-35 set who have fueled the fever. Named for the city that has Brazil's liveliest Luso-African cultural scene, Bahía offers a menu full of allusions to the Creole tradition, whether you order chicken and cashews in a yucca sauce or roast pork stuffed with vegetables, bacon, and olives. The nightclub down the block may seem quiet if you pass by on your way to an early dinner; it won't if you take another look after 10:00 P.M. Tel: 626-3306.

In 1984 Ann Harris, wife of California beef king Jack Harris, opened **Harris'**, 2100 Van Ness at Pacific Avenue, reintroducing steak-house gentility to a San Francisco that was ready for just such a traditionalist revival. In a dining room outfitted with leather booths and paneled in rich woods, a first-rate staff serves the finest dry-aged beef the state has to offer. The expertly grilled steaks can be accompanied with deep-fried onion rings, garnished baked potatoes, and creamed spinach, or with plain steamed potatoes and unadorned vegetables for waistline watchers. Tel: 673-1888.

Hayes Street Grill, at 324 Hayes, was the first upscale dining option to take root within a short stroll of the city's Performing Arts Center. Simplicity is its menu's defining characteristic. Each day about a dozen fresh-fish selections appear on the blackboard; your choice is grilled and then served with an array of sauces that may range from the classic béarnaise to an innovative Southeast Asian creation. The Grill's owners also run a small eatery at 201 Ivy Street, directly behind the restaurant, where California-style pizza and calzone are served. Tel: 863-5545.

Located at 1115 Polk Street, half a dozen blocks north of the Civic Center proper, **Maharani** is one of the city's most popular Indian restaurants. Its Punjabi cooks are especially adept at the subcontinent's northern dishes, turning out outstanding examples of tandoori meats and breads; but, this being California, they are also more than willing to vary the tandoori formula with such distinctly un-Punjabi items as salmon and prawns. There is a conventional front room, nicely appointed to meet middlebrow tastes, and a back-room done up in Mogul-style booths lined with pillows and hung with veils. Tel: 775-1988.

Miss Pearl's Jam House (601 Eddy Street at Larkin) offers West Indian food with a California-cuisine twist. The young, sometimes boisterous crowd that packs this lively bar and restaurant in the evenings is infatuated with the cross-cultural results, served in small plates that add up to a Caribbean version of Spanish *tapas*. The menu boasts some 30 choices, from Jamaican jerk chicken to deep-fried catfish. At lunch on sunny days you can eat alongside the swimming pool; Tel: 775-5267. Miss Pearl's is installed in **The Phoenix**, once a ticky-tacky motel that has since become a trendy downtown inn decorated in the pastel mode of Malibu; Tel: 776-1380.

For years Bruce Cost guided San Franciscans through the exotic maze of Asian cuisines with his weekly newspaper column, two best-selling books on the Orient's larder, and heavily booked cooking lessons. Then in 1989 he opened **Monsoon** in the Opera Plaza at 601 Van Ness. This updated version of an Asian restaurant marries extraordinary Postmodern decor to an ever-changing menu of Chinese and Southeast Asian specialties. Don't expect a chop suey dinner check: The emphasis is on labor-intensive methods and the highest-quality ingredients. A classy wine cellar rounds out the attractions of this unique—and uniquely San Francisco—spot. Tel: 441-3232.

The Civic Center area borders on the Tenderloin District, where thousands of Indo-Chinese refugees have settled; they're responsible for the scores of Southeast Asian restaurants that line the surrounding blocks of the Van Ness corridor. The bright, airy **Thanh Long Larkin Restaurant**, 500 Larkin at Turk Street, is a modest dining room that offers some of the most unusual Vietnamese fare in the neighborhood, ranging from braised goat with chrysanthemum leaves and rice noodles to eel prepared in a curried coconut-milk sauce. Ask the staff for help in translating the Vietnamese-language menu, which expands considerably on the English version.

Nearby at number 607 is **Pacific Restaurant**, the best of many neighborhood restaurants specializing in the Hanoi-style dish called *pho*—a fragrant broth filled with rice noodles and beef, in the form of thin, rare slices, well-cooked brisket, tripe, or meatballs. The huge bowls arrive with a plate of raw bean sprouts, coriander, green chiles, and lemon wedges, to be added as desired. It will set you back half the price of a movie ticket.

Spuntino, 524 Van Ness near McAllister Street, is a *tavola calda*—an Italian fast-food spot—the ideal place for a quick pizza, *panini,* or pasta before settling in for an evening of Verdi across the street. The routine is streamlined: Make a choice, order at the counter, and take a seat. Your brick oven–cooked pizza Margherita will be delivered in no time at all.

Jeremiah Tower, one of the granddaddies of California cuisine, wore the top toque at a number of Bay Area restaurants before christening his own phenomenally popular **Stars**, at 150 Redwood Alley, near Polk Street, in 1984. This is a place to see and to be seen, a hangout for society matrons and rising politicos, accomplished *tenori* and incurable foodies. You can join them in a pricey full dinner, a more proletarian bowl of chili, or a plate of raw oysters; both the food and the experience will be memorable. Tel: 861-7827.

The **Zuni Café**, another landmark of California cuisine, stands a quarter mile west of City Hall at 1658 Market Street, near Franklin. In an inviting setting of white walls, a long copper bar, and snowy table linens, chef Judy Rodgers steers the kitchen on a creative course through Italy and southern France, using the finest fresh ingredients of Northern Califor-

nia. Her menu crosses the traditional culinary boundaries
with great sophistication, offering assortments of the freshest shellfish, pizza topped with oil-cured olives and ancho-
vies, and sausage with creamy polenta. You can start your
day here with breakfast, or stop by at noon for a Gorgonzola-
crowned hamburger and some of the best *pommes frites* in
the city. Reservations are *de rigueur* for the dinner hour; Tel:
552-2522.

The Mission and South of Market
San Francisco's Hispanic soul resides in the busy, colorful
streets of the Mission District Although the prevailing spirit
is Latin American, the legacy of Mother Spain can be explored at **El Oso**, 1153 Valencia near 22nd Street, where you
enter through a handsome, dark-wood bar area, walk past a
musical combo playing variations on *Granada,* and wind up
in a plaza-sized dining room patroled by tuxedoed waiters.
They carry a complete range of hot and cold *tapas* and great
metal pans of steaming paella.

Fueled by more than a decade of unrest in Central America, the city's Salvadoran population has steadily grown
through the 1980s and into the 1990s, as have the numbers
of Salvadoran restaurants. One of the oldest of these establishments is still one of the best. Located at 3522 Twentieth
Street, near Mission, the friendly, casual **El Tazumal** serves
hearty portions of the dishes that expatriate Salvadoreños
long for. There is buttery beef tongue in a richly seasoned
tomato sauce and *carne deschilichada* (shredded meat
cooked with vegetables and eggs). In a storefront right next
door, the Tazumal cooks dish out *pupusas* (griddle-fried
cornmeal rounds stuffed with cheese and/or meat) that are
the Salvadoran answer to the American burger.

Twenty-fourth Street, between Mission and Potrero, is not
only the liveliest stretch of the barrio, but also offers some of
its most serious eating. **La Victoria**, at the corner of 24th
Street and Alabama, is a combination Mexican bakery and
restaurant. Breads and sweets are sold inside the 24th Street
entrance and full meals are served in the dining room
located at the back, reached through an Alabama Street door.
Longtime customers swear by the *birria* (goat stew) and
chiles rellenos. This is a cash-only operation.

For decades Jaliscan-born Josie Reyes and her sister Marga-
rita ran a small diner in the Mission, where they were among
the neighborhood's most popular restaurateurs. In late 1988
they launched **Los Jarritos**, 901 South Van Ness at 20th Street,
decorating the cheerful dining room with hundreds of the

tiny earthenware cups (*jarritos*) that Jaliscan men traditionally use for tequila. The sisters offer a full menu of Mexican
classics, from *carnitas* garnished with onion, tomatoes, and
fresh coriander to *carne asada* piled high on a pair of
handmade corn tortillas. No credit cards.

Nicaraguans dine seven days a week at 3015 Mission, near
26th Street, where the simply decorated **Nicaragua Restaurant** specializes in the dishes of their homeland. Two versions of the Mesoamerican tamale are served here: the
featherlight *yoltamal* of pure cornmeal and the *nacatamal*
stuffed with seasoned shredded beef. There are fried plan-
tains and cream, steamed yucca crowned with crisp *chic-
charones,* and whole fried Pacific snapper. The menu even
includes a list of traditional drinks, from *pozol* (hominy and
milk) to tamarind, and the jukebox pulses with a steady Latin
beat. No credit cards.

The brightly lit, practically furnished **Taquería San José**,
2830 Mission at 24th Street, turns out a true taco—not the
mass-produced version found in shopping malls, but a pair
of soft corn tortillas stacked with grilled beef, pork, or a
variety meat—tongue, head, brains—and fresh chile-laden
salsa. The package is expanded to burrito form with a large
flour tortilla, beans, and rice.

The straightforward Latin food of the Mission barrio is in
stark contrast to that of the adjoining SoMa (South of Market)
neighborhood, where restaurant trends (and clichés) define
the landscape. Attracting a mostly young, professional crowd,
the low-rise district regularly sprouts new restaurants and just
as regularly sees them close. One of the most dependable
establishments in this constantly changing dining scene is the
South Park Café, 108 South Park Avenue on the north side of a
small square in what was once a neighborhood of stately
Victorian mansions. Most of the grand homes long ago gave
way to light industrial buildings, which have subsequently
been converted to office space. At lunchtime, workers from
these surrounding structures fill South Park Café's charm-
ingly Gallic dining room to feast on grilled *boudin* accompanied with sautéed apples and thin, crisp *pommes frites.* A rack
of French newspapers and the occasional French-speaking
waiter add to the overall Parisian ambience. Tel: 495-7275.

In 1988 Yahya Salih took over a former truck stop at
Eighth and Harrison streets and transformed it into **Yaya**,
where California meets the Middle East. In an open, white-
tiled kitchen, Salih prepares appetizers of tender grilled
eggplant with a pomegranate-and-cream sauce and smoked
salmon with cucumber salad. Main courses of grilled, mari-

nated meats and fish are evidence of the Iraqi-born chef's considerable mastery of both the pantry and the charcoal fire. Tel: 255-0909.

Western Addition and Japantown

Tucked away in the southern reaches of the Western Addition, in a neighborhood that is experiencing a restaurant renaissance, the **Indian Oven**, 237 Fillmore, near Haight Street, delivers a fresh perspective on the food of the subcontinent. Flanked by a tandoor and an ebony grand, a mostly young crowd dines on specialties from Kerala and Mysore, the Punjab and Goa. The kitchen has a real flair for contemporary interpretations, such as goat cheese–stuffed peppers. Parsi-style chicken with potato straws and apricots and a tandoor-cooked rack of lamb are just two of the superb classics offered here. Tel: 626-1628.

Just down the block at the corner of Fillmore and Waller reigns one of Thai cuisine's finest local outposts: **Thep Phanom**. Maintaining this enviable reputation almost since the day it opened in 1986, Thep Phanom has kept the intimate, attractive dining room full every night of the week, with a waiting line curving out the door. The *keang ped,* served in lovely blue-and-white bowls, combines roast duck in a rich curry enlivened with fresh Asian basil leaves. Try the flavorful coconut-based soups, barbecued meats, or banana leaf–wrapped grilled fish. Tel: 431-2526.

A cross section of Japanese dining can be enjoyed at a single site in the city, a two-story center in Nihonmachi, (Japantown). Called the Kinkei-Kintetsu Mall after the Honshu-based railroad line and conglomerate that built it, it houses exactly the sorts of places that you'd find on the island of Honshu where Kintetsu's tracks run. Located on the center's first floor, **Mifune**, a branch of a well-known Osaka restaurant, dishes up huge portions of house-made buckwheat *soba* and spaghetti-like *udon* noodles, served hot or cold in some two dozen combinations. Just across the street from the mall at 1728 Buchanan Street is Mifune's sister restaurant, **Iroha**, which concentrates on yet another favorite Japanese noodle, the thin wheat *ramen*. Next door to Mifune, at serene, booth-lined **Misono**, genial waitresses cater to a large clientele of Japanese businessmen with a full selection of Tokyo's traditional dinner plates.

Mitoya, on the second floor of the Kintetsu Mall, is a *robata-ya* (grill house) where fresh fish, meats, and vegetables are arranged on a ice-lined counter. Point to what you want and the *robata* man will grill it over a charcoal fire. Steps away from Mitoya, at a tiny *sushi-ya* called **Kame-sushi**, a husband-and-wife team oversee an eight-seat counter topped by a glass case filled with some of the freshest, finest raw fish in town. Japanese authenticity at Kame-sushi extends right down to its no-tipping policy.

North of Japantown, at 1915 Fillmore Street, near Bush, is **Oritalia**, where the name says it all: one-half Orient, one-half Italy. The menu backs up the claim with such wildly innovative dishes as linguine with Japanese *unagi* (eel), and sweet potato topped with crème fraîche and flying-fish roe. A very contemporary decor of faux marble, abstract art, and shining brass fixtures reflects owner Nori Yoshida's experimental spirit. Tel: 346-1333.

A kindred spirit resides at **Rasselas**, 2801 California at Divisadero Street, thanks to the top-flight jazz musicians who perform in its lounge. The dining room, by contrast, is a decidedly traditional haven for the cuisine of Rasselas's Ethiopian proprietors. Spicy vegetarian dishes and braised meats arrive atop a large round of *injera,* the soft, almost spongy national bread that doubles as plate and silverware. Accompany the meal with a bottle of honey-based Ethiopian wine. Tel: 567-5010.

North of Golden Gate Park

In the 1980s the broad boulevards and avenues north of Golden Gate Park—Clement, Geary, and others in the Richmond District—blossomed with scores of new restaurants, many of them serving the cuisines of the neighborhood's large and growing Asian-American population. One clear sign of this demographic trend was a mushrooming of *bulkogi-jips,* dinner houses that grill spicy Korean meat dishes right at the diners' charcoal pit–equipped tables. A fine example is the **Kyung Bok Palace** at 6314 Geary, set a mite incongruously in the shadow of the onion-domed Russian Orthodox cathedral (Soviet emigrés have also settled here in large numbers). Along with grilled meats, Kyung Bok provides an unusually ample spread of *kim chee,* the small plates of prepared vegetables and seafood that accompany every Korean meal. This is fiery stuff, not the choice for those with second thoughts about the merits of the chile pepper.

Hong Kong Flower Lounge arrived in the Bay Area as the American cousin of a multibranched Hong Kong restaurant family; today, with two locations near the San Francisco International Airport and a third at 5322 Geary, near 17th Avenue, the cousin is raising quite a clan of its own. Its hallmark is seafood, with great importance attached to preparations that do not disguise the natural flavors of ingredients. Its steamed fish, poached prawns, and stir-fried Dungeness crabs will transform the perspective of anyone who thinks Cantonese food means sweet-and-sour pork. Reservations are absolutely essential. Tel: 668-8998 or 878-8108.

Before the Avenues were Asian, they were heavily Irish—and as far as the pub culture goes, they still are. **Pat O'Shea's Mad Hatter** is an immensely popular example, crammed nightly with fans of World Cup soccer and Guinness stout. Under the direction of Nancy Oakes, its kitchen developed a following for strictly American beef stew and meatloaf. When Ms. Oakes grew more ambitious, she leased the quarters next door at 3854 Geary, near Third Avenue, and opened **l'Avenue**. The menu in this warm, intimate bistro bespeaks the innovative nature of California cuisine: its influences draw, in varying measures, from the regional United States, the Mediterranean, and, occasionally, the Orient. Tel: 386-1555.

Burmese food was put on the San Francisco map by **Mandalay**, 4344 California Street, near Laurel, which converted the former stage space of the Asian-American Theater into a quiet, art-lined dining room. The national dishes of Burma, *panthe kaukswe* and *mohinga* (respectively a chicken curry with rice noodles and a rich fresh-water fish soup), both come off handsomely here, as do a number of highly unusual "salads" that combine such ingredients as fresh ginger, tea leaves, ground nuts, dried shrimp, and tropical herbs; Tel: 386-3895. The theater group, incidentally, now occupies an old Masonic Hall at the corner of Clement and Arguello.

Almost everywhere in Southeast Asia, ethnic Chinese are the chief restaurateurs, serving both indigenous and Chinese dishes. **Narai**, 2229 Clement near 23rd Avenue, is in that sense one of the most authentic Thai restaurants you'll ever patronize, because it frankly offers both Thai and Chao Zhou Chinese specialties. In the former category, its chefs excel at a tart and chile-laden squid salad and a claypot of fresh mussels cooked in a lemongrass-scented broth. The Chao Zhou braised duck, served at room temperature with a vinegar and garlic dip, is worth twice the modest price it fetches. Tel: 751-6363.

If you ask, the chef at **San Wang**, 2239 Clement, will be delighted to demonstrate one of the grand mysteries of China: *la mian* (hand-pulled noodles), in which a ball of dough is twisted and pulled until it magically self-separates into a perfectly uniform skein. This dish's source is the highly sophisticated Chinese school of Shandong, which sent chefs to the imperial kitchens of Beijing for centuries. Another of its secrets is the pedestrian-sounding "sautéed pork with two pieces of skin," which is in fact a remarkable platter of seafood delicacies, spun bean-thread ribbons, pork, and vegetables under a mustard sauce. There's a full bar equipped with fireplace if you have to wait for a table.

The chef at the **Straits Café** (3300 Geary near Commonwealth Avenue) is a Nonya, a scion of a fascinating culture on the Malacca Strait that blends Malay and Chinese influences. In her San Francisco kitchen, the possibilities—which in Singapore or Penang may run to hundreds of dishes—have been narrowed to a couple of dozen, but they are executed to perfection. Highlights include *otak-otak* (fish mousse steamed in banana leaves), a searing coconut noodle soup called *laksa,* and green beans sautéed with a mixture of garlic, chiles, and shallots. The decor is also a creative mixture of California chic and Southeast Asian shophouse. Tel: 668-1783.

Of the six Chinese cuisines represented in these selections, Hakka is probably the least known outside of Asia. The term *hakka* translates as "guest" and refers to a once-nomadic people who wandered into southern China centuries ago. The Wongs, proprietors of **Ton Kiang**, wandered into the Bay Area in the late 1960s, eventually making one Hakka dish—salt-baked chicken—so popular that it's nearly taken on the identity of a San Francisco mainstay. There are two Ton Kiang locations, at 3148 Geary, near Spruce Street, and 5827 Geary, near 22nd Avenue; the former is larger and somewhat fancier than the latter. If salt or chicken aren't to your taste, try the superb stuffed bean curd or one of the wine-flavored dishes.

The Marina and Cow Hollow

After a walk along the yacht-filled harbor that gives this district its name, health-conscious strollers can head right into America's best-known vegetarian restaurant. Founded and run by the San Francisco Zen Center, **Greens** is to the meatless meal what wine is to grape juice. In a spacious former army-transport pier shed at Fort Mason, diners sit before enormous windows that yield a spectacular view of the Golden Gate Bridge and Sausalito. The accent is California cuisine, and among the things that bring diners back again and again—whatever their attitudes on meat—are small pizzas from a wood-fired oven, pastas, and mesquite-grilled tofu brochettes. Tel: 771-6222.

It's entirely likely that there are more Cambodian restaurants in the Bay Area than there are in Phnom Penh—about a dozen at last count, from Berkeley to San Jose. At **Angkor Palace**, located in the heart of the motel strip at 1769 Lombard, near Laguna Street, diners can recline like royalty on pillow-strewn banquettes. Fresh-water fish, caught in the great lake known as Tonle Sap, are the glory of the Cambodian table; at Angkor Palace, Sacramento Delta catfish fill the role with delicious results. A meat dish, pork sliced and sautéed with banana blossoms and black mushrooms, is also sensational. Tel: 931-2830.

Izzy's Steak & Chop House, 3349 Steiner, near Chestnut Street, is all-American, from the vintage advertising art that covers its walls to the old-fashioned creamed spinach and scalloped potatoes that arrive on its plates. The big draw here is beefsteaks, especially thick New York strips. You can sauce them up from a choice of literally hundreds of prepared condiments. For those who don't want beef there are pork and lamb chops, plus grilled chicken breast and fish filet. The name Izzy, by the way, refers to the famous old Pacific Street barkeep, Izzy Gomez, whose history is told in newspaper clippings displayed in the restaurant. Tel: 563-0487.

Chestnut Street is the heart of the Marina, six blocks of family-run shops, markets, restaurants, and delis that evoke the Italian origins of many of the district's residents. **La Pergola**, 2060 Chestnut near Steiner Street, stakes its claim to their allegiance with a chef whose own origins lie on the shores of Lake Garda, west of Venice. His *mezza luna* (half-moon–shaped raviolis stuffed with squash and served in a butter-and-sage sauce) are cogent reminders of the traditional northern Italian menu's delicacy. A more creative touch goes into his superb risotto with smoked salmon, when it's available; the menu changes frequently. Tel: 563-4500.

In the mid-1980s Cow Hollow's **Balboa Café** (3199 Fillmore Street near Union Street) and **Perry's** (1944 Union Street near Buchanan) were among San Francisco's strongest magnets for the faddish singles set. On Friday and Saturday nights hundreds of young doctors, lawyers, and MBAs would squeeze into these bar–restaurants to meet and mix with their fellow professionals. Except for a highly touted hamburger served at the Balboa (created by the café's then chef, the now-famous Jeremiah Tower), little attention was paid to the American saloon–style fare turned out at either establishment. Today, although the crowds have thinned somewhat, both the Balboa Café and Perry's remain popular, albeit still more for their social opportunities than for their culinary efforts.

—*Sharon Silva*

BARS AND NIGHTLIFE

Since the gold seekers and fortune hunters rushed here to get rich in 1849, San Francisco has been a good-time, boisterous town. The combination of new found wealth, customs from around the world, and geographical isolation created an unmatched diversity of entertainment and nightlife. What other city prohibited local police from entering gambling saloons or brothels after sunset?

But the nightlife slowed in the late 1970s, the culmination of a trend that started after World War II, which brought a new aura of respectability to the city in tandem with the pervasive influence of television. And perhaps people needed a rest from the turbulent 1960s and early 1970s. But since the SoMa nighttime scene began in the late 1980s, and with the recovery of The Haight, the San Francisco nightlife tradition has been rediscovered and is again roaring with a wide variety of entertainment—from a club with three live bands playing simultaneously in different rooms to bars and restaurants resembling everything from a Caribbean jungle to Casablanca in 1941 to Medieval Russia to a 1930s speakeasy.

There are five major areas of nightlife activity in San Francisco—North Beach, South of Market, Downtown, Cow Hollow, and The Haight—where you can visit a comedy or jazz club, go to the theater, check out a gay club, or have a late-night meal. And for those who want something more refined, San Francisco is dedicated to romance.

North Beach

The heart and soul of nighttime San Francisco is North Beach. For more than a decade it shook a world that for the most part only wanted it to go away. Back in the elsewhere-sanitized 1950s, "the Beats" (Jack Kerouac, Allen Ginsberg, Neal Cassady, Gregory Corso, Lawrence Ferlinghetti, et al.) deliberately dropped out of the success track to explore the unexplored. Donning black garments, smoking marijuana, and saying "weird" things ("Look me in the eye." "Which I?"), they sparked a cultural renaissance. Nightclubs featured Lenny Bruce and Mort Sahl (see the Comedy section below), who were called Communists because they dared to say something different. Artists flocked to San Francisco, and, on October 13, 1955, when Ginsberg read his soon-to-be-famous *Howl,* San Francisco's reputation as the "Left Bank of the West" was affirmed. By the following year the authorities were punishing these same people; legal suits proliferated, and *Howl* was judged obscene. But the movement could not be stopped; the free-thinking Beats had laid the groundwork for the Summer of Love and the student protests that eventually affected the entire world.

By the early 1960s, however, the spotlight in North Beach was on breasts, as topless dancing on the Broadway strip became the latest rage—not surprisingly, because North Beach had always had a racy past. (This is where the Barbary Coast originated, and terms such as "to shanghai," "hoodlum," and "Mickey Finn"—named after a disreputable pharmacist— were coined.)

North Beach has slowed a little today, but there are still plenty of cafés and some of the best bars in the city to keep it vibrant. And that's not all it is. North Beach is alive with fresh-ground coffee aromas, opera singing at the Caffè Trieste, murals on the streets, and the melodic and vibrant sound of Italian being spoken.

If you're not within walking distance of North Beach take a cab (parking is very difficult) to Grant and Vallejo, where you'll find **Caffè Trieste**, a North Beach institution with an Old World spirit and a youthful feel. (Perhaps it's the patrons—artists, poets, writers, and their imitators—who manage the blend.) The café's history goes back to the Beat Era (check out the wall photos), and the place is almost always filled to capacity. The church across the street, St. Francis of Assisi, was the only building standing on Columbus after the 1906 earthquake and fire.

Walk downhill on Grant as far as Columbus Avenue, where you should cross Broadway and start following Columbus. Halfway down the block you will find **Spec's 12 Adler Museum Café**. This is a colorful hangout for locals, but everyone is welcome. You'll find it in a tiny alley at 12 Adler. No credit cards. **Tosca's** (242 Columbus), almost next door to Spec's but worlds apart in feeling, is a late-night wateringhole for San Francisco's Hollywood clientele. Its jukebox is full of Italian opera.

Continue south on Columbus as far as Pacific, cross to the west side of the street, and you're at the very comfortable microbrewery/bar **San Francisco Brewing Company** (155 Columbus), located almost in the shadow of the Transamerica

Pyramid. This perfect example of a traditional San Francisco drinking emporium has a handsome solid mahogany bar, dark decor to match, and even wooden ceiling fans. The various beers brewed here are named after historical figures or places. Try an "Emperor Norton," coined for the wealthy rice merchant of the Gold Rush era, who, after losing all his money and his mind, declared himself "Emperor of the United States and Protector of Mexico." He was such a likeable character that nearly every merchant in San Francisco honored the scrip he issued. When the Emperor died in 1880, just weeks before his 20 years of scrip was to be repaid, more than 10,000 cheerful mourners attended his funeral; Mark Twain wrote a commentary on his life. Even today the anniversary of his death is commemorated by hundreds of members of the jolly pioneer fraternity E Clampus Vitus, who parade out to his gravesite. The San Francisco Brewing Company is open until midnight on weekdays and 1:30 A.M. on Fridays and Saturdays.

Backtrack north on Columbus one block to **Vesuvio's** (255 Columbus), a bar with a history. Since 1949 this has been a haunt of locals and a home away from home for many beatniks and artists. The exterior walls are worth a read and the interior ones are filled with art.

Next door is **City Lights Booksellers and Publishers** at number 261, the granddaddy of the paperback bookstores and a North Beach cultural shrine. Founded by Lawrence Ferlinghetti (he published *Howl*) in the early 1950s, the store carries books and magazines few others stock; City Lights tilts toward the arts, especially poetry, and left-wing politics. It is the spiritual center of what the Beat Generation was all about. Chairs invite you to browse, sit, and relax, and patrons mirror the diversity of San Francisco; open until midnight.

When you reach the corner of Broadway and Columbus cross the street and head east on Broadway. At number 493 is **Rumors**, where there might be live jazz, salsa, funk, or poetry. This is a place where a performer's creativity is valued and applauded—you may catch the next Woody Allen or Barbra Streisand at a new talent showcase on Thursdays. This violet-lit room, reminiscent of old North Beach, serves the best hamburgers in town and is open for food until 10:00 P.M. (the bar closes at 2:00 A.M. Wednesdays through Sundays).

At 506 Broadway, **Finocchio's** has presented a drag show nearly 50 years running, still a kick if you've never seen female impersonators; be prepared to put up with the many large groups brought here on bus tours.

Return to Columbus and head north where, at number

411 on the west side, is **Caffè Puccini**, the coffeehouse where the locals hang out (especially in the early parts of the day). You might see Lawrence Ferlinghetti or former mayor Joe Alioto conferring with daughter Angela, now a local politician herself. This is a place where there is no hurry, so try the grenadine mixtures and enjoy the people-watching.

Continue north on Columbus and make a left on Union to the **Little City Antipasti Bar** (673 Union), an upscale bar and restaurant where the bartenders are as friendly as the denizens. The *antipasti* dishes are wonderful—try the brie and garlic, heated in a cast-iron skillet, then spread on delicious bread. Food is available until about midnight and the bar closes at 2:00 A.M.

Across the street to the north is the **Washington Square Bar and Grill** (1707 Powell), a sophisticated but comfortable spot for the movers and shakers of San Francisco as well as national media celebrities (Tom Brokaw and Art Buchwald have both been spotted here). It's a place to see or be seen, but also still very much a bar where people like to drink. The bartenders are excellent. At the corner of Columbus and Union is the **Bohemian Cigar Store** at number 566, an old-time North Beach haunt where you can get a dose of local flavor as well as some excellent sandwiches, and the **Portofino Caffè** at number 520, a wine-and-beer bar that is home to sailors and elderly Italians.

Continue east on Union (you'll pass **Caffè Malvina**, a wonderful spot for gelato) and reach **Silhouettes** at number 524, one of the first dance bars to have a 1950s motif and features lots of memorabilia. **North Beach Pizza** at Grant and Union has the best late-night pizza around and a usually eclectic crowd that dresses up a rather plain interior. There is another branch of this pizzeria two blocks away, but somehow it doesn't have the same pizzazz, so make sure you catch this one (open until 3:00 A.M. on weekends, 1:00 A.M. otherwise).

When you enter or leave the pizzeria, take a look up the hill, where you can see over a dozen houses that were saved from the fire created by the 1906 earthquake. In a most ingenious fashion, the Italian inhabitants doused their bedding with red wine and placed it against the houses's outer walls to protect them from the flames. From here it is well worth a walk up the hill on Union for some marvelous bay views. Turn left and continue on Montgomery, which leads to the apex of the hill—you'll pass a beautiful white-and-silver Art Deco apartment house that was part of the 1947 Humphrey Bogart and Lauren Bacall movie, *Dark Passage*. The

street ends at the next block with the approach to Julius Castle
(see Romantic San Francisco below).

Head south on Grant and you'll see **Quantity Postcard**, a
one-of-a-kind store that can get you off the hook with all
those people at home you forgot to get a present for. The
thousands of theme choices include 1950s, movie, humorous, antique, and geographic—including postcards from
nearly every state in the Union and worldwide. Open until
11:00 P.M. every night.

Savoy Tivoli at 1434 Grant has an open-air seating area
(with roof if needed) and is a good place to have a *latte* (bar
drink) and people-watch. There's truth in advertising at **The
Schlock Shop** (1418 Grant), which has a bit of everything,
including a decent selection of men's full-brimmed hats.

Head west on Green and at number 574 is **Caffè Sport**,
which has very good Italian food if you don't mind crowds
and insulting waiters. At least walk by and stick your head in
to see the remarkable number of garish decorations and
ornaments that have been crammed into such a tiny space.

If you're in the mood for a late-night snack, make a left on
Columbus and at number 430 is **Calzones**, a newer, hip
restaurant that has good food and is open until 1:00 A.M.,
although when it's crowded it tends to feel packed.

Caffè Roma at 414 Columbus is a fancier type of coffee-
house/restaurant—in interior, atmosphere, and price. If
you're in the mood for pizza, try the pesto one. Open until
1:15 A.M. on weekends, 11:15 P.M. weekdays.

South of Market

The area south of Market Street, also known as SoMa, is
currently the site of the hottest night spots in town. Once the
home of working-class Irish and industrial San Francisco,
SoMa until recently housed many artists who moved here to
take advantage of the cheap rents. Now it seems a new
nightclub opens every day. SoMa covers a large geographical
area, but is one neighborhood where you could walk comfortably (weather permitting).

Start with **Julie's Supper Club** (1123 Folsom, between
Seventh and Eighth streets), an enjoyable place to down a
drink and people-watch. At first you may be unimpressed by
the ambience, described by one of the owners as "1950s
Jetsons," but give it a few minutes—this is a fun place. Stars
photos from the 1950s (Marilyn Monroe, Annette Funicello,
Elizabeth Taylor, Steve Allen) line one wall, along with
bowling pins and other period kitsch. The best music of the

1950s energizes the attractive, professional crowd, few of whom wear the all-black uniform that SoMa has popularized. The appetizers are excellent—try the beer-batter catfish. Julie's is a prototypical SoMa club, where comfort, filling food and drink, and an exciting group of people mix. It's open Tuesdays through Saturdays, with last call at 1:00 A.M.

Across the street is a meeting place for the 1990s—the Brain Wash, which is a combination a café/laundromat. Just up the block is **Eddie Jack's Tap Room Bar**, a pleasant and intimate spot decorated with photos of old tap dancers and featuring live jazz on Wednesdays and Thursdays. Keep going west up the street and you'll see Rausch Alley, where the **Half-Shell Seafood Bar and Grill** is located. The bar here, down the long entranceway to the right, has a happy hour on weekdays between 5:00 and 7:00 P.M., with complimentary appetizers and oysters at 50 cents a pop. It's a friendly place with a tropical atmosphere.

If you return to Folsom Street and head for number 1190, you'll find the **South Side**, with the sounds of inspired, live Motown and a tuxedoed doorman sporting a stylized, slicked down hairdo. Brick walls surround a long, handsome bar and comfortable table seating. There's some dancing in a small spot in front of the band, and plenty more in the back room, where a disc jockey works his art. Sixty years ago this would have been an upscale speakeasy; today this spot attracts a trendy crowd that is well-dressed on the casual side. Open Wednesdays through Saturdays, the cover is $5 to $7.

Continue up Folsom past downscale, minimalistic **Limbo** and the relaxed **Kaffe Kreuzberg**, and head to the club hub of South of Market—11th and Folsom. The **Oasis** here, one of the originals of the SoMa club scene, is a lunch spot with swimming pool by day, and club haven with a dance floor that slides out over the pool by night. When the weather is good this is an open-air dance palace; when it rains a portable roof keeps the elements away. The cover charge varies, depending on whether there is live music.

Also at the corner of 11th and Folsom is the **Paradise Lounge**, which offers three rooms of live entertainment. The music's diversity (anything from country to punk; poetry readings on Sundays) is matched only by that of its patrons, who move freely between rooms. The Paradise is a creative mecca on the San Francisco nightlife scene, and creativity in this case can mean something absolutely incredible to something nearly dreadful (you can always move to the next room). The employees here are all working-to-make-it musicians, and admission is charged only on weekends or if a special act is booked. The Paradise closes at 2:00 A.M.

At 333 Eleventh is a premier San Francisco nightclub that books big names and seats only 500. But even more important than the statistics is that **Slim's** maintains an integrity about its product—blues and roots music. This is the place where musicians go for a busman's holiday, and with good reason: It's owned by Boz Scaggs and Huey Lewis's manager. Headliners like Elvis Costello, Laurie Anderson, Rickie Lee Jones, and Simply Red (as well as Boz and Huey) have performed here, and there's a large video screen for entertainment between live acts. The cover varies from $7 to $29; call ahead for times and roster; Tel: 621-3330.

If you want to stretch your legs, make a final stop at the **DNA Lounge**, 375 Eleventh Street. The pulse here begins at 9:00 P.M. and doesn't end till 3:30 or 4:30 in the morning depending on the night. This is a place where black attire reigns and where the "smart, weird, and hip professionals play," according to the doorman. (The basic-black room with flashy art strives for a subterranean post-apocalypse feeling.) Thursdays are free for those with student I.D.s, and weekend covers range from $8 to $10. Occasionally there's live music.

If food is what you're after, there are a couple of good spots in the area to try. For an upscale bite try **Undici's**, across the street from the DNA Lounge at 374 11th Street. Here you'll find excellent Southern Italian cuisine amid a throng of "beautiful people." Open until 11:00 P.M., closed on Sundays. Reservations are helpful; Tel: 431-3337. Up the block from the Oasis, at 1582 Folsom, is the SoMa institution **Hamburger Mary's**, a popular haunt that tends to fill up with a denim-loving crowd. The interior is a veritable museum of pop culture, the bar is open until 2:00 A.M., and yes, there really is a Mary—she bakes the desserts. Cross to the other side of Folsom, head back east, and you'll pass the **Ace Café**, a simple but good eatery at number 1539, open until 1:00 A.M. on the weekends.

There's a large new dance club with a 1950s-style drugstore-fountain motif in SoMa. At **Boppers**, 650 Howard, the waiters regularly gather onstage to perform pelvic gyrations to the piped-in music—often to the enjoyment of the younger women in the audience; open until 2:00 A.M., with a small cover charge. **Club DV-8** at 55 Natoma (between Mission and Howard streets) is as near a theme park as any rock club in San Francisco. If you spend an evening at this club, created by a keen self-promoter now known as Dr.

Winkie, it's likely to begin in the darkened downstairs room, done in basic black with seating all around the dance floor. Miniskirts are prevalent here and dress is trendy/formal. When this room fills, you'll be directed to a street-level room with Copacabana-style seating and atmosphere, including chandeliers and Picasso-like wall paintings created by the late Keith Haring.

But all this pales next to Dr. Winkie's latest invention: the **Caribbean Zone**, located in the back lot of the club, where an unimpressive, corrugated-sheet-metal exterior gives way to a tropical-theme bar/restaurant with reggae music. The centerpiece is a vintage plane, displayed as if it had crashed in the jungle; its exterior holds the bar's liquor bottles, and, if it's not crowded, you can enjoy a drink inside the plane. This is definitely a place to see—but not during prime hours on Fridays or Saturdays. It's just too popular now; open until midnight on weekends.

If you're looking for a bit of understated elegance, try the full-sized bar at the **Fly Trap** at 606 Folsom (near Third Street). This bar and restaurant is a legend reincarnated— the original turn-of-the-century restaurant was located near a horse-drawn trolley line and the owner was forced to put a piece of fly paper on each table. Having relocated to the SoMa area in 1989, chef Craig Thomas now offers a wonderful blend of traditional fare from the original menu (try the Hangtown Fry) as well as many less-filling but equally delicious salads. Open until 11:00 P.M. on Saturdays, 10:00 P.M. on weekdays. Closed Sundays.

If you're missing that country feeling, check out the **Hotel Utah** (500 Fourth Street), a no-nonsense, nontrendy working-class/cowboy bar. **The Ramp** on 855 China Basin Street (along the industrial waterfront) is a friendly place to dance alfresco to a Brazilian-style or rock band. The club is open until 1:15 A.M. on Fridays and Saturdays, there is no cover charge and the bar itself is located indoors, so you can still have a good time if the weather is bad. **Dolphin P. Rempp** is a romantic treat even if only for a drink. This exquisitely decorated ship of highly polished wood and brass, which once carried wine from France to northern Europe, has now found a resting place high on land at Pier 42 off the Embarcadero. The grounds around the ship are worth exploring in daylight.

That's Ritch (333 Ritch, between Third and Fourth streets off Townsend) is a new club that is a throwback to the basic hip, steak-and-potatoes nightclub of about 20 years ago. The plain brick interior and conventional tables allow you to concentrate on the performers—there's not a bad seat in the house and there's plenty of elbow room. You can dance to live jazz/rock/blues on the ample dance floor until 5:00 A.M., so dress for comfort. There's a mimimal cover charge.

Townsend, at number 177 on the street of the same name, is another new club, this one focusing on dancing, with decor that reminds you that SoMa was once an industrial center. The hip clientele comes here for the heavy bass beat, the large dance floor, and the strobe lighting.

Downtown

Downtown includes the Financial District and Union Square. The Financial District closes up early on weekdays (usually no later than 11:00 P.M.), and is just about closed altogether on weekends, but the Union Square area is geared for nightlife (see Romantic San Francisco for bars here with a view).

Named after an 1850s bar, **The Bank Exchange Saloon and Restaurant** (600 Montgomery in the Financial District) replaces the historic Monkey Block building that stood here more than a hundred years. Mark Twain and his friend, fireman Tom Sawyer, were frequent visitors, and the father of modern China, Sun Yat-sen, drafted his country's first constitution in an office here. Today the bar is in a brightly lit ground floor of the Transamerica Pyramid; filled with wood and stained glass, it turns into a disco at night. **Regina's** (490 Geary) is an exciting Creole restaurant catering to theater patrons before and after performances. Its bar is a comfortable place for a drink; open until 1:00 A.M. on weekends and midnight on weekdays.

Northeast of Union Square toward the waterfront (eight or ten blocks), the Embarcadero Center is four skyscrapers with three levels of shops and restaurants and bars at its base. This is a fun place to start an evening by browsing or watching the office workers stream out on their way home. If you are here after sunset, the beautifully lit Ferry Building can be seen from Building Four. **Harrington's** at 245 Front Street nearby, the **Royal Exchange** at 301 Sacramento, and **Schroeders** at 240 Front across the street, are all traditional San Francisco bars.

Near Union Square, **Kuleto's** at 221 Powell, **Lascaux** at 248 Sutter, **The Maltese Grill** at 20 Annie (off Market), and **PosTrio** at 545 Post are all new and excellent restaurants where you can get a drink at the bar and watch the beautiful people. The bar at the Maltese Grill has its own separate area with piano player. Also in this neighborhood, **The Iron**

Horse (19 Maiden Lane) is a traditional San Francisco bar frequented by traditional San Francisco businesspeople.

West of Union Square (about eight blocks), **The Great American Music Hall**, 859 O'Farrell, is a great place to see a wide variety of the best talent in America, ranging from country music's Jerry Jeff Walker to jazz legend Maynard Ferguson. This old-time music hall is so small you're always close enough to really watch the performers at work. Tickets for the shows vary depending on who's playing and start at $10. A kilted bagpiper may greet your entrance on a weekend night at **Edinburgh Castle** at 950 Geary. The premier Scottish-British pub in town, the Castle, like all good pubs, creates an atmosphere of comfort and congeniality. Have your first drink at the bar to gaze at the array of Scottish memorabilia displayed, and take a cab to get to these last two spots, as the neighborhood is not the best.

The Plush Room at 940 Sutter is an intimate place to see excellent cabaret entertainment. There is a varying cover charge and two-drink minimum (call to see who's playing; Tel: 885-6800). Also on Sutter, **Penny Farthing Pub** at number 679 and the **White Horse Taverne** at number 637 will quench your thirst for Mother England. The food at Penny Farthing is recommended.

Cow Hollow

Union Street west of Van Ness is the main street in the area known as Cow Hollow. There were, in fact, dairy farms here until the 1880s, and women brought their clothes here to wash them in the nearby streams and lagoon (now filled in). Now Union Street is likened to New York's Upper East Side for both its boutique flavor and the difficulty in parking. Nightlife in this area is centered on Union Street and the streets that lead off of it.

Travelling east to west along Union Street, with detours north and south along the way, you could begin with a thoroughly enjoyable time at **Pasand** (1875 Union), a relaxed and intimate Indian restaurant that features melodic live jazz every night until 1:00 A.M. **Perry's** at number 1944, once synonymous with Union Street nightlife, is still a popular wateringhole/restaurant with a fair share of movers and shakers. The tile floor combines with a wood-and-brass bar to offer a clean but warm feeling. The restaurant is open until midnight and the bar closes at 2:00 A.M.. Across the street at number 1979, **Blue Light Café** is a dimly lit but attractive Tex-Mex restaurant/bar owned by native Texan Boz

Scaggs. Open until 1:30 A.M., this is a hangout for the chic and hip of Union Street. Up the block at number 2000 is **Prego**, a classy Italian eatery, open until midnight, that caters to a clientele similar to that of Perry's.

Balboa Café (3199 Fillmore near Union) has taken over the role of hottest spot in the area; its dull-white exterior opens into a handsome wood, glass, and brass decor that is *the* place to be seen (and to make a fashion statement). Try their good hamburgers (food is served until 11:00 P.M.), but stay away on Friday and Saturday nights—Balboa is packed and the immediate area is filled with other bars catering to hundreds of college-age kids discovering drink for the first time.

Le Montmartre at 2128 Lombard (parallel to Union a few blocks north) is a dance club featuring Brazilian music as well as rock; the English pub–style **Monroe's** (number 1968) is a favorite among San Franciscans who are serious about having a good time, particularly those who appreciate superb martinis; and farther west is **Liverpool Lil's** (2942 Lyon adjacent to the Presidio), whose dark wood and dim lighting gives it the flavor of an English pub. This fun, friendly bar and restaurant serves food until midnight and drink up to 1:00 A.M.

A block north of Lombard Street in the Marina District is **Windows On Chestnut** (2241 Chestnut), a friendly, casual neighborhood bar, where you can strike up stimulating conversations with its varied, mostly upper-income patrons. Almost next door is the **Chestnut Street Bar and Grill**, which has a more sophisticated ambience and garden dining in warm weather. Two blocks east at number 2024 is **The Horseshoe**, another neighborhood treasure where you can hear the best big-band jukebox in town. Also in the Marina is **Mulhern's**, which has decor and clientele similar to North Beach's Washington Square Bar and Grill and Perry's on Union. Upholding the best in traditional San Francisco eating and drinking, Mulhern's is at 3653 Buchanan, and its bar is open until 2:00 A.M. Mondays through Saturdays.

The Haight

You can see it all on Haight Street, located in the geographical center of the city: from suits to suede, from shaved heads to Day-Glo orange-and-pink hairstyles. Home of the Summer of Love, Haight-Ashbury has fallen and risen again since the peace and love era of the 1960s, when it served as a refuge for tens of thousands of wannabe hippies. Where once all you could see were boarded-up storefronts and fallen, drug-laden bodies in the streets, now there is some gentrification and prosperity. Window shopping among the vintage-clothing stores, galleries, and even a store with high-tech furniture has become a visual treat, but even in this evolution, Haight Street retains its wild and unpredictable nature. Street people are prevalent at night, and only on weekends do the rougher edges soften a bit; this is a place for the adventurous who want to see the various permutations of the human species.

You are invited to take a trip back in time to the era of *Casablanca* at the **Persian Aub Zam Zam Room**. Through the Moorish entrance to this bar at 1633 Haight an oasis from the hectic street pace awaits. The near-room-size semi-circular bar, surrounded by dim red lights, sports a local mixed-dressed crowd, and the jukebox is filled with big-band music. Bruno, the owner, also tends bar, dressed in formal bartender attire. He serves the best $1.75 martini in town and is known to throw out anyone he doesn't like, but if he approves of your manners take a seat around the solitary table in the main room and prepare to be over-whelmed by the dropped circular ceiling and decorations around the bar.

Full Moon Saloon at 1725 Haight has live music ranging from rock to blues. Here, the ample dance floor is sur-rounded by videos and a huge wall painting of the waxing and waning moons; the next-door pizzeria delivers food through a hole in the wall. Open until 2:00 A.M. daily. The **I Beam** at number 1748 is one of the better-known New Wave clubs in San Francisco, with live or recorded music depending on the night, and a black-leather, pink-hair crowd. The cover charge here can be up to $12; open daily until 2:00 A.M.

Kezar (900 Cole at the corner of Carl) is a fun neighbor-hood bar and restaurant three blocks south of Haight Street and worth a visit. You'll pass some beautiful Victorian man-sions as you head into the wealthier part of the Haight to this bar, filled with local professionals and good conversation, ample drinks, and delectable food (try the Mexican Pot Roast). Open until 2:00 A.M. every day; the kitchen closes at 11:00 P.M. Across the street is the **101 Bakery Café** (101 Carl), serving homemade pastries in surroundings filled with local artists' work.

Back on Haight Street, **Rockin' Robin's** at number 1821 is a 1950s and 1960s–style rock 'n' roll/sports bar with a good-size dance floor. Parts of old cars of the era protrude from the walls, which are also covered with scores of photos—

mainly of sports and rock legends. The jukebox has a good selection, and occasionally there's live music and even weekly dance lessons. Given video games, big-screen television, and even dominoes here, the crowd is in its glory; open daily until 2:00 A.M. Farther west on Haight, **Park Bowl**, at number 1855, is the home of "Rock 'N' Bowl." This popular bowling alley displays music videos above the lanes and offers dancing between frames. It's open until 11:30 P.M. most nights, but call ahead for its weekend schedule; Tel: 752-2366.

Elsewhere in San Francisco

In addition to the five areas above, there are other spots in the city for nighttime fun. From hot samba to jazz and ballads, **Bahia Tropical** at 1600 Market Street has Brazilian music every night of the week. This large club attracts a high-energy crowd that packs the place on the weekends to hear the authentic music and to dance. (Whether you dance or just enjoy the scene, this is a feel-good place.) Informal dress, with a cover charge ranging up to $10 on weekends, when Bahia swings until 2:00 A.M.

The **Buena Vista Café** at 2765 Hyde (near Ghirardelli Square) began serving Irish Coffee in the United States in the early 1950s. This is a very popular wateringhole for both natives and visitors.

César's Latin Palace, for the enthusiastic dancing aficionado, is owned by perennial mayoral candidate César Ascurrunz and located at 3140 Mission; open until 6:00 A.M. on weekends, 2:00 A.M. weekdays.

For those looking for a non-alcohol environment, **Club Soda** (250 Napoleon), **Studio Brasil** (50 Brady), and **The Third Wave** (3316 Twenty-fourth Street) are all alcohol-free clubs. **The Elite Café** (2049 Fillmore) and **Harry's on Fillmore** (2020 Fillmore) are two fine restaurants with bars where you can enjoy conversing with the urban professional folks over a good drink.

Li Po at 916 Grant Avenue is a kick. For more than half a century this dimly lit room with American music on the jukebox has been a way for Westerners to experience a Chinese bar. You'll usually find a jovial crowd here. **Lou's Pier 47** is a premier music spot for those with sophisticated tastes—some of the best Bay Area musicians (Mark Naftalin, Nick Gravenites) play this very comfortable Fisherman's Wharf spot at 300 Jefferson. New Orleans Zydeco music is popular here along with the blues—or, to put it another way, any music that makes you tap your feet or moves your spirit.

Walk through the doors of the **Russian Renaissance Bar and Restaurant** (5241 Geary) to enter a world of myth and fairy tales, Russian style. Dozens of exquisite dolls stand regally, surrounded by wall and ceiling murals depicting a Russia of centuries ago; the more time you spend in this room, the more alive it becomes. For the last 32 years owner Boris Vertloogin has offered an extensive list of Russian cocktails as well as authentic Russian cuisine. (Ample drinks are a custom, and Boris as bartender always has an appropriate story or two.) On Fridays and Saturdays a classical pianist adds even more flavor to this extraordinary place. Open daily until 11:00 P.M.

The bars at the very trendy **Stars** (150 Redwood Alley), **Speedo 690** (690 Van Ness), and **Harry's Bar and American Grill** (500 Van Ness) are excellent places to people-watch the sometimes-rich and ersatz-famous in the early evening.

Zuni Café (1658 Market) is a restaurant/bar with Southwestern decor and a mixed crowd. Much of the excellent food is mesquite grilled. Open until midnight with reservations recommended (closed Mondays); Tel: 552-2522.

Late-Night Eating

If it's late-night munchies you want, try: **International House of Pancakes** (2299 Lombard; open 24 hours), **La Rondalla**, for Mexican fare (901 Valencia; open until 4:00 A.M.), **Yuet-Lee**, for Chinese food (1300 Stockton; open until 3:00 A.M.), and **Zim's** (corner of Sutter and Powell and 1498 Market; both open 24 hours). For Italian food try **Basta Pasta** (1268 Grant; open until 2:00 A.M.). **Clown Alley** (Columbus at Jackson), a hamburger joint, is open until 3:00 A.M.; its other location at 2499 Lombard is open 24 hours. **Cala**, a supermarket chain, is open 24 hours at Fifth Avenue and Geary, and also at Hyde and California.

—Mark Gordon

ENTERTAINMENT

Comedy

San Francisco and the Bay Area are considered by many to be the birthplace of modern stand-up comedy. Much of the credit should go to Enrico Banducci, who engaged Mort Sahl in the 1950s to play for months at Banducci's world-famous hungry i nightclub when precious few other clubs in the country would book him. Banducci was truly a point of light in the gray-flannel-suited decade, introducing to the world such unknowns as Woody Allen (who shared a double bill with Barbra Streisand), Bill Cosby, Phyllis Diller, the Smothers Brothers, Dick Gregory, and Mike Nichols and Elaine May. Lenny Bruce got his break at a North Beach lesbian club called Ann's. (A good deal of notoriety and a lawsuit followed Bruce's comedic bit here about a black hipster auditioning for "The Lawrence Welk Show.")

This tradition of ground-breaking comedy continued through the 1980s with Robin Williams, Whoopie Goldberg, and Dana Carvey, who also began their careers here. Today small clubs still exist, including **Holy City Zoo** (408 Clement in the Richmond district), the city's oldest comedy club, and the spot where Robin Williams got his first break. Williams still drops in unannounced around town to try out his new material. In addition to Holy City Zoo, some good places for laughs are **Cobb's** (2801 Leavenworth near Fisherman's Wharf), **The Improv** (40 Mason), and the **Punchline** (444A Battery).

Jazz

Some of the very best jazz clubs in the country are located in San Francisco. Many jazz greats, such as Stan Getz, Bobby Hutcherson, and Pharaoh Sanders, live in the Bay Area, so call to find out if a favorite of yours is playing, or just drop by—you won't be disappointed. Some good places to try are **Kimball's** (300 Grove), **Milestones** (376 Fifth Street), **Pasand** (1875 Union Street), **Pearl's** (256 Columbus), **Pier 23 Café** (Pier 23 along the Embarcadero), **Rasselas** (2801 California), and **Rolands** (2513 Van Ness).

Theater

When San Francisco was just a toddler of a city, it rated second only to New York as a theater town. Aside from gambling and womanizing, there was not much to do in the Gold Rush era besides take in a show; from opera to burlesque, isolated San Franciscans were thirsty for nearly every form of entertainment. Luisa Tetrazzini, a famous turn-of-the-century opera singer, was so enamored of San Franciscans she gave a free public performance on Market Street on Christmas Eve, 1910, to a reputed crowd of 250,000, when the city's population was not much greater. San Francisco maintained its edge as the theater capital of the West Coast until both Los Angeles and television grew up in the middle of this century.

Today's theaters (with several exceptions) cluster just west of Union Square, within the rectangle of Post and Geary, Powell and Taylor streets. The **American Conservatory**

Theater (ACT), one of North America's finest resident companies, presents the best of classical and modern dramatic theater. Displaced from its home in the ornate 1909 Geary Theater at 415 Geary Street when the walls came tumbling down in the 1989 earthquake, ACT now plays out its October to May season in various venues all over town while rebuilding proceeds; for current venues, Tel: 749-2200. The **Cable Car Theater**, 430 Mason Street at Post, is an informal, 140-seat theater in a former speakeasy, where popular long-run shows such as *Greater Tuna* are presented; Tel: 771-6900.

The **Curran Theater**, 445 Geary Street, was the last major theater constructed downtown, in 1922. Although opera and ballet have shared its stage with straight plays, today's diversions usually fall within the Best of Broadway series that showcases musicals en route to or from Broadway; Tel: 474-3800 (box office) or 392-SHOW (Ticketron ticket agency).

Eureka Theater Company, away from theater row at 2730 16th Street and Harrison in the Mission district, was established in 1972 to present a much-needed series of contemporary (and some classical) plays that deal with current and continuing political and social questions; Tel: 558-9898.

Grandeur returned to the 1922 **Golden Gate Theater** (in a less-than-grand neighborhood, however) following a recent face- and body-lift. The big bands of the 1940s and headliners from Carmen Miranda to Shirley Maclaine have kept the Golden Gate aglitter. (For a while, this was even a first-run movie house.) Today, too big for most plays, it's employed mostly for musicals, at 1 Taylor Street, Golden Gate Avenue at Market; Tel: 474-3800. **Marines Memorial Theater**, on the second floor of the classic Marines Memorial Building at 609 Sutter Street, has featured one award-winning hit after another; Tel: 771-6900.

Located in a former cabaret, the **Mason Street Theater**, at 340 Mason Street and Geary, offers dramas and minimusicals, such as the long-running *Bar None,* in which the audience participates in the outcome of the whodunit; Tel: 861-6985. At 1192 Market Street, corner of Hyde (Civic Center), the **Orpheum**, inheritor of a vaudeville tradition, today relies mostly upon musicals, such as the endlessly reproduced *The King and I;* Tel: 474-3800.

San Francisco Mime Troupe is a sassy, smart-alecky, politically oriented company that's anything but silent on the issues or anything else. In summer they perform free shows in various regional parks; you'll find them at home in an area few travellers visit, 855 Treat Avenue at 21st Street (Mission district); Tel: 285-1717. **Theatre Rhinoceros** at 2926

Sixteenth Street and South Van Ness, founded in 1977, is the most important gay ensemble around, and produces such shows as *Gertrude Stein and a Companion;* Tel: 861-5079.

Theatre on the Square, in a lovely old building of vaguely Mediterranean persuasion at 450 Post Street, offers locally written plays as well as Off-Broadway vehicles. It seats 650 people in an elegant setting of gold leaf, wrought iron, and tile; Tel: 433-9500. In the reworked Mason Temple at 25 Van Ness Avenue (Civic Center), the **Zephyr Theater** doesn't limit itself to a single genre, presenting children's plays, dance, revues, and more; Tel: 861-6895.

San Francisco's wackiest, most endearing, zaniest, and perennial theatrical production is *Beach Blanket Babylon,* in its present incarnation as *Beach Blanket Babylon Goes Around the World,* at the **Club Fugazi**, 678 Green Street. In its 16th year, it's not to be missed; Tel: 421-4222. **On Broadway** runs a narrow and funny gambit from lighter-than-fluff musicals to parlor dramas to female-impersonation shows in its house at 435 Broadway. You always have to check; Tel: 391-9999. In addition to the above, there are perhaps 20 other small stages in town.

The ultimate theatrical adventure may be riding on a city bus while performers entertain with music, comedy, and even dance. **Showbus, Inc.** offers a variety of entertainment packages: Showbus on Location, which visits five decades of movie locations in the city (from 1927's *The Jazz Singer* to 1988's *True Believer*); Showbus Goes Shopping, a loud, lively, discount-shopping spree; and Showbus Nightlife Adventures, which visits San Francisco's hottest nightclubs. Call for dates and departure times; Tel: 775-SHOW.

Other than the individual theaters' box offices, try **City Box Office**, Sherman Clay & Co., 141 Kearny Street, 94108 (Tel: 392-4400); and **St. Francis Theater and Sports Tickets,** Westin St. Francis Hotel, Union Square, 94102 (Tel: 362-3500).

BASS (Bay Area Seating Service) ticket centers include STBS on Union Square; Supermail, Four Embarcadero; Headlines, 838 Market Street; The Emporium, 835 Market Street; and Tower Records, Bay Street and Columbus Avenue; Tel: 762-2277 (charge by mail) or dial TELETIX (recorded calendar listings).

Ticketron centers in San Francisco include Rainbow Records, Stanyan and Geary streets, and Downtown Center Box Office, 325 Mason Street (located in the Downtown Center Parking Garage, the best spot to park in the theater district).

STBS provides day-of-performance tickets for selected music, dance, and theater events at half price. They also handle advance, full-price tickets to many events in the neighbor-hoods and outlying areas as a BASS outlet. Cash sales only are accepted, and no reservations or telephone orders are taken. STBS, on the Stockton Street side of Union Square, is open from noon to 7:30 P.M. and closed Sundays and Mondays; Tel: 433-STBS.

To see what's playing at the moment, check the Sunday newspaper's Pink Section, a good guide to nearly all the performing arts and entertainment in the Bay Area. A section at the front of the Yellow Pages phone directory will show you the seating plan of each of the major theaters. (The free guides given out in the streets or at many hotels may be good for the latest goings on, but they are mostly self-promotions with listings not necessarily related to quality.)

—*Georgia I. Hesse and Mark Gordon*

Theater District Dining

Grand dining and great theater do not mix well: A fine meal is theater enough in itself, and can last as long as a performance of *Les Misérables*. Some of the finest chefs in the city are within a sole's throw of the theater district but deserve to have their cuisine enjoyed without curtain pressure. Below, some rewarding compromises.

Kuleto's, in the Villa Florence Hotel at 225 Powell Street, serves continually from 11:00 A.M. to 11:00 P.M., so there's time for an early meal as well as one to last the entire evening. Plenty of delicious tastes can be enjoyed that won't put you to sleep during the second act; Tel: 397-7720.

Regina's in the Regis Hotel at 490 Geary Street could not be handier to the major theaters. It opens at 6:00 P.M. for early diners, but as the French-Creole or haute Louisiana cooking is anything but skimpy, you might prefer to go following the show to try the "After the Arts" menu served until 1:00 A.M.; Tel: 885-1661. Inventive cooking can be a perfect pre-theater solution when lightness is of the essence; try **Post Street Café and Bar**, 632 Post (Tel: 928-2080).

Trader Vic's is an institution, and, considering the quality of younger restaurants in the city, not to be taken seriously for its food alone. However, it's a great people-watching place for before-theater snacks and before-bed drinks and snacks. It's at 20 Cosmo Place, off Taylor; Tel: 776-2232.

Bardelli's is one of the oldest (1909) and was one of the most prestigious restaurants downtown (243 O'Farrell Street). The beautiful stained-glass panels and cozy seating area near the bar recommend it to traditionalists. Go early and slip into your seat to be relaxed by the time warp; Tel: 982-0243.

Christophe, at 320 Mason Street, is right across the street from the Downtown Center Garage, very handy for drivers. Its French menu can be chic, light, and quick, especially when you arrive early (it opens at 5:30 P.M.) and explain that you have theater tickets; Tel: 433-7560.

Corona Bar & Grill at 88 Cyril Magnin Street (adjoining the Monticello Inn) may serve the best Mexican cooking you've ever tasted. It's open continually from 11:30 A.M., so you can arrive early or take a light meal at the bar; Tel: 392-5500.

The **English Grill** at the St. Francis Hotel opens at 6:00 P.M. and is used to serving up fresh seafood and other light specialties for its theater-bound guests; Tel: 774-0233.

La Mère Duquesne is a French confection in precisely the right place, at 101 Shannon Alley off Geary, and a few yards from the top theaters. It's elegant and simple at the same time, and the serving staff knows all about your timing; Tel: 776-7600.

If you want it quick, casual, simple, and inexpensive, choose **La Quiche**, a tiny bistro that features, what else, quiche. It's at 550 Taylor Street; Tel: 441-2711.

Lefty O'Doul's, at 333 Geary, is a landmark as much as a restaurant. It was founded by the famous ex-Yankee ball player. Service is cafeteria style, and the laid-back sports bar attracts a nostalgic crowd; Tel: 982-8900.

Should it get really late and should you be really hungry, step into **Lori's Diner** at 336 Mason Street and back into the 1950s, where hamburgers and old-fashioned, familiar diner fare is served 24 hours a day; Tel: 392-8646.

It's cavernous, the servings gigantic, and the atmosphere nonexistent, but for filling (if nondramatic) meals there's little more satisfying than a down-to-earth, San Francisco–Italian dinner. You can put your elbows on the table at **New Joe's**, 347 Geary Street, until 1:30 A.M.; Tel: 989-6733.

For decades **David's Delicatessen-Restaurant** at 474 Geary Street, right across from the Curran and Geary theaters, has been packing them in to the only true Jewish deli in town. It's open until 1:00 A.M. for a lot of late-night noshing; Tel: 771-1600.

—Georgia I. Hesse

Classical Music Performances

The always-sold-out openings of the symphony and the opera seasons, held in the same week in early September, are the beginning of high society's social season—these are *the* places to be seen. Many observers of the human species hang around outside the Opera House and Symphony Hall to watch the show outside the show. Among the many cultural venues are the **San Francisco Ballet** (Tel: 621-3838; January–May season), **San Francisco Chamber Orchestra** (Tel: 552-3656; January–April season), **San Francisco Symphony** (Tel: 431-5400; September–May season), and the **San Francisco Opera** (Tel: 864-3330; September–December season). See also Civic Center section earlier in chapter.

The **Chamber Symphony of San Francisco** performs classical and modern chamber works at Herbst Theater (Civic Center) from January to May; Tel: 552-3656. The **Philharmonia Baroque Orchestra** also plays at Herbst Theater, with a season usually running from February to April; Tel: 552-3656. **San Francisco Contemporary Music Players** give occasional concerts in the Green Room of the Museum of Modern Art (Civic Center), with preconcert discussions of new and avant-garde works; Tel: 558-0447. **San Francisco Performances** is an umbrella for chamber music, jazz, and dance staged at Herbst Theater (Tel: 552-3656).

Noted local artists and faculty as well as the Conservatory Orchestra appear at Hellman Hall, **San Francisco Conservatory of Music**, 19th Avenue and Ortega Street; Tel: 665-0874. Year-round classical concerts are presented at **Old First Presbyterian Church**, Van Ness Avenue at Sacramento Street (Tel: 474-1608); at Masonic Auditorium (Nob Hill) and Herbst Theater by **Today's Artists Concerts** (Tel: 398-1324); in the Florence Gould Theater of the Palace of the Legion of Honor by Chevron Museum Concert Series; and in Grace Cathedral (Nob Hill) with its superb acoustics in the Cathedral Concert Series (Tel: 776-6611). Free noontime concerts are offered on Tuesdays at 12:30 P.M. at **Old St. Mary's Church**, 660 California Street in Chinatown; Tel: 255-9410.
—Georgia I. Hesse and Mark Gordon

GAY NIGHTLIFE

The central gay district is Castro Street between 17th and 19th streets, where restored Victorians thread their way in and around the bars, bookstores, restaurants, and a magnificent Art Deco movie theater. At 401 Castro you'll find **Twin Peaks**, a popular drinking establishment with an attractive antique bar. After a walk around Castro Street, return to Market and visit **Café San Marcos** (2367 Market), complete with a two-tier dance floor. If it's not too crowded, try the terrace seating for a perch above the colorful street scene. Cross Market Street and head east until you reach the **Metro Bar and Restaurant** (3600 Sixteenth Street at Market); this second-floor oval bar, handsomely decorated with just a dash of violet neon, offers another of view street life. If you cross the street and continue east, you'll encounter **Café Flore** (2298 Market), a garden-like indoor/outdoor sidewalk café. The pervasive aroma of coffee here, along with marvelous desserts, makes this a pleasant place for good conversation and people-watching.

Out in Pacific Heights awaits the cozy **Lion Pub** (Sacramento and Divisadero), **JJ's**, a fun piano bar at 2225 Fillmore, and the elegant **Alta Plaza** at 2301 Fillmore. The *San Francisco Sentinel* and the *Bay Area Reporter* are free weeklies distributed throughout the city that will give you the latest information on the gay scene.

ROMANTIC SAN FRANCISCO

A century-old description of San Francisco as "the cool, gray city of love" is appropriate for the city even today, where the physical beauty serves as a stunning backdrop for a romantic evening. Modern-day skyscraper view-rooms and waterfront restaurants make it easier and more comfortable than ever for lovers to enjoy the lush hills, the water, and the necklace of lights strung across the Golden Gate Bay Bridges.

Start by enjoying a sunset from the **Marin Headlands**, a view guaranteed to thrill even the most hard-hearted (check beforehand to make sure the bridge and surrounding area aren't enshrouded in fog). To get there, drive or take a cab across the Golden Gate Bridge (try to avoid 4:00–6:00 P.M. rush hour and keep to the right-hand lane); take the Alexander exit right off the freeway almost immediately after Vista Point on the northern side of the bridge. Turn left at the stop sign and follow the road west until you reach the Golden Gate National Recreation Area/Marin Headlands; from here follow the twisting road up the hill. You can stop at any of the numerous gravel parking areas for a magnificent view of the bridge, the bay, and the city. If you want to continue, the climb eventually surpasses the height of the top of the bridge towers (746 feet above sea level). To return to the city using the same route, follow the road until it ends at the stop sign, where you should turn right onto the bridge (be aware of fast-paced oncoming traffic).

If you make a left turn instead, you will wind your way down toward Sausalito, where there are many restaurants with spectacular views. The best of the bunch is the **Casa Madrona Hotel** located at 801 Bridgeway on the main street, but elevated above the hustle and bustle; Tel: 331-5888. Although the interior of the **Alta Mira Hotel**, 125 Bulkley, isn't as lush, the meals are more moderately priced than those at the Casa Madrona and the view is better. Reservations at either restaurant should be made well in advance; Tel: 332-1350 for the Alta Mira.

For an even more romantic time, take a Red & White ferry from Pier 43½ across the bay to Tiburon (to check the time and place of departure, call 546-BOAT; a Champagne Cruise is also available, and some ferries serve drinks). After you arrive at Tiburon, you can choose to stay aboard and return directly to the city, or else disembark and have an outdoor dinner at any of a variety of local restaurants, and return on a later ferry. Situated immediately next to the ferry mooring is **Guaymas**, an upscale Mexican restaurant. Take the time to stroll through Tiburon on Main Street, which is reminiscent of Sausalito before it became a tourist mecca. You'll find **Sam's Anchor Café** along the way, an institution among locals.

If you return to the city without having eaten, try the **Mandarin** in Ghirardelli Square and request a table with a view. The Szechwan cuisine of the Mandarin, a favorite among Chinese-food fans, is expensive but worth the price, especially the crispy fried-chicken salad. Another romantic dining spot with waterfront views is **Julius Castle** (1541 Montgomery)—it's hard to find and up a few "only in San Francisco" steep streets (see North Beach nightlife for directions). The panoramic view of the bay and the interior of this Continental restaurant are exquisite, although the food doesn't quite match. The same can be said for the **Waterfront** (Pier 5) and **Sinbad's Pier 2 Restaurant** along the Embarcadero. A dining room that once sailed the seas, the **Dolphin P. Rempp** on Pier 42 has both good views and good food. If you visit San Francisco around Christmastime, another maritime treat is a walk around the outskirts of Pier 39 (the truck-loading areas) to see the decorated sailboats.

A very special place to catch the sunset or, better yet, to see the bright lights of the nighttime skyline from a perfect distance is **Treasure Island**. Drive (or take a cab) east on the Bay Bridge, exit at Yerba Buena Island (right-hand exit), then circle right toward Treasure Island, the man-made island that was the home of the 1939–1940 World's Fair. (It is now a military base.) Just before you arrive at the main gate, make a U-turn that will lead you to a parking area for a one-of-a-kind view. On the ride home, keep to the right-hand lane for the best view of the city. Turn off into the downtown area (first exit from the right-hand lanes) and head for the Westin St. Francis hotel located on Union Square, where a nightcap at the **Compass Rose** will place your feet firmly on land but put your spirit into flight. This grand room features two-story Corinthian columns, art from around the world, and a jazz trio that plays favorites from the 1930s and 1940s beginning at either 8:00 or 9:00 P.M. There is no cover charge, but the drinks and appetizers are very expensive.

If your desire for panoramas is still not sated, there are plenty of glorious skybars that can accommodate you. The **Carnelian Room** atop the Bank of America building at California and Kearny has a view that softens even sophisticated San Franciscans. The lounge closes between 11:30 P.M. and midnight; a jacket and tie are required and drinks are expensive. When the **Top of the Mark** at the Mark Hopkins Hotel opened in 1936, it was the world's pinnacle of skyrooms. Today it shares the honors with the Fairmont's **Crown Room**, across California Street, which boasts the highest elevation of any of the skyrooms. If you're on Nob Hill, stop in at the bar of the **Big Four Restaurant** in the Huntington Hotel, where the feeling is rich and comfortable, and photos and memorabilia are displayed throughout. Be sure to have a look at the area outside the bathrooms where the telephones are located: A 270-degree series of photo blowups is mounted on the circular wall showing late-19th-century San Francisco before the 1906 devastation. Especially note the single-family dwellings on Nob Hill in the foreground. (The Big Four Restaurant is named after Stanford, Huntington, Hopkins, and Crocker, who turned a $7,000 investment into hundreds of millions by building the western section of the railroad that tied the country together economically.

The Hyatt Regency Hotel features the **Equinox**, a bar and restaurant revolving full circle every hour. It has delicious vistas and is expensive, as are the public top rooms of the Sir Francis Drake, the Holiday Inn at Union Square (480 Sutter Street), and the new downtown Marriott (Fourth and Mission streets). For the best bargain "room with a view" and privacy to boot, try the **Sky Club** atop the Marines Memorial Club and Theater at 609 Sutter. When you enter the building, turn right directly to the elevators: This building is a private hotel for Marines and club members, but the theater and Sky Club are open to the public. Drinks are cheap, the employees are very informal, and there is nearly always a seat by the window as the hour nears midnight. The view, with some exceptions, is one of San Francisco of 50 years past; open until 1:00 A.M. every day.

Rivaling the Compass Rose is the **Redwood Room** in the Four Seasons Clift Hotel. Wall panels of redwood along with the tremendous height of the ceiling only serve to increase the opulent feeling associated with this traditional San Francisco room. Lighting is romantic, and the chances are a pianist with the last name of Scales will enhance the mood.

At 1500 Sutter near Gough, **Café Majestic**'s classy horseshoe bar and surrounding tables won't win prizes for views, but they make a perfect atmosphere for lovers; check out the butterfly collection.

For outdoor vistas, anyone would have to include the ever-popular **Twin Peaks** (south of The Haight), the second-highest site in the city at just over 900 feet. The Indians thought the two peaks were a husband and wife who were separated by lightning because of their constant bickering, while the Spanish renamed the area Breasts of the Maiden. But no matter the name, the time of day or night (as long as it's not foggy), this view will stun as you gaze past the Golden Gate over to Marin and to the East Bay, and south down the Peninsula. (Be warned: If it's windy, this is one of the coldest spots in all of San Francisco and right in the middle of a fog belt.) Informational displays at the parking zone will help in getting a fix on what you're seeing.

Another favorite spot is **Outer Broadway**, in the 2800 and 2900 blocks of Broadway in Pacific Heights. Walk along the two most expensive blocks of residential real estate in San Francisco and admire the view of the Marina district and the bay. Gorbachev slept at the Soviet consul's residence (2820 Broadway) while in San Francisco during mid-1990. For even more superlative views, there's always **Coit Tower** and the top of **Lombard Street**. Or avail yourself of San Francisco's luxurious and romantic but pricey evening dining cruises from Pier 33; Tel: 394-8900.

—Mark Gordon

SHOPS AND SHOPPING

For dedicated consumers, San Francisco is the most important shopping destination in the northwestern United States. The city boasts an impressive variety of boutiques, specialty and department stores, shopping malls, and neighborhood shops, many stocking exclusive merchandise not likely to be found elsewhere, in several venues: a thriving downtown area, a growing bargain-hunter's mecca in the South of Market (SoMa) district, and ethnic neighborhoods that provide shopping experiences akin to being in another country. In such a highly competitive market, merchants go to great lengths to attract customers by emphasizing exceptional service (this is particularly true of the downtown department stores). Some shops and malls offer entertainment, many stores keep evening hours, and many are open seven days a week, although there is little consistency to the opening and closing hours in any neighborhood. Most of the downtown stores are open by 10:00 A.M., although some open as early as 9:30 A.M..

North and South of Union Square

The focal point of downtown shopping is Union Square, a pleasant oasis of greenery filled with pigeons, noontime lunchers, sun worshippers, and more recently, some homeless people, surrounded by some of the most prestigious stores in town as well as many boutiques with international reputations. It is bordered by Geary Street to the south, Powell to the west, Post to the north, and Stockton to the east.

The largest store on the square is **Macy's**, next door to I. Magnin on Geary, near Stockton Street. This department store, a West Coast branch of the famous New York Macy's, carries a vast variety of mid-to-upper-price-range merchandise for the home and all members of the family. Fashion lovers should head for the shop-within-a-store dedicated to ultrachic designer clothing. Across the street, at Stockton and O'Farrell streets, is a second Macy's, this one filled with menswear.

In a building with a handsome white marble façade at the corner of Geary and Stockton streets, **I. Magnin**, a long-established store with a wide selection of upscale fashions and one of the poshest ladies' powder rooms in town, should be your next stop. Across the street, at the corner of Geary and Stockton, is **Neiman Marcus**, the San Francisco branch of the famed Dallas specialty store. The huge stained-glass dome inside the store is all that is left of the City of Paris department store, which was demolished over many protests to accommodate the present building. Within the store is the **Rotunda** restaurant, a comfortable place to have lunch.

Marithé & François Girbaud/Paris, at 17 Stockton Street, specializes in French sportswear for those who like to be on the cutting edge of youthful fashion. Across and up the street at number 48, a fellow in a toy-soldier's costume greets customers as they pass **F. A.O. Schwarz**, the famous toy store that occupies three floors here.

North Beach Leather (not in North Beach at all, but occupying another corner of Geary and Stockton streets) features high-style leather clothing, while **Gucci**, at 200 Stockton, offers you a luxurious wood-and-marble interior in which to make costly choices in clothing and accessories. Right next door, **Hermès of Paris**, with some of the highest prices in the city, draws an enthusiastic clientele that covets the Hermès scarves, gloves, and ties. Farther up the same side of the street at number 238, **Bally of Switzerland** carries costly, conservatively designed shoes, clothing, and leather goods for men and women. On the next block is **Scheuer Linens**, operated for three generations by the same family and specializing in fine accoutrements for the bedroom, bathroom, and dining room. Nearby, the **Waterford/Wedgwood Shop** stocks a complete collection of these renowned Irish and British imports. **Alfred Dunhill of London**, at the corner of Stockton and Post, is famous for its smokers' supplies and leather goods.

On the north side of the square, at 340 Post Street, is **Bullock & Jones**, with high-quality conservative menswear and a line of Aquascutum rainwear and women's apparel, and at 360 Post is Northern California's only branch of **Tiffany & Co.**, which moved to this new location in September, 1990. At the corner of Post and Powell streets is **Saks Fifth Avenue**, a handsome branch of the reputable specialty store that dresses New York fashionables.

West of Union Square

Moving on to the west side of the square: Within the St. Francis Hotel at 335 Powell Street is **MCM**, filled with accessories and travel gear from Munich, imprinted with the manufacturers' status logo. Farther west along Post Street you'll find several interesting little shops, among them **Swaine Adeney**, at 434 Post, the only branch of this "veddy" British shop, where horsewhips, umbrellas, riding gear, and other accessories fit for royalty can be purchased. Take a few more footsteps and you'll come to **La Ville du Soleil**, where you can purchase gifts and home accessories, mostly imported from France, which are displayed in an environment dressed to look like a stage set for a French provincial production. On the same block is **Bazaar Cada Dia**, with its charming selection of handcrafted items from South and Central America. Close by, at number 460, is the delightful **La Parisienne**, where French costume jewelry and vintage posters are fancifully displayed in antique French showcases.

One street north, at 524 Sutter Street, is the **Pasquale Ianetti Gallery**, which has a substantial collection of prints by Old Masters and contemporary artists. Nearby, **Pierre**

Deux at number 532 offers a splendid array of French provincial fabrics and home furnishings. If you are ready for a rest at this point, you might appreciate the services of **La Belle Skin and Body Care Salons**, one of which is at 575 Sutter Street, offering pedicures, facials, body massage, and other pampering services. Those who don't mind strolling just a little farther on will find **Obiko**, 794 Sutter, a fine little boutique specializing in unique clothing, some of which could double as works of art and most of it fashioned by local designers.

East of Union Square

Along Geary Street, at 1 Union Square, you will find **Joan & David**, a sleek contemporary shop selling their fine footwear and leather accessories for men and women. A little farther on, at 156 Geary, are the high style and high prices of the **Ted Lapidus** boutique, which features clothing by the famous French designer. **Kris Kelly**, 174 Geary, is a delightfully fragrant three-level shop specializing in very romantic linens and giftware, while **Britex Fabrics**, at number 146, carries just about everything any seamstress would ever need on several well-stocked floors. **Bottega Veneta** at 108 Geary, sells high-status handmade Italian leather goods and accessories, and next door **N. Peal Cashmere** is the place for shoppers with a soft spot in their hearts for this very luxe knitwear, especially sweaters and socks. **Gallery Paule Anglim** at 14 Geary Street is best known for exhibiting works of famous contemporary American artists, as well as evolving new talents.

One block north is Post Street and the chance to explore several worthwhile stores. At 272 Post is **Jaeger**, specializing in fine English sportswear. **Gump's** is nearby, a local institution founded in 1865 and known far and wide for its pearls and jade, fine Oriental decorative arts, and a vast collection of the highest quality china and crystal. At number 251 is the **Allrich Gallery**, which deals principally in contemporary California artwork, and on the same block is **Cartier**, the jewelry house.

The dramatic block-long **Crocker Galleria** at 50 Post Street, modeled after Milan's elegant Galleria Vittorio Emanuelle, is a handsome collection of shops on several levels, but in general the merchandising thrust lacks real excitement. Among the more compelling of the Galleria's stores are **Japonesque** (well-chosen treasures from Japan) and, **Gianni Versace**, **Marimekko**, and **Ralph Lauren** for label collectors.

One street north, at 345 Sutter Street, is the **Stephen Wirtz Gallery** of contemporary photography and artwork. At number 353 **Jessica McClintock** stocks a sugary assortment of romantic clothing created by this San Francisco designer. **Wilkes Bashford**, on the same side of the street, has high-ticket, high-fashion designer apparel for men and women, while just across the way **Diagonale** specializes in men's and women's clothing, mostly by Italian designers. **Jeanne Marc**, at 262 Sutter, is named for two local designers (she's Jeanne, he's Marc) who have carved a national reputation for themselves with their colorful, whimsical clothing for women. There are several galleries at 250 Sutter Street, among them the **Brauntein/Quay Gallery** on the third floor, specializing in contemporary works on paper, and sculpture and painting, and **871 Fine Arts**, which carries modern California artwork.

Maiden Lane

It's hard to believe that this charming, historic byway, running east from Union Square, parallel with Post and Geary, and bordered by pricey shops, was a seedy enclave of bordellos until the earthquake and fire of 1906. At 34 Maiden Lane is **Orientations**, a serene place to find tasteful Asian furnishings. At number 77 is **Ralph Davies**, an ultramodern shop that carries innovative European fashion for men and women. The **Circle Gallery**, at 140 Maiden Lane, may attract you for its contemporary art, but it's best known because the building it's housed in was designed by Frank Lloyd Wright, and the ramp leading to the upper floor served as a prototype for New York's Guggenheim Museum. **Diane Freis**, 120 Maiden Lane, sells one-size-fits-all dresses in variegated patterns, and the mirrored and sparkling **Chanel Boutique** at number 155 is one of the most beautiful—and expensive—clothing shops in the city.

Grant Avenue

One block east of Stockton Street (the eastern border of Union Square) is Grant Avenue, crammed with shops all the way down to its intersection with Market Street. Starting north of Sutter Street: **Teuscher of Switzerland**, 255 Grant Avenue, is a good place for a Swiss-chocolate break; **Jasmin**, a by-appointment-preferred boutique next door, deals very personally with fashion-conscious customers who are interested in upscale, designer clothing; **Maude Frison** at number 249 sells dramatic and high-priced footwear, designed in France and made in Italy; and the **Erika Meyerovich Gallery** at number 231 carries some of the greatest names in contemporary art on its three levels. **Malm**, a luggage-and-leather-accessories shop founded in 1856, is still run by the same family at 222 Grant Avenue.

Some of the city's best-known galleries are housed at 228 Grant Avenue, including the **Berggruen Gallery**, dealer in some of the biggest American art names, and the **Micher/ Wilcox Gallery**, which handles conceptual and minimalist work by American and European artists. For a change of pace, number 256 is **Banana Republic**, where it's always fun to poke around the safari-inspired sportswear. Across Grant Avenue is tiny Tillman Place, with several small boutiques.

For a bit of the delicious, head down the street to the **Candy Jar**, 210 Grant, which sells sensational egg-shaped truffles made by Joseph Schmidt, a local genius who works in chocolate. **Fogal**, next door, has a wonderful line of very unusual and pricey hosiery; **Tom Wing & Sons**, at the corner of Post Street and Grant Avenue, offers fine jade jewelry. Across the street is San Francisco's oldest retail store, **Shreve & Co.**, a not-to-be-missed showcase of fine jewelry, silver, and crystal displayed in a historic shop full of marble columns. For conservative menswear, you can't miss with **Brooks Brothers**, across from Shreve's. A branch of **Christofle** silversmiths is one of the newest shops in the area at 140 Grant.

At **Crate & Barrel**, 125 Grant Avenue, there are well-designed buys in home accessories, dishes, and glassware; number 55 is home to the **Fraenkel Gallery**, which specializes exclusively in fine 19th- and 20th-century photography. **Eileen West**, 33 Grant Avenue, is the only retail outlet for the dresses, sleepwear, and linens created by this local designer; and the **Jeremy Stone Gallery**, a few doors down, shows drawings and paintings by emerging artists. At the foot of the street, a landmark building (once a bank) houses **Cable Car Clothiers**, primarily a menswear store, at 1 Grant Avenue.

Powell and Market Streets

If you head west on Market Street from Grant, you'll find many shops of no particular distinction, but keep going. The big shopping reward is the **San Francisco Centre**, across from the huge Woolworth's at the intersection of Market, Fifth, and Powell streets. This shopping facility is San Francisco's first downtown mall, and most of its shops are prestigious clothing boutiques purveying labels by well-known designers and manufacturers. A distinctive element of the shopping experience here is the stacked and spiraling escalator that carries you through the oval atrium. **Nordstrom**, a famous retailer known for its service and quality merchandise, occupies the top three floors of the building and includes a beauty spa and four restaurants, where weary shoppers can refresh themselves. Nordstrom offers its customers valet parking at the Fifth Street entrance, but it's really just as easy, and cheaper, to park at the Fifth and Mission Street garage.

Adjoining the new San Francisco Centre is the **Emporium**, a long-established department store that carries an excellent selection of mid-priced merchandise; the store's lower level includes several snack bars and a counter for take-out food. A few doors away at 821 Market Street is the **Pacific Center/ Apparel Mart**, a building filled with wholesale showrooms open to the public on the second and fourth Fridays of each month (and a haven for bargain hunters who search for the great savings in sample sales).

Bibliophiles might want to make a fast detour to 48 Turk Street (west of Hallidie Plaza at the foot of Powell) to visit the disorganized display at **McDonald's Bookstore**, which carries more than a million records, books, and magazines, many of them out-of-print editions. The block is seedy, but browsing amid the literature and erotica can be amusing. Near the cable-car terminus, upstairs at 41 Powell Street, is the **Hatley/Martin Gallery**, predominantly contemporary art by Californians.

Chinatown

Chinatown is not to be missed, although it will soon become apparent to you that while stores are plentiful, many carry the same merchandise. Nonetheless, it's a great place to find small, interesting, and inexpensive items. Stockton Street between Bush and Broadway (through a long tunnel north of Union Square) is where the day-to-day commerce of Chinatown is concentrated, and the street is usually full of housewives taking care of family shopping at bustling fish and poultry markets.

A block east, Grant Avenue caters to visitors in search of souvenirs; many shops are open until 10:00 P.M. every night. **Tai Nam Yang**, with stores at 438 and 408 Grant Avenue, carries decorative objects and rosewood furniture, and, to the north, **Dragon House**, a tiny, poorly lit shop at 315 Grant Avenue, stocks some choice Asian antiques. As you continue north you'll find one of Chinatown's most upscale stores: the **City of Shanghai**, at number 519, where you will discover some exquisitely made silk robes and lingerie from China. The shop also does custom tailoring. There are usually good prices on hand-embroidered Chinese linens at **Imperial**

Fashion, 564 Grant Avenue, a little bit of everything at the **Canton Bazaar**, 616 Grant, and playful souvenirs at the **Chinatown Kite Shop**, at number 717.

If you're looking for an exotic cure, herb shops abound, and **Che Sun Tong Herb Shop**, 729 Washington Street (just off Grant), has the added attraction of being run by a man who speaks English. The **China Trade Center**, 838 Grant Avenue, carries a wide representation of Chinatown's wares on several shopping floors; **Chew Chong Tai & Co.**, 905 Grant, deals in calligraphy supplies and claims to be Chinatown's oldest shop; the **Ten Ren Tea Co., Ltd.**, at number 949, is the place to find exotic teas and ginseng; a small factory, **Golden Gate Fortune Cookies**, 56 Ross Alley (a narrow street running from Jackson to Washington west of Grant), will supply you with some nontraditional cookies with naughty messages.

Embarcadero Center

At the eastern end of the Financial District (also east of Chinatown) is Embarcadero Center, a handsome complex with stores concentrated along Clay and Sacramento streets between Battery and Drumm, in Buildings One, Two, Three, and Four. Some, but not all, stores are open Sundays. Most shops are located on the street, lobby, and podium levels of these contemporary interconnected buildings, and you'll find plenty of places along the way to dine or snack.

For the fashion-forward male there's **The Hound**, in the West Tower, 275 Battery Street; in Building One is the **STBS** outlet, where half- and full-price theater tickets are sold in a space designed to look like the interior of a theater; **Papyrus**, in Building Two, has some beautiful cards and wrapping papers; Building Three is home to **Jolin**, one of the most chic women's-wear shops in the center; and **The Nature Company** in Building Four, carrying everything from books to toys, is a sheer delight for anyone with ecological interests. **Confetti**, also in Building Four, carries fine, unusual chocolates and is a good place to stop for an espresso; on the Parkway between the Hyatt Hotel and Building Four is **Techsis**, a high-tech shop full of interesting, often playful contraptions and gizmos; and nearby is **Lotus**, a tiny but well-stocked earring boutique.

Jackson Square and North Beach

The historic Jackson Square district, bounded by Washington, Pacific, Columbus, and Sansome streets, contains many buildings that date from the mid-1850s; thus, it is fitting that the area now is home to some of the finest antiques galleries in the city. **Robert Domergue & Co.**, 560 Jackson Street (at the corner of Columbus Avenue), carries European (especially French) furniture from the 18th and 19th centuries and high-quality architectural prints and drawings; **Dillingham & Co.**, 470 Jackson, is known for its 18th-century English furniture; and, a few shops away, **Norman Shepherd, Inc.**, at 458 Jackson, offers Oriental, English, and Continental furnishings (the owner also has a shop on Long Island in New York). **Challiss House**, just across the road, has a mixed stock of furniture and English porcelains, and **Foster-Gwin**, at number 425, sells English and Continental furnishings. **Daniel Stein Antiques**, 701 Sansome Street, offers a nice selection of masculine English pieces that would look right at home in an office or a den; **Prints Etc.** at 494 Jackson Street carries prints and also does framing; **William Stout & Associates**, 804 Montgomery, is a marvelous store with an emphasis on architectural books; and **Arch**, 407 Jackson Street, is where you can find fanciful paper goods, art supplies, and unusual small gifts.

North beyond the borders of downtown and Chinatown, Grant and Columbus avenues belong to North Beach, where the shops cater to offbeat and bohemian tastes. **City Lights Booksellers and Publishers**, 261 Columbus Avenue, owned by poet Lawrence Ferlinghetti, stays open until the wee hours and is a bibliophile's heaven. Works by many of San Francisco's best-known Beat Generation writers are featured on the bookshelves. For a broad selection of new and used readables at discount prices, try **Columbus Books**, at 540 Broadway. On the next block, **Biordi Italian Imports**, 412 Columbus, stocks a good selection of ornate decorative and practical ceramics.

A few blocks east of Columbus, between Washington Square and Coit Tower, you'll find **The Schlock Shop**, at 1418 Grant Avenue, filled with all sorts of fanciful headgear to enable you to fulfill any fantasies you might harbor about dressing like a seaman, cowboy, or flying ace. A few doors away at number 1422 is the **Primal Art Center**, the place to find primitive art and sculpture. Across the street is **Quantity Postcards**, where you'll discover thousands of collectible and current postcards, ranging in price from a few cents to big bucks. Nearby, at 478 Union Street, is a novel little shop called **Yoné**, with a connoisseur's collection of beads and buttons. Back on Grant and up the street at number 1543 is **Slips**, which carries clever custom-made slipcovers suitable for folding and director's chairs, made by the shop's owner.

Fisherman's Wharf Area

In the Fisherman's Wharf neighborhood, **Cost Plus**, 2552 Taylor, is a great place to browse and purchase inexpensive decorative and practical goodies, ranging from teak trays and straw baskets to edibles. Footsteps away, at number 2598, is the **Cost Plus Wine Shop**, which has a fine selection of domestic and imported bottlings at attractive prices.

Along the water, at the intersection of Beach Street and the Embarcadero, is **Pier 39**, a wonderful place to visit with children, because entertainment is regularly scheduled at several spots along the pier; shops are open from 10:30 A.M. to 8:30 P.M. Many of the businesses in this 45-acre, two-level complex are highly specialized, such as the **S. Claus** store, where it's Christmas all year long; **Mike's Puzzle People** shop, which offers brain-straining challenges to kids and adults through their wooden puzzles; or **Animal Country**, which stocks animal-theme toys and clothing. **Cartoon Junction** carries licensed cartoon-character merchandise; **The Disney Store** is like being in Disneyland without the rides (its stock is all licensed Disney merchandise); **Kite Makers of San Francisco** has a collection of kites from all over the world; **Puppets on the Pier** deals in hand puppets and marionettes; **Wound About** is the place for a wide variety of moveable toys that get their impetus from batteries or windup keys; and there are bears galore at **Ready Teddy**.

For adults the Pier offers mobiles and sculpture by local artists at **Designs in Motion**, Native American arts and crafts (including custom silverwork) at **Indian Village**, movie memorabilia at **Hollywood U.S.A.**, and California country crafts and gifts at **Country San Francisco**. **Behind the Wheel** carries gifts for auto buffs, **Left-Hand World** deals in items for southpaws, and **Magnet P. I.** is where you can pick from thousands of refrigerator magnets.

Walk six blocks west along Jefferson Street from Pier 39 and you'll come to **The Cannery**, 2801 Leavenworth, a handsome square-block collection of shops, galleries, restaurants, and entertainment offerings in brick buildings that functioned as a peach packing plant around the turn of the century. Frequently there's free entertainment in the courtyard, and always a variety of intriguing shops, including **Aerial**, with architectural books and prints as well as high-quality accessories; **Candles to Burn**, stocking candles and original wax sculptures; **The Gold Rush Store**, a great resource for early California artifacts; **Gourmet Guides**, with one of the largest selections of cookbooks and travel guides to be found anywhere; **Kachina** for Native American crafts and jewelry; **Peter Robins** for all manner of music boxes; **Play**, a colorful shop filled with kites and other toys; and **Past & Present**'s lovely assortment of home accessories, mostly handmade by local and foreign artisans. On the first floor is a large gourmet market full of tempting edibles and interesting wines and beers.

From The Cannery's Beach Street exit, it's just a one-block stroll west to **Ghirardelli Square**, a complex of rambling brick buildings that has National Historic Register status, and that served at various times as a woollen mill and a chocolate factory. Wonderful for browsing and strolling, and you can usually find free entertainment around the patio level. In summer, shops are open 10:00 A.M. to 9:00 P.M. Mondays through Saturdays (until 6:00 P.M. on Sundays); in the less touristy winter months, stores are generally open until 6:00 P.M., except those on the main plaza, which stay open until 9:00 P.M.

Almost the entire second floor of the Cocoa Building is occupied by **Xanadu**, a gallery that carries Asian, African, and folk art. **Royal Regiment** (on the Beach Street side) specializes in traditional European sportswear for men; **Goosebumps** inspires chuckles with its amusing contemporary gifts; and **something/ANYTHING** (in the West Plaza) is a fine place to find a piece of jewelry or crafts made in California.

Cow Hollow

Named for the dairy farms that once characterized this neighborhood, Cow Hollow has been transformed into a chic district that incorporates a seven-block shopping area along Union Street from Van Ness west to Steiner, and down Fillmore from Union to Lombard. Many of the shops are hidden in courtyards.

The Enchanted Crystal, 1771 Union, sells all kinds of crystal geegaws from the practical to the mystical; **Loui De No** at number 1749 has wonderful outré leather and fabric clothing, designed by the husband-and-wife proprietors. Across the street, the tiny **Edward Davidson Antiques** offers silver and silver-plated *objets* and lots of flatware. Nearby, the fragrance emanating from **L'Essential de Provence** lures customers who love the soaps, skin-care products, and aromatherapy supplies sold in this charming store.

Smile, 1750 Union Street, is a gallery overflowing in fanciful, whimsical objects. Behind the gallery and down a passageway is **Argentum/The Leopard's Head**, one of the largest silver dealers outside of New York (their specialty is antique Early American, European, and English flatware collections and collectors' pieces). **Saint Eligius**, in the same complex of shops, sells gems and original jewelry designs made by the two European-trained goldsmiths who work on the premises. On the same side of the street is a delightful shingled building in which you'll find the **Kundus Gallery** at number 1782, a treasure trove of ethnic rugs, baskets, and decorative textiles from Central Asia and West Africa. Downstairs is **Images of the North**, another gallery, but this one of Eskimo and Native American arts.

On the next block is **Familiar**, the first U.S. mainland branch of a Japanese chain of quality children's clothing shops; in the back of the store is a garden maze, where children can play while the adults shop. **Ogetti**, 1846 Union Street, carries sensational Italian paper goods. **Lucy de Marchant**, located next door in a courtyard, has a loyal clientele that loves her hand-crocheted dresses and sportswear. **Bauer Antiques**, at number 1878, is the oldest antiques shop on Union Street—its specialties are French antiques from the 18th century onward, and Italian painted furniture and accessories. **Yankee Doodle Dandy**, on the next block, has one of the largest collections of pre-1935 quilts in the country. Innovative women's clothing by American designers from Los Angeles and New York is carried at **JLC**, at 2124 Union Street. Within a nearby courtyard at 2166 Union and up a ramp, you'll find **UKO Japanese Clothing** for men and women.

Turn down Fillmore Street and you'll find many more interesting shops, among them, **Artifacts**, for contemporary art and crafts, and the **Silk Route**, with a marvelous selection of tribal rugs, clothing, carved masks, and jewelry from all over the world. If you are intrigued by hardware shops, **Fredericksen's**, 3029 Fillmore, has been pleasing do-it-yourselfers since 1896. Back on Union Street, at number 2254, is **Coco's Italian Dreams**, which carries women's one-size-fits-all, romantic, washable, handmade Italian clothing. The creations are all lacy, whipped-cream fantasies, designed by a German and manufactured in Italy. **Masquerade**, 2237 Union Street, the only vintage-clothing shop on the street, has a great stock of Hawaiian shirts from the 1930s to 1950s. If you have something more elegant in mind, there's **Ofelio**, 2213 Union, where the merchandise is refined menswear, most of it from Italy. **Three Bags Full**, at number 2181, is a wonderful sweater shop, and nearby **Tampico** is part of a complex of courtyard stores. The specialty at Tampico is handmade, natural-fiber clothing, and antique and vintage jewelry. On the next block, carrying dramatically styled women's clothing, is **Farnoosh**; its next-door neighbor, **Shaw**, focuses on pricey, high-fashion shoes. **Annalisa Antiques**, 1861 Union Street, offers a handsome selection of German country-pine and Biedermeier furnishings.

Haight-Ashbury

This particular part of San Francisco between Golden Gate Park and Civic Center caught the public's eye during the psychedelic 1960s, and although the mood is substantially more subdued now, this remains one of the most intriguing shopping areas, still much favored by the counterculture. It boasts a remarkable concentration of used-clothing stores and many shops that deal in esoterica. **Living Art**, 1317 Haight Street, deals in live reptiles, fish, and rodents for those eccentric visitors who would like to pick up a living souvenir of their visit. On the same block is **Bound Together**, an anarchist bookstore, and **Recycled Records**, which trades in rare records, tapes, and compact discs. Close by, at 1157 Masonic Street, is **The Ritz**, where you'll discover a remarkable cache of costume jewelry and collectible objects from the 1950s. Art Deco pieces and vintage dresses get the spotlight at **Sugartit**, 1474 Haight Street, while those interested in magic should check out **Touch Stone**, 1601 Page Street, and **Tools of Magick**, at number 1915 (where the proprietor will also do card readings). **Artery**, 1510 Haight Street, carries a striking collection of primitive art; **Dharma**, 1600 Haight, is where you'll discover the ethnic fashions favored by present-day hippies; and an old theater at number 1660 has been turned into a used-clothing shop called **The Wasteland**. On the next block, **Forma** carries an intriguing selection of useful and fanciful art objects. Across the street, the **Holos Gallery** has a fascinating variety of those three-dimensional laser photographs called holograms. Talismans, jewelry, rocks, and stones are traded at **Bones of Our Ancestors**, 624 Shrader Street.

Japantown

The focal point of San Francisco's Japanese community is Japan Center, a shopping-dining-entertainment complex that covers three square blocks bordered by Post, Geary, Laguna, and Fillmore streets. The Center has never managed to be as interesting as many people had hoped it might be, so it's worth a look only if you have the time—don't make it a high priority. The **Kinokuniya Book Store** (upper level, West Building) has books, records, and magazines about Japan; **Kinokuniya Stationery & Gifts** (Kinokuniya Building) carries imported cards and paper; **Asakichi** (Kinokuniya Building) has decorative items and *tansu* chests; and **Mikado** (Kintetsu Building) stocks everything you need to properly dress in a kimono.

Beyond the Japan Center are **Mr. Dandy** and **Oshare Corner**, both at 1737 Post Street, carrying clothing for men and women in small sizes. In the next block you can accessorize your purchases at **Jolyet Shoes**, which also caters to small sizes. **Soko Hardware**, 1698 Post Street, is a wonderful place for exotic cookware and gardening equipment, and if you walk over to 190B Fillmore Street you'll find **Narumi Antiques**, which has some lovely pieces—especially stained glass and 18th- and 19th-century Japanese dolls.

Sacramento Street

Most visitors don't know about this shopping area, which stretches west to east from approximately Spruce to Baker streets south of the Presidio, but if you are interested in smart, upmarket boutique merchandise, you will find it worth a trip. Home accessories and tableware of distinction can be found at **Sue Fisher King**, 3067 Sacramento Street. A few doors away is **V. Breier**, a gallery dedicated to whimsical American decorative pieces. In the next block is **American Pie**, a delightful general store that sells a variety of goods suitable for impulse shoppers; **Brava Strada** at number 3247 is a beautiful shop full of stunning leather goods and accessories at upscale prices; **Forrest Jones** is a fine place to shop for kitchenware; Turkish carpets are the specialty at **Return to Tradition**; and **Robert Hering & Associates**, 3307 Sacramento Street, is the magnet here for 18th- and 19th-century English antiques and accessories. **Elaine Magnin Needlepoint**, at number 3310, has supplies for those handy with a needle; **Phoenix Gallery**, at number 3391, has a noteworthy selection of Asian artifacts; and American handmade crafts delight shoppers at **Cottonwood** at number 3461. At nearby **Santa Fe**, the emphasis is on Southwestern design and both antique and contemporary Native American crafts; **The Littlest Mouse** deals in doll houses, miniature furnishings, and a charming selection of beautifully outfitted mice; **Vignette**, in the next block, carries exquisite accessories for the well-dressed home; and **Dottie Doolittle** at 3680 Sacramento stocks clothing for privileged kids.

South of Market

Popularly known as SoMa, this heavily industrialized part of town south of Market Street is a bargain hunter's heaven, chock-full of outlets selling everything from toiletries to household wares. In general it's a no-frills shopping experience—dressing rooms are oftentimes communal, and bare-bones decor is the usual rule—but savings can be substantial. Because the outlets are spread over a wide area, the shopping can be tiresome unless you're driving; otherwise, try to restrict yourself to what's offered within a few blocks.

If you have limited time you can find a number of outlets under one roof at **Yerba Buena Square**, 899 Howard Street, where a dozen stores are clustered (the largest is the **Burlington Coat Factory**). Numerous outlets are also concentrated in one building at **660 Third Street** (at Townsend), where a variety of merchandise from jewelry to ladies- and menswear can be found. Nearby is the **Aca Joe** outlet, at 148 Townsend, a good place to find classic, natural-fiber casual wear, and for good buys on cosmetics and fragrances there's **New York Cosmetics and Fragrances**, 318 Brannan Street and 674 Eighth Street. A **Van Heusen Factory Store** at 601 Mission Street has a great selection of shirts and other men's casual wear.

Those who like frilly, romantic clothing will find a wide selection at the **Gunne Sax Outlet**, 35 Stanford (off Second Street, between Brannan and Townsend streets), with labels such as Gunne Sax, Jessica McClintock, and Scott McClintock. Nearby is **AHC Apparel**, 625 Second Street, for men's and women's washable silk sportswear with the Go Silk label. Comfortable, youthful cotton separates are plentiful at **Simply Cotton**, 610 Third Street, and **Carole's Shoe Outlet**, 350 Brannan, is the spot for designer shoes and handbags at discount prices. For artificial flowers and plants, try **Ssilkss**, 635 Brannan Street. One of the most attractive and largest outlets is **Espirit**, at 16th and Illinois streets, where you'll discover a huge selection of youthfully styled unisex sportswear, and, next door, a café where shopping energies can be recharged.

—Bea Pixa

DAY TRIPS FROM SAN FRANCISCO

BERKELEY, OAKLAND, MARIN COUNTY, THE COAST, PALO ALTO

By Carole Terwilliger Meyers

Carole Terwilliger Meyers, a native San Franciscan, lives in Berkeley. She is the author of the award-winning Weekend Adventures for City-Weary People: Overnight Trips in Northern California *and* San Francisco Family Fun. *She writes a weekly column on travel in Northern California for the* San Francisco Examiner. *In the past she has covered Bay Area special events and restaurants for* California *magazine.*

Although San Francisco itself provides enough to see and do to last a lifetime, even natives like a change of scene once in a while, and, even more than a change of scene, they like a change of weather. Sunshine and warmer temperatures are as easy to find as a freeway out of the city.

To the north across the Golden Gate Bridge is Marin County, with its inviting beaches and natural wonders. Majestic redwood groves are just a few minutes away from spectacular rugged coastal scenery and Southern California–style beaches. The weather here is reliably sunny; it is the place to go when you've had your fill of chilly winds and foggy afternoons.

To the south are yet more rugged vistas and beaches. Inland is Stanford, the area's leading private university, and the sophisticated town of Palo Alto, which serves the needs of the university community.

To the east across the Bay Bridge is the always-fascinating community of Berkeley. Home to the University of California, the state's most prestigious public university, it is a study in contrasts, where both informal coffeehouses and acclaimed restaurants are plentiful. Nearby, you can experience the area's more conservative, middle America personality in Oakland.

When exploring these surrounding communities in your car, your morning trip out of San Francisco and your return later in the afternoon should be easy—commuter traffic will be going against you. But if you'd rather not drive, alternatives are the ferry to Sausalito or Tiburon in Marin County, or to Oakland's Jack London Square; CalTrans down the Peninsula to Palo Alto; and rapid-transit BART trains' convenient service to Berkeley and Oakland.

MAJOR INTEREST

Berkeley
University of California
Telegraph Avenue
The "Gourmet Ghetto"
Tilden Regional Park

Oakland
Lake Merritt
Oakland Museum
Historic Paramount Theatre
Jack London Square

Marin County
Sausalito
Tiburon
The Mountain Play

North Coast
Muir Woods National Monument
Stinson Beach
Point Reyes National Seashore

South Coast
Princeton-by-the-Sea
Miramar Beach
Half Moon Bay
Año Nuevo State Reserve

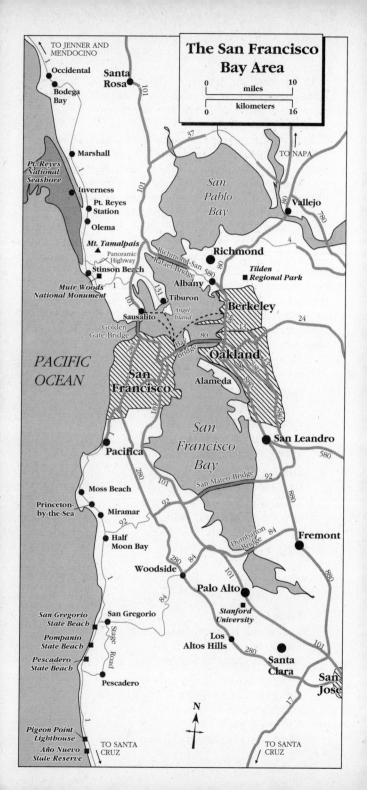

BERKELEY

Visitors to Berkeley arrive with a mixture of expectations. Some are looking for the intellectual climate associated with a community built around a great university, while others expect to see weird people and hippie communes. Those who know their food come seeking what is generally touted as the best available in the area, and those who know one of the town's nicknames, Berserkeley, expect to see a bit of that. Then there is the well-known ultraliberal political climate, in which someone who would be referred to as a liberal elsewhere is here considered to be a conservative, and thus comes another nickname—the People's Republic of Berkeley. In reality, Berkeley is all these things, and, making any stereotype impossible, it is also the place where the word "yuppie" was coined.

University of California

Because the University of California campus is the town's focal point, it is a good place to begin a visit. You reach the campus by taking the University Avenue exit off Freeway I-80 and following it east to Oxford Street, where the university boundary begins. Street parking around the university can be difficult; a reasonably priced city parking lot, the Sather Gate Garage, is at 2450 Durant near Telegraph Avenue (for which see below).

The foremost attraction at the university is, of course, higher learning. Known for academic excellence, it boasts a faculty distinguished by ten Nobel Prize winners. Many noteworthy facilities on the 1,200-acre campus are open to the public, and a good way to get an overview is by taking the free guided tour that leaves every weekday at 1:00 P.M. from the visitors' center in University Hall, located at the intersection of Oxford Street and University Avenue. A self-guiding tour brochure is available here as well.

The landmark **campanile** stands approximately in the center of the campus. Rising 307 feet (30 stories), it was modeled after the slightly taller campanile in St. Mark's Square in Venice. When classes are in session, concerts are hand-played on its 61-bell carillon three times each day (at 7:50 A.M., noon, and 6:00 P.M.). A 45-minute recital is given each Sunday at 2:00 P.M.—a good time to enjoy a picnic on the inviting grass surrounding the tower.

The **Lowie Museum of Anthropology**, to the south toward Bancroft Way, has been part of the campus since 1901 and stores the largest anthropological research collection in the western United States. Public exhibits change regularly.

Across from the Lowie, the architecturally dramatic **University Art Museum** displays its permanent collection of modern and Asian art. It also boasts a large collection of paintings by Modernist Hans Hofmann and an attractive sculpture garden. **The Swallow**, a casual cafeteria-style restaurant, operates in the museum's basement. Run by a collective, this Very Berkeley operation prepares sandwiches, creative salads, and homemade soups. When the weather is good you can dine alfresco in the sculpture garden. Also in the basement, the **Pacific Film Archive** is internationally known for its film exhibition and scholarship. Public programs are presented daily.

Just behind the museum, the **Hotel Durant** is a good lodging choice and is particularly popular with parents in town to visit their children at the university.

Strawberry Canyon to Grizzly Peak

A drive through lush Strawberry Canyon, to the east of campus on Centennial Drive, takes you past fraternity and sorority houses and Memorial Stadium before you reach the **Botanical Garden**. This "library of living plants" covers over 30 acres and contains over 8,000 different types of plants organized into 16 collections according to geographic origin, taxonomic affinity, and economic value. Of special interest are the herb garden, rhododendron dell, redwood grove, California native-plants area, and a Chinese medicinal herb garden stocked with over 90 rare plants. Recent additions include a pygmy forest of miniature plants and the Garden of Roses.

Continuing north on scenic Centennial Drive brings you to the celebrated **Lawrence Hall of Science**. Located high in the hills just below Grizzly Peak Boulevard, this participatory museum was established by the university in 1958 as a memorial to Ernest Orlando Lawrence, developer of the cyclotron and the university's first Nobel laureate. Of special interest to school-age children, this button-pusher's paradise is filled with educational games, an Earthquake Information

Center, a seismograph, and a miniplanetarium. The snack bar provides an absolutely magnificent panoramic view of the bay and San Francisco and has a computer keyed to the menu that allows you to score the nutritional value of your food choices.

Telegraph Avenue

This famous, or perhaps infamous, avenue runs south from the campus. Probably best known for its role as a gathering spot and point of confrontation during the 1960s Free Speech Movement, it has now slipped into a more peaceful state.

On weekdays rushing students crowd its sidewalks, on weekends visitors crowd its many boutiques. Strolling up and down "the Ave," as it is nicknamed, along the four blocks between Bancroft (the street forming the campus's southern boundary) and Dwight ways, takes you by a psychedelic "head shop" left over from the turbulent 1960s. You'll also see thoroughly modern shops such as Mrs. Field's Cookies and The Gap, which were controversial when they first opened because they displaced older mom-and-pop-type businesses.

In the 2400 block, bookstores include **Moe's** and **Shakespeare & Co.**, good choices for picking up obscure used editions, and **Cody's**, which holds Wednesday evening poetry readings and stocks new obscure tomes as well as the latest best sellers. A stop for cappuccino at **The Med** makes for an atmospheric break. The decor is extremely casual, maybe even slovenly, but the shop is now an institution that seems to have been serving coffee to students forever. Don't miss their mean chocolate layer cake with rum custard filling.

For a solid meal, make a stop at **Larry Blake's** (2367 Telegraph). A campus hangout since 1940, it is known for its hamburgers and steaks and also serves an excellent barbecued beef sandwich. In the evening blues performances are often scheduled in its funky rathskeller. Or, if you prefer, make your way to the **Berkeley Thai House**, off Telegraph at 2511 Channing Way, where you can savor well-prepared ethnic specialties on a pleasant, sheltered upstairs deck.

At Telegraph's intersection with Bancroft Way (where Telegraph ends at the campus) you can pick up a quick, inexpensive lunch at one of the food stalls that appear here on weekdays; they dispense an assortment of international fast foods (burritos, falafel) and student favorites such as smoothies (a blended mixture of fruit and juice) and soft pretzels. This famous intersection also attracts all manner of performers—jugglers, musicians, revivalists. On weekends enjoy the informal, free musical performances that take place in the lower Sproul Plaza.

The "Gourmet Ghetto"

The area of town surrounding the intersection of Shattuck and Vine, northwest of campus, is not only home to the celebrated restaurant **Chez Panisse** but has sprouted a veritable garden of gourmet food shops as well.

The famous restaurant at 1517 Shattuck Avenue, opened in 1971 by U.C. graduate Alice Waters as a hangout for her friends, is worth the trouble of making reservations. They are essential and may be made up to one month in advance; Tel: 415-548-5525. The expensive and small downstairs dining room serves a different fixed-price menu each evening, prepared with the freshest of ingredients and considered to be the definitive California cuisine. An upstairs café is less expensive, though not less popular. Lunch reservations are only accepted for the café on the same day; no dinner reservations are accepted, and after 6:00 P.M. you should expect a long wait.

Across the street a Berkeley collective operates the **Cheese Board,** which sells freshly baked breads and hundreds of kinds of cheeses. One block north on Shattuck, the original **Cocolat** shop dispenses the rich, path-paving chocolate truffles for which it is famous. This extremely successful enterprise was begun in 1976 by another U.C. graduate.

East down Vine Street, **Peet's Coffee** offers an impressive variety of coffee beans and teas. Coffee freaks gather at this Berkeley institution in great numbers each morning, spilling right out into the street with their hot cups of java. This is a good spot to observe the interesting mix of people that populate Berkeley: you'll often see people in three-piece suits chatting with others in blue-collar work clothes. In Berkeley it sometimes seems that almost everyone, no matter what kind of work he does, has a curious, educated mind.

Mirabelles, located on the corner of Shattuck and Cedar, is a newcomer to the Berkeley restaurant scene. Its French-trained owner-chef runs the kitchen, producing European cuisine and some delightfully unusual sauces. Regional French dinners are served every Wednesday, and Spanish *tapas,* accompanied by live flamenco music, are the specialty every Thursday night. Lunch and weekend brunch are also available. Reservations are suggested; Tel: 841-2002. A few doors away, **Cha-Am** is the current leader in the informal ongoing competition for the city's best Thai restaurant. Though its front dining room can be drafty in winter, many of the dishes are spicy enough to make up for it. Prices are rock bottom, keeping the restaurant jammed.

Across the street, the European-modern **French Hotel** is another popular spot to enjoy an espresso while watching the world go by. It is also a convenient, moderately priced place to spend the night. The hotel has only 18 rooms, each with a private patio, so the staff can treat guests to plenty of personal attention.

Next door the upscale Andronico's supermarket has replaced the failed consumer-owned Co-op. Things change.

Berkeley's trendy food ghetto has an outpost on Hopkins Street, which runs northeast from the corner of Cedar Street and San Pablo Avenue. Here the unpretentious **Monterey Market**, at 1550 Hopkins, presents an amazing assortment of fresh produce. Locals come here to buy baby vegetables, unusual melons, and exotic wild mushrooms, and to reap the unexpected benefit of low prices. This market also supplies many of the area's finer restaurants; you might see chefs in aprons here selecting the day's ingredients for their menus.

Also on Hopkins, **Made to Order** abounds in wonderful deli fare, including freshly prepared salads and sandwiches. A coffee store, fish market, bakery, and poultry shop complete this European-style row of food shops. Plan a visit here to put together a picnic to enjoy up in the hills in magnificent Tilden Park. (To get there from the "gourmet ghetto" outpost, follow Hopkins Street east to Sutter Street, turn left and then jog immediately to the right up Del Norte. Cautiously enter the traffic circle and exit up Marin, Berkeley's steepest street. Take a left on Grizzly Peak and at the first stop sign, turn right onto Canyon Drive; follow it into the park to Central Park Drive.)

Tilden Regional Park

Exemplifying the wealth of natural beauty the Bay Area enjoys, this magnificent 740-acre regional park to the northeast of the campus is overflowing with relaxing options. The **Environmental Education Center**, with its informative programs and natural-history exhibits, is a good place to get oriented and obtain information about park attractions. In addition to pony rides and a 15-inch-gauge miniature train ride, the park is home to an antique carousel—one of only four in northern California. Across the street from the carousel, Tilden's **Botanic Garden** features native plants and makes an ideal spot for a leisurely, quiet walk. A scenic 18-hole golf course is nearby, as is the wonderfully low-key swimming area of Lake Anza: Ten miles of hiking trails wind through the park.

Exiting the park at Grizzly Peak Boulevard and heading south to Claremont Avenue provides a refreshing drive through less-populated areas of the city. Situated where Claremont meets Ashby Avenue, the elegant **Claremont Resort & Spa**, a Victorian hotel built in 1915, is located in the middle of an enclave of architecturally interesting homes. It provides all the amenities of a resort in an urban setting: Olympic-size swimming pool, tennis courts, and modern spa. It also has an elegant restaurant with a good bay view (some rooms have wonderful views as well); Sunday brunch here is a buffet extravaganza.

Across the street from the hotel, Domingo Avenue is home to a small shopping area. Of special note here is the **Bread Garden Bakery**, where superb French baguettes and cinnamon-flavored butter cookies are available daily.

OAKLAND

Though this much-maligned city usually loses in the struggle with San Francisco for media attention, it does have a "there there." (Although Gertrude Stein, who lived here as a child, is often quoted as having said about the city, "There is no there there," in reality it seems that she was referring to what remained of her demolished childhood home.)

You reach Oakland from San Francisco by simply crossing the Bay Bridge. Then, from Highway 580 take the Harrison Street exit and follow it west to lovely **Lake Merritt**, at the center of Lakeside Park and the hub of a variety of activities. (From Berkeley, take Telegraph Avenue south to Grand Avenue, turn left and follow it to the lake.) On the lake's west edge near 14th Street, the 1876 Italianate-style Victorian **Camron-Stanford House**, which has been restored and furnished in period fashion, is open for tours on Wednesdays and Sundays. A short film on Oakland's history is also presented. Nearby, the Sailboat House rents a variety of vessels, including rowboats and sailboats, or you may want to board the replica Mississippi sternwheeler *Merritt Queen* for a 30-minute tour of the lake. In the park's center, near Bellevue Avenue, you'll find the oldest wildlife refuge in the U.S. Dating from 1870, the **Lake Merritt Waterbird Refuge** is the winter home of all kinds of migrating fowl, including brown pelicans, bay ducks, and, occasionally, the rare tufted duck from Europe. A highlight in the spring and early summer is the nesting colony of egrets. The birds are fed each day at 3:30 P.M. In the evening, a lovely necklace of lights circles the lake.

Not far away, at Oak and 10th streets, the beautifully designed tri-level **Oakland Museum** focuses on the art, natural sciences, and history of California. Built in 1969, it is celebrated both for its architecture and for its innovative shows. One permanent exhibit provides a walk across a miniature representation of the state, complete with appropriate plant and animal life.

A few blocks north of Lake Merritt, the grand Art Deco–style **Paramount Theatre** at Broadway and 21st Street is worth going out of your way to visit. Built in 1931, the renovated theater is at its best during an actual performance; try to come for the Organ Pops series (October, January, March, April, June, July), when silent films are accompanied live by a magnificent old Wurlitzer organ, or for the Hollywood Movie Classics series (January, March, April, June, August, October, November), which features the best of the old movies. Tours are given on the first and third Saturdays of each month; Tel: 465-6400 or 893-2300.

Situated on the inlet of the Oakland Estuary and easily reached by following Broadway southwest to its terminus, the **Jack London Square** area borders the town's huge commercial shipping area. Come here to stroll the spacious, modern walkways and to stop in at a variety of shops. **Jack London Village**, an attractive shopping mall, is at the square's eastern end. Among the many restaurants in the area, two stand out: Upscale **Scott's Seafood Grill & Bar** (Tel: 444-3456) has an extensive menu of fresh seafood and window tables overlooking the estuary, and nearby **Il Pescatore** (Tel: 465-2188), situated inside a boat-shaped building, offers a variety of Italian seafood dishes. Reservations are necessary at both. An informal, funky bar, **Heinolds' First and Last Chance Saloon** pays tribute to the area's waterfront past. Jack London, a longtime Oakland resident, was a regular customer during the period when he was an oyster fisherman here. Though somewhat menacing in appearance (it is impossible to see in through the thick windows), the saloon makes a good spot to wet your whistle.

Informative free boat tours of the Port of Oakland, which in volume is the fourth-largest container-shipping port in the U.S. (in physical size it is the largest on the West Coast), are available May through August. Reservations are necessary; Tel: 272-1200.

If you've ever wondered what it would be like to spend the night on a luxury yacht, here's your chance to find out. **Bayside Boat & Breakfast** rents out yachts anchored in the estuary that are not being used by their owners, including one with a private Jacuzzi, for example, and a view of San Francisco. A Continental breakfast is included, and arrangements can be made for dinner on board as well.

MARIN COUNTY

Across the Golden Gate Bridge from San Francisco, spectacularly scenic Marin County is composed of prosperous bedroom communities. It is home to numerous rock stars and Beautiful People, such as *Star Wars* filmmaker George Lucas, who built his studios in the hilly back country.

Books and films have teased the generally upscale residents about their stereotyped easygoing, laid-back approach to life, about the decadence of having nothing better to do than tickling each other with peacock feathers while soaking in a hot tub, and about their New Age flakiness. The reality of Marin is for you to discover.

Consistently fair weather makes this area a popular destination with locals, especially when other areas are covered with fog.

Sausalito

Sausalito is the first exit off Highway 101 after you cross the Golden Gate Bridge and is also easily reached by ferry from San Francisco. Tiny waterfront Sausalito, known as a magnet for artists and tourists, remains a pleasure for both. Set in the hilly area above **Bridgeway**, the main shopping street, the village's splendid homes and gardens make a delightful scene. The street fronts the bay, allowing for terrific views of San Francisco. A climb up Princess Street (just south of the ferry terminal) will give you an overview of both the houses and the bay.

A stroll along Bridgeway is the best way to see most of the shops, galleries, and restaurants. Unusual among the many boutiques is the **Village Fair** multi-level shopping enclave, once a parking garage. This indoor center houses 35 shops and features a curvy, steep "Little Lombard" path to the upper floors. On the fourth floor, the **Café Madrona and**

Bakery serves home-style sandwiches, soups, and pastries, and offers panoramic views of the Sausalito yacht harbor and San Francisco.

You can pick up picnic supplies in several stores along Bridgeway. For invigorating alfresco dining, just cross the street and find a spot to sit on the shoreline rocks, where passing boats and seagulls provide free entertainment.

If you prefer fine dining and an even more magnificent view, try **Casa Madrona**, nestled in the hills above Bridgeway. The food is California-style, the mood elegant and romantic. You can spend the night in one of the individually decorated rooms that are sprinkled down the hillside, each with a good view, or in one of the rooms in the older Victorian house located in back.

Another special restaurant, the **Alta Mira**, is in the hills above town at 125 Bulkley Avenue. Refined, reserved, and expensive, it serves traditional Continental cuisine and is a lovely spot to enjoy a leisurely lunch or Sunday brunch, especially on the terrace, which commands an excellent bay view. Reservations are highly recommended; Tel: 332-1350. Twenty-eight quiet guest rooms and cottages, many with bay views, are available for overnight stays.

The small and quaint **Sausalito Hotel**, located next to the ferry landing right off Bridgeway at 16 El Portal, has 15 rooms decorated with Victorian antiques. The Marquis of Queensberry Room holds a bed that, it is claimed, was once occupied by General Grant.

To see the real Sausalito, continue north on Bridgeway from the ferry terminal and turn left onto **Caledonia Street**. This back street is where the town's everyday business takes place. Of special interest is the spacious **Real Food Company** grocery at 200 Caledonia, which stocks an overwhelming variety of the health foods this area helped make trendy.

Great Szechwan food is served up at the tiny **China Station** restaurant at 47 Caledonia. Portions are generous and attractively presented. About a half mile north on Bridgeway, the U.S. **Army Corps of Engineers Bay Model** welcomes visitors. Located on the site of a shipyard that turned out World II tankers and Liberty ships—built to replace cargo ships being sunk in huge numbers by enemy submarines and used to transport troops and supplies—it is a working hydraulic scale model of the Bay Area and Delta estuary systems. As big as two football fields, it was built to simulate bay water conditions for research. A computerized slide show and interpretive displays help make this complex scientific project understandable to the layman. The model operates irregularly, so be sure to call for upcoming dates; Tel: 332-3870.

A few blocks farther north, at 400 Gate 5 Road, **Heath Ceramics** sells "seconds" of its fine contemporary ceramic tableware at reduced prices.

Farther north at Waldo Point is a private houseboat colony. Containing both the funky and the exquisite, it provides an interesting sight. Visitors are not welcomed by residents but are legally permitted to view the area if they respect posted trespassing signs. If you'd like to get a really close look by spending the night on one of the houseboats, it can be arranged through **Bed & Breakfast International**, which books guests onto several high-quality, upscale boats in the colony (see Accommodations Reference at the end of this chapter).

To get to Sausalito from San Francisco, you can take the Golden Gate Transit ferries (Tel: 332-6600) from the Ferry Building at the foot of Market Street, or the Red & White Fleet (Tel: 546-2896), which operates ferries from Pier 43½, near Fisherman's Wharf. Both routes land in Sausalito just east of Bridgeway at El Portal.

Tiburon

Often missed by visitors to San Francisco, this town is smaller and less well known than Sausalito. Its tiny **Main Street** is sprinkled with a variety of boutiques and galleries. Locals usually visit Tiburon with a restaurant in mind. Two of the most popular are casual **Sam's Anchor Café**, which attracts a singles crowd after hamburgers and Sam's famous Ramos gin fizz, and **Guaymas**, which serves unusual regional Mexican fare and attracts a somewhat trendier crowd. A few doors down, the inexpensive **Sweden House Bakery** is the place to go for a delightful dessert pastry.

If a picnic with a view sounds appealing, hasten to **McKegney Green**. Located on the outskirts of town on Greenwood Beach Road off Paradise Drive, this flat expanse of grass overlooks the bay and San Francisco. Pick up your picnic fare from **Let's Eat**, nearby at 1 Blackfield Drive in the Cove Shopping Center, where delicious salads and made-to-order sandwiches are packed to go. And you won't want to miss the fine desserts available a few doors down at **Sweet Things**.

Not far away, at 376 Greenwood Beach Road, the 11-acre **Richardson Bay Audubon Center & Sanctuary** shelters a variety of birds and animals and offers a self-guided nature trail leading to a rocky beach and lookout spot with sweep-

ing views of San Francisco. The oldest Victorian home in
Marin County, the 1876 **Lyford House**, is located here, and is
open for tours on Sunday afternoons; Tel: 388-2524.

The ferry to **Angel Island** leaves from a dock located
behind Main Street's restaurants (for schedule information,
call 435-2131) or you can take the Red & White Fleet from
San Francisco. This 740-acre island in the middle of the San
Francisco Bay is perfect for a picnic or a hike—it has about
12 miles of well-marked trails and paved roads so you can
completely circle it. Some paths lead to old military ruins,
reminders of the island's past: It has been a prison for Native
Americans, a holding camp for quarantined immigrants (the
island was once called the Ellis Island of the West), a
prisoner-of-war camp, and a missile defense base.

The Mountain Play

If you are lucky enough to be in the area in May or June, save
time for the Mountain Play. Presented annually since 1913 in
the natural outdoor amphitheater atop **Mount Tamalpais**, the
plays have run the gamut from the obscure to Shakespeare
to well-known Broadway musicals; for ticket and parking
information, call 383-1100. In the old days people came on
burros, by stagecoach, or on the old Mount Tamalpais Scenic
Railway, known also as the Crookedest Railroad in the World.
Now many audience members ride the free shuttle buses up
the mountain, and then after the performance participate in
an enjoyable four-mile hike partway down, to a point where
they can board a shuttle bus for the rest of the journey back
to the parking area. You'll see Marinites on the mountain's
hiking trails year-round.

To reach Tiburon by car from San Francisco, cross the
Golden Gate Bridge and continue on Highway 101 to the
Tiburon Boulevard exit; follow it east into town. (From
Sausalito, take Highway 101 north and follow the same
route.) If you'd rather take the ferry from San Francisco, the
Red & White Fleet services this route from the Ferry Build-
ing during the morning commute and from Pier 43½ begin-
ning at 11:20 A.M.

NORTH COAST

Heading north from San Francisco to the west of Marin
County allows an escape into a quieter, less-populated area
(cross the Golden Gate Bridge via Highway 101 and take the

exit to Highway 1). Highway 1, a two-lane road, winds through fragrant eucalyptus groves, then rustic countryside rife with wildflowers in spring and for long stretches hugs oceanside cliffs. Good beaches add to the appeal, as does a spectacular national seashore.

Note, however, that this road can become quite congested on those sunny summer days when San Franciscans, like everyone else in the area, want to head to a spot where they can soak up some of that famous California sunshine that can be so elusive in the city.

Take the Highway 1 exit 5 miles after you cross the Golden Gate Bridge; a few miles before you arrive at Muir Woods the **Green Gulch Farm** Zen retreat is reached by a sharp downhill turnoff from the highway. The retreat offers public meditation programs on Sundays, when visitors are also welcome for lunch and informal afternoon walks in its organic garden, which supplies the herbs and vegetables for Green's Restaurant in San Francisco. Lodging is available nightly in a peaceful Japanese-style guesthouse, and meals may be taken with the residents.

About one mile on, the Muir Beach Overlook provides panoramic coastline views and is a good spot from which to watch the winter whale migration. From here the winding road drops like a rollercoaster into **Muir Beach**, reached by turning left off the highway down a leafy, blackberry-lined lane just before The Pelican Inn. Swimming is unsafe but sunning and people-watching are excellent, and picnic tables are available.

If you're looking for a pleasant stop for afternoon tea, try **The Pelican Inn**. Sheltered by towering pines and alders, it is a persuasive reconstruction of a 16th-century English Tudor inn. It has a cozy, wood-paneled bar area, and lunch and dinner are served every day but Mondays. Several snug rooms, complete with canopied beds, are rented out upstairs. It was in this area (the exact spot is still disputed) more than 400 years ago that Sir Francis Drake beached the *Golden Hinde,* formerly known as the *Pelican,* and claimed California for Queen Elizabeth I. After the Pelican, fantastic views begin to loom ahead as you approach the turnoff for Muir Woods.

Muir Woods National Monument

Coast Redwood trees have a normal life span of 400 to 800 years, but have been known to live for more than 2,000 years. They are found only in a 540-mile-long by 30-mile-wide strip of the Northern California coast. Located just off Highway 1 and enveloping 560 acres, Muir Woods National Monument, a fragrant redwood forest, provides a convenient opportunity to see these majestic trees. Among its six miles of walking trails is an easy paved Main Trail with interpretive exhibits, and there are also seven unpaved trails, which are more challenging and lead away from the crowds. (This is the exception to the area's promise of escape from the masses—over one million people visit Muir Woods each year. Only a visit early or late in the day provides the hope of some solitude.) Naturalist John Muir, for whom the forest was named, said of it, "This is the best tree-lover's monument that could be found in all the forests of all the world." No matter what time of year, bring along warm wraps since the dense forest lets in very little sunlight, and the weather is usually damp, foggy, and cold.

From here you can backtrack a few miles on Highway 1 to pick up the Panoramic Highway over **Mount Tamalpais**. (You can stop at "Mount Tam," as the mountain is affectionately nicknamed, to hike some of the 200-plus miles of trails leading past creeks, waterfalls, and spectacular views.) The Panoramic Highway is steep and winding, but currently is the only available route to Stinson Beach and the coast in this area since the 1989 earthquake tumbled a three-mile section of Highway 1 into the sea.

Stinson Beach

Among locals this seems to be everyone's favorite beach. This magnificent stretch of sand, at the end of the Panoramic Highway west of Muir Woods, offers a small taste of the Southern California type of beach scene immortalized by the Beach Boys. Unlike at most Bay Area beaches, summer visitors may actually swim here, although the water is still quite cold and lifeguards are not always on duty. When the rest of the Bay Area is lost in fog, this small area can be warm with sunshine. Should you wish to check the weather at Stinson before setting out, call for a report; Tel: (415) 868-1922.

Spending the night in one of the beach houses fronting the ocean here is a fantasy most people indulge in while sunbathing on the sand. The **Stinson Beach House** here is a privately owned, million-dollar mansion that *can* be rented for two or more nights, for a price. It is claimed that the four windows in its dramatic front room cover such a wide horizon that you can actually see the curvature of the earth. Most people would prefer to spend just one night in Stinson

Beach, however, with some pampering included. Then the lodging of choice is the relatively new Mediterranean-style **Casa del Mar**, where a full breakfast is served to guests each morning. Perched on a hill above town, it has four rooms, some of which have gorgeous ocean views. In fact, with balcony doors ajar, the sound of the breaking surf can be heard quite clearly. The inn's garden, obviously loved by the owner and dating back to the 1930s, was used as a teaching garden by the University of California's School of Landscape Architecture in the 1970s. Now guests are welcome to pinch and prune, should the mood strike them.

There is little commercial lodging in town, so spending the night here is a pleasure few have known. Bulging with tourists during the day, the town quiets significantly by sunset, when the busy, congested highway becomes calm and empty. Best of all, spending the night allows early access to the beach—which usually becomes crowded on sunny weekends—so you can stroll the ocean's edge in peace, in search of shells. At night there isn't much to do in town. Dinner at the casual, comfortable **Stinson Beach Grill** is about it, but that's enough because the food here is quite good. The eclectic menu includes a well-executed Greek salad and fresh fish, and the chef isn't afraid of spices. The bar dispenses a large variety of beers from Northern California microbreweries, plus many more from around the world. On sunny days lunch can be enjoyed on a roadside deck. Reservations are suggested on weekends; Tel: 868-2002. Note that there is no gas station in town. According to a local resident, "It disappeared one night and didn't come back."

Point Reyes
National Seashore

About 15 miles farther up Highway 1 is the entrance to Point Reyes National Seashore, which stretches over approximately 25 miles of spectacular coastal land. Known for its beaches and hiking trails, the area has a wealth of interesting things for visitors to do.

Many activities are clustered around the park headquarters, a half mile west of Olema (Tel: 663-1092). A visitors' center houses a working seismograph and a variety of nature displays. A short walk away is **Kule Loklo**, a replica Miwok Indian village that was re-created using the same tools and materials that the Miwok used. Demonstrations of weaving, arrowhead-making, and other crafts are sometimes scheduled. At the adjacent Morgan Horse Ranch, pack and trail animals for the national parks are raised and trained.

Numerous hiking trails begin near the headquarters, including the self-guided Woodpecker Nature Trail; the mile-long, self-guided Earthquake Trail, which follows the infamous San Andreas fault; and the popular 4.4-mile Bear Valley Trail, which winds through meadows, fern grottoes, and forests before ending at the ocean. Point Reyes also has more than 70 miles of equestrian trails, and horses may be rented at Five Brooks Stables, 3 miles south of the park headquarters on Highway 1.

Twenty miles west of the park headquarters is the **Point Reyes Lighthouse**, where, it is claimed, winds have been recorded blowing at 133 miles per hour—the highest rate in the continental U.S. The bottom line is that it gets very windy, cold, and wet at this scenic spot. The lighthouse, reached by hiking 300 steps down the side of a steep, rocky cliff, is a strategic spot in winter for viewing migrating gray whales; open Thursdays through Sundays, 10:00 A.M. to 5:00 P.M.

At the northern end of Point Reyes, wide, level **Drake's Beach** is a good spot for taking a walk. An informal café here serves inexpensive fare such as home-style soup, hamburgers, and barbecued oysters. In the style of California cuisine, most items are prepared using fresh ingredients, many of which are obtained locally. The exceptional quality is a surprise in such rustic surroundings.

Within the park area you can view the various stages of the commercial oyster-farming process at the scenically situated **Johnson's Drakes Bay Oyster Company.** (Oysters are also available for purchase.) There are more oysters several miles north on Highway 1 in the rustic town of Marshall, where the house specialty at informal **Tony's Seafood** is oysters barbecued in their shells. They also offer deep-fried oysters and fresh fish entrées.

Many day-trippers end their excursions to this area with a casual dinner at the **Station House Café** in the town of Point Reyes Station on Highway 1. Moderately priced fare includes fresh fish, local oysters, and beef from organically fed cattle raised at the nearby Niman-Schell ranch. Breakfast and lunch are also served daily. Reservations are suggested on weekends; Tel: 663-1515. The informal **Chez Madeleine**, also in Point Reyes Station, specializes in French country-style cuisine. Dinner is the only meal served, and the restaurant is closed on Mondays and Tuesdays. Reservations are suggested on weekends; Tel: 663-9177.

There are many charming little bed and breakfasts in this area; **Inns of Point Reyes** can provide information on them (P.O. Box 145, Inverness, CA 94937; Tel: 415-663-1420). One standout is the **Holly Tree Inn**. Located just beneath the Inverness Ridge in its own valley complete with a picturesque stream running through, it offers lots of space and attractively appointed rooms.

On the return drive from Point Reyes, Sir Francis Drake Boulevard east from Olema (2 miles south of Point Reyes Station) takes you through different terrain; winding east through the coastal hills, it passes through several towns and Samuel P. Taylor Park, ending at busy Highway 101. Then it's a scenic 12-mile drive back down 101 to the Golden Gate Bridge and San Francisco.

Or you can continue north from Point Reyes Station on Highway 1 to the fishing village of **Bodega Bay**, where Alfred Hitchcock filmed *The Birds*. You can watch local fishermen bring in their catch at the wharf and a moderately priced seafood restaurant offers casual waterside dining. About ten miles farther up, the tiny town of Jenner occupies the scenic site where the Russian River empties into the Pacific Ocean. Here you can begin your journey back to San Francisco by taking Highway 116 east. Plan a stop at **Duncans Mills**, about ten miles inland. Once a lumber town, this tiny village is now home to a number of cute shops and several inexpensive restaurants. Continue on Highway 116 through Sebastopol and back to Highway 101 for your return to San Francisco.

SOUTH COAST

Like the north coast area, the coast south of San Francisco along Highway 1 is strikingly scenic. Leave San Francisco via 19th Avenue, which turns into Highway 1 south of the city. After passing ridges of boxy houses in pastel tones (referred to as "ticky-tacky" by folk singer Malvina Reynolds in her 1960s song *Little Boxes*) and the beach town of Pacifica, Highway 1 winds to the ocean through a eucalyptus-lined gap in the coastal foothills.

A stretch of this road known as **Devil's Slide** hugs cliffs that drop steeply into the sea. In fact part of the road itself occasionally drops off. Though many people make informal stops here to take pictures, it can be unsafe and restraint is in order until you find an obvious parking zone. Once the road passes through these hills, it turns inland (although just a few minutes from the ocean) and becomes flatter and straighter.

This area is often covered by fog in the morning, but the fog tends to burn off by noon. In fact, on many late summer and early fall days, when San Francisco is completely fogged in, this area is at its most beautiful. The spectacular unspoiled beaches are a popular destination any time, but especially then, when the weather is usually warm and clear. Be cautious, though, about going in the surf, as tides can be dangerous. Check with a ranger station or lifeguard before swimming or even wading.

Princeton-by-the-Sea

About 25 miles south of San Francisco on Highway 1, the scenic fishing village of Princeton-by-the-Sea makes an inviting stop. Famed as a haven for bootleggers during Prohibition, it is now known more for surfers—who can usually be observed enjoying their sport—and for its seafood restaurants.

Situated inside a Cape Cod–style structure built on the site where a speakeasy once stood, the **Shore Bird** specializes in serving fresh local fish in a refined atmosphere. Steaks, ribs, and pasta dishes are also on the menu and the restaurant takes pride in its dressings, chowders, and desserts.

Across the street the more modest **Fish Trap** beckons with a moderately priced fresh fish menu and casual dining on a glassed-in deck overlooking the harbor.

Fishing charters leave from Princeton harbor, and whale-watching boat trips are scheduled January through April. They are sponsored by both the Oceanic Society (Tel: 474-3385) and the Whale Center (Tel: 654-6621) and trips cost from $23 to $28 (advance reservations are necessary).

Located about 5 miles north of Princeton, the **James Fitzgerald Marine Reserve** in Moss Beach is considered one of the best spots on the West Coast to explore the tidepools. Call ahead (Tel: 728-3584) to check the tide schedule; low tides provide the best opportunity for seeing unusual specimens, and free walks led by naturalists are scheduled then.

Miramar Beach

Two miles south of Princeton, a turn toward the sea on Magellan Avenue brings you to peaceful Miramar Beach. Off the beaten path, it provides a chance to view the area as the luckier local residents do.

The beach is reached by climbing down a breakwater constructed with large boulders. From there, it's a pleasant place to watch the brown pelicans and scurrying sandpipers.

Lodging is available in the comfortable and attractive new **Cypress Inn**. Located on the quiet frontage road, it claims to be the only beachfront inn for 50 miles in either direction, with magnificent ocean views available from every room, and delicious afternoon snacks and a complete breakfast included in the rate.

Just a few doors away, at 312 Mirada Road, the **Bach Dancing and Dynamite Society** presents classical concerts on Friday nights and jazz on Sunday afternoons. Reservations are not accepted, but it is a good idea to call ahead for the lineup and performance times; Tel: 726-4143.

A few doors farther down, the **Miramar Beach Inn** serves fresh seafood and steak dinners. Though the menu is on the pricey side, dinner on a Friday or Saturday night gives you a 50 percent reduction in the cover charge for their 10:00 P.M. rock show. Reservations are highly recommended; Tel: 726-9053.

Half Moon Bay

Oldest of the coastal towns in this area, Half Moon Bay has an interesting Main Street, which, uncutesied, looks much as it has for a century. Two shops are noteworthy: **Feed & Fuel**, a modern-day takeoff on the old-time general store, sells farm, pet, and garden supplies to locals, and has plenty of chicks, ducklings, bunnies, and other small farm animals for petting and purchase; in a more artistic vein, the **Cavanaugh Gallery** displays a large selection of spare Amish-style furnishings and country art.

Good use is made of local seafood and produce in the kitchen of the **San Benito House**. This attractively appointed dining room is part of an inn. Guest rooms upstairs feature solid walls, high ceilings, and bathrooms with old-fashioned tubs. A formal English garden invites relaxing contemplation, and a croquet lawn satisfies competitive urges. A deli supplies picnic fare, and a lively Western-style saloon provides the perfect spot for a nightcap.

You also can put your picnic together at the quaint **Cunha Country Store**, which has been in the same building for over 50 years, and the **Half Moon Bay Bakery**, which is still using its original brick ovens and is known for its French bread and Portuguese sweet bread. To enjoy all this good food, head west for Dunes Beach, a pleasant spot for beach picnicking.

South of here on Highway 1, which now passes through bucolic, rich farmland, there is a string of other special beaches. Picturesque and popular, **San Gregorio State Beach** often has sunshine when there is none elsewhere along this stretch of coast. An "unofficial" nude beach is located just to the north. Pomponio State Beach and Pescadero State Beach are also good choices; the latter has large sand dunes and a 210-acre waterfowl refuge with hiking trails.

In the town of San Gregorio, a half-mile drive inland via La Honda Road to Stage Road, you'll find the **Peterson and Alsford General Store**. Built in 1899, it is an old-fashioned country emporium stocking rural wares and picnic supplies, where locals gather around its long bar to chew the fat. Take Stage Road south for a 7-mile drive through the quiet coastal back country that ends almost in front of family-run **Duarte's Tavern**—a favored spot for a casual home-cooked meal—in the tiny agricultural town of Pescadero. Of special note are the restaurant's grilled fresh local fish and artichoke dishes, prepared using produce fresh from the local fields. (Artichokes are so plentiful in this area that a local high school has a cheer, "Artichokes to the left, artichokes to the right, stand up, sit down, fight, fight, fight!")

Eight miles south from Pescadero on Highway 1 is the **Pigeon Point Lighthouse**. Named after the first big ship that crashed on the rocks here, the lighthouse now houses a hostel, where inexpensive rooms are available to anyone willing to put up with the inconveniences associated with hosteling. Built in 1871, this is the second-tallest (115 feet) freestanding lighthouse in the U.S. Public tours are given on Sundays from 10:00 A.M. to 3:00 P.M.; call 879-0633 for reservations.

Año Nuevo State Reserve

Continuing south a few more miles brings you to Año Nuevo State Reserve, one of only two mainland breeding colonies in the world for the northern elephant seal. The huge seals return to this beach each year to bear their young and to mate again. Docent-guided tours, lasting two and a half hours and covering three miles, take visitors close enough to observe the seals basking in the sun or sleeping. Usually that is the extent of the activity to be seen, but occasionally one of the two-ton bulls roars into battle with a challenging male.

Though the seals look fairly harmless, they are unpredictable and can be dangerous—males are especially irritable—so the law dictates that visitors may get no closer than 20 feet.

The season runs something like this: The males arrive in early December (this is when most of the battles occur), the females arrive in January, and the pups begin to arrive in late January. (Birthing can sometimes be observed.) Mating occurs in February, when the population peaks, and then the seals begin to leave. Reservations are required; Tel: (800) 444-7275.

About 15 miles south of the reserve is Santa Cruz (see The Central Coast chapter).

PALO ALTO

Stanford, California's premier private university, stretches into the foothills at the edge of the sophisticated town of Palo Alto. With large tree-lined streets and impressive mansions on its outlying boulevards, the city historically has been home to upper-class residents, many of whom are affiliated with the university. More recently it has become known for being the heart of that nebulous area known as Silicon Valley.

Stanford University

Founded by Leland Stanford in 1885 on what had been his family's horse farm, Stanford University is dedicated to the memory of Stanford's son, who died of typhoid fever at the age of 15. It is now home to approximately 13,000 students.

Entry to the campus off busy El Camino Real (from San Francisco take Highway 101 and exit at the University Avenue exit, or take Highway 280 and get off at the Page Mill Road exit) is down aptly named Palm Drive, at the end of which you'll find the main quadrangle. The oldest part of the 8,180-acre university, this area features buildings of mission-style architecture, with thick stucco or sandstone walls and red-tile roofs. Hour-long campus tours, led by students, leave from the Visitor Information Booth daily at 11:00 A.M. and 2:15 P.M. during the school year. A self-guiding map is also available. Tours of the medical center (Tel: 723-4000) and the two-mile-long linear accelerator (Tel: 926-3300) are available by appointment.

Hoover Tower, Stanford's shorter version of the University of California's campanile, rises east of the main quadrangle. Standing 285 feet tall, it affords a panoramic view of the area and a visual orientation to the campus from its top. Its 35-bell carillon can be heard most days at noon and 5:00 P.M. A museum at the tower's base, part of the Hoover Institution on War, Revolution, and Peace, honors Stanford graduate Herbert Hoover and includes among its artifacts a couch and chair owned originally by President Abraham Lincoln and ultimately by Hoover.

Back down Palm Drive and to the west on Museum Way you'll find the **Stanford University Museum of Art**. Built in 1892 it is the oldest museum west of the Mississippi. It was also the first building to be built of structurally reinforced concrete. In spite of this reinforcement, it suffered severe damage in the 1989 earthquake and has been closed temporarily for repairs. (It is expected to remain closed into 1991. To check the status, call before visiting; Tel: 723-3469, or 723-4177 on weekends.) When open, the museum offers interesting California Indian exhibits, among them a canoe carved by the Yuroks from a single redwood log. Its eclectic collection also holds the gold spike that marked the meeting of the two sections of the transcontinental railroad in 1869.

An adjacent one-acre **Rodin Sculpture Garden** remains accessible. Tours are given on Wednesdays and Saturdays; call the museum for times. Together the museum and garden hold the world's second-largest collection of Rodin sculpture. (The largest is in Paris.)

Convenient lodging in the campus area can be found at the **Palo Alto Holiday Inn**, centrally located and offering the amenities typical of this chain. In addition to a large pool, which is particularly enjoyable here because of the generally good weather, it has an attractively landscaped garden area with a large *koi* pond.

The fashionable **Stanford Shopping Center**, the only shopping center in the world owned by a university, is located north of the main campus, just west of El Camino Real. Among its 150 shops are the Oakville Grocery, filled with esoteric foods; Smith and Hawken, an innovative California-based garden store; Gleim Jewelers, where the "world's largest emerald" is sometimes on display; and Schaub's Meat, Fish, and Poultry, where a unique "black steak" is available. The unusual **Tribal Eye** offers African antiquities and handicrafts (its only other branch is in Nairobi, Kenya), and six major department stores are also represented. Several restaurants here attract crowds even when the stores are closed. **Babbo's Pizzeria Restaurant** serves up the trendiest of pizza, and **Max's Opera Café** dishes up deli sandwiches ("ham" is provided by the servers, who double as opera-singing entertainers).

Beyond the shopping possibilities, the architectural design and landscaping of the center itself is of interest as is the art on display, which reflects the center's philosophy of making art accessible, easy to understand, and fun for viewers. After passing through the arched entrance, known as The Portico, turn right into vine-covered Palatine Court—named after one of Leland Stanford's prized racehorses. Avenues off of this area are named after more racehorses, and each is identified with a description of the champion and its bloodlines. Just beyond the soaring stone Wall Fountain at its end is a collection of exclusive boutiques known as the Inner Circle. Sprinkled in this area are bronze sculptures of people and animals by contemporary local sculptor Albert Guibara. Trees, flower planters, and 200 hanging baskets add to the landscaping.

Downtown Palo Alto

Follow Palm Drive east out of the campus and cross El Camino Real (where Palm Drive becomes University Avenue) to the center of the charming town of Palo Alto. Park your car and walk up one side of University Avenue, the main drag, and down the other along the brick-inlaid sidewalk. Most spots of interest are located on University in the six blocks between High Street and Webster Street. The side streets running off University also hold pleasant surprises.

As would be expected in a university town, bookstores are plentiful. Both **Stacey's** and the **Stanford Bookstore** have an extraordinary collection of technical computer books, from esoteric computer-science subjects to PC programming books. (One of the most unusual sights is the **Barbie Hall of Fame** at 460 Waverly Street. Opened in 1984 on the Barbie doll's 25th birthday, it is packed with over 7,000 dolls and accessories.)

Restaurants on this busy street are varied and casual. **The Good Earth** is a popular natural-foods coffee shop open daily for breakfast, lunch, and dinner. Specialty coffees and pastries can be found at **Il Fornaio**, where sidewalk seating is available in good weather. A few doors away, **Suzanne's Muffins** offers a different selection each day from among over 100 breakfast, dessert, and savory varieties. Nearby **Liddicoat's Market** houses a variety of ethnic food stalls and is home to the original Mrs. Field's Cookies stand.

Trendy Italian food is available at always-jammed Il Fornaio restaurant, just off University at 520 Cowper, cousin to the aforementioned café. Rustic pizzas are served here either the elegant interior or the sunny, peaceful courtyard in back. Reservations are highly recommended; Tel: 853-3888. The attractive Garden Court Hotel operates on the two floors above the restaurant and matches it in quality.

Several movie theaters on University are also worth mentioning. The Stanford Theater has been meticulously restored to its 1925-era grandeur by former Classics professor David Packard, son of computer tycoon David Packard. Plush red seats and elaborate ceiling paintings help take audiences back in time as they view classic Hollywood films shot before 1950. Silent films are often accompanied by an organist on the theater's Wurlitzer. Another old-time movie palace, the attractive mission-style Varsity Theatre, operates a few blocks away and features first-run movies.

Silicon Valley

Since the silicon chip was invented in a warehouse in Mountain View, it seems that everyone wants to see the Silicon Valley named after it. This isn't easy to do because it is an amorphous place. Unless you are extremely determined to see something in particular, you should avoid venturing into the morass of traffic jams that occurs farther into the heart of the area, which is around Santa Clara. Though partly populated with computer-related millionaires, this rapidly growing area has been unable to keep its population as neatly laid-out and bug-free as a good computer program.

You can get an easy and representative view of the many computer firms by driving on Page Mill Road, at the southern perimeter of the Stanford campus. There you will have a chance to see the boxy low-rise architecture and expansive lawn landscaping typical of these big-name, world-famous electronics firms. Stretched out along this road are Alza, Varian, IBM, and Hewlett-Packard. Because of the secretive and competitive nature of the electronics business, none offers public tours.

Should you wish to learn more, visit the Foothill College Electronics Museum in Los Altos Hills for historic and interactive exhibits. Take the Los Altos Hills/El Monte Road exit west off Highway 280 to the northwest corner of the Foothill College campus. Hours are Thursdays and Fridays from 9:30 A.M. to 4:30 P.M. and Sundays from 1:00 to 4:00 P.M., but it is best to double-check the hours by calling ahead; Tel: 960-4383.

Farther south on Highway 280 is the sprawling metropolis of **San Jose**, home to several interesting attractions. The **Rosicrucian Egyptian Museum**, at Park Avenue and Naglee, holds a collection highlighted by mummies, fine jewelery, and a full-size reproduction of a 4,000-year-old rock tomb— the only such tomb in the United States. The surrounding grounds are stunning, perfect for a stroll. The **Winchester Mystery House**, at 525 South Winchester Boulevard, seems to have grown in sympathy with its city. The story behind it is that Sarah Winchester, heir to the $20 million Winchester rifle fortune, believed that to make amends for a past wrong-doing she had to build additions to her home continuously, 24 hours a day. Her eccentric ideas resulted in some unusual features: asymmetrical rooms, narrow passageways, zigzag staircases, and doors opening into empty shafts. The tour takes in 110 rooms, climbs more than 200 steps, and covers almost a mile.

Filoli Estate

West of Palo Alto, in the wealthy suburban village of Wood-side, is the Filoli Estate. Under the protection of the National Trust for Historic Preservation, this 654-acre country king-dom features a 43-room modified Georgian mansion. Built in 1917 by architect Willis Polk, its ballroom is gilded with 200 pounds of gold extracted from the original owner's Empire Mine in Grass Valley (see The Gold Country chap-ter), but it is now best known as the exterior of the Carring-ton home shown at the beginning of TV's "Dynasty."

Tours of the 16 landscaped acres of mature formal gar-dens include such delights as two herbal gardens, a garden designed to resemble a stained-glass window at Chartres cathedral in France, and a practical cutting garden. Tours are scheduled Tuesdays through Saturdays, February through November. Reservations are required (Tel: 366-4640 or 364-2880), and children under 12 are not permitted.

GETTING AROUND
From San Francisco you can reach Marin County by car by crossing the Golden Gate Bridge. This area is also served by Golden Gate Transit ferries from the Ferry Building to Larkspur and Sausalito (Tel: 332-6600), and Red & White Fleet ferries from Pier 43½ to Sausalito and Tiburon (Tel:

546-2896). Gray Line offers bus tours to Sausalito and Muir Woods (Tel: 558-9400), and Golden Gate Transit (Tel: 453-2100) provides public bus service.

You can reach the Peninsula south of San Francisco by car by taking either coastal Highway 1 from 19th Avenue or inland routes 280 or 101. Palo Alto is also served by CalTrans (Tel: 557-8661), with a stop in Palo Alto at the eastern end of University Avenue, and SamTrans (San Mateo Transit System) buses (Tel: 761-7000), with a stop at the Stanford Shopping Center.

The East Bay is across the Bay Bridge from San Francisco. It is served by BART (Tel: 465-2278), with stations in Oakland near Lake Merritt (19th Street, 12th Street, and Lake Merritt stations) and in Berkeley near the University (Berkeley/downtown station). A.C. Transit buses run here (Tel: 839-2882) and a Red & White Fleet ferry operates from the Ferry Building to Jack London Square.

ACCOMMODATIONS REFERENCE
The area code for the Day Trips area is 415.

▶ **Alta Mira Hotel.** 125 Bulkley Avenue (P.O. Box 706), **Sausalito**, CA 94966. Tel: 332-1350; Fax: 331-3862.

▶ **Bayside Boat & Breakfast.** 40 Jack London Square, **Oakland**, CA 94607. Tel: (800) BOAT-BED.

▶ **Bed & Breakfast International.** 1181-B Solano Avenue, **Albany**, CA 94706. Tel: 525-4569.

▶ **Casa Madrona Hotel.** 801 Bridgeway, **Sausalito**, CA 94965. Tel: 332-0502 or (800) 288-0502; Fax: 332-2537.

▶ **Casa del Mar.** P.O. Box 238 (37 Belvedere Avenue), **Stinson Beach**, CA 94970. Tel: 868-2124.

▶ **Claremont Resort & Spa.** Ashby & Domingo avenues, **Oakland**, CA 94623. Tel: 843-3000 or (800) 323-7500.

▶ **Cypress Inn.** 407 Mirada Road, **Miramar**, CA 94019. Tel: 726-6002 or (800) 83-BEACH.

▶ **French Hotel.** 1538 Shattuck Avenue, **Berkeley**, CA 94709. Tel: 548-9930.

▶ **Garden Court Hotel.** 520 Cowper, **Palo Alto**, CA 94301. Tel: 322-9000.

▶ **Green Gulch Farm.** Star Route, **Sausalito**, CA 94965. Tel: 383-3134.

▶ **Holly Tree Inn.** P.O. Box 642, **Point Reyes**, CA 94956. Tel: 663-1554.

▶ **Hotel Durant.** 2600 Durant Avenue, **Berkeley**, CA 94704. Tel: 845-8981; in California, (800) 5-DURANT; outside California, (800) 2-DURANT.

► **Palo Alto Holiday Inn.** 625 El Camino Real, **Palo Alto**, CA 94301. Tel: 328-2800 or (800) HOLIDAY; Fax: 327-7362.

► **The Pelican Inn.** Star Route, **Muir Beach**, CA 94965. Tel: 383-6000.

► **Pigeon Point Lighthouse Hostel.** Pigeon Point Road (P.O. Box 477), **Pescadero**, CA 94060. Tel: 879-0633.

► **San Benito House.** 356 Main Street, **Half Moon Bay**, CA 94019. Tel: 726-3425.

► **Sausalito Hotel.** 16 El Portal, **Sausalito**, CA 94965. Tel: 332-4155.

► **Stinson Beach House.** P.O. Box 162, **Forest Knolls**, CA 94933. Tel: 488-9721.

THE WINE COUNTRY

By Tom Horton

Tom Horton, author of Super Span: The Golden Gate Bridge *and contributor to* The Penguin Guide to Hawaii, *is a ten-year resident of San Francisco. He owns a restaurant in the Bay Area.*

Although wine grapes are now grown in every region of California, with more than 770 bonded wineries producing 91 percent of the wine made in the U.S. and accounting for 72 percent of all the table wine consumed in America, the undisputed heart of California's Wine Country is Napa–Sonoma, two contiguous counties an hour's drive north of the Golden Gate Bridge. California's best wines are made here, and this is where you can do the most enjoyable wine touring. You'll see beautiful countryside dotted with historic wineries rising from the vineyards like European château, with old farmhouses and rustic brick buildings dolled up as Victorian bed-and-breakfast inns, with small towns full of fashionable restaurants, and with a multitude of other road-side or village diversions that make Napa–Sonoma Wine Country an enormously popular destination for Bay Area residents as well as millions of other U.S. and international visitors. (The Anderson Valley, a rising star on the wine scene, is an excellent route to the Mendocino coast and is covered in The Redwood Country chapter.)

It has become the style of this region to make more of

wine than the wine they make—wine has grown to represent a way of gracious living, where the fruits of the harvest
include fine food, art, music, fashion, architecture, and that
supremely Californian art of pursuing whatever is in vogue
with the utmost intensity while trying to appear completely
at leisure. Those from the San Francisco Bay Area who can
afford it, as well as increasing numbers from outside California and the U.S., have adopted Napa–Sonoma, most particularly the gold-plated Napa Valley, as the *très chic* address for a
country home. The rest of us must be content with a day, a
weekend, or a short vacation to sample the civilities of the
Wine Country.

MAJOR INTEREST

Winery tours and tastings
Restaurants
Early California history

Napa Valley
Yountville, St. Helena, Calistoga
Highway 29 wineries
Silverado Trail wineries
Calistoga mineral and mud baths
The Wine Train
Hot-air balloon rides

Sonoma County
Sonoma Plaza
Early California mission history
Sonoma Valley wineries
Jack London State Park
Russian River Valley wineries

NAPA VALLEY

State Highway 29 runs straight through the heart of the Napa
Valley. This heavily travelled road extends 29 miles north
from the sprawling, uninteresting town of Napa, the county's
urban business center, to the fashionably rural hamlets of
Yountville, St. Helena, and Calistoga, which attract the greatest attention and provide most of the valley's overnight
accommodations. Wineries are lined up along both sides of
this two-lane highway, as are many state historic landmarks
dating from the birth of the California wine industry here in
the Gold Rush era of the 1850s. Vineyards grow in all direc-

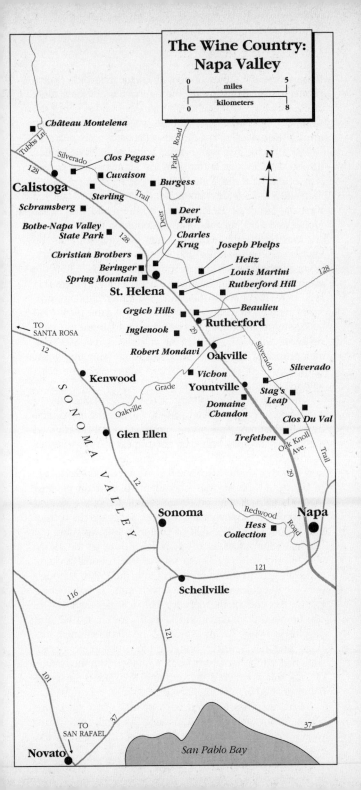

tions across the valley floor and up the hillsides. Tasting rooms are usually open daily throughout the year from about 10:00 A.M. to 4:30 P.M., although hours can vary in congested summer months and in wintertime, when vines are dormant, tourists are scattered, and the valley becomes more peaceful.

The romantic lure of the grape, however, has transformed the Napa Valley into a four-seasons attraction. The perfect port of entry for the Wine Country, Napa Valley is 34 miles long and 5 miles wide, with mountain ranges on the east and west and Mount St. Helena at the northern end. The Pacific Ocean and San Francisco Bay air-condition the valley with sea fogs during the summer, when the vineyards may be enveloped in a cool morning fog that burns away as afternoon temperatures climb toward 100 degrees F. On the average, however, neither heat nor humidity is excessively high here, and rain is unknown in summer, although normally plentiful in winter (an exception being the 1985–1990 succession of drought years). Spring and fall are the most delicious times. The soil left by volcanic eruptions is rich and deep and, by global standards, quite youthful; when Europeans first saw it, they knew immediately the Napa Valley was meant to make wine.

"The wine is bottled poetry," wrote Robert Louis Stevenson, who toured Napa Valley in 1880 and became intoxicated by its "crystal mountain purity." Prohibition in 1919 blighted the valley's fortunes, and even after repeal in 1933 wineries continued to fail, until a mere 25 remained by 1960. Then a new breed of vintners, schooled in the advanced technology of American wine making—and not unskilled in the modern methods of packaging an image to sell a product—joined the Prohibition survivors and led Napa Valley into its current era of fine wines. The rest of California followed, and the national wine renaissance was in full flower by the 1970s.

California wines began to receive international acclaim, and sales growth was unprecedented in the 1980s. Although the pace of California's $6 billion wine industry was sputtering by the end of the decade, with U.S. per capita wine consumption declining gradually each year since 1982, and despite growing health concerns, neo-Prohibitionist stirrings, and rising prices bringing more economic gloom, wine had still become as strongly identified with the glamor of California as beaches and sunshine. Nowhere is the image better defined than in the Napa Valley.

Napa Valley has matured into America's first viticulture region, in the style of the Bordeaux, Burgundy, and Champagne regions in France. The number of Napa wineries has grown from a couple dozen to more than 200, with 31,000 acres planted in grapes, compared to little more than 18,000 acres ten years ago. Growing along with the vineyards, at a rate that alarms conservationists who fear it will bury the natural charms of the valley, is Wine Country tourism. Although no accurate count of the number of visitors is possible, a widely accepted claim—or criticism—is that Napa Valley is second only to Disneyland as a California tourist attraction. Visitors no longer come just to tour wineries and taste free samples, but to eat in the highly publicized restaurants, sleep in the Victorian atmosphere of country inns, and shop for tee-shirts, picnic goods, knicknacks—anything with the look or taste of Wine Country.

Because the Napa Valley and the adjacent Sonoma Valley are an easy one-hour drive from San Francisco, the Wine Country is a popular day trip for visitors staying in San Francisco hotels. Napa Valley, where so many wineries are concentrated along one 20-mile stretch of Highway 29, is more suitable for such a day trip than Sonoma, where there are fewer wineries scattered over a much larger area. With an early-morning start from San Francisco you can spend an enjoyable day in the Napa Valley and still return to your San Francisco hotel at a reasonable hour. Although the valley is more crowded during the summer months, this is still the best time of year for day trips because of the extra hours of sunlight during Pacific Daylight Saving Time (from the first Sunday in April to the last Sunday in October).

A long day in the Napa Valley, beginning when most tasting rooms open at 10:00 A.M., could include short tasting-room stops at several of the wineries along Highway 29 and at least one winery tour (one tour is enough for a day), and still leave time for lunch or early dinner at one of the many fine restaurants in or near the small valley towns of Yountville, St. Helena, and Calistoga. Visitors who want to have lunch or dinner in the best known Napa Valley restuarants, including most of those recommended in this chapter, should call as far in advance as possible to book a reservation—the most popular restaurants here are hard to get into almost any weekend of the year, and any day or night during the summer months.

While you can enjoy the scenery and an introductory taste of Napa Valley on a day trip, this does not mean that the Wine Country is primarily a day-trip experience. On the contrary, you cannot fully appreciate all that this region has to offer unless you spend a number of days and nights exploring it. How many days you might want to devote depends on the depth of your interest in wine and how much you prefer a country atmosphere to the attractions of a city such as San Francisco. A real wine enthusiast could easily devote a whole one- or two-week vacation to touring Napa–Sonoma Wine Country, while the average traveller might be quite satisfied with a two- or three-day stay.

The recommended route to Napa Valley from San Francisco is across the Golden Gate Bridge and north on the U.S. 101 freeway through Marin County. Eight miles past the town of San Rafael (marked by freeway exit signs), take the Vallejo-Napa exit off U.S. 101 onto State Highway 37. Continue on Highway 37 seven miles until the Sonoma turnoff onto State Highway 121, which leads north and then east 11 miles to the junction with State Highway 29, the road to and through the Napa valley.

Touring the Wineries

The larger wineries offer free guided tours and tastings; some smaller wineries have tasting rooms (not always complimentary), but no guided tours, while others welcome visitors to the winery and the retail sales room but offer no tastings or tours without appointments. Many of the most elite and out-of-the-way wineries can be toured, and wines tasted, by calling ahead for appointed hours, and it is worth the effort if you have more than a casual interest in wine (such places are discussed in detail below). You will find that part of the charm of the small wineries is that the person working the tasting or sales room may be one of the owners, or the owners' son, daughter, niece, or nephew.

Unfortunately, a reliable formula is that the size of the crowds will be nearly in direct proportion to the size and accessibility of the winery. Some of Napa's most historic wineries, and small new wineries with strategic locations, have become the Wine Country counterpart to San Francisco's Fisherman's Wharf, drawing hordes of tourists into tasting rooms that are equally devoted to overpriced merchandise bearing some relationship, however farfetched, to wine. Governing authorities have tried to stem the tide of one-acre wineries, situated primarily to cash in on the souvenir shoppers, by passing legislation requiring all new wineries to be no more than an "agricultural facility for the fermenting and processing of grape juice into wine," and ordering that all wines produced here contain a minimum of 75 percent Napa grapes.

Even the wine is no longer a good buy at most wineries, as retail wine shops in Napa and throughout the Bay Area offer enormous selections of premium wines at prices lower than what you will find at the wineries. Serious wine collectors, however, may find special varieties and rare vintages sold at the wineries that are not commonly available elsewhere.

Despite these drawbacks, selective touring and tasting of the Napa Valley can be as relaxing, invigorating, or educational as you care to make it. The country air is a natural tonic for the urbanized condition, and even those who arrive without any incumbent interest in wine are likely to leave with a new understanding of how and why it is made: to be enjoyed, in moderation and in the company of good food.

Many of the oldest, most famous wineries are immediately accessible off Highway 29, which is where you will encounter the full parking lots and tasting rooms. But take any of the little roads off Highway 29 in either direction and they will lead you to the smaller wineries tucked away in quieter pockets of the valley and on the hillsides. Another alternative to Highway 29 is the Silverado Trail, a two-lane highway looping along the eastern flank of the valley. Numerous wineries are located near this less-congested artery (we discuss the Trail after Calistoga, at the head of the valley).

Keep in mind that it is impossible to visit more than a few wineries in the same day, at least in any civilized fashion, and that after one or two winery tours you may have seen more than enough grape crushers and steel fermenting tanks. A selective mix between the big wineries, with impressive history on display, and the smaller, out-of-the-way wineries that occupy historic sites and make small lots of high-quality wines, will give you an overview of 130 years of Napa Valley wine making.

Entering the Valley

After you pass through the town of Napa, driving north on Highway 29, one of the first side roads you will see is Redwood Road. Turn left, and after about 20 tree-shaded curves, you will arrive at 4411 Redwood Road, site of the unusual **Hess Collection Winery**, perhaps the most striking example of Napa Valley's penchant for art in the vineyards, as well as wealthy Europeans' fondness for buying up Napa Valley land.

The winery tour is perfunctory, but save at least an hour for viewing the Hess Collection of more than 130 provocative works of contemporary art by well-known American and European painters. The 13,000-square-foot art gallery, three-story stone winery originally built in 1901, and 900 acres of hillside vineyards are the property of European entrepreneur Donald Hess, who made his fortune in real estate and Swiss Alps mineral water, then spent a nice piece of it converting these historic buildings on the slopes of Mount Veeder into a winery best known for its art collection.

Back on Highway 29, about 2 miles north of the town of Napa at 1160 Oak Knoll Avenue (between Highway 29 and Silverado Trail), **Trefethen Vineyards** is one of the finest of the small family wineries. Surrounded by nearly 600 acres of vineyards, the tasting room is inside an 1886 wooden building that is the oldest three-story gravity-flow wooden winery in Napa. (Gravity-flow wineries eliminated the need for pumps by starting the process on the third floor of a building where the grapes are crushed, letting gravity move the juice to second-floor tanks for fermentation, and then to the ground floor for aging and storage.)

Yountville

Yountville, a small town that serves as a gateway to the Napa Valley, is a concentration of inns, restaurants, and shops, with a defunct train station at one end of town, an old graveyard at the other, and vineyards all around. **Vintage 1870** incorporates the town's major shopping into one location, an old brick winery remodeled as a complex of boutiques, art galleries, and antiques stores. Shops such as **Basket Bazaar** and **Vintage Country Treasures** specialize in country-style gifts and foods, and for a soothing interlude in between shops you can enjoy the romantic slide show of the Wine Country with classical music in the Keith Rosenthal Theatre.

Your best restaurant choices in Yountville are all on the same few blocks of Washington Street. Begin with **The Diner**, the place for breakfast and a source of wholesome, inexpensive meals throughout the day and early evening, serving everything from traditional diner food to excellent Mexican dishes. Another local favorite is the **French Laundry**, every bit as unusual as its name: An old French laundry in a tiny stone-and-redwood structure has been converted to a family restaurant serving the kind of French country food that keeps the little place packed; Tel: 944-2380. Garlic lovers are directed to **Piatti**, a trendy trattoria with an open kitchen serving distinctive Italian meals of pasta, grilled meats and fish, oven-baked breads and pizzas, and daily risotto specials; Tel: 944-2070. **California Café**, a Bay Area chain of super-slick bar-and-grills, specializes in California cuisine served in a neon-bright dining room or at outdoor tables; Tel: 944-2330. **Washington Street Restaurant** offers contemporary food in a red-brick atmosphere, or you can sit outdoors on a patio overlooking one of the few patches of open green space that hasn't been planted in grapes; Tel: 944-2406. A good break from wines and the ubiquitous California cuisine is Mexican food with beer and margaritas at the festive **Compadres**. For eating alfresco, **Gerhard's Sausage Kitchen** makes the kind of exotic sausages that give a picnic basket a real lift, and the **Groezinger Wine Company** is a good place to shop for wine.

One of the Napa Valley's largest and most luxurious country inns, the **Vintage Inn** in Yountville is an example of the trend toward blending modern comforts into a country environment. There are 80 guest rooms, including two-story villas, clustered amidst three acres of gardens and man-made babbling brooks fed by numerous fountains. All the rooms have wood-burning fireplaces as well as air-conditioning, antique-style ceiling fans, color cable television, and mini-refrigerators. There are also tennis courts, a heated lap pool, and rides at dawn in the inn's own hot-air balloon. **Magnolia Hotel,** built in 1873, is a fashionable stone-and-brick bed and breakfast in the center of town that welcomes the 20th century with a pool and Jacuzzi. Romantic couples will also find intimate bed-and-breakfast accommodations inside the brick walls of the **Bordeaux House** and **Burgundy House**, both downtown as well. Other possibilities are the comfortable **Napa Valley Lodge**, a modern, reasonably priced, well-managed motel with large rooms and a nice pool area on the edge of town adjacent to Highway 29, or **The Webber Place**, a red farmhouse with a homey atmosphere, on the outskirts of Yountville. Three miles south of town, **Oak Knoll Inn** is one of the valley's ultraelegant bed-and-breakfast inns.

A short distance south of Yountville, on the west side of Highway 29, is **Domaine Chandon**, a notably successful California-French hybrid. Tastings are not free here—the product is expensive sparkling wine—but you can purchase flutes of Chandon and enjoy them on a sunny patio. Tours give an excellent short course on *méthode champenoise,* the traditional French method of making Champagne, or sparkling wine, which is how the French insist we identify any sparkling wine made outside the province of Champagne. Möet-Hennessy of France, producers of some of the world's great Champagnes, was a pioneer of European investments that have led to widespread purchases of vineyards and construction of multi-million-dollar wineries and showcase

estates throughout Napa–Sonoma. Möet-Hennessy invested
$12 million in this 900-acre vineyard, which began produc-
ing sparkling wine in 1977; millions more have been spent
since on expansion.

Chandon also helped raise the level of dining in the Napa
Valley, which was rarely notable until **Domaine Chandon
Restaurant** opened. This elegant, expensive restaurant is
one of the loveliest places to dine in the valley, with an open-
air view of the vineyards that makes lunch a delight and with
superb service that goes well with the refined dinner atmosphere and the California-French cuisine. Reservations are
essential; Tel: 944-2892.

A mile's drive north of Yountville, and easy to spot on the
west side of Highway 29, is **Mustards Grill**. Reservations are
generally needed at all of Napa Valley's better restaurants, but
Mustards seems to have been fully booked since its opening.
(This was one of the early triumphs for the Real Food Group,
which went on to open the wildly successful Fog City Diner in
San Francisco and Tra Vigne in St. Helena, among others.)
Dining at Mustards is like finding the most popular bar and
grill in any large city—but on the side of a country road. The
upbeat mood is crowded, noisy, and still comfortably casual,
with a big open kitchen that uses wood-burning grills and
ovens to cook delicious ribs, chops, Sonoma rabbit, and West
Coast and Hawaiian fish; Tel: 944-2424.

From Yountville
to St. Helena

Vichon Winery, owned by the Robert Mondavi family, is
north of Yountville and a short drive west off Highway 29 on
the Oakville Grade Road. This top-quality small winery is
high enough to give its visitors a grand view of the valley
below; picnic tables under shady oak trees are the perfect
place to share the view with a bottle of Vichon's trademark
wine, Chevrignon. The ultimate in picnic supplies can be
purchased at the **Oakville Grocery**, a 19th-century crossroads general store and valley landmark that remains a
grocery in name only; dusty pickup trucks may be parked
here, but Mercedes are just as common at this store that is
country on the outside, foie gras and quail eggs on the
inside. Since 1975 Oakville Grocery has satisfied the valley
taste for the finest French pâtés, Sonoma cheeses and sausages, crusty loaves of French bread, and an assortment of
fancy foods from regional farms and foreign lands.

Oakville is Cabernet country, and two of the best producers of that variety are **Groth**, with tours and tastings by
appointment (Tel: 255-7466), and **Silver Oak**, which has daily
tours by appointment (Tel: 944-8808) and a $5.00 charge for
the tasting room on Oakville Cross Road east of town.

From Oakville north to Rutherford and on to St. Helena,
you will pass winery after winery. Among the most popular
for guided tours and free tastings is **Robert Mondavi**, a
powerful draw for the name as well as for the excellence of
the tour and the artistic merits of the winery; **Inglenook**,
for the history preserved in this high, handsome, ivy-
covered winery built in 1879 by Finnish sea captain Gus-
tave Niebaum (where casks of wine are still aged in the
caves originally dug into the slope of the Mayacamas foothills); **Beaulieu**, makers of renowned Cabernet Sauvignons
since 1900, who provide one of the most informative of all
the winery tours; and **Grgich Hills**, where French owner–
wine maker Mike Grgich is famous for his Chardonnays
and is now trying to establish his Cabernets on an equal
level. **Louis Martini** also merits a stop, if only to toast the
family that has been making fine Napa Valley wines since
1933 without losing sight of the Martini philosophy of wine
making: good wine that pairs well with food, made so you
can drink it right away, and priced so you can afford it.

At the other end of the spectrum, the roadside tasting room
of **Heitz Wine Cellars**, a small family winery, looks mundane,
with no visible reason for a visitor to be impressed—unless
you arrive with foreknowledge of Joe Heitz and his Heitz
Martha's Vineyard Cabernet Sauvignon, perhaps California's
most prestigious wine. Older vintages command hundreds of
dollars per bottle, and when the 1985 Martha's Vineyard
Cabernet was released for public sale in January 1990, a line
began forming outside the Heitz tasting and sales rooms
before dawn. By noon there was a traffic jam, and customers
waited up to three hours to buy meager allotments of the $50-
a-bottle vintage that was gone by the end of the day.

St. Helena

St. Helena is large enough to have a real Main Street,
complete with ordinary shops, cafés, and hardware stores
occupying turn-of-the-century stone buildings, but small
enough to retain its easygoing personality while all around it
the resident population steadily grows apace with the tourist
traffic and the requisite supply of new places to eat, sleep,
and shop. There is a classic old Main Street hotel, **Hotel St.**

Helena, refurbished in the Victorian style. The public library houses the **Napa Valley Wine Library** and the **Silverado Museum's** Robert Louis Stevenson memorabilia, but St. Helena would be just another small town where farmers buy supplies and farmers' wives shop, except the crop being farmed here is thousand-dollars-a-ton wine grapes and little St. Helena is the hub of the prosperous Napa Valley wine community.

Among the ever-growing number of pricey restaurants that have sprung up to serve visitors to the valley, **Tra Vigne,** another of the Real Food Group's string of hits, is a star. A massive brick building and courtyard of almost baronial proportions at 1050 Charter Oak Avenue, once cold and overbearing, has been transformed by the exuberant Italian style of food and wine into a backdrop as dramatic as grand opera. Soaring ceilings and huge arched windows overlook a cavernous dining room flooded with unusual lighting and hung with strings of garlic and brightly colored peppers. The open kitchen delivers hearty Tuscan-style food: chewy breads, wonderfully flavorful *antipasti,* bold pizzas, unusual salad combinations, veal, grilled meats, and seafood. It's expensive but worth it; Tel: 963-4444.

Trilogy, by contrast, is small, intimate, and light on the palate, with nouvelle California-French cuisine, brass chandeliers, and classical music, as well as courtyard dining in good weather; it's at 1234 Main Street. Tel: 963-5507. The latest darling of the food critics is **Terra** (1345 Railroad Avenue; Tel: 963-8931), thanks to owner-chef Hiroyoshi Stone's unusual dishes, made with an imaginative mixture of Japanese-Italian and other European-Asian touches, while **Miramonte,** one of the valley's first great restaurants, remains a special place. Miramonte, at 1327 Railroad Avenue, is small but has both stunning decor and food, California-French cuisine in the atmosphere of an exclusive little hunting lodge; Tel: 963-3970.

If you are planning a picnic (and many of the wineries will welcome you), **Napa Valley Olive Oil Manufacturing Co.,** which has been making olive oil for nearly a century, is also a good place to buy cheese, salami, and Italian foods. **Model Bakery's** brick oven delivers marvelous breads and daily pizza specials; cheese and other gourmet picnic items are also available. **V. Sattui Winery,** in addition to its wines, has a large deli shop featuring some 200 different cheeses, and **St. Helena Wine Merchant** and **The Bottle Shop** are two of the valley's best wine shops.

There are several notable inns in St. Helena if you wish to

stay overnight. **Ambrose Bierce House**, a luxury bed and breakfast built in 1872 and within walking distance of downtown, was the California author's occasional home until 1913, when he vanished in Mexico. Although the **Creekside Inn** is in the heart of St. Helena, its three guest rooms are sheltered by large oaks, and White Sulphur Creek meanders past the garden patio.

Many of the best St. Helena lodging choices are just outside town. **Harvest Inn**, built among vineyards off Highway 29, is a sprawling, lavish hostelry with an antique English Tudor look and all the modern conveniences of luxury-size rooms with fireplaces and TVs, a pool, and a Jacuzzi. **Villa St. Helena** has only three guest rooms, but they're elegant, as is the wood-paneled library and parlor, the manicured lawn, large pool, and the orchid solarium. Verandahs offer splendid views of the grounds, with their flower gardens, and of the valley. The larger **Wine Country Inn** offers 25 antiques-decorated rooms with country views, some with fireplaces, private balconies, and patios. **Bartel's Ranch**, secluded in a quiet valley, has the natural charm of country surroundings, and provides just three guest rooms, which have the comforts of private baths, views, and a pool with Jacuzzi. **Zinfandel Inn**, an English Tudor–style home surrounded by vineyards, has three rooms with private baths and antique touches such as brass and four-poster beds. And in a Victorian vein, **The Farmhouse** is a bed and breakfast in the Joseph Phelps vineyards featuring a spring-fed swimming pool and the chance to hike or jog through the Phelps vineyards.

St. Helena Wineries

Some of the valley's most historic wineries are located in St. Helena or north of town. **Beringer**, built north of town in 1876 by German immigrants Jacob and Frederick Beringer, is the oldest continuously operated winery in Napa Valley—and continuously crowded with visitors who are led through the wine caves that tunnel deep into the limestone hillside, and then are welcomed to the spectacular Rhine House, Frederick's gorgeous gingerbread mansion now serving the multitudes as the Beringer tasting room and gift emporium.

Charles Krug was the valley's first winery, founded in 1861 by the Frenchman Charles Krug, who died in 1902. The winery was revived in 1943 when Cesare Mondavi bought it to make wine with his two sons, Peter and Robert, who years later would engage in one of the valley's nastiest family feuds. Robert Mondavi left the family-owned winery in the early 1960s, built his own several miles down the valley (near Oakville, as mentioned), and quickly became one of the biggest names and dominant personalities in California wine, followed in turn by his two sons who now help run the Robert Mondavi Winery. Peter Mondavi and his two sons still own and operate Charles Krug, which has gone on to become one of Napa's largest producers.

Spring Mountain is a nice destination for a drive through the hillside vineyards above St. Helena on Spring Mountain Road. The original 1885 Victorian home has been faithfully restored and an impressive new winery built out from the hillside tunnels; the wines are first rate, and, last but certainly not least in the eyes of some visitors, Spring Mountain is the location used for the popular TV series "Falcon Crest." **Christian Brothers**, back on Highway 29 north of St. Helena, has been making wine in Napa Valley since 1930, and since 1888 **Greystone Cellars** has been one of the valley's most impressive monuments. Built as the largest stone cellar in the world, Greystone is still used as the Christian Brothers' aging cellars (the modern wine-making facility is located south of St. Helena), while serving as a magnet for visitors who are awed by volcanic stone walls three stories high and heroic Roman arches rising above some three acres of cellar space. Enhancing tours of Greystone is one of the better displays of wine history, including Brother Timothy's famous collection of antique corkscrews.

Farther north, **Schramsberg**'s location atop Diamond Mountain, near Calistoga, dates from 1862 and was given lasting literary fame in 1880 when Robert Louis Stevenson wrote romantically of Jacob Schram's "cellars dug far into the hillside, and resting on pillars like a bandit's cave—all trimness, varnish, flowers, and sunshine, among the tangled wildwood." Jack Davies revived the defunct historical landmark in 1965 and for several years has made here what many consider to be California's best sparkling wine. The natural charms that enthralled Stevenson have been carefully protected, and although Schramsberg is not normally open to the public, guided tours can be arranged by appointment (Tel: 942-4558).

Sterling Vineyards nearby is a different trip indeed: You pay $5.00 to ride an aerial tram to the top of a bluff high above the valley, where there's a self-guided tour of Sterling's gleaming white monastic buildings that make up one of Napa's most unusual wine-making facilities. Almost in Calistoga, **Clos Pegase**'s excellent wines have been less controversial than its winery. Opened in 1987, this architectural curiosity, a structure of massive proportions, has upset the valley's old-timers and startled many a wide-eyed visitor.

Calistoga

Calistoga is the one town in the Napa Valley that could stand on its own merits without wine as the *raison d'être*. There's a certain crusty flavor to Calistoga akin to an Old West town where the main street is lined with white, two-story wood-frame buildings, dusty boots and crumpled cowboy hats are not out of place, and at the end of town there's a train depot. And, of course, there are the hot mineral springs and the mud baths. Perhaps because it rests where the valley ends, with Mount St. Helena and surrounding hills rising up sharply to the north, Calistoga has an identity of its own apart from the Napa Valley. For all that, it is also a fun place to hang your hat after a grueling day in the valley's tasting rooms.

The hot springs have been Calistoga's chief visitor attraction since the 1860s, when San Francisco's flamboyant Gold Rush millionaire Sam Brannan, looking to increase his fortune, decided to make this the Saratoga of California. The apocryphal version of history is that Sam got his tongue twisted on Champagne, and his boastful forecast came out "Calistoga of Sarafonia." It had a nice ring to it, so the name stuck.

There are spas in and all around town, most of them with overnight lodging similar to motel accommodations, but you can also drop in for a quick mineral or mud bath, facial, and invigorating body rub. Notable are **Dr. Wilkinson's Hot Springs**, **Calistoga Spa Hot Springs**, **Golden Haven Hot Springs**, and **Nance's Hot Springs**. Northern California's two top producers of bottled mineral waters, Calistoga Mineral Water Company and Crystal Geyser, also do business here: Calistoga Mineral Water is bottled at a plant on the Silverado Trail, and Crystal Geyser's plant is in town and open to visitors.

You can find deluxe accommodations without the hot springs in the middle of town at the Art Deco **Mount View Hotel**, which has a nice pool area, as well as impressive California cuisine in the **Mount View Restaurant** and some after-dark action in the hotel's cocktail lounge. **Brannan Cottage Inn**, within walking distance of town, is an award-winning restoration of Sam Brannan's 1862 Greek Revival guesthouses, with six air-conditioned rooms and private

baths. **Wayside Inn** and **Wine Way Inn**, both close to downtown, are among the numerous bed-and-breakfast choices.
Calistoga Country Lodge is a restful haven in the hills north
of town, and **Larkmead Country Inn**, south of Calistoga, is
another quiet retreat.

Napa Valley's fashionable dining trend has yet to fully
assert itself in Calistoga. **Calistoga Inn**, which operates its
own brewery with outdoor beer garden, serves the town's
best dinners, with an emphasis on fresh seafood. **All Seasons
Café** is the Calistoga version of a provincial French bistro
with an impressive, unusually low-priced wine list, and **Silverado Restaurant and Tavern** is the local favorite, a spirited
gathering place known for its outstanding wine list but not
for its food.

Chateau Montelena, about 2 miles north of Calistoga off
Highway 29 at 1429 Tubbs Lane, is rich in history and graced
by a little lake ideal for picnics. This well-preserved 1882
stone winery is a small French-designed castle built into the
slope of a hill, where, in charming contrast, it faces a tranquil
setting of Chinese origins—Jade Lake, the heritage of a
former owner who built bridges in zigzag patterns (to con-
fuse evil spirits) to two small islands adorned with bright
red teahouse pagodas.

Silverado Trail

Silverado Trail begins northeast of Calistoga, then winds
south along the lower mountain slopes to the southern end of
the Napa Valley, giving you a peaceful alternative to Highway
29. Or, for a bit of both, there are numerous crossroads that
make it easy to alternate between Highway 29 and Silverado
Trail as you work your way up and down the valley. Commercialism is not intrusive on the Trail, and interesting wineries
are located along this road, which is high enough to provide
panoramic views of the valley. The Trail is the link to a new
wave of wineries and vineyards that have taken to higher
ground in the last 20 years as land on the valley floor became
unavailable or prohibitively expensive.

Cuvaison, just south of Calistoga, was built in 1970 and is
recognized as one of Napa's finest labels. This Spanish
mission–style winery of bright white walls and red-tile roof
is a striking centerpiece in a panorama of vineyards, and a
perfect place to picnic is its landscaped grounds. If you are
serious about visiting out-of-the-way wineries, take twisting
Deer Park Road to **Burgess Cellars**, a small family winery
near the top of Howell Mountain. This classic 1880s stone-

and-redwood winery has cellars tunneled into the hillside and vineyards planted down the slopes. A short distance below it on the same road is **Deer Park Winery**, a 1980s revival of the type of stone gravity-flow wineries that were built throughout the Napa hillsides in the late 19th century.

Two miles east of St. Helena is **Meadowood Resort**, which receives the highest recommendation for the ultimate in deluxe Napa Valley lodging. The resort occupies 256 heavily wooded acres that resemble a secret emerald green forest. The 58 guest rooms and suites, all luxurious, are well distributed among several small lodges nestled among the trees and provide a choice of views of the nine-hole golf course, the tennis courts, the pool, or the croquet courts. The serenity is complemented by superb nouvelle California cuisine in the romantic **Starmont Restaurant**, where you would be well advised to book a dinner reservation regardless of where you are spending the night; Tel: 963-3646.

Joseph Phelps, a winery on Taplin Road, occupies the lower slope of the hills above Silverado Trail. Founded in 1974, Phelps makes a number of consistently high quality wines. Farther south along the Trail, on Rutherford Hill Road, the **Rutherford Hill Winery**, founded 1976, has interesting tours of the more than 30,000 square feet of caves bored into the hillside and now filled with wine aging in French oak barrels.

Just south of Rutherford Hill Winery you will see the rustic elegance of **Auberge du Soleil**, one of the valley's most fashionable retreats for dining or lodging. Built at considerable cost on the side of the mountain, thereby giving guests spectacular views of the valley, the Auberge has 48 expensive rooms and suites, where natural wood is matched with leather furniture, and terra-cotta tile floors lead to private decks. The showpiece restaurant, designed by an architect and an interior decorator from the ranks of San Francisco society, has a Southwestern earth-tone color scheme and striking architectural flourishes. The food here is a Wine Country version of haute cuisine, better known for the high level of prices than the quality, but the views are the best of any restaurant in the valley; Tel: 963-1211.

Silverado Vineyards, well signposted and easily accessible on the west side of the Trail, commands a high piece of ground and a lofty reputation built swiftly by wine maker Jack Stuart. Owned by Walt Disney's widow (see if you can find the portrait of Mickey hiding in the stained glass), the ultramodern winery, built in 1981, is housed in an early-California–style structure and is now the home of outstanding Cabernets, Merlots, and Chardonnays. The reception inside Silverado's tasting room is most pleasant and the views from the sunny verandah are wonderful.

Two miles south of Yountville, **Stag's Leap Wine Cellars**, a small family winery just east of Silverado Trail in a grove of oak trees, is a sight to make Cabernet lovers' hearts beat faster. Its vineyards planted in 1970 and its winery completed two years later, Stag's Leap has been a bench mark of great Napa Valley Cabernet Sauvignon ever since. Indeed, we're crossing serious red wine country now, for not a mile later, on the same side of the road and still within the Stag's Leap viticultural area, is **Clos Du Val**. Founded in 1972 and still owned and operated by French wine maker Bernard Portet, the winery produces Cabernets, Merlots, and Zinfandels that are among California's best. In contrast to Napa Valley's 19th-century architectural and wine-making heritage, Clos Du Val offers an authentic taste of the traditional French approach. The Clos Du Val tour (by appointment; Tel: 252-6711) followed by guided tastings is an enjoyable way to take an excellent lesson in wine-making philosophy. **Silverado Resort and Country Club**, at the southern end of the Trail, is a toney resort that tries its best to identify with the Napa Valley wine scene but is mainly an attraction for golfers. Deluxe accommodations are available in modern condominium-style units, from studios to three bedrooms.

Other Napa Valley
Activities

The controversial **Napa Valley Wine Train** was universally damned from inception by the valley's old guard but has received rave reviews from paying passengers since it finally overcame legal roadblocks and inaugurated service in the fall of 1989. The train tour was the brainstorm of determined San Francisco millionaire Vincent DeDomenico (he also gave America Rice-A-Roni). DeDomenico took some of the millions Quaker Oats paid for his company and bought Southern Pacific's near-defunct Napa Valley line, which dated back to the 1860s when trains carried tourists to the Calistoga mineral baths. DeDomenico improved the roadbed, bought turn-of-the-century Pullman cars and 1950s diesel streamliners, and stood his ground against a great public outcry from opponents who said diesel fumes would pollute the air and foul the vineyards, trains crossing country roads would cause traffic jams and accidents, and, worst of all, the train would bring more tourists into a valley already overcrowded with them. Protesters succeeded in derailing the original plans for the train to make scheduled stops at selected wineries, and the organized opposition has not abandoned its hope of completely stopping the train service. For now, however, the Napa Valley Wine Train is providing one swell ride.

Prices range from $25.00 per person for a lunch excursion to $45.00 for a dinner ride (wines are available but not included in the price). You board at the Main Depot, 1275 McKinstry Street in the town of Napa and then spend two and a half to three and a half hours, depending on whether you've chosen lunch or dinner, riding the rails in nostalgic luxury. The Pullman cars are plushly carpeted and lavishly decorated with velvet curtains, etched glass, and chandeliers; good food and wine is served at linen-covered tables set with fine china, Sheffield silver, and crystal stemware. But all this soon takes a back seat to the panorama of Napa Valley passing in review outside your window. The train rolls nonstop (but at a leisurely speed, never exceeding 20 miles per hour) from the northwest edge of Napa to St. Helena, where the engines are unhooked and reconnected for the trip back. There is one seating for dining on the way to St. Helena and a second seating on the return, with an inviting lounge where you may sip your pre-meal wine or relax afterwards. The Wine Train has been heavily booked in advance, especially during summer months and weekends; Tel: (707) 253-2111.

Hot-air balloons have long been a popular way to see the Napa Valley from a different perspective. Because afternoon winds are too strong, balloons are launched at sunrise. The gondola, or basket, holding up to seven passengers, soars for about an hour in magnificent silence above the valley, and the landing is traditionally followed with a Champagne celebration. Balloon companies are numerous, so the most convenient way to go is with the one that launches closest to wherever you're staying; Adventures Aloft at Yountville's Vintage 1870 shopping plaza (Tel: 707-255-8688), Napa Valley Balloons (Tel: 707-253-2224), which launches from the Domaine Chandon winery, and Once In a Lifetime (Tel: 707-942-6541) at 1546 Lincoln in Calistoga, are recommended. Be sure to phone first: They launch from different sites depending on several conditions. Glider and bi-plane rides are also a popular valley thrill offered by the Calistoga Soaring Center (Tel: 707-942-5592) at 1546 Lincoln. Napa

Valley has also become one of California's premier destinations for bicyclists, who love the network of country roads (rentals are available throughout the valley).

While the whole valley seems to resemble one giant picnic venue, there are two state parks available: **Bothe–Napa Valley State Park** above St. Helena, with picnicking, camping, swimming, and hiking trails (one of which leads to the nearby Old Bale Grist Mill, a flour mill with a spectacular water wheel built in 1846 and restored to working condition); and **Robert Louis Stevenson State Park**, north of Calistoga on Highway 29 near the summit of Mount St. Helena, with picnicking and hiking.

A variety of special events such as wine auctions, music festivals, and cooking workshops brightens the Napa Valley scene throughout the year, but mainly from June to early October. The Napa Valley Wine Auction, held annually in June at Meadowood Resort, is the valley's premier event; Tel: (707) 963-5246. Other annual attractions include the Concours d'Elegance vintage motor car show in June at Silverado Resort and Country Club, June music concerts at Domaine Chandon, the Summer Jazz Festival at Robert Mondavi Winery in July and August, and the Charles Krug Winery harvest festival in September. The Napa Valley Conference & Visitors Bureau can supply information; Tel: (707) 226-7459.

SONOMA COUNTY

Sonoma, in contrast to a compact Napa Valley that is devoted almost entirely to vineyards and wine making, is a large, sprawling, agriculturally diversified county to the west of the Napa Valley that extends all the way from the Sonoma Valley north to Mendocino County and west to the Pacific Ocean. There are actually two primary wine regions here, the Sonoma Valley (west of the Napa Valley on the other side of Sugarloaf Ridge) and the Russian River Valley (northwest of the Sonoma Valley), but neither has the exclusive concentration of vineyards, wineries, and wine-related pleasures aligned in the tight, convenient order of neighboring Napa Valley. There is far more territory to be covered in any tour of Sonoma Wine Country, but it is a rewarding journey for anyone who can enjoy a leisurely drive through lovely countryside with an occasional stop at a winery or a shrine of early California history. Although some population centers are struggling with explosive growth, principally the towns of Sonoma and Santa Rosa, the rest of Sonoma County

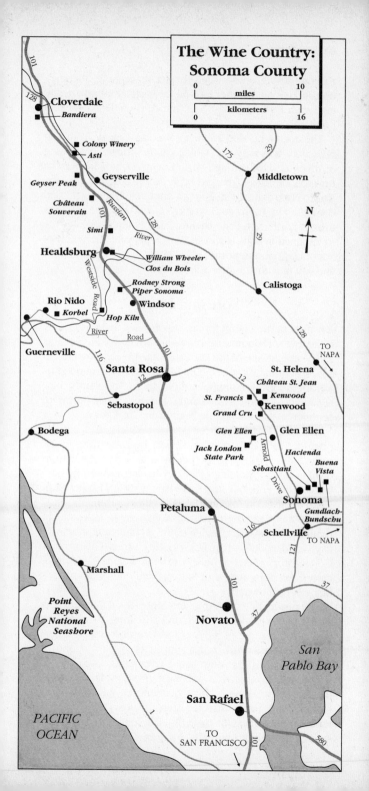

The Wine Country: Sonoma County

miles
0 ——————— 10

kilometers
0 ——————— 16

N

Cloverdale
Bandiera

Colony Winery
Asti

Geyser Peak

Geyserville

Middletown

Château
Souverain

Simi

Healdsburg

William Wheeler
Clos du Bois

Rodney Strong
Piper Sonoma

Windsor

Rio Nido
Korbel

Hop Kiln

River Road

Guerneville

Santa Rosa

Sebastopol

Bodega

Calistoga

TO NAPA

St. Helena

Château St. Jean

St. Francis
Kenwood
Kenwood

Grand Cru

Glen Ellen
Glen Ellen

Jack London
State Park

Hacienda

Sebastiani

Buena
Vista

Sonoma

Gundlach-
Bundschu

Petaluma

Schellville

TO NAPA

Marshall

Point
Reyes
National
Seashore

Novato

San
Pablo Bay

San Rafael

PACIFIC
OCEAN

TO
SAN FRANCISCO

retains a strong, unvarnished country atmosphere. Sonoma's ever-increasing number of vineyards still must share the land with fruit orchards, beef and dairy cattle, sheep, and poultry.

The recommended route to Sonoma County from San Francisco is across the Golden Gate Bridge, continuing north on U.S. 101 through Marin County. Eight miles past the town of San Rafael (marked by freeway exit signs), take the Vallejo-Napa exit off U.S. 101 east onto State Highway 37, and continue on Highway 37 seven miles until the Sonoma turnoff north onto State Highway 121. Follow Highway 121 to its junction with Highway 12 at Schellville, just south of Sonoma. Continue north on Highway 12 for 4 more miles and you're at the historic Sonoma Plaza.

Sonoma Plaza

A natural starting point for any trip through Sonoma County is the town of **Sonoma**, near the southern end of the Sonoma Valley and the site of the last California mission (founded in 1832). Sonoma Plaza is an Old World piazza surrounded by historic adobe buildings, modern shops and stores, new restaurants, antiques-filled inns, and the varied forms of commerce necessary to the heart of any small town.

A young Mexican officer, Mariano Vallejo, laid out the plaza in 1835, and American settlers began arriving in the early 1840s. Prohibited by the Mexican government from owning land or holding office, Americans inspired by Captain John C. Frémont staged the famous Bear Flag Revolt of 1846, seizing control, imprisoning Vallejo, raising the Bear Flag in the plaza, and declaring California an independent republic, Texas-style. The life of the republic was short—25 days—and ended when U.S. troops claimed California as U.S. territory. General Vallejo exhibited remarkable resilience, becoming mayor of Sonoma and one of the valley's first vineyard owners.

The history of that colorful era is preserved here in many of the original adobe, basalt, and false-front Western-style buildings; in some of the Mexican troop barracks and servants' quarters, which remain much as they were; and in other structures that now house restaurants, fashion boutiques, shops, and inns. A walking tour of the plaza includes the two-story adobe built as quarters for Vallejo's Indian servants and a reconstructed structure from the general's Casa Grande estate; Toscano Hotel, a combination general store and lending library dating from 1886; a large adobe that served as Vallejo's troop barracks; and a restoration of the original St. Francisco Solano Mission of 1832 that includes an exhibit of adobe building techniques and mission artwork, notably Chris Jorgensen's watercolors of all the California missions, painted in the early 1900s.

Alongside the Mission history is the plaza's heritage of native food shops. The culinary tour features the **Old Sonoma Creamery**, where you will find locally made mustards, Sonoma wines, and deli assortments; **Sonoma Sausage Company**, with 60 kinds of sausage; **Sonoma Cheese Factory**, where you can see the delicious Sonoma Jack cheese being made and choose from a variety of fresh cheeses, wines, and deli items; **Vella Cheese Company**, a smaller but much-loved old-time maker of Sonoma Jack; and **Sonoma French Bakery**, known for crusty loaves of sourdough and other oven-baked delights.

Interesting shops abound, among the most notable **Champagne Taste**, a chic women's clothing boutique; **Viva Sonoma**, with an eclectic inventory of treasures from California country clothing to Central and South American folk art; **Sign of the Bear**, for fancy kitchenware, gadgets, and baskets; and **Old City Pottery**, where artisans fashion pots, mugs, and vases.

The grandly refurbished **El Dorado Hotel**, a plaza landmark originally built by General Vallejo's brother, is now one of Sonoma's deluxe places to eat and sleep. Elaborate remodeling undertaken by Claude Rouas, the owner of Napa Valley's prestigious Auberge du Soleil, has gracefully highlighted El Dorado's Spanish heritage, and each of the 27 tastefully decorated rooms comes with four-poster bed and private bath, some with private balcony. The hotel's **Ristorante Piatti** has an attractive dining room and a flower-filled courtyard dominated by a lovely old fig tree; its hearty Italian menu features pasta, risotto, grilled meats and fish, and a variety of soups and salads. Tel: 996-2351.

Directly across the street, the three-story **Sonoma Hotel** is classic Victorian with an easygoing atmosphere. A variety of rooms and suites offer private or shared baths, views of the plaza, brass beds, and claw-foot bathtubs. The hotel bar and dining room have the same unpretentious style, serving good regional foods and wines at pleasing prices. Similar bed-and-breakfast accommodations are available at the **Hidden Oak**, **Thistle Dew Inn**, and **Victorian Garden Inn**.

Sebastiani Vineyards, one mile northeast of the town plaza, is one of Sonoma's major producers and has been a colorful mainstay of the town history since Samuele Sebastiani arrived from Italy in the early 1890s and purchased vineyards that had been planted in 1835 by General Vallejo. Samuele started his winery in 1904, but it was his son, August Sebastiani, who led the family winery to national prominence by expanding production beyond a million cases a year. The antithesis of today's self-important set who cloak wine in a mystic aura, August wore striped overalls, smoked cigarettes with his Cabernet, and insisted he was just a simple farmer growing grapes to make good everyday wine, although he was in fact a very astute businessman and one of the great characters in the history of the California wine industry. After August's death in 1980, command passed to his son, Sam Sebastiani, an outstanding wine maker who successfully strived for a higher level of premium vintages as well as a higher profile for himself. But in another of those family bloodlettings that play out like a TV soap opera, Sam lost a power struggle with his younger brother Don and was unceremoniously fired from the family winery by his mother, Sylvia Sebastiani, August's widow and, not incidentally, the majority stockholder in Sebastiani Vineyards. Don Sebastiani, who also managed to become a controversial state legislator for a short term, remains in charge at the family winery, while Sam has built an impressive new estate winery of his own in the Carneros region south of Sonoma. You will only encounter selected parts of this provocative family history on the otherwise excellent tour that includes Sebastiani's famed collection of original wine-barrel carvings done by a local artisan in the Old World tradition.

A short drive east of the Sonoma Plaza, at the end of Old Winery Road, **Buena Vista** is California's oldest surviving winery, founded in 1857 by the Hungarian colonel Agoston Haraszthy, who imported the first major plantings of European grape varieties and is known as the father of California viticulture. Born in European splendor, California's first winery survived fires, diseased vines, and high taxes, only to have its stone cellar collapse during the 1906 earthquake. The winery was essentially defunct until World War II, when a gradual revival of its fortunes began, culminating with the present ownership by a German company that has established Buena Vista as one of Sonoma's finest wine makers. You can enjoy self-guided tours of the limestone caves, free tastings inside another of the original stone winery buildings, and spacious, shaded picnic grounds. (While the caves here are still used as aging cellars, Buena Vista's vineyards and modern wine-making facility are located in the Carneros area.) In the foothills east of Sonoma are two smaller modern wineries with tasting rooms situated on historic, scenic sites:

Hacienda and **Gundlach-Bundschu**, the latter a prize-winning revival by descendants of the founders of the enterprise more than a century ago.

Sonoma Valley

The Sonoma Valley is a 17-mile-long greenbelt extending north from the crossroads town of Schellville (where highways 12 and 121 intersect), through the town of Sonoma, and on to the hamlet of Kenwood, at which point you are only a few miles from the outskirts of the booming city of Santa Rosa, the largest community in Sonoma County. Santa Rosa and the entire Sonoma Valley have been experiencing a population boom fed by newcomers who commute to jobs in San Francisco, occasionally making traffic on Highway 12, the main artery through the valley, heavy. But for the most part, the gentleness of the country still fills the air.

Sonoma Mission Inn and Spa is this region's premier luxury resort, a pink temple devoted to healthful indulgence in a supremely relaxing fashion. In the tradition of the Native Americans who once enjoyed the therapeutic waters of the nearby Boyes Hot Springs and Agua Caliente (literally "hot water"), this serene resort two miles northwest of Sonoma via Highway 12 offers its jet-set clientele indoor and outdoor Jacuzzis and a heated pool, both part of a spa that offers a number of rejuvenating treatments including their herbal wrap. You can register for the full spa program or simply spend a night or more as a pampered guest with access to tennis courts and an Olympic-size pool. **The Grille Room** at the inn is one of the valley's finest restaurants, a health-oriented spot serving grilled fish and chicken, pasta with vegetables, crisp crab cakes, and regional specialties; Tel: 938-9000. More of a country atmosphere can be found in Sonoma Valley's bed-and-breakfast inns and ranch-style guesthouses such as **Beltane Ranch**, **Gaige House Inn**, and **Stone Tree Ranch**, all in Glen Ellen.

Glen Ellen Winery, in the little town of Glen Ellen, five miles northwest of Sonoma on Arnold Drive west of Highway 12, is an 1860s winery that was revived in 1980 by the Bruno Benzinger family. Their inexpensive Glen Ellen wines have done extremely well, and they have added an upgraded line carrying the Benzinger name. There's a self-guided tour of this friendly winery that is a throwback to the 19th-century days of family wine making, and odds are good that some member of the large Benzinger clan will be present to introduce you to their wines.

Not far beyond Glen Ellen Winery is the entrance to **Jack London State Park**, where the nomadic author settled in 1904, intending to build his dream home in what the Indians had christened the Valley of the Moon. **Wolf House**, a three-story structure of massive rock quarried in the Sonoma hills and hauled by four-horse teams, was completed in 1913 but destroyed by fire before London and his wife could occupy it. Three years later, Jack London died at age 40; the charred ruins of Wolf House still stand among the redwoods. A second house, occupied by London's widow until her death in 1955, bears the ironic name, **House of Happy Walls**. Inside is a wealth of memorabilia from London's world travels and his prolific writing, including original manuscripts and even a well-preserved stack of rejection slips.

Grand Cru Vineyards, tucked away on a country lane (Vintage Road, behind Dunbar School), a short distance off Highway 12 northwest of Glen Ellen, was founded in 1970 when a modern winery was built making partial use of 1886 cellars and stone-and-concrete fermenting tanks. There's a tasting room and a scenic picnic area under large oak trees. **Kenwood Vineyards**, north and off Highway 12 at the roadside settlement named Kenwood, is a top-flight Sonoma producer that can be classified as a veteran in a county populated by so many new wineries. Kenwood started in 1970, converting a 1906 winery into a modern facility where a variety of fine wines are made. **Kenwood Restaurant** (no relationship to the winery), one of the best eating stops along Highway 12, is an airy, city-style bistro with contemporary art and views of the countryside. The regularly changing menu may feature roast duck, Sonoma rabbit, venison, sweetbreads, and summer salads, with an emphasis on locally grown foods; Tel: 883-6326.

A hideaway for a leisurely lunch in an enchanting setting is **Oreste's Golden Bear Lodge**, on Adobe Canyon Road in Kenwood. Dating from the 1920s, the Golden Bear presents a modest front alongside a winding country road, but there's a cozy dining room and, behind that, the main attraction: outdoor, tree-shaded tables overlooking a meandering country stream. The Italian menu features pizzas, pastas, seafood ravioli, and Sonoma sausage with grilled polenta; Tel: 833-2327.

After lunch you can visit two more wineries, on opposite sides of Highway 12, before leaving the Kenwood environs. **St. Francis Winery**, which counts a superior Merlot among its varietals, has operated since 1979, although its vineyards were first planted in 1910. **Château St. Jean** looks and sounds French, but it had a thoroughly modern stateside beginning and is now owned by the giant Suntory International, Ltd. of Japan. Founded in 1974 by a group of California businessmen, the winery was named for an owner's wife, Jean, thus the American pronunciation applies. St. Jean quickly built a reputation for outstanding Chardonnays and other white varietals. A self-guided tour gives an excellent view of state-of-the-art wine-making technology, the tasting room is in the French-style villa that was part of a 1920s country estate, and there's a beautifully maintained picnic area.

Highway 12 continues north a few miles to Santa Rosa, where you can continue to the Russian River Valley or return to San Francisco via U.S. 101 in about two and a half hours.

Russian River Valley

What could be more Californian than Wine Country with a highway? U.S. 101, carrying traffic from the Golden Gate Bridge to the Oregon border, cuts through the heart of the Russian River Valley section of Wine Country that begins just north of the city of Santa Rosa and extends across 40 miles of open country to Cloverdale and the Mendocino County line. If you have limited time, you can make exclusive use of the highway in visiting wineries that are easy to find on the old frontage roads that parallel both sides of U.S. 101, but there are more than 60 wineries operating throughout the Russian River region, and most of them can only be found by deciphering the maze of narrow roads twisting back well into the countryside. As always throughout Napa–Sonoma Wine Country, it is the searching that sometimes can be as memorable as the finding.

Although wine grapes have been growing in this part of Sonoma since Prohibition, it wasn't until the wine boom of the late 1960s that full-scale investment in new vineyards and wineries gained serious momentum. Now you will find clusters of wineries up and down the Russian River watershed, and some of California's finest wines of every variety are identified with this region's distinct viticultural areas, such as Alexander Valley, Dry Creek, and Chalk Hill.

Four miles north of Santa Rosa at 4350 Barnes Road (take the River Road exit off Highway 101) are the deluxe **Vintner's Inn** and **John Ash & Co.** restaurant in the middle of 50 acres of vineyards. John Ash & Co. built a reputation as one of the most creative restaurants in all of the Wine Country while functioning for several years in a Santa Rosa shopping center. Now that the restaurant is suitably placed among the vineyards, which you can view through huge windows from the two-tiered dining area or from the terrace, its prices are predictably higher, but John Ash continues his devotion to cooking with a flair the freshest fish, fowl, and produce available from surrounding areas; Tel: 527-7687. Vintner's Inn is in the elegant European country style, with unusually large guest rooms in two-story town houses separated by piazzas and generous landscaping.

River Road, which turns west off U.S. 101 four miles north of Santa Rosa, is an easy-to-follow, 14-mile scenic route to **F. Korbel and Bros.**, a winery founded in 1882 by the three Korbel brothers from Bohemia and owned since 1954 by the Heck family. Korbel is one of California's largest producers of sparkling wine using the classic *méthode champenoise*. An added highlight to the excellent tour and elegant tasting room is a walk through the famous Korbel rose gardens.

River Road continues another few miles to the little towns of **Rio Nido** and **Guerneville**, which are the hub of the Russian River resort area, with inexpensive cabins and motels overlooking the river—a popular summer destination for rafting, canoeing, and kayaking.

The Russian River resort area has also become known as a popular gathering place for gays, and many of the area's lodges, bars, and restaurants are owned and operated by gays. Although this area is an inexpensive alternative to the higher-priced attractions of Napa Valley and the best parts of Sonoma County, it also has far less to offer in the way of quality restaurants, first-class accommodations, and other amenities that will attract you to the better-known regions of the Wine Country.

Several small wineries are scattered along the back roads on both sides of the Russian River as it snakes its way south from Healdsburg (north of Guerneville) before turning west and reaching the Pacific Ocean at Jenner. Take Westside Road northeast from Guerneville to one of the most unusual of these Russian River wineries: **Hop Kiln**, about midway between Guerneville and Healdsburg. A contender for Sonoma's most-photographed winery, Hop Kiln recalls part of a 19th-century hop kiln used in beermaking, leaving the winery with a soaring roofline that looks like three giant, upside-down funnels. There's a handsome tasting room at this tiny family winery, a registered California Historical Landmark.

If, instead of exploring the smaller roads alongside the

Russian River, you do return to U.S. 101 to continue north, you'll see **Piper Sonoma Cellars** and **Rodney Strong Vineyards**, parts of an architecturally striking complex not far off 101 on Old Redwood Highway, five miles south of Healdsburg near the small town of Windsor. Piper Sonoma began as a 1980 partnership between the prestigious French Champagne maker Piper Heidsieck and the Sonoma winery that featured the highly regarded Rodney Strong as wine maker. Now operated separately, Piper Sonoma concentrates on sparkling wines, while Rodney Strong produces a full line of varietal wines. Both wineries are worth viewing for their distinctive designs. Piper Sonoma also provides one of the most elaborate tours imaginable of the sparkling wine–making process, while the Rodney Strong tasting room is a rare visual experience, high above and overlooking the enormous wine cellar below.

Healdsburg and Environs

Though it lacks the instant appeal of more scenic Wine Country towns, Healdsburg (pronounced "HEELDS-burg") has nonetheless become "the St. Helena of Sonoma County" and the center of the Russian River Valley wine region. Situated about 70 highway miles from San Francisco, this was for years a dusty, sleepy little town surrounded by fruit orchards, including enough prune trees to make Healdsburg known as "the buckle in California's prune belt." During the last two decades, thousands of acres of peaches, apples, pears, cherries, and, yes, prunes have been replaced by grapes. Still, local produce remains so bountiful that the Saturday morning farmers' market outgrew the town square and moved to a larger space down the street. Shaded by redwoods and palm trees, graced with fountains and benches, Healdsburg is a small farming town dressing in new styles to greet its growing number of guests.

The town jewel is **Madrona Manor**, a sturdy three-story gingerbread Victorian where you can gather around the music room's 100-year-old carved rosewood piano, sip wine in front of a roaring fireplace, dine in high-ceilinged rooms overlooking the terrace, and retire to canopied beds. There's a resident ghost: a lady in a long black dress with a high white collar who wanders the hallways at night—usually on the second floor, where the best rooms are located—but disdains being seen near the Manor's swimming pool. The **Madrona Manor Dining Room** also qualifies as the best restaurant in town; each night a different menu features fresh produce, poultry and meats from Sonoma, fresh fish from not-too-distant waters, pizza from wood-burning brick ovens, fruits and vegetables from the Manor's own orchards and gardens, and delectable trout, duck, and other wonders from the smokehouse out back. Tel: 433-4231. If you can't get a room at the Madrona Manor, try the **Belle de Jour**'s four attractive farmhouse cottages or the **Grape Leaf Inn**, a gracious Queen Anne Victorian with eight bed-and-breakfast rooms with private baths. Two Healdsburg wineries open for tastings and tours by appointment, **Clos du Bois** (Tel: 433-5576) and **William Wheeler** (Tel: 433-8786), exemplify the modern wave of top-rated Sonoma wines.

Northeast of Healdsburg is the **Alexander Valley** wine-growing region, home to several small wineries and fine Chardonnays; even more are found northwest of Healdsburg in the **Dry Creek** region, which is noted for superior Zinfandel. **Simi Winery**, north of Healdsburg (take the Dry Creek Road exit off U.S. 101 east to West Healdsburg Avenue and continue one mile north), is one of this area's oldest wineries, built in 1890 by Giuseppe and Pietro Simi. Their original stone winery is still used as Simi's aging cellars, and every afternoon the train still rolls through on the Southern Pacific tracks that run between the winery and the tasting room.

A destination that can serve as a worthy conclusion to a trip up the Russian River Valley is **Château Souverain**, six miles north of Healdsburg and right off U.S. 101. Souverain, built in 1972 by the Pillsbury Company, was given a soaring architectural style specifically designed to give you exceptional views of the inner workings of a modern winery; you'll find more grand views from their tasting room. **Château Souverain Restaurant**, where first-rate food is served in a beautiful open-air dining room with views of terraced vineyards and the distant countryside, is a pleasant way to finish off a day of Sonoma Wine Country touring; Tel: 433-3141. If you prefer to push on, you will find a few more wineries at the northern end of the U.S. 101 wine trail: **Geyser Peak**, just north of the small town of Geyserville; the historic and quite colorful **Colony Winery** at Asti, known as Italian Swiss Colony for nearly 100 years (its TV commercials featured the "little old Italian wine maker" in the days before California wine became sophisticated); and **Bandiera**, the last stop, at Cloverdale, a winery founded after Prohibition and enjoying a modern revival that began in the 1980s.

GETTING AROUND

The best way to tour the Wine Country is by private car, giving you the flexibility to set your own schedule. However, there are some options for non-drivers. Gray Line offers bus tours from San Francisco (Tel: 415-558-9400 or 800-556-5660), as does Starline Tours (Tel: 415-582-2223). Viviani Touring Company in Sonoma offers customized wine-oriented touring (Tel: 707-938-2100) and Stage-a-Picnic arranges visits to wineries in a stagecoach (Tel: 707-857-3619). Two invaluable sources of information are the Napa Valley Conference & Visitors Bureau (1556 First Street, Napa, CA 94958; Tel: 707-226-7459) and the Sonoma County Convention & Visitors Bureau (10 Fourth Street, Suite 100, Santa Rosa, CA 95401; Tel: 707-575-1191).

ACCOMMODATIONS REFERENCE

Weekends and warm-weather months, from about April to the end of the crushing season in October, are naturally the most difficult times for reservations. Lower rates for midweek and winter reservations often apply. Travellers should be aware that many of the bed-and-breakfast establishments do not allow children and have strict no-smoking policies. The area code for the Wine Country is 707.

▶ **Ambrose Bierce House.** 1515 Main Street, **St. Helena**, CA 94574. Tel: 963-3003.

▶ **Auberge du Soleil.** 180 Rutherford Hill Road, **Rutherford**, CA 74573. Tel: 963-1211.

▶ **Bartel's Ranch.** 1200 Conn Valley Road, **St. Helena**, CA 94574. Tel: 963-4001.

▶ **Belle de Jour.** 16276 Healdsburg Avenue, **Healdsburg**, CA 95448. Tel: 433-7892.

▶ **Beltane Ranch.** P.O. Box 395, **Glen Ellen**, CA 95442. Tel: 996-6501.

▶ **Bordeaux House.** 6600 Washington Street, **Yountville**, CA 94599. Tel: 944-2855.

▶ **Brannan Cottage Inn.** 109 Wapoo Avenue, **Calistoga**, CA 94515. Tel: 942-4200.

▶ **Burgundy House.** 6711 Washington Street, **Yountville**, CA 94599. Tel: 944-0889.

▶ **Calistoga Country Lodge.** 2883 Foothill Boulevard, **Calistoga**, CA 94515. Tel: 942-5555.

▶ **Calistoga Inn.** 1250 Lincoln Avenue, **Calistoga**, CA 94515. Tel: 942-4101.

▶ **Calistoga Spa Hot Springs.** 1006 Washington Street, **Calistoga**, CA 94515. Tel: 942-6269.

▶ **Creekside Inn.** 945 Main Street, **St. Helena,** CA 94574. Tel: 963-7244.

▶ **Dr. Wilkinson's Hot Springs.** 1507 Lincoln Avenue, **Calistoga,** CA 94515. Tel: 942-4102.

▶ **El Dorado Hotel.** 405 First Street West, **Sonoma,** CA 95476. Tel: 996-3030.

▶ **The Farmhouse.** 300 Taplin Road, **St. Helena,** CA 94574. Tel: 963-3431.

▶ **Gaige House Inn.** 13540 Arnold Drive, **Glen Ellen,** CA 95442. Tel: 935-0237.

▶ **Golden Haven Hot Springs.** 1713 Lake Street, **Calistoga,** CA 94515. Tel: 942-6793.

▶ **Grape Leaf Inn.** 539 Johnson Street, **Healdsburg,** CA 95448. Tel: 433-8140.

▶ **Harvest Inn.** 1 Main Street, **St. Helena,** CA 94574. Tel: 963-9463.

▶ **Hidden Oak.** 214 East Napa Street, **Sonoma,** CA 95476. Tel: 996-9863.

▶ **Hotel St. Helena.** 1309 Main Street, **St. Helena,** CA 94574. Tel: 963-4388.

▶ **Larkmead Country Inn.** 1103 Larkmead Lane, **Calistoga,** CA 94515. Tel: 942-5360.

▶ **Madrona Manor.** 1001 Westside Road, **Healdsburg,** CA 95448. Tel: 433-4231.

▶ **Magnolia Hotel & Restaurant.** 6529 Yount Street, **Yountville,** CA 94599. Tel: 944-2056.

▶ **Meadowood Resort.** 900 Meadowood Lane, **St. Helena,** CA 94574. Tel: 963-3646; in California, (800) 862-7272; outside California, (800) 345-3457.

▶ **Mount View Hotel.** 1457 Lincoln Avenue, **Calistoga** CA 94515. Tel: 942-6877.

▶ **Nance's Hot Springs.** 1614 Lincoln Avenue, **Calistoga,** CA 94515. Tel: 942-6211.

▶ **Napa Valley Lodge.** Highway 29 and Madison Avenue, **Yountville,** CA 94599. Tel: 944-2468 or (800) 368-2468.

▶ **Oak Knoll Inn.** 2200 East Oak Knoll Avenue, **Yountville,** CA 94599. Tel: 255-2200.

▶ **Silverado Resort and Country Club.** 1600 Atlas Peak Road, **Napa,** CA 94558. Tel: 257-0200 or (800) 532-0500.

▶ **Sonoma Hotel.** 110 West Spain Street, **Sonoma** CA 95476. Tel: 996-2996.

▶ **Sonoma Mission Inn and Spa.** P.O. Box 1447, **Sonoma,** CA 95476. Tel: 938-9000 or (800) 862-4945.

▶ **Stone Tree Ranch.** 7910 Sonoma Mountain Road, **Glen Ellen,** CA 95442. Tel: 996-1114.

► **Thistle Dew Inn.** 171 West Spain Street, **Sonoma,** CA 95476. Tel: 938-2909.

► **Victorian Garden Inn.** 316 East Napa Street, **Sonoma,** CA 95476. Tel: 996-5339.

► **Villa St. Helena.** 2727 Sulphur Springs Avenue, **St. Helena,** CA 94574. Tel: 963-0262.

► **Vintage Inn.** 6541 Washington Street, **Yountville,** CA 94599. Tel: 944-1112 or (800) 351-1133.

► **Vintner's Inn.** 4350 Barnes Road, **Santa Rosa,** CA 95403. Tel: in California, (800) 421-2584; outside California, (800) 575-7350.

► **Wayside Inn.** 1523 Foothill Boulevard, **Calistoga,** CA 94515. Tel: 942-0645.

► **The Webber Place.** 6610 Webber, **Yountville,** CA 94599. Tel: 944-8384.

► **Wine Country Inn.** 1152 Lodi Lane, **St. Helena,** CA 94574. Tel: 963-7077.

► **Wine Way Inn.** 1019 Foothill Boulevard, **Calistoga,** CA 94515. Tel: 942-0680.

► **Zinfandel Inn.** 800 Zinfandel Lane, **St. Helena,** CA 94574. Tel: 963-3512.

THE REDWOOD COUNTRY

By Georgia I. Hesse

In the deep, still shade of old-growth groves in Redwood National Park, north of Eureka, you can't hear a pin drop; even your own footfalls are silenced, buried in the duff of the forest floor. The ticks of time and life themselves are muted: Water drips, somewhere beyond your seeing, through beds of moss and sprays of giant ferns; little winds wail high in the thick, green vault; you start at the sudden, sharp staccato of a woodpecker.

The drama that began in prehistory can give the thoughtful traveller chills.

In the Jurassic period, about 160 million years ago, when dinosaurs ruled the earth and mammals were just being born, a sturdy plant sprouted and began its steady growth into giant forests, the ancestors of the redwoods. Eras passed, flying reptiles became extinct, insects and flowering plants and primates appeared, and by about 20 million years ago, redwoods as we know them today stood in tall parade around the globe, from western Canada to the Atlantic, from France to Japan.

Then came the great glacial ages. Arctic ice sheets crept inexorably south over lands and seas. When eventually they retreated, the tall trees had vanished almost everywhere—except in a slice of Northern California and in a remote region of China (where they were identified only as recently as 1946).

Today's redwoods have been classified by botanists into

three species: *Sequoia sempervirens* (the Coast Redwood; sempervirens means "evergreen"), *Sequoiadendron giganteum* (Giant Sequoia), and *Metasequoia glyptostroboides* (China's Dawn Redwood). The redwoods were baptized *sequoia* by Hungarian botanist Stephen Endlicher, who wished to honor a Cherokee Indian named Sequoyah who had invented an alphabet for his people.

The Coast Redwood is the titan, towering over all other living things: One overachiever in Redwood National Park is the tallest tree in the world, topping out at 367.8 feet. Exceptional giants may reach a height of 350 feet, a diameter of 20 feet, and an age of about 2,000 years; such a one is the Founders' Tree in Humboldt Redwoods State Park, a mere sprout when Christ was born.

When Europeans first arrived in California, the coastal redwood belt stretched about 450 miles from a pinch of southern Oregon to the south tip of Monterey County and the Santa Lucia Mountains, and into the hills behind what is today Oakland. Forests blanketed much of today's San Mateo, Santa Cruz, and Marin counties, but now most of those old trees have been cut except the ones preserved in the Big Basin, Portola, Butano, Cowell, Mount Tamalpais, and Samuel P. Taylor state parks, and much-visited Muir Woods National Monument north of San Francisco. The most dramatic stands today are found in Humboldt and Del Norte counties farther north, part of what we call the Redwood Country.

The redwoods are rulers of a varied empire: a few towns that serve as toeholds of civilization; fine, burgeoning vineyards; sunny uplands; a wave-battered, now brilliant, now fog-shrouded coast; and still enough wilderness to soothe the city-strangled soul.

Like the traveller who starts in San Francisco, we will wander it from south to north (on the major inland highway) and back (on the scenic coastal highway).

MAJOR INTEREST

The Redwood Highway
Anderson Valley wineries
Small town flavor of Ukiah, Willits, and Garberville

Humboldt Redwoods State Park
Avenue of the Giants
Founders' Grove Nature Trail
Rockefeller Forest

Eureka and Region
Eureka's Old Town, Carson Mansion
Ferndale and the Lost Coast
Coastal towns from Arcata to Orick

Redwood National Park
Tall Trees Trail
Lady Bird Johnson Grove
Prairie Creek Redwoods State Park (Fern Canyon)

Del Norte County
Alder Basin Trail
Damnation Creek Trail
Crescent City
Jedediah Smith Redwoods State Park

Coastal Highway 1, Mendocino Coast
Fort Bragg (Skunk Train, Jug Handle State Park)
Mendocino (art colony, coastal activities)
Coastal towns of Little River, Albion, Elk, Gualala
Sonoma County Coast

THE REDWOOD HIGHWAY

It is physically possible to spin north from San Francisco to
Eureka (or perhaps even to Crescent City on the Oregon
border) and back in two or three days—but all you will
experience is exhaustion. At least a week or ten days are
demanded if you wish to appreciate the natural majesty and
the cultural quirks of this compelling country.

The best plan is to follow an itinerary that runs north of
San Francisco on the Redwood Highway (U.S. 101), through
Leggett to Eureka and beyond to Crescent City (359 miles
from the Golden Gate Bridge), returns to Leggett, then
winds south on coastal State Highway 1. A dozen satisfying
detours may be made along the way.

A first stop might be made in Santa Rosa or Healdsburg
(about 70 miles north of San Francisco) in Sonoma County,
both with rewarding inns, restaurants, vineyards, and other
attractions (see the Wine Country chapter).

Beyond Cloverdale, north of Healdsburg, commuter com-
munities yield to farmland and vineyards; just north of town,
State Highway 128 leaves 101 to snake northwest into
Mendocino County and Anderson Valley.

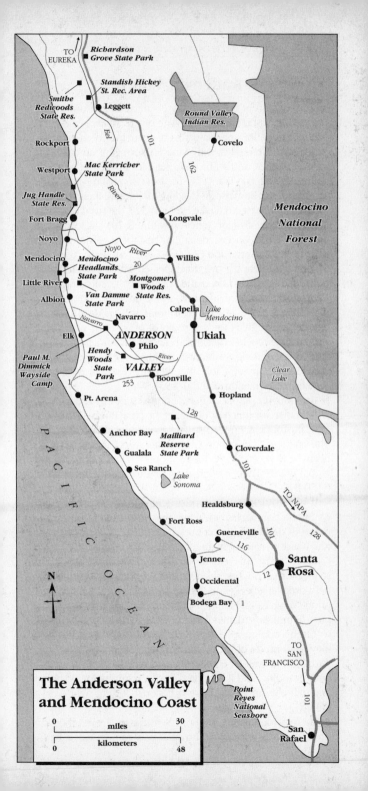

The Anderson Valley
and Mendocino Coast

TO EUREKA

Richardson Grove State Park

Standish Hickey St. Rec. Area

Smithe Redwoods State Res.

Leggett

Round Valley Indian Res.

Rockport

Eel

Covelo

Westport

Mac Kerricher State Park

162

Jug Handle State Res.

Fort Bragg

Longvale

Noyo

Noyo River

Mendocino National Forest

Mendocino

Mendocino Headlands State Park

Willits

20

Little River

Montgomery Woods State Res.

Van Damme State Park

Calpella

Lake Mendocino

Albion

Navarro

Navarro

ANDERSON

Ukiah

Elk

Philo

VALLEY

Clear Lake

Paul M. Dimmick Wayside Camp

Hendy Woods State Park

River

Boonville

253

Hopland

Pt. Arena

128

Anchor Bay

Mailliard Reserve State Park

Cloverdale

Gualala

Sea Ranch

Lake Sonoma

101

TO NAPA

Healdsburg

128

Fort Ross

Guerneville

116

101

Jenner

Santa Rosa

Occidental

12

Bodega Bay

1

TO SAN FRANCISCO

N

PACIFIC OCEAN

101

Point Reyes National Seashore

1

San Rafael

0	miles	30
0	kilometers	48

Anderson Valley

Traditionally remote, isolated, self-sufficient, and unfriendly to outsiders, the wide-spot towns of the valley—Yorkville, Boonville, Philo, and Navarro—are stirring in their afternoon naps these days, with wineries springing up like California poppies, and with one restaurant that alone is worth the drive from San Francisco, the New Boonville Hotel.

Indeed, San Franciscans heading for long weekends on the Mendocino Coast often take Highway 128, the rural road that runs northwest from its junction with U.S. 101 at Cloverdale, easing in an unconcerned manner past the stately redwoods of **Mailliard Reserve** and **Hendy Woods State Park** (pleasant ambles in redwood groves interspersed with the twisted red-gold madrones that echo the shades of the sun, and with Douglas firs, California laurels, and deer ferns), on through the shady silence of **Paul M. Dimmick Wayside Camp**, to emerge suddenly at the sea south of Albion (for which see South of Mendocino later in the chapter). Dimmick is mainly for day use (hiking, swimming, fishing, etc.); a few primitive camping sites are available, though limited in off-seasons; for the latest information, call (707) 937-5804.

In **Boonville**, about 25 miles northwest of Cloverdale, you should plan for lunch or dinner at the **New Boonville Hotel**, a creaky-looking wooden structure on the wide main street. The emphasis here is on California cuisine, featuring fresh herbs and vegetables, Sonoma County baby lamb, and regional wines. There's open-air dining in good weather; Tel: (707) 855-2210.

If you're lucky, you may hear someone "harping Boont," otherwise known as speaking the private local language called Boontling, a dialect preserved in a handy guide to the town and its native tongue entitled *A Slib of Lorey* (A Bit of Folklore). Try this example: "The shoveltooth was at a sharking match when the telef rang, calling all kimmies to help dreek a jeffer" (The doctor was playing cards when the phone rang, calling all men to help put out a fire). The 700-plus "kimmies," "dames," and "tweeds" (men, women, and children) of Boonville don't all harp Boont perfectly, but they're all proud of it. Boontling originated in the 1880s, it is said, so that tweeds could converse without their parents' understanding, and it delighted the backcountry folk to harp unintelligibly in front of the occasional "bright light" (city dude).

There's not total joy in Boonville these days, even though since the New Boonville arrived, you can "gorm a bahl gorm" (eat a good meal). The "posy tweeds" (hippies) have gone, sure, but they have been succeeded by the environmentalists and "Gold Dome kimmies" (men from the state capital), who are irritating the "croppy kimmies" (sheepmen) with too many regulations.

Despite its determined rusticity, Anderson Valley stands ready to soothe the slowed-down driver with two retreats: the small, fashionable **Toll House Restaurant and Inn**, just east of Boonville on Highway 253, and **Bear Wallow Resort**, 4 miles west of town on Mountain View Road. In addition there's the neat, seven-room **Anderson Valley Inn** in Philo, a few miles north on 128.

Toll House was built in 1912 to serve as headquarters of the vast Miller family ranch, where tolls were charged the mule-skinners who hauled redwood logs to the inland lumber mills. Today it's a four-room escape commanding 360 acres, with hiking, riding, and fishing available. The restaurant serves its own organically grown vegetables and locally produced veal, lamb, beef, and free-range chicken. Room rates are moderate by city standards.

Bear Wallow's one- and two-bedroom cabins sit on 40 acres of redwoods, offering fireplaces, decks, and kitchens. The Dinner House (closed in midwinter) features barbecued steaks, fresh seafood, and regional wines. All considered, prices are moderate, even modest.

Should you be in the neighborhood in late April, plan to attend the colorful Annual Wildflower Show at the Boonville Fairgrounds. The Mendocino County Fair & Apple Show is held late in September at the same arena.

Anderson Valley wineries are sparking statewide nods, even from tasters who've never heard of Boonville. They are clustered around Philo: try Husch Vineyards (tours are available), Scharffenberger, Navarro, Greenwood Ridge, and Handley. Each offers daily tastings and is just a few yards off Highway 128 to the left or right, clearly signposted.

Hopland to Leggett

Wine enthusiasts who don't detour into Anderson Valley may want to stop around Hopland, about 15 miles up 101 from Cloverdale, especially at the **Fetzer** winery, which has been producing since the 1970s at 1150 Bel Arbes Road (there's a tasting room and tours by appointment only; Tel: 744-1298). Fetzer's organic acres, Valley Oaks Garden, produce apples, vegetables, and herbs to accompany meals at nearby **Sundial Grill** (reserve by calling 744-1328). **Milano Winery**, just south of town, is a good place to buy a picnic-suitable Zinfandel.

Drivers who detoured into Anderson Valley can return to the freeway race north of Hopland via Highway 253. Highway 101 then hurtles past **Ukiah**, a pleasant wide-street town with a vaguely Midwest air suggestive of the thwack of Saturday afternoon Little League baseball games. At 431 South Main Street here, the **Grace Hudson Museum** (open daily except Mondays and holidays) is installed in Sun House, home of John Hudson and his wife, Grace Carpenter Hudson, a painter of the primitive, little-known Pomo Indians. "My desire is that the world shall know them as I know them, and before they vanish . . . before the opportunity is no more," the artist wrote in 1934. In Hudson's day her work was considered sentimental and trivial, but today it is recognized as a genuine record of a day and people long since gone.

A good choice for dining in town is the **Coach House**, serving old-fashioned American cooking, at 131 East Mill Street; for Italian-American food, try lively **Basilio's**, 1090 South State Street. Late in May and into June, Ukiah stages the Hometown Festival, a combination rodeo, regatta, marathon, and food show spiced with tours of Victorian homes in the area; the Redwood Empire Fair comes to town late in August.

Just north of Ukiah, **Parducci Cellars**, a longtime producer of premium wines, offers tastings and tours; Tel: 462-3828. Beyond Calpella in the town of Redwood Valley, **Weibel Vineyards** has a tasting room; the winery's headquarters in Mission San Jose south of Oakland were established by Leland Stanford, California's governor and founder of Stanford University. Five miles northeast of Ukiah is **Lake Mendocino**, which provides sports facilities especially suited to families—swimming, waterskiing, boating, fishing, hiking, picnicking, and camping; Tel: (707) 462-7582. For information and regional maps, stop by or write to the Mendocino County Convention & Visitors Bureau, 320 South State Street, Ukiah, CA 95482; Tel: (707) 462-3091.

North of Ukiah, about 10 miles south of Willits, is Black Bart Rock, a large stone outcrop dedicated to one of Northern California's favorite rogues who practiced in this area a century ago. Black Bart didn't drink or smoke, he fussed about his personal linen, his breast pocket held a silk handkerchief, and his head bore a proper topper. When he robbed Wells Fargo stagecoaches (27 of them), he donned a flour-sack mask and a linen duster and spoke politely as he demanded (in resonant

tones, they said) the strongbox. Then he left behind delightful
doggerel: "I've labored long and hard for bread—/For honor
and for riches—/But on my corns too long you've tread,/You
fine-haired sons of bitches."

Black Bart's colorful career came to an end in the autumn
of 1883, when, following a holdup, he dropped a silk handkerchief that was traced by its San Francisco laundry mark to
one Charles C. Bolton, a mining engineer and, some histories say, a former Wells Fargo clerk. Released after a five-year
residence in San Quentin prison, Black Bart soon vanished.
It is not known whether he ever returned to his faithful wife
in Illinois, who claimed he was a good and tidy man.

Willits, 23 miles north of Ukiah, was until recently a city in
search of instant identity; it lacked a Golden Gate Bridge or
an Eiffel Tower. In 1990 though, the town gained a symbol—
the famous old arch that once identified Reno, Nevada, as
"the Biggest Little City in the World." It now proclaims
"Gateway to the Redwoods."

Willits is known by most tourists solely as the eastern
terminus of the famous **Skunk Train**, which chugs for 40
miles through ranch country and redwood groves from Fort
Bragg on the coast to Willits and back again (see Fort Bragg
below). This little town of 4,000 is worth a stop in itself,
however, chiefly for the **Mendocino County Museum** on
East Commercial Street (open Wednesdays through Sundays), a repository of artifacts and crafts from the regional
Pomo Indian culture and items illustrative of pioneer history. "In early times nothing was as you see it now," a Pomo
legend reads. "Coyote was let down from the zenith by
Spider after he had created both of the upper worlds. In his
hunting sack he carried the sun, moon, clouds, water, and a
small bit of earth . . . He told Spider to spin some more web.
Then he spread the earth upon the web, and that is how the
land was made."

Willits's annual **July 4 Frontier Days Rodeo** is the oldest
regularly held rodeo in the state, a fine occasion for
countrified whoop-de-doo. Then, or anytime, consider a
long, laid-back weekend at **Brooktrails Lodge**, 3.5 miles
northwest on Sherwood Road. The 20 motel rooms and 19
one- to two-room cottages nestle in a setting of tall redwoods, with access to an informal café, large swimming
pool, tennis courts, and nine-hole golf course, all at quite
moderate prices.

Drivers who have decided not to make the trek to the
really big trees farther north can take Highway 20 west from
Willits across the Coast Range to Noyo, through scenery

similar to that seen aboard the Skunk; the drive is about 42 miles. (For Noyo, see The Mendocino Coast below.)

"Covelo . . . is the gathering place for a rude population which rides in on mustang ponies whenever it gets out of whiskey." So a traveller wrote in *Harper's* in 1873. That particular pastime may have changed, but **Covelo** and the Round Valley Indian Reservation (50,000 acres) echo the Old West (or, more properly, Hollywood's classic adult Westerns) along State Highway 162, which cuts east off 101 around Longvale, north of Willits. Few travellers will take the time to poke around here, but you may like to ponder its history as you continue north to Leggett and the Smithe Redwoods State Reserve.

In the mid-1880s some 20,000 Yuka Indians lived in Round Valley. As Stuart Nixon describes its aspect today in *Redwood Empire:* "The great white oaks and lush green pastures of Round Valley's big ranches suggest the manorial estates of Surrey or Shropshire, but Covelo, all dusty streets and false fronts, proposes Dodge City or Deadwood. In time, the last hunted Yuka would tell an Army agent: 'We have lost faith in everything but death.' "

If you do take time for a detour to Covelo, visit the Tribal Center with displays of Native American crafts and jewelry; the All-Indian Rodeo is held in September.

The Big Trees Begin

Leggett, where 101 meets the northern end of Highway 1 running inland from the coast, is really the entryway to the northern redwoods, just south of Humboldt County. It's a natural spot in which to take a break, although, unless you're camping, probably not to stay the night. **Standish-Hickey State Recreation Area** on the south fork of the Eel River here is a handy place for a picnic; a comfortable hiking trail leads to the Captain Miles Standish Tree, 225 feet tall, and the rugged five-mile Mill Creek Loop leads south to a superb overlook.

Just north of here the highway slips through Smithe Redwoods State Reserve (old-growth redwoods) and Richardson Grove State Park. Touristy shops (many selling coffee tables and other objects made of redwood burl) and diversions abound all through here, including a Drive-Thru Tree (but wait for the one at Myers Flat).

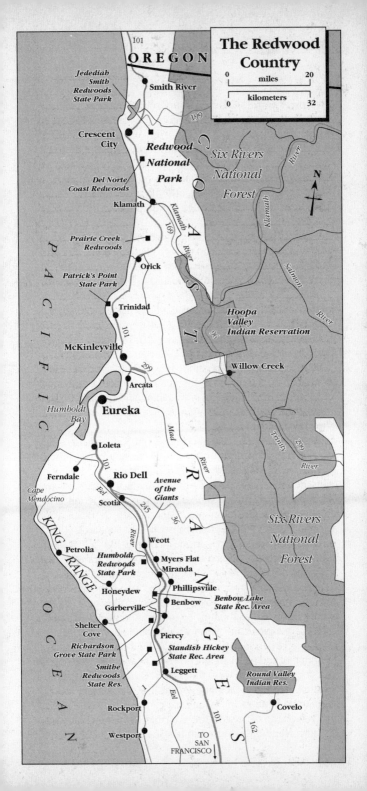

The Redwood Country

| miles | 0 — 20 |
| kilometers | 0 — 32 |

Benbow Lake

Five miles north of Richardson Grove, Benbow Lake State Recreation Area consists of 786 forested acres and a six-mile lake created by a seasonal dam from May through September. In season there are campfire programs, hiking and horse-riding trails, outdoor theater, non–power boat rentals, swimming, fishing, and camping. A huge outdoor Arts and Crafts Fair is staged in June, and the annual Benbow Lake Shakespearean Festival brings the Bard to the Big Trees in August.

Motels abound in the immediate region, but for style, atmosphere, warm welcome, and good food the grateful traveller settles down in **Benbow Inn**, two miles south of Garberville. In partially timbered Tudor, Benbow commands a bow in the south fork of the Eel; it is a place for deep, relaxed breathing and a sense of having arrived at the proper place at the end of a long day (particularly if it's the first overnight stop from San Francisco). The lobby is a cozy, eclectic sitting area of vaguely Victorian persuasion, with a fire blazing whenever possible; on pleasant afternoons and evenings you can retreat to the outdoor terrace. A nine-hole golf course, putting green, lawn games, and reading are the diversions of choice; at night wonderful old movies are shown.

Gourmands and even gourmets from San Francisco frequently are critical (and justly so) of cooking beyond their city limits. Benbow, however, does not disappoint. From the eggs Benedict at brunch to the roast duck *à l'abricot* or shrimp scampi sauté at dinner, dining is an experience in excellence. Unlike most inns, Benbow is a destination in itself; slightly expensive, though not by city standards.

Benbow should serve as headquarters for a day-long meander through Humboldt Redwoods State Park (see below), the largest of its kind in California and one very likely to make you trip over your own adjectives. Although there are informal cafés and snack spots along the route, those who choose to match dining to scenery should ask Benbow to prepare a picnic luncheon with suitable beverages.

Little Garberville, just north of Benbow, is mainly a jumping-off and provisioning point for redwood park visitors and for excursions west to Shelter Cove, nearby fishing streams, wilderness camping, and the like. Although the aforementioned Benbow Inn is the clear choice when rambling in this region, a few motels are available in Garberville: **Best Western Humboldt House Inn** has 56 modestly priced units and a swimming pool; **Garberville Motel**, with restaurant, provides special facilities for winter salmon/steelhead fishermen at reasonable prices; and the inexpensive **Rancho Motel** has a swimming pool. Yet another choice can be found 8 miles south of Garberville at Piercy, where the 62 cabins of **Hartsook Inn** sit on 30 redwood-shaded acres along the Eel River, next to Richardson Grove State Park. Diversions include river swimming, lawn games, and hiking. The well-regarded dining room (American cuisine) has no liquor license, but you may bring your own wine.

HUMBOLDT REDWOODS STATE PARK

Through fog of summer and rain of winter, with bursts of sun searing through, the forests of Humboldt have stood (with trillium and sorrel and ferns at their feet) since the bubonic plagues ravaged Europe; winds have whispered in their crowns since Charlemagne and the Vikings and the birth of Cairo. Sounds are muffled; time appears a permanent twilight; hoary age rules. "This is the forest primeval . . .": The druids of antiquity could certainly have sheltered here; maybe they still do.

Take the signposted turnoff south of Phillipsville to slip into the shadows of the 31-mile-long **Avenue of the Giants** (Scenic Route 254). It parallels 101, returning to that raceway just south of Scotia.

Your first stop should be at **Chimney Tree**, where hunters who had camped near a great redwood in 1914 left their fire unextinguished. For days, perhaps weeks, it burned inside the giant trunk. When the tree's top was sheared off in a mighty windstorm, a living chimney was created. This is a superb example of the redwoods' regenerative powers, as new growth continues to seal old cracks and hundreds of shoots sprout from the old tree.

Just a hop north of Phillipsville on this route at Miranda, the Avenue of the Giants Association supplies information on redwoods, camping, lodging, dining, biking, and summer recreation; Tel: (707) 943-3108. At Miranda the 16 cottages of **Miranda Gardens Resort** are sheltered in the forest, some having fireplaces and whirlpools. There's a heated pool and campfires are held nightly in summer; rates range widely according to the size of and facilities in the cabins.

A little farther on at Myers Flat the **Shrine Drive-Thru Tree** was struck by lightning centuries ago, creating a fire that ate away at its base for years. Today visitors drive their cars through the resulting hole in the 2,000-year-old trunk and photograph each other doing it. You can also park your car on a log that weighs 100 tons.

Along the winding way, visitors will note signs that identify more than 570 memorial groves, such as the Garden Club of America Grove or the Franklin K. Lane Grove, which are a result of the Save-the-Redwoods League's efforts (begun in 1918) to purchase redwood lands from local owners in order to create the park.

South of Weott, near Burlington Campground, the **Humboldt Redwoods State Park Visitor Center** houses worthwhile exhibits on natural history and sells publications about the big trees and the various parks. Inquire about the summer campfire interpretive programs, ranger-guided walks, children's Junior Ranger program, and more.

Just north of Weott there'a a parking lot for the **Founders' Grove Nature Trail**, a gentle, short, and level walk that begins at the foot of magnificent Founders' Tree, 40 feet in circumference and 346 feet high. (It was thought to be the world's tallest tree until the Libbey Tree in Redwood National Park—see below—was measured.) Pick up a self-guiding brochure and follow the trail past an upturned tree with its exposed root system, the mammoth Dyerville Giant, and many other spots of interest. Early in May some 2,000 runners from the U.S. and Canada join in the Avenue of the Giants Marathon, cruising a course beneath the soaring redwoods; it begins at the wide spot named Dyerville.

Directly opposite Founders' Grove, a marked turnoff under Highway 101 leads into **Rockefeller Forest** (named for the signature on the check), often called the world's finest forest. Turn off your car's engine at Bull Creek Flat, about five miles from Dyerville Bridge, and listen to the silence. Superb specimens in the woods include the Tall Tree (359 feet high), the strangely shaped Flatiron Tree, and many fallen giants.

When you can bear to move on, turn back the way you came and then continue north along the Avenue of the Giants to Redcrest, north of which you may wish to make short stops at the Eternal Tree and the Immortal Tree. Both are ancient (Eternal is 70 feet around) and demonstrate the redwoods' resistance to fire and disease.

To sleep in the deep dark of Humboldt is a special experience available at three family campgrounds. Reservations should be made eight weeks in advance; Tel: (800) 444-PARK.

For information on other lodgings, restaurants, grocery stores, and guides, contact the Avenue of the Giants Association; Tel: (707) 943-3108.

The Avenue of the Giants re-joins Highway 101 just south of Rio Dell and Scotia, which face each other across the Eel River. The **Pacific Lumber Company** of Scotia, the world's largest processor of redwood, offers interesting self-guided mill and museum tours. A traditional spot for a meal in town is **Scotia Inn**, which opened in 1888 and serves dinners Wednesdays through Sundays. (Early settlers and lumbermen imported the name of their home, Nova Scotia, for the town.)

FERNDALE AND CAPE MENDOCINO

About 2 miles north of Fortuna, Highway 211 takes an abrupt swing southwest off 101 and makes a short run through dairy farms to **Ferndale**, the self-proclaimed Victorian Village, a State Historical Landmark, and the prettiest little cow town in Northern California.

The rich agricultural community of Ferndale was settled in the 1860s by prosperous Swiss-Italian and Portuguese farmers. Later a welcome was extended to Danes forced to leave Denmark during the battles with Prussia over Schleswig-Holstein, adding to the human cultural cocktail. The village seems to have stepped intact out of the 19th century, smart and sparkling with freshly painted façades, outstanding examples of ornately decorated gimcrack and gingerbread Victoriana. The local architectural styles—Italianate, Roman-Renaissance, Carpenter Gothic, Gothic Revival, Stick, Queen Anne, Eastlake—demand an extensive walking tour, chiefly along Main and Ocean streets, camera in hand.

After you have ogled the houses, a natural stop is the **Ferndale Museum and Gift Shop** at Third and Shaw streets, where the town's heritage is displayed in cameo settings, exhibits of antique farm and logging equipment, and more. If you want to stock up on the past, stop by **Golden Gait Mercantile** at 421 Main Street to buy such latter-day essentials as Dr. Kilmer's Swamp-Root, red suspenders, long johns, straight razors, fish-eye tapioca, and even horehounds.

Of the several galleries in Ferndale, the most curious and compelling is **Hobart's Galleries**, also on Main Streeet; it was Hobart Brown who fathered the local madness known as the

Great Arcata-to-Ferndale Cross-Country Kinetic Sculpture Race, staged annually on Memorial Day weekend in May. The point is to drive, push, or otherwise encourage an engineless, wheeled artwork over land, water, beaches, and highways for 35 miles south from Arcata. Other less loony local celebrations include June's Portuguese-inspired Holy Ghost Festival; the Humboldt County Fair, early to mid-August; and the unusual Scandinavian Mid-Summer Festival in mid-June. This last celebrates Scandinavia's midnight sun and the settlement of Scandinavians on the Humboldt County coast; you'll find dances, food stalls, arts, crafts, soccer matches, and parades.

Some travellers choose to settle down here for two or three days to explore the countryside at a measured pace. Others headquarter in Eureka (see below) and visit Ferndale on a day trip. In town on Berding Street, **The Gingerbread Mansion**, an 1898 mansion with nine guest rooms, is an unusually attractive hideaway with lavish baths, antique furnishings, parlors, an English garden, and bicycles for loan; the quality justifies the room rates.

Three other stylish inns are **Ferndale Inn** (three bed-and-breakfast rooms that share a bath), **Shaw House Bed-and-Breakfast Inn** (five bedrooms in a gabled, Gothic Carpenter house built in 1854 by Ferndale's founder), both on Main Street, and **Victorian Village Inn** (12 rooms in an 1890 Victorian building, with an auto museum and a restaurant-bar) on Ocean Avenue.

Most restaurants are located on Main Street: **Fern Café** (for lunch), a deli at **Ferndale Meat Company**, **Roman's** (Mexican and American cuisine), pasta at **Koblick's**, and **Guadalajara** (meals with a Mexican accent).

A primitive area of 105 acres, **Russ Park**, in the southeast corner of town off Bluff Road, is a refuge and breeding place for over 60 types of birds that's open daily for walking, horseback riding, and picnicking.

A delightful, hand-drawn brochure, "Visitors' Guide and Walking Tour," is available at most inns and shops in town or at the Ferndale Chamber of Commerce, 248 Francis Street (a continuation of Main Street).

Cape Mendocino

To wander magnificent country rarely traversed even by seasoned California travellers, take Mattole Road (Route 211), which meanders southwest from Ferndale toward Cape Mendocino, passes through wide spots called Petrolia and Honeydew, then continues inland and eastward back into the Rockefeller Forest and Dyerville (Founders' Grove). From there it's possible to make a speedy return to Ferndale on 101 or to continue on to Eureka.

On this and similar backcountry outings throughout Northern California, check your gasoline gauge before setting out, and stop by a deli for picnic supplies; you won't find any charming country inns or service stations along many of these routes.

The Mattole Road runs almost into the sea at Cape Mendocino, the most westerly point of the continental United States, named to honor Don Antonio de Mendoza, a 16th-century viceroy of New Spain. The name Mendocino later was given to the county immediately to the south and to the town there that has become a popular weekend retreat for San Franciscans—see The Mendocino Coast below.

It remains uncertain which Spanish explorer first spotted the monumental point, but surely it was around the mid-16th century when the Manila galleons plied the wild sea lanes from Asia across the Pacific to Acapulco and New Spain. The annual Manila-to-Mexico crossing was called "the longest and most dreadful of any in the world," taking six to eight months and sometimes ending in disaster: Between 1565 and 1815, thirty Manila treasure ships were lost on the crossing, many pounded into pieces on these rocks.

For 250 years the Spaniards sailed the route, and many a famous explorer marked his course by the rocky tip: Sir Francis Drake in 1579 on his voyage around the world; Sebastián Rodríguez Cermeño in 1595, while hunting a port for the galleons; Sebastián Vizcaíno in 1602 and 1603, while charting the coast; and Captain George Vancouver, sent by England in 1792 to report on the Spanish possessions along the Pacific coast.

The wind shrieks, the sea swells, on inland pastures the sheep huddle into their woollen coats as you strain to imagine the galleons, blown in from the Far East with their luxurious cargoes of gold and spices and silks bound for the Old World via the New.

The Lost Coast

The only place that can claim the title of town in this country is skimpy **Petrolia**, near the banks of the Mattole River where oil was discovered in the 1860s. Originally the land had been called, rather pompously, New Jerusalem, but on the occasion of California's pioneer oil strike by Governor Leland Stanford's Mattole Petroleum Company in 1865 it became Petrolia. Collectors of trivia will pause to photograph the commemorative marker. Mattole Road bends sharply inland at Honeydew, where there's a post office and general store.

Much of this unknown land is known as California's Lost Coast; part of it is officially the **King Range National Conservation Area**, a riot of peaks, valleys, and shoreline barely scratched by logging roads. The first inhabitants in this wilderness were the Whilkut, Sinkyone, and Mattole Indians, who used the land for hunting and gathering for more than 2,000 years; they have been gone for more than a century. Two major trails, the King Crest and the Chemise Mountain, may be hiked, but walkers should carry drinking water, tell friends where they are going, and be aware that rattlesnakes abound in driftwood and rocky areas. For maps and information on hunting, camping, etc., call the U.S. Bureau of Land Management's office in Ukiah; Tel: (707) 462-3873.

Few people make a living along this isolated, forbidding coast except those who farm marijuana. Tourist authorities don't like it, but marijuana is, at this writing, the leading cash crop in Humboldt County. If you're hiking, be careful to stay on marked paths and trails and off private property.

If you return to Ferndale and then back to 101 and continue north toward Eureka, stop in the small town of Loleta (off 101) for a visit to the family-run **Loleta Cheese Factory**, which produces 14 types of cheeses, from creamy Monterey Jack to smoked salmon Cheddar.

EUREKA
Humboldt Bay

Humboldt Bay, the only fine large harbor between San Francisco and Puget Sound, escaped discovery even longer than did San Francisco Bay, having eluded the eyes of Juan Rodríguez Cabrillo, Bruno Heçeta, Sir Francis Drake, and George Vancouver, all of whom sailed by without spotting it.

Named (as was the county) for the great German naturalist and traveller Baron Alexander von Humboldt, the bay was first found in 1806 by Captain Jonathan Winship, an American hired by the Russian-American Fur Company to hunt seals along the coast. He named it the Bay of the Indians because of the many villages around its shore, and it was christened for von Humboldt in 1850. (The explorer would have been pleased; he once remarked, "There are three stages in the popular attitude toward a great discovery: First, men doubt its existence, next they deny its importance, and finally they give the credit to someone else.")

It was the year 1850 when one James Talbot Ryan, a descendant of the earls of Shrewsbury and at the time a surveyor in the employ of the Mendocino Exploring Company, came to the shores of Humboldt Bay in search of the proper site for a lumber-shipping port. "Eureka!" he is supposed to have cried, hence the name of the major town on the bay. At first the settlement waged small struggles for "top town" with Humboldt City and Uniontown (now Arcata), but Eureka soon proved to have the finest site, not too far from the bay's entrance and unimpeded by mud flats. By 1853 a post at Fort Humboldt had been built within the city limits as defense against the surrounding tribes.

Surely the most notable man to serve at Fort Humboldt (no one would have believed it at the time) was Captain Ulysses S. Grant, who arrived in 1854 to find the foggy bay a dreary duty. Soon he discovered the whiskey barrel at Ryan's Store; not long after he was requested to resign. The day he departed Eureka for Ohio and civilian life, the future president told post surgeon Jonathan Clark, "My day will come, they will hear from me yet."

"By 1854," writes Stuart Nixon in *Redwood Empire,* "nine mills were sawing fir and pine on Humboldt Bay. But not redwood. Everyone suspected profits lay in the big trees, but nobody cared to tackle 400 tons of tree. Finally in 1856 a New Brunswicker, William Carson, took the plunge. Using a leased mill, Carson sawed and shipped the first redwood lumber across Humboldt Bay. In no time, redwood was the rage in San Francisco. Its elegant color and its rot-resistance commanded premium prices."

The days of "mining" red gold had begun. By 1881 twenty-two sawmills were at work in Humboldt County alone. Spans of oxen, as many as seven at a time, towed the enormous logs over a slip of lesser logs laid crossways: From this arrangement the term "Skid Road" evolved (now corrupted to Skid Row). Then came steam "donkey" engines that snaked logs out of the forests with a manila line; they were faster and complained less than oxen. Rails were laid for logging locomotives.

The 200-foot-tall redwoods didn't give up easily: Every one that fell with a thunderous crash cost five days' exhausting labor for two "choppers." Even the Paul Bunyans who leveled the monarchs respected them. As one old logger sighed, gazing at the green tangle high above his head (quoted by Stuart Nixon): "She sure makes a big hole in the sky."

Today debates rage between the preservation-minded ecologists, along with other adherents of the current green movement, and the remaining lumber companies, their employees, and adherents who see no economic future in Northern California without such industry. Offshore oil drilling comes into the arguments, too. Anyone who doubts the tenacity with which the two sides stick to their guns should start a discussion some night in a Eureka saloon.

Old Town

Eureka, with a population of almost 25,000, is the largest city in the state north of Sacramento, and its fishing fleet is second only to San Francisco's. Along 101 (which becomes Broadway in town), traffic seethes in summer, but elsewhere there's a wide-street, low-rise tranquillity reminiscent of an old Midwestern town.

As in so much of the state, tourism is the real growth industry. Sensing its importance a few years ago, city fathers encouraged restoration in and around Old Town, which had been allowed to slip into seediness. The result is a remarkably attractive (and not too cute) collection of specialty shops, promenades, art galleries, antique nooks, restaurants, and saloons in exuberant Victorian settings.

Just in back of the Humboldt waterfront, Old Town proper extends between 1st, 2nd, and 3rd streets, running east and west, and C to G streets, running north and south. This historic heart is a spruced-up, partially pedestrian area with a waterfall, gazebo, sculptured benches, and a trolley that runs shopping tours from May through September and during the Christmas season. There are also horse-and-buggy tours of Old Town. A first stop might be at the Eureka/Humboldt County Convention & Visitors Bureau at 1034 2nd Street, which can supply information on the entire region; Tel: (707) 443-5097 or (800) 338-7352; outside California, (800) 346-3482.

There are several art galleries and museums worth visiting in Old Town. At 3rd and E streets, regional history, antique firearms, Victorian relics, and a superb collection of Karuk, Huma, and Yurok Indian baskets are lures to the **Clarke Memorial Museum**, housed in the former Bank of Eureka building, which is an example of what's locally called Roman Renaissance Revival style. Nearby on 2nd Street the **Romano Gabriel Wooden Sculpture Garden** displays a whimsical collection of sculptures created over a period of 30 years from wooden discards and scraps by Gabriel, a local carpenter-artist. About a block away at 422 1st Street, the **Humboldt Cultural Center** occupies an 1875 loft-style brick building with a cast-iron storefront; delights include changing exhibitions as well as pottery, jewelry, and gift shops. The **Indian Art Gallery** at 241 F Street was established by the Northern California Indian Development Council to provide artists an opportunity to show and market their works in a gallery setting; there's also a gift shop here featuring handcrafted items. A few doors away, the **Old Town Art Guild** is a cooperative venture of many North Coast artists, with one-person shows held monthly.

When hunger strikes in Old Town, seek solace at **Lazio's**, 327 2nd Street (between D and E streets), or **The Landing**, at the foot of C Street, right off Humboldt Bay. Both are renowned for seafood, some of which has just swum in. All that noise you hear is the happy sound of gregariousness.

A three-block walk from Old Town, **The Eureka Inn** adds another traditional style to the cityscape: English Tudor. Eureka's major hotel, at 7th and F streets, offers 105 rooms in a 1922 structure that's now a National Historic Landmark, complete with heated pool, whirlpool, saunas, and minibars. This is the kind of place for reading in a deep chair before the fireplace. A local clientele, which includes everyone from loggers to attorneys, breakfasts and lunches in the **Inn Café**; the **Rathskeller** is a German-style pub, and the **Rib Room** serves international cuisine, local seafood, and, of course, prime rib. On the other hand, should a Mexican mood strike, try **Luna's** at 1134 5th Street; Tel: 445-9162.

Half a dozen blocks in the other direction, on the corner of 4th and V streets, the **Red Lion Inn** is another leading hotel, with 180 reasonably priced rooms, a pool, and the well-regarded **Misty's Restaurant**.

Victoriana in Eureka

Gingerbread Gothic sweeps to its glorious pinnacle in the **Carson Mansion** at 143 M Street, one of the most photographed homes in California. Completed in 1886 to the order of aforementioned redwood king William Carson, it employed a hundred carpenters and artisans to create a fantasy in three stories, with spacious porches and balconies, 18 rooms, arched recesses, soaring staircases, carved panels, stained glass, and outbursts of onyx in the fireplaces.

Unfortunately Carson Mansion must be enjoyed—and

photographed—only from the outside, since it is now the very private property of the select Ingomar Club. Still, you won't want to miss this joyful explosion of creamy spinach-colored finials, gables, friezes, parapets, and roofs as pointed as witches' hats.

The Eureka Chamber of Commerce, 2112 Broadway (Tel: 442-3738 or 800-356-6381) issues a brochure on a self-guided "Victorian Architectural Tour of Eureka," which will direct you to 26 of the most interesting houses; there are almost a hundred others. Prominent among the styles are Eastlake, Queen Anne, Carpenter Gothic, and French Empire.

Fortunately, it's possible to sleep here in a Victorian mansion. **Old Town Bed-and-Breakfast Inn**, dating from 1871, was Carson's original home; it offers five rooms, an evening social hour, and full breakfast to guests. **Carter House Bed-and-Breakfast Inn**, near the entrance to Old Town, is a splendid 1982 re-creation of an ornate San Francisco Victorian, vintage 1884. Furnished with antiques, Oriental rugs, marble fire-places (one suite boasts its own whirlpool), and exuding an air of old-fashioned hospitality, Carter House is as winning as Eureka itself. Catty-corner from Carter House, the 20-room **Hotel Carter** is owned by the same family and offers the same warm welcome; it was modeled after Old Town's classic Cairo Hotel, now vanished. Both inns have a no-smoking policy.

A few blocks from Old Town, the restored Queen Anne Victorian home now called **Iris Inn** joins antiques to contemporary art in happy proximity. Guests of the four rooms enjoy a full breakfast, afternoon tea, use of the library, and a nightcap in the parlor. At 8th and J streets, just on the edge of downtown and within walking distance from Old Town, **Craddock Manor** has been restored to its 1904 Colonial Revival style; the bath is shared and rates are quite reasonable.

Not a Victorian but a Swiss-Tyrolean, the two-room **Chalet de France**, 10 miles east/southeast of town, commands 160 acres overlooking 30-mile views of the Pacific. Rates include full breakfast, French gourmet meals, massage, use of the swimming pool, and more; it's not expensive, considering what you get. Reservations are essential year round.

Sights and Tours in Eureka

For a special long-lasting memento of Redwood Country, stop by **North Coast Concepts** at 233 Manzanita Street; this timber nursery sells Coastal and Sierra Redwood seedlings in an Adopt-a-Redwood plan. If ships and sailors are more to your fancy, you'll find the seafaring tradition of the North

Coast beautifully displayed at the **Humboldt Bay Maritime Museum**, 1410 2nd Street.

Fort Humboldt State Historic Park sits just off Broadway (Highway 101) and Highland Avenue southwest of downtown. Within the complex (much of it under restoration), the walk-through **Logging Museum** is regarded by knowledgeable enthusiasts as one of the best in the country. Tours and picnicking are available, but it's wise to check on details; Tel: 445-6567.

Forty-six acres of redwoods surround **Sequoia Park and Zoo** at Glatt and W streets in the south of town, near the Municipal Golf Course. A duck pond, gardens, trails, children's playground, snack bar, and picnic facilities make it popular with families.

In a most unusual circumstance, a historic local lumbering operation doubles as a dining experience that's all but a requirement for travellers in Eureka. The **Samoa Cookhouse** is the last surviving lumberjack cookhouse in the West, operating in the small company town of Samoa, near the Louisiana-Pacific plywood mill.

To reach this relic of the 1885 rough-and-ready lumberjacks and millhands, take the Samoa Bridge off R Street, in northern Eureka, and follow the signs to the Cookhouse. Be hungry, and prepare for Paul Bunyan–size flapjacks, soups served in tub-size tureens, beef roasts King Henry VIII would have envied, and plates of potatoes that could serve a whole squad of ravenous loggers. The decor might be called Early Oilcloth, and the prices are about that old-fashioned, too. Adjoining, the Cookhouse Historical Museum of Lumbering is open daily.

From mid-June to mid-September, **Eureka Image Tours**, 2112 Broadway, offers a five-hour bus trip around the city on Tuesdays and Thursdays that includes visits to Fort Humboldt, Sequoia Park and Zoo, and Clarke Museum; a Humboldt Bay cruise; and lunch at the Samoa Cookhouse. Reservations are necessary; stop by at 2112 Broadway or call 442-3738.

Humboldt Bay Harbor Cruise operates 75-minute sailings aboard the M.V. *Madaket,* once the Eureka–Samoa ferry, from the foot of C Street. They run daily from June through September, weekends in May; Tel: 444-9440 or 442-3738.

To leave the road signs behind, board the **North Coast Daylight** passenger train for a serpentine ride between Eureka and Willits along Eel River Canyon. Completed in 1914, the line was one of the most expensive engineering feats of its age. Service declined with the construction of highways and the train was discontinued in 1971, but now it's alive again with 1950s-vintage equipment. The trips last from 8:00 A.M. to 5:30 P.M. in each direction, with breakfast and luncheon served in the dining car for coach-class and parlor-class passengers. Trips of one, two, three, and seven days are available; Tel: 442-7705 and (800) 544-3763 within California.

Sport fishing, especially for salmon, tuna, and rockfish, is offered through **King Salmon Charters**, 5333 Herrick Road (Tel: 707-442-FISH), and through **Celtic Charter Service**, Woodley Island Marina (Tel: 707-442-7580).

Major celebrations in Eureka include the Rhododendron Festival & Parade during the last week of April and first week of May; Fourth of July Celebrations; September's Food Fair; and October's Oktoberfest and Redwood Art Fall Exhibit.

Eureka's Backcountry

Back roads wiggle and twist around the vast, little-populated country to the east of Eureka. This is empty, rugged land where, in the shadows of Douglas fir trees, you may stumble across the path of Big Foot, the huge, hairy humanoid occasionally seen in the deep woods, particularly within Six Rivers National Forest. Big Foot is known as Sasquatch along Canada's west coast and invites comparison with the Himalayan yeti (the Abominable Snowman). From time to time, spottings of Big Foot are cited in newspapers from Eureka to San Francisco and even Los Angeles. In 1958 a tractor driver in the wilderness beyond Bluff Creek found a series of 16-inch, human-looking footprints that indicated a creature weighing from 600 to 800 pounds with an average stride of four feet. Since then seven people claim to have glimpsed Big Foot, and 38 findings of footprints have been recorded, all of which have been judged not to have been made by an animal. Skeptics should join the debates in the hamlets along the Trinity and Klamath river valleys.

Following Highway 101 north from Eureka for 10 miles and then turning eastward on State Highway 299, you will drive 40 winding miles to reach **Willow Creek**, nestling in the heart of the world's largest virgin stand of Douglas firs. In Gold Rush days this was a distribution point for mining supplies; today Willow Creek introduces outsiders to the wonders of the great outdoors with white-water trips, rafting and tubing, horseback riding, fishing, hunting, camping, hiking, cross-country skiing, and even golf.

Trinity River Rafting Center on Star Route #5 can tailor raft trips to beginners (even four-year-old children) or experienced white-water runners (ratings Class IV and V). Rafting is on the Upper and Lower Trinity rivers, the Lower and Upper Klamath, and the Salmon. Backpacking and rafting combos take you through the cool fern grottoes and forests of Douglas fir, incense cedar, and ponderosa pine; Tel: (916) 629-3646. White-water trips, an evening dinner cruise in the company of osprey (with candles and linen in the primitive canyons), and day excursions for those on a short detour from Eureka are offered by **Bigfoot Outdoor Co.** at the Mountain Provisioner Deli in downtown Willow Creek; Tel: (916) 629-2967. At least five motels operate in Willow Creek; ask for details at the local Chamber of Commerce, P.O. Box 704, Willow Creek, CA 95573; Tel: (916) 629-2963 or 629-2019.

About a 20-minute drive north of Willow Creek via State Highway 96, the settlement at the **Hoopa Valley Indian Reservation** on the Trinity River is worth a call because of the excellent Native American basketry, weaponry, and arts on display at the **Hoopa Tribal Museum.** Tours of nearby Hoopa villages can be arranged; Tel: (916) 625-4110.

Watered by the Klamath, Smith, Eel, Trinity, Van Duzen, and Mad rivers, the more than a million acres of **Six Rivers National Forest** provide excellent fishing, hunting, camping, and picnicking north of Hoopa. For information on lodgings, fees, licenses, and the like, check with the Forest Supervisor's Office, 507 F Street, Eureka CA 95501; Tel: (707) 442-1721.

HUMBOLDT COUNTY

You face a dilemma here: Whether to remain headquartered in Eureka, to stop at one of the neighboring towns or coastal resorts, or to roar onward to the north to Orick and Redwood National Park. While it's only 41 miles from Eureka to Orick, that means an 82-mile round trip, and it's impossible to see much of the park in one day. That dilemma will probably be solved by the time at your disposal and which of the following attractions prove intriguing to you.

Arcata and McKinleyville

In 1850 a party of 30 men from San Francisco founded a citysite on Humboldt Bay and called it Uniontown, which in 1853 became the seat of newly organized Humboldt County and eventually the busy center of mule pack trains that carried goods over mountain trails to the mines. As mining faded and lumbering took the spotlight, Eureka, with its deep-water site, became county seat in 1856 and Uniontown substituted the Native American name for its spot, Arcata.

In 1857 the frontier poet Francis Bret Harte, out of pocket after a stay in the Sierra mines and in San Francisco, stepped ashore to stay with his sister Maggie and her husband while looking for a paying job. A year later Harte became editor of the local weekly, *Northern Californian,* an entry into the literary world to which he would eventually contribute some of pioneer America's best stories, such as "The Outcasts of Poker Flat."

Today Arcata's Victorian homes, wide streets, green lawns, and flower gardens center around Town Plaza, which is watched over by a stern memorial of President William McKinley. The best way to gain a sense of Arcata is by taking a self-driven **Architectural Homes Tour**, a 45-minute swing past 21 structures of note. A driving map and other information is given out by the Arcata Chamber of Commerce, 780 7th Street, Arcata, CA 95521; Tel: (707) 822-3619.

In 1857 one Augustus Jacoby built the first sturdy business building in Arcata at 8th and H streets off the plaza. It's still here, as **Jacoby's Storehouse**, today housing 11 shops and restaurants.

Enthusiastic birders enjoy a literal field day within the 154 acres of **Arcata Marsh and Wildlife Sanctuary**, headquartered at the foot of I Street. It's an outstanding achievement in the use of treated wastewater, with aquaculture projects including a fish hatchery, salt marshes, and sloughs, frequented today by more than 200 species of birds. The Audubon Society conducts nature walks on Saturdays at 8:30 A.M., and the park is open daily from sunrise to sunset.

In addition to parks open to the public for all kinds of sports, the University Center at **Humboldt State University** offers bi-monthly one-day outings from June through September that take participants rafting, canoeing, windsurfing, and sailing; Tel: (707) 826-3358 or 826-3011.

Arcata has lured several accomplished new restaurateurs, and one of the best has opened **Abruzzi**, at 791 8th Street. Breads and pastas are fresh daily, as is locally caught seafood, and the prices are moderate; Tel: 826-2345. Healthy and heart-conscious Mexican cuisine may seem an oxymoron, but it exists at **Casa de Que Pasa**, 854 9th Street, where flavors riot, servings are the size of a hacienda, and prices are reasonable. Musicians appear from time to time, with endearing Mexican irregularity; Tel: 822-3441.

Not long ago, anything other than steak and potatoes was

considered international, even exotic, cuisine in Arcata. Now Ottavio and Kahish Sabia have brought a mix of Greek, Hungarian, Italian, French, Thai, and Chinese cooking with refreshing prices to **Ottavio's**, 686 F Street; Tel: 822-4021. **Youngberg's**, in Jacoby's Storehouse, continues its long popularity (there's a bakery right on the premises); Tel: 822-1712.

Pastoral serenity is the theme at **The Plough and the Stars Country Inn and Croquet Club**, a most uncommon retreat on two acres within city limits on 27th Street. Named for the work by Irish playwright Sean O'Casey, it's an introduction to the homey, historical interests of proprietors Bill and Melissa Hans. An air of casual hospitality permeates the place, with its five guest rooms (three with private bath, one with Franklin stove and outdoor deck), outdoor hot tub, horseshoe pit, croquet and lawn games, and midnight hors d'oeuvres for those who've gone to dinner in Eureka. Prices are quite reasonable, considering the quality. In the north of town on Valley West Boulevard, the **North Coast Inn** maintains 78 modern rooms, a pool, spa, coffee shop, restaurant, and lounge.

McKinleyville, about 4 miles north of Arcata on Highway 101, was one of many towns across the United States named after President William McKinley following his assassination in 1901. Its main attraction, aside from the Hammond Trail, which follows the route of an historic railroad now used by hikers, bikers, and equestrians, is the **Azalea State Reserve**. Here some 30 acres glow pinkish-white from April into summer; turn off 101 on North Bank Road. At 1100 Griffith Road, the **Fairyland Begonia and Lily Garden** hybridizes and develops new lilies and begonias; visitors are welcome to tour the nursery and greenhouses the year round and to purchase the unique varieties.

McKinleyville is highly residential in nature, though **Bella Vista Motel** does offer 16 modest and informal family units in a pretty rural setting overlooking the Pacific. Dining above the ocean is the lure at **Merryman's Dinner House**, north of town on Moonstone Beach. Seafood and steaks are the specialties, and reservations are accepted only for banquets; open Fridays through Sundays only between October 1 and April 1.

Trinidad

It was Holy Trinity Sunday, June 9, 1775, when explorers Juan Francisco de la Bodéga and Bruno Heçeta sailed into Humboldt Bay and named the site in honor of the day (*La*

Santisima Trinidad in Spanish). Its foggy, rocky headland then rested undisturbed for 18 years until Captain George Vancouver landed here to find the rough-hewn cross erected by the Spaniards.

Trinidad is the oldest town along the northern coast, founded in 1850 as a trading post for the mining camps. By the following year it had boomed to a population of perhaps 3,000 residents; today it has less than 400.

The glory days of gold have gone now, but the rugged meeting of waves and wooded headlands creates another kind of riches. **Trinidad Head Trail** is one of the most spectacular scenic walks on the entire California coast, allowing you views of migrating whales as you amble from redwood-topped cliffs to coves filled with lacy ferns. Sea lions sun on offshore rocks, hummingbirds pirouette in garden ballets, and hawks swoop and soar on coastal waves of air. Most visitors whiz right by on Highway 101. Instead, take the Westhaven Drive exit and follow along Main Street to Trinity, then turn right on Edwards and follow the signs to the trail parking lot. Keep on the trails and roads here, as everywhere, because poison oak is omnipresent.

Anyone with an interest in marine life will be fascinated by the **Humboldt State University Marine Biology Lab** south of town; take College Cove Beach Access. There's a good self-guided tour.

A restaurant that's pulling in diners from all around the area, **Larrupin' Café**, 1658 Patrick's Point Drive, is small and elegant with cuisine to match: barbecued cracked coastal crab with mustard-dill sauce, and chicken breast in phyllo with artichokes, just for starters; Tel: 677-0230.

Nearby on Patrick's Point Drive one mile off the Redwood Highway, **The Lost Whale Bed and Breakfast** is a cozy Cape Cod–style inn with four spacious suites overlooking the ocean. When sea lions bark and fog blankets the Pacific, shrug into a sweater and stroll into Patrick's Point. On a sunny morning, breakfast on the inn's deck (home-baked goods and locally smoked salmon, for instance) before hunting agate and jade on the beach. **Trinidad Bed and Breakfast** is another Cape Cod home (with four rooms) above Trinidad Bay on Edwards Street, within strolling distance from shops, restaurants, beaches, parks, and trails.

A rustic cluster of cottages, **Bishop Pine Lodge** is a long-time favorite of wanderers along the North Coast who appreciate quiet and seclusion. The 13 cottages have one, two, or three rooms; ten are equipped with kitchens. Picnic tables, grills, an outdoor fireplace, and a children's playground are available; a café is nearby. Take the Trinidad exit northbound or the Seawood Drive exit southbound to Patrick's Point Drive.

Patrick's Point State Park

Five miles north of Trinidad, Patrick's Point State Park is a splendid introduction to stands other than redwoods: Waves may batter offshore rocks, but here you are sheltered in forests of fir, pine and hemlock, Sitka spruce, red alder, and cypress. The floor is as intricate as an Oriental carpet: azaleas, blackberry, fairy bells, huckleberry, false lily-of-the-valley, salmonberry, rhododendrons, thimbleberry, and trilliums. Rim Trail is a comfortable walk from the Agate Beach parking area to Palmer's Point, from which six other steep, short trails lead to the shoreline. For information on camping, call 677-3570.

North of Patrick's Point, the Redwood Highway enters dramatically diverse **Dry Lagoon Beach State Park**. Fifteen miles of sandy beaches, lagoons, and rocky headlands are backed by an eye-popping parade of rolling farmlands, mountainous outcrops, and cool, shaded, old-growth forests where rays of sun filter down to illuminate outbursts of shrubs and wildflowers. Unfortunately, in midsummer the beaches are almost obscured from view by campers and RVs parked tailgate-to-tailgate along the edges of the road.

REDWOOD NATIONAL PARK

On a glorious autumn day more than 20 years ago, President Lyndon B. Johnson signed into being a richness of 50,000 acres north of Eureka to form the Redwood National Park, and Lady Bird Johnson dedicated the handsome nature trail that today bears her name. It was October 2, 1968. Ten years later, following a decade of struggle between conservationist forces led by the Save-the-Redwoods League on one side and lumbering interests on the other, President Jimmy Carter signed the Redwood National Park Expansion Act, increasing the size of the National Park to 106,000 acres. In a curious geographical amalgamation, Redwood National encloses three *state* parks: Prairie Creek Redwoods, Del Norte Redwoods, and Jedediah Smith Redwoods. These 28,000 acres are administered by the California Department of Parks and Recreation. Although there are political squabbles over the administration of the various parks (as ever), as a casual traveller you will probably be unaware of it as you pass from one entity to another.

The original inhabitants of these great reaches were, among the major regional tribes, the Karok (meaning "up-river people"), the Yurok ("down-river"), and the Hoopa, who (as we have seen) lived around the confluence of the Klamath and Trinity rivers. The tribes kept their cultures distinct: Stuart Nixon says a man could wander from one tribal region to the next and never come upon the same language twice.

It is said that the Spanish explorers were regarded as strange gods. In most ways they left the natives alone, but the Yankee arrivals were less respectful. By 1851 the so-called Indian Wars had begun, and raged sporadically until about 1870. (The fiercest of these encounters was the Bridge Gulch Massacre of 1852, which took place near Weaverville in Trinity County.)

Seeing the Forest

Surrounded by an army of soaring giant-trunked redwoods, you come upon a mysterious gathering: trees of respectable size and age in a ring around—what? Sometimes it's a mere circular slump in the forest floor; less often, it may be a ragged stump, broken apart like a bad tooth.

This is a "family circle," a grouping of three or even four generations, paying court to their ancestral tree. When it was toppled, by nature or loggers, and its stump returned to the earth from which it had arisen, a second generation sprouted from the still-living root crown. Members of the second generation that were logged produced a third, and if you peer closely you may see the sprout of yet another generation. The latest young have to fight to survive, since their still-mighty elders shut out the life-giving sun. (Most conifers reproduce only by seeds and cones, not by sprouting, thus giving the Coast Redwood a family advantage.)

Look for the "goose pen," the hollowed-out stump or trunk resulting from natural or man-made fires. (The Chimney Tree near Phillipsville is a prominent example.) The name results from the pioneers' practice of penning poultry within the hollows. Another phenomenon is the "penthouse," a clutch of new growth taking root far up in a tall trunk, its top having been sliced off by lightning or even a big wind.

Trees that would be giants anywhere else stand tall here: the massive Oregon white oak, the regal California black oak, the coast hemlock, the stately Douglas fir, and the noble Sitka spruce, in addition to big-leaf maples and cedars. Note also the shorter, twisted madrone and the California laurel (also known as bay, myrtlewood, or pepperwood), popular for its leaf used in cooking.

Sadly, a recent import in the woods is the invisible protozoan called giardiasis, which inhabits streams and lakes. Even the clearest waters may swarm with these microscopic creatures that when ingested produce chronic diarrhea, abdominal cramps, bloating, fatigue, and loss of weight in human victims. Only treatment by a physician who recognizes the symptoms can effect a cure. Walkers, hikers, and campers always should carry water canteens or flasks in addition to canned or bottled beverages to avoid drinking from potentially contaminated waters.

Even in summer, coastal areas and high altitudes can be cool; you would be wise to carry coats, jackets, or sweaters in your car. Breaking storm waves and high tides can sweep away not only swimmers but also beach and cliff walkers. Never turn your back on the ocean. Also, poison oak (similar to poison ivy) abounds. Stay on trails and/or wear high-topped sneakers or boots, and do not pluck strange foliage.

No lodging is available in Redwood National Park proper (a version of Yosemite's Ahwahnee Hotel would be much appreciated), and there are no federally developed camp-sites, although nearly 400 sites exist within the three state parks. Thus you should decide well in advance where you wish to headquarter, depending on whether you are choosy about accommodations or, on the other hand, want to avoid long, daily round trips. The choices are those described above in Trinidad, about 21 miles south of Orick and the park entrance; in Orick itself (modest accommodations); or in Klamath, 20 miles north of the park's entrance in Del Norte County (see below).

Orick

Little Orick is an essential stop for the **Redwood Information Center**, near Redwood Creek at Freshwater Lagoon just west of Highway 101. It's the headquarters for all national park information, state park camping, maps, nature walks, and special summer programs. Some horseback trail rides begin here, and ocean-facing decks allow whale watching in season. The center is open daily except on Thanksgiving, Christmas, and New Year's Day; Tel: (707) 488-3461. Horseback rides in Redwood National Park, ranging from one hour to all-day or overnight trips, can be arranged in summer through **Lane's Pack Station**. For information and reservations, write P.O. Box 31, Orick, CA 95555; Tel: (707) 488-5225 or 488-5325.

Aside from the center, the only attraction south of town is **Stone Lagoon Schoolhouse Museum**, a one-room building built of redwood in 1893 that houses Native American artifacts and regional memorabilia.

Orick has standard motels, modest to moderate in facilities and prices, each with kitchens in some units: try **Park Woods Motel; Green Valley; Palms**, with a small pool and playground; and **Prairie Creek** (ten units and a café). They are mentioned here for the convenience of those who may not want to make round trips each day from Klamath or Trinidad or the Eureka area to the park.

Exploring the Park

From Tall Trees trailhead in Redwood National Park you gaze down and into the past where, just over a mile away and 680 feet below, the world's tallest tree (so far as is known) lofts its head high into the sky above Redwood Creek. Howard Libbey Tree, reaching 367.8 feet, is only one in a family of giants, born about the time the Magna Carta was signed, before the days of Joan of Arc. As the Tall Trees Trail (with interesting signposts en route) twists toward the river, plants inexplicably enlarge, as if you were entering a primordial universe and peregrine falcons might become winged reptiles. (It is best to be alone with your imagination on this trail, or at least with companions not compelled to be chatty.) Giant, feathery ferns bow gently over sorrel (like fat, outsized clover), trillium holds out its three leaves, here each about the size of a human hand. The trail abuts a large earth bank—but it isn't a bank. It is the body of a sleeping giant, a redwood returning to the soil from which it arose, in a slow decaying process that may last for centuries.

Eventually you stand at the foot of the **Libbey Tree**, but its top eludes your view, closed in as it is by those of other titans. The sign at its base reads, simply and cautiously, "Tall Tree." (Tall Trees Grove was "discovered" and measured by a joint expedition of the National Geographic Society and the National Park Service in 1964. There is reason to believe some even taller tree might be found some day.)

Approximate hiking time on Tall Trees Trail is four hours (contemplation time unknown). It's rated as a Class 5 hike on a scale running from Class 1 (the easiest) to Class 6 (most difficult, steep grades with switchbacks). In high season a shuttle bus transfers hikers between the Redwood Information Center in Orick and the trailhead, with sprightly, educational commentary by the driver.

Even the least athletic explorer will be stirred by the stroll (Class 1) along the **Lady Bird Johnson Grove Nature-Loop Trail**, a one-mile circle near Little Lost Man Creek that can be ambled in 30 minutes. The well-marked turnoff from 101, slightly north of Tall Trees Trail, leads two miles inland on Bald Hills Road to a parking area. From there you cross a footbridge and follow an old logging trail through mature forest. This is a fine experience (with self-guided brochure) for those who because of health, age, or lack of time, cannot negotiate a longer, more difficult trail. Be on the lookout for "widow-makers" (lower branches the size of small trees that can come striking down as a result of winter storms), and keep your eyes peeled for sprouts at the base of a mother tree, "goose-pens," delicate forest lace, toothy tan oak, and showy, wild rhododendron (California Rose Bays).

In May 1982, Redwood National Park was dedicated as a World Heritage Site. It's a park undergoing restoration, some 39,000 of its acres having been logged off (clear cut) before they were added to the park in 1978. Some 200 to 300 miles of abandoned logging roads and 2- to 3,000 miles of crisscrossing tractor trails remain to be rehabilitated as the natural forest land recovers. A century or more may pass before the land and streams return to their natural state.

Prairie Creek Redwoods State Park

About 10 miles north of Orick, a grassy meadow spreads out along U.S. 101 in which wild iris blooms, herds of Roosevelt elk roam, and a sign alerts you to turn the car's radio dial to A.M. station 1610 for recorded information. You have arrived in Prairie Creek Redwoods State Park. At the northern edge of the meadow, follow the marked road left toward the small visitors' center and museum that serve the 12,544-acre park, where hiking on more than 55 miles of trails, camping, fishing, and picnicking may be enjoyed among redwood groves or on broad, sandy beaches. (Avoid the elk!)

One of the most fascinating trails in all Redwood Country begins near the visitors' center: the circular, 1-mile **Revelation Trail** (Class 1). It's a self-guided nature walk for the blind and handicapped, dedicated to the proposition that many senses other than sight may contribute to an understanding of the woods. Superbly designed, it is lined by a guide rope on which plastic balls have been placed, indicating the presence of a Braille marker at which one should stop, smell, listen, and "read" the Braille message. (The sightless who don't know Braille may borrow an explanatory tape cassette at the visitors' center.)

Revelation comes even to the sighted, calling attention at 17 stops to the textures of tree barks, the pungent odor of bay leaf, the splash of Prairie Creek roiling its bed through the woods. The walk takes about 45 minutes.

Too many travellers skip **Fern Canyon** on the west (sea) side of the park because the narrow, winding, unpaved Davison Road into it is time-consuming. The route runs west from U.S. 101 at a well-marked point about halfway between Orick and the Prairie Creek headquarters.

En route to the canyon you'll pass Gold Bluff and Gold Beach, names recalling the 1850s, when gullible fortune-seekers swarmed to sands said to be glittering with gold and panned themselves into penury. Today a beach campground nestles into the sand dunes and the only gold twinkles in the sky at twilight. The road ends at a wooded picnic area near Home Creek, which bubbles out of Fern Canyon. The canyon itself is a gash more than a mile long through the coastal bluffs, its 50-foot walls draped with ferns that seem to be dense, green waterfalls.

Fern Canyon Trail, a loop of less than a mile (Class 2), wiggles up the creek to a prairie where a small mining town once sat. Whether or not you know a fern from a *fritillaria,* you'll be enchanted by the intricate intertwinings of five-fingered ferns (used to create those black designs in Native American baskets), sword ferns (complete with hilts), feathery lady ferns (they might fit on Sunday bonnets), and giant horsetails, looking today exactly like their fossils, millions of years old. Fern Canyon is a fine place for a pensive picnic.

If you want to hike into Fern Canyon rather than drive, you can do so from the Prairie Creek Visitors' Center along James Irvine Trail (Class 3), which takes about three hours one way.

DEL NORTE COUNTY

The saying "Redwoods follow the fog" is nowhere better proven than in Del Norte County, where nature often mimics the rain forests of Washington's jungle-like Olympic Penin-

sula. Rhododendrons in this blooming land grow to 30 feet
in height.

Klamath Country

For about ten miles north of Prairie Creek Park, U.S. 101 runs
through memorial groves, crosses the Del Norte County line,
then debouches onto the flood plain of the Klamath River,
across a bridge guarded by the statues of four golden grizzly
bears, symbols of the state. (If you haven't stopped to drive
through a redwood before, there's another chance here at the
northern end of the bridge. The **Tour-Thru Tree**, some 700
years old, was damaged by fire about 300 years ago. Most cars,
vans, and even pickups can negotiate the passage.)

The Klamath area was long a wild mystery, its vastness all
but impenetrable. The diary of explorer Peter Skene Ogden
(for whom Ogden, Utah, was named) is the earliest account
of the visits of Europeans into the country north of Mount
Shasta. It was the course followed by Jedediah Smith (see
Jedediah Smith Redwoods State Park below) and his band of
trappers in the spring of 1828 when he blazed the trail down
the Klamath River from the Sacramento Valley into Oregon.

Klamath

Klamath is a phoenix, having been wiped out and rebuilt at
least twice. Established near the mouth of the Klamath River
in 1851 by miners with great expectations, it was shortly
deserted because of the ocean's shifting sandbars. Later, with
the rise of farming and small, regional industries, it came
back into existence, only to be erased by the devastating
floods of 1964.

Repositioned to higher ground today, Klamath is a burgeoning town that bills itself as "the Steelhead [trout] Capital
of the World" and makes its living off outdoor activities,
camping, and retirement-vacation homes. In summer the
pilots of **Jet-Boat Cruises** take thrill seekers on a 64-mile, six-
hour escape up the Klamath River from ocean to wilderness;
Tel: (707) 482-4191.

Four miles north of town, **Trees of Mystery**, announced by
a winking, 49-foot figure of Paul Bunyan flanked by faithful
Babe the Blue Ox, appears at first to be a garish tourist trap.
Not so: Its **End-of-the-Trail Indian Museum** houses one of
the West's outstanding collections of Native American artifacts, basketry, costumes, masks, and jewelry. The items of-

fered for sale are choice, not souvenirs. Trees of Mystery itself is a theme park featuring the story of Bunyan, as carved from redwood by the chainsaw sculptor Kenyon Kaiser, as well as a natural reserve of Douglas firs, cedars, spruces, and redwoods.

One mile west of U.S. 101 on Requa Road, historic **Requa Inn** offers 16 pleasant guest rooms from March to October and on weekends in winter; its dining room is geared to steaks and seafood for the public as well as guests; Tel: 482-8205. Across 101 from Trees of Mystery, **Motel Trees** has 23 units with cable TV, tennis courts, lounge and restaurant; rates are very moderate.

Del Norte Redwoods State Park

Much of Del Norte Redwoods State Park, the northern part of Redwood National Park, is dense, virgin forest; it's certainly the least developed of any of the redwood parks. There's splendid, scenic hiking along about 28 miles of trails, including Alder Basin Trail and Damnation Creek Trail.

The short, easy walk known as **Alder Basin Trail** exemplifies the care that has been taken to make the redwoods accessible to visitors of all ages. It's a Class 1, two-mile round trip that takes about 45 minutes through alder forest and maple and willow groves and is especially pretty in autumn.

On the distinctly opposite hand, **Damnation Creek Trail** (only 2.5 miles but it consumes at least three hours) is a trek for serious walkers, taking you from old-growth trees and a hidden sea cove at the bottom of a steep trail through an oceanside spruce forest. The trailhead is on U.S. 101, north of False Klamath Cove, a wide turnout on the oceanside near U.S. 101 marker 16.0.

Crescent City

Just north of Del Norte Park and about 18 miles south of the Oregon line, Crescent City tends to think of itself as the little metropolis of the northern redwoods, which is overstating the case a bit. Its first settlers arrived in 1853 from San Francisco aboard the schooner *Pomona* and by the summer of 1854 had set up 300 buildings and a supply center for the gold miners of southern Oregon and Siskiyou and Trinity counties.

Those were heady days. The first newspaper made its debut in 1854, and two years later the first drama appeared on the local boards: "The Toodles and Paddy Miles, the Limerick Boy." Crescent City, small, chilly, and inaccessible during winter, was nonetheless proposed as the new capital of California. A county history regales us today: "What an immense amount of ignorance must have been concentrated in that legislative body of the days of '55! But the Crescentarians were buoyant with life and energy, and the news of the failure was but a passing cloud across their bright hopes and expectations. No doubt, as the principal men of the place discussed the matter over their wine and cigars, new speculations and day-dreams of future greatness served to 'solace the hopes that ended in smoke.' "

Diggings and diggers came and went, along with the occasional tragedy. On July 30, 1865, the side-wheeler *Brother Jonathan,* plying offshore toward Oregon during a severe storm, struck St. George's Reef with (according to A. J. Bledsoe, author of *Indian Wars of the Northwest*) "such force that her foremast went through the hull, her foreyards resting across the rails . . . the ship was fast sinking in the embrace of the hungry waves, and short time was left to prepare for death." Today **Brother Jonathan Cemetery**, at Pebble Beach Drive and 9th Street, shelters 203 of the 232 people aboard who were drowned.

On Good Friday of 1964 a tsunami wave created by the gigantic Alaskan earthquake smashed Crescent City's business district to bits. Crescent has since called itself Comeback City, U.S.A.

Chiefly a research center, **Del Norte County Historical Society Main Museum** at 577 H Street displays exhibits of local pioneer history and artifacts of the Yurok and Tolowa tribes.

The northernmost **Redwood National Park Headquarters and Information Center** is located at 1111 2nd Street. Like the center at Orick, it offers informational brochures and maps and sells books, postcards, and souvenirs.

Battery Point Lighthouse, constructed in 1856, now houses a small museum of seafaring. Visitors are admitted several hours a day at low tide, when you can approach on foot across the ocean floor. In town you might stop at **Rumiano Cheese Company**, the largest producer of Dry Monterey Jack in California, at 9th and E streets, to see the cheese being made and to sample their imported and domestic cheeses.

Of the handful of motels available in the area, **Best Western Ship Ashore Resort** should be considered first. It's 16 miles north on the Redwood Highway in Smith River and offers 50 units, suites, and a penthouse (some rooms with kitchens). Also on hand are a hairdressing salon, a whirl-pool, fishing guides, and a museum in a converted yacht—rather eclectic accommodations, at reasonable prices. If you're in Smith River in July, be sure to enjoy the annual Easter-in-July Festival, a celebration of the midsummer harvest of blooming lily plants. Smith River is the Easter lily capital of the country, supplying 90 percent of the nation's lily bulbs.

On 101 immediately north of Crescent City, two lodging choices are **Pacific Motor Hotel** and **Crescent Travelodge**. Or, **Best Western Northwoods Inn** is just south of town, across 101 from the ocean. Also south on 101 is **Curly Redwood Lodge**, constructed of rare wood from a single redwood tree. The best café in Crescent City is **Harbor View Grotto**, specializing in seafood; what else?

Jedediah Smith
Redwoods State Park

The 9,560 acres of Jedediah Smith Redwoods State Park stand as a memorial to one of the sturdiest pathfinders in California's history, Jedediah Strong Smith. Mountain man and fur trader driven out of California by the Mexican authorities, Smith completed an arduous journey down the Klamath River to the Pacific, which is detailed in his comrades' journals. As quoted by Stuart Nixon: "Sometimes the party made only a mile a day. Animals tumbled into the wild gorges. Armed Indians harassed the party constantly, shooting the horses which they mistook for a new kind of elk."

This was not easy country. As reported in *Historic Spots in California*, "Trails had to be blazed over steep and rugged mountains, while progress was often impeded by heavy fogs. The scarcity of wild game, which was almost their only food, added to their hardships." Handily, en route to Crescent City, 10 to 15 Indians visited the Smith camp, "bringing with them a few Muscles [*sic*] and Lemprey [*sic*] Eels and some raspberries." Camped in the vicinity of Crescent City on June 19, 1828, Smith discovered the river that today bears his name. As Smith's party pushed north from Crescent City into Oregon, the Umpqua Indians massacred all except Smith and three companions. Smith was killed three years later by Comanches on the Cimarron River. His remarkable coastal trail north was followed in later years by trappers of the Hudson's Bay Company.

To enter Jedediah Smith Park, take 101 north from Crescent City to its junction with U.S. Highway 199 and then follow 199 nine miles east to the park entrance. Or look for Elk Valley Road south of Crescent City, which then branches off onto unpaved but scenic Howland Hill Road.

Howland Hill is a beautiful introduction to the park, paralleling the old stagecoach road for part of its length. Pull off at the indicated parking area for Stout Memorial Grove, a sanctuary presented to the state in 1929 as the first of the park's memorial groves. It preserves the park's largest measured redwood, 340 feet high and 22 feet in diameter.

The Stout Grove Trail (Class 1), about a circular mile, shows off several other spectacular sights along Mill Creek, including the upturned base of a giant tree that reveals its surprisingly shallow root system.

Off the Highway 199 entrance, the Hiouchi Ranger Station (open except in winter) hands out trail maps, supplies interpretive programs, presents exhibits, and stocks interpretive publications.

You can emerge from the mystery of the redwoods and travel south to the beauty and tranquillity of the Mendocino Coast by following Highway 101 south from the park to Leggett, then turning west onto Highway 1 all the way to the coast.

THE MENDOCINO COAST

In 1913 J. Smeaton Chase described the decaying settlement of Navarro, in a deep valley at the river mouth that opened upon the sea. "Most of the buildings were out of plumb; the church leaned at an alarming angle; and a loon, swimming leisurely in the middle of the stream, seemed to certify the solitude of the place." That Navarro has vanished, but its name lives in the little town 14 miles up the Navarro River in Anderson Valley.

"The solitude of the place": It is that, almost as much as the dramatic meeting of land and sea, that lures today's traveller to the Mendocino Coast. Only in the very small town of Mendocino itself has tourism made real inroads, and they are relatively tasteful. North and south, and east into forest stands and along narrow riverbeds where no roads run, there remains that rare commodity in the United States of the 1990s: room to be alone.

On a clear day sun glitters golden on the blue Pacific and you look west toward the horizon of Asia, half a world away. On other days, when fog swaddles the sharp, black, offshore rocks, the coast turns in on itself like a cat, sheltering in its own warmth, aloof. The lone walker braves the beaches and knows that nature is indifferent.

Nature aside, there are no demanding sights along this compelling coast: no cathedrals, no great museums, no antique monuments. Laziness soon seduces the wanderer; there is time and space for stretching in the grass, for picnicking on a rock-ribbed headland, for sipping wine in the sun and reading before the fireplace.

A corollary is that accommodations take on an unusual importance here. A hotel-motel room must be more than a respite from the business and the busyness of the day. It should serve as retreat, as solace; be it an aerie above the sea or a snuggery beneath the trees. Hence the many country inns that have arisen during the last decade and the space we devote to them here.

If you wish to motor directly from San Francisco's Golden Gate Bridge to Mendocino, you have several choices. You may follow Highway 101 to the Russian River turnoff at Cotati (Highway 116), emerging at the sea at Jenner; take 101 farther north to the Cloverdale turnoff, then continue on Highway 128 through Anderson Valley and Boonville to the sea south of Albion; or travel north as far as Willits on 101, turning west onto Highway 20 and following it west to meet the sea at Noyo. The distance will be 150 to 200 miles.

A caution: The beautiful, long route from the Golden Gate Bridge, then west at Mill Valley to Muir Beach and north to Stinson Beach before continuing all the way to Mendocino on Highway 1 is now impossible and impassable because of massive sinking of the roadbed on the bluffs south of Stinson Beach, triggered by the 1989 earthquake. Authorities say the portion of the road between Muir Beach and Stinson Beach may never be reopened, despite pleas from local landholders.

Rockport, Westport, and Cleone .

In 1851 a vessel loaded with silk and tea bound for San Francisco was battered onto the Mendocino beaches at the mouth of the Noyo River. Men sent to salvage the freight first saw the timber along this coast and reported to mill owner, lumberman, and alderman of San Francisco, Harry Meiggs. The trees were so tall they hid the sky, Meiggs was told, and they were so broad 20 men with outstretched arms couldn't span one.

By the following year, Meiggs had arrived with heavy

machinery and set up a sawmill to mine the "red gold." During the height of the felling fury a mill could be found up every creek or river. Ships were loaded by chutes on which lumber plummeted down from the cliffs; early photographs show wharfs and wire networks that look as if Rube Goldberg had invented them.

Towns and hamlets sprang up: Rockport, Hardy Creek, Westport, Cleone, Fort Bragg, Noyo, Caspar, Mendocino City (briefly Meiggstown), Little River, Albion, Navarro, Greenwood, Elk River, and Gualala.

Today's Rockport, Westport, and Cleone were all but abandoned by the end of World War I; now they are small scatters of wooden houses, waiting patiently for the gods (or perhaps tourism) to push them into prosperity once again. All share the wild seascape and the mountainous sand dunes built up during winter storms.

In his *Northern California,* Jack Newcombe reports that in 1881 Westport boasted "three hotels, six saloons, two blacksmith shops, three stores, and two livery stables," and that 50 schooners had docked in town between April and December.

Today's visitors make their own action: surf fishing, picnicking, hiking, and more. **Westport–Union Landing Beach**, southeast of Leggett and south of Rockport, has opened five new access trails and offers restrooms and camping. The **Westport Community Store** sells groceries and gas and houses the post office.

Those who mean it when they say they want to be alone can hide out in atmospheric comfort up here, far from city chic. The **Howard Creek Ranch Inn**, 3 miles north of Westport on Highway 1, named for the rancher who established it in the 1870s, comprises an inn and cabins in a pleasant valley near the beach. An unheated swimming pool, hillside hot tub, and sauna add to the welcome.

Cleone Lodge, on five and a half acres near the beach in Cleone, offers 11 rooms, including AsLan House, a cottage with two suites available. (Some cottages have kitchens; all have fireplaces, private deck, and balconies.) Picnic tables and a grill are available for the use of guests, and prices are moderate (even for suites, considering their facilities).

Most historic of the hostelries is Westport's former Cobweb Palace, built of redwood in the 1890s and one of a dozen or so inns where lumbermen once bellied up to the bar and the table. It has metamorphosed into the **Pelican Inn**, now spruced up so much you'd like to call it home (that is, if you have a full bar in your living room). There are six rooms in the inn and a house completely outfitted for families; it can sleep six. The full restaurant is open daily, except Mondays and Tuesdays, to the public as well as guests; vegetables are homegrown. Rooms are quite reasonably priced, as is the house.

South of Cleone and 3 miles north of Fort Bragg, **Mac-Kerricher State Park** offers campsites, biking, fishing, and trails for hikers and horseback riders; there's also a designated underwater diving area.

Fort Bragg

The metropolis of the Mendocino coast, relatively speaking, Fort Bragg was born not as a lumber town (though it soon became one) but, in 1857, as a military post on the Mendocino Indian Reservation. It was named to honor one General Braxton Bragg, a hero of the Mexican War. Both reservation and fort were abandoned in 1867 when the Indians were moved to Covelo, and the town settled down to decay.

A history of the place, written in 1880 (and quoted by Mendocino's Barbara Dorr Mullen) said, "Long years ago the paint and whitewash had been washed off the buildings by the fogs of summer and the rains of winter, and their places had been taken by a coat of green moss . . . The plaza, once so smooth and nicely kept, is now overgrown with a heavy crop of dog fennel and chickweed."

But in 1885 one Charles Russell "C.R." Johnson raised money in his native Michigan for the construction of a wharf and a mill at Fort Bragg and founded what became the Union Lumber Company, now owned by the Georgia-Pacific Corporation. Fort Bragg bounced back. The mill and much of the town were leveled by the San Francisco earthquake of 1906, but demand for lumber to rebuild San Francisco restored business. The little city has prospered since as a lumber, agricultural, recreational, and fishing center.

The driver who accelerates along Fort Bragg's Main Street (Highway 1), probably late for lunch in Mendocino, sees an unexceptional town with the usual complement of grocery stores, banks, gas stations, drug stores, general merchandise outlets, and the like. But along the back streets, away from the through traffic, you find a quieter, prettier Fort Bragg, where houses and even barns and fences have been handsomely restored, where beautiful gardens (wild and manmade) and several nurseries glow with fuchsias, rhododendrons, trillium, ceanothus, broom, lupine, and other lovely blooms. A pamphlet illustrating the self-guided **Historic Outdoor Fort Bragg Walking Tour** is available from motels, inns, or the Chamber of Commerce at 322 North Main Street. It begins at the Skunk Railroad Depot.

In summer old coast hands often prefer staying in unpretentious, accommodating Fort Bragg to dealing with the increasing tourist trauma of Mendocino. Even a few artists have left that scene to settle here in what one called "a more honest atmosphere." In fact, there's now a **Fort Bragg Center for the Arts**, with changing exhibits on the mezzanine of Daly's Department Store.

The three-story Victorian home of the aforementioned lumber baron C.R. Johnson became the Union Lumber Company's guesthouse from 1912 to 1969. Today it's the **Guest House Museum** at 343 North Main Street, open Wednesdays through Sundays to display photographs of old-time logging operations, artifacts, and some donkey engines and locomotives. The house itself is worth the visit, with its 12-foot ceilings, stained-glass windows, marble-top bathroom basins, and other luxuries rare on the frontier.

Whale-watching is a major diversion for locals and visitors alike from December to April as the pods of California grays migrate north and south just off the coast. A **Whale Festival**, with watch-tours and cruises, films and other activities is staged in late March (call Eureka Convention and Visitors Bureau for what's available; Tel: 707-443-5097). Other annual events include the Rhododendron Show in May; the Salmon Barbecue at Noyo Harbor in early July; and Paul Bunyan Days, with logging competitions, a parade, and a fuchsia show over the Labor Day weekend.

The Skunk Train

It was busy lumber titan C. R. Johnson who in 1885 pushed a logging railroad line from Fort Bragg through the dark, dense woods for 40 miles east to **Willits**. Steam passenger service began in 1904 and was extended to Willits in 1925, when the self-powered, yellow Skunk rail cars were inaugurated. (They were nicknamed for their original gas engines; the saying was, "You can smell 'em before you can see 'em.") Now, as then, travel on the line is casual, with frequent stops en route for deliveries of mail and groceries in areas inaccessible by car. (For Willits, see above in the Redwood Highway section.)

Over today's tracks, California Western Railroad also operates **Super Skunks**, a line powered by historic diesel and steam logging locomotives featuring open observation cars. Two kinds of trips operate in each direction: Full-day trips between Fort Bragg and Willits, starting at either point, and half-day round trips from either terminus to Northspur, the halfway point on the line. In either case, a snack or outdoor luncheon is served at Northspur.

Travelling east, the route passes along Pudding Creek from Fort Bragg, then along sleepy Noyo River in the redwood shadows. If you want to make the all-day trip and stay over at one terminus, assign one of your group to follow Highway 20 through Jackson Demonstration State Forest (firs, redwoods, hemlocks, bishop pines) to meet you at the terminus. The Fort Bragg depot is just off Main Street and Laurel Avenue, and reservations are advised; Tel: (707) 964-6371. (The Willits depot is off Main and Commercial streets.)

Fort Bragg's best restaurant, **The Restaurant**, at 418 North Main Street, opposite the Skunk depot, is chef-owned, specializing in seasonal dishes, fresh salmon, and in-house baked goods. There is no smoking in the dining room, and the house is closed on Wednesdays; Tel: 964-9800.

Staying In Fort Bragg

A most unusual bed and breakfast is the **Grey Whale Inn**, a weathered redwood structure that once served as the Redwood Coast Hospital, built in 1915. Because of their medical past, most of the 13 rooms are unusually spacious for a bed and breakfast. Travellers who dislike the forced friendliness of many such inns can find privacy here; the rates are moderate, considering the amenities. The toll-free reservations line also may be used to request a brochure from the Mendocino Coast Innkeepers' Association; Tel: (800) 382-7244, in California.

Near the Skunk Train depot at 700 North Main Street, **Pudding Creek Inn** consists of two Victorian homes built in 1884 and connected by a garden court. Of the ten rooms, two have working fireplaces; rates are reasonable. The **Glass Beach Inn**, just down the road, has nine rooms, some with fireplaces, and a hot tub. Or try the **Blue Rose Inn**, also near the Skunk Train depot at 520 North Main.

Old-fashioned windows, wainscoting, wallpapers, and sloping ceilings accent the restored redwood warmth of the **Country Inn Bed and Breakfast**, with eight rooms, appointed throughout with watercolors and photographs by the owner.

Visitors who prefer motels to bed and breakfasts may select from **Harbor Lite Lodge** with 70 rooms, many with a harbor view; **Pine Beach Inn**, 51 rooms and suites, a café, tennis courts, and some private patios; and **Surf Motel**, with

54 rooms, picnic tables, and a horseshoe pit. All rates are eminently reasonable.

Around Fort Bragg

Two miles south of Fort Bragg, in a coastal pine forest and on sea-cresting headlands, the **Mendocino Coast Botanical Gardens** show off 17 acres of native and planted species—rhododendrons, azaleas, fuchsias, heather, hydrangeas, daisies, ferns, and trees. Even if you are completely ignorant of botany you'll find the stroll along these paths and trails spectacular. Picnicking is allowed on coastal meadows or in the fern canyons.

A nursery, shop, and pleasant café are near the parking lot just west of Highway 1. Restrooms and main trails are now accessible by wheelchair, and two electric wheelchairs are available to the handicapped at no charge.

On weekdays from April through November, Georgia-Pacific's **Forest Tree Nursery** in town welcomes visitors to its miniature woods, with three million redwood and Douglas fir seedlings destined for reforestation projects on regional timberlands. Facilities on Walnut Street include a visitors' center, nature trail, and picnic tables; Tel: 964-5651.

One of the early lumber towns, Noyo today is a photogenic fishing village called **Noyo Harbor**, immediately south of and contiguous with Fort Bragg. It's a center for charter sport-fishing boats as well as commercial ones, and a pleasant spot for lunching with a view of dock action. **Casa del Noyo**, an inn under the cypress trees on short Casa del Noyo Drive, is cozy on chilly nights. **Noyo River Inn**, South Harbor Drive, bustling at lunch and at happy hour, serves local seafood, prime rib, and pastas. Dinner reservations are suggested; Tel: 964-6341. **The Wharf** at 780 North Harbor Drive prides itself on its seafood, great prime-rib sandwiches, clam chowder, baking done on the premises, and a superb view; Tel: 964-4283.

Noyo Harbor is the site of the roasting facility of **Thanksgiving Coffee Company**, producers of one of America's finest coffees, well recognized in wine and redwood country but little known elsewhere. Top bed and breakfasts in Mendocino County serve Thanksgiving; specialty packages make good gifts and may be found locally in groceries, supermarkets, and delis.

You can see one of the most remarkable natural phenomena in the state, or the nation, at **Jug Handle State Reserve**, 5 miles south of Fort Bragg and slightly north of Mendocino. Here, over half a million years, forces of climate and geology have created five seaside terraces—the Ecological Staircase—climbing out of the sea and back from the ocean at a remarkably even rate, each approximately 100 feet lower and 100,000 years younger than the one above it. Five terraces and 500,000 years: The newest terrace is forming under the roiling waters of the Pacific.

Walk half a million years back in time. The trees of the first terrace are the Bishop pine and the Monterey pine. On the second terrace, 200,000 years old, Bishop pines are joined by grand fir, Sitka spruce, western hemlock, and the plants that love the redwood shade.

By the third terrace, and the fourth and fifth, you have reached the strange world of the pygmy forest, where the podzolization process (well explained in the self-guiding brochure) has reduced a cypress (which might reach 100 feet elsewhere) to a stunted dwarf; you are a giant. The sand on the third terrace is the beach half a million years old that has washed down from the fifth terrace.

The Ecological Staircase may be climbed year round, although it's not recommended on stormy days; on Saturdays at 10:00 A.M., a much-recommended ranger-conducted walk is available. The round-trip hike to the third terrace (the fourth and fifth are similar) takes about three hours.

Just south of Jug Handle, Highway 1 skirts Caspar, a clutch of creaky frame houses as yet unawakened by tourism, and enters Mendocino.

MENDOCINO

A straggle of Victorian houses and water towers set back from wave-battered cliffs, Mendocino is the very model of an antique eastern coastal town, set on a stern (at least in winter) and rockbound coast as rugged as any in Maine. So close is the resemblance, indeed, that the little city has become the stand-in for the New England hamlet of Cabot's Cove in the television series "Murder, She Wrote."

The town began, like its coastal sisters, as a lumber port at the mouth of Big River (the Pomo Indians' Booldam), just to the south. Settlers began to arrive in the 1850s: State-of-Mainers and other Yankees, Nova Scotians, and New Yorkers. Surely they wanted to build a town that looked as much as possible like those they left and expected never to see again, and so they did. (Chinese, Portuguese, and representatives of many other peoples followed, but they had little effect on the look of the place.) There was no architectural restraint.

Differing styles here have been classified as Gothic Revival, Saltbox, Gingerbread, Rustic, Pointed Cottage, Carpenter's Gothic—an overall description might be Redwood Rampant. These are the houses of the 1840s to 1860s; in distinct contrast is the town's sentinel, the Presbyterian Church, pristine, stiff, almost accusing in its whiteness.

As Dorothy Bear and Beth Stebbins put it in their *Mendocino,* "There was formed a definite social structure based on the mores of the 19th century. The elite ... kept within their own groups. They owned the mill, the banks, the mercantile stores. The others worked for them.

" 'Fast houses,' pool halls and saloons seem to have been plentiful. During the height of the lumber industry it is reported there were 19 saloons ... So-called Fury Town was a district in east Mendocino ... When the loggers came to town from the logging camps, the idea was to have a good time; and according to their tastes they did. . . "

Even before World War I, however, the lumber business was moving from boom to dust. The *W.P.A. Guide to California* tells how the town appeared in the depressed 1930s: ". . . a jumble of weathered, gabled wooden buildings fronting dirt streets, edged by the gloomy pine woods of encircling hills."

It was poverty that preserved Mendocino, kept old buildings from being "improved," and tempted no tract developers. Looking at a photograph of Main Street taken in 1862, you can identify many houses as they stand today: Bever's Temperance House (1878), for instance (no liquor served to boarders), which became the Central Hotel and is today the smart Mendocino Hotel (definitely not a temperance house).

In the 1960s artists (some said hippies) and their celebrators, fleeing what they felt was the confinement and commercialization of Carmel, Sausalito, and San Francisco's North Beach, found Mendocino. Fortunately they liked it just as it was (though local loggers and fishermen didn't like *them* much) and proceeded with paint, nails, plumbing, and elbow grease to bring the old beauty back to life.

One can't help but notice today a creeping cuteness, a hint of the quaint. Still, Mendocino is small by California art colony standards (population about 2,000), and her spectacular setting remains untrammeled.

Downtown Mendocino

A helpful first stop in town is the **Ford House Visitor Center** at 735 Main Street, built by Jerome Bursley in 1854, which offers exhibits and information on natural and cultural history of the coast.

The town's major hostelry is the aforementioned **Mendocino Hotel**, right across the way, a landmark with 51 rooms (38 with bath), some with balconies, fireplaces, and ocean views; the **Garden Café and Bar** is particularly pleasant for lunch. The rates will remind you of the expensive antiques around.

On the corner of Main and Evergreen, the **Mendocino Village Inn** offers 12 rooms in an 1882 Queen Anne Victorian, built by town physician W. A. McCornack. It's locally called the House of the Doctors, having been occupied successively by four village doctors. The breakfasts are particularly notable (blue-cornmeal banana pancakes), and the rates inexpensive to moderate. Yet another place to sleep on Main Street is **Sears House Inn**, an 1870 Victorian "main house" with cottages and a water tower behind. Some of the eight guest rooms boast fireplaces and kitchens.

The menu at **Bay View Restaurant** (where Brannon's Whale Watch used to be), in a water tower on Main Street, is nothing if not eclectic, featuring fresh seafood, crab, clam chowder, but also stir-fries, nachos, and escargots. Everything's good; Tel: 937-4197.

One of the most highly acclaimed chefs in Northern California is Margaret Fox, whose **Café Beaujolais** at 961 Ukiah Street is highly praised for the originality and imagination devoted to the use of local produce in dishes of American, French, and California inclination. Breakfast and lunch are served daily, dinners May through November (but closed January 4 to March 10). Reservations are always advised; Tel: 937-5614.

One of the most pleasant occupations in Mendocino is what the trendies call "hanging out," and a good place to do so is the **Sea Gull** at Ukiah and Lansing streets, across from the Masonic Hall. Sea Gull serves good old-fashioned American cooking, fresh seafood, and pasta. Don't miss the **Cellar Bar** (it's upstairs); Tel. 937-2100.

After you're sated, cross the street to snap the signature picture every traveller takes before leaving, that of the Mendocino Masonic Temple. The lodge was formed by the hardy pioneers of the country in 1866 and crowned by the landmark sculpture of Father Time and the Maiden, carved from a single redwood log by the lodge's builder, Eric Albertson.

Little Lake and Albion Streets

The practice of crafts and instruction in them goes on at the **Mendocino Art Center and Gallery**, 45200 Little Lake Street, four corners north from Main. For show and for sale are the examples of glass-staining, painting, photography, pottery- and print-making, and more. The gallery is open daily year round (except Christmas and New Year's) and exhibits the works of some 180 artist-members. In addition drama, dance, and musical performances are presented and fairs staged here in midsummer and at Thanksgiving; Tel: 937-5818. The Mendocino Performing Arts Company is on the grounds of the center and presents six plays a year.

The Art Center occupies the site of the Denslow-Morgan-Preston mansion where Elia Kazan shot *East of Eden* in 1954; it burned in 1956. (Angela Lansbury's house in "Murder, She Wrote" is nearby on the corner of Little Lake and Ford streets.) Farther east on Little Lake, where there's a turnoff from Highway 1, Joshua Grindle from Maine built a handsome Italianate home in 1879. Today it's the ten-room **Joshua Grindle Inn**, one of the finest along the coast. There is also one cottage, as well as three rooms in the water tower. Despite the impeccable taste in decoration, rates are moderate.

The **Kelley House Historical Museum & Library**, at 45007 Albion Street, occupies a home constructed in 1861 for William H. Kelley, a native of Prince Edward Island and one of the original men who arrived aboard the brig *Ontario* in 1852. Intriguing old photos of the town and coast, historical shows, and gardens with century-old plantings are open to the public daily, afternoons only.

Just across the street, **MacCallum House Inn** ranks among the top bed and breakfasts in the area, especially respected for its fine dinners. One of the prettiest houses in town, it was built by Kelley for his daughter Daisy MacCallum in 1882. Some of the 20 rooms are located in the grounds' Carriage House & Water Tower, Greenhouse, and Gazebo Playhouse & Barn. Rates range from reasonable to expensive; some rooms have fireplaces. Nearby, at 44950 Albion, is the **Headlands Inn**.

In the next block west on Albion, the 1882 **Temple of Kwan Tia** is one of two remaining joss houses (Chinese temple for a cult figure) in Northern California. It may be visited by appointment only; Tel: 937-4506 (evenings).

Around Mendocino

Yet another bed and breakfast, **Whitegate Inn**, on Howard Street, occupies an elegant 19th-century house overlooking the **Mendocino Headlands State Park**, which partially surrounds the town. Its five moderately priced guest rooms are handsomely appointed. Palette Drive's **Hill House Inn** offers 44 rooms, four suites, a café and bar, a library, and some private patios and balconies. It overlooks the ocean and soothes with privacy those who find a bed and breakfast slightly confining. A good inn to try is **Agate Cove Inn** on Lansing Street.

Just north of Mendocino is Larkin Road, a loop off the highway to the east. Here you'll find a 13-room lodge, spread out with units that resemble old Western storefronts. This is **Blackberry Inn**, in a serene setting where an old inn was demolished and a brand-new one built in 1981. The result is larger rooms, bathrooms superior to those found in the traditional bed and breakfast, many fireplaces, and ocean views throughout.

Just to the south of town across Big River is an unusually attractive resort on ten acres of private grounds. **Stanford Inn by the Sea (Big River Lodge)** offers 25 rooms in a redwood lodge that stretches out above the sea, allowing luxury-size units with ocean views, wood-burning fireplaces, spacious decks, cable color TVs, and bicycles on loan. It's rather expensive, and worth it. The nearby **Mendocino Yacht & Canoe Club** can arrange canoeing along Big River through a narrow canyon forested with redwoods and firs; it's the habitat of great blue herons, ospreys, wood ducks, and beavers, to name a few of the living treasures that abound here. The club will recommend swimming holes and picnic spots; Tel: 937-0273.

Also right at hand near Stanford Inn, the Comptche–Ukiah Road is a wonderfully rugged run east through the woods that eventually winds back to Highway 101 at Ukiah. At a point on the upper Big River, it splits into Low Gap Road and Orr Springs Road; the latter passes through Montgomery Woods State Reserve.

SOUTH OF MENDOCINO

Little River, Albion, Elk, and several other settlements along this coast are called "dog hole" ports, from the complaint of an early lumber schooner captain that "the ports are so narrow and tight only a dog could turn around in them."

Little River

Among these ports was Little River (just south of Big River), a pleasant, rural hamlet described in 1912 by equestrian author J. Smeaton Chase as "a pretty, straggling village of high-gabled houses with quaint dormer windows, and red roses clambering all about." Today it's just as pretty, not much busier, but a prosperous little hub of inns and restaurants.

Just north of the village, Van Damme State Park is a pleasant detour inland. Stop at a marked parking area for the Pygmy Forest, especially if you missed Jug Handle.

Little River Inn has sat here, just off the highway and near the sea, for nearly a century and a half, famous for its cozy cottages and dining room; many people drive down for dinner from Mendocino. There are 56 moderate-to-rather-expensive units in the inn, annex, and cottages, as well as lighted tennis courts and a nine-hole golf course. The welcome is warm, the style rustic.

Queen of all the coastal resorts and a pacesetter among country inns, **Heritage House**, west of the highway on the coastal cliffs, was built in 1877 for the lumber-rich Pullen family, when the cove below was called Pullen's Landing. In 1949 Loren Dennen, the builder's grandson, opened the original farmhouse as an inn. It was an immediate hit, perhaps because of Dennen's refusal to regiment his guests: "No one is going to hound you to play games," he proclaimed.

Today Heritage has 70 units, some perched high on cliffs over the pounding Pacific. The inn operates on the Modified American Plan (includes breakfast and dinner), has no TV or telephones, accepts no credit cards, and may seem expensive until you consider that the dining experience is included. It's closed in December and January, and reservations are required for dinner and for lodging; Tel: 937-5885.

Inns and bed and breakfasts have sprung up along this route like California poppies, and this area is so compact that you can easily find any of them. **Victorian Farmhouse** was built in 1877, by the John Dennen of Heritage House, with six rooms and private baths; **Glendeven**, an 1867 farmhouse, has decor from antique to abstract modern; and **Rachel's Inn** features owner-created etchings and tapestries. Another favorite is **Stevens Wood** on Shoreline Highway.

Little River Restaurant (not to be confused with Little

River Inn) is a tiny place squeezed next to the Little River Post Office. You won't believe the quality of the California-French cuisine served at the seven tables Fridays through Tuesdays in high season, Fridays through Mondays in winter. Reserve for seatings at 6:00 and 8:30 P.M. It's fairly expensive and well worth it; Tel: 937-4945.

Ledford House at 3000 North Highway One serves what might be called California Current cuisine, ravioli stuffed with ricotta cheese, say, or duck-liver pâté with Granny Smith apples, capers, roasted garlic, and goat cheese. There's a little straining for elegance; Tel: 937-0282.

Travellers who want the independence and hands-off attitude of motels should enjoy the **S.S. Seafoam Lodge**, three miles south of Little River. It has 29 reasonably priced rooms, some with fireplaces, decks, refrigerators, or porches, and offers fine ocean views over a grassy lawn.

Albion

Named for ancient Britain, Albion, just a skip south of Little River, grew up around a lumber mill started in 1853. The aforementioned J. Smeaton Chase in his *California Coast Trails* (1912) wrote, "The piece of coast between Albion and Little River, seemed to me almost the finest I had seen. Such headlands, black and wooded, such purple seas, such vivid blaze of spray, such fiords and islets, a painter would be ravished by it."

Not much has happened in Albion since the last "lokey" (a Baldwin locomotive) hauled the last logs out of the forest and loaded them by wire chutes onto bobbing schooners—and that's just the way the whale-watching weekenders like it. What has happened is that **Albion River Inn**, long recognized for fine dining (seafood, pasta, veal, and wines from nearby Anderson Valley vineyards), now offers lodge rooms in addition to oceanfront bedroom suites and cottages (rather expensive). You should reserve for dinner; Tel: 937-1919. Another choice is the **Fensalden Inn** on Navarro Ridge Road.

Elk

Even by Highway 1 standards, Elk (once Greenwood) is little more than a wide spot on the coast—but what a photogenic one! Offshore, the ocean beats itself white against great black sea stacks, pointed as broken teeth. A wooden fence decays, wildflowers growing over its body. The wind seems to whistle with the curses of mule skinners, the creaks of the lumber chutes. There is nothing to do in Elk but to stroll the surf-scalloped shore and the wind-whipped headlands, to sip Scotch or wine before a fireplace, to speak softly with friends, and to read a big book.

Fortunately, there are inns in this tiny spot that allow you all that. A traditional old place is **Harbor House**, an inn built in 1916 as an executive residence and guest lodging by the Goodyear Redwood Lumber Company. Rates for the ten units and four cottages include breakfast and dinner. Lawn games, library, and a private beach add to the sense of cosseted privacy.

The first bed and breakfast along the North Coast is believed to have been **Elk Cove Inn**, the property of German-born Hildrun-Uta Triebess, with nine rooms in an 1890s Victorian with sweeping ocean views, some fireplaces, gardens, and a library; rates are moderate to expensive.

Greenwood Pier Inn is gaining in popularity with San Franciscans and others in the region for its outstanding service and excellent cooking. The 11 rooms occupy contemporary cottages with views of the ocean, fireplaces, gardens, and decks. You can even be served breakfast in bed.

Two other tranquil escapes are the 1920s cottages at **Greenwood Lodge**, with ocean and garden views, and the redwood interior of the **Sandpiper House Inn**, and the inn's garden.

Point Arena

About 15 miles south of Elk, Punta de Arenas (Sandy Point) was once the most thriving town between San Francisco and Eureka, with gardens and houses sheltering from the wind behind inland-curved cypresses. In 1870 a lighthouse was erected on the point in reaction to the many shipwrecks along this stormy coast; on the one night of November 20, 1865, ten vessels had been blown ashore within a few miles of the point. The early lighthouse was ruined by the 1906 shaker in San Francisco, but was rebuilt and still functions at **Point Arena Light Station**. It is open to the public from about 11:30 A.M. to 3:00 P.M. except on Thanksgiving and Christmas, and gives sensational views of the coastline to those who climb the almost 150 steps. The Fog Signal Building (1869) houses historical artifacts. Point Arena today is only a drive-through town otherwise, not worth an overnight stay with so many good inns to the north and south of it.

Anchor Bay

Off tiny Anchor Bay in September of 1938, the S.S. *Dorothy Wintermote* smashed up on the rocks, bringing a pleasant bounty to the Depression-downed town south of Point Arena. The town mostly subsisted for a decade on the ship's 1,400 tons of coffee, shortening, and soap. Today a clutch of mobile homes sullies the wooded valley at the northern edge of town, which supports a general store and a couple of cafés.

Also north of Anchor Bay, however, you will round a curve to come upon a surprising sight, a dramatically contemporary clutch of buildings radiating out from a central, hexagonal house, built in the 1970s by an architectural designer to be his second home. It seems every bit as suited to its blufftop spot as the aging Victorian up the road, the 18-room **Whale Watch Inn**, on a protected inlet with sandy beaches. Adults only are admitted to this seaside sanctuary to enjoy spacious decks, fireplaces, four rooms with kitchens, some with spas, others with private patios. It looks expensive, and it is.

Gualala

This is where the road ends (or begins) in Mendocino County. South lie the seductions of Sonoma County (see below and Wine Country chapter) and the return to San Francisco.

Gualala, where a curving beach at the mouth of the Gualala River meets the sea, boomed in the 1860s and 1870s, but by the 1930s apparently had a population of only 15. A little more than a decade ago, when you rented a cottage or house at nearby Sea Ranch (just south in Sonoma County), you had to ice and carry your own meat with you in order to have edible supplies for the weekend. No more. Gualala (pronounced "wah-la-la", probably Pomo Indian for "water coming down place") is today's boom town, with 600 residents—hundreds of second-home part-time citizens, a Surf Supermarket, delis, inns, ye olde gifte shoppes—all the comforts of home away from home. It's not spoiled; it has merely come of age.

The locals and their visitors go fishing for steelhead and silver salmon, canoe, swim, and camp. In town, the **Gualala**

Hotel, which used to look (and probably smell) exactly like the hotel in "Gunsmoke," now has 19 rooms (but only five with private bath; tradition lives); its Italian dining room has always been popular. Prices are exceedingly and befittingly modest. **North Coast Country Inn** on Highway One has only four kitchen units, but they feature hot tub, refrigerators, fireplaces, private decks, and all such requirements.

When someone says "you can't miss it," you know you can—except for **St. Orres**, 2.5 miles north of Gualala, which appears to be a fantasy Russian dacha with an onion dome. It has eight tiny rooms and nine cottages (nine of the rooms or cottages have private baths and range from inexpensive to expensive). For pure luxury, request the Tree House. The restaurant is highly regarded throughout the area; Tel: 884-3335.

SONOMA COUNTY COAST

Sonoma County's rugged shoreline, backing up against the mountains of the Coast Range, presents a very different aspect from bucolic, inland Sonoma (see the Wine Country chapter). Highway 1 curls and weaves south from Gualala through Sonoma (said to have been the name of an Indian chief baptized by the mission fathers in 1824), occasionally straying inland into wooded coves and out along windy promontories, followed by sheep and grass and the smell of the sea.

South of Gualala and the wide, sandy mouth where the Gualala River meets the sea (super for driftwood collecting), you will begin to notice homes of a distinctive style, cresting the hills and sitting in the meadows, of non-intrusive, weathering wood suited to the play of wind and wave. This is **Sea Ranch**, a second-home community designed not to look like a single cohesive complex that commands 5,500 acres of a former Mexican land grant, although that is what it is. About 12 miles south of the river's mouth, the **Sea Ranch Lodge** sits on a seaside bluff to the east of Highway 1, a two-story inn with 18 rooms (some fireplaces) and smashing views of the sea, a good restaurant, and a bar. Guests have the use of the Ranch's two heated swimming pools with saunas, spunky nine-hole golf course, and tennis courts; not inexpensive but a worthwhile escape.

From Stewarts Point, a couple of miles south of Sea Ranch, the fairly rough but beautiful Stewarts Point-Skaggs Springs Road crawls up and over the ridges east to Highway 101, affording a freeway return for those in a hurry to reach San Francisco.

If you take it, however, you'll miss a coastline studded with natural and historic diversions. Just south of that turnoff, for example, **Kruse Rhododendron State Reserve** is a 317-acre glory of the tall, pink plants, in bloom usually from early April into June; Tel: 865-2391. Slightly farther south, two dramatic coastal areas are open to the public: Salt Point State Park (miles of wave-sculpted shoreline, hiking, riding, fishing, and campsites), and Stillwater Cove Regional Park (redwood trails to the beach, fishing, hiking, and beachcombing).

Fort Ross

Ten miles south of the Kruse Reserve, you round a curve and drive into old Russia. In 1741, Russian Admiral Vitus Bering, following the watery paths of the fur seal, discovered the white wastes of Alaska and the sea today named after him. Following his lead, the Russian-American Fur Company was firmly established in the north by the close of the 18th century, but came to require more fertile soil and a warmer growing climate in order to supply its colonists with food.

Pushing down the coast, the fur-seekers found this site in 1811, where they negotiated with the Indians for 1,000 acres, began building a log fort, and by the next year dedicated their settlement, complete with cannon, blockhouses, Orthodox chapel, officers' quarters and other buildings inside a palisade, and 50 buildings outside the enclosure. They called it Fort Ross, an ancient name for Russia.

The community flourished, not only shipping supplies to the Alaskan colonies, but also trading with their Spanish neighbors, which was officially forbidden but winked at in practice. Then, in December 1823, came the promulgation of the Monroe Doctrine, which brought an end to any aim of Russia's to acquire California. The colony at Ross, however, continued to prosper until 1840, when the sea otter had become almost extinct. In 1841, Czar Nicholas I ordered the return of his people from California, and the whole property was sold (for an estimated $30,000) to Captain John A. Sutter.

After World War II, the state park system began constructing **Fort Ross Historic Park**, which today—despite two arson fires throughout the years—is an intriguing grouping of redwood structures closely copying the originals: stockade, blockhouses, Orthodox chapel, officials' barracks, water well, and two houses. The new Visitors' Information Center near the highway offers interpretive displays, meeting rooms, library, and book and souvenir sales. There's also a picnic area; Tel: 847-3286.

Two miles north of Fort Ross (but, confusingly, with a mailing address in Jenner, 14 miles south), **Fort Ross Lodge** has 24 motel-type units with ocean views, fireplaces, TVs and VCRs, a hot tub, and sauna; rates range from moderate to expensive, with special mid-week prices.

Just a handful of miles inland via Fort Ross Road, **Timberhill Ranch** is one of the most stylish country resorts in the state, set on 80 acres of woods atop a 1,100-foot ridge. Opened in 1984, it was awarded membership in France's prestigious Relais & Chateaux group in 1990, one of only 21 such inns in the United States. Rustic outside, luxurious inside, it consists of a ranch house reworked into a splendid lodge, and ten cottages, swimming pool, Jacuzzi spa, and tennis courts. Meals of a gourmet persuasion are included in the understandably rather expensive rates.

The pretty fishing village of **Jenner**, south of Fort Ross where the Russian River flows into the Pacific, is a popular hesitating or stopping-over spot for drivers headed up or down Highway 1, usually to take a meal at either **Murphy's Jenner by the Sea** or **River's End**, a roadside general store that has become a stop notable for good cooking with a German accent. Jenner is a handy place for refilling your gas tank. Jenner is also the gateway for the inland Russian River resorts (see the Wine Country chapter); here we keep to the coast road.

Bodega Bay and South

It was October 3, 1775, when explorer Juan Francisco de la Bodega y Cuadra sailed his schooner Sonora into the bay and protected harbor today bearing his name, about 10 miles south of Jenner. Nothing much happened for years after, except that an expedition led by Captain George Vancouver came ashore in 1793 and a small Russian fur station was set up in 1809.

Today, the 300-plus residents of Bodega Bay watch for migrating gray whales (in season), catch crab and fish commercially, operate charter fishing boats, and enjoy a slow but steady increase in tourism. Of the various dine-in and take-out places, the best is **Lucas Wharf Restaurant and Bar**, right on the water; a most attractive place to spend a night or two is **Inn at the Tides**, which attracts some San Franciscans who don't want to drive farther to spend a weekend by the sea. It is a smart place with 86 rooms (some with fireplaces and/or patios), an indoor-outdoor pool, sauna, good restaurant and lounge; a golf course is nearby.

On a handsome bluff-top setting, the **Best Western Bodega Bay Lodge** offers 78 units, exercise area, some refrigerators and fireplaces in rooms, and a heated pool. It's more informal than Inn at the Tides; neither one could be called inexpensive.

From Bodega Bay, detour inland to tiny Bodega, a village still snoozing in the 19th century, where Victoriana lives in St. Teresa's Catholic Church (1861), and a schoolhouse that played a role in Alfred Hitchcock's *The Birds*.

A town devoted almost solely to the consumption of Italian cuisine is **Occidental**, inland and slightly north of Bodega Bay about nine miles via Bodega and Bohemian highways. In the late 1880s it was established as a rail terminus, but nothing much came of that, and the population flowed away, leaving in its ebb three loud, lively restaurants dedicated to serving the crowds who haven't had a good family-styled meal since they left San Francisco's North Beach. **The Union Hotel, Fiori's**, and **Negri's** (all on five-block Main Street) serve up enough spaghetti, ravioli, tagliarini, and other temptations to make a Neopolitan weep.

South of Bodega, Highway 1 turns out to the coast again, running through hamlets such as Tomales and Marshall, across Tomales Bay from Point Reyes National Seashore (see Day Trips From San Francisco).

To avoid congested Sir Francis Drake Boulevard between Olema and San Rafael to Highway 101 (now carrying all the traffic that used the Highway 1 route before it collapsed as a result of the 1989 earthquake), you might consider returning to San Francisco from Marshall over the Marshall-Petaluma Road and Novato Boulevard, a pleasantly rural route that puts you back on Highway 101 near Novato, 20-some miles north of the Golden Gate Bridge.

GETTING AROUND

The most practical as well as the most enjoyable way to explore Redwood Country is by private car. From San Francisco's Golden Gate Bridge, Highway 101 (the Redwood Highway) is the most direct route north to points of interest in Marin, Sonoma, Mendocino, Humboldt, and Del Norte counties. Via Highway 101 it's 359 miles to Crescent City, just south of the Oregon state line.

On one leg of the round trip, we recommend you drive coastal Highway 1, a slower, narrower, and more scenic road. If you can afford the time for them, several routes across the high country of the Coast Range are recommended: State Highway 128 from north of Cloverdale (on 101) to Navarro Point south of Albion (on 1); similarly, State Highway 20 from Willits to Noyo, and State Highway 211 from 2 miles north of Fortuna to Cape Mendocino and beyond (see the Humboldt County section).

If a fly-drive itinerary suits your schedule better, consider service out of San Francisco International Airport to various cities to the north. American Eagle Airline flies from SFO to Santa Rosa and Eureka (Tel: 800-433-7300), while United Express Airline serves Santa Rosa, Eureka, and Crescent City (Tel: 800-241-6522). All the airport facilities include rental-car pickup.

All major towns along the route are served by Greyhound/Trailways Bus Lines; for information, Tel: (415) 558-6730.

Several companies offer regional bus and/or van services in both Mendocino and Humboldt counties. For details and current schedules, call Mendocino Transit Authority, Coast Van, Tel: (707) 884-3723; Mendocino Stage, Tel: (707) 964-0167; Arcata–Mad River Transit System, Tel: (707) 822-3775; Redwood Transit Eureka Service, Tel: (707) 822-0836; Redwood Transit, Orick–Scotia service, Tel: (707) 443-0826; Redwood Empire Lines, Eureka–Redding service, Tel: (707) 443-9923.

For details on the Skunk Train of California Western Railroad, Tel: (707) 964-6371; for trips on the North Coast Daylight Railroad, Tel: (707) 442-7705.

At this writing, directors of the Golden Gate Bridge and other transit authorities are considering a project to create a 151-mile-long commuter train route from San Rafael, 17 miles north of San Francisco, to Willits, 137 miles north of San Francisco in Mendocino County.

Backroads Bicycle Touring of Berkeley arranges weekend or week-long vacations (camping or inns) along the coast and in the redwoods; Tel: (415) 527-1555 or (800) 533-2573 (outside California).

For further information: A map of Marin, Sonoma, and Mendocino counties with listings of motels, bed and breakfasts, and other lodgings, recreation and real estate firms, etc., is published in Gualala; it's extremely helpful. Send $1.00 for the packet to The Porters, Gateway 1990, P.O. Box 999, Gualala, CA 95445.

ACCOMMODATIONS REFERENCE
The area code for Redwood Country is 707.

▶ **Agate Cove Inn.** 11201 Lansing Street, **Mendocino**, CA 95460. Tel: 937-0551.

▶ **Albion River Inn.** 3790 North Highway One, **Albion**, CA 95410. Tel: 937-1919.

▶ **Anderson Valley Inn.** P.O. Box 147, **Philo**, CA 95466. Tel: 855-3325.

▶ **Bear Wallow Resort.** Box 533, **Boonville**, CA 95415. Tel: 895-3335.

▶ **Bella Vista Motel.** 1225 Central Avenue, **McKinleyville**, CA 95521. Tel: 839-1073.

▶ **Benbow Inn.** 445 Lake Benbow Drive, **Garberville**, CA 95440. Tel: 923-2124.

▶ **Best Western Bodega Bay Lodge.** Coast Highway One, **Bodega Bay**, CA 94923. Tel: 875-3525 or (800) 368-2468; Fax: 875-2428.

▶ **Best Western Humboldt House Inn.** 701 Redwood Drive, **Garberville**, CA 95440. Tel: 923-2771.

▶ **Best Western Northwoods Inn.** 655 U.S. 101, **Crescent City**, CA 95531. Tel: 464-9771.

▶ **Best Western Ship Ashore Resort.** 12370 Highway 101 North, **Smith River**, CA 95567. Tel: 487-3141.

▶ **Bishop Pine Lodge.** 1481 Patrick's Point Drive, **Trinidad**, CA 95570. Tel: 677-3314.

▶ **Blackberry Inn.** 44951 Larkin Road, **Mendocino**, CA 95460. Tel: 937-5281.

▶ **Blue Rose Inn.** 520 North Main Street, **Fort Bragg**, CA 95437. Tel: 964-3477.

▶ **Brooktrails Lodge.** Sherwood Road, **Willits**, CA 95490. Tel: 459-5311.

▶ **Carson House Bed-and-Breakfast Inn.** 4th and M streets, **Eureka**, CA 95501. Tel: 433-1601.

▶ **Hotel Carter.** 301 L Street, **Eureka**, CA 95501. Tel: 444-8062.

▶ **Carter House Bed-and-Breakfast Inn.** 1521 Third Street, **Eureka**, CA 95501. Tel: 445-1390.

▶ **Casa del Noyo.** 500 Casa del Noyo Drive, **Fort Bragg**, CA 95437. Tel: 964-8045.

▶ **Chalet de France.** 17687 Kneeland Road, **Eureka**, CA 95549. Tel: 443-6512 or 444-3144.

▶ **Cleone Lodge.** 24600 North Highway 1, **Fort Bragg**, CA 95437. Tel: 964-2788.

▶ **Country Inn Bed and Breakfast.** 632 North Main Street, **Fort Bragg**, CA 95437. Tel: 964-3737.

▶ **Craddock Manor.** 814 J Street, Eureka, CA 95501. Tel: 444-8589.

▶ **Crescent Travelodge.** 725 Highway 101 North, Crescent City, CA 95531. Tel: 464-6106 or (800) 255-3050.

▶ **Curly Redwood Lodge.** 701 Redwood Highway South, Crescent City, CA 95531. Tel: 464-2137.

▶ **Elk Cove Inn.** P.O. Box 367, Elk, CA 95432. Tel: 877-3321.

▶ **The Eureka Inn.** 7th and F streets, Eureka, CA 95501. Tel: 442-6441.

▶ **Fensalden Inn.** 33810 Navarro Ridge Road, Albion, CA 95410. Tel: 937-4042.

▶ **Ferndale Inn.** 619 Main Street, Ferndale, CA 95536. Tel: 786-4307.

▶ **Fort Ross Lodge.** 20705 Coast Highway One, Jenner, CA 95450. Tel: 847-3333.

▶ **Garberville Motel.** 948 Redwood Drive, Garberville, CA 95440. Tel: 923-2422.

▶ **The Gingerbread Mansion.** 400 Berding Street, Ferndale, CA 95536. Tel: 786-4000.

▶ **Glendeven.** 8221 North Highway 1, Little River, CA 95456. Tel: 937-0083.

▶ **Glass Beach Inn.** 726 North Main Street, Fort Bragg, CA 95437. Tel: 964-6774.

▶ **Green Valley Motel.** P.O. Box 67, Orick, CA 95555. Tel: 488-2341.

▶ **Greenwood Lodge.** 5910 South Highway One, Elk, CA 95432. Tel: 877-3422.

▶ **Greenwood Pier Inn.** 5926 South Highway One, Elk, CA 95432. Tel: 877-9997.

▶ **Grey Whale Inn.** 615 North Main Street, Fort Bragg, CA 95437. Tel: 964-0640 or (800) 382-7244 in California.

▶ **Gualala Hotel.** Box 675, Gualala, CA 95445. Tel: 884-3441 or 785-2146.

▶ **Harbor House.** Box 367, Elk, CA 95432. Tel: 877-3203.

▶ **Harbor Lite Lodge.** 120 North Harbor Drive, Fort Bragg, CA 95437. Tel: 964-0221.

▶ **Hartsook Inn.** 900 Highway 101, Piercy, CA 95467. Tel: 247-3305.

▶ **Headlands Inn.** 44950 Albion Street, Mendocino, CA 95460. Tel: 937-4431.

▶ **Heritage House.** 5200 North Highway 1, Little River, CA 95456. Tel: 937-5885.

▶ **Hill House Inn.** 10701 Palette Drive, Mendocino, CA 95460. Tel: 937-0554.

▶ **Howard Creek Ranch Inn.** 40501 North Highway 1, Westport, CA 95488. Tel: 964-6725.

▶ **Inn at the Tides.** 800 Coast Highway One, **Bodega Bay,** CA 94923. Tel: 875-2751 or (800) 541-7788.

▶ **Iris Inn.** 1134 H Street, **Eureka,** CA 95501. Tel: 445-0307.

▶ **Joshua Grindle Inn.** 44800 Little Lake Road, **Mendocino,** CA 95456. Tel: 937-4143.

▶ **Little River Inn.** 1853 North Highway 1, **Little River,** CA 95456. Tel: 937-5942.

▶ **The Lost Whale Bed and Breakfast.** 3452 Patrick's Point Drive, **Trinidad,** CA 95570. Tel: 677-3425.

▶ **MacCallum House Inn.** 45020 Albion Street, **Mendocino,** CA 95460. Tel: 937-0289.

▶ **Mendocino Hotel.** 45080 Main Street, **Mendocino,** CA 95460. Tel: 937-0511.

▶ **Mendocino Village Inn.** 44860 Main Street, **Mendocino,** CA 95460. Tel: 937-0246.

▶ **Miranda Gardens Resort.** P.O. Box 186, **Miranda,** CA 95553. Tel: 943-3011.

▶ **Motel Trees.** P.O. Box 309, **Klamath,** CA 95548. Tel: 482-3152.

▶ **North Coast Country Inn.** 34591 South Highway One, **Gualala,** CA 95445. Tel: 884-4537.

▶ **North Coast Inn.** 4975 Valley West Boulevard, **Arcata,** CA 95521. Tel: 822-4861.

▶ **Old Town Bed-and-Breakfast Inn.** 1521 Third Street, **Eureka,** CA 95501. Tel: 445-3951.

▶ **Pacific Motor Hotel.** Box 595, **Crescent City,** CA 95531. Tel: 464-4141.

▶ **Palm Motel.** 21130 Highway One, **Orick,** CA 95555. Tel: 488-3381.

▶ **Park Woods Motel.** P.O. Box 62, **Orick,** CA 95555. Tel: 488-5175.

▶ **Pelican Inn.** 38921 North Highway One, **Westport,** CA 95437. Tel: 964-5588.

▶ **Pine Beach Inn.** P.O. Box 1173, **Fort Bragg,** CA 95437. Tel: 964-5603.

▶ **The Plough and the Stars Country Inn and Croquet Club.** 1800 27th Street, **Arcata,** CA 95521. Tel: 822-8236.

▶ **Prairie Creek Motel.** P.O. Box 265, **Orick,** CA 95555. Tel: 488-3841.

▶ **Pudding Creek Inn.** 700 North Main Street, **Fort Bragg,** CA 95437. Tel: 964-9529.

▶ **Rachel's Inn.** 8200 North Highway 1, **Mendocino,** CA 95460. Tel: 937-0088.

▶ **Rancho Motel.** 987 Redwood Drive, **Garberville,** CA 95540. Tel: 923-2451.

▶ **Red Lion Inn.** 1929 Fourth Street, Eureka, CA 95501. Tel: 445-0844.

▶ **Requa Inn.** 451 Requa Road, Klamath, CA 95548. Tel: 482-8205.

▶ **St. Orres.** 36601 South Highway 1. Gualala, CA 95445. Tel: 884-3303.

▶ **Sandpiper House Inn.** P.O. Box 49, Elk, CA 96432. Tel: 877-3587.

▶ **Sea Ranch Lodge.** Box 44, The Sea Ranch, CA 95497. Tel: 785-2371.

▶ **Sears House Inn.** 44840 Main Street, Mendocino, CA 95460. Tel: 937-4076.

▶ **Shaw House Bed-and-Breakfast Inn.** 703 Main Street, Ferndale, CA 95536. Tel: 786-9958.

▶ **S.S. Seafoam Lodge.** Highway 1, Little River, CA 95456. Tel: 937-2011.

▶ **Stanford Inn by the Sea (Big River Lodge).** P.O. Box 487, Mendocino, CA 95460. Tel: 937-5615.

▶ **Stevens Wood.** 8211 Shoreline Highway, Little River, CA 95460. Tel: 937-2810.

▶ **Surf Motel.** P.O. Box 488, Fort Bragg, CA 95437. Tel: 964-5361.

▶ **Timberhill Ranch.** 35755 Hauser Bridge Road, Cazadero, CA 95421. Tel: 847-3458.

▶ **Toll House Restaurant and Inn.** P.O. Box 268, Boonville, CA 95415. Tel: 895-3630.

▶ **Trinidad Bed and Breakfast.** P.O. Box 849, Trinidad, CA 95570. Tel: 677-0840.

▶ **Victorian Farmhouse.** 7001 North Highway 1, Little River, CA 95456. Tel: 937-0697.

▶ **Victorian Village Inn.** 400 Ocean Avenue, Ferndale, CA 95536. Tel: 725-6227.

▶ **Whale Watch Inn.** 35100 Highway 1, Gualala, CA 95445. Tel: 884-3667.

▶ **Whitegate Inn.** 499 Howard Street, Mendocino, CA 95460. Tel: 937-4892.

NORTH-EASTERN CALIFORNIA

By Barry Anderson

A third-generation Californian, Barry Anderson has written about California for more than 30 years, first as a Sunset Magazine *editor, then as a free-lance writer of magazine and newspaper articles and guidebooks. He has contributed to many publications, including the* Los Angeles Times *and the* World of Travel *series.*

Head northeast out of the San Francisco Bay Area on Interstate 80 and pick up Interstate 505, then I-5, through the broad, agricultural Sacramento Valley. Somewhere beyond the town of Willows you begin to notice the snowcapped tip of a large mountain poking above the intervening foothills. By the time you reach Red Bluff, 223 miles north of San Francisco, 14,162-foot Mount Shasta, the signature landmark of north-central and northeastern California, dominates the horizon.

If you could perch atop Shasta for a bird's-eye view in every direction, you'd see some of the loveliest and least-visited country in California. To the west the heavily forested mountains of the Coast Range stand between the hot, dry interior and the cool, moist coast. To the southeast the rugged Sierra Nevada punctuates the horizon and, in the foreground, rocky volcanic landscapes and the cone of 10,357-foot Mount Lassen spread at your feet. To the east and northeast, jumbled hills and valleys, studded with manzanita and pine and cut by clear rushing streams, gradually give way to the high sagebrush desert of the Great Basin that seems to stretch away forever.

You'd also notice that there are few signs of civilization in this vast mountain and desert corner of the state—few towns, few barns and ranches, and, beyond the interstate, only a handful of roads.

Californians call this last part of Northeastern California the Lonely Corner. As the state and its visitor attractions become more crowded, this area is becoming increasingly attractive as a destination that offers plenty of untrammeled nature as well as a measure of solitude that is increasingly rare.

Among the trade-offs you must make to savor all this quietude and natural beauty are elegant accommodations and gourmet dining. With some exceptions, accommodations are conventional motels. The term "resort" is used rather broadly in this region and usually means rustic cabins or housekeeping accommodations, sometimes bordering on the primitive—you select them for their location, not their amenities. Where accommodations choices are unremarkable, we've included a range for various budgets. As for dining, with the exception of ethnic specialties, restaurant menus typically include several beef entrées, chicken, and fish or shellfish, but usually not anything to write home about.

MAJOR INTEREST

Unspoiled natural beauty
Mount Shasta for skiing and hiking
Shasta Lake for houseboating and camping
Lassen Volcanic National Park
Fall River Mills for fly fishing
Lava Beds National Monument
Klamath Basin bird-watching

THE I-5 CORRIDOR
Red Bluff and Redding

Red Bluff is the smaller, but historically more interesting, of these two small cities at the top end of the Sacramento Valley, about 136 miles north of Sacramento. Detour off the interstate at Red Bluff to **William B. Ide Adobe State Park**, the restored homestead of the leader of the Bear Flag Revolt that

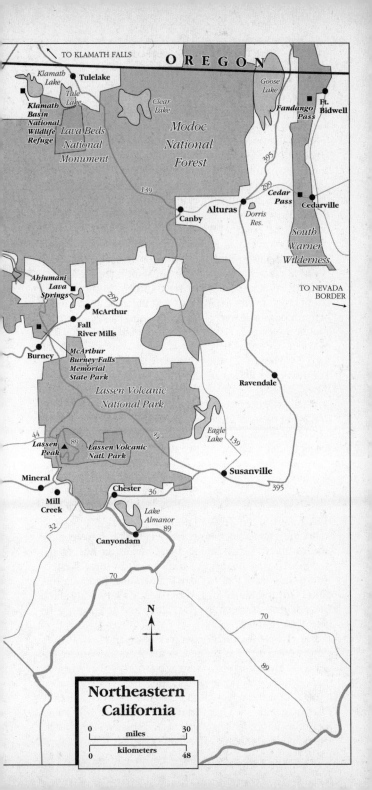

briefly made California an independent republic in 1846. With big shade trees beside the Sacramento River, it's a lovely spot for a picnic, especially on those summer days when the thermometer exceeds 100 degrees F, as it frequently does in July and August. Red Bluff is also a treasure house of Victorian architecture, with dozens of ornate residences and business and public buildings dating from 1870 to 1890 scattered around downtown; the chamber of commerce distributes driving maps that identify many of them. **The Kelly-Griggs House Museum**, a classical Victorian gingerbread design, is open to the public. **The Faulkner House** offers bed-and-breakfast rooms in an 1890s Victorian home, and **The Victorian** operates as a restaurant in the downtown area.

The Sacramento River, lifeblood of the valley, is also the focus of recreation in these river towns. **City River Park** offers broad lawns sloping down to the river, picnic tables beneath big shade trees, boat rentals, and band concerts on summer weekends. A couple of miles south a diversion dam provides a salmon-viewing plaza where you can watch salmon climbing fish ladders on their way upstream to spawn. The **Riverside Restaurant** has outdoor dining overlooking the river.

Once you get beyond the interstate more than a few miles to the east or west, accommodations and restaurants are few and far between, yet the essence of this region is precisely the splendid scenery, historical sightseeing, and outdoor recreation that are remote from I-5. Both Red Bluff and Redding have a wide choice of facilities, so consider basing yourself in either city and making day trips to Lassen Volcanic National Park, to the three big lakes, and to the backcountry to the west and northeast.

Redding, about 30 miles north of Red Bluff, has a population of about 50,000 and is the commerical hub of the region. A string of quality chain lodgings—**Best Western Hilltop Inn, Days Inn, Holiday Inn-Redding, Red Lion Inn, Motel Orleans, Motel 6**—is conveniently located on Hilltop Drive, just off the freeway. (The Hilltop and Red Lion are the best of these choices.)

The Shasta-Cascade Wonderland Association, 1250 Parkview Avenue, and the Redding Convention and Visitors Bureau, 777 Auditorium Drive, are good sources of information on the city and all of the surrounding area. The convention bureau furnishes a map detailing three driving tours of the city that include such historic architecture as the 1879 **James McCormick Residence** and the classic Mission Revival–style **Hotel Redding**. Other stops of interest include Caldwell Park, adjacent to the river, with its **Carter House Science Museum** (children's exhibits), and the **Redding Museum and Art Center** (Native American, pre-Columbian, and local art). The newly opened **Sacramento River Trail** provides a paved loop of nearly five miles on both sides of the river through park-like surroundings. This walk is especially appealing in the early morning when the riverbanks are alive with birds.

You can make an unusual excursion from Redding to **Lake Shasta Caverns**, limestone caves high on a hillside above Shasta Lake. The three-hour round trip includes a boat-crossing of the lake and a guided walking tour of the lighted caverns, where you view flowstone, bacon rind, popcorn, and other formations typical of limestone caves via a route that is somewhat steep and rough.

Redding has a delightful variety of restaurants, including Chinese, Japanese, French, Italian, and Mexican establishments. Recommended are **El Papagayo** (Mexican) at 460 North Market, **Nello's Place** (Italian) at 355 Bechelli Lane, **River City Bar and Grill** (Cajun/Creole) at 2151 Market, **Maxwell's** (upscale American/Continental), also on Market, and **The Hatchcover** (seafood) at 202 Hemstead Drive.

Mount Shasta

North of Redding I-5 crosses an arm of Shasta Lake (see Big Lake Country below) and begins to climb; the broad highway swings wide on curves and winds its way through the mountains. Far below, the Sacramento River cuts a steep brush-covered canyon, and the Southern Pacific Railroad, route of Amtrak's Coast Starlight, crisscrosses the river on spindly bridges and plunges into tunnels through the mountains.

Three stops on this stretch of highway are worth considering if you have the time. **Castle Crags State Park** features dramatic granite spires towering more than 4,000 feet above the river. The park has camp- and picnic sites, hiking trails, naturalist programs, and good photo vantage points for the crags and Mount Shasta. The historic California–Oregon Toll Road passes through the park. Just beyond, **Railroad Park Resort** houses guests in 20 railroad cabooses that have been remodeled as bedrooms. A few miles farther north on Interstate 5 is **Dunsmuir**, a ramshackle old railroad town squeezed in stair-step fashion into the narrow river canyon; its venerable downtown is in the National Register of Historic Places.

If you want to steep yourself in the atmosphere of this railroad town, stay the night at the **Dunsmuir Bed & Breakfast Inn**. This inn in the heart of town, formerly a Southern

Pacific Railroad rooming house, comes complete with old-fashioned claw-foot bathtubs and an ice cream parlor serving ice cream sodas the way they used to be. In the evening, stroll the old streets down to the depot.

From Dunsmuir I-5 climbs steeply out of the Sacramento River Canyon and comes face-to-face with the massive white bulk of 14,162-foot Mount Shasta. Depending on the time of year you're here, the mountain may be glittering in sunshine or truncated, with its summit lost in the clouds.

Shasta is a major recreation area, with skiing and snowmobiling in the winter and climbing, hiking, and mountain biking the rest of the year. **Mount Shasta Ski Park** is modest, with just two high-speed triple chairlifts serving 22 runs that drop from the 6,600-foot elevation to 5,500 feet at the day lodge, but what it lacks in sophisticated facilities, Mount Shasta makes up for as a low-key, uncrowded, and affordable family winter-sports area. Here you can cross-country ski, snow-board, sled, snowshoe, or toboggan, and not have to fight the crowds. In summer, ski runs become mountain-bike trails and the lifts take cyclists and sightseers up the mountain.

There are no accommodations at the ski area itself, but **Mount Shasta City**, on the west flank of the mountain, has a cluster of motels. Among the best are **Swiss Holiday Lodge**, with just 21 units and fine views of the mountain, and the **Best Western Tree House**, a large establishment with landscaped grounds, indoor pool, and restaurant.

While you're in town, stop at the **Sisson Museum**, a combination of the oldest trout hatchery in the country and displays covering wildflowers, geology, weather, and other natural history. Another way to explore the Shasta area is to join the **llama-packing trips** that travel Shasta's trails from June through September. You walk, your docile llama follows closely behind carrying your pack. Try **Rainbow Ridge Ranch** (P.O. Box 1079, Mount Shasta, CA 96067; Tel: 916-926-5794) or **Shasta Llamas** (P.O. Box 1137, Mount Shasta, CA 96067; Tel: 916-926-3959). **Shasta Mountain Guides** (1938 Hill Road, Mount Shasta City, CA 96067; Tel: 916-926-3117) leads climbs of Mount Shasta and Castle Crags as well as glacier seminars, photography workshops, and cross-country ski treks. A short distance to the west, Lake Siskiyou, a dammed section of the Sacramento River, has swimming beaches, camping, and water sports. **Sisson-Callahan National Recreation Trail** here follows the river for nine miles to Deadfall Summit and ranks high for its spectacular views of Mount Shasta, Castle Crags, and the Trinity Alps.

From Mount Shasta detour 10 miles east on California 89

to **McCloud**. Once a wholly owned lumber company mill town, it's now doing a thriving business as a recreation center. Massive log buildings on the side streets once housed lumber company offices. The original home of the company president now serves as **The McCloud Guest House**, an elegant 1907 country inn and upscale restaurant that lists among its guest activities, "mountain and cloud gazing." **Stoney Brook Inn**, another country bed and break-fast on the south shoulder of Mount Shasta, nestles among the pines. The McCloud River and nearby Lake McCloud are noted for their fine trout fishing; three modest waterfalls on the river plunge into a sheer-walled gorge south of town. **Ah-Di-Na**, south of McCloud, is the remains of an Indian settlement and the ruins of the historic homestead of the William Randolph Hearst family.

As you continue north on I-5 you'll pass the nearly perfect volcanic cinder cone of **Black Butte**, a fairly young (about 10,000 years old) crater. The two-and-a-half-mile trail to the summit, built by the Civilian Conservation Corps in the 1930s, makes a nice respite from driving, and the view from the 6,325-foot summit is spectacular. You can see all the way to Mount McLaughlin in Oregon on a clear day.

Weed, Yreka, and the Klamath River Country

In addition to enjoying breathtaking views of Mount Shasta to the southeast, **Weed**, a few miles north of Black Butte on I-5, lies at the junction of two of the three major routes to the Pacific Northwest (the third is the Redwood Country's U.S. 101). Interstate 5 continues north on the west side of the Cascade Mountains via Oregon's Rogue and Willamette river valleys to Portland and Seattle. This route is faster and gener-ally enjoys better winter driving conditions, although it also tends to be wetter, cloudier, and cooler in the summertime. U.S. 97 takes the eastern path alongside the Cascades, passing through ranch and recreation country around Bend, Oregon, crossing the Columbia River east of Mount Hood, and tran-siting Washington's Yakima Valley wine country. Access to Portland is via the Columbia Gorge and to Seattle via the Cascade mountain passes. This route is warmer and drier in summer, colder in winter.

Weed offers a cluster of standard motels and restaurants close to the freeway. Nearby **Lake Shastina** has a full-fledged golf resort, with fairways flanked by pines and dominated by

Mount Shasta, less than a dozen miles away. Lakeside houses and condominiums are available through **Lake Shastina Accommodations** (see Accommodations Reference).

North of Weed, I-5 crosses a lovely high valley dotted with ranches, where cattle graze beside the road. **Yreka** (pronounced why-REE-ka) is worth considering for your overnight stop. This historic little town at the foot of the Siskiyou Mountains has good, conventional accommodations, a couple of rather unusual restaurants for this part of the world, and some intriguing things to see and do. The only serious barrier to north–south travel in winter is the crossing of the Siskiyou Mountains between Yreka and Ashland, Oregon. Several times each winter, snowstorms close 4,466-foot Siskiyou Summit for several hours or more—enough to make Yreka a welcome haven.

Shortly after the discovery of gold at Coloma, the much-sought-after element was found near Yreka, in 1851, and enough prospectors had gathered by 1857 to justify giving the settlement a name: Thompson's Dry Diggings. Begin your exploration of Yreka at the **Siskiyou County Museum**, an outstanding, small collection of Gold Rush exhibits, Native American displays, a stagecoach and other pioneer vehicles, and a typical miner's cabin. At 311 Fourth Street, the county courthouse displays a dazzling array of gold nuggets taken in the area. Much of 19th-century downtown Yreka is preserved in a historic district bounded by Lane, Lennox, Third, and Gold streets; the old business blocks on Miner Street are especially photogenic. The **Miner Street Deli** features wall murals painted in 1910 by a local Russian immigrant and is reputed to be the oldest meat market in California.

From Memorial Day through Labor Day the **Blue Goose Short-Line Railroad** provides passenger excursions on a three-hour round trip to the old railroad town of Montague. On weekdays a diesel leads the train, on weekends a venerable steam engine chuffs its way up the steep grade east of town.

Good choices among Yreka's lodgings are **Klamath Motor Lodge**, **Miner's Inn**, or **Motel Orleans**—all three conveniently located just off the freeway, all with swimming pools. Most of Yreka's dining establishments are within walking distance of the city's motels: **Ming's** serves a variety of Chinese dishes in a dimly lit atmosphere; **Grandma's House** has an American menu served in an 1890s home; and **The Diner** serves hamburgers in an old railroad observation car still sitting on its track.

The **Klamath River** leaves Upper Klamath Lake in Oregon, swings southwestward into California, and cuts through Klamath National Forest, north of Yreka, to the sea. The Klamath, one of California's premier recreational rivers, plunges in white-water cataracts through rocky canyons and dense forest, offering superb rafting and canoeing, excellent fishing for steelhead and trout, and a pristine environment for hiking, camping, and wildlife viewing. Just north of Yreka, California Route 96 leaves I-5 to follow the Klamath's north bank, then crosses over and hugs the south bank for most of the way west to the coast, where the river empties into the sea at Klamath (see the Redwood Country chapter).

Several recreational vehicle parks and rustic resorts are scattered along the river, including **The Sportsman's Lodge**, **Oaks RV Park**, **Big Foot Resort**, **Beaver Creek Lodge**, **Rainbow Resort**, **Steelhead Lodge**, and **Hawk's Roost**. Accommodations are simple and typically include housekeeping facilities with grocery, laundromat, gasoline, and fishing-tackle shops nearby. The emphasis here on river activities—fishing, rafting, boating, swimming—makes this a good choice for families who want a vacation strong on outdoor recreation. Sportsman's Lodge has the only restaurant in the area. **Bigfoot Recreation** (30841 Walker Road, Horse Creek, CA 96045; Tel: 916-496-3313) offers guided fishing trips. **Orange Torpedo Trips** (P.O. Box 1111, Grants Pass, OR 97526; Tel: 503-479-5061) schedules rafting trips down the river.

BIG LAKE COUNTRY

Drive north through the Sacramento Valley on any warm-weather weekend and you'll follow a procession of trailer-mounted boats—sleek racing boats, elegant cabin cruisers, modest fishing craft, and an occasional sailboat. They're heading for the Shasta country north and northwest of Redding.

Water—lots of it—is the reason most Californians come to this region. You'll find more recreational water here than any place north of San Francisco Bay, and, with the exception of Lake Tahoe, more than anywhere else in the state.

Shasta Lake

In the late 1930s, toward the end of the Great Depression, President Franklin Roosevelt's administration embarked on a series of vast hydro projects. In Northern California a huge concrete dam—Shasta—plugged the Sacramento River as it emerged from its river canyon just above Redding. Shasta Dam, completed in 1945, is the centerpiece of the Central Valley Project, a massive complex of dams, canals, and power and pumping plants that irrigate more than five million acres of the state's Sacramento and San Joaquin valleys and has made this region the richest farmland in the country. However, recreational demands on Shasta Lake, the lake created by the dam, are so great that they compete with hydroelectric and irrigation needs during periods of low water, when there's not enough for everybody.

Shasta Lake, the largest man-made lake in the state, is surrounded by steep red-clay hills covered with pine, manzanita, and chaparral. Lake waters back up into the Sacramento, McCloud, and Pitt rivers, plus Squaw Creek and dozens of smaller tributaries; the result is a many-armed lake, ideal for houseboating, exploring by boat, and waterside camping at scores of secluded coves, inlets, and beaches. The steep hills and labyrinthine waterways have another benevolent effect for boaters: They tend to break up any wind, making the lake unusually calm for its size.

Houseboating and power boating are the favorite activities on this lake, and at least ten firms rent boats (both the Shasta-Cascade Wonderland Association and the Redding Convention and Visitors Bureau furnish lists). Houseboating veterans wax enthusiastic about mooring in a remote cove that you have all to yourself, jumping over the side to swim in the cool waters of the lake, and cooking up a family barbeque on an evening when a big full moon climbs above the ridge and lights a path on the lake.

The popular houseboats sleep 5 to 18 people and come fully equipped with kitchen, toilet and shower, linens, and utensils. Most have a gas barbecue, rooftop sunning deck, and covered bow deck, while some even come with television, VCR, and stereo tape deck. Prices between mid-May and mid-September range anywhere from $1,200 to $2,000 per week, somewhat less in other seasons. Among the largest firms renting houseboats are **Seven Crown Resorts**, located at Bridge Bay and Digger Bay marinas (P.O. Box 1409, Boulder City, NV 89005; Tel: 800-PLAY-NOW); **Lakeshore Resort and Marina** (Star Route Box 760, Lakehead, CA 96051; Tel: 916-238-2301); **Holiday Floatels**, at Packers Bay Marina (P.O. Box 336, Redding, CA 96099; Tel: 916-221-5666); and **Sugarloaf Marina Resort**, at the Sugarloaf Recreation Area near Lakeshore (P.O. Box 599, Redding, CA 96099; Tel:

916-243-4353). All of these marinas also rent power boats for fishing or cruising. The single motel on the lake is **Bridge Bay Resort,** located just off I-5 about 12 miles north of Redding. Seven other marina-resorts around the lake offer cabins, and eight lakeside resorts have full-hookup recreational vehicle camping.

Shasta and its neighbors, Whiskeytown and Trinity lakes (see below), constitute the **Whiskeytown-Shasta-Trinity National Recreation Area.** The U.S. Forest Service maintains several waterside campsites around the lake, most of them accessible by road, as well as boat-launching ramps. Shasta has an open season year round for fishing the 19 species that inhabit the lake, including rainbow and brown trout; silver salmon (landlocked); largemouth, smallmouth, and spotted bass; bluegill; crappie; and catfish. **Shasta Dam Visitor Center** (just off I-5) has displays depicting the construction of the dam and its hydroelectric generating plant as well as the Central Valley Project. Guided tours of the galleries inside the dam and the powerhouse at the base of the spillway are sometimes available; inquire at the visitors' center.

Whiskeytown Lake

Spreading over 38,780 acres in the brush-covered hills eight miles west of Redding, Whiskeytown is the smallest of the three lakes in the recreation area, and, unlike the other two, it remains nearly full during the heavily used summer months. For the visitor Whiskeytown is quieter than Shasta and is best suited for swimming, sailing, canoeing, windsurfing, and fishing for trout, bass, and kokanee (landlocked sockeye salmon). A visitors' center perches on a bluff overlooking the lake; ranger-guided walks, gold-panning demonstrations, and illustrated evening programs are scheduled at Oak Bottom Amphitheater during the summer months. There are two campgrounds beside the lake and two in the hills to the south, as well as several picnic sites and sandy beaches ideal for sunning or swimming.

President John F. Kennedy dedicated Whiskeytown Dam in 1963, and if you're a Kennedy admirer you will want to detour the mile from the visitors' center to the dam to hear tape-recorded excerpts from his speech and view the bas-relief plaque that details the accomplishments of his administration. Just beyond the western end of the lake, **Tower House Historic District** consists of abandoned Gold Rush–era mine workings, the 1852 Camden House, and the site of an early hotel. Detour three miles north to **French Gulch**, a photogenic, ramshackle old settlement from the 1850s, situated on the original California–Oregon Trail.

Shasta and Weaverville

The 47-mile drive west from Redding to Weaverville, via California 299, is loaded with historical sightseeing of the Gold Rush era. Barely six miles beyond Redding, the red-brick walls and iron-shuttered doors of **Shasta** (also called "Old Shasta" to avoid confusion with Shasta City) flank both sides of the highway. There isn't much left of the old town, but what's there is well worth stopping to explore. If you're a photographer, try to arrive early in the morning or late in the afternoon, when long shadows throw the rugged old walls into bold relief.

Now preserved as a State Historic Park, Shasta began as a boomtown named Reading Springs after the discovery of gold nearby in 1848 by Major P. B. Reading. Because it lay astride the main wagon-and-stage route north to Oregon, it thrived until the railroad bypassed it with a route through Redding in the 1870s.

Many of the dozen or so buildings are roofless relics but have signs to identify them. Litsch Store still operates as a museum store, its shelves stocked with vintage top hats, axe handles, stove pipes, barrels of whiskey, and patent medicine. Across the street the Masonic Hall, California's oldest lodge, chartered in 1852, still holds meetings. The highlight of the old town is the 1855 Shasta County Courthouse, a well-preserved building operated as a museum by the state parks department. In addition to the completely furnished courtroom and basement jail, the museum displays one of the best collections of California landscape paintings in the state, including works by Frederick Shaefer, Charles Hittell, and Charles Christian Dahlgren. One curiosity is the pistol used by abolitionist John Brown in his raid on the Harper's Ferry Arsenal in 1859.

Beyond Shasta the highway passes Whiskeytown Lake, then climbs its tortuous way over Buckhorn Summit. Twisting and turning as it ascends, the road provides splendid views of the surrounding countryside. You can almost hear teamsters cracking whips and urging on the teams of horses and mules that struggled over these hills carrying supplies to the gold miners. After driving this route to Weaverville, you shouldn't be surprised that Trinity County boasts it has no freeways and no traffic signals.

Weaverville has a bit more bustle than it did a century ago, and the strip of fast-food restaurants and other brightly signed businesses south of town is beginning to change the look of the place. Still, the false-front buildings and covered sidewalks in the heart of town look very similar to those in California's Mother Lode. The town was founded in 1849, the year after gold was discovered on the Trinity River by the same Pierson B. Reading after whom Reading Springs (Shasta) was named. More than four dozen homes and public and business buildings date from the 19th century. You can pick up a free walking-tour map at the Chamber of Commerce, 317 Main Street.

Weaverville Joss House State Historic Park is the most unusual and most popular attraction in town. Set in the trees just off Main Street, the ornate wooden structure is typical of many Chinese houses of worship built to serve Chinese miners in the Gold Rush country in the last century. It's the oldest continuously used Chinese temple in California and is considered the finest historic temple remaining in North America. A ranger-guided tour leads you into the dimly lit interior for an explanation of the shrines, banners, and symbols. One of the extremely rare "dogs of foo" (small idols in the shape of lion-like dogs), stolen from the joss house many years ago, has recently been returned anonymously.

Just down the street, J. J. Jackson Memorial Museum features pioneer and gold-mining displays, a large collection of old bottles, a miner's cabin, and a restored, steam-operated stamp mill. Other attractions include the Highlands Art Center; Trinity County Courthouse, dating from 1857, the oldest courthouse in continuous use in the state; and the ornate Weaverville Bandstand, built in 1902 and still used on the Fourth of July and other civic occasions. If you're a fan of old-fashioned ice-cream concoctions the way they used to make them (especially ice-cream sodas), stop in **The Confectionery** on Main Street, in continuous operation since 1891. Among their specialties are the sinfully rich, multilayered Weaver Bally and Bully Choop.

If it's lunchtime, consider the **Pacific Brewery Café**, serving salads and sandwiches in an 1855 brick brewery, **The Mustard Seed**'s eclectic breakfast and lunch menu that ranges from quiche to Mexican dishes, or, adjacent to the bandstand, **The Village Station**, which offers soup and sandwiches.

The best among the town's handful of conventional motels are **The 49er** and the newly constructed **Weaverville Victorian Inn**. For bed and breakfast in a 19th-century house, try **Granny's House**, or **The Old Yellow House**.

Trinity Lake and the Trinity Alps

North of Weaverville, California Route 3 runs for about 100 miles through some of the most rugged and wildly beautiful country in the state to return you to I-5 at Yreka. This is a scenically rewarding route, but the road is two lane all the way, narrow and steep in spots; plan to spend the better part of a day en route. **Trinity Alps Wilderness Area**, the third largest in California, flanks the highway to the west and is a destination for hiking and horse- and llama-packing trips that depart from the tiny towns of Trinity Center, Etna, and Fort Jones. No motorized vehicles are permitted in this vast mountain and forest region.

Trinity Lake, the third lake in the national recreation area, is actually two adjoining lakes—Clair Engle and Lewiston— that usually are referred to by the single title, Trinity. Both lakes are even prettier and quieter than either Shasta or Whiskeytown. Deep, cold, and ringed by steep, conifer-clad hillsides, Lewiston is a bit chilly for swimming, but trout love it. Clair Engle (named for the late senator) is warmer and an outstanding smallmouth bass fishery. Bounded by California 3, Lewiston's western shore is dotted with vacation homes, campgrounds, and small, rustic resorts. Houseboat rental firms operate at the town of Trinity Center, but in recent years, low water levels in Clair Engle Lake have made house-boating an iffy proposition. (Check with the Shasta-Cascade Wonderland people in Redding—see above—before you go.) The town of Lewiston dates from the mid-1800s and still has several historic wooden buildings standing.

Trinity Center, the small community at the northern end of Clair Engle Lake, features the Scott Museum, with small but excellent pioneer, Native American, and barbed-wire collections. The **Carrville Inn** here dates from 1917 and now offers bed-and-breakfast accommodations. **Wyntoon Resort**, on the lake, has housekeeping cottages, RV campsites, and rental boats. Other rustic resorts nearby include **Coffee Creek Chalet**, **Bonanza King Resort**, and **Coffee Creek Guest Ranch**, all on Coffee Creek to the north of Clair Engle Lake, and **Ripple Creek Cabins**, on Ripple Creek overlooking Trinity River. All are the kind of quiet, cozy places you might build for yourself as a vacation cabin in these mountains. **Josephine Creek Lodge** is a small, remote adult resort that emphasizes hiking, fishing, and solitude at 5,300 feet.

Scott Valley, a lovely 28-mile-long valley of pastures full of fat cattle, big barns, and stacks of newly mown hay, lies at the northern end of California Route 3. **Etna**, originally called

Rough and Ready, is the largest town in the valley and seems frozen somewhere in the early part of this century. The town is loaded with venerable architecture to tempt your camera; pick up a free guide pamphlet at Scott Valley Drug, 511 Main Street. At Fort Jones stop at the Fort Jones Museum for its excellent collections of Native American basketry and stone mortars and pestles. Nearby, the Doll Museum displays more than 6,000 dolls from many different countries. Just south of Fort Jones, **Marlahan Ranch House** is a bed-and-breakfast inn in a ranch house built in 1899 within sight of the Oregon–California Stage Road. Yreka and the intersection with I-5 are a few miles north of Fort Jones.

LASSEN VOLCANIC
NATIONAL PARK

When Washington's Mount St. Helens blew its top on May 18, 1980, it shocked the nation. The awesome spectacle of nature beyond control unnerved many because of where it happened—in the continental United States. Mainland Americans are comfortable with volcanic eruptions in Hawaii, which seems distant and exotic—not in their backyards. Yet, for many people, the memory of another volcano eruption is still alive–one that blasted the skies of Northern California. Between 1914 and 1921 Mount Lassen erupted almost continually, first in flows of hot lava and mud that washed down its flanks into the valleys below, then, on May 22, 1915, in explosions that leveled trees and sent a towering mushroom cloud of ash more than 40,000 feet aloft. Today Lassen and the national volcanic park that surrounds it are quiet; the volcano is not extinct, just dormant, as the dozens of hot springs, steam vents, and boiling mud pots in the park testify.

Lassen is a gentle park, the mountain's scarred slopes covered with brush and trees, its meadows deep with grass and wildflowers, its streams running clear. The rehabilitation that has taken place over the past three-quarters of a century is really quite remarkable and provides a preview of what may eventually happen at Mount St. Helens.

There are a number of reasons for scheduling a trip to Lassen. The park offers excellent outdoor recreation—fishing, horseback riding, hiking, camping—and its volcanic features make for fascinating sightseeing. But one of the strongest incentives is its relative serenity compared to other Western national parks. In 1988, for example, just half a million people visited Lassen compared to more than three million for Yosemite.

Two state highways lead to the park's north and south entrances. From Red Bluff it's 47 miles east via California 36 to Mineral and park headquarters. It's exactly the same distance to the north entrance from Redding east via California 44. There are no conventional accommodations in the park (other than Drakesbad Guest Ranch in a remote eastern valley; see below), and motel facilities near the entrances are somewhat limited. Still, if you find everything booked up on a busy summer weekend you can easily base yourself in Red Bluff or Redding and make the park a day trip. Both approaches from the west climb gradually into the foothills through stands of pine and hillsides covered with manzanita and past ruins of mining operations.

California 89, the Lassen Park Road, loops through the western third of the park from both the north and south entrances, encircling all but the western side of this 10,457-foot mountain. Pick up a copy of the road guide at either entrance station; it provides mile-by-mile driving information keyed to 67 numbered roadside markers (numbered from the south entrance). Some caution is required: the road is wide but steep and winding in places with sharp drop-offs, and you can encounter patches of ice in the shady places as late as June. It's 29.5 miles through the park and 34 miles between Route 89's junctions with routes 36 and 44. Allow a minimum of one and a half hours for this drive with no stops, a bit more if the road is busy with sightseers on a midsummer weekend. But, as with most national parks, the key to enjoying Lassen is to get out of your car and walk or hike the trails to its attractions.

From the southwest entrance, the road climbs more than 1,400 feet in the first six miles. You'll have barely shifted out of first gear before you reach the first attraction, **Sulphur Works**. Perfuming the air with the smell of rotten eggs, a sulphur-laden mist emerges from dozens of vents in the ground. A short signed nature trail leads to bubbling hot springs, gaseous fumaroles, and plopping mud pots. In the next several miles the road twists and turns to give you fine views of the landscape to the south, west, and northwest; this stretch is one of the best in the park for photos. In addition to Lassen, you'll see 9,235-foot Brokeoff Mountain, Little Hot Springs Valley, and Mill Creek Canyon. Pristine Emerald Lake and Lake Helen, at 8,000 feet and 8,162 feet respectively, lie right beside the road; fishing for trout is permitted on Lake Helen.

One of the park's most popular sights is **Bumpass Hell**, an outstanding area of geothermal activity, the largest in the park. From the parking lot a 1.5-mile self-guiding nature trail leads to a Dante-esque scene of hot springs, steam vents, and mud pots. The trail is an easy one, climbing about 500 feet and descending about 250 feet en route, crossing the flank of ancient Mount Tehama for excellent views westward.

After covering about 7.5 miles from the entrance you reach the parking lot and trailhead for the **Lassen Peak Trail**. This 2.3-mile trail to the top, one of the best hikes in the park, is not difficult, but it does climb about 2,000 feet on a steady grade; you should allow half a day if you're going to take it. Once on top you have sweeping views of the vast volcanic landscape stretching away on all sides. During the summer rangers are often on hand at the peak and at Bumpass Hell to explain the geologic features you are viewing. In this case you can see an example of each of the four types of volcanoes found in the world from Mount Lassen's summit.

As you continue driving toward the summit of the park road you encounter more and more vegetation, especially red fir, lodgepole pine, and western pine. At several places the road opens out for top-of-the-world views of Warner Valley and Lake Almanor to the east. Dersch Meadows is bright with wildflowers in July and August and is one of the best places in the park to spot deer, in contrast to the Devastated Area, the most visible evidence of the 1915 eruption, where you can still see some of the old tree trunks felled by the blast (all pointing away from the crater). Just beyond, at Hot Rock, rests a huge boulder, measuring 10-by-15 feet and weighing 300 tons that was thrown five miles down the mountain by the 1915 blast and was still scalding hot 40 hours later. The road descends the last few miles to the north entrance, through stands of white fir, Jeffrey pine, incense cedar, ponderosa pine, and manzanita, to **Manzanita Lake**, a favorite destination for anglers and canoeists.

The Backcountry

The eastern two-thirds of the park is wilderness, studded with a lovely chain of lakes and laced with good hiking trails. No matter when you go, you're likely to have this back-country mainly to yourself. One of the best overnight routes begins at Summit Lake, proceeds to Twin Lake, and ends at Echo Lake, for eight miles filled with beautiful wildflowers, terrific views, and excellent lakeside stopping spots. A paved spur road enters the park at the southeastern corner and reaches Juniper Lake, largest and deepest of the park's lakes at an elevation of 6,792 feet. At the northeast corner, Butte Lake, reached via a dirt road from California 44, is noted for its fine rainbow trout fishing.

Lassen offers eight developed campgrounds, none with recreational-vehicle hookups. The campgrounds at Manzanita and Summit lakes are the most popular and often fill up early in the day in summer. There's fast-food service at Lassen Summer Chalet, at the southwest entrance, and fast food, groceries, and camping supplies available at the store at Manzanita Lake.

Other than campgrounds, **Drakesbad Guest Ranch**, in Warner Valley at the southeastern edge of the park, is the only overnight accommodation in Lassen. The venerable ranch, which, with its galvanized-roof ranch house and pole fences, looks as if it belongs in a Western movie, has been in operation for more than a century and offers horseback riding, pack trips into the backcountry, a swimming pool filled from hot springs, and hearty meals served on the American Plan. Rooms are modest, some without electricity, but the ranch is quite popular; reservations, as much as a year in advance, are advised (the ranch only operates from mid-June to mid-September). Warner Valley itself, with its timber-lined trails, soft meadows, and Boiling Springs Lake, is a bit of a Shangri-la in this park; it's also accessible to campers.

Lassen Off Season

Lassen operates year round, but the main park road is closed by snow from November until snowplows can complete clearing it, usually by Memorial Day. Park nature programs, which include hikes, campfire talks, star-gazing programs, children's activities, and nature and cultural demonstrations, get into full swing in mid-June and continue through Labor Day weekend.

For seekers of solitude, September and October are delightful, with their warm sunny days and cool crisp nights, when park trails are nearly empty and fall foliage, especially at lower elevations, provides a bright backdrop. On winter weekends, **Lassen Park Ski Area**, at the southwest entrance, operates a chairlift and surface tows; facilities include a rental shop, instruction, and a cafeteria. For the adventurous, the park's snow-covered roads and trails offer ideal cross-country skiing conditions. Several signed routes begin from Manzanita Lake and from Lassen Summer Chalet and wind through stunning park scenery mantled in white. On weekends rangers lead snowshoe walks and programs on winter wildlife and survival techniques.

South of Lassen

Overnight accommodations on California 36 southwest of the park entrance include **Lassen Mineral Lodge**, a motel with pool, restaurant, store, and tennis courts; **McGovern's Vacation Chalets**; and **Lassen Lodge Cabins**. **Volcano Country Camping** on this route has RV hookups.

Following California 36 six miles east from Mineral, south of the park's southern entrance, you reach Mill Creek and the best choice of lodging near the park: **Child's Meadows Resort**, **Mill Creek Resort**, **Fire Mountain Lodge** (built of logs, with a big stone fireplace, it also has detached cabins), **Deer Creek Lodge**, **Black Forest Lodge** (offering 14 rooms and excellent views), and **St. Bernard Lodge** (a seven-room chalet that has been operating since 1929). Good choices for dining include St. Bernard Lodge (locally famous for its three-quarter-pound hamburger on a homemade bun), Fire Mountain Lodge, and Black Forest Lodge, which specializes in German cuisine.

Lake Almanor, and its little resort town of **Chester**, is the most significant water-recreation area east of Lake Shasta. Situated at a summer-cool 4,500 feet, fringed with pine forest, and dotted with rustic resorts and vacation homes, Lake Almanor is a popular summer destination for fishing and boating. It's near enough to Lassen National Park to make it a good choice for a base from which to combine aquatic recreation and park sightseeing. The 52-square-mile lake boasts a summertime surface temperature in the mid-70 degrees F, making it comfortable for swimming, and local fishing tackle shops will tell you where to rent a boat and give you advice on the best techniques for catching the lake's trout, kokanee, bass, catfish, and perch. In Chester, **Antlers Motel**, **Seneca Motel**, and **Cinnamon Teal Bed and Breakfast** are modest but good choices for lodging. Lakeshore accommodations (suitable for families) include **Plumas Pines Resort**, **Harbor Lights**, **Lassen View Resort**, and **Almanor Lakeside Lodge**—all tucked away in the woods on the east shore. For unusual surroundings for dinner, try the **Timber House**, constructed of huge wooden blocks; beef and seafood entrées are featured, and there is entertainment on weekends.

From here it's about 35 miles east on Highway 36 to Susanville, the gateway to the Lonely Corner (see below).

NORTH OF LASSEN
Burney and Old Station

About 50 miles east of Redding, California Route 299 crests at 4,368-foot Hatchet Mountain Pass, revealing a lovely mountain valley below, and the little town of Burney. Burney's focus has always been the lumber industry, but because it lies near the intersection of east-west Highway 299 and north-south Highway 89 from Lassen, it thrives on vacationers, both those just passing through and those who use it as a base for the superb fishing and hiking country in Burney Basin that surrounds it, especially in Lassen National Forest and the Thousand Lakes Wilderness to the south. The Chamber of Commerce (Caldwell's Corner, Highway 299 in Burney) distributes a walking-and-driving tour guide that describes nine separate tours in the area. **McArthur–Burney Falls Memorial State Park** features a 129-foot waterfall along Burney Creek that plunges over a mossy rim into a narrow, rocky gorge below. Theodore Roosevelt, never at a loss for superlatives, called the falls one of the wonders of the world—a bit of an overstatement, but they are lovely. A mile-long, signed nature trail takes you down to the base of the falls, which are often enveloped in mist and rainbows. They face northward and are shaded most of the day, making photography difficult except on overcast days, but try for early-morning light.

The site of the California Stage Company's Hat Creek Station in the 1850s, **Old Station** (south of Burney on Highway 89) is the location of the University of California Radio Astronomy Observatory, whose dish antennas you can see on a nearby hill. Other points of interest at hand include Subway Cave, an underground lava tube, common in these parts, but this one is noteworthy for its "lavacicles," pendants of lava that dripped from the ceiling and solidified (it's not illuminated, so take a flashlight), and Spattercone Trail, which departs from Hat Creek Campground north of town and leads about two miles through scenes of fairly recent volcanic activity.

Fall River Mills

Not much more than a wide spot in the road northeast of Burney on 299, Fall River Mills takes the honors as the fly-fishing capital of this part of California—the fishing here is legendary, drawing eager anglers from all over the West. Not surprisingly, the town boasts several fly shops where you can hire a local guide to take you to the best spots and recommend what flies to use. The four buildings of Fort Crook Museum display Native American artifacts, antique furniture, a blacksmith's shop, and an old jail. **Ahjumawi Lava Springs State Park,** 3 miles north of McArthur (just up the road from Fall River Mills), is a most unusual state park: It cannot be reached by road, only by boat (available at Rick's Lodge and the Fall River Hotel—see below). Its 6,000 acres of wilderness encompass Big Lake, Ja-She Creek, and the Tule, Fall, and Pit rivers. As you'd expect of a park that is so well protected, the wildlife is abundant and is one of the primary reasons visitors make the extra effort to get here. Birds include bald eagles, ospreys, and herons, and large herds of deer forage along the lake shoreline.

Rick's Lodge, a rustic getaway nine miles northwest of Fall River Mills on County Road A-19, specializes in fishing vacations, offering a fly shop, guide service, boat rentals, fly-fishing school, and a fly-tying bench in every room (there are 12). To get to Rick's, take A-20 five and a half miles north of town to reach A-19. In town the **Fall River Hotel**'s dining room serves hearty meals and will make arrangements for licensed fishing guides and boats.

The climatic and topographic changes in this part of California can be abrupt. Within a score of miles east of the cool, forested country around Fall River Mills you enter open, rolling sagebrush rangeland and near-desert, where summertime temperatures are scorchers. The gateway to this area, however, is not Burney/Fall River Mills, but Susanville, to the area's south, about 35 miles east of Chester and Lake Almanor on Highway 36.

THE LONELY CORNER

Once a rough-and-tumble town of the 19th century, **Susanville** is now devoted to the cattle-and-sheep industry, and is becoming increasingly popular as an outfitting and jumping-off spot for fishing, hunting, hiking, horse packing, and backcountry exploring in nearby Lassen National Forest and the Caribou Peak Wilderness, adjacent to Lassen Volcanic National Park. It is also the gateway to the so-called Lonely Corner, the far northeastern part of the state.

Eagle Lake, one of the largest natural lakes in California, is
16 miles north of Susanville; situated at the 5,000-foot level
in an isolated valley, it's a favorite destination for anglers,
who come to catch the native trout that thrive in its alkaline
waters and can weigh up to 11 pounds. The lake is also a
paradise for wildlife viewing, with mule deer, antelope,
porcupine, and small animals often observed along the
shore, and for bird-watching, including grebe, pelicans,
gulls, Canada geese, and ospreys—which—perch high in
the trees and swoop down to the lake surface to grab a
glistening trout in their talons.

In Susanville, **Roop Fort and William Pratt Memorial
Museum** has pioneer, Native American, and logging exhibits
housed in a small wooden fort constructed during local
skirmishes in 1854. For hikers there's the **Bizz Johnson Trail**,
which follows the old grade of the Fernley and Lassen
Railroad through tall timber to the little mill town of Westwood, 21 miles west.

Adequate motels in Susanville include **Best Western
Trailside Inn**, **River Inn Motel**, and **Super Budget Motel**. The
Hotel Mt. Lassen dates from 1927, was restored in 1950, and
includes an old-fashioned Western saloon with stained-glass
windows and a restaurant specializing in Italian cuisine. **Roseberry House Bed and Breakfast** offers three guest rooms in a
1902 residence. **Spanish Springs Ranch**, northeast of Susanville on U.S. 395, offers a guest-ranch experience on a
working cattle ranch, including participation in cattle drives,
pack-train trips, and nights in remote historic homesteads.

Exploring the Lonely Corner

At Susanville the demarcation line between forested mountain environment and sagebrush desert is sharply drawn.
Within a half-dozen miles you descend from cool pine
forest, pass through Susanville heading east, and emerge
onto bunchgrass rangeland that soon gives way to less hospitable sagebrush country. If you squint your eyes against the
sun and look east, you'll see the terrain flattening out into
the Great Basin. Those white patches you see 20 or more
miles away are alkali flats backdropped by a haze of purple
mountains on the horizon. This is mind-expanding country,
the kind of wide open spaces where you can drive for hours
and seldom encounter a town worthy of the classification.
Drive north on U.S. 395 from Susanville to Alturas, for
example, and you'll find the traffic so sparse you can ease up

to within 50 yards of a herd of pronghorn antelope standing beside the road without startling them.

This is also cowboy country, with vast ranches sprawling across thousands of acres of rangeland. If you're lucky you may encounter one on horseback following a fence line or herding cattle, but don't be disappointed if the cowboys you see are driving pickup trucks instead of riding horses: Still, they're plying their outdoor trade on these ranches with the same skills they've used for more than a century.

The other figure indigenous to this landscape is the sheep-herder, for this is also sheep-ranching country. As you travel along, you may encounter bands of woollies grazing along a hillside followed by a solitary man and a black-and-white dog. The man is probably Basque; the dog, a Border collie.

The Basques came to the West from their native home in the Pyrenees in search of gold, but most came after the great bonanzas were over and instead turned to the vocation they knew best, sheepherding. For generations they lived in curious canvas-covered wagons while on the range (you can see one preserved in the Klamath County Museum in Klamath Falls, Oregon), but these days they're likely to live in small travel trailers pulled behind battered pickup trucks. Some of the best places to see them and their herds are along U.S. 395, in the 110 miles between Susanville and Alturas, and along California Route 139, southeast of the town of Tulelake (see below).

Alturas and Surprise Valley

Modoc County has lots of elbow room. Northeasternmost of the 58 California counties, it covers a land area of a little more than 4,373 square miles—with a county population of about 9,500. That makes a population density of about two people per square mile; Alturas, the county seat, accounts for about 3,400 of those residents.

Situated in the broad valley of the Pit River, Alturas, 104 miles north of Susanville via U.S. 395, is a town with a Western flavor. Saturday mornings the curbs are lined with pickup trucks as ranchers come to town to shop, and restaurants tend to serve extra-large portions, heavy on the beef. Focusing on that Western heritage, the **Modoc County Historical Museum** features a large collection of firearms and cattle brands in addition to a steam locomotive and memorabilia from the Modoc War (discussed below).

Basque cuisine covers a broad range but typically includes lamb (sometimes boiled, sometimes barbecued), soups, stews, sausages, beans, and the traditional sheep-herder's bread. You can try Basque food—and the spicy Basque Picon punch—served family style at the **Brass Rail** in Alturas. The frontier-style **Niles Hotel** includes a traditional cowboy saloon, historic photos on the walls, an arcaded sidewalk outside, and prime rib and steak. Alturas is not big enough to have a wide variety of accommodations, but the **Best Western Trailside Inn** and the **Dunes** offer reasonably priced, conventional motel accommodations. **Dorris House** has bed-and-breakfast rooms in a 1912 ranch house on the shore of nearby Dorris Lake.

From downtown Alturas you can look east and see the snow-capped peaks of the Warner Mountains, at the extreme eastern edge of the state. Just beyond the mountains lies **Surprise Valley**, named by westward-bound pioneers be-cause its lushness came as such a pleasant surprise after crossing the trackless miles of Nevada desert. If you have a day to spend exploring, consider driving a 98-mile round trip from Alturas east over 6,350-foot Cedar Pass to Surprise Valley, returning west via 6,250-foot Fandango Pass, 14 miles of which are unpaved road, but usually in good condition; inquire locally.

Cedarville, the largest settlement in Surprise Valley, looks as if it hasn't changed much in this century; several of its well-maintained residences date from the 1880s. Stop at the Cressler and Bonner Trading Post, the 1865 log cabin that housed the first mercantile store in the county, then head north 25 miles to Fort Bidwell, a former cavalry post estab-lished in 1862. The **Fort Bidwell Hotel and Restaurant**, circa 1906, operates as a bed-and-breakfast inn, with a restaurant open to non-guests. A portion of the Warner Mountains is protected as the South Warner Wilderness, an alpine area studded with mountains over 8,000 feet high and laced with trails. **Modoc Wildlife Adventures** (P.O. Box 1882, Alturas, CA 96101; Tel: 916-233-3777) leads backcountry horse-packing trips into the wilderness.

Lava Beds National Monument

One of the most tragic stories in Western history was played out in the 1870s in what is now Lava Beds National Monu-ment. A band of Modoc Indians, under a leader named Kientpoos (also called Captain Jack), unable to live with their traditional enemies, the Klamaths and the Paiutes, on the Klamath Indian Reservation, fled to the jumbled terrain of Lava Beds. In the ensuing negotiations with the U.S. Army for their surrender, the Modocs killed the negotiators, General Canby and Reverend Thomas. For nearly five months the Modoc band, which never numbered more than 55 men, plus women and children, managed to hold off an army of more than 1,000 troopers equipped with modern weapons and artillery, but the end result was inevitable. The Modocs managed to escape from Lava Beds, only to be caught two months later; Captain Jack and several of his lieutenants were hanged, while other survivors were sent to a reservation in Oklahoma where their identity as a tribe ceased to exist. As one old Modoc chief put it, "Once my people were as the sand along the shore. Now I call to them and only the wind answers."

The National Monument combines the history of the Modoc War with the unusual geology of vulcanism in a primeval and dramatic landscape that brings to mind the earth's beginnings. Located on the northern flank of a shield volcano known as Medicine Lake Volcano, the monument is significant geologically for the many different volcanic phenomena you can see in such a small area (only about 47,000 acres).

Follow California 299 west from Alturas 19 miles to its junction with California 139 at Canby, then take 139 northwest about 50 miles to the entrance of the park south of Tulelake. Driving the main park road is the easiest way to get an overview of the monument in the space of about two hours, but if you have more time, stop and walk the short trails to natural attractions that interest you. Beginning at the northeast entrance off California 139 south of the town of Tulelake, follow the paved route 22 miles to the north entrance, then cut across the lava fields to exit at the southeast entrance, where the visitors' center is located. Signs along the way describe the historic and geological highlights.

The first (northern) stretch of road concerns Native American history and connects the main sites of the Modoc War. Immediately inside the entrance, a graded dirt road leads to a large group of prehistoric Indian petroglyphs—many recognizable as stick figures, circles with rays, and wiggly lines that probably portray snakes or worms—carved in rock over an area of about two city blocks. At Captain Jack's Stronghold you can follow trails leading into the lava beds to reach what was the Modoc vantage point in the conflict. Canby's Cross marks the spot where the two negotiators were killed.

As the road swings south, you pass beneath steep lava bluffs, then climb to a viewpoint above Devil's Homestead

Lava Flow, where you can see the great river of molten rock that poured downhill into Tule Lake. The road continues to wind through lava beds, climbing for a while, then descending to cross lava flows before climbing again. One of the most remarkable of the monument's features are the lava tubes, caves that lie beneath much of this surface-of-the-moon landscape. Formed when the surface of a molten lava flow cooled more rapidly than the still-liquid interior, these interconnected caves are sometimes several miles in length. There are more than 200 in the monument, 25 of which are open to the public. Cave Loop Road takes you past the only electrically lighted cave, Mushpot, plus at least a dozen others; rangers conduct cave walks as well as orientation and evening interpretive programs from Memorial Day through Labor Day.

At first encounter, Lava Beds may seem like an empty desert of rocks, uninhabited and uninhabitable, but stay a while and this harsh environment will begin to grow on you. Rocky Mountain mule deer, pronghorn antelope, coyote, fox, weasel, skunk, and badger inhabit the monument, and yellow-bellied marmots are ubiquitous. They're especially plentiful along the north boundary road, and you may first encounter one as a large, blond ball of fur scurrying in front of your car or as a fat lump sunning on a flat rock. Several varieties of squirrels, chipmunks, cottontail, and jackrabbits are also common. Large colonies of bats inhabit some of the caves in summer, emerging at dusk to feed at nearby Tule Lake. There are 225 species of birds in the monument; some are residents, some come as visitors. You can pick up a checklist at the visitors' center.

Klamath Basin Birding

For bird watchers the **Klamath Basin National Wildlife Refuges** are prime destinations. Straddling the California–Oregon border north of Lava Beds, lakes and marshes scattered across the basin host one of the largest concentrations of migrating waterfowl in North America. In November, when the greatest concentrations occur, thousands of ducks and geese make brief rest and feed stops here before continuing south along the Pacific Flyway. It can send shivers of delight up your spine to watch skeins of high-flying geese dotting the sky from horizon to horizon, the leaders honking their distinctive calls to keep their flocks together.

The best place to start is the refuge headquarters, five miles west of Tulelake, where you can view interpretive exhibits that will help you understand what to look for. The refuge provides free checklists to the more than 254 species that regularly stop here, as well as maps to help you find your way around the various ponds and marshes.

If you're visiting Lava Beds and the wildlife refuges, you'll probably want to find accommodations and a place to dine a few miles north in Klamath Falls, Oregon, as motels and restaurants close to the California attractions are virtually nonexistent. **Best Western Klamath Inn, Thunderbird Motel**, and **Molatore's Motel** all offer good, standard motel facilities. **Thompson's Bed-and-Breakfast Inn by the Lake** has three bed-and-breakfast rooms with spectacular views of Upper Klamath Lake and visiting waterfowl. In the dining department at Klamath Falls, **Fiorella's** features northern Italian fare, **Chez Nous** serves excellent Continental cuisine in a former residence, and **The Stockman's Social Club** concentrates on beef and seafood, Western decor, and country-western music.

GETTING AROUND

The most practical means of exploring northeastern California is with your own vehicle or a rented car; Redding is about a four-hour drive from San Francisco via Interstates 80, 505, and 5. Public transportation systems serving the entire region do not exist. United Express (Tel: 800-241-6522) and American Eagle (Tel: 800-433-7300) feeder airlines have frequent service from San Francisco International Airport to Redding Airport. Hertz, Avis, National, and Budget rental car systems have offices in the Redding airport.

ACCOMMODATIONS REFERENCE

▶ **Almanor Lakeside Lodge.** 3747 Eastshore Drive-Highway 147, **Lake Almanor**, CA 91637. Tel: (916) 284-7376.

▶ **Antlers Motel.** P.O. Box 538, **Chester**, CA 96020. Tel: (916) 258-2722.

▶ **Beaver Creek Lodge.** Klamath River, CA 96050. Tel: (916) 465-2331.

▶ **Best Western Hilltop Inn.** 2300 Hilltop Drive, **Redding**, CA 96002. Tel: (916) 221-6100 or (800) 528-1234.

▶ **Best Western Klamath Inn.** 4061 South Sixth Street, **Klamath Falls**, OR 97603. Tel: (503) 882-1200 or (800) 528-1234.

▶ **Best Western Trailside Inn.** 343 North Main Street, **Alturas**, CA 96101. Tel: (916) 233-4111 or (800) 528-1234.

▶ **Best Western Trailside Inn.** 2785 Main Street, **Susanville**, CA 96130. Tel: (916) 257-4123 or (800) 528-1234.

▶ **Best Western Tree House.** I-5 and Lake Street, **Mount Shasta City,** CA 96067. Tel: (916) 926-3101.

▶ **Big Foot Resort.** 30841 Walker Road, **Horse Creek,** CA 96045. Tel: (916) 496-3313.

▶ **Black Forest Lodge.** Route 5, Box 5000, **Mill Creek,** CA 96061. Tel: (916) 258-2941.

▶ **Bonanza King Resort.** Route 2, Box 4790, **Trinity Center,** CA 96091. Tel: (916) 266-3305.

▶ **Bridge Bay Resort.** 10300 Bridge Bay Road, **Redding,** CA 96003. Tel: (916) 275-3081.

▶ **Carrville Inn.** Star Route 2, Box 3536, **Trinity Center,** CA 96091. Tel: (916) 266-3511.

▶ **Child's Meadows Resort.** Route 5, Box 3000, **Mill Creek,** CA 96061. Tel: (916) 595-4411.

▶ **Cinnamon Teal Bed and Breakfast.** Highway 36 and Feather River Drive, **Chester,** CA 96020. Tel: (916) 258-3993.

▶ **Coffee Creek Chalet.** Star Route 2, Box 3969, **Trinity Center,** CA 96091. Tel: (916) 266-3235.

▶ **Coffee Creek Guest Ranch.** Route 2, Box 4940, **Trinity Center,** CA 96091. Tel: (916) 266-3343.

▶ **Days Inn.** 2180 Hilltop Drive, **Redding,** CA 96002. Tel: (916) 221-8200 or (800) 325-2525.

▶ **Deer Creek Lodge.** Route 5, Box 4000, **Mill Creek,** CA 96061. Tel: (916) 258-2939.

▶ **Dorris House.** P.O. Box 1655, **Alturas,** CA 96101. Tel: (916) 233-3786.

▶ **Drakesbad Guest Ranch.** California Guest Services, Inc., Adobe Plaza, 2150 Main Street, Suite 7, **Red Bluff,** CA 96080. Tel: ask long distance operator for Drakesbad Toll Station #2, operator route 028-181 in Susanville, for reservations; Tel: (916) 529-1512 for information.

▶ **Dunes.** 511 North Main Street, **Alturas,** CA 96101. Tel: (916) 233-3545.

▶ **Dunsmuir Bed & Breakfast Inn.** 5423 Dunsmuir Avenue, **Dunsmuir,** CA 96025. Tel: (916) 235-4351.

▶ **Fall River Hotel.** P.O. Box 718, **Fall River Mills,** CA 96028. Tel: (916) 336-5550.

▶ **The Faulkner House.** 1029 Jefferson Street, **Red Bluff,** CA 96080. Tel: (916) 529-0520.

▶ **Fire Mountain Lodge.** Mill Creek, CA 96061. Tel: (916) 258-2938.

▶ **Fort Bidwell Hotel and Restaurant.** P.O. Box 97, **Fort Bidwell,** CA 96112. Tel: (916) 279-6199.

▶ **The 49er.** P.O. Box 1608, **Weaverville,** CA 96093. Tel: (916) 623-49ER.

▶ **Granny's House.** P.O. Box 31, 313 Taylor Street, **Weaverville**, CA 96093. Tel: (916) 623-2756.

▶ **Harbor Lights.** 300 Peninsula Drive, **Lake Almanor**, CA 96137. Tel: (916) 596-3208.

▶ **Hawk's Roost. Seiad**, CA 96086. Tel: (916) 496-3400.

▶ **Holiday Inn-Redding.** 1900 Hilltop Drive, **Redding**, CA 96002. Tel: (916) 221-7500.

▶ **Hotel Mt. Lassen.** 28 South Lassen Street, **Susanville**, CA 96130. Tel: (916) 257-6609.

▶ **Josephine Creek Lodge.** Star Route 2, Box 5702, **Trinity Center**, CA 96091. Tel: ask long distance operator for Toll Station 4677 in Sawyer's Bar (area code 916).

▶ **Klamath Motor Lodge.** 1111 South Main Street, **Yreka**, CA 96097. Tel: (916) 842-2751.

▶ **Lake Shastina Accommodations.** 6030 Lake Shastina Drive, **Weed**, CA 96094. Tel: (916) 938-4111.

▶ **Lassen Lodge Cabins.** Route 5, Box 65, **Paynes Creek**, CA 96075. Tel: (916) 597-2944.

▶ **Lassen Mineral Lodge. Mineral**, CA 96063. Tel: (916) 595-4422.

▶ **Lassen View Resort.** 7457 Highway 147, **Lake Almanor**, CA 96137. Tel: (916) 596-3437.

▶ **Marlahan Ranch House.** 9539 North Highway 3, **Fort Jones**, CA 96032. Tel: (916) 468-5527.

▶ **The McCloud Guest House.** 606 West Colombero Drive, **McCloud**, CA 96057. Tel: (916) 964-3160.

▶ **McGovern's Vacation Chalets.** 563 McClay Road, **Novato**, CA 94947. Tel: (916) 595-4497.

▶ **Mill Creek Resort. Mill Creek**, CA 96061. Tel: (916) 595-4449.

▶ **Miner's Inn.** 122 East Miner Street, **Yreka, CA** 96097. Tel: (916) 842-4355.

▶ **Molatore's Motel.** 100 Main Street, **Klamath Falls**, OR 97603. Tel: (503) 882-4666.

▶ **Motel Orleans.** 2240 Hilltop Drive, **Redding**, CA 96002. Tel: (916) 221-5432.

▶ **Motel Orleans.** 1804 B Fort Jones Road, **Yreka**, CA 96097. Tel: (916) 842-1612.

▶ **Motel 6.** 1640 Hilltop Drive, **Redding**, CA 96097. Tel: (916) 221-1800.

▶ **Oaks RV Park. Klamath River**, CA 96050. Tel: (916) 465-2323.

▶ **The Old Yellow House.** 801 Main Street. **Weaverville**, CA 96093. Tel: (916) 623-2274.

▶ **Plumas Pines Resort.** 3000 Almanor Drive, **West Canyon Dam**, CA 95923. Tel: (916) 259-4343.

▶ **Railroad Park Resort.** 100 Railroad Park Road, **Dunsmuir**, CA 96025. Tel: (916) 235-4440.

▶ **Rainbow Resort. Hamburg**, CA 96045. Tel: (916) 496-3242.

▶ **Red Lion Inn.** 1830 Hilltop Drive, **Redding**, CA 96002. Tel: (916) 221-8700 or (800) 547-8010.

▶ **Rick's Lodge.** Glenburn Star Route, **Fall River Mills**, CA 96028. Tel: (916) 336-5300 (April–November); (916) 336-6618 (November–April).

▶ **Ripple Creek Cabins.** Star Route 2, Box 3899, **Trinity Center**, CA 96091. Tel: (916) 266-3505.

▶ **River Inn Motel.** 1710 Main Street, **Susanville**, CA 96130. Tel: (916) 257-6051.

▶ **Roseberry House Bed and Breakfast.** 609 North Street, **Susanville**, CA 96130. Tel: (916) 257-5675.

▶ **St. Bernard Lodge.** Route 5, Box 5500, **Mill Creek**, CA 96061. Tel: (916) 258-3382.

▶ **Seneca Motel.** P.O. Box 504, **Chester**, CA 96020. Tel: (916) 258-2815.

▶ **Spanish Springs Ranch.** P.O. Box 70, **Ravendale**, CA 96123. Tel: (916) Dial 102880 and ask for Ravendale 30.

▶ **The Sportsman's Lodge.** 20502 Highway 96, **Klamath River**, CA 96050. Tel: (916) 465-2366.

▶ **Steelhead Lodge. Hamburg**, CA 96045. Tel: (916) 496-3256.

▶ **Stoney Brook Inn.** 309 W. Colombero, **McCloud**, CA 96057. Tel: (916) 964-2300.

▶ **Super Budget Motel.** 2975 Johnstonville Road, **Susanville**, CA 96130. Tel: (916) 257-2782.

▶ **Swiss Holiday Lodge.** 2400 South Mount Shasta Boulevard, **Mount Shasta City**, CA 96097. Tel: (916) 926-3446.

▶ **Thompson's Bed-and-Breakfast Inn by the Lake.** 1420 Wild Plum Court, **Klamath Falls**, OR 97601. Tel: (503) 882-7938.

▶ **Thunderbird Motel.** 3612 South Sixth Street, **Klamath Falls**, OR 97603. Tel: (503) 882-8864.

▶ **Volcano County Camping.** P.O. Box 55, **Mineral**, CA 96063. Tel: (916) 595-3347.

▶ **Weaverville Victorian Inn.** 1709 Main Street, **Weaverville**, CA 96093. Tel: (916) 623-4432.

▶ **Wyntoon Resort.** P.O. Box 70, **Trinity Center**, CA 96091. Tel: (916) 266-3337.

THE GOLD COUNTRY

AND YOSEMITE

By Eloise Snyder

Eloise Snyder, formerly a reporter at the San Francisco Examiner, *is a free-lance writer based in Jackson, California.*

Linking the unspoiled villages, the ghost towns that survive only with a marker, and the neon-lit main streets of thriving county seats is the highway that courses through the history of the Gold Rush and marks the way to Yosemite National Park. It is, appropriately, Highway 49. For 318 miles it climbs from 200 to 6,000 feet in altitude up roller-coaster hills, through pine forests and oak stands and into plunging canyons. It is the route from the Northern to the Southern Mines once travelled by the legendary grizzled prospector by jackass, by stagecoach, or on foot.

For the fast-track traveller, one day devoted to a couple of Gold Rush sites is possible—but superficial. For searching for the offbeat, learning to pan for gold, and listening to some tall tales take three days to a week.

In communities that recognize the extraordinary value of tourism, chambers of commerce outdo each other with comprehensive maps, carefully designed self-guided walking tours, schedules of seasonal events, and volumes on colorful local history.

While the name Mother Lode is applied generously along the Highway 49 Golden Chain, it was first used in 1851 to designate a vein of enormous richness that stretched for about 100 miles midway between the Northern and Southern Mines areas. Today lofty headframes mark some of the great mines closed by presidential order during World War II. Others remain unmarked, but there is a growing awareness of the importance of preserving what is meaningful and significant from the Gold Rush era: Cities seek the status of National Historic Landmarks as a measure of conservation, and communities unite to save the old stone general store bearing massive iron shutters.

Those iron shutters are integral to the architectural styles of the Gold Country that speak of the origins of those who swarmed to California in 1849. Along Highway 49 you will see prim New England cottages, soaring church steeples, and verandahs of the Old South. (If you travel Highway 49 in summer, when the temperature climbs, you will recognize the value of double balconies to screen against the sun.)

Traffic is at its densest in summer. Spring promises warm days, cool nights, green hills, and brilliant poppies. In fall the sun turns mellow, toyon bushes produce scarlet berries, and in the High Country of Yosemite aspen and maples glow warm bronze and shimmering gold.

The distance from Sacramento, born of the Gold Rush and two rivers, to the Northern and Southern Mines is short in mileage but long in contrasts. Each surviving community, once a ragtag cluster of tents and wooden shacks, now struggles as it grows to preserve the feeling of a time that produced an aura of romance—a feeling that the grizzled prospector, the true 49er, would never have understood.

We begin east of San Francisco in Sacramento, travel northeast to Auburn, and then head north on Highway 49 to the Northern Mines towns of Grass Valley and Nevada City. Returning south of Auburn along Highway 49, we head into the Southern Mines area and more gold-mining communities, including Placerville, Sutter's Mill (where the discovery of gold started it all), Jackson, and Calaveras County. (The Southern Mines area is also one of California's finer wine-producing areas.) Finally, we turn east to Yosemite National Park.

MAJOR INTEREST

Sacramento
Historic buildings
River cruises

Northern and Southern Mines
Gold Country communities
Gold panning

Exploring caves
Wine tasting
Western architecture
Museums
Steam-train trips

Yosemite National Park
Hiking
Yosemite Valley's beauty
Natural magnificence of the High Country
Seasonal sports activities
Photography

SACRAMENTO

The grand dome of the state capitol building, which once dominated the skyline of Sacramento, is hedged today by tall buildings that speak eloquently of the city's surge toward major metropolitan status. Comfortable little "River City" is up-tempo and making a statement of its own to get out from under the shadow of San Francisco, a 90-minute drive to the west on Highway 80.

There is still small-town pride in California's capital city, where urban dwellers can thank early settlers for planting protective shade trees along every street to combat the torrid summers. Sacramento today says it has more trees than Paris (nobody is challenging the claim). Another source of pride is its designation as "Camellia City." More than a million camellia bushes transform the city into a veritable garden every March, when the city celebrates its blossoms with a formal ball and a parade.

Along with new growth has come pride in restoration. A good place to get acquainted with the city is in the historic **Old Sacramento** section on the east bank of the Sacramento River, now a State Historical Park, west from the capitol building. Before the truck and the automobile quelled river travel, the Sacramento River was famous for its luxurious steamboats, and had an enormously profitable river trade. Today a paddle wheeler takes passengers up the river for a few miles, from Raley's Landing across from Old Sacramento. You can purchase tickets at the Old Sacramento Schoolhouse.

In addition to browsing in shops that sell everything from cotton candy to leather boots to quality paintings, you may be interested in exploring the many carefully renovated

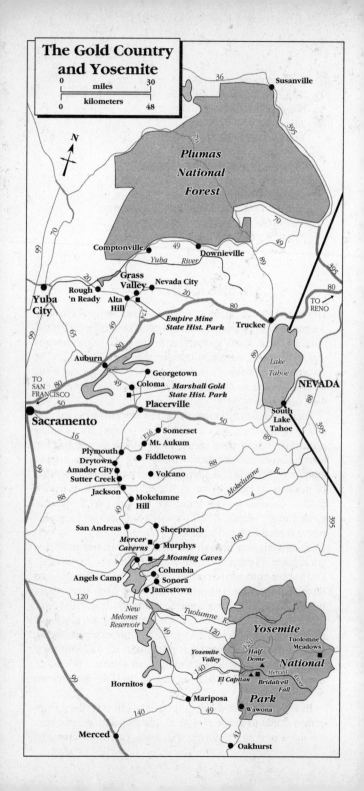

The Gold Country and Yosemite

0 — miles — 30
0 — kilometers — 48

N

Susanville

Plumas National Forest

70

36

395

Comptonville
49
Downieville
Yuba River
89
49

Grass Valley
Nevada City
Rough 'n Ready
Alta Hill
20
20
80
Empire Mine State Hist. Park

Yuba City
70
99

Truckee

TO RENO
80
395

Lake Tahoe

NEVADA

Auburn
80
49

Georgetown
Coloma
Marshall Gold State Hist. Park
Placerville

TO SAN FRANCISCO
80
50
65
99

Sacramento
16
50

South Lake Tahoe
88
89
395

E16
Somerset
Mt. Aukum
Fiddletown
Plymouth
Drytown
Amador City
Volcano
Sutter Creek
Jackson
Mokelumne Hill
88
Mokelumne R.
4

San Andreas
Sheepranch
Mercer Caverns
Murphys
Moaning Caves
Columbia
Angels Camp
Sonora
Jamestown
120

108

New Melones Reservoir
Tuolumne R.
49
120

99

Hornitos
Mariposa
140
49
Wawona

Merced

140

Oakhurst
41

Yosemite
National
Park
120
Half Dome
Tuolumne Meadows
Yosemite Valley
El Capitan
Merced River
Bridalveil Fall

buildings here, just north of Capitol Mall. The **History Center**, at Front and I streets, is a re-creation of the town's first city hall and waterworks building of 1854; exhibits tell the story of how the city survived the tumultuous growth brought on by the Gold Rush, as well as getting through two devastating floods and a depression.

The showplace of Old Sacramento for both train buffs and those who have never set foot on one is the extraordinary **Railroad Museum**, an impressive collection of railroad memorabilia displayed as fine art. Sounds and mirrors give the sensation of rumbling through the night on one of these old beauties. Vintage locomotive, passenger, and freight cars are polished and lovingly restored. A visit is highly recommended.

Along with revolving contemporary exhibits, **Crocker Art Gallery**, on the other side of Capitol Mall at Second and O streets, evokes nostalgia with its splendid collection of classic Old West paintings. The oldest art gallery and museum west of the Mississippi, it is an expansion of the architecturally distinguished home of railroad magnate Charles Crocker, who founded the gallery in 1873 after the Crockers returned from a trip to Europe.

You can't miss the **Capitol dome** at the end of Capitol Mall, which leads east from Old Sacramento and the river. The recently restored building, which dates from 1874, stands in a cherished park with hundreds of species of trees, each carefully designated, and platoons of friendly squirrels. The real show is inside the Capitol, where the glorious rotunda dome has been painted in pastels and trimmed with plaster decoration and sparkling lights on a gold background. The first floor has museum rooms complete with original furnishings looking much as they did in 1906; stop by the office of then-Governor Pardee, maintained as it was left the day after the San Francisco earthquake. Free guided tours are offered daily on the hour, or you can wander on your own. Be sure to peek in on the senate and assembly chambers if the legislature is in session.

Drive or take J Street bus number 30 or 31 east several blocks to **Sutter's Fort**, at 26th and L streets, site of the fort built by John August Sutter, owner of the Coloma mill where gold was discovered. Sutter's dream of building a city named Sutterville at the site of the fort was crushed in the wake of the Gold Rush, but it's all been put back together here—carpenter, cooper, and blacksmith shops ring the courtyard; inside are guest quarters, guards' quarters, and Captain

Sutter's office. An Indian Museum around the corner from the fort entrance displays an impressive basket collection.

Sacramento's reputation for attractive restaurants and good dining reflects a growing demand for ethnic variety. You don't have to stray from the downtown area to find a price and a menu to suit your tastes. On the moderate end, **Paragary's**, at 28th and N streets, lures fans of carpaccio, polenta, veal chops, and mushroom salad (don't neglect the excellent wine list). Gumbo and kibbeh put the accent on Caribbean at **Celestin's**, 2516 J Street. Upscale **Biba**, at 2801 Capitol Avenue, is where regulars relish tortellini and green lasagna, and **Chanterelle**, at 1300 H Street, serves California cuisine from seafood sausage to Frangelico soufflé.

For overnighters the **Ponderosa Motor Inn**, three blocks from the capitol on H Street, is convenient for city sightseeing and dining. The **Holiday Inn Capitol Plaza** is only a minute from Old Sacramento on J Street, and top-floor dining there provides a fine view of the city and its surroundings. Or, if new and grand is your style, the **Hyatt Regency**, on L Street directly across from the capitol, is a good bet.

Just off Highway 80 on the fast track east to the Gold Country is **Red Lion Inn**, on West Point Way. It's about ten minutes from downtown and has a shuttle service to the airport, two pools, and two restaurants.

THE NORTHERN MINES

Less than an hour's drive northeast of Sacramento on Interstate 80 is **Auburn**, a Gold Rush town experiencing the clutches of urbanization. Between Auburn and rugged little Downieville, about 72 winding miles north on Highway 49, are the Northern Mines. This is a region of contrasts: bustling communities determined to preserve some of the flavor of a romantic past, and, beyond them, unspoiled miles of pine forests, oak woodlands, and streams that invite gold panning.

How much time you have available will determine how far up Highway 49 you go, but Auburn, where Highway 49 intersects with I-80, is a convenient and pleasant starting place. At the gateway to Old Auburn, you'll find a stone sculpture of Claude Chana, the man who discovered the first three nuggets and stayed to found the city in 1848. Auburn's Old Town and all of its Gold Rush structures have been collectively designated as a National Historic Landmark. Don't miss the four-story red-and-white firehouse; it's irresistible to photographers.

Nevada City

For fast relief from high-speed I-80, take the turnoff to the west for Highway 174, north of Auburn, to Grass Valley and Nevada City. Plunge deep into the past on gravel U-Bet Road, which makes a loop east off of Highway 49 and passes You Bet and Red Dog, historic hydraulic mining towns. (All that's left in Red Dog now are a few old frame buildings and a small cemetery.) Curving west, U-Bet Road rejoins Highway 49 in Nevada City, restoration gem of the Gold Country, with white church steeples and turreted Victorians sparkling on its seven pine-clad hills.

Today's primly charming homes and public buildings cloak Nevada City's boisterous past. From a primitive camp in 1849, the city grew to challenge San Francisco and Sacramento in the 1850s as third-largest city in the state. What lured a peak population of 10,000 were accounts of miners pulling a pound of gold a day—gold for gambling, whiskey, bawdy ladies, and an occasional pipe of opium—from Old Coyote Ravine. Murders over claim-jumping were routine.

As gold-seeking gave way to commerce, conservative easterners brought their families and built the gingerbread Victorians that are primary tourist attractions more than a century later. Queen Anne, Italianate, and Gothic Revival styles, most dating from the 1870s, stand behind white picket fences and boast steep roofs, turned posts, and stained-glass windows. Some have been classified as historic landmarks, but are still private residences. Walking-tour brochures leading you to these gems are available from the Chamber of Commerce at 132 Main Street in the downtown section (a designated Historical Preservation District).

Nevada City's twisting streets glow with gaslights in the evenings, and horse-drawn-carriage tours add the appropriate authenticity. Old-timers still tell tall tales in city saloons, where the spirit of Madame Moustache lurks. A fashionably turned-out young woman who stepped off the stagecoach in Nevada City in 1854, Madame Eleanor Dumont opened a *vingt-et-un* parlor that became famous the length of the Mother Lode. She dealt games for a couple of years, becoming famous as "Madame Moustache," a reference to the dark line on her upper lip, but as gold discoveries dwindled she moved on. Where she went from Nevada City is unknown, but the guess is that she combed the West for boomtowns and bistros open to Twenty-One and a female dealer.

To tour the town, start a block from the Chamber of Commerce at the splendidly face-lifted Nevada Hose Company No. 1 firehouse. Built in 1861 of whitewashed brick and capped with a highly embellished bell tower, the building serves as the **Firehouse Museum** and is operated by the Nevada County Historical Society. Inside you'll find relics from the tragic Donner Party and an altar from a Chinese joss house (temple). Along Broad Street a restoration standout is the state's oldest theater building, the 1865 Nevada Theater, site of historic stage presentations by Mark Twain and Jack London, as well as current community events.

Nearby, the **National Hotel**, resplendent with Victorian antiques, opened its doors nine years before the theater and is the oldest continually operating hotel west of the Rockies. Where government currency buys refreshments today, nuggets and gold dust were once exchanged for beer and whiskey at the polished bar that was shipped here via Cape Horn and San Francisco.

Up the street is the 1880 New York Hotel, now a collection of shops and galleries and home to the Museum of Ancient and Modern Art (actually a gallery of local art). At **Main Street Antiques**, old and rare books, old toys, and primitives draw collectors. **Mountain Pastimes**, on Spring Street, specializes in toys for "thinking grown-ups" and in puzzles for fanciers of all ages.

Across the street is the **Nevada City Winery**, located only a few blocks from its original site of a century ago and center of the northernmost of the Sierra foothills' wine-producing regions. Call (916) 265-WINE for tasting times, when you can sample Chardonnays and Zinfandels bearing the Nevada City Winery label.

The pioneer cemetery is out on West Broad Street, as is a big boulder considered by Native Americans to have healing powers. On top of the Indian Medicine Stone are hollows where the ill sought cures and took the sun in ancient times.

Restaurants and cafés in Nevada City reflect the historic ethnic mix of the Gold Rush. A short stroll from the winery at 211 Spring Street, **Bit of England** serves crumpets, scones, sandwiches, and Devonshire cream; there's also a pub here with a long list of British beers. For traditional Mexican fare (and very fresh tortillas), stop at long-established **Casa Gonzalez**, 405 Gracie Road.

Country Rose, at 300 Commercial Street, features patio

dining on Country French fare; **Coach House** is a longtime favorite with a conventional Continental menu; family-oriented **Northridge Inn** can be found at the Nevada Street exit; and **Apple Fare**, 307 Broad Street, is the place for breakfast.

The Gold Country is witnessing a boom in bed-and-breakfast inns at popular traveller destinations, and in Nevada City the mood is frequently Victorian. **Red Castle Inn**, on Prospect Street overlooking the city, is a 125-year-old Gothic Revival mansion and well established locally. Century-old **Downey House**, on West Broad Street, has a lovely garden with a lily pond, and **Grandmère's**, on Broad Street, is a three-story Colonial Revival with an inviting garden. The **Northern Queen Inn**, on Railroad Avenue, is a comfortable motel with a café.

Grass Valley

Although the Gold Rush was the genesis of both Nevada City and Grass Valley, the two cities, four miles apart on Highway 49, are more cousins than twins. Where Nevada City was able to preserve its architectural treasures despite a disastrous fire, Grass Valley burned to the ground in 1855 in a blaze that consumed 300 buildings in 90 minutes. It was probably the most calamitous of the many fires that roared through tent camps and collections of wooden shacks all over the Mother Lode.

Historians say the rebuilding of the city, using heavy masonry walls and ponderous iron shutters, influenced the character of Mother Lode architecture. Downtown Grass Valley has a decidedly contemporary air today, but the winding back streets tell a different story.

Probably the most famous of the surviving residences of the great fire is the **cottage of Lola Montez**, at 248 Mill Street. Authentically restored, the cottage is now the headquarters of the Nevada County and Grass Valley Chamber of Commerce; walking-tour brochures are available here.

The names of singer-dancer Montez and her young student Lotta Crabtree, once famous throughout the mining camps, are a part of the history of the Northern Mines. Sensational Lola (born Eliza Gilbert in Ireland) and her husband bought the Grass Valley cottage in 1852 as a retirement haven after a disappointing national tour. She brought to the Gold Rush town a penchant for big parties and a scandalous reputation as an ex-mistress of King Ludwig I of Bavaria and as an intimate of Franz Liszt and Victor Hugo.

What titillated the mining townspeople most was that she installed her own bathtub. Visitors can see it on the front porch today (although you can only imagine the grizzly bears and monkeys Lola kept as pets).

Restless Lola became acquainted with her neighbor Lotta Crabtree when the seven-year-old girl stopped by for a visit. Soon Lola was tutoring her in singing and dancing, thus beginning Lotta's successful lifelong theatrical career; she made her debut at age eight at a local tavern and left an estate of $4 million when she died in 1924. Lola Montez was not so fortunate. After a disappointing attempt to revive her career, she went on the lecture circuit, never to return to Grass Valley. She died in New York at the age of 43.

Grass Valley's main street since 1849 has been Mill Street, a fragment of a trail that led to a nearby mine site. Little remains of that exciting past on the main street today except for long wooden awnings over the sidewalks. Over on South Church Street, built on land donated by a mining company, you can visit the oldest Episcopal house of worship in California. First opened for services in 1858, Emmanuel Episcopal Church is one of only two area churches that date from the Gold Rush days. At Church and Chapel streets, early Irish settlers are buried in St. Patrick's Cemetery, marked by towering cedar trees. Gravestones date from 1853, many girdled by ornate iron fences.

Back in town the **Holbrooke Hotel** on West Main Street, now into its second century, was rebuilt in 1862 after the fire; its guest register bears the names of such well-known guests as Mark Twain, presidents Ulysses S. Grant and Grover Cleveland, and the notorious robber Black Bart. Rooms at the hotel today are furnished with original period pieces and named after Gold Rush personalities of fame or notoriety.

If you're feeling hungry and want to sample some local cooking, Cornish pasties are staples on more than one menu in town and are special favorites, along with scones, at the annual Cornish Christmas celebrations, when gas-lit streets are closed to vehicle traffic and replaced by horse-drawn carriages and wagons. There has long been a strong Cornish influence in Grass Valley; in 1910, people with ties to Cornwall were estimated to make up two-thirds of the city's population, bringing with them the hard-rock mining skills of their native England (and the introduction of the invaluable pump that kept the mines dry—and boosted the city's output). The miners back then carried pasties in their lunch pails, and today the pasties make splendid picnic fare for a gold-panning expedition or a side-road foray to a nearby creek.

Marshall's, at 203 Mill Street, or **Mrs. Dubblebee's**, at 251 South Auburn, produce the authentic vegetable- and meat-filled varieties for the enjoyment of all. For more formal dining in a Gold Rush atmosphere, try the **Empire House**, at 535 Mill Street, or **Main Street Café**, at 213 West Main, featuring wild game in season, and fresh seafood for lunch and dinner. **Tofanelli's** is "family friendly," at 302 West Main. Most local markets operate delicatessens for picnic-minded travellers, and **Gregory's**, at 11426 Sutton Way, has a wine-tasting bar as well.

Look into **Something Different** on Mill Street if you are interested in handwork by local artisans; here you'll find footstools and pine-needle baskets in addition to more conventional crafts.

Within walking distance of central Grass Valley is one of several bed-and-breakfast inns: Lovingly decorated **Murphy's Inn**, on Neal Street, was built in 1866 by a railroad and mine magnate. Downtown is the **Swan-Levine House**, on Church Street, a three-story restored Victorian that caters to artists by offering studio space and art instruction. **Annie Horan's**, on West Main, is elegantly Victorian, with breakfast on the patio. Two other choices are the **Alta Sierra Resort**, a contemporary-style inn with pool, golf, and tennis, and the **Golden Chain Resort**, on Highway 49, away from the town center in a park-like setting with picnic facilities.

Around Grass Valley

Where the charm of neighboring Nevada City lies in its dedication to maintaining a strong historical presence today, Grass Valley's significance in Gold Rush history lies in its gold. Here gold mining developed into a major industry, not with picks and panning, but with heavy machinery that set a precedent for other Mother Lode mining operations. A visit to the Northstar Mining Museum and the showplace Empire Mine State Park, 1.5 miles east of town on Empire Street, clearly illustrates Grass Valley's place in Mother Lode history.

It all started modestly, so the story goes, and by accident. Local historians say the big hard-rock mining boom was sparked when George McKnight stubbed his toe on a rock while pursuing an errant cow one night. The rock gleamed in the moonlight, and when McKnight crushed it he found gold flecks. A discovery marker on Jenkins Street memorializes this occasion.

Beyond lower Mill Street at the **Northstar Mining Museum** is one of the finest collections of hard-rock mining equipment and artifacts in the nation. The star attraction here is the giant 1896 Pelton wheel, which—at 30 feet in diameter and weighing ten tons, the largest Pelton wheel in the world when installed—still awes visitors. This waterwheel used turbine principles to produce power and was invented by Lester Pelton of nearby Camptonville. There is a creekside picnic area near the museum.

About a mile and a half east of the museum on East Empire Street is the **Empire Mine State Park**, site of the oldest and most profitable hard-rock gold mine in California. More than $960 million in gold was removed over a period of 107 years from shafts that plunge 11,000 feet and tunnels that burrow for 360 miles underground. Scattered over the large park area are restored buildings, including the baronial home of the mine owners, the Bourne Cottage, flanked by formal gardens.

The Empire Mine State Park is open daily, with programming and hours governed by the season. Check the schedule for the movies and slide shows as well as the self-guided and docent tours of the cottage, grounds, and mine yard. The antique rose garden is a draw when it's at its peak in color and fragrance; June is a fairly safe bet, but nevertheless it depends on the weather. For information, call (916) 273-8522.

Rough 'N Ready

West of Grass Valley a few minutes off Highway 49, along the Rough 'N Ready Highway (also known as Highway 20), is the town of Rough 'N Ready, a thriving little village named during the Gold Rush by a band of Mexican War veterans in honor of their ex-commander, General Zachary Taylor and his nickname. Rough 'N Ready seceded from the Union in 1850 when a mining tax outraged the locals. Then, after having elected their own president and having adopted a constitution, the new republic reversed its engines and saluted the Union flag at a Fourth of July celebration. It was not until 1948, however, that the secession was officially ended and the federal government gave its blessing to a local post office. Send a postcard, because collectors prize the unusual postmark.

Surviving buildings of interest from the 1850s include the Fippin blacksmith shop, Grange Hall, and the Old Toll House, which charged 25 cents for passage for a man on horse and $3.00 for a flock of geese. For browsing or shopping, **Bertie's Nest** is the antiques haven in Rough 'N Ready.

On the way back to Highway 49, take time to scan the wall mural at Lyman Gilmore School, on the stretch of the Rough 'N Ready Highway before it becomes West Main Street in Grass Valley. It honors the colorful local for whom the school is named—reputedly California's first aviator. The present school site, covering 20 acres, is located on the first commercial airfield in the United States. There is evidence that Gilmore built and flew his own aircraft a year before the Wright Brothers became celebrated at Kitty Hawk in 1903. Gilmore, little known to the world at large, was a Grass Valley celebrity until he died in 1951.

North to Downieville

From Grass Valley and Nevada City, Highway 49 curls and curves up toward the Yuba Pass. This stretch is not heavily travelled, and, except in winter, supplies another kind of Gold Rush flavor to a flexible itinerary.

It is about 45 miles to **Downieville**, a true survivor of 49er days with crooked streets and 1860s brick-and-frame buildings. The town sprawls on both sides of the rushing Yuba River and climbs pine-thick hills. You may want to stop at the Sierra County Museum, housed in a building with walls of schist, on Main Street, or ask at the store for the best gold-panning locations.

A few blocks from the museum is the site of the original town gallows, where the hanging of a woman named Juanita brought notoriety to this Sierra outpost. Many historians agree it was self-defense when the dance hall girl killed a miner with a knife, but frontier "justice" prevailed.

If you're going to be in this region in spring, you'll find yourself surrounded by dogwood blossoms and cascading waterfalls. Autumn, on the other hand, is mellow, with clear skies and colors like slashes of gold and bronze against a wall of evergreens.

Follow Highway 49 as it wanders south from Downieville through Camptonville and North San Juan, skirting Nevada City and Grass Valley on the road to the Southern Mines and you'll pass through communities whose populations once numbered in the thousands but now are sparsely populated.

Camptonville has two monuments at the west end of town. One is in memory of Lester Pelton, inventor of the Pelton wheel that brought prosperity to Grass Valley, and the other is dedicated to William "Bull" Meek, who was, as the monument says, a stage driver, Wells Fargo agent, teamster, and merchant. Meek deserves attention because he was allegedly the only regular stage driver in the area to escape holdups. Locals say it is because he carried supplies to a Downieville bawdy house, and the influence of those fancy ladies produced a pact with the robbers that protected him.

THE SOUTHERN MINES

Mother Lode is the name attached to much of the California Gold Country, but the precious primary vein the Mexican miners called *Veta Madre* extends from Auburn south about 100 miles along the Highway 49 corridor to Melones. Melones is only a memory beneath a reservoir, but thriving communities that were once scattered tents—and the region's silent ghost towns—draw most travellers to the Southern Mines. Not only visitors, but retirees and young families are flocking to the Sierra foothills here to settle where restless miners sought their fortune before moving on to the next glory hole, as they called any profitable concentration of the precious mineral.

From Auburn's Old Town to Coloma, the original glory hole, the highway winds and twists south through pastures and rolling hills, green year round with ponderosa pine and live oak, then plunges a thousand feet into the American River canyon. It is a slow 20 miles to Coloma and the bronze statue of James Marshall, which marks the site of the discovery that brought the world to California. A stop at **Sierra Nevada House III** on Highway 49 will be an appropriate moodsetter. It is the third inn built on this location since the Gold Rush, and offers a restaurant, bed-and-breakfast accommodations that operate seasonally, and a soda parlor that is a cool haven on hot summer days.

Coloma

Just a mile farther south of Sierra Nevada House III on the highway is Coloma, on the bank of the American River. Here John August Sutter naively instructed his lumber-mill construction workers to keep secret John Marshall's discovery in the mill tailrace on January 24, 1848. The news was out in days.

The entire town of Coloma is now James Marshall Gold Discovery State Historic Park. Rangers have detailed maps, and you'll find plenty of comfortable picnicking areas in shady groves. Authentically restored interiors of picturesque stone buildings include a Chinese store and a blacksmith shop. You can also wander through a reproduction of a mine tunnel and poke into a meticulously equipped assay office. A reconstruction of the rough cabin where Marshall lived after he discovered gold illustrates the spartan lifestyle of the 49er.

Marshall himself became a miserable recluse, living on handouts and sales of his autograph after a $100-a-month state pension was cut off in 1876. The man who sounded "Eureka" died in tiny, nearby Kelsey in 1885. Miner friends packed the body in ice and transported it to Coloma for a wake and burial near his old cabin.

Sutter's Mill has been reconstructed on the river using the original techniques of hand-hewn beams and mortise-and-tenon joints. The sawmill operates seasonally on weekends, and there is an ore-crushing stamp mill nearby.

Once a rowdy collection of 10,000 souls, Coloma has experienced violence in its history. A bizarre double hanging, which occurred in 1855 after most miners had moved on, was the occasion for entertainment by a brass band from nearby Placerville, but it was two convicted murderers who were center stage. A school teacher named Crane marked his final exit by singing a song of his own composition that ended abruptly with "here I come," and bad man Mickey Free danced a jig. His gravestone is in the Coloma cemetery.

If you want to try your luck, gold panning is permitted in a recreation area of the American River across from the bronze statue of Marshall. For an overnight stay, Victorian-style guest rooms, a restaurant, and a reputation for being haunted distinguish historic **Vineyard House**, on Cold Springs Road. **Coloma Country Inn**, a restored 1852 country home, is two blocks from Sutter's Mill. The inn can arrange hot-air ballooning and white-water rafting.

Placerville

Jagged cliffs ripped by hydraulic mining mark the approach to Placerville, about 10 miles south of Coloma. The second-largest of all Gold Rush cities, it is a high-growth area with burgeoning residential developments serving commuters to fast-growing Sacramento.

Once just a branched-out version of Coloma called Dry Diggin's, Placerville was also known as Hangtown after a series of lynchings in 1849. One was a triple hanging; the usual plaque on Main Street marks the site of the tree. The city was also a stop on the pony express and overland mail routes and commemorates this every June with an abbreviated memorial run.

One person who took advantage of Placerville's Gold Rush prosperity to "build a poke" (build up a bank account) and go on to better things was J. M. Studebaker, who harvested profits from building wheelbarrows for the miners. He returned to the Midwest and founded the wagon factory that became the Studebaker Corporation. Meat packer Phillip Armour once ran a butcher shop in Placerville, and financier and railroad builder Mark Hopkins was a grocer here.

City-owned **Goldbug Mine** is one mile east of town off busy Highway 50. There are scheduled tours of the historic park, a real gold mine, which, with its special lighting, is worth exploring. Or check out a gold pan and try your luck in the sands of a nearby creek. Picnic facilities and hiking trails make possible a pleasant extended visit.

Wine making in the Sierra foothills has been a tradition ever since some of the early settlers opted for grapes over gold. Small family-owned-and-operated vineyards and wineries are producing award-winning vintages 150 years later. Most wineries here are north and southeast of Placerville, off Highway 50 along Carson Road and off Mt. Aukum Road. A few are open daily, most on weekends. An informative brochure with a map is available at the Placerville Chamber of Commerce, 542 Main Street.

The tasting room at **Boeger Winery**, on Carson Road, is housed in a stone cellar built in 1872 and listed on the National Register of Historic Places. You can picnic under ancient fig trees on the rambling grounds. **Fitzpatrick Winery**, on Fairplay Road in Somerset, about 20 miles east of Placerville, offers a bed and breakfast in **Fitzpatrick Lodge**, a replica of a hand-peeled log lodge. The rooms are upstairs, a country kitchen and tasting room downstairs.

For city bed-and-breakfast accommodations, **James Blair House** is within walking distance of Placerville's Main Street. A preserved Queen Anne Victorian with a three-story turret and a skylighted conservatory, it is furnished appropriately with antiques. **Rupley House**, on Highway 50 in the Apple Hill area, is near the wineries and also near a gold-panning area and has an acre of gardens. The **Broadway Motel** and **Gold Trail Motor Lodge** are located downtown on Broadway.

Browsers for antiques will find old post office boxes and pie safes, sepia portraits of early settlers, and potbellied stoves in shops in downtown Placerville.

Smokehouse 1898, located at 311 Main Street, is well known for its informality and good food. **La Casa Grande**, in the next block, and the **Carriage Room**, on Broadway, are also popular for their casual, relaxed atmospheres and excellent meals. It's worth the three-mile drive east of Placerville to Smith Flat Road for the linen-and-crystal hospitality and the extensive menu at **Historic Smith Flat House**, situated in a beautiful country setting. It's wise to reserve, especially on weekends; Tel: 621-0667.

Seasonal cultural events in Placerville include "Celebrate the Arts," a county-wide festival featuring local artists (the third week in May), and the Annual Hangtown Jazz Jubilee in October. Little-theater fans will enjoy the spring and winter productions at Discovery Playhouse on the county fairgrounds. Ask about the schedule at the Chamber of Commerce; Tel: 621-5885.

Amador County

About 25 miles south of Placerville, in neighboring Amador County's sensuous hills, are the mines where half the prodigious wealth of Mother Lode gold was extracted. In this region, about midway along the 318-mile stretch of Highway 49, are the mines that helped Leland Stanford finance the Central Pacific Railroad, Stanford University, and a political career. Millions of dollars from this area amplified the resources of Wall Street's Hetty Green, who was known as "the richest woman in the world" in her day and who, for a time, owned the Old Eureka Mine near Sutter Creek.

Landmarks along Highway 49 in Amador County include the headframes of the Keystone Mine at Amador City and the Argonaut and Kennedy mines at Jackson. The latter had some of the deepest vertical shafts in the world—at 5,000 feet—before closing in 1942.

In Jackson pack your picnic basket at the **Mother Lode** deli on Main Street and head for a tour of local wineries and tasting rooms in the Shenandoah Valley (take Shenandoah Road east off Highway 49 at the Plymouth intersection). Local wine makers, many of them students of enology who moved to the area in the early 1970s, have made vineyards and the fruits of the vine an important economic asset to the county.

More than a dozen wineries have opened in the last 20 years, and the traditional, robust, local Zinfandel now shares the tasting roster with Sauvignon Blanc, Chardonnay, Chenin Blanc, and Cabernet Sauvignon. Most wineries schedule tastings on weekends; ask the Chamber of Commerce at the intersection of Highways 49 and 88 for a brochure and a map.

A reminder of the importance the Chinese have had in the history of the region can be found in a dozing village called **Fiddletown,** six miles east of the Highway 49–Plymouth junction on Fiddletown Road. Here remains one of the few rammed-earth adobe buildings in the state from the 1850s. Once the shop of an herb doctor, **Chew Kee Store** has been restored by state and private funding. Now a museum, its interior and the amazing collection of sale items from the past constitute a visible time capsule: There are tiny pots of herbs, medicines, an abacus, cooking implements, tools, and stamps, all of which have been catalogued and returned to their original places.

Why the name Fiddletown? Elder Missourians, who settled here in 1849 to farm, found younger men "always fiddling." Later this name offended a dignified local judge who prevailed on the legislature in 1878 to change Fiddletown to Oleta. But the "damage" was already done: He had become known as "the man from Fiddletown," and Bret Harte's "An Episode in Fiddletown" had fixed the name firmly. Cooler heads officially restored it in the 1920s. There's a post office, if you collect postmarks.

"Founded in 1849," announces more than one community in this Mother Lode region. Tiny **Drytown** is a year older. It possesses no famous mine but is the first village you'll encounter after Highway 49 curves sharply east past Plymouth in Amador County. Once a tent camp with a raucous collection of 26 saloons and 10,000 miners, Drytown today is down to a solitary saloon, pegged "the only wet spot in Drytown." In a small cluster of buildings on the west side of the highway as it climbs up from Dry Creek is the store where publisher William Randolph Hearst's father, George Hearst, operated a printing press in his mine office.

A few minutes beyond is Amador City, which once laid claim to being the smallest incorporated city in the United States; its population now hovers around 200. Snacks, antiques, quilts, and period fashions are tucked along the abbreviated main street, Highway 49.

Recently restored, the tasteful **Imperial Hotel,** situated where the road curves, is operated as a bed-and-breakfast inn. It has a mellow bar and an excellent restaurant where you can catch up on local gossip. Also popular with Gold Country regulars is the **Mine House Inn,** complete with pool and framed against a hillside just above the city overlooking the headframe of the Keystone Mine.

Rambling stone walls (most often constructed by Chinese laborers on their day off from mining), classic barns with sagging roofs, fat grazing cattle, and spreading California oaks provide special photo opportunities on this section of Highway 49.

Sutter Creek to Jackson

The contrast to this purely Western landscape makes your first glimpse of **Sutter Creek** at the end of a sweeping curve even more surprising—it has the appearance of a New England village, with trim white cottages, green shutters, church steeples, and cherished gardens.

Spring in Sutter Creek is an extravagance of azalea and camellia blossoms and flowering fruit trees, but gardening is not of historical significance in the founding of this city—it was a pine and cedar forest on a nearby ridge that in 1846 sparked a tent city in the pleasant little valley straddling what is now Sutter Creek.

Before long, seven mines were operating within two miles of Main Street (Highway 49), one of which was the Lincoln Mine, partly owned by Leland Stanford. A major mining company is now exploring the land adjacent to the old Lincoln, and with new technology, both new and old gold mines are opening and reopening in more than one Mother Lode community. Engineers believe the Gold Rush only hinted at the wealth of minerals that still exists.

A walking tour of Sutter Creek's winding, shaded back streets is included in a useful Visitor's Guide put out by the Amador County Chamber of Commerce, and which can be obtained from most merchants. Sutter Creek has an abundance of antiques; everything from four-poster beds to stained-glass art to funky old postcards are displayed in the shops.

The first and most luxurious of the Sutter Creek bed-and-breakfast inns, flanked by green lawns and towering shade trees, is **Sutter Creek Inn**, behind a white picket fence on Highway 49. Adjacent is **Foxes**, which boasts individually designed rooms, carefully chosen furnishings, and a Victorian flavor. Both inns serve splendid breakfasts.

Nothing could be farther from prim and proper Victorian than rugged and unspoiled little **Volcano**, a half-hour side trip east off Highway 49 from Sutter Creek on Sutter Creek–Volcano Road. The miners thought this spot looked like a crater dwarfed by pine-covered circling hills, so "Volcano" it was. Some old-timers say it is the torrid summer weather that inspired the name, and there is probably truth in both stories.

There are more tales to be told at the tiny bar in Volcano's **St. George Hotel**. Built in 1862, this simple, comfortable lodging (with shared baths) still retains its traditional second-story balconies and vine-shaded verandah. Dinners in the restaurant are hearty prime rib, steak, or chicken, depending on the day of the week. It's strictly home-style cooking—and highly recommended. Reservations are necessary; Tel: 296-4458.

Photographers find Volcano worth the film for its sleepy Main Street stone buildings and for "Old Abe," one of the oldest 19th-century bronze cannons in the United States, used by the Volcano Blues in the Civil War. In addition to the 40 saloons, three breweries, and fandango halls, Volcano claims some California "firsts": a public library, private law school, and little-theater group. The Volcano Community Pioneer Theatre Group carries on the thespian tradition with weekend performances from mid-April through mid-October in the charming Cobblestone Theatre.

For a longer look back in the history of the region, plan to spend some time at **Chaw Se**, a few minutes south of Volcano on the Pine Grove–Volcano Road. The 40-acre state park is a showcase for a limestone outcropping covered with more than 300 Native American petroglyphs and more than a thousand mortar holes. It was here that the Miwok Indians pulverized acorns and other nuts, seeds, and berries. Among the authentically reproduced structures in the park are a roundhouse for religious gatherings, a conical bark dwelling, and an Indian "football" field. There is also a museum with artifacts and Miwok crafts; for tours call (209) 296-4788.

From Volcano take Highway 88 southwest to return to Highway 49 and a stop at the busy county seat of **Jackson**, where you'll find **Amador County Museum**, dedicated to another era; it's located two blocks up from Main Street in one of the oldest homes in the community. Mother Lode memorabilia is the attraction in this 1859 building centered among lawns with scattered picnic tables. There is an extraordinary scale model of a stamp mill, the towering Kennedy Mine tailings wheels and headframe, and an amusing collection of household appliances used by homemakers more than a century ago.

Just below the museum is a full-scale replica of a narrow-gauge railroad locomotive, a model of the kind of machine that opened the West that has appeared in movie and television productions.

Almost as much a landmark for Jackson as the Kennedy tailings wheels is **St. Sava Serbian Orthodox Church**, mother church of the denomination in North America and a gem of pristine design. Lit at night, it is visible from many areas of the city and to the east from Highway 49 as the highway curves down into the city.

If you wander by St. Patrick's Catholic Church, a block south of the museum, you will discover that the founder of Columbus Day was a Jackson native named Angelo Noce. A monument in front of the 1868 church building honors him.

In recognition of Jackson's ribald past, there is a sidewalk plaque on Main Street in front of a venerable bar memorializing the ladies of the evening once headquartered in the "female boarding houses" on Jackson Creek, the city's lively recreation area of those bygone days.

Rinky-tink piano and community singing often erupt evenings from the commodious bar in the old **National Hotel** at the end of Main Street. An early stage stop, the hotel is still in operation. There are motels along busy Highway 49 as it borders the city, although the **Country Squire** on North Main is a quieter exception. In the bed-and-breakfast category are **Court Street Inn**, two blocks up from Main Street, and **Gate House Inn**, on a narrow creek off Jackson Gate Road.

Calaveras County

Bret Harte and Mark Twain celebrated the Mother Lode in chronicles and fiction as they drifted in and out of Calaveras County, where Highway 49 bends south from Jackson through a continuing corridor of the Southern Mines. The haunts of the two writers extend from the Mokelumne River in the north to the Tuolumne River in the south, where tall tales of bad men and big nuggets in the Gold Country still find an avid audience.

If you take a jog off Highway 49 you'll come upon small but spirited **Mokelumne Hill**. This city, whose population ballooned after 1849 to the point where claims were limited to 16 square feet, is proud of its I.O.O.F. Hall, the first three-story building in the Mother Lode.

A chance encounter with a local historian sipping beer under the high ceiling fans of the old **Hotel Leger** bar in Mokelumne Hill, a few minutes south of Jackson, will verify an account of the Perkins Nugget, which reportedly was taken from a mine a few miles to the south in 1854 and assayed at 190 pounds. At the time its $40,000 worth was a fortune—and no single larger nugget has since been found in the United States. Another beer may prompt the tale of the ghost of George Leger, allegedly a regular visitor to the saloon, who was assassinated at the hotel in 1879.

At **Sky Eyes Indian Arts and Outfitters** on Main Street in Mokelumne Hill, Jesse "Sky Eyes" Clark, winner of national tribal competitions, creates authentic Native American costumes, headdresses, and ornaments. A few doors down, Rod Hanchett hand-throws and fires stoneware and porcelain pottery for both decorative and kitchen use in a kiln on the premises.

In **San Andreas**, south of Mokelumne Hill, drop in at the local museum, which maintains a broad collection of minerals, Native American handicrafts, and Gold Rush treasures. And mosey on over to the old jail behind the courthouse to see the cell marked "Black Bart Slept Here." This most famous stage robber of them all postdated the peak of the Gold Rush but remains associated with the era because of the 28 robberies he staged between 1877 and 1883. Always polite, wearing a flour sack over his head with holes cut for eyes, the invariable request to stagecoach drivers was: "Throw down the treasure box, *please,*" backed by a menacing shotgun. Bart's career ended when a handkerchief he dropped near Copperopolis was traced by a laundry mark to a San Francisco location: Black Bart turned out to be Charles E. Bolton, respected citizen and prominent socialite. He was tried in San Andreas and served less than six years in San Quentin. History loses him after his release.

Black Bart Inn in San Andreas has modern hotel accommodations and a comfortable Victorian-style dining room (the Friday night seafood buffets here are legendary). For bed and breakfast try the **Robin's Nest**, a Gold Rush–era mansion restored to its original charm on St. Charles Street.

Nothing much happens today in Altaville, where Highways 49 and 4 intersect south of San Andreas, but the town is remembered as the birthplace of a mammoth hoax in the Gold Country involving a skull found in a mine at Bald Mountain. The find was proclaimed in 1866 to be the "Pliocene skull," the remains of a prehistoric man, but 50 years later it was pronounced to be the skull of an Indian, and the whole episode was dismissed as a practical joke. Bret Harte wrote a poem "To the Pliocene Skull"—a fraud nobody ever admitted to masterminding.

For a round of local wine tasting, take Murphys Grade Road east from Highway 49, before Angels Camp, to **Stevenot Winery**, the largest producer in the Sierra foothills, three miles beyond the community of Murphys. You'll also find other wineries open weekends for tasting; check for the schedules at **Murphys Historic Hotel**. Said to have been described by Bret Harte in "A Night in Wingdam," the hotel retains its old iron shutters and second-story balcony with iron railing, not to mention the bullet hole in the doorframe. The hotel, which has hosted such notables as J. Pierpont Morgan and Mark Twain, has a restaurant and saloon along with lodgings. A walking-tour map of small, well-preserved Murphys has an astonishing 55 listings.

In addition to the hotel, bed and breakfast is available at **Dunbar House 1880**, an Italianate-style Victorian establishment in century-old gardens. They've got air-conditioning for hot summers and wood stoves for crisp fall weather.

For a different perspective of the Mother Lode, go underground for exploring instead of mining at **Mercer Caverns**, one mile north of Murphys up Highway 4 on Sheep Ranch Road. A tour of this subterranean setting with its dazzling crystalline formations and "curtains" takes 45 minutes. The maze of passageways is still being explored more than 100 years after prospector Walter Mercer discovered the caverns.

If one cavern is not enough for you, there are two more in the vicinity. **California Caverns Park**, a few miles north of Murphys, offers Wild Cave expedition tours lasting two to four hours, led by experienced guides. You can explore, crawl, and climb with ropes and ladders, or take a tour that crosses crystal lakes on rafts. There are also family tours that follow in the footsteps of naturalist John Muir and, of course, Harte and Twain. Reservations are recommended; Tel: (209) 736-2708.

Moaning Cave is California's largest public cave, off Highway 104 as it turns south toward Columbia State Park from Highway 4. At Moaning Cave visitors can rappel almost 200 feet into the huge main chamber, which is vast enough to store the entire Statue of Liberty and more. Studies show that the cave was a burial place 13,000 years ago, and bones preserved here by mineral-rich waters are considered possibly the oldest human remains found in North America.

Where Highway 4 joins Highway 49, **Angels Camp**, memorialized by Bret Harte in "Luck of Roaring Camp," straddles a creek and climbs wooded hills. Near the creek is Angels Hotel, where Mark Twain reportedly heard the jumping frog story. The city remembers both celebrities with a monument to the frog on Main Street and a statue to Mark Twain in a park alongside Highway 49. There's an annual Frog Jump competition in May.

Columbia and Sonora

A short distance to the south, just over the border into Tuolumne County and a jog north off Highway 49, is a truly living Gold Rush town. **Columbia** was once the "gem of the Southern Mines" and is now Columbia State Historic Park. A clamorous community of 5,000 within a month of gold discovery in 1850, Columbia missed being the state capital by a scant two votes in the legislature. After $87 million in gold was shipped out by 1858, things quieted down, but Columbia never became a ghost town. Since 1945 its park status has preserved the historic buildings as a living museum, somewhat like Colonial Williamsburg.

You can stroll the shaded street where the only traffic is an occasional horseman or a stagecoach. Don't be turned off by a veneer of commercialism: the people costumed in the style of the Gold Rush era here do make their living in Columbia and live inside the park. The sweet shop and the harness shop, the blacksmithy, the saloon, and the trading post operate today as they did more than a century ago.

There are opportunities here to pan for gold, taste wine, take a stagecoach ride, or visit a mine—or you may prefer to find a shady spot and settle for a moment to envision 15,000 obstreperous miners, slick gamblers, men of commerce, camp followers, and the ubiquitous fancy ladies. The **Columbia City Hotel** is a salute to them all. Upstairs rooms are remarkably restored and open to overnight visitors. On the main floor is an award-winning restaurant featuring a classic French menu and a selection of mesquite-grilled meats and seafood; the What Cheer bar adjoins.

The **Fallon Hotel** in Columbia is a bed-and-breakfast–style, Victorian jewel with flocked wallpaper, tall ceilings, and lace-trimmed lampshades. The nearby Fallon House Theater is the setting for Columbia Actors' Repertory productions September through May.

What was once a main street of adobe, rough plank, canvas, and tin shacks is now heavily trafficked Washington Street in **Sonora**, just south of Columbia on Highway 49. The Queen of the Southern Mines now claims the busiest main street in the Mother Lode and is in the grasp of phenomenal growth.

Where horse races and bull-and-bear fights were once on the entertainment agenda, today you'll find gift shops and commerce and the seat of county government. But a block or so off the main street there are strong echoes of earlier times.

Beside proudly restored Victorian homes stands the **St. James Episcopal Church**, a landmark since 1860 and one of the most photographed of Gold Rush churches because of its impressive steeple and fine stained-glass windows. If you are looking for the Tuolumne County Museum, at 158 Bradford Avenue, you'll find it in the Old County Jail, listed on the National Register of Historic Places. Walking-tour maps and information are available weekdays in the same building from the Chamber of Commerce.

To satisfy your hunger, **Hemingway's Café and Restaurant** on Stewart Street serves up California cuisine with emphasis on fresh produce, innovative sauces, and creative presentations, and offers a good wine list. Family-oriented, 24-hour **Europa Coffee Shop**, on Washington Street, has been a local favorite for 70 years (especially for its homemade biscuits). **Kyoto House** is a well-established Japanese restaurant on Washington Street downtown.

Barretta Gardens Inn, within walking distance of downtown Sonora, is a bed-and-breakfast accommodation in a restored Victorian farmhouse with an assortment of elegantly furnished parlors. Country English is the theme at **La Casa Inglesa**, two miles out of town on a wooded gold-mine site on Lime Kiln Road. Llamas are for petting at **Llamahall Guest Ranch**, in a forested, creekside setting on Wards Ferry Road. Near the town center, **Gunn House** is a local historic hotel furnished with antiques.

Jamestown and South

Serious gold seekers and steam-train buffs will find **Jamestown** a welcome stopover. West of Sonora and just off Highway 49, "Jimtown" is the spot where gold was discovered by a prospector searching for his lost jackass. (He found gold nuggets and a thousand ounces of gold in Jackass Gulch.) In those days the amount of gold dust you could hold between thumb and finger was valued at a dollar, a wineglass full was $100, and a tumbler $1,000. In 1985, when a couple entered a Jamestown shop carrying 11 pounds of gold nuggets in a shopping bag, their value was placed at $140,000. The couple refused to say where they discovered the gold and refused to give their names, but you can see it all as it happened on a videotape shown at the Old Livery Stable on Main Street.

Jimtown offers opportunities for gold-prospecting expeditions and for polishing up gold-panning, sluicing, and other prospector techniques on trips that can last anywhere from two hours to five days. You can get information about these trips and about helicopter and white-water raft runs at the Old Livery Stable on Main Street, where **Gold Prospecting Expeditions** is headquartered. Or call ahead; Tel: (209) 984-4653.

Nostalgia is the draw for the **Railstown steam-train rides** offered weekends from the Sierra Railway Depot on Fifth Avenue. A five-acre California State Historic Park and launching spot for a variety of theme trips, Railstown schedules train rides on weekends April through November. There are also roundhouse tours and picnic grounds. A full rundown on steam-train rides is available at the park or by calling (209) 984-3953.

Jamestown's historic **National Hotel**, operating since 1859, has beautifully restored guest rooms with shiny brass beds and patchwork quilts, and a saloon with a glossy, 19th-century redwood bar. Fresh seafood, veal, and pasta are turned out with skill from the hotel's kitchen, and dinners are served under a cool grape arbor in warm weather. Reservations for dining are advised; Tel: 984-3446. **Jamestown Hotel**, a bed-and-breakfast inn on Main Street, is elegantly restored in Victorian fashion and serves a Continental breakfast.

Bedar and **Coyote Gallery**, behind the Jamestown Hotel, displays and sells the work of 20 artists, mostly California Native Americans. Graphic arts focus on dance, religion, stories, and traditions; basketry, jewelry, and weaving are also exhibited. In addition to local artists, the galleries include samplings from Native American communities throughout the United States.

From San Andreas to Sonora to the most southern of the Southern Mines (near Mariposa), you'll find historical markers and plaques memorializing the legendary Joaquin Murieta. A bandit hero of the "take from the rich and give to the poor" school, he is the Gold Rush Robin Hood, and whether or not he actually existed, Joaquin is the subject of books, paintings, and innumerable tall tales. He adopted his lifestyle, the story goes, to avenge the killing of his family and the rape of his wife by Yankee marauders. In some quiet San Andreas saloon, you may hear the anecdote of the man who fashioned a bulletproof vest for Murieta and took a shot from the bandit to prove its worth.

In tiny Hornitos, west of Highway 49 toward Mariposa, is an underground tunnel that was reputedly used more than once by Murieta as an escape route from the self-styled "wildest and most wicked city of the Southern Mines." The entrance is marked on a corner of this sleepy little town.

Was it the real Murieta who was hunted down by a lawman

who cut off his head for proof and claimed a $5,000 reward? That's questionable. Some historians believe Murieta is more myth than legend, but he remains a romantic figure of a romantic time.

As Highway 49 continues on the home stretch toward its terminus in Oakhurst, it passes through Mariposa. A suitable final stop for a Gold Country tour is a visit to the **Mariposa County Fairgrounds**, where an expansive collection of precious minerals that for years was in the Ferry Building in San Francisco, is now on exhibit. Much of what you will see is pure gold.

YOSEMITE NATIONAL PARK

Yosemite is a magnet for three million visitors a year from around the world. Its unparalleled natural beauties have lured the solitude-seeker and the gregarious summer camper for more than a century.

An easy three-hour drive south from Sacramento (via Highways 16 and 49 through Sonora to Moccasin, then Highway 120 to the park; via Highway 49 to Mariposa and then Highway 140; or on Highway 49 to Oakhurst, where you can pick up Highway 41), or four hours from San Francisco (take the Bay Bridge to Highway 580, south to Highway 50, then east to Manteca; from there take Highway 120 to Yosemite), the park's approaches converge from three entrances when they reach **Yosemite Valley**. The valley is nature's preeminent example of a canyon carved by a primordial river of ice. The seven-mile, U-shaped valley floor area, dominated by shouldering masses of granite, is both goal and getaway point for rock climbers and wilderness backpackers, anglers and horseback riders, skiers and ice skaters in winter, day-trippers and vacation campers spring through autumn.

Narrowing your choice to a season and its unique attractions is the key to a rewarding visit. One day to explore Yosemite's wonders would be only a tantalizing introduction to granite monoliths, towering waterfalls, and giant sequoias. A stay of three days or more is not overdoing it. Yosemite's 1,200-mile sprawl comprises altitudes that climb from 2,000 to 13,000 feet. In the High Country you will find the serenity of open meadows and pine forests, solitary lakes and challenging peaks; in the valley there are easily accessible waterfalls and rewarding hiking trails. Whatever your destination, you can reach it via 800-plus miles of marked trails or 360 miles of paved roads. Reservations are strongly advised for all park accommodations, from the valley's venerable and luxurious Ahwahnee Hotel to the Curry Village tent cabins and High Country dormitory-style housing.

The Yosemite Valley

Whether you are travelling independently in a private car or by public transportation, abandon the wheels once you arrive in the valley. Plan to walk or take the free shuttle buses to shops and trailheads. Open-air trams operate seasonally, and there are commercially guided tours of Yosemite Valley and beyond that range from two to four hours. During full-moon weeks spring through fall, the enchanting mystery of the valley at night can be experienced on open-air moonlight tours.

Even a one-day excursion is a dramatic revelation of 500 million years of evolutionary process that began when the Sierra Nevada lay beneath an ancient sea. As sediment merged with molten rock, granite was formed and then exposed by erosion. Where summer visitors today picnic and sun on Merced River's beaches in the park, an ancient Alpine glacier cut through weaker granite and enlarged the canyon. What remains are the stunning monoliths—El Capitan, Half Dome, Cathedral Rocks, and their sisters.

Rare for most travellers is the opportunity to learn basic rock-climbing techniques as beginners or to polish up advanced skills. The prestigious Yosemite Mountaineering School teaches daily classes from May through September at Tuolumne Meadows, 55 miles by road north of Yosemite Valley. You will learn hand- and footholds and the use of belays and rappels. Classes move back to the valley in the fall.

Climbers come to Yosemite from around the world to scale the face of **El Capitan**, guardian of the valley entrance and the largest single granite rock in the world. More than three times as high as Australia's Ayers Rock, it is almost 4,000 feet from summit to base. From a turnout along El Capitan Meadow in summer, climbers can be glimpsed as tiny moving dots on the sheer surface. These great brooding blocks of stone generated superlatives in a newspaper article as early as 1855, from one of the park's early visitors nine years before Abraham Lincoln signed the Yosemite Grant— an act that laid the foundation for all succeeding national and state parks.

Unlike others of the nation's parks, Yosemite's activity

agenda is controlled by changing seasons. At two visitors' centers in mid-valley, maps and backcountry information are available. A video program illustrating "One Day in Yosemite" and a helpful staff will contribute toward planning an itinerary. The invaluable, free, fact-packed Yosemite Guide lists every scheduled program and activity in the park. Write Yosemite Association, P.O. Box 230, El Portal, CA 95318, or call general information for the park at (209) 379-2646.

Summer is predictably the peak-activity and peak-crowd period. Accommodations can be limited or nonexistent on holiday weekends, so be sure to plan ahead. Summertime is for swimming in the beautiful but chilly Merced River at the eastern end of the valley, and river rafts, life jackets, and paddles are available for rent in early summer at Curry Village in the valley. Hazardous rapids put a limit on the safe rafting area, but rafting here is an exciting adventure nonetheless.

Gear up for a guided saddle ride if you're in the park any time from early spring through November (weather permitting). At a leisurely pace, savor valley meadows carpeted with spring wildflowers and flowering shrubs and ride through lush oak woodlands and cedar forests. With luck you can spy a mule deer, a black bear, or a glorious orange-and-black monarch butterfly in a field of lupine. Look for the pale-gold mariposa lily and the pink-crimson shooting star. Your horse has the right-of-way on all trails, something to remember as well if you are a hiker. Parents of small children can rent gentle ponies to take along on walks. Horses are rented at Yosemite Valley Stables at the upper end of the valley. Reservations are necessary; Tel: (209) 372-1248.

Hiking and climbing shoes and sports gear are the practical merchandise offered by Yosemite Valley shops. For the browser as well as the collector with an interest in Native American jewelry and handicrafts, visit the Ahwahnee Hotel shop and the Indian Shop at Yosemite Lodge (see below for both). Original photographs by Ansel Adams, who glorified Yosemite for almost 70 years, are on display at the **Ansel Adams Gallery**, where staff photographers conduct free workshops and lead camera walks in spring and fall.

The Yosemite Guide's rating and timing chart of hikes to almost a dozen popular Yosemite attractions is a valuable planning tool for the novice as well as the dedicated mountaineer. The scale ranges from easy to very strenuous, and the times range from 20 minutes to 12 hours. Half Dome and Bridalveil Fall are two popular hikes.

Incomparable **Half Dome**, perhaps the most photographed and easily identified of the ice-carved giant granites, is rated very strenuous—a 10- to 12-hour 17-mile round trip. If you opt for a view from the base, look for the profile of an Ahwahnee Indian princess on the vertical surface.

Less taxing is a 20-minute round-trip walk to Lower Yosemite Falls from a valley-floor start at a shuttle bus stop. Upper Yosemite Falls is demanding, with a trail climb of 2,700 feet in 3.5 miles, and is a six to eight hour round trip. The reward is a memorable view of the highest of North America's falls (most dramatic in May and June). Linked by an intermediate cascade, the Yosemite Falls plunge 2,425 feet.

Bridalveil Fall, in the western part of the valley, was *Pohono* (spirit of the puffing wind) to the Yosemite Indians, because swirling drafts often force the frothy water sideways in billowy surprise. But after mid-August the falls are a disappointment because they become nearly or completely dry.

How the falls and Half Dome were formed over half a billion years of Yosemite's existence is the subject of a film shown evenings in the theater at the visitors' center. Check the Yosemite Guide for this and other nature films.

Little changed in the wondrous valley that became the heart of the park between the time the first people arrived 10,000 years ago and the 1868 arrival of famed naturalist John Muir, whose indefatigable efforts set the tone for preservation awareness that has endured in the succeeding years. An introduction to the descendants of the first people, the Miwok and Paiute Native American tribes, is the centerpiece of the **Yosemite Museum** and the **Indian Cultural Exhibit** at the visitors' center. Displays and a re-created Ahwahnee Indian village show aspects of the life of a people who gathered and ground acorns, hunted with bows and arrows, and developed basketry to a high art.

It was an expedition aimed at subduing Indian hostility to gold miners in the early 1850s that brought the volunteer Mariposa Battalion of soldiers face-to-face with the magnificence of the valley, and began the revelation of its wonders to outsiders. Later two Native Americans served as guides for the first tourist, James Hutchings, whose impassioned adjectives in a newspaper article, as we have seen, encouraged 42 tourists to make their way to Yosemite Valley in 1855. That was the beginning.

The High Country

In a park bigger than the state of Rhode Island, there is still escape from high-season crowds: in the High Country, reached by daily bus service or private car. The summer-only Tioga Road has turnouts for sublime views of lakes, domes, and crags that were under glacial ice 10,000 years ago. (The road leads east from the entrance to the park at Big Oak Flat, which is about an hour east of Sonora.) One of the most beautiful of the Sierra lakes, Tenaya, is in this area and deserves a stop.

As you drive east you will come to Tuolumne Meadows Visitor Center, just south of Tioga Road a few miles before the Tioga Pass crests at 9,900 feet. Tioga is the highest of California's vehicle passes through the Sierra and is closed in winter.

From **Tuolumne Meadows**, trails wheel off in all directions into the wilderness. Maps at the visitors' center will direct day-hikers toward Lembert Dome and Elizabeth Lake, both splendid treks for becoming acquainted with the largest subalpine meadow in the entire Sierra Nevada range. Information is also at hand about four-day guided hiking trips offered by both the Yosemite Mountaineering School and Yosemite Association.

Early summer promises an abundance of wildflowers and wildlife activity in that brief, warm growing season at 8,500 feet. Mark Twain called the air here "bracing and delicious and why shouldn't it be? It is the same the angels breathe." Icy lakes and ponds reflect emerald meadow borders or chains of granite crags, and attract the mule deer, the wily black bear, and the elusive coyote. More elusive still are the California bighorn sheep. Once facing extinction in Yosemite National Park, herds of the sheep are being reintroduced and can be sighted occasionally along the eastern park edge beyond Tuolumne Meadows. During mating season in late October the macho rams, bearing magnificent antlers that can weigh up to 30 pounds, butt heads with crashes audible almost a mile away. Celebrated for its song and its eccentricities is the Sierra ouzel; the fortunate hiker should be alert to this gray, wren-like bird that walks on pool and stream bottoms to search for food. It is capable of underwater flight when the current is swift.

Staying in Yosemite

If your focus in Yosemite is on the High Country, you can rent tent cabins at **Tuolumne Meadows Lodge** from summer to fall. Breakfast and dinner are served in a rustic tent within sight and sound of the Tuolumne River. Reservations for dinner are required; Tel: 372-1313. Backpackers have a pick of five High Sierra camps, each in an area selected for its nature interests and mountain grandeur. Accommodations are dormitory style and morning and evening meals are included in the price.

White Wolf Lodge is just north of Tioga Road, about halfway between Yosemite Valley and Tuolumne Meadows; day-hikers value its proximity to Lukens and Harden lakes. If you are planning a longer stop, tent cabins are available. Dinner reservations are advised; Tel: 372-1316.

Summer-camp simplicity is not a hallmark of the **Ahwah-nee Hotel** in Yosemite Valley. A National Historic Landmark, this recently refurbished luxury hotel opened in 1927 and has maintained its reputation for elegance, comfort, and fine cuisine through the succeeding years. Framed by nature with the granite Royal Arches at the north end of the valley, the hotel has rooms with TVs, mini-bars, and hairdryers, as well as vistas of thick forests and of the meadow. Towering dining room windows set the stage for meals served with distinctive china, silver, and crystal. Casual is acceptable for breakfast and lunch, but dinner is dressy—no denims, no shorts. Dinner reservations are required; Tel: 372-1489.

In mid-valley **Yosemite Lodge** occupies the site where Fort Yosemite, headquarters of the U.S. Army Cavalry, once stood. The Army was responsible for administration and protection of the park from 1906 to 1914 (the National Park Service took over two years later). Rooms are scaled from deluxe-with-balcony to bath-down-the-hall to rustic cabins. The lodge is open all year and offers three choices of dining: a cafeteria, which serves three meals daily; the **Four Seasons Restaurant**, where family dining is the key; and the **Mountain Room Broiler**, where broiled steak and chicken are the menu hits at dinnertime.

Glacier Point overshadows **Camp Curry** on torrid summer days in the valley. At this, the oldest establishment in the park, tent cabins and hotel rooms are available from spring to fall.

An hour's drive south of Yosemite Valley on the way to the Mariposa Grove, the largest of the three giant Sequoia stands in the park, is the charming Victorian **Wawona Hotel**. Like the Ahwahnee, it is a National Historic Landmark and is also recognized by the California Trust for its meticulously restored interior. The rambling, white-balconied Wawona (a Native American word thought to mean "big tree") is circled by lawns and a nine-hole golf course, where players share the greens with grazing deer herds. Time your evening meal for sunset in the hotel dining room, memorable for its views as well as its cuisine. Dinner reservations are required; Tel: 375-6556.

Other Sights in Yosemite

From the Wawona Hotel a historic covered bridge leads to **Pioneer Yosemite History Center**, a collection of relocated historic buildings and horse-drawn carriages. Ranger-led walks, stagecoach rides, and living history programs focus on the people who shaped events in Yosemite's history.

Another 15-minute drive farther south from Wawona is **Mariposa Grove**. The history of the giants here parallels that of the Western world. The average mature *Sequoiadendron giganteum* is 20 feet in diameter; the largest, 35 to nearly 40 feet. As you stand beneath their crowns, towering 200 to 300 feet above, you can't help feeling not only dwarfed, but also awed and uplifted.

Private vehicles are not allowed beyond the grove parking area; walk or take the tram ride May through October. It is less than a mile from the lot to the foot of dominating Grizzly Giant, thought to be the oldest of the Sequoias at 2,700 years. These trees are cousins of the taller Coast Redwoods (*Sequoia sempervirens*), which tower up to 367 feet but whose girth is only 20 to 22 feet in diameter.

One of the perversities of the Sequoias' survival mechanism is a need for fire to assure reproduction, so the National Park Service sets prescribed fires to simulate natural ones and encourage growth. You'll find smaller groves at the Tuolumne stand near Crane Flat and at Merced, off Big Oak Flat Road near the northwest entrance to the park.

Winter in Yosemite

Winter is a different world in Yosemite. The Merced River flows along snowy banks decorated with icicles then, and the snow-covered valley floor is stark against the circles of deep-hued evergreens and bare-branched trees. Weather is generally mild here, where the visitor count dwindles along with the rates.

You can ski at **Badger Pass**, 40 minutes southwest of the valley, with 90 miles worth of trailheads and roads for cross-country and downhill skiing, or you can ice skate—at the only outdoor rink in California—at the Curry Village complex in the valley against the spectacular backdrop of snow-blanketed Half Dome and Glacier Point. Snow may close most valley hiking trails in winter, but there are other activities. Park Service naturalists lead a daily snowshoe interpretive walk on a moderate 3-mile course in the Badger Pass Ski Area. No experience is necessary and you can rent snowshoes. If seeing an animal in the wild excites you, the chances of spotting a bobcat or coyote multiply in winter, when wildlife tracks are easier to pick out in the snow. Or, head for the snow-play area on Southside Drive in the valley.

Fine-food addicts and wine connoisseurs find the winter season here attractive for its annual Vintners' Weekends and Chefs' Holidays at the Ahwahnee Hotel. They are pricey but worth the indulgence. The Yosemite Winterfest is a traditional winter carnival at Badger Pass, complete with slalom racing and other forms of ski competition. The Winter Hotline has all the information for these events and takes reservations for them; Tel: (209) 454-2000.

No reference to the glories and delights of Yosemite is complete without mention of the ten-year planning effort by the National Park Service to return Yosemite Valley to its natural state in the face of an overwhelming surge of visitors. Progress has been made in backcountry cleanup and in restoring one of the park's meadows—and there's still more on the agenda. Some critics, though, call the plan unrealistic for including proposals to remove primitive tent cabins and, eventually, prohibit all private vehicles. Budget constraints are blamed for the lag in "de-urbanizing" the Incomparable Valley.

Although millions who visit every year glow with memories, there are some to whom nature is not benevolent. Tragedy can result unless hikers stick to marked trails and roads and realize that rivers, streams, and waterfalls can look inviting but may prove treacherous. Feeding wild animals is not only inadvisable, it will subject you to a Park Service fine. Fines also apply to any failure to store food properly in designated lockers provided to outwit black bears—they look brown, but they are indeed black bears—and they are no fools. Bears know the connection between ice chests and food and may break into containers whether food is present or not. Canny Yosemite bears figured out long ago the tenderfoot backpacker technique of hanging food in one tree and tying it with a rope to another tree. Chewing through the rope and waiting for the food to drop was no puzzle to the bears. So far, a counterbalance method has been bear-proof, but no one is taking any bets.

GETTING AROUND

Sacramento Metropolitan Airport is only 20 minutes from downtown Sacramento by cab or shuttle bus. Rental cars are available from the airport or at downtown locations, and some hotels have courtesy transportation. Most points of interest are within easy walking distance from Old Town. Sacramento has an efficient bus and light rail system, but there is also a Sacramento Sightseeing Service with daily tours of one or three hours; Tel: (916) 442-7564.

Once outside the metropolitan area, driving yourself is the only real option, because public transit systems in the Gold Country are purely local and limited. Driving distances are manageable; driving times will depend on the byways you want to follow.

While "rush hour" in the Gold Country may seem mild to the average urban dweller, there are areas where the traffic light is still unknown. Plan your long hauls between the morning and evening traffic crunch.

The Golden Chain map of Highway 49 is a detailed guide geared to Gold Rush history and interests. Any Chamber of Commerce in the area should be able to supply you with one. County maps may also be helpful, because road signs do not crop up on every corner, and you could find yourself with a picnic basket and no park table.

Ask for activities schedules wherever you plan a stopover. Art and little-theater festivals are popular the length of Highway 49, with many taking place during summer or in early fall.

Few gas stations in small Gold Rush towns are open 24 hours a day, so plan your purchases accordingly. If you venture north to Downieville, go with a full tank.

Dress for comfort in the Gold Country. Tank tops and shorts are acceptable in summer, jeans and shirts when it's cooler. Remember, the first Levi's were made here during the Gold Rush from tent material. That is one fashion that hasn't changed.

Yosemite National Park can be reached from Oakland (across San Francisco's Bay Bridge) by daily Amtrak service, which stops in Merced and connects there to the Yosemite Gray Line tour (daily from Merced year round); for Amtrak information, Tel: (800) 872-7245; for Gray Line information, Tel: (209) 383-1563 (Merced is about 40 miles west of Mariposa, one of the last Highway 49 Gold Rush communities in the Southern Mines area.)

ACCOMMODATIONS REFERENCE

▶ **Ahwahnee Hotel.** Yosemite Park & Curry Company, **Yosemite National Park**, CA 95389. Tel: (209) 252-4848.

▶ **Alta Sierra Resort.** 135 Tammy Way, **Grass Valley**, CA 95945. Tel: (916) 273-9102.

▶ **Annie Horan's.** 415 West Main Street, **Grass Valley**, CA 95945. Tel: (916) 272-2418.

▶ **Barretta Gardens Inn.** 700 South Barretta Street, **Sonora**, CA 95370. Tel: (209) 532-6039.

▶ **Black Bart Inn.** 55 West Saint Charles Street, **San Andreas**, CA 95249. Tel: (209) 754-3808.

▶ **Broadway Motel.** 1332 Broadway, **Placerville**, CA 95667. Tel: (916) 622-3124.

▶ **Camp Curry.** Yosemite Park & Curry Company, **Yosemite National Park**, CA 95389. Tel: (209) 252-4848.

▶ **Coloma Country Inn.** 2 High Street, **Coloma**, CA 95613. Tel: (916) 622-6919.

▶ **Columbia City Hotel.** Main Street, **Columbia**, CA 95310. Tel: (209) 532-1479.

▶ **Country Squire Motel.** 1105 North Main Street, **Jackson**, CA 95642. Tel: (209) 223-1657.

▶ **Court Street Inn.** 215 Court Street, **Jackson**, CA 95642. Tel: (209) 223-0416.

▶ **Downey House.** 517 West Broad Street, **Nevada City**, CA 95959. Tel: (916) 265-2815.

▶ **Dunbar House 1880.** 271 Jones Street, **Murphys**, CA 95247. Tel: (209) 728-2897.

▶ **Fallon Hotel.** Main Street, **Columbia**, CA 95310. Tel: (209) 532-1470.

▶ **Fitzpatrick Lodge.** 7740 Fairplay Road, **Somerset**, CA 95684. Tel: (209) 245-3248.

▶ **Foxes.** 77 Main Street, **Sutter Creek**, CA 95685. Tel: (209) 267-5882.

▶ **Gate House Inn.** 1330 Jackson Gate Road, **Jackson**, CA 95642. Tel: (209) 223-3500.

▶ **Gold Trail Motor Lodge.** 1970 Broadway, **Placerville**, CA 95667. Tel: (916) 622-2906.

▶ **Golden Chain Resort.** 13363 Highway 49, **Grass Valley**, CA 95945. Tel: (916) 273-7279.

▶ **Grandmère's.** 449 Broad Street, **Nevada City**, CA 95959. Tel: (916) 265-4660.

▶ **Gunn House.** 286 South Washington Street, **Sonora**, CA 95370. Tel: (209) 532-3421.

▶ **Holbrooke Hotel.** 212 West Main Street, **Grass Valley**, CA 95945. Tel: (916) 273-1353.

▶ **Holiday Inn Capitol Plaza.** 300 J Street, **Sacramento**, CA 95814. Tel: (916) 446-0100 or (800) 465-4329.

▶ **Hyatt Regency.** 1209 L Street, **Sacramento**, CA 95814. Tel: (916) 443-1234 or (800) 233-1234.

▶ **Imperial Hotel.** Highway 49, **Amador City**, CA 95601. Tel: (209) 267-9172.

▶ **James Blair House**. 2985 Clay Street, **Placerville**, CA 95667. Tel: (916) 626-6136.

▶ **Jamestown Hotel**. Main Street, **Jamestown**, CA 95327. Tel: (209) 984-3902.

▶ **La Casa Inglesa**. 18047 Lime Kiln Road, **Sonora**, CA 95370. Tel: (209) 532-5822.

▶ **Llamahall Guest Ranch**. 18169 Wards Ferry Road, **Sonora**, CA 95370. Tel: (209) 532-7264.

▶ **Mine House Inn**. 14400 God's Hill Road, **Amador City**, CA 95601. Tel: (209) 267-5900.

▶ **Murphys Historic Hotel**. 457 Main Street, **Murphys**, CA 95247. Tel: (209) 728-3444.

▶ **Murphy's Inn**. 318 Neal Street, **Grass Valley**, CA 95945. Tel: (916) 273-6873.

▶ **National Hotel**. 2 Water Street, **Jackson**, CA 95642. Tel: (209) 223-0500.

▶ **National Hotel**. Main Street, **Jamestown**, CA 95327. Tel: (209) 984-3446.

▶ **National Hotel**. 211 Broad Street, **Nevada City**, CA 95959. Tel: (916) 265-4551.

▶ **Northern Queen Inn**. 400 Railroad Avenue, **Nevada City**, CA 95959. Tel: (916) 265-5824.

▶ **Ponderosa Motor Inn**. 1100 H Street, **Sacramento**, CA 95814. Tel: (916) 441-1314 or (800) 528-1234.

▶ **Red Castle Inn**. 109 Prospect Street, **Nevada City**, CA 95959. Tel: (916) 265-5135.

▶ **Red Lion Inn**. 2001 West Point Way (off Business Loop 80), **Sacramento**, CA 95815. Tel: (916) 929-8855.

▶ **Robin's Nest**. 247 West St. Charles Street, **San Andreas**, CA 95249. Tel: (209) 754-1076.

▶ **Rupley House**. 2500 Highway 50, **Placerville**, CA 95667. Tel: (916) 626-0630.

▶ **St. George Hotel**. Main Street, **Volcano**, CA 95689. Tel: (209) 296-4458.

▶ **Sierra Nevada House III**. P.O. Box 496, Highway 49 and Lotus Road, **Coloma**, CA 95613. Tel: (916) 622-0777.

▶ **Sutter Creek Inn**. 75 Main Street, **Sutter Creek**, CA 95685. Tel: (209) 267-5606.

▶ **Swan-Levine House**. 328 Church Street, **Grass Valley**, CA 95945. Tel: (916) 272-1873.

▶ **Tuolumne Meadows Lodge**. Yosemite Park & Curry Company, **Yosemite National Park**, CA 95389. Tel: (209) 252-4848.

▶ **Vineyard House**. Cold Springs Road, **Coloma**, CA 95613. Tel: (916) 622-2217.

▶ **Wawona Hotel.** Yosemite Park & Curry Company, **Yosemite National Park**, CA 95389. Tel: (209) 252-4848.

▶ **White Wolf Lodge.** Yosemite Park & Curry Company, **Yosemite National Park**, CA 95389. Tel: (209) 252-4848.

▶ **Yosemite Lodge.** Yosemite Park & Curry Company, **Yosemite National Park**, CA 95389. Tel: (209) 252-4848.

LAKE TAHOE AND FAR WESTERN NEVADA

By David Toll

David W. Toll is the author of The Compleat Nevada Traveler. *He is a publisher and journalist and lives in Gold Hill, Nevada.*

Nevada is not like California. Despite being next-door neighbors, with interwoven social and economic ties, these two very Western states are quite distinct from each other. To oversimplify: California is the leading edge of the 21st century, and Nevada is the last remnant of the 19th.

California, with the seventh-largest economy in the world, is the tip of the United States arrow, a world leader in social and political innovation. Nevada is the seventh-largest state in the nation, more than a half-million square miles of mostly undeveloped scrub-forested mountains and broad brushy valleys. Its two urban areas, Reno and environs in the north and Las Vegas in the south, contain 80 percent of the state's population.

You will experience a subtle sense of dislocation as you travel from California into Nevada when the pine forests of California's High Sierra suddenly drop away and plunge down 3,000 feet into the desert vastness of Nevada, land of hidden treasures.

Lake Tahoe buttons these two unlikely neighbors together

at the border. The magnificent natural landscapes of Tahoe and far western Nevada combine with their hell-raising histories and with the luxuries and comforts of modern resort hotels and gambling casinos to form a beguiling mix that attracted more than seven million visitors in 1988.

Nevada's northern metropolitan area—the other, larger one is based in Las Vegas nearly 500 miles to the south, and we do not cover it in this guidebook—is centered on the connected cities of Reno and Sparks, with a western lobe at Tahoe and a southern lobe containing Virginia City, Carson City, and the Carson Valley.

Reno, once a rambunctious little railroad town at Lake's Crossing, has outgrown its naughty youth and begun at last to live up to its Roaring Twenties brag as the Biggest Little City in the World. Sparks, Reno's near neighbor on the east side of the Truckee Meadows, has developed an energetic reputation of its own as an industrial city. Carson City, the old Territorial capital, has lately become a manufacturing center, and the smaller towns of the region, almost all of them dating from the pioneer period, reflect their adventurous beginnings on the far Western frontier.

Base yourself in Lake Tahoe's High Country if you can, and make day trips down to Reno, Carson City, Virginia City, and the other nearby communities. They have much to offer, but none of them can match Tahoe for sheer physical beauty.

MAJOR INTEREST

Lake Tahoe
Casinos
Ski resorts
Truckee

Carson City
Carson Valley
Virginia City

Reno and Sparks
Casinos
Pyramid Lake
Washoe Valley

LAKE TAHOE

Mark Twain called Lake Tahoe "the fairest picture the whole earth affords." He had visited Lake Tahoe in 1863, just 19 years after the first visit to Tahoe from the East Coast, by John C. Frémont in 1844. Twain set up camp at what is now Marla Bay in an attempt to establish a timber ranch; unfortunately, a mishap with the campfire set the forest on fire, and he had to row out into the lake to save his life as his camp—and half the mountainside—was consumed by the raging flames. He then pursued other career opportunities, first as a quartz miner at Aurora, then as a newspaper reporter at Virginia City, but that's another story.

It was also in 1863 that stagecoach tycoon Ben Holladay built a vacation retreat at Emerald Bay. Lake Tahoe has been a favorite vacation getaway ever since.

In those early times and in the dreamy summers that followed, vacationers came to Tahoe by stagecoach and later aboard the train that chugged up the Truckee River canyon from the main line at Truckee to Tahoe City. They rested in luxury at enormous resorts like the Glenbrook Inn and Tallac House and glided out across the lake from pier to pier in graceful steamers named *Tahoe* and *Governor Stanford.* A string of small communities grew up on the north and south shores of the lake.

As a modern visitor to Tahoe, you can fly or drive into the basin, most likely from Northern California, to stay in high-rise hotel-casinos, in the dozens of less expensive motels, or—if you have reserved your campsite ahead of time—in public campgrounds. You can choose from among dozens of excellent eating places, take to the lake on everything from boogie boards to many-decked glass-bottomed excursion boats, play tennis and golf, and lounge around swimming pools in which the water is considerably warmer than the chilly lake. Ski resorts, unheard of at Tahoe until after World War II, attract enthusiastic winter visitors from around the world. Through all this expansion, the small settlements of the 19th century have grown larger and denser, and, at the South Shore in particular, peak summer weekends are positively urban with crowds and traffic jams. Still, even on a hot July weekend, once you are off the main thoroughfares the lake and its surrounding mountains provide a perfect vision of beauty, majesty, and peace.

The best ways to experience the lake are to make the spectacular 72-mile drive around its perimeter, to hike the forest trails, and to take to the water. Lake cruisers maintain regular schedules from May through October. The stern-wheeler **Dixie** (Tel: 702-588-3508) and the trimaran **Wood-wind** (Tel: 702-588-3000) embark from Zephyr Cove Marina on the Nevada shore, the **Tahoe Queen** (Tel: 916-541-3364)

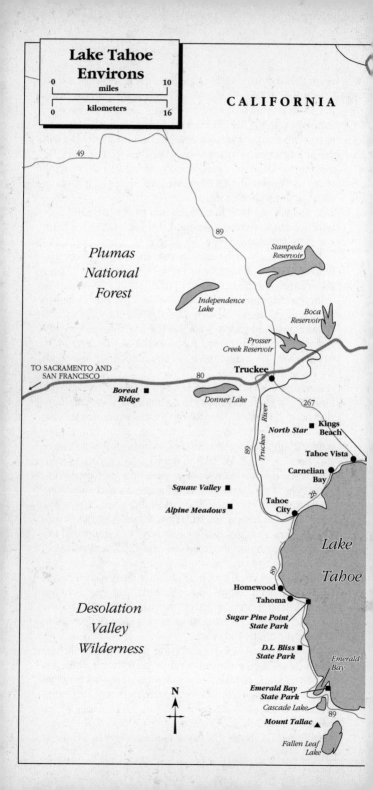

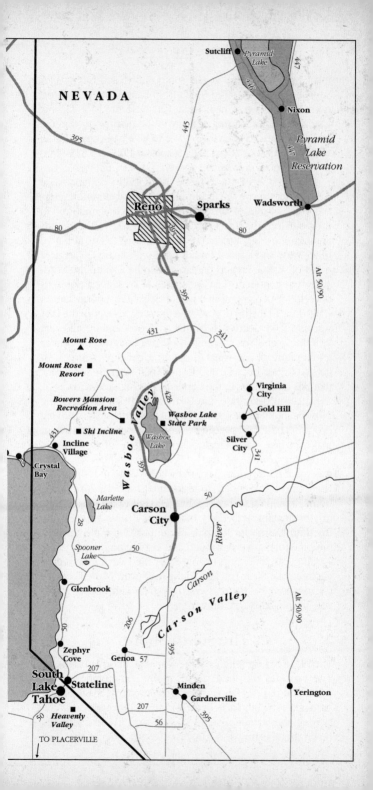

from Ski Run Marina at the South Shore, and the smaller **Sunrunner** (Tel: 916-583-0141) from Tahoe City on California's North Shore. Small boats can be rented for fishing, water-skiing, or cruising at many of the marinas around the lake, and there is even a seaplane to take passengers for an air-and-water tour at **Cal Vada Seaplanes** (Tel: 916-525-7143) in Homewood, on the west shore.

The surface of Lake Tahoe is officially designated at 6,226.95 feet above sea level, although actual elevation varies according to the season and the amount of water allowed to flow out into the Truckee River for the use of the Nevada communities and agriculture downstream. Tahoe, about 12 miles wide and about 22 miles long, with nearly 200 square miles of surface area, is the largest Alpine lake on the North American continent, 1,645 feet deep at its deepest point. Its pure (99.9 percent) water would cover the entire state of California 14 inches deep. While the surface layer of the lake warms to 68 degrees F by the end of summer, allowing swimming and water-skiing in relative comfort, the winter temperature of the water drops to a chilly 39 degrees. (It gets so chilled because it's mostly runoff from the snow pack that lies motionless in the depths at this high elevation.)

Statistical data aside, the Lake Tahoe Basin is one of the most beautiful places on the face of the earth, with a thriving economy based on pleasing visitors. Perhaps the best way to make the lake's acquaintance is by taking the drive around it, a trip that leads to so many different possibilities for enjoyment that it's best to devote the whole day to it. It's possible (but not recommended) to make the drive in less than three hours, assuming you're resolute enough to avoid stopping, but by making it a day's outing you'll give yourself the freedom to stop for food, drink, and to take walks through the pine forests as your mood and inspiration dictate.

Although you will probably enter the Lake Tahoe region via Interstate 80 at Truckee, to the northwest of the lake, our circular tour begins and ends on the South Shore, where you are most likely to be staying.

The South Shore

The blaze of bright lights at the Nevada-California boundary line provides the focal point for the communities at the south end of Lake Tahoe collectively known as South Shore, particularly South Lake Tahoe on the California side of the border, and Stateline, on the Nevada side. These enormous resort hotel–casinos, all on the Nevada side of the line, provide employment to many of Tahoe's full-time residents. To the customers who patronize them and play the gambling games, they provide entertainment—often featuring major stars—comfortable accommodations, and food varying from a cup of snack bar coffee to a lavish gourmet feast. **Harrah's,** for example, has, in addition to its over 500 guest rooms, a snack bar, a deli sandwich shop, a 24-hour coffee shop and restaurant, a steak and seafood restaurant, a brunch and dinner buffet, a gourmet dining room, and a showroom where meals are served as a part of the first show of the evening. **Caesar's Tahoe** has seven restaurants and 440 rooms. **Harvey's** has six restaurants and 638 rooms, and the **High Sierra** maintains five restaurants and 540 rooms. Their best is among the very best at the lake.

In contrast to the international style of the casinos, a variety of local and regional cuisines are represented on the South Shore—including American food. In the town of South Lake Tahoe the **Dory's Oar** (Tel: 916-541-6603) presents a New England seafood menu, **Dixie's Cajun & Creole Cuisine** (Tel: 916-541-0405) represents the Old South, and at **Nepheles** (Tel: 916-544-8130) it is California cuisine, complete with hot tubs for after-dinner relaxation. The **89th St. Bar & Grill** (Tel: 916-544-2556) on Highway 89 serves an American menu, and at **Evan's Gourmet American Café** (Tel: 916-542-1990), two blocks away, the name says it all.

There are numerous other dining places worth considering. For the views and the ascent—getting there is half the fun—dine at the **Top of the Tram** at Heavenly Valley (Tel: 916-541-1330; in summer, 544-6263). The dinner cruises aboard the *Tahoe Queen* (Tel: 916-541-3364) from Ski Run Marina and M.S. *Dixie* (Tel: 702-588-3508) from Zephyr Cove make a most glamorous experience on a silky summer's night, what with the bands that play for dancing after dinner. Or reserve a table at the **Eagle's Nest** (Tel: 702-588-6492), on Needle Peak Road via the Kingsbury Grade (Highway 207). This elegant inn is situated in the crags high above the lake, and the view from the dining room is sublime.

And that's just the beginning. The care and feeding of visitors is the leading local industry, with more opportunities around the lake than even most residents have tried yet, and even the least pretentious of them is good. **Izzy's Burger Spa,** for example, is just a little hamburger stand beside the lake, but the burgers here are memorable.

The **Lake Tahoe Museum** (Tel: 916-541-5458), adjacent to

the Chamber of Commerce on Highway 50 in South Lake Tahoe, provides a brief glimpse into Tahoe's past and includes a small exhibit of Native American artifacts.

The six miles of lakefront on the California side of the state line are heavily built up with small businesses of every description, but from the junction where State Highway 89 turns north along the lake's western shore (U.S. 50 continues west to Placerville and Sacramento), the bustling traffic of town is left behind.

The West Shore

Tahoe's west shore is what remains of the old classic era of Lake Tahoe's gilded age. Most of it is still relatively unchanged since that earlier era when only a favored few could afford lodges, chalets, and cabins for the summer, and only two or three dozen people toughed it out through the long, deep winters.

A few miles past the junction with Highway 50, just north of the Fallen Leaf Lake turnoff on Highway 89, is the U. S. **Forest Service Visitor Center** (Tel: 916-573-2674). Camping and hiking information is available here for the entire Tahoe Basin; guided walks and boat tours are also offered. One of the highlights of the visitor's center is the stream-profile chamber on Taylor Creek, an underground room built so that its "windows" provide a trout's-eye view of the stream and its aquatic life. Fascinating at any season, the chamber is especially colorful when the kokanee salmon are spawning in the autumn. Rangers also conduct campfire programs at the Lake of the Sky Amphitheater near the center.

Not far away is the **Tallac Historic Site**, where the mansion-size stone-and-log "cabins" of the Pope and Baldwin estates hark back to long Sunday afternoon picnics with parasols and boater hats. They are now maintained by the forest service, which offers tours during the summer months; also in the warm months, events such as August's Great Gatsby Festival, a Roaring Twenties celebration with Dixieland music and classic cars and boats, and the Starlight Jazz & Blues Festival (in August and September) are offered.

Along with an exhibit devoted to pioneer tycoon-gambler Elias "Lucky" Baldwin, a Native American museum is open Saturdays and Sundays on the grounds of the adjacent **McGonagle Estate**. Native Americans inhabited the Tahoe Basin for some 10,000 years before its discovery by the white man, and you will see evidence of their activities—grinding stones, for example, where they crushed and pulverized the seeds they gathered—all around the lake.

The Washo tribe were the dominant people to live here in the 19th century, coming up from the valleys to the east in spring and departing again with the onset of the snows; they spoke the Hokan language, a tongue unrelated to the Uto-Aztecan languages spoken by the Nevada Shoshone and Paiute tribes to the east. The name Tahoe is derived from the Washo words *Da ow* (meaning "big water"—not "grasshopper soup," as Mark Twain explained it).

Barely 20 years after Frémont's sighting of Tahoe, the Washo were being written off by these newcomers. In 1866 the superintendent of Indian Affairs reported, "There is no suitable place for a reservation in the bounds of their territory, and in view of their rapidly diminishing numbers and the diseases to which they are subject, none is required." By 1870 the Washo population had diminished to about 500 people. One of them, a young woman named Dat-So-La-Lee, learned the traditional survival skills of her tribe and excelled in basket making. In the 1890s, the baskets she made attracted the attention of Abe Cohn, a Carson City merchant and Indian trader, whose promotion and sponsorship of Dat-So-La-Lee brought recognition to the beauty and artistry of her baskets. Today the examples of her handiwork are considered priceless works of art; the Washo Tribe is now based near Gardnerville in the Carson Valley, their traditional homeland.

Highway 89 continues north from the museum through thick pine forests with meadows and glades and gives access to D. L. Bliss and Emerald Bay state parks. Mount Tallac, the lake rim's tallest peak, bears a snowy cross—an *X*-shaped feature that can be seen all around Tahoe Basin until the last of the snow melts in the spring. The mountain towers over the pine-forested western shore of Tahoe and Cascade and Fallen Leaf lakes.

The lovely and much-photographed **Emerald Bay** is a few miles farther north. Emerald Bay encloses Tahoe's only island, Fanette Island, sometimes known as Dead Man's Island because Ben Holladay's caretaker drowned here while rowing back from Tahoe Tavern on the west shore during a storm. Emerald Bay is also the site of the mighty 38-room Scandinavian-style stone castle called **Vikingsholm**, which you can reach by a one-mile walk down from the parking lot on the highway. Vikingsholm is the replica of a 1,200-year-old Viking castle that was owned by a millionairess, built in one summer by a crew of 200 craftsmen, and furnished with exact replicas of antique Scandinavian furniture. Estimated cost of construction in 1928: $500,000 (not including the wildflowers growing in the sod roof). Tours are conducted during the summer months.

At Sugar Pine Point State Park, about five miles farther north, the 1902 **Ehrman Mansion** (Tel: 916-525-7982) provides another glimpse of vanished glories. It's open for touring in summer and has a park for swimming and picnicking. The **Alpenhaus** (Tel: 916-525-5000) at nearby Tahoma is an Old World country inn with a Swiss menu—except for the Basque dinners it serves two nights a week—and it also functions as a bed and breakfast.

Homewood, a few meandering miles farther along, is one of Tahoe's venerable resort areas. **Sunnyside Lodge** (reservations are essential) is a very contemporary resort here serving a modern clientele with the lake's traditional stock in trade: comfortable accommodations, fine food and drink, and natural splendor all around. The pleasing view from the deck looks across the lake to the sparkling lights of the casinos at South Shore, and the bar and restaurant are open to all. The **Firesign Café** (Tel: 916-583-0871) across the highway serves breakfast and lunch with an emphasis on natural foods and home-style cooking. Mountain Bob's **Old Tahoe Café** on West Lake Boulevard (Tel: 916-525-5437) represents the rustic Tahoe tradition, while the **West Shore Café** (Tel: 916-525-5200) maintains a somewhat more contemporary ambience with outside tables at lakeside.

At **Tahoe City**, two miles farther north, the lake spills over its banks to form the Truckee River, which you will cross on the famous Fanny Bridge, so named because of the way folks like to rest their elbows on the rails along each side, peering out over the edge and down into the river at the schools of enormous trout undulating in the current. The Gatekeeper's Cabin, a recently built replica of the structure that stood here from 1909 until 1978 when it burned, is now maintained as a museum by the local historical society and is open to visitors without charge in the summer months.

You'll see a big roadside sign advertising horses for trail riding, and when the Truckee is in flood stage (usually in spring), you can rent a raft at Fanny Bridge to float down the more than four miles (about a two-and-a-half-hour cruise) to the **River Ranch** (Tel: 916-583-4264), where partying boaters fill the sunny riverside deck by day and diners sample the casual Continental menu by night (for more nearby dining choices see The North Shore, below). Mountain bikes can be rented at Tahoe City, and the bicycle trail beside the Truckee River has been paved from the city to River Ranch.

Highway 89 leaves the Lake Tahoe shore at Tahoe City and continues north along the banks of the Truckee to join I-80, just west of Truckee. Both **Alpine Meadows** and **Squaw Valley** ski areas are to the west off this twisting canyon road. Alpine Meadows, three miles west into the mountains from River Ranch, is the starting point for hiking trails into Sherwood Forest. A few miles farther north, Squaw Valley, which made Tahoe synonymous with the best of skiing, is transformed into a self-contained summer resort when the ski season is finally over in the spring. The 150-passenger cable cars and six-passenger gondolas carry sightseers up the sheer mountain face for walking and dining at the top of the runs. The views are unforgettable. (See Lake Tahoe Ski Areas below for details on ski-season facilities.)

Truckee

Less than 20 miles north of Tahoe City on Highway 89 is Truckee, once the ugly duckling of the Sierra, built to accommodate the logging industry's need for railroad access, now an attractive community of considerable distinction and charm. Truckee's architecture ranges across the whole spectrum of 19th-century aesthetic, from the brooding, heavy-shouldered Truckee Hotel bulked up against the deep and heavy snows of winter, to the lightest and airiest of filigreed Victorian mansion houses, all framed by the pine forest and Sierra summits.

The railroad still passes through Truckee, but it is no longer the crucial link with the rest of the country that it once was. After World War II, U.S. 40 took over the importance the railroad once had, eventually becoming Interstate 80, which passes Truckee on the north and provides the town's main connection with the outside world.

One of the great tragedies of the Western frontier occurred just three miles west of town, on the shores of **Donner Lake**. In 1846, as the great national migration westward was just beginning to stir, an "uncohesive assemblage of individuals" (as one historian describes them) set out from Illinois, bound for a better life in California. The Donner Party, as it is now forever known (named for its leader, George Donner), got this far after weeks of wandering in the Nevada desert and suffering six deaths. Here 37 more people died, men, women, and children, starved and frozen, held captive in this foodless place by the freezing temperatures and the deep snows.

Some who survived reportedly ate some of those who didn't, and some of the dead may have been killed for meat. The horror of cannibalism hung over the lake for many years afterward as other wagon trains crossed the Sierra for the more hospitable regions of California. Thus there is a special irony in the 154-site campground operated here by the state park system.

Some other travellers had passed through here only two years before the Donner Party, and their experience was considerably happier. Led by Elisha Stevens, they came upon a Paiute Indian, Truckee (later Captain Truckee and then Chief Truckee), who agreed to show them the way over the summits. The grateful pioneers named the river, as well as the trout that swam in it, in his honor. It was also Truckee's Lake that the Donner Party camped beside, although it has been Donner Lake since 1846. The town of Truckee was called Gray's Station when it was a log-cabin trading post in 1863; renamed Coburn's Station a while later, it was finally named Truckee in the chief's honor when the rails were spiked down here in 1868.

The building of the railroad attracted many people to the area, including a large Chinese population to fill the labor force. All through the 1870s gangs of railroaders, loggers, and others raided the Chinatown that grew when the railroad came through. It was burned four times, and in 1886 all the Chinese residents were forced out of their homes and out of Truckee for good. Truckee's tough reputation persisted into the 1920s as economic stagnation and its relative isolation preserved its frontier character.

The 1960 Winter Olympics, held nearby at Squaw Valley, provided a reawakening for the town, and now Commercial Row, the little city's main street, is an attractive collection of shops and restaurants serving an all-season clientele of highway travellers, Tahoe visitors, and local folks.

Staying and Dining in Truckee

Nightlife and dining out are almost synonymous in Truckee, and despite the town's modern attitudes, the sidewalks tend to roll up early, even in summer. The **Bar of America**, the **Capitol Saloon**, and a few other drinking houses provide such after-dinner excitement as Truckee offers, except on special occasions. Dinner itself is another matter. Several excellent restaurants cater to local customers as well as to the skiers and summer vacationers who make Truckee a stopping place on their Lake Tahoe vacations.

The **Passage Restaurant** (Tel: 916-587-7619) in the Truckee Hotel offers an ambitious California-cuisine menu in tasteful surroundings. **The Left Bank** on Commercial Row (Tel: 916-587-4694) specializes in seafood, with lots of garlic. (That there is an emphasis on garlic in the Truckee culinary tradition stems from a now-departed French chef who attracted an international clientele from among visitors to Lake Tahoe; his legacy lives on at **Pop's**, where the garlic-chip pizza is a highlight.)

Fermin's Copa de Oro serves authentic Mexican food, and the **Cottonwood**, decorated with railroad ties and heavy timbers harking back to Truckee's youth, offers an intriguing menu featuring Cajun and Italian specialties, as well as a welcoming view of downtown.

The Beginning is especially inviting for its family-style approach, featuring homemade bread and entrées such as pot roast and meat loaf. At the **Truckee Brewing Company** at the junction of Highway 89 and Donner Pass Road the attraction is less the pizzas and submarine sandwiches than the beer brewed on the premises. The Company's boast as "the highest brewery in the U.S." is probably safe from contradiction.

Busby's Café is a local favorite for breakfast and lunch; the **Coffee And** is a classic coffee shop seemingly frozen in time about 40 years back, with delectable homemade fruit pies; and cappuccino and espresso are served at **The Cookery Deli** on Commercial Row.

Several motels serve travellers in Truckee, as does the **Truckee Hotel** at the corner of Bridge Street and Commercial Row. This is the largest residential structure in Truckee, built in 1868, the year of Truckee's founding. Rates are moderate for the renovated rooms. Bed-and-breakfast accommodations are also available in Truckee at **Richardson House** on Spring Street, the **Blue House Inn-on-the-River** on Highway 89 south, and on weekends at the **Donner Country Inn** on the west shore of Donner Lake.

You can return to the shores of Lake Tahoe from Truckee via two all-weather highways. Highway 267 runs southeast to King's Beach and serves Northstar. Highway 89 follows the course of the Truckee River and provides access to Squaw Valley on the way to Tahoe City. Both cross beautiful forested highlands.

The North Shore

Tahoe City is at the southwestern end of the 15-mile string of small California and Nevada communities collectively called the North Shore. These small towns, extending north-eastward across the state line as far as Incline Village, Nevada, are noticeably quieter and slower-paced than the bright band of lights far across the lake at the South Shore. But for all their calmer qualities, these towns provide numerous enticements to visitors, from lodgings to boat rentals to good food. And while there are many activities available, such as hiking, tennis, and golf, the greatest attraction is still the mountain lake itself. Parks, recreation areas, and public beaches are accessible from the highway at many places along the way, and no matter which way you turn a delightful experience awaits you.

The North Shore offers a wide variety of dining places, from the cozy and colorful to the most sophisticated, often with evening entertainment.

Sunday brunch is a tradition at Lake Tahoe, and there are any number of wonderful places to serve you. Pick from **Emma Murphy's Avalanche Sushi Bar** (Tel: 916-583-6939) at Tahoe City, **GarWood's Grill & Pier** (Tel: 916-546-3366) at Carnelian Bay, the **Tahoe Biltmore** (Tel: 702-831-0660) and the **Cal Neva Lodge** (Tel: 702-832-4000) at Crystal Bay (for more on which, see below) and, in Incline Village, **Hugo's Rotisserie** (Tel: 702-831-1111) at the Hyatt Regency, or **Spatz** (Tel: 702-831-8999) on Ski Way Boulevard. All include Champagne. The casinos in Crystal Bay also serve splendid Friday night seafood buffets.

For breakfast on the other days of the week, the **Wildflower Restaurant** (Tel: 702-831-8072) in Incline Village and the **Log Cabin Caffè** (Tel: 916-546-7109) in King's Beach are local favorites. And in Tahoe City the **Cobblestone Café** (Tel: 916-583-2111) and **Rosie's Café** (Tel: 916-583-8504) start the morning off right within a few blocks of each other on North Lake Boulevard. You'll find moderate prices, informal atmosphere, and California casual cuisine at all of these cafés.

For French cuisine try **Le Petit Pier** (Tel: 916-546-4464) in Tahoe Vista, **Soule Domaine** (Tel: 916-546-7529) in King's Beach, or **Marie France** (Tel: 702-832-3007) and **La Fondue** (Tel: 702-831-6104) in Incline Village. Mexican food is the delight at the long-established **Cantina de los Tres Hombres** (Tel: 916-546-4052) in King's Beach and at **Hacienda de la Sierra** (Tel: 702-831-8300) in Incline Village. Italian entrées are featured at **Azzara's** (Tel: 702-831-0346), **Chianti**

Ristorante (Tel: 702-832-4040), and **Ferrari's Testarosa** (Tel: 702-831-8878), all in Incline Village.

Highway 267 connects the town of King's Beach here on the North Shore with Truckee and leads to **Northstar**, a modern ski resort that provides a variety of amenities and temptations in warmer seasons as well. Take advantage of their shops, restaurants, 18-hole golf course, tennis courts, swimming pool, horse and mountain-bike rentals, hiking trails, and a restaurant serving lunch at the **Day Creek Lodge**, accessible by taking the gondola lift. (See Lake Tahoe Ski Areas below.)

If you are a golfer, the venerable nine-hole Brockway golf course, now called **Wood Vista**, is at the junction of Highways 28 and 267 near Tahoe Vista, and there's another nine-hole course at Tahoe City right on North Lake Boulevard. At Incline Village the Robert Trent Jones–designed **Championship course** overlooks the lake, as does the shorter Executive course, both 18 holes.

A bright cluster of small casinos is gathered at the state line, which actually bisects the venerable **Cal Neva Lodge Resort** at the great fireplace in the old lobby, continues across the floor, and outside through the swimming pool. This is the hotel that Frank Sinatra owned a share of in the 1960s until his gambling license was rescinded by the Nevada Gaming Commission for having unsavory playmates; now under new ownership, the Lady of the Lake has been restored to its original elegance and charm and offers cabins, chalets, and lakeview hotel rooms. The **Tahoe Biltmore**, the **Crystal Bay Club**, and the **Tahoe Mariner**, all lined up on the Nevada side of the state line, also offer gambling, as does **Jim Kelly's Nugget**, a small casino that still maintains the local tradition of closing for the winter.

East of Crystal Bay is the community of **Incline Village**, which has long since outgrown its roots in 19th-century logging and is now a modern, attractive settlement of homes and small businesses set off by the **Hyatt Lake Tahoe**, a larger and more ample hotel-casino than most of its North Shore neighbors. Even the Hyatt, despite its relative size, maintains a quieter presence than any of its South Shore relatives.

Highway 431, the Mount Rose Highway, departs Lake Tahoe at Incline Village and heads north for Reno and Virginia City. A short distance up this road, stop to take in the stunning view, and if you're hungry head over the summit and the **Christmas Tree** (Tel: 702-849-0127), a steak house about halfway to Reno.

The **Ponderosa Ranch**, an amusement park devoted to

television's "Bonanza," is located at the east end of Incline Village. Hayrides are offered every morning from 8:00 to 9:30 A.M., with a pancake breakfast served afterward, from Memorial Day to Labor Day. The area beyond the Ponderosa around the east side of the lake to Glenbrook is largely undeveloped. **Sand Harbor State Park** is the principal exception, with swimming beaches and a boat-launching ramp as well as picnic sites and parking. In August the annual **Shakespeare at Sand Harbor** (Tel: 916-583-9048) is presented in a natural lakeside amphitheater. Spectators bring their own picnic dinners and spread blankets on the sand for performances of *Twelfth Night, A Midsummer Night's Dream,* and occasionally plays by other authors such as Rostand's *Cyrano de Bergerac.* You can find other swimming beaches along the east shore, some difficult to reach, with very limited roadside parking.

Highway 28 follows the east shore of the lake past the former Whittell Estate, once the home of an extensive private zoo (and not open to the public), to its junction with U.S. 50 at Spooner Lake. This little lake was once a stagecoach station and sawmill site and is now a small park and trailhead for the beautiful 5-mile hike (with spectacular views) into Marlette Lake, located high above Lake Tahoe.

Glenbrook, south of Marlette Lake, was once a bustling lumber town graced by an exclusive lakeside resort and served by daily steamers; now it is now a modern developed community with a nine-hole golf course open to the public. Highway 50, which leads north to Carson City, continues south past Zephyr Cove, where the M.S. *Dixie* and the trimaran *Woodwind* depart, to Round Hill and the par-72 **Edgewood Tahoe Golf Course** (Tel: 702-588-3566).

From Edgewood it's only a short distance to the South Shore casinos at Stateline, where we started. The turnoff for the Kingsbury Grade (Highway 207), which connects Lake Tahoe with the Carson Valley (see below), is on the way, and a detour here will give you a wonderful bird's-eye view of the valley below. This road approximates the route once taken by the Pony Express (1860 to 1861), which served Tahoe at Friday's Station, not far from the modern-day Harrah's, where the station is commemorated by a larger-than-life bronze sculpture of a rider dashing westward. Friday's was the home station for Pony Bob Haslem, who made the greatest ride in the history of that spectacular organization—380 miles through hostile Indian country, where stations were burned and relief riders and horses were run off into the desert. His heroism, and the cruel events of the frontier that prompted it, now seem very long ago and far away in contrast with the comforts and conveniences of this vacation paradise.

Lake Tahoe Ski Areas

In the 1850s a Norwegian gold seeker changed his occupation by agreeing to carry the mail between Placerville and the small settlement at Genoa, Nevada. "Snowshoe" Thompson, as he came to be known, used long oak skis to make the winter crossing of the Sierra and created a legend in the process. His example was unique, however, and he was regarded as something of a curiosity, virtually the only skier in the West until the 1860s, when the residents of a few isolated mountain communities turned to skiing as a winter diversion. Settlements like La Porte and Whiskey Flat challenged one another to downhill ski races between town teams, and local champions developed new techniques and secret concoctions of wax to speed them down the slopes.

Their activities did not attract others to the sport, however. Just the opposite: Skiing was considered a sport for hillbillies and was scorned by the swells who vacationed at the mountain resorts in summer and abandoned them when the snow began to fall. In the 1930s a few students at the University of Nevada were making ski trips to Mount Rose, but it wasn't until World War II, when U.S. combat units were trained to fight in the deep snows of winter here, that skiing began to take on a wider appeal. After 1945 a few small ski areas were developed in the Sierra, and in 1960 resort developer Alex Cushing made an almost impertinent invitation to hold the Winter Olympics at Squaw Valley. Winter sports began to be taken seriously in the Sierra.

Today the Lake Tahoe region has the greatest concentration of ski areas in the United States, with 15 major resorts offering alpine (downhill) and nordic (cross-country) skiing, as well as snow-play areas and all the amenities associated with winter recreation. Most years the ski season extends from Thanksgiving through Easter and is enhanced by an average 350-inch snowfall (double that of the Swiss Alps), pleasant temperatures (25–45 degrees F), and often sunny days. The terrain varies from gently sloping meadows to the most challenging expert runs, which vary according to elevation and degree of difficulty. Some resorts offer a limited number of lifts and modest base facilities, while others operate a wide array of lifts including gondolas and cable cars, with entire self-contained communities at the base. Most resorts run shuttles from base lodges to the casinos, with exact routes and schedules changing each year. Here are the leading Tahoe ski areas:

- **Alpine Meadows** (Tel: 916-583-4232), on Highway 89 six miles north of Tahoe City, prides itself on maintaining the longest ski season in the Tahoe region and on the family orientation of its slopes and services. The area covers 2,000 acres and is served by 13 lifts, with top elevation at the 8,637-foot summit of Ward Peak. The longest run is 2.5 miles. Terrain is rated 25 percent beginner, 40 percent intermediate, and 35 percent advanced. There are daily lessons, private and group, for skiers ages three and up and for handicapped skiers. All base facilities are available, including one of California's largest rental shops. Ski shuttle service is available daily to the North Shore and midweek to the South Shore.
- **Boreal Ridge** (Tel: 916-426-3663), on I-80 at the Castle Peak exit, offers night skiing until 10:00 P.M. every night except Christmas Eve. This long-established resort operates nine lifts to a 7,800-foot summit, with a 600-foot drop to the base lodge. Terrain is rated 30 percent beginner, 60 percent intermediate, and 10 percent advanced.
- **Diamond Peak** (Tel: 702-832-1177; 24-hour Ski Line: 831-3211) is at Ski Incline on Tahoe's North Shore. The 8,540-foot summit of Diamond Peak is served by seven lifts, has an 1,840-foot drop, and offers exquisite views of Lake Tahoe. Terrain is rated 19 percent beginner, 48 percent intermediate, and 33 percent advanced. There's a Child Ski Center here, and most of the terrain is served by a computerized snowmaking system. A free shuttle operates to the North and South shores.
- **Heavenly Valley** (Tel: 916-541-1330) is the largest ski area in the U.S., with nine summits in 20 square miles of ski slopes straddling the California–Nevada state line above the South Shore of Lake Tahoe. Twenty-four lifts take skiers to summit elevations of over 10,000 feet, some with drops of 3,600 feet. Six day lodges provide amenities, including the Top of the Tram restaurant, and the longest run is 5.5 miles. Instruction is available. Terrain is rated 25 percent beginner, 50 percent

intermediate, and 25 percent advanced. Free shuttle service is provided to the South Shore. Access
to the Nevada slopes is via Highway 207 (Kingsbury Grade) and Benjamin Road; on the California
side, Ski Run Boulevard leads to the base lodge
from South Lake Tahoe.

- **Kirkwood Meadows** (Tel: 209-258-6000) is a little
off the beaten track, about 30 miles south of Lake
Tahoe on Highway 88 (closed from the east during
the winter, when you must approach from the west
via Stockton). Kirkwood's 65 runs traverse 2,000
acres. Eleven lifts carry skiers 2,000 feet to the
9,800-foot summit from the highest base elevation
of any California ski resort. With five bars and restaurants and 104 condominium units, Kirkwood
has been developed as a self-contained destination
resort. A cross-country ski area with groomed
meadow and mountain trails provides for all experience levels. Terrain is rated 15 percent beginner,
50 percent intermediate, and 35 percent advanced.
- **Mount Rose** (Tel: 702-849-0704) is on the east
slope of the Sierra overlooking Washoe Valley,
about 11 miles northeast of Incline Village via Highway 27 and 22 miles southeast of Reno, also via
Highway 27. Its base elevation of 8,260 feet is the
highest in the Lake Tahoe region, and snowfall av-
erages 400 inches a year. Five lifts serve 900 acres
with drops of 1,450 feet, and the longest run is 2
miles in length. Terrain is rated 30 percent beginner, 35 percent intermediate, and 35 percent advanced. A daily shuttle serves Reno.
- **Northstar-at-Tahoe** (Tel: 916-562-1113) is another
self-contained community development centered
around skiing in the winter but with a variety of
recreational opportunities in other seasons. It is located on Highway 267 about midway between
King's Beach and Truckee. Eleven lifts, including a
six-passenger gondola, carry skiers 2,200 feet to
the summit of Mount Pluto. The longest run on the
1,700 acres is 2.9 miles, and in addition to the
downhill skiing, sleigh rides and more than 25
miles of cross-country ski trails are offered. Terrain
is rated 25 percent beginner, 50 percent intermediate, and 25 percent advanced.
- **Sierra Ski Ranch** (Tel: 916-659-7453, or 659-7475
for ski information) is on the west slope of the

Sierra, southwest of the Tahoe Basin at Twin Bridges on U.S. 50, about 15 miles west of its junction with Highway 89. The area contains three mountainsides in its 2,000 acres, with a top elevation of 8,852 feet. Nine lifts carry skiers from the 6,640-foot base lodge. Terrain is rated 20 percent beginner, 60 percent intermediate, and 20 percent advanced. Shuttles operate to the South Shore.

- **Squaw Valley** (Tel: 916-583-7226, for the resort; 583-3451 for accommodations) was the site of the 1960 Winter Olympics and is one of the world's leading ski areas. Thirty-two lifts, including a 150-passenger cable car and a six-passenger gondola lift, carry skiers to a summit elevation of 9,050 feet. Base and upper-mountain facilities at the 8,300-acre resort are highly developed, with a variety of restaurants, bars, and shops. The longest run is three miles, and a cross-country area is adjacent to the alpine runs. Terrain is rated 25 percent beginner, 45 percent intermediate, and 30 percent advanced.

CARSON CITY

Carson City, about 15 miles east of Lake Tahoe's Glenbrook on Highway 50, no longer announces itself as the nation's smallest state capital—in fact, there are nine others that are smaller now. But much of the simplicity and charm of its frontier past are still very evident in this pleasant community, where the Sierra Nevada towers against the western horizon.

Carson City was a rough settlement of a few dozen small structures when it was proclaimed capital of the Nevada Territory in 1861. By the time statehood was achieved three years later—Lincoln so urgently needed Republican votes and Comstock silver that population standards were ignored—Carson City had begun to exhibit some of the charm that characterizes its large downtown historic district today.

Much of the largely residential district at the center of town west of Carson Street remains unchanged from a century ago, when the homes were built to house prosperous frontier merchants, politicians, lawyers, and bankers. Begin a half-hour stroll through the tree-shaded Victorian streets at the 1870 silver-domed Capitol building, meander westward as far as the Governor's Mansion on Mountain Street—Robinson Street between Mountain and Division streets is especially rich in architectural treasures—and then continue northeast to conclude at the **Nevada State Museum**, which occupies the imposing stone building that once housed the U.S. Mint. The stamps that transformed gold and silver bullion from the mines of the Comstock Lode into coins of the realm are still here and are still used to produce commemorative coins from time to time. Exhibits from the animal, vegetable, and mineral kingdoms complement the historical artifacts displayed, and the basement has been transformed to replicate the underground workings of a silver mine.

The **Carson City Nugget**, a long-established casino at the center of town on Carson Street, displays an extraordinary collection of gold specimens collected from around the world. In addition to large nuggets discovered in streambeds, you'll see ribbons, wires, threads, and crystals of native gold formed in the cracks and crevices of the quartz veins. There are even twigs and leaves of gold, created when the original organic materials decomposed and left voids in the rock in which gold was later deposited.

On the south side of town, the **State Railroad Museum** occupies a complex of modern and historic structures beside the highway. Some of the buildings were built to house the collection of rolling stock rescued from the scrap pile and from the Hollywood movie studios, others are former depots and section houses moved here from original sites elsewhere in the state. Trains are fired up for display and to move around the short sections of track, and plans are in place for extending the rails to carry passengers into Carson City's historic district and back.

The **Roberts House** museum on Carson Street is a residence from pioneer days restored to give a glimpse of the mundane realities of frontier home life.

There is another small museum on the second floor of the stone firehouse at Musser and Curry streets, where the Warren Engine Company No. 1 (Carson City's venerable fire department) still maintains a roster of volunteers in addition to the paid staff. The museum is open to visitors in the afternoons and displays historical firefighting tools, gear, clothing, and other unusual artifacts—even segments of the redwood water mains that once served the city.

An **Indian Museum** occupies the former superintendent's residence at the Stewart Indian School on Snyder Road, east of U.S. 395, once a boarding school for children from Western tribes. When the school closed in 1980 after 83 years of operation, students from 20 tribes were enrolled. The stone school buildings, built by Indian craftsmen, are enrolled on the National Register of Historic Places, and the exhibits of Native American arts and crafts are exceptional. A small store stocks Native American art, jewelry, pottery, rugs, basketry, and beadwork, and the school grounds—now devoted to a variety of state uses—are the site of an annual powwow in June that brings together Native Americans from around the Western states, many of them alumni and descendants of alumni. You will see craftsmen, such as the Zapotec weaver who sets up his loom on the front porch in July, at their traditional work.

Staying and Dining in Carson City

Since the frontier period when shootings and stabbings were common, nightlife has not been much of a priority in Carson City, which was, with very few exceptions, a charming community of homebodies. Today, though, the situation is considerably improved, with quite a variety of first-class restaurants catering to visitors and residents alike.

The **Carson City Nugget** and the **Ormsby House**, Carson City's principal casinos on Carson Street, each offer 24-hour coffee shops and dining rooms much patronized by the local residents, and the Nugget has a small oyster bar as well. The **Carson Station**, the **Senator**, and a small handful of other gambling houses also provide simple fare. The elegance of Carson City's Victorian past is represented at **Adele's**, perhaps the city's most refined dinner house, in a bandbox Victorian home on Carson Street. A Basque restaurant, **Irrintzi**, occupies the imposing Rinckel Mansion a block west of Carson Street; **Marrone's**, in a shopping center on the north side of town, serves Italian specialties and offers diners the opportunity to order any combination of pasta and sauce; and **Stanley's**, a little farther north, is another local favorite that offers a Continental menu.

Bodine's, at the junction of Highways 50 and 395 south of town, is a nostalgic visit to the 1960s with its barnwood decor and steak-lovers' menu. A half-dozen Chinese restaurants maintain the Nevada tradition; for example, **Genghis Khan** serves Mongolian sautés at 260 East Winnie Lane just east of Carson Street.

El Charro Avitia on Carson Street at the south end of town is a popular Mexican restaurant, as are **Mi Casa Too** on Carson Street at the north end of the city, **Tito's** two blocks east of Carson near the center of town, and **La Raza** a few miles east on U.S. 50, just across the line in Lyon County. The

Miramar, also on Carson at the south end of town, is Carson City's first Thai restaurant, and **Amimoto**, in the nearby Silver City mall, serves Japanese food.

Two casino-hotels, the **Ormsby House** and **Carson Station**, are next-door neighbors on South Carson Street, and a large number of motels also provide accommodations. **The Edwards House** is a four-room Victorian bed and breakfast at 204 North Minnesota Street in the historic district.

Carson City is especially lively during the summer and fall months, when a series of public events take place. The very best of them is the Nevada Day Parade that celebrates Abraham Lincoln's creation of the state—a brilliant show every October 31. Another colorful interlude is provided by the Mountain Man encampment—a gathering of wilderness buffs dressed in buckskin and beads—in the great park on the east side of town in June.

CARSON VALLEY

After a grueling trip west by mail wagon, Horace Greeley entered the Carson Valley in July 1859. "I had previously seen some beautiful valleys," he wrote in a dispatch to his newspaper in New York, "but I place none of them ahead of the Carson. . . . This valley, originally a grand meadow, the home of the deer and the antelope, is nearly inclosed by high mountains, down which, especially from the north and west, come innumerable rivulets, leaping and dancing on their way to join or form the Carson [River] . . . producing an abundance of the sweetest grass, and insuring bounteous harvests also of vegetables, barley, oats, etc. . . . I may never see this lovely valley again—it is hardly probable that I ever shall—but its beauty, its seclusion, its quiet, the brightness of its abundant rivulets, the grandeur of its inclosing mountains, the grace and emerald verdure of their vesture of pines, have graven themselves on my memory. . . ."

The splendor of the towering peaks of the Sierra Nevada rising steeply up out of the lush valley pasturelands makes a profound impression, even if you haven't bounced and bumped across Nevada in a mail wagon. The valley lies just south of Carson City (which, confusingly enough, is situated in Eagle Valley) on U.S. 395. It can also be reached by way of the Kingsbury Grade from the southeast corner of Lake Tahoe, the route that Greeley followed when he continued west, which provides a breathtaking view of the valley as it descends.

Each of the Carson Valley's three communities has its distinctive character, and all three are growing rapidly as population spills over the summits from Lake Tahoe and south from Reno in search of affordable housing.

About 10 miles south of Carson City is **Genoa** (Juh-NO-uh), established at the base of the Sierra Nevada as a trading post by Mormon pioneers from Salt Lake City in 1851, two years after California achieved statehood. Take Highway 57 west off Highway 395 to reach Genoa, Nevada's first permanently settled community, which comprised 40 or 50 houses when Horace Greeley passed through and which was the seat of government for Carson County, Utah Territory. The reconstructed Mormon Fort is now the centerpiece of a small state park, and the former Douglas County Court House (Genoa lost the county seat to Minden in 1916) is now a historical museum.

Several of the pleasantly rambling old residences have been converted to restaurants. The **Pink House** is a celebrated dinner house, and the **Wild Rose Bed and Breakfast** offers accommodations. Nevada's first saloon, **The Genoa Bar**, still slakes the thirst of travellers here. Genoa's stunning setting—the Sierra rises steeply up behind the town—and Victorian charm have attracted moviemakers in recent years, and the Candy Dance, an autumn fundraiser for the local volunteer fire department, attracts many visitors.

A few miles south of Genoa, **Walley's Hot Springs** caters to visitors as it has for more than a century—with hot water pools, overnight accommodations, and a restaurant of considerable distinction (Tel: 702-883-6556). The resort was a favorite among the wealthy residents of Carson City and Virginia City when it was located on the main line of travel; then, after some years of decline, the original resort burned to the ground. The modern Walley's was built a few years ago, a 20th-century version of the original available for a brief swim or a week's indulgence.

Gardnerville, a few miles southeast of the Genoa turnoff on Highway 395, was established as the farming and ranching center of the valley, growing to prominence as Genoa declined after the 1860s. It is best known to visitors for the family-style Basque restaurants that have served generations of diners: the **J T**, the **Overland Hotel**, and the **Carson Valley Country Club** south of town, where the restaurant (you can select steaks, shrimp scampi, or lamb chops as your entrée) adjoins the golf course. Each of the Basque restaurants has a bar where, along with the usual fare, you can order the favorite Basque cocktail, Picon Punch (American Picon and brandy are the principal ingredients).

Every Nevada town has at least one local casino, and **Sharkey's** in Gardnerville is famous for its huge prime rib dinners, the boxing and buckaroo memorabilia displayed on the walls, and the lavish Eastern Orthodox Easter feast given to the community by proprietor Sharkey Begovich.

Minden, one mile north of Gardnerville, is the youngest of the Carson Valley's three communities. In 1905 the Virginia & Truckee (V&T) Railroad was deprived of its main revenues by the depletion of the Comstock mines and the construction of a new Southern Pacific spur line that severed the V&T's connection to the Tonopah and Goldfield mines far to the south; the V&T Railroad turned to the vegetable kingdom to make up the income by shipping the harvest from the Carson Valley. The V&T made its last run in 1950—its brick depot is a café now—but Minden's pleasant downtown area still reflects a turn-of-the-century small-town atmosphere, with a park at its center, complete with velvety lawn, charming gazebo, and shade trees all around. The old Minden Inn, where Clark Gable once married, is closed, but the new **Carson Valley Inn** at the center of town beside the highway provides accommodations, dining, and a casino. In an unusual and welcome variation, the inn's dinner house, **Fiona's**, is located in its own building away from the frenetic casino environment.

VIRGINIA CITY AND THE COMSTOCK LODE

In the 1860s and 1870s, Virginia City was the gaudiest and brawniest city in the West, rivaling San Francisco with its wealth and abandon. Today most of the wealth of the gold and silver mines of the Comstock Lode has been depleted and spent, but Virginia City, although its population has dwindled and many of its fine mansions now stand empty, is still the dowager queen of the Old West, an open-air, three-dimensional museum a little more than a half-hour's drive southeast of Reno and an even shorter drive northeast of Carson City.

From Carson City take U.S. 50 east about 7 miles, then turn left onto Nevada Highway 342. Four miles farther along you'll reach Silver City, once a bustling mining town, now a venerable collection of homes and a post office. The highway continues north through Devil's Gate, an eroded volcanic flow that once plugged the narrow canyon, and climbs the steep old wagon road through Gold Hill to Virginia City.

The highway from Reno climbs the pinyon- and juniper-stippled Virginia Range to an 8,000-foot summit, providing pleasing panoramic views of the cities in the Truckee Meadows below and of the Sierra Nevada farther west.

The Comstock Lode was discovered at Gold Hill, a settlement just south of Virginia City, in February 1859, when the famous Red Ledge was uncovered by prospectors from a camp a few miles down in the canyon. A second discovery of astonishing richness followed in June at what is now the northwest corner of Virginia City, and for 20 years the drama of discovery and development was unceasing.

In October 1875, when Virginia City had swollen from the primitive tents and shanties of its beginnings to a major modern city of more than 20,000, it burned in a catastrophic fire. Two-thirds of the city was destroyed, including much of the business district on B and C streets. So rich were the ores being brought out of the seemingly inexhaustible mines, however, that rebuilding began immediately, and as a consequence the city stands today as a showplace of Western Victorian architecture. As tourism has replaced mining as the economic mainstay, most of the important buildings—particularly those on C Street, the main commercial center—are open to visitors.

The V&T Railroad, once the richest (and crookedest) short line in the world, is being restored as far as Gold Hill and takes passengers daily in Virginia City from May through October. The depot car is parked in a siding on F Street in Virginia City—listen for the whistle.

Saint Mary's-in-the-Mountains, on D Street, is a celebrated monument to the Victorian period, a spired and steepled Gothic brick Roman Catholic church still in everyday use. Its interior reflects the richness of its origins, with soaring ceilings above the altar and choir loft, and a baptismal font brought from Paris more than a century ago.

Similarly, the **Storey County Court House**, with its unusual unblindfolded Justice over the entrance, offers a rare opportunity to step into the past. County business is conducted here in the same offices as it was in the glory years and in the long decline that followed.

Piper's Opera House, a block north of the Court House, is intriguing for its raked stage (slanted downward toward the footlights so that the audience had unobstructed views from the level-floored hall) and for its distinguished roster of players, including the incomparable Jenny Lind.

The **Fourth Ward School**, at the south end of C Street, is the only remaining schoolhouse from the bonanza period (there were four others this size, and a sixth in Gold Hill). It was preserved as much by inertia and neglect—the signatures of its last graduating class (1936) are still scribbled in chalk on the blackboards—as by more recent restoration financed by a whiskey distiller and by the owner of the county's brothel. It is now maintained as a museum.

Some of the palatial private homes are also open to visitors. **The Castle**, on D Street, was built with silver doorknobs for a mining superintendent before serving as the residence of a leading banker for many decades. It is still furnished and appointed exactly as it was in the glory days—even the lace curtains that flutter in the vagrant breeze are original.

Other bonanza-era mansions—the Mackay Mansion and the Chollar Mansion on D Street—are open for tours, and some have been converted to bed and breakfasts (see below).

Virginia City clings to the eastern flank of Sun Mountain, and on its rumpled northeastern outskirts, the old cemeteries—nine of them—combine to make a substantial burying ground. Celebrities like Indian fighter Edward Storey and Fire Chief K. B. "Kettle Belly" Brown lie beside paupers and babies in such a confusion of headstones and burial plot enclosures that the burying ground almost seems lively. Virginia City's most famous murder victim, Julia Bulette, was a prostitute so beloved by the community that her strangled body was conducted to its grave by a civic parade led by the Volunteer Fire Department. She was not permitted to spend eternity within the regular cemeteries, however, and her lonely gravesite is barely visible on a hillside far to the south.

C Street is Virginia City's lone remaining commercial district, two lively rows of saloons, cafés, shops, and restaurants facing each other across their wooden sidewalks. The **Bucket of Blood** and the **Delta** saloons at the center of town once feuded over the patronage of Lucius Beebe (the late newspaper columnist and railroad writer who, for a time, owned the weekly *Territorial Enterprise*) and his St. Bernard, T-Bone Towser. Like most of the drinking emporia along the street, their walls bristle with memorabilia. Photographs of the mines, the railroad, and the city decorate every interior surface along C Street, so that even a pause for refreshment is also a museum visit.

There's a banjo-strumming jazz band at the Bucket of Blood, and the **Silver Stope** maintains a long-standing tradition of jazz jam sessions on Sunday afternoons. At the **Union Brewery** the excellent beer is brewed downstairs in the basement, where a small Nevada beer museum has also been installed.

Virginia City tends to be quite crowded in the summer, far from the ghost town you might expect, and if swarms of sno-cone eaters are not your preferred milieu you'll prefer the late afternoons and evenings when the family vacationers have swept their school-age offspring back down to Reno and Carson City. Crowds are thinner in spring and fall, and in the winter you're apt to have the saloon to yourself at any given moment and actually experience the ghostliness.

There are some interesting events in Virginia City each year, most notably the exciting spectacle of the Camel Races held in September (with real camels). A Dixieland Band festival and a John Philip Sousa festival fill the city with sound on summer weekends, and St. Patrick's Day is celebrated here with special vigor in tribute to the thousands of Irish miners who labored underground. August's Fireman's Muster is a major spectacle, as fire fighters and their gleaming antique trucks and pumpers come from several states to congregate and compete in the uproarious contests.

Closed in 1942 as nonessential to the war effort, few of the great mines of the Comstock Lode ever reopened. Most mining since then has been the open-pit variety at odds with the historic nature of the district, and only one company is now at work underground with a small-scale operation. You can get a glimpse of the mines by taking one of the offered tours. The Chollar Mine is at the south end of D Street, or the back door of the Ponderosa Saloon on C Street opens into an extension of the underground workings that honeycomb the mountain beneath Virginia City. Tours are available at both.

Another interesting visit is to the basement workrooms of the **Territorial Enterprise building**, where the old presses and type library gather dust, and Mark Twain's copy desk sits like a shrine.

Staying and Dining in Virginia City

You'll find snacks and light lunches easily available up and down C Street during the day. Basque-style dinners are served at the **Sharon House** (Tel: 702-847-9495), and steaks are the enticement at the **Silver Stope** (Tel: 702-847-9011). Gold Hill,

a mile down the canyon toward Carson City, offers two region-
ally celebrated dining places: **The Gold Hill Hotel** (Tel: 702-
847-0111), a pioneer hostelry recently restored and enlarged,
with an ambitious European menu, and **Joe Conforte's Cabin
in the Sky** (Tel: 702-847-0733), half a mile down Main Street,
serving steaks and Italian cuisine.

Because so many of its summer visitors are day-trippers,
Virginia City's long summer evenings belong to those who
take accommodations in the two motels and the handful of
bed-and-breakfast inns—**Edith Palmer's Country Inn** on Virginia City's B Street, the bonanza-era **Chollar Mansion**, the
House on the Hill in a modern Victorian mansion in Gold
Hill, and **The Hardwicke House** on Main Street in Silver City,
two miles closer to Carson City and Lake Tahoe. This last is a
monumental stone structure on Silver City's main street that
has been a general store and (downstairs) a stable. Now it
caters to overnight visitors as a cordial bed-and-breakfast
inn. The **Gold Hill Hotel** also takes guests in both older and
modern rooms, all decorated with antiques. (These accommodations are all easily visible from the highway.)

WASHOE VALLEY

This valley at the eastern foot of the Sierra between Reno
and Carson City, parallel to the Virginia City area, is traversed
by Highway 395, a modern freeway that bypasses the attractions that make the valley more than just a beautiful drive.
The **Bowers Mansion** is accessible via Franktown Road exit
on the west side of the valley; Washoe Lake State Park is
accessible only from Lakeside Drive on the east.

When Sandy Bowers struck it rich as one of the original
discoverers of the Red Ledge in Gold Hill he married his
landlady, Eilly Orrum, and the two of them set out to live as
grandly as Sandy's newfound fortune permitted, building
this grand cut-stone mansion at the edge of the pine forest
and travelling to Europe to furnish it. They had money
enough "to throw at the birds," in Sandy's memorable
phrase, and they spent it lavishly, shipping furniture around
Cape Horn for their new home.

But Sandy died within a few years of striking it rich, and
Eilly lived on long after the money had all been spent. She
progressively closed off more and more of the great stone
house until at last she could not afford to live there even on
the most meager scale. So she sold this monument to grandeur and moved back to Virginia City, where she eked out a

slender living as the Washoe Seeress, telling fortunes to a gullible clientele until she died, broke.

The house she and Sandy built passed through a number of hands—it acquired a steamy reputation as a roadhouse during Prohibition—before being acquired and restored to something like its original splendor by the Washoe County Park District. Tours are conducted and the grounds are available for picnics.

A few miles south along Franktown Road you can see what is left of the town of that name, which was settled as a sawmill site, developed as an ore milling center, and served by the V & T Railroad—the old water tank marks the depot site—when its fruit and vegetable farms fed the miners in Virginia City. A little farther south stands a log cabin, barely visible through the pine trees from the road, in which Will James wrote "Smoky" and other stories that established his reputation as a Western storyteller.

Washoe Lake State Park is on the other side of the valley. Its main attraction is to boaters, but there are fine beaches and even small dunes on the east side that may invite you to stroll in good weather.

The **Cattlemen's Restaurant**, with a menu strong on beef, is located beside the highway near the center of the valley at the old settlement of Ophir.

RENO

Reno, 20 miles north of Carson City on Highway 395 or 25 miles northeast of Truckee via Interstate 80, was a child of the railroad, a patch of lots in the sagebrush bottom of the Truckee Meadows sold at auction when the Central Pacific pushed through in 1868. A homely little burg, it prospered as the shipping point for the rich Comstock mines, as well as for other nearby mining districts and for Carson City. With the slowing of production from the gold and silver mines in Tonopah and Goldfield after 1910, Reno transformed itself into the commercial and financial center of Nevada. As prosperity overtook the roughneck little railroad town, trees were planted to give the city an inviting and charming air, and gambling was made illegal.

But in 1931, when four successive drought years combined with the Depression to break the Nevada agricultural and mining economy, the state legislature relegalized gambling, the purpose being to put the licensing fees into the public treasury, instead of the pockets of "cooperative" sheriffs and district attorneys who allowed the gambling to continue underground. It succeeded, and in the process created a mechanism for regulating what had until then been outlaw enterprises. The statute has succeeded so well that "gaming" (as gamblers call gambling when it becomes an industry) has far overshadowed ranching and mining in Nevada, both economically and politically, for most of two generations now.

Since the recession of the early 1980s, the state government has earnestly promoted industrial development to mitigate the overwhelming reliance on casino slot machines and on other forms of tourism for jobs and tax revenues. The success of this program can be seen in the prospering new industrial parks east and south of the Reno airport and in Sparks, where increasing numbers of businesspeople, engineers, and managers have joined the population of lawyers, card dealers, cowboys, Indians, and other colorful folks who give Reno its flavor.

Exploring Reno

Most of Reno's casinos, entertaining gamblers for more than a century, are centered in the heart of the city, which is bisected by the Truckee River, flowing from west to east, and Virginia Street, the main north–south boulevard. Fourth Street (once U.S. 40) is the main east–west artery connecting Reno and Sparks, but most crosstown drivers use the freeways (I-80 east to west and U.S. 395 north to south).

Reno's history reflects the individualism of the Western frontier, a historical moment at which independence and self-sufficiency were highly prized qualities. The frontier has lingered longer in Nevada than elsewhere, and as a consequence men like Harold "Pappy" Smith and Bill Harrah who came here in the 1930s to operate storefront bingo parlors stayed to create the gambling industry that now leads the economy of the state.

The high-rise Harrah's is a fitting monument to Bill Harrah's business sense, but this highly individualistic man left a legacy on his personal side as well. At his death, Harrah, an eager collector of antique and classic automobiles, left three warehouses stuffed with 1,400 cars, plus a $3 million research library and a fully staffed and equipped restoration garage.

When Bill Harrah's casinos were acquired by the Holiday Inn chain of hotels, the collection was whittled down to the crème de la crème, and these 175 cars were donated to the

National Automobile Museum, at Lake and Mill streets. Other cars have since been acquired by the museum, and now more than 200 painstakingly restored antiques and classics are displayed in showroom condition in exhibit space designed to emphasize the automobile's impact on American life and culture, both as artifact and as icon. Video presentations, a handful of small shops, and the Roadhouse Café supplement the automotive displays, where you can also view the restoration workshop. Make sure you stop by to see the Thomas Flyer that won the 1908 New York-to-Paris race, the 1948 Tucker Sedan, Buckminster Fuller's 1934 Dymaxion, the one-of-a-kind 1938 Phantom Corsair, and James Dean's 1949 Mercury from *Rebel Without a Cause*. Other delectable celebrity cars include Al Jolson's 1933 Cadillac phaeton and Elvis Presley's 1973 custom white-on-white Eldorado coupe.

The Truckee River is Reno's most enduring landmark, and a walk west along its banks from the auto museum is a pleasant way to make the city's acquaintance. Follow a path that has been created along the riverbank to connect Wingfield Park downtown, with its free summertime band concerts, to Idlewild Park, about one and a half miles west, with its nationally acclaimed rose gardens and broad green lawns. The 20-minute walk leads through the Reno of the 1920s and 1930s, the "city of trembling leaves" that Walter Van Tilburg Clark wrote about in his novel of that name: gracefully porched Victorian and Edwardian mansions (some of them serving in earlier years as boardinghouses for six-week divorcées—women taking advantage of Nevada's lenient law requiring only a six week residence in the state to file for divorce) on quiet, tree-shaded streets.

The **Sierra Nevada Museum of Art** occupies two near-downtown locations. The E. L. Weigand Museum at 160 West Liberty Street offers an array of travelling exhibits from modern works to paintings of the 16th and 17th centuries; The Hawkins House, a Neo-Georgian mansion at 549 Court Street, on the south side of the river, has exhibits of 19th- and 20th-century American art.

North of the city center, the University of Nevada campus maintains a busy schedule of art exhibits at the **Sheppard Galleries** in the Church Fine Arts complex on Virginia Street, and you can walk through the campus to view the Gutzon Borglum sculpture of Comstock Lode mining magnate John Mackay. The university also offers an active schedule of theater and music performances throughout the year. On the north side of the campus, the **Nevada State Historical**

Society maintains an archive for research and a museum, part of which is devoted to a historical overview of Nevada and part to changing exhibits on various themes and topics.

Across from the Historical Society is another monument left by one of Nevada's supreme individualists, Major Max Fleischmann. A prime incentive for wealthy outsiders to settle in Nevada has been its low tax rate, particularly the absence of state income and inheritance taxes. Of the many monied men and women who settled here to take advantage of this benign climate was the scion of the Fleischmann's Yeast family fortune who came here in the 1930s. Fleischmann fell in love with Nevada—not uncommon among people who live here—and in the years before his death he established the Fleischmann Foundation to contribute funds to many community projects around the state. The **Fleischmann Planetarium** (Tel: 702-784-4811 for recorded show information and 784-4812 for reservations), a part of this legacy, plays a 60 to 70 minute double feature that combines a planetarium star show (such as one on UFOs) with a hemispheric wraparound movie in the Cinema-360 film format (such as one on arctic light). A small museum presents exhibits about the solar system and outer space, and free public sky-gazing sessions are offered regularly throughout the year.

At the **Rancho San Rafael**, a few blocks west of the campus, is yet another memorial to a wealthy Nevada transplant— Wilbur D. May, a member of the May department store family. Before going on a year-long safari in 1929, May, a devoted big-game hunter, sold his stock portfolio and invested in government bonds. When he returned—with some of the wildlife trophies exhibited here—he had escaped the catastrophe of the stock market crash and emerged with his wealth intact. He used it to travel around the world and to support a leisurely lifestyle on the Double Diamond Ranch a few miles south of Reno. Since his death in 1980, the Wilbur D. May Museum has displayed the eclectic collections of this charmed life—T'ang dynasty horses, West African musical instruments, and Lalique vases among them—with a major emphasis on big-game trophies.

A big part of Reno's appeal to visitors is the series of major public events that take place throughout the year. The September Reno Air Races attract visitors from all over the world, the Reno Rodeo in June is a big-league cowboy show, and Hot August Nights is an enjoyable romp and reunion with the 1950s and 1960s.

As enjoyable as Reno's parks and public places can be, the

main attraction for visitors is still the casino-hotels, most of which are clustered at the center of the city. This is where Pappy Smith, Bill Harrah, and other pioneers built little bingo parlors into the huge casinos known around the world. Today the casinos are bigger and brighter than ever, but few of them are operated by single owners any longer; most have corporate owners now and reflect a smoother, less idiosyncratic management style. The Smith family sold Harold's Club to Howard Hughes's Summa Corporation in the 1960s, and Harrah's has been part of the Holiday Inn company since Bill Harrah died in 1978.

Sparks

Sparks, like Reno, was originally created by the railroad. When the Central Pacific came through in 1868, the division point for this section of the road was located at Wadsworth, about 30 miles east. Shortly after the turn of the century, though, the repair shops and crew facilities were moved to a new community at Harriman (named for the railroad tycoon), just east of Reno in the Truckee Meadows. Once the railroad was established, Harriman changed its name to Sparks, in honor of Nevada's governor John Sparks, and the town began amassing a long and uneventful history as a slowly growing one-industry town. By the 1950s, when the railroad's influence and economic importance began to wane, Sparks had grown westward and Reno eastward so that the two communities intertwined.

Despite their interconnections, Reno and Sparks have maintained quite separate identities, with Sparks developing as a city of light industry in contrast with Reno's casino- and tourism-based economy. Recently, the old downtown district on B Street has been transformed, first by the expansion of **John Ascuaga's Nugget**, a major casino-hotel with more than 600 rooms and suites in its new tower, then by the construction of the Disneyesque **Silver Club** across the street, and finally by the transformation of B Street itself into **Victorian Square**. The 90-year-old business houses of Harriman, refurbished with Victorian motifs, have achieved a splendor they never actually had when new, and the square, with its fountain and bandstand gazebo, serves as a focal point for community celebrations throughout the year.

Besides the attractions of its downtown core, Sparks also offers you a refreshing respite from the summer heat at **Wild Waters Water Fun Resort**, on Sparks Boulevard just north of the I-80 freeway. Open from May through September, the recreation area offers thrilling descents, daredevil plunges, lazy floats, and plenty of sunshine, with food and drink available into the evening.

Staying in Reno and Sparks

All of the hotel-casinos in Reno and Sparks are alike in offering comfortable accommodations, dining that is exceptional in quality or price or both, and more or less identical gambling games. But there are differences too. **Bally's Reno** was the largest casino-hotel in Nevada when it opened in 1979 as the MGM Grand, and its size and splendor made it one of the favored destinations for high rolling gamblers. High rollers have since become something of an endangered species, but the ambience lingers on for ordinary mortals to enjoy at Bally's. The gambling floor is the size of two football fields, an arcade of shops offers items ranging from simple souvenirs to Native American art and artifacts and clown paintings by Red Skelton, and seven restaurants cater to every dining mood. Accommodations range from generic upscale hotel rooms to the most lavish celebrity suites.

Harrah's and the **Flamingo Hilton**, both downtown, and the **Peppermill Hotel Casino** on South Virginia Street also cater to the public in the high style that was once reserved only for elite players. The food and the amenities reflect the highest standards. At **John Asquaga's Nugget** in Sparks the hotel tower is a relatively recent addition to this long-established casino famous for its food. Trader Dick's, a Polynesian restaurant, was once the Nugget's most exotic offering, but now it is only one of seven or eight excellent restaurants in the casino complex. The Nugget is also the last word in accessibility, as the I-80 Freeway is built through the property, right across the roof of the casino, with two offramps giving onto immense parking lots. At Fourth and Virginia streets in downtown Reno, the **Eldorado Hotel & Casino** has also established a reputation for fine food, and its restaurants are popular with local people as well as with visitors.

The **Comstock Hotel & Casino** is interesting as one of the first "theme" hotels in Reno, modeling its decor after the famous Comstock Lode and the mines beneath Virginia City. It caters to a mixed clientele of visitors and locals who appreciate its down-home Nevada atmosphere and modest prices. The **Virginian**, the **Sundowner**, the **Sands**, the **Riverboat**, and **Fitzgerald's** all project their own distinct styles and offer moderately-priced accommodations. The **Ponderosa**

Hotel & Casino proclaims itself the world's first non-smoker's hotel-casino, and the **Holiday Hotel**, on Center Street beside the river, originally opened as Reno's premiere non-gaming hotel, although it has a small casino now. The most unusual of Reno's hotel-casinos is **Circus Circus**, an extraordinary combination of gambling house and carnival midway, with aerialists, performing dogs, jugglers, high wire artists, and other traditional circus acts doing their routines above the crowded carnival games. This is one casino-hotel where you are likely to see infants in strollers at the registration desk and teeny-boppers in the elevators.

Standing like monuments to the pioneer past are two of the most wonderful of Reno's casinos: the Mapes and the Riverside. Both have lively histories—the Riverside dates back almost to Reno's 19th-century beginnings. The great brick building opened as the first hotel in the state during the dark period in the 1920s when gambling was illegal, and in the 1930s served as home base to a generation of divorcées who found the out-of-town dude ranches too confining. It is now closed, as is the Mapes, which was the first hotel-casino built after World War II and one of last Art Deco structures built in the U.S.—the plans had been drawn up in 1938, but construction was delayed by the war. Today they loom like ghosts in the glare of the bright lights on Virginia Street.

The term "one-armed bandit," once a jocular synonym for the slot machine that helped build Reno's reputation, is obsolete now. Some slot machines have no arms at all but are operated by pushbuttons; others are not traditional slot machines with spinning reels, but video poker and keno games. There are some slots that have handles but then have video displays instead of reels. And even the machines that combine the traditional handle on the right side with spinning reels are actually computer-driven—the handle is painstakingly designed to give the impression that it operates mechanically, resisting the pull as if an internal spring were tensing, but the flexing is just for effect. The handle simply engages a switch to activate a tiny computer that commands an electric motor to spin the reels and display a result randomly chosen by the computer.

That may not sound like a lot of fun, but the popularity of the machines proves that many still enjoy them. Increasingly, casinos devote expensive floor space to slot machines and less to the table games—craps and blackjack—that a whole generation of young men learned to play in army barracks and aboard navy ships during World War II. Today's volunteer army simply doesn't provide adequate training in throwing the dice to make these games the attractions they once were.

The clubs still serve free drinks to active players, and entertainment is still a mainstay of the casino experience, although not quite on the lavish scale as in the past. Today some of the spectacle that was once supplied by big-name stars is provided by the architecture and by the food.

Dining in Reno and Sparks

Typically each casino-hotel offers a wide variety of dining options under its roof, from a snack bar serving coffee and hot dogs to a gourmet restaurant priding itself on lavish cuisine and service. Thus, as you might expect, some of Reno's finest dining is found at the casinos.

Spectacular buffets have become a staple of the Nevada casino, almost an indigenous art form, and they are well represented in Reno. The breakfast buffet at the Eldorado, at Fourth and Virginia streets, is especially highly regarded and often has a line of eager locals waiting when it opens at 8:00 A.M. For lunch or dinner the buffet at the Peppermill, 2707 South Virginia Street, provides a tropical decor as exotic as the food, and the mountain of shrimps may be worth the entire price. The **Rotisserie Restaurant & Buffet** at John Ascuaga's Nugget in Sparks provides another impressive spread, and the brunch at Bally's, 2500 East Second Street, about a mile east of downtown Reno via either Mill or Second streets, is a Sunday tradition. Served in the casino's Restaurant Row, the buffet features 13 entrées and complimentary Champagne. None of the buffets is expensive, yet each projects an air of an extravagant feast.

Another casino staple is the bargain special. They change often, but are well-advertised and range from a 99-cent breakfast at the **CalNeva Club**, Second and Center streets, to a $5 full-course prime rib dinner at the Sands, 345 North Arlington. The specials change, but there is seldom a day without one or two to attract bargain hunters.

Yet another casino standby is the gourmet restaurant: No self-respecting casino manager can function comfortably without a European-trained chef directing a squad of white-hatted perfectionists in the preparation of culinary delights. The **Top of the Hilton** at the Flamingo Hilton, Second and Sierra streets, is a particularly elegant example of this kind of dining; the service is impeccable, the food delectable, and the view from the 21st floor—especially when the sun is setting beyond the white-capped Sierra and the lights of the city are twinkling below—is superb.

Other casino dinner houses of distinction are the **Steak House** at Harrah's, **Le Moulin** at the Peppermill, and the **Café Gigi** at Bally's.

Casinos don't offer the only dining options, but they have elevated the general level of taste considerably above what might be expected in a state traditionally dominated by miners and cowboys. Reno and Sparks offer an astonishing number and variety of exceptional restaurants without gambling attached. If Nevada can be said to have a native cuisine other than that of the Paiute Indians or the casino buffets, it is—of all things—Basque boardinghouse fare.

Each spring and autumn in the late 19th and early 20th centuries, large flocks of sheep moved between Nevada's high-mountain summer grazing lands and the broad desert valleys where they spent the winter. To manage these flocks of sheep, Scottish, Chinese, and eventually Basque herders were employed. These Basques, recruited from the Pyrénées mountain districts of France and Spain, came to take the demanding job of moving with the sheep, keeping them safe and unscattered with the help of a dog or two. For months at a time they roamed the solitary wilderness with the animals, and when they took a week off or bunked up in town—Elko, Winnemucca, Ely, Gardnerville, Reno—between jobs, they stayed at boarding hotels kept by their fellow countrymen, where hearty meals were served family-style. Inevitably diners other than Basques were attracted to the table as well, and over the years the Basque hotels have become popular local dining places in many Nevada communities. In Reno there are three exceptional and quite different examples of the genre. The **Pyrenees Bar & Grill** (Tel: 702-329-3800), in the porched and pillared old Hardy mansion at Flint and California streets, and **Louis' Basque Corner** (Tel: 702-323-7203), at Fourth and Evans, are actually dinner houses of some elegance, with specialty entrées and steaks. At the **Santa Fe Hotel** (Tel: 702-323-1891), 235 Lake Street, the style is simpler. Tureens, bowls, and platters are passed up and down the long tables, and the house red wine is served in water tumblers. Be sure to bring a sheepherder's appetite.

Another popular mainstay in Reno is seafood: **The Rapscallion Seafood House** (Tel: 702-323-1211), 1555 South Wells Avenue, **Famous Murphy's Restaurant and Oyster House** (Tel: 702-827-4111), 3127 South Virginia Street, and **MacKay's** (Tel: 702-348-6222), 336 Mill Street, feature seafood and pleasing surroundings. **The Oyster Bar** at John Ascuaga's Nugget (Tel: 702-356-3300) is also a favorite for seafood concoctions, especially the New York pan roasts.

Some unusual dining places: **The Liberty Belle** (Tel: 702-825-1776), 4250 South Virginia Street, is a fine specimen of a saloon with a magnificent back bar and hearty lunch and dinner fare. It is operated by Marshall and Frank Fey, the grandsons of the man who invented the slot machine. Examples of their illustrious ancestor's handiwork—most notably the original five-cent piece's Liberty Belle—are on display. **Ichiban Japanese Steak House & Sushi Bar** (Tel: 702-323-5550), 635 North Sierra Street, features the astonishing Teppanyaki-style tableside cooking involving dancing knives and flashing smiles. Try the traditional Japanese dishes as well as the steaks and lobster.

For a one-of-a-kind experience, **Landrum's** (Tel: 702-322-5464), at 1300 South Virginia, is a Reno institution. This eight-stool diner opened for business in 1937 and has been satisfying customers 24 hours a day with standard favorites like chicken fried steak and chili omelettes ever since. There are newer Landrum's farther south on Virginia Street and in Sparks, but the tiny original is a uniquely satisfying and totally authentic diner.

Lunch at the **Board of Trade** (Tel: 702-322-7183), at 425 South Virginia, served at tables, at booths, and at the bar, is a boisterous and lively exercise, a favorite with downtown professionals and almost undiscovered by tourists. Its convivial atmosphere is a part of the attraction—the food is good, too.

Pyramid Lake

This extraordinary desert lake, a remnant of the inland sea that once covered much of the Great Basin (Utah's Great Salt Lake is another), is a little more than a half-hour's drive north from Sparks via Pyramid Way (State Highway 445).

Fed by the Truckee River, which is fed in turn by Lake Tahoe, Pyramid Lake is contained within a Paiute Indian reservation. It is the antithesis of Lake Tahoe, with an absolute minimum of development and no glamor at all. There are no pine forests, no casinos, and no tours (other than the brief look at the fish hatchery that maintains the populations of Lahontan cutthroat trout and *cui-ui,* a species unique to Pyramid). There is only the lake and its desert setting. Cupped by chalky pink, tan, and gray hills, Pyramid's water is such a brilliant iridescent blue under the summer sun that it can sizzle your eyes just to gaze upon it, so dark and cold to look at in winter that it freezes eyeballs in their sockets.

The principal attraction for visitors is the otherworldly beauty of the lake itself and the sport provided by the cutthroat trout (the minimum size that you can keep is 19 inches). Tribal permits are available for fishing and boat launching at the ranger station at Sutcliff, as is and information for hiking and exploring by car. At The Needles, near the northern end of the lake, warm pools fed by hot springs provide a sort of prehistoric pleasure.

Nixon, the reservation's main town, is on the southeast shore of the lake. The road from Nixon south to Wadsworth (Highway 447) parallels the Truckee and passes by the site of the battle in which the Paiutes annihilated an invading force from Virginia City in 1860. At Wadsworth you can pick up Interstate 80 to return to Reno.

GETTING AROUND

The Reno-Cannon International Airport is served by major airlines (American, US Air, United, Delta, and America West) with flights to and from metropolitan centers around the United States. Shuttle connections are available from the airport to hotels in Reno and to hotels and ski areas at Lake Tahoe. American Airlines flies from San Francisco and southern California to the airport at South Lake Tahoe.

There is local bus service in Reno and Sparks and in some towns at Lake Tahoe; Greyhound buses link these communities to each other and to Carson City. That makes public transportation a possibility, but if ease, comfort, and convenience are considerations, a remote one. There is no substitute for travelling by car around the far western part of Nevada, and if your visit is in winter, late fall, or early spring, make it four-wheel drive. Reno, Carson City, and Lake Tahoe offer plenty of taxicabs, and limousines are available at short notice, but there is nothing better than the simplicity and flexibility of getting around by car.

Amtrak sends a train a day in each direction between Chicago and San Francisco across the Sierra, with stops at Truckee and Reno (Tel: 800-872-7245).

Highway access to this part of Nevada is by Interstate 80 from San Francisco and Sacramento to the west and from Salt Lake City and northern Nevada to the east. From the west I-80 passes through Truckee, where Highways 89 and 267 proceed, respectively, to Tahoe City and King's Beach at the North Shore of Lake Tahoe; and through Reno. U.S. 395 connects Reno, Carson City, and the Carson Valley, continuing south along the east slope of the Sierra through the Owens Valley to southern California and north to northeastern California and Oregon. U.S. 50 connects the South Shore of Lake Tahoe with Placerville to the west, and to the east continues through Carson City, central Nevada, and (eventually) Baltimore, Maryland.

Summers are hot and thronged with visitors throughout the region; winters are cold and brisk and especially busy at Lake Tahoe, where the ski resorts provide the major attraction. Despite the unpredictable weather, spring and fall are perhaps the most beautiful seasons, with wildflowers blooming in May and June and the cottonwood trees blazing brilliant yellow in October.

Because pleasing visitors is the major industry in this part of the West, there are squadrons of organizations you can call when you have a question. They are devoted to helping you find your way around, and they welcome the opportunity to assist you with current information: Nevada State Commission on Tourism, Tel: (702) 885-4322, 885-3636, or (800) 237-0774; Lake Tahoe Visitors Authority (South Shore), Tel: (916) 544-5050; Incline Village/Crystal Bay Visitors & Convention Bureau (North Shore, Nevada side), Tel: (800) GO-TAHOE or (702) 831-4440; Tahoe North Visitor & Convention Bureau (North Shore, California side), Tel: (800) 824-6348 or (916) 583-3494; Reno-Sparks Convention & Visitors Authority, Tel: (800) FOR-RENO or (702) 827-RENO; Reno Downtown Visitors Center, Tel: (702) 329-3558; Sparks Downtown Visitors Center, Tel: (702) 358-1976; Carson City Convention & Visitors' Bureau, Tel: (800) 634-8700 or (702) 883-7442.

ACCOMMODATIONS REFERENCE

▶ **Alpenhaus.** P.O. Box 262, **Tahoma**, CA 95733. Tel: (916) 525-5000.

▶ **Bally's Reno.** 2500 East Second Street, **Reno**, NV 89505. Tel: (702) 789-2000 or (800) 648-5080.

▶ **Blue House Inn-on-the-River.** 7660 Highway 89 South, **Truckee**, CA 95734. Tel: (916) 582-8415 or (800) 548-6526.

▶ **Caesar's Tahoe.** P.O. Box 5800, **Stateline**, NV 89449. Tel: (702) 588-3515 or (800) 648-3353.

▶ **Cal Neva Lodge Resort.** P.O. Box 368, **Crystal Bay**, NV 89402. Tel: (702) 832-4000 or (800) 225-6382.

▶ **Carson Station.** 900 South Carson Street, **Carson City**, NV 89701. Tel: (702) 883-0900.

▶ **Carson Valley Inn.** 1627 Highway 395, **Minden**, NV 89423. Tel: (702) 882-0822.

▶ **Chollar Mansion.** P.O. Box 889, **Virginia City**, NV 89440. Tel: (702) 847-9777.

▶ **Circus Circus Hotel & Casino.** P.O. Box 5880, 500 North Sierra Street, **Reno**, NV 89513. Tel: (702) 329-0711.

▶ **Comstock Hotel & Casino.** 200 West Second Street, **Reno**, NV 89501. Tel: (702) 329-1880.

▶ **Donner Country Inn.** 9 Green Valley Drive, Lafayette, CA 94549 (mailing address). Tel: (916) 587-5574 or (415) 938-0685.

▶ **Eagle's Nest Inn.** P.O. Box 5250, **Stateline**, NV 89449. Tel: (702) 588-6492.

▶ **Edith Palmer's Country Inn.** P.O. Box 758, **Virginia City**, NV 89440. Tel: (702) 847-0707.

▶ **The Edwards House.** 204 North Minnesota Street, **Carson City**, NV 89703. Tel: (702) 882-4884.

▶ **Eldorado Hotel & Casino.** P.O. Box 3399, 345 North Virginia Street, **Reno**, NV 89505. Tel: (702) 786-5700 or (800) 648-5966.

▶ **Fitzgerald's Casino-Hotel.** Box 40130, 255 North Virginia Street, **Reno**, 89504. Tel: (702) 785-3300 or (800) 648-5022.

▶ **Flamingo Hilton.** 225 North Sierra Street, **Reno**, NV 89502. Tel: (702) 322-1111 or (800) 445-8667.

▶ **Gold Hill Hotel.** P.O. Box 304, **Virginia City**, NV 89440. Tel: (702) 847-0111.

▶ **The Hardwicke House.** P.O. Box 96, 99 Main Street, **Silver City**, NV 89428. Tel: (702) 847-0215.

▶ **Harrah's.** 210 North Center Street, **Reno**, NV 89502. Tel: (702) 329-4422 or (800) 648-3773.

▶ **Harrah's.** P.O. Box 8, **Stateline**, NV 89449. Tel: (702) 588-6606 or (800) 648-3773.

▶ **Harvey's.** P.O. Box 128, **Stateline**, NV 89449. Tel: (702) 588-2411 or (800) 648-3361.

▶ **High Sierra.** P.O. Box C, **Stateline**, NV 89449. Tel: (702) 588-6211 or (800) 648-3322.

▶ **Holiday Hotel.** P.O. Box 2700, Mill and South Center streets, **Reno**, NV 89505. Tel: (702) 329-0411.

▶ **House on the Hill.** P.O. Box 625, **Virginia City**, NV 89440. Tel: (702) 847-0193.

▶ **Hyatt Lake Tahoe.** P.O. Box 3239, **Incline Village**, NV 89450. Tel: (702) 831-1111 or (800) 233-1234.

▶ **John Ascuaga's Nugget.** P.O. Box 30030, **Reno**, NV 89502-0030. Tel: (702) 356-3300 or (800) 648-1177.

▶ **Ormsby House.** 600 South Carson Street, **Carson City**, NV 89701. Tel: (702) 882-1890 or (800) 648-0920.

▶ **Peppermill Hotel Casino.** 2707 South Virginia Street, Reno, NV 89502. Tel: (702) 826-2121.

▶ **Ponderosa Hotel & Casino.** 515 South Virginia Street, Reno, NV 89501. Tel: (702) 786-6820 or (800) 228-6820.

▶ **Richardson House.** P.O. Box 2011, **Truckee**, CA 95734. Tel: (916) 587-5388.

▶ **Riverboat Hotel & Casino.** 34 West Second Street, **Reno**, NV 89501. Tel: (702) 323-8877 or (800) 888-5525.

▶ **Sands Hotel Casino.** 345 North Arlington Avenue, **Reno**, NV 89501. Tel: (702) 348-2200.

▶ **Sundowner Hotel & Casino.** 450 North Arlington Avenue, **Reno**, NV 89503. Tel: (702) 786-7050.

▶ **Sunnyside Lodge.** P.O. Box 5969, **Tahoe City**, CA 95730. Tel: (916) 583-7200.

▶ **Truckee Hotel.** P.O. Box 884, **Truckee**, CA 95734. Tel: (916) 578-4444.

▶ **Walley's Hot Springs.** P.O. Box 36, **Genoa**, NV 89411. Tel: (702) 883-6556.

▶ **Wild Rose Bed and Breakfast.** P.O. Box 256, **Genoa**, NV 89411. Tel: (702) 782-5697.

THE CENTRAL COAST

MONTEREY BAY TO SAN LUIS OBISPO

By Jacqueline Killeen

A native San Franciscan and fourth-generation Californian, Jacqueline Killeen has written about the state since 1968 for a number of guidebooks, as well as regional and national magazines. Currently a contributing editor and restaurant critic for San Francisco Focus *magazine, she is the author of the guidebook* Country Inns of California.

"The greatest meeting of land and water in the world." So wrote poet Robinson Jeffers of California's central coast—a land of awesome beauty, where high mountains plunge abruptly into the sea, and a region with a vivid past, which has inspired writers from Richard Henry Dana to Jack Kerouac. Its history encompasses the settlement of California by Spanish soldiers and missionaries, the era of Mexican rule when rich *rancheros* and Yankee traders made Monterey "Queen of the West," and the boisterous saga of whalers and fishing boats that plied the coastal waters. Later chapters involve the bohemian colonies in Carmel and Big Sur, the struggles of migrant workers in John Steinbeck's "Long Valley," and the castle of William Randolph Hearst, who brought the glitter of Hollywood to a hilltop above San Simeon.

The Central Coast is also one of the world's fabled playgrounds, with diversions ranging from golf and polo to deep-sea excursions, and from sightseeing to shopping, dining, and wine touring. The best way to explore this area is in a circular itinerary south along the ocean from Santa Cruz at the south base of the San Francisco Peninsula, through the Monterey Peninsula and Big Sur, down to Hearst Castle and San Luis Obispo. You can then return quickly back north to San Francisco via Highway 101, the inland route (mostly freeway) through the Salinas Valley.

This central section of the California coast is enormously popular with visitors and locals alike and thus can become unpleasantly crowded on peak-season weekends. If possible, plan your trip for a midweek visit to the coast, especially during the summer months.

MAJOR INTEREST

Monterey Peninsula
Historic buildings of Monterey
Cannery Row and the Monterey Bay Aquarium
Golf, tennis, polo, and deep-sea excursions
Seventeen Mile Drive and Pebble Beach
Carmel Mission
Shops and galleries of Carmel
Dining and wine tasting
Point Lobos State Reserve
Big Sur scenery

San Simeon to San Luis Obispo
Hearst Castle
Shops and galleries of Cambria
Surfing and deep-sea fishing
San Luis Obispo and its Mission

The Inland Route
Wineries
Old missions
Steinbeck House and Library in Salinas
San Juan Bautista's early Californiana

THE COASTAL ROUTE TO MONTEREY

From San Francisco, State Highway 1 follows the Pacific coastline all the way south to Monterey, but it's a long drive

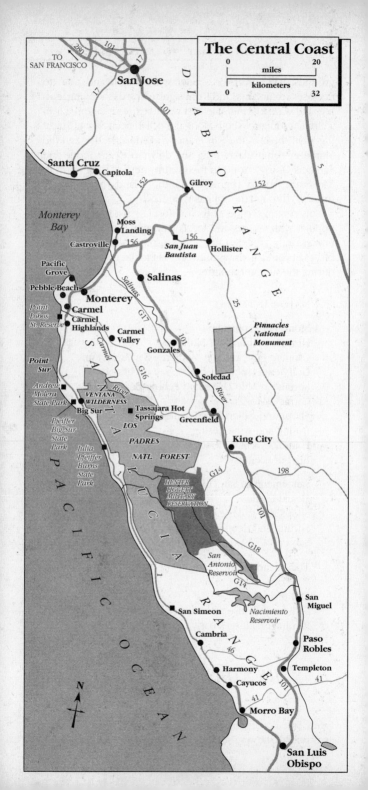

and traffic on the two-lane road north of Santa Cruz is often congested (see Day Trips From San Francisco for the coast from San Francisco down to Santa Cruz). A faster and equally scenic route is from San Jose across the heavily forested Santa Cruz Mountains on State Highway 17, which meets Highway 1 in Santa Cruz, about 80 miles south of San Francisco and 43 miles north of Monterey.

Santa Cruz

In 1791 Spanish priests founded Santa Cruz Mission on the north end of Monterey Bay to convert the Ohlone Indians who lived in the area; only a replica of the Mission's chapel remains. A hundred years later, the town blossomed into a popular beach resort with a boardwalk, casino, and Victorian mansions along the shore. The **Santa Cruz Beach Boardwalk** still exists—complete with its landmark 1911 merry-go-round and its Giant Dipper roller coaster—the sole survivor among California's old-time seaside amusement parks. Unfortunately, many historic buildings in the downtown area did not survive the earthquake of 1989, which hit Santa Cruz particularly hard, but one of the city's weirdest attractions remains: **The Mystery Spot**, at 1953 North Branciforte Drive, where, by deceptive construction, the laws of gravity are seemingly reversed—balls roll uphill and the like; daily tours are conducted.

If you want to tarry a while in the area, consider a visit to **Roaring Camp** in nearby Felton, a re-creation of a 19th-century logging town where you can ride through the redwoods in a steam-powered narrow-gauge railroad (Tel: 408-335-4484). Or, enjoy Santa Cruz's many facilities for pier and deep-sea fishing; **Stagnaro's Fishing Trips** at the Municipal Wharf offers daily seven-hour excursions. Tel: (408) 425-7003. You'll also find fine beaches here and in the nearby resorts of Aptos and Capitola. (Capitola is the site of the **Antonelli Begonia Gardens**, at 2545 Capitola Road, whose blooms reach their peak in late summer.)

Santa Cruz is also an important center for the performing arts. Of note are **Shakespeare Santa Cruz**, a company based at the University of California campus here whose year-round performances are highlighted by a six-week summer festival (Tel: 408-459-2121), and the **Cabrillo Music Festival**, an internationally acclaimed two-week event in July, which features classical and serious contemporary music (Tel: 408-662-2701).

For an overnight stay in Santa Cruz, your best choices

include two bed-and-breakfast inns: **Chateau Victorian**, a beautifully restored and tastefully decorated Victorian near the boardwalk, and the **Babbling Brook Inn**, a wooded retreat beside a waterfall and creek; decorated in frilly country style, most of its rooms have decks and Franklin-type stoves.

For dinner or a weekend brunch, one local favorite is romantic **Shadowbrook**, at 1750 Wharf Road in Capitola, which, located beside a small river at the base of a cliff, is reached by funicular; Tel: 475-1511. A fine place for lunch is **The Farm**, 5555 Soquel Drive; this complex, set among extensive gardens, includes a restaurant with outdoor patio dining and several little shops.

Below Santa Cruz, Highway 1 becomes freeway for a while, then narrows as it winds along the shore of Monterey Bay past the fishing village of **Moss Landing**; consider a stop here for antiques hunting, for lunch at the **Moss Landing Oyster Bar**, or for bird-watching at **Elkhorn Slough**, a 1,300-acre wildlife sanctuary. Beyond town the road crosses the artichoke fields of Castroville and finally skims along the sand dunes past the army base of Fort Ord to Monterey, a 40-mile drive in total.

MONTEREY

The various communities of the Monterey Peninsula–Big Sur area are bound only by their proximity—in looks and character, each is as different from the others as a family of adopted children: in order going down the coast, historic Monterey, flaunting its Spanish-Mexican heritage; modest Pacific Grove, in the process of shedding its prim Victorian upbringing; stately Pebble Beach, looking down its aristocratic nose at the others; quaint Carmel, clinging to its image as a picturesque artists' colony; chic Carmel Valley, fighting the encroachment of suburbia; and the renegade child Big Sur, basking in its isolation and bohemian tradition.

Throughout the year, numerous cultural and athletic events occur on the Monterey Peninsula; for a calendar, write to the Monterey Peninsula Chamber of Commerce, P.O. Box 1770, Monterey, CA 93942. On your arrival in the area, pick up a free copy of the *Monterey Peninsula Entertainment & Dining Review* for a comprehensive listing of what's happening that week.

Nestled along the hilly southern shore of Monterey Bay, the

town of Monterey flourished as the political, economic, and cultural capital of Alta California under Spanish-Mexican rule (1770 to 1846), when San Francisco was scarcely more than a village. The wealthy *rancheros* built their homes here, as did the Yankee sea captains and merchants who made fortunes trading at the bustling seaport. In *Two Years Before the Mast* (1835), Richard Henry Dana described Monterey as "decidedly the pleasantest and most civilized-looking place in California." But under U.S. rule in the latter half of the 19th century, Monterey declined: The state capital was moved north, eventually to Sacramento, and San Francisco became the major port of entry. After the turn of the century the town was revived by a thriving fishing industry and then immortalized by John Steinbeck in *Cannery Row,* but the sardines have long since departed and tourism is now the mainstay of Monterey.

Old Monterey

The best way to get a historical perspective of Monterey is along the Path of History Walking Tour, a self-guided, two-mile itinerary marked by golden tiles set in the sidewalk and plaques at some 40 historic sites. Many of these adobe structures are now operated as museums with regular guided tours; during the summer actors portray historic characters in some of them. Many of them are associated with the **Monterey Historic Park**, which puts out maps, brochures, and booklets describing the route that can be picked up or purchased at Pacific House on Custom House Plaza near Fisherman's Wharf (see below) and also appear in many tourist-oriented magazines here. (For more information, Tel: 408-649-2836.) Following, in quasi-chronological order, are some highlights.

Monterey's oldest building, **The Royal Chapel**, marks the site of the mission and presidio (fort) that Father Junípero Serra and Don Gaspar de Portola founded in 1770, as Spain's second outpost (after San Diego) on the California coast; the following year Serra moved the mission to Carmel. Mexican and Indian craftsmen built the present chapel in 1795 to replace an earlier structure destroyed by fire.

In 1822 Mexico won its independence from Spain and encouraged foreign trade with Alta California, making Monterey the official port of entry. The Mexicans collected the lucrative port duties at a waterfront **Custom House**, which now displays items from a typical ship's cargo of the 1830s. Richard Henry Dana described his own ship's store as "everything that can be imagined. From Chinese fireworks to English cart wheels . . ." For an in-depth view of this seafaring era, stop at the **Allen Knight Maritime Museum**, which exhibits nautical art and artifacts, along with ship models and Chinese junks.

The new California trade attracted Yankees, who built two-story, balconied adobe homes during the 1830s and 1840s in a beguiling blend of New England and Spanish architecture, now known as Monterey Colonial. One of the best examples is the **Larkin House** (now a museum), built by New Englander Thomas Oliver Larkin, who became a wealthy merchant and United States consul to California. Another notable home of this era is the **Cooper-Molera Adobe**, built by Larkin's half-brother, a sea captain and trader known as Juan Bautista Cooper, who adopted Mexican citizenship and married the sister of General Vallejo. Exhibits in the house and gardens depict life in 19th-century Monterey. **Casa Soberanes** is called the House with the Blue Gate, another handsome adobe that is furnished with a mix of modern Mexican folk art and pieces from New England and the China trade. An 1840s residence has been renamed **The Stevenson House** because an impoverished and not-yet-famous Robert Louis Stevenson rented a room here in 1879 while courting his future wife, Fanny Osbourne, and writing his essay "The Old Pacific Capital." Today the house serves as a museum of Stevenson memorabilia.

Mexican rule of California came to a halt on July 7, 1846, when Commodore John Drake Sloat of the U.S. Navy raised the Stars and Stripes over the Monterey Custom House. California was administered by U.S. military governors until the new state's constitution was drafted and signed in 1849 at **Colton Hall**, now a historical museum. Also on the property is the **Old Monterey Jail**, which Steinbeck fans will recognize as the spot frequented by Big Joe in *Tortilla Flat*. In 1847 the Yankees erected **Pacific House** for the army quartermaster corps and held Sunday bull-and-bear fights in the rear walled garden. Later this large adobe was used for such disparate purposes as a tavern and headquarters of a temperance society; today it displays exhibits of California's history and Native American artifacts. In the same period, **California's First Theater** was built as a boardinghouse and tavern, and in 1850 a group of U.S. Army officers started staging plays here. The theater was reopened in 1937, and 19th-century melodramas are still performed regularly.

The mercantile center of Monterey in the 1850s was

Joseph Boston and Company, later known as the **Casa del Oro** because of the gold supposedly stashed away in its safe. One of its employees in those days was a canny young Scotsman named David Jacks, who wound up owning the store—and most of Monterey County—when he and a partner purchased town lots and thousands of surrounding acres at a city auction in 1859—for $1,002.50. Jacks, however, might be best known for his marketing of Monterey Jack, the cheese made by his tenant farmers. **The Boston Store** now sells items representative of that heyday as well as dried herbs from its garden.

In the heart of old Monterey, but not listed on the Path of History tour, is the **Monterey Peninsula Museum of Art**, 559 Pacific, where collections and exhibits focus on the art of California, Asia, and the Pacific Rim, as well as international folk and tribal art. At the **Castro Adobe**, the museum also displays work by regional artists as well as decorative arts.

Fisherman's Wharf

To handle the heavy traffic of trading ships, Monterey built a new pier across from the Custom House in 1846. In the 1850s this wharf was home to whaling ships and later to commercial fishing vessels, which now dock at the nearby Municipal Wharf, leaving the old wharf to tourists. But even if you're turned off by the predictable array of curio shops, there are several good reasons for a stop here: One is the din of barking sea lions and seals who hang out near the end of the pier; you can buy fish to feed them at nearby stalls.

Surprisingly, you can also feed yourself well on the wharf, another good reason to stop here. Try **Café Fina**, an upscale new eatery, for grilled seafood, seafood pastas, and pizzas. Lovers of squid should check out **Abalonetti**, an old-time favorite that fixes calamari in every imaginable way. Near the wharf—but a world away in atmosphere—is one of Monterey's finest dinner houses: **Fresh Cream**, a quiet, intimate restaurant in the Heritage Harbor building at 99 Pacific offers light French fare based on seasonal ingredients. Reservations are advised; Tel: 375-9798.

Back on the pier: **The Wharf Theater** draws on local talent to stage productions several nights a week; these are mostly musicals ranging from *Cabaret* to Gilbert and Sullivan classics; Tel: (408) 649-2332. Across the street from the wharf, in the Custom House Plaza, **Monterey Bay Theatrefest** presents a seven-week midsummer festival of free entertainment: live music, clown troupes, poetry readings, improvisational theater, intermezzo opera, light comedy, and more. These productions are sponsored by **Grove-Mont Theater**, which stages avant-garde plays year round at its Arts Center at 320 Hoffman; Tel: (408) 649-6852.

Cannery Row

John Steinbeck would be horrified by much that has happened to his beloved Cannery Row, just half a mile west of Fisherman's Wharf. From the early 1900s until the 1950s the great silver sardine boom was a boon to Monterey's economy, reaching its apex in 1945's catch of 235,000 tons. When the sardines vanished, the hulking canneries along the waterfront shut down, later to reopen as honky-tonk shopping complexes, catering primarily to collectors of flashy tee-shirts and plastic porpoises; there's even a wax museum. Amid the hurly-burly, however, nostalgia buffs will discover a few gems such as the handcrafted turn-of-the-century carousel in the **Edgewater Packing Company** complex; behind this cannery a wealth of railroad memorabilia awaits collectors at **The Caboose**. Some of the former canneries also house tasting rooms for Monterey County wines, where you can sip the varietals of the Monterey Peninsula Winery, Bargetto, and Paul Masson. Steinbeck might still recognize a few of his old haunts: The building at 800 Cannery Row was the Pacific Biological Laboratories of his real-life friend and fictional hero "Doc" Edward Ricketts; the Old General Store across the street was Lee Chong's Heavenly Flower Grocery; and the structure that is now the Cannery Row Antique Warehouse was cast as a bordello in several Steinbeck novels.

Steinbeck and Ricketts probably would approve of Cannery Row's biggest attraction: the **Monterey Bay Aquarium**, which draws nearly two million visitors annually. Located in a multi-million dollar reconstruction of the former Howden Cannery, the aquarium is home to 6,500 specimens of marine life, representing 525 species of fish, mammals, birds, and plants whose natural habitat is the two-mile-deep canyon under Monterey Bay. Notable among the exhibits are a 28-foot-high kelp forest (the world's tallest aquarium exhibit), re-creations of Monterey Bay marine habitats, and a 55,000-gallon tank where you can observe the antics of the resident sea otters. These adorable creatures, once preyed upon for their valuable pelts, were believed to be extinct until they mysteriously reappeared along the Central Coast in 1938. Within the aquarium is the **Portola Café**, which combines a cafeteria and a full-service restaurant with a splendid bay view.

A block above Cannery Row, on Wave Street, two rather pricey dinner houses evoke the area's robust past. Especially appealing for its turn-of-the-century nautical atmosphere is the Captain's Room of the **Sardine Factory**, which specializes in foods of the area prepared with an Italian flair; Tel: 373-3775. Mesquite-grilled fresh seafood is the forte of **Whaling Station Inn**, which occupies a former Chinese grocery store of the Steinbeck era; Tel: 373-3778.

Staying in Monterey

Monterey has no dearth of places to stay: Most of the major hotel chains are represented, and a string of moderately priced motels lines Munras Avenue. But many discriminating—and well-heeled—travellers opt for **Old Monterey Inn**, a Tudor mansion set in lush gardens on a wooded hillside above the town. You'll find neither television sets nor telephones in the ten exquisitely decorated bedrooms, just heaps of reading material, fireplaces, skylights, canopied beds, and garden views. A lavish breakfast is served on the patio or in the formal dining room.

There is one exceedingly romantic spot on Cannery Row: **Spindrift Inn**, a small luxury hotel that echoes a pre-cannery epoch, when this beach area was a seaside resort. Wood-burning fireplaces and views of the hills or the bay grace the elegant rooms, as do European antiques and Oriental rugs. Breakfast in bed on a silver tray? Of course. If you prefer a homey bed and breakfast to a hotel, consider **The Jabberwock**, a towered and turreted former convent with a charming garden, on the hillside above Cannery Row. Named after the poem from Lewis Carroll's *Alice in Wonderland,* the hotel carries the poem's themes throughout the inn—from breakfast, which might include "razzleberry flabjous," to a volume of the famous work next to your bed.

Exploring Shore, Sea, and Air

Monterey is a pedaler's paradise: A fine bicycle path runs along the edge of the bay, with bike rental shops en route. On Cannery Row try **Bay Bikes**, at 640 Wave, which also rents mountain and tandem bikes, bicycles built for two, and four-wheel surreys; Tel: 646-9090. Over at 299 Cannery Row, **Adventures by the Sea** rents bikes (with free hotel pickup and delivery), as well as roller skates and kayaks. Its kayak tours are a novel way to see the waterfront by sea—don't be surprised if a friendly otter jumps on your lap or a harbor seal escorts you back to shore; Tel: 372-1807. And if you want a look under the sea, **Aquarius Dive Shop**, 2240 Del Monte Avenue, provides skin- and scuba-diving instruction, tours, and equipment rentals; Tel: 375-1933.

More conventional seagoing tours are found at sport-fishing outlets based near the end of Fisherman's Wharf. Year-round deep-sea fishing and winter whale-watching cruises can be booked at **Monterey Sport Fishing**, Tel: (408) 372-2203, and **Randy's Fishing and Whale-Watching Trips**, Tel: (408) 372-7440. On weekends Randy's also conducts two-hour sea-life tours narrated by naturalists.

Western Hang Gliders, on the sands at the town of Marina, offers hang-gliding lessons northeast of Monterey. Reservations and payment are required 24 hours in advance; Tel: (408) 384-2622. If that's a bit too adventurous, you can still enjoy the beautiful breezes at the weekend kite flies on the dunes near Monterey, organized by **Windborne Kites**, 585 Cannery Row; call (408) 373-7422 for a schedule. Windborne will happily sell you a kite or windsock from its inventory of more than 500 models, but even kiteless participants can usually find kiters willing to lend one of theirs.

Jazz in Monterey

The mammoth musical event in this part of the world is the **Monterey Jazz Festival**, where Oscar Peterson, Dizzy Gillespie, and the Pancho Sanchez Latin Band have appeared on the same program in recent years. Held each September, the festival sells tickets only for the entire three-day package, with a June deadline for orders: P.O. Box Jazz, Monterey, CA 93942; Tel: (408) 373-3366. Less structured is **Dixieland Monterey**, a three-day festival held the first weekend in March, when roughly a dozen bands converge to play in various hotels and cabarets. Beyond these events, on any night of the year some form of pop music—from swing to rock—can be heard in the clubs of Cannery Row and at Monterey's hotels.

PACIFIC GROVE

In marked contrast to the Roman-Catholic roots and bawdy seafaring past of Monterey, the heritage of neighboring Pacific Grove, to the west, of Monterey, is puritanically Protestant. The town was founded just west of Monterey in the 1870s as a Methodist campground on acreage donated by land baron David Jacks, whose deed prohibited gambling or consumption of alcohol on the property, and who also contributed some $30,000 toward its improvement—about 30 times what he had paid in 1859 for the entire city of Monterey. In 1879 Pacific Grove became the site of the first Chautauqua Assembly in the western United States, an annual gathering for summer education until the outbreak of World War I. During these decades, many Victorian mansions were built as boardinghouses for conference goers; other vacationers built elaborate summer homes along the rocky shore.

If you come to Pacific Grove for no other reason, at least drive or cycle along **Ocean View Boulevard** around the rim of the peninsula, where you'll catch glimpses of sea otters, seals, and, in winter months, perhaps a migrating whale. From Monterey's Cannery Row, the road heads west, passing Stanford University's Hopkins Marine Station on China Point, once the home of a large Chinese community and the location of Chin Kee's Squid Yard in Steinbeck's *Sweet Thursday*. From here the road leads past Pacific Grove's Victorian mansions to **Lighthouse Point Park** where a small cove shelters one of the area's few safe swimming beaches. In winter look for the swarms of monarch butterflies that migrate annually to Pacific Grove.

To learn more about them and other wildlife, detour into town to the **Pacific Grove Museum of Natural History**, at 165 Forest Avenue, which was founded by the Chautauqua Assembly in 1881. Nearby, at 222 Central, the headquarters of the **John Steinbeck Arthurian Society** are located in a Victorian house that belonged to the author's grandparents; he built and lived in the cottage next door during the 1930s. In both buildings Steinbeck memorabilia mingle with objects relating to the King Arthur legends that fascinated him throughout his life; for tour information, call (408) 373-6976.

Beyond town Ocean View Boulevard swings around Point Pinos Lighthouse, the state's oldest continuously operated beacon. Here the road becomes Sunset Drive to cross the sand dunes of **Asilomar State Beach**—a fine spot for picnicking or observing marine life in the tidal pools. At the end of the beach, among pines and cypress, is **Asilomar Conference Center**, an architectural gem you should not overlook. Julia Morgan (the architect of Hearst Castle) designed the older buildings from 1913 to 1928 in a woodsy arts-and-crafts style for YWCA conferences. Now owned by the state, Asilomar is still used for meetings, but independent travellers also can book budget-priced rooms; the furnishings are spartan, but the wooded seaside setting is glorious.

Many Victorian houses in Pacific Grove have been converted to bed-and-breakfast inns. Two of the loveliest, **The Green Gables Inn** and **The Gosby House Inn**, are owned and meticulously operated by the Post family, who make sure you are treated to all the extras: fresh flowers and fruit in your room; pretty, frilly furnishings; and wine and hors d'oeuvres in the afternoon. Built in the 1880s, both inns have fireplaces in most rooms, and Green Gables has a dazzling view of the bay.

For most of this century, David Jacks's prohibition of the ingestion of alcohol in Pacific Grove inhibited the growth of restaurants, but after the ruling's repeal some restaurants began to attract diners from throughout the Monterey area. Here are three of the newest among an abundance of choices: **Central 1-5-9**, at 159 Central Avenue, occupies a small bungalow with a fireplace and, from some tables, a view of Monterey Bay. The California-style cooking of chef-owner David Beckwith is creative and original, with dishes on an ever-changing menu ranging from crab cakes with jicama "slaw" to grilled rabbit served with polenta and hoisin sauce; Tel: 372-2235. At **Melac's**, 663 Lighthouse Avenue, French-born Jacques Melac and his Cordon Bleu–trained wife, Janet, offer a lively menu that is basically French, with Latin and Asian overtones. The presentation of the food is as picture-pretty as the mirrored, flowery setting; Tel: 375-1743. Finally, **Fandango**, at 223 17th Street, emulates a country *auberge*—stone fireplace, bouquets of flowers—and serves a mix of Mediterranean fare from paella to cassoulet to cannelloni; Tel: 373-0588.

PEBBLE BEACH

A mention of Pebble Beach evokes many images: the wind-swept Lone Cypress on its isolated perch on the shore, the storybook homes of the very rich along the Seventeen Mile Drive, and some of the world's most challenging golf. But Pebble Beach's gilt-edged present was begotten in a humble past. The 5,300 acres of Del Monte Forest, on the southwest tip of the Monterey Peninsula (now owned by the Pebble Beach Company) southwest of Monterey and Pacific Grove, were once part of the ubiquitous David Jacks's holdings until

1898, when he sold the property for five dollars an acre to Southern Pacific Railroad's Pacific Improvement Company, which grazed its cattle there. At the turn of the century Southern Pacific built a rustic log lodge on the pebbled beach of Stillwater Cove. Chinese fishermen harvested abalone where Southern Pacific built this beach retreat for vacationers at S.P.'s swank Del Monte Hotel in Monterey—a 17-mile excursion over dirt roads.

Samuel F. B. Morse (grandnephew of the telegraph inventor) forged the destiny of so-called Pebble Beach by buying Del Monte Forest. In 1919 he built the Pebble Beach Golf Links along Stillwater Cove, as well as the most lavish showplace of the era: Del Monte Lodge, now known as **The Lodge at Pebble Beach.** Recently renovated, the lodge is still every bit the grand resort of yesteryear; its traditionally furnished rooms have wood-burning fireplaces, private balconies or terraces, and picture-postcard views across the cove to Carmel and Point Lobos. (Less expensive rooms face the forest.) But if you don't care to exchange your family jewels for a room here, you can still experience the mystique of Pebble Beach at tea by the massive fireplaces in the lobby or with a drink or sandwich in the club-like **Tap Room**, where photos of golf's greats peer down from the walls. Of several restaurants at the Lodge, the best is **Club XIX.** This intimate French spot is formal and a bit stuffy at night, but it's terrific for lunch, when less expensive bistro-style fare is served informally on a terrace above the fabled 18th hole of the Pebble Beach links; Tel: 624-3811.

The only other place to stay within Del Monte Forest is **The Inn at Spanish Bay**, the Pebble Beach Company's large new resort complex beside the sand dunes on the northwest edge of the forest. It is slightly more affordable than the lodge; a stay at the Inn still allows you to use all of the lodge facilities. The rooms are decorated in a contemporary style and are equipped with gas-burning fireplaces, wet bars, and decks or balconies. Rates are based on the view—there's a $100 difference between the rooms overlooking the ocean and those by the parking lot. Spanish Bay has several restaurants with ocean views, including **The Dunes**, which serves breakfast, lunch, and dinner on an oceanfront terrace and in a glass-walled dining room. But the culinary jewel is **The Bay Club**, which turns out memorable northern Italian dinners with some most creative touches: calamari vinaigrette served in a radicchio cup, saffron risotto with lobster, and spinach cannelloni with a basil-salmon stuffing, to name a few. The check will be big, but so will the pleasure; Tel: 647-7500.

Guests at the Pebble Beach Resorts may use the athletic facilities at two private clubs, which have tennis courts, large swimming pools, and full fitness centers.

Sports at Pebble Beach

Golf, of course, is king at Pebble Beach, and the reigning monarch is **Pebble Beach Golf Links**, which many regard as the world's premier public course for its cliffside fairways and holes at the water's edge. But golfers pay a king's ransom to play here—well over $150, including greens fees and mandatory cart or caddy. Substantial discounts and preferential tee times, however, are granted to guests at the Pebble Beach Resorts, as well as at the company's other less expensive championship courses: **Spyglass Hill Golf Course** near Seal Rock and the new **Links at Spanish Bay**. Reservations for all courses are advised; Tel: (408) 624-3811. The Pebble Beach Company also owns the **Del Monte Golf Course** in Monterey, where the fees are about one-third of the charge at the least expensive courses in Del Monte Forest; Tel: (408) 373-2436. Also open to the public in Del Monte Forest is the championship 18-hole **Poppy Hills Golf Course**; Tel: (408) 625-2035. Many golf tournaments are held at Pebble Beach throughout the year, but the granddaddy of them all is the famous **AT&T National Pro Am** (formerly the Crosby), which pairs top pros with political and show-biz celebrities each January.

Pebble Beach is also a haven for the horsey set. **The Pebble Beach Equestrian Center** (Tel: 408-624-2756) conducts trail rides daily through Del Monte Forest and periodically sponsors horse shows and dressage shows, and **Collins Polo Field** is the site of some major meets. Other annual events at Pebble Beach include dog shows, rugby matches, and regattas at Stillwater Cove, but since 1950 one of the biggest draws has been the **Concours d'Elegance**, an August conclave of vintage and classic cars plus classy imports at the lodge; a new highlight is a Christie's auction of rare antique autos.

The Seventeen Mile Drive

This scenic drive winds along the rocky shores of Del Monte Forest from Pacific Grove to Carmel. Visitors are charged an admission fee (and given an annotated map), but the fee will be refunded if you eat at one of the Pebble Beach Resorts along the drive or pick up picnic makings at the **Company Store** behind the lodge.

From the Pacific Grove gate and Spanish Bay the road follows the edge of several private golf courses (including ultraexclusive Cypress Point). Along the way are the **seal and bird rocks**, home to numerous shore birds and herds of sea lions and harbor seals. There is a picnic area here and at Spanish Bay. From here you'll reach Cypress Point Lookout; gawk at the view down the coast to Point Sur Lighthouse 20 miles south. Along the coast are the famous cypress trees, which Robert Louis Stevenson described as "ghosts fleeing before the wind." From here you'll pass palatial seaside villas, most of which were designed in the 1920s by leading architects of the era, including Bernard Maybeck, Julia Morgan, and Palm Beach's Addison Mizner, in styles from Byzantine and Romanesque to Spanish Colonial Revival. You'll also see the lodge and the public swimming beach at Stillwater Cove.

CARMEL-BY-THE-SEA

Every nook and cranny of this wooded village, just west off Highway 1 south of Monterey, or at the south end of 17 Mile Drive, whose picturesque architecture ranges from Mediterranean to Hansel and Gretel, seems to be crammed with quaint cottages and inns, eateries, shops, and galleries—and with visitors. It's hard to imagine that only 90 years ago Carmel was just a stretch of windswept sand dunes south of Pebble Beach waiting to be developed. At that time the Mission (see below) had been abandoned, leaving only a few farms near the Carmel River. Then, at the dawn of the 20th century, land developers started selling lots on the dunes for $250 apiece. One of the first takers was poet George Sterling, who built a bungalow here in 1905 and soon was joined by many of his literary cronies. Mary Austin, Jack London, Upton Sinclair, Sinclair Lewis, and many lesser-known or never-known writers and artists were among the members of the "Carmel Colony." But this bit of bohemia already was breaking up in 1910 when the *Los Angeles Times* headlined a spoof on Carmel: "Hotbed of Soulful Culture ... the Most Amazing Colony on Earth." After the literary heavies had fled Carmel, however, a number of major writers and artists settled here in later years, among them Lincoln Steffens, Robinson Jeffers, Edward Weston, and Ansel Adams.

Today Carmel carefully preserves its artsy-craftsy village-like character with strict ordinances. Neither high buildings nor glitzy signs—not even street numbers—mar the landscape, and no buses are allowed in town. For a scenic overview, drive or cycle down Ocean Avenue, the flower-bedecked main street, to the cypress-edged white sand dunes above Carmel Beach. From here Scenic Road, paralleled by a bike path, leads south on a bluff above the beach with no obstructions on the seaward side except **The Walker House**, a low-slung stone residence designed by Frank Lloyd Wright. Just beyond, at Carmel Point, is **Tor House**, the stone cottage and adjacent Medieval-looking tower that Robinson Jeffers built in 1918. Until his death in 1962, he wrote most of his major works here, including his play *Medea*. Tours of the house are conducted on Fridays and Saturdays by reservation only; Tel: (408) 624-1813. Around the point the road clings to the cliffs, then leads by Carmel River State Beach, a lagoon, and a bird sanctuary before reaching the Mission.

Carmel Mission

Mission San Carlos Borromeo del Río Carmel is the second oldest, and unquestionably the most important, of California's missions. In 1771 Spanish-born priest Junípero Serra moved this mission from Monterey to the fertile lands at the mouth of the Carmel River. This became his home, and from here he and his successors established the string of 21 Franciscan missions that stretches—each a day's foot-journey apart—from San Diego to Sonoma; thus Carmel became known as the Mother Mission. Father Serra lived here until his death in 1784 and is buried in the church (now a basilica). In 1988, after visiting here, Pope John Paul II beatified Serra, the final step before his canonization as a saint.

The original wooden Mission buildings were gradually replaced with adobe; the present sandstone church with its Moorish tower was completed in 1797, when the Mission reached the height of its prosperity with a Christianized Indian population of over 900. Then, in 1834, Mexico abruptly secularized the missions and civil officials granted most of the lands (which Spain, before Mexico became independent, had intended to return to the Indians) to favored friends of the government. The Carmel Mission was abandoned and gradually collapsed into ruins. Although attempts at preservation were made, serious renovation did not begin until 1931 when Harry Downie, a Catholic layman, became curator of the restoration—a project that lasted 50 years.

Today you should plan to loiter a while. Enter through a lovely courtyard, which is filled with flowers, cacti, and larger-than-life statues of saints, to the interior of the church, where a vaulted stone ceiling and carved altar tower over Serra's tomb. Museum exhibits are devoted to the history of the area and the Mission; of special interest are the re-creations of the padres' living quarters: dining room, library, kitchen, and the cell-like room where Serra lived in ascetic simplicity.

Shopping on Ocean Avenue

As a shoppers' mecca, only San Francisco outranks Carmel in Northern California. Conveniently, most of the town's myriad shops and galleries are located along a five-block stretch of Ocean Avenue (from Junípero to Monte Verde) and its side streets; here you will find plenty of high-quality and unusual collectibles, clothing, antiques, jewelry, artwork, crafts—you name it—from all over the world. What follows is a mere sampling.

At the head of Ocean Avenue, **Carmel Plaza** houses branches of many major stores: I. Magnin, Peck & Peck, Saks Fifth Avenue, Banana Republic, Laura Ashley, and Brentano's Bookstore. In between are some smaller shops like **Thinker Toys** (just what it says) and **Mickey and Friends** (Donald, Minnie, et al.).

A stroll down Ocean Avenue leads to some fine clothing stores: **Derek Rayne, Ltd.** (Carmel's oldest shop with a classy and classic selection for men and women), **Scotch House** (sweaters from Scotland), and **Hilda, Ltd.** (knitwear from Iceland). Custom-made cotton clothing in prints from Provence is the forte of **The French Collection**, along with provincial accessories for wardrobe and home. Even more awaits Francophiles at **Pierre Deux** (French country clothing, fabrics, tablewear, bedding, and such). For cookware check out **Carmel Bay Company** (which also carries gifts and posters) and **Dansk II** (a factory outlet that handles the full Dansk line at substantial discounts). Ocean Avenue haunts for collectibles include **Quilts, Ltd.** (handmade American patchworks, plus quilted apparel and gifts), **The Impulse Shoppes** (miniatures, dollhouse furnishings and accessories), and **Kris Kringle of Carmel** (bewitching ornaments, Santas, stockings, illuminated villages, and the like).

Prowl the side streets for more boutiques, many tucked into little arcades south of Ocean Avenue. Worthy of stops on San Carlos are **The Owl's Nest** (a tiny shop brimming with a huge menagerie of artist-made teddy bears), **Joan Winters Boutique,** (handmade beaded, sequined, and feathered gowns), and **Lockwood Antiques** (classic, elegant

pieces from England). A block down on Dolores look for
Conway of Asia (two bazaars full of Oriental rugs, furnishings, jewelry, and objets d'art), and **Gepetto's Workshop**
(fanciful toys for kids of all ages). Lincoln Avenue holds
even more treasures: **Anderlé Gallery** (a discriminating
collection of primitive and Far Eastern art, wall hangings,
and furnishings), **Peter Rabbit & Friends** (clothing, stuffed
animals, china, silver, and books for the friends of Beatrix
Potter), **Carousel of Carmel** (paintings, etchings, music
boxes, posters, and full-size horses for merry-go-round
fanciers), and **Carmel Doll Shop** (antique French and German china-headed dolls, Storybook and Madame Alexander
dolls, old-fashioned puppets, paper dolls, and teddy bears).

Fewer shops are located on the side streets north of
Ocean Avenue. On Mission **Koala Blue** carries bold, colorful
apparel from Australia. On San Carlos **For Car Buffs** sells
everything car lovers might crave, from automotive accessories to posters and jewelry. On Dolores a duffer's dream is
Village Golf Shop, for knickers and other clothing, golfing
gifts and equipment.

The streets north of Ocean Avenue hold many of Carmel's
art and crafts galleries. A good start for a gallery tour is the
Carmel Art Association Galleries, on Dolores near Fifth,
where works by more than 100 local professionals are
exhibited in eight rooms. You can also pick up a copy of the
Carmel Gallery Guide here, which describes the type of
work (from Neo-Impressionist to contemporary to copies of
Old Masters) shown in over 60 galleries, both in town and in
Carmel Valley. Some highlights on or near Dolores include
First Impressions (watercolors, etchings, posters, and wood-
cuts of noted contemporary artists), **Cheppu from Himalaya**
(artifacts, clothing, and jewelry from Tibet, Nepal, and
Sikkim), and **Handworks** (jewelry, ceramics, glassware, weav-
ing, and furniture by more than 300 American craftspeople).
Not to be missed are **The Photography West Gallery** and the
Weston Gallery, which display the work of such distin-
guished photographers as Edward and Brett Weston and
Ansel Adams.

Dining in Carmel

For a picnic, tote your basket to the following food stores
and take cash; none accepts credit cards. You'll find most
everything you need at **Mediterranean Market**; located at
Ocean and Mission, this superb deli, grocery, and wine shop
has a fine selection of sandwiches, cheeses, cold meats (even

prosciutto from Parma), and seafood, pasta, and fruit salads. For crusty sourdough bread and luscious pastries, head down Ocean to **Monterey Baking Company**; an adjoining deli sells croissant sandwiches. And just down the street the New York–style **Dilli Deli** puts together a huge selection of hearty sandwiches.

If you need a lunch or teatime break during a shopping spree, make your way down Dolores, south of Ocean, to ye olde English tearoom, the tiny **Tuck Box**, which is justifiably famous for its scones, muffins, and homemade jams and marmalades. You can buy a terrific breakfast here, too, but expect to wait in line. From morning through teatime, **Patisserie Boissiere**, in Carmel Plaza, indulges with Belgian waffles, fruit-filled crepes, sandwiches, and a dazzling array of French pastries.

For alfresco meals at any time, a top choice is the patio at **Casanova**, a charming bistro serving the foods of Italy and France, at Fifth near Mission. Another spot for breakfast, lunch (on the terrace), or dinner is the **Spyglass Restaurant**, at La Playa Hotel (see below). Under the aegis of chef Bryan Carr, a star on the rise, Spyglass now offers some of Carmel's most creative cooking, although it remains based on classic technique. A buffet brunch on Sunday is a big event here; for reservations, call (408) 624-4010. The Monterey Peninsula is not noted for its Asian food, but for lunch or dinner, **Shabu Shabu**, in Carmel Plaza, offers with the romantic atmosphere of a Japanese country inn and traditional one-pot dishes cooked at your table; Tel: 625-2828.

Carmel's better dinner houses tend to be French or Italian, intimate, and fairly expensive; reservations are advised. A local classic for Italian cooking is **Raffaello**, the enterprise of a distinguished family of Florentine restaurateurs. Remo d'Agliano is host and his mother, now in her 70s, is in charge of the kitchen, turning out homemade pastas and *secondi piatti* such as garlicky prawns and tangy veal piccata. The dining room, at Mission south of Ocean, is quite formal, and jackets are required; Tel: 624-1541. At Fifth and Junípero, you'll find French haute cuisine at **The French Poodle**, owned and operated for some 30 years by Michele and Marc Vedrines. In the candlelit dining room, there's taped classical music, illuminated oil paintings, and a menu that goes by the book—Escoffier's; Tel: 624-8643. **Creme Carmel**, at San Carlos and 7th, offers a more contemporary approach to French dining. The decor in the narrow, wood-ceilinged dining room is low key, with mostly banquette seating and a smattering of graphics on the wall, and the cooking of owner-chef Craig Ling is decidedly Franco-Californian, with light sauces and many daily specials to reflect the seasonal bounty (Tel: 624-0444).

Hotels and Inns of Carmel

In most vacation locales only a few places stand out as exceptional among a run-of-the-mill gaggle of look-alike motels and hotels. Not so in Carmel—each of the 50-plus lodging places here is distinctive, with not a single carbon-copy branch of a chain in the lot. The diversity of these accommodations, plus the town's central location in the hub of the Monterey Peninsula, make Carmel the base of choice for many visitors.

Carmel's oldest hostelry, **Pine Inn** opened in 1902 to attract prospective real-estate buyers. Located smack on Ocean Avenue, the hotel has grown to occupy most of a block, with shops, restaurants, and a cozy bar off its turn-of-the-century lobby. Though small, the moderately priced rooms in the original building mirror the Victorian spirit. **La Playa Hotel,** a small resort a few blocks from the beach, is the grande dame of Carmel hotels, with beautiful gardens surrounding a pool. (A massive face-lift in the 1980s rescued this place from a dowdy middle age.) But the rates—and the accommodations—are more modest than other luxury resorts on the Monterey Peninsula (about half the tariff at Pebble Beach). Request a room with a view of the bay, or, if you're travelling with a family or another couple, consider one of La Playa's newly renovated cottages. These have wood-burning fireplaces, private gardens, and more pizazz than the rooms in the hotel; most also have full kitchens.

Many budget-oriented travellers to Carmel favor historic **Mission Ranch**, a 20-acre resort (with tennis courts) overlooking a meadow of grazing sheep where Carmel River enters the bay. Purchased and spruced up in 1987 by former Carmel mayor Clint Eastwood, the ranch was once part of a large dairy farm; the original farmhouse now offers bed-and-breakfast accommodations. Outbuildings have been converted to housekeeping cottages with kitchenettes, some with views of Point Lobos. Room rates for these somewhat rustic units and other larger motel rooms include a Continental breakfast.

Breakfast is also included at the following small inns, as is afternoon wine or tea. At **Sea View Inn** the breakfast is served by candlelight in this 1920s Maybeck-style shingled house, which probably once had a view that is now blocked by pines.

The eight bedrooms (some with private baths and window seats tucked in alcoves) are decorated in country chic. In the center of the shopping area, **Cypress Inn**, also dating from the 1920s, might well be mistaken for the Mission because of its ornate tower and Moorish-Mediterranean façade; its 20 rooms cluster around a tiled, flower-banked courtyard and offer modern comforts such as TV, phones, and private baths. You'll also find these amenities in the rooms at **Cobblestone Inn**, along with fireplaces, refrigerators stocked with soft drinks, bowls of fruit, and flowery country furnishings.

North of Ocean Avenue, another small inn echoes Carmel's literary past. Don Blanding lived at **Vagabond's House** during the 1940s, although no one is certain if he wrote the poem of that name here. Nevertheless it's a poetic setting with rooms (most with fireplaces) overlooking a courtyard that's shaded by a giant gnarled oak and abloom with flowers. Guests are served breakfast here, and in turn can feed the battalion of squirrels that inhabits the tree.

All of the preceding small inns are located in the heart of Carmel village, an easy walk from the shops. Away from town at Carmel Point, **Sandpiper Inn At-the-Beach** is a favorite of visitors from abroad; the guest book of the multilingual owners shows names from over 70 countries. The inn is indeed at the beach, and many of the antiques-filled rooms offer fine bay views as well as fireplaces.

The Performing Arts in Carmel

The Monterey Peninsula's oldest and best-known musical event is the July **Bach Festival**. Concerts, recitals, lectures, and symposia relate not only to Bach but to other Baroque luminaries; even opera and ballet are included. The highlight of the festival is a candlelit concert in the Carmel Mission basilica; other performances are held at the Sunset Cultural Center. Book well in advance: P.O. Box 575, Carmel, CA 93921; Tel: (408) 624-3996.

The Monterey County Symphony also performs at Sunset, as do the Chamber Music Society and the Carmel Festival of Dance. Nearby, the open-air Forest Theater mounts productions that range from 20th-century plays to an autumn Shakespeare festival. For information on both theaters, call Sunset Cultural Center at (408) 624-3996. Finally, if your taste is Baroque and you miss the Bach Festival, check out **Hidden Valley Music Center** in Carmel Valley for year-round chamber music, opera, and dance performances; Tel: (408) 659-3115.

CARMEL VALLEY

East of the village of Carmel-by-the-Sea, the Carmel River flows from the Santa Lucia Mountains to the Pacific for a dozen miles through a long, narrow valley. The sun usually shines here on those many days when fog veils the coast, making Carmel Valley a desirable place to live and to visit. Among those who have built homes on the oak-studded hillsides are several émigrés from Hollywood: Doris Day, Clint Eastwood, and Merv Griffin. And the green turf of golf links—dotted with tennis courts and tiny lakes—now covers former dairy lands on the valley floor. Some of the golf and tennis centers are semiprivate clubs, but others are open to the public; check out the two 18-hole courses and modest greens fees at **Rancho Canada Golf Club** (Tel: 408-624-0111) and the tennis courts and fitness center at **Carmel Valley Racquet Club** (Tel: 408-624-2737).

Carmel Valley has also become a wine-producing area in the years since William Durney planted the first vineyards in the surrounding mountains in 1968 and started producing varietal wines in 1977. Although the Durney winery and several others in the area are not open to the public, **Chateau Julien** on Carmel Valley Road has become a major visitor's attraction. The winery's Swiss-style château is open daily for tasting of its award-winning varietals and for tours; Tel: (408) 624-2600.

The Barnyard and
The Crossroads

Don't dismiss as suburban sprawl the stretch of shopping malls and apartments along Highway 1 at the foot of the valley; tucked behind the parking lots are two of the peninsula's finest shopping centers. **The Barnyard**, in a garden setting, is a complex of rustic barn-like structures with over 50 shops and restaurants. Barnyard is also home to **Thunderbird Bookshop**, a giant that claims to have the greatest inventory on the West Coast and frequently hosts book-signing events. Within the shop a café offers soups, sandwiches, pastries, full lunches, and dinners—with outdoor seating, too. Another spot for an alfresco lunch is **Silver Jones**, which cooks up lively, eclectic California cuisine. The Barnyard's boutiques are a treasure trove of unusual jewelry, home accessories, tableware, fine arts, and collectibles. Meriting special mention are **Total Dog** (gifts for dogs, cats, and their owners), **Holly Berry** (handmade Christmas ornaments and miniatures), **Hudson & Company** (English riding apparel and tack, plus equestrian gifts), and **Succulent Gardens** (more than 500 cacti and other succulents, "living" wreaths made from succulents, innovative planters, and an extraordinary selection of wind chimes).

About 100 establishments occupy **The Crossroads**, which was built to resemble an English village with streets and mews bordered by trees and flowers. This is the locale of the **Rio Grill**, one of the peninsula's most popular eateries—and deservedly so. The ever-changing menu highlights the cooking of the American Southwest, with creative dishes such as quesadilla with almonds and smoked tomato salsa or grilled marinated rabbit with black beans; Tel: 625-5436. Hunters of collectibles will find a wide range of choices in the shops. Just for starters you might try **Willow Tea Room Studio** (Art Nouveau antiques), **Sea Fantasies** (seashells, coral, and objects made from them), **International Showcase** (native crafts and miniatures from around the world), **Classic Cat** (for feline fanciers), **Holiday Hutch** (decorations, toy soldiers, nativities, and ostrich-egg figurines), and **Gepetto's Collectibles** (Raggedy Anns, hand puppets, and music boxes, among the barrage of dolls and stuffed animals).

The Resorts of Carmel Valley

From Highway 1, Carmel Valley Road (route G 16) leads east past a number of resorts. In the lower valley, the 245-acre, beautifully landscaped grounds of the Carmel Valley Golf and Country Club, **Quail Lodge** provides luxuriously appointed rooms and suites (many with fireplaces) set in one- and two-story buildings. Guests here (and members of other golf clubs with agreements with Quail Lodge) may use the club's championship 18-hole golf course, tennis courts, and swimming pool. (Inquire about the specially priced golf packages.) Also at the lodge is **The Covey**, an elegant, intimate dinner house facing a little lake; for reservations, call (408) 624-1581.

Midway up the valley, **Carmel Valley Ranch Resort** sits among the oaks on a hillside above Carmel Valley Ranch Golf Club. The units are one- or two-bedroom deluxe suites with fireplaces, broad decks, wet bars, cathedral ceilings, and stylish contemporary furnishings. Some rooms have private hot tubs on the decks and most have views of the valley. As at Quail Lodge, guests at the resort are welcome to use the links of the golf club and the pool and courts of the Carmel Valley Ranch Tennis Club.

Most of the lower reaches of Carmel Valley were developed during the last two decades, but the upper valley is a step back in time. The weathered buildings of the tiny Carmel Valley Village resemble a town of the Old West, and nearby **Los Laureles Lodge** revels in its history. The lodge occupies part of a large Mexican land grant where the recipe for Monterey Jack cheese was supposedly developed. Early in this century cabins were built on the property for guests of Monterey's Del Monte Hotel, who came to the valley to hunt and fish. (The lodge's main building was once the home of Muriel Vanderbilt Phelps, who raised racehorses here in the 1930s.) Although the lodge was extensively renovated in 1990, it retains its rustic country charm and very reasonable room rates. Its dining room and Victorian-era bar are open to the public.

One of California's most extraordinary inns is secluded in 330 acres of mountainous terrain at the top of Carmel Valley. **Stonepine** was the equestrian estate of the Henry Potter Russells (he was a noted breeder of racehorses and she was the granddaughter of Big Four railroad magnate Charles Crocker). They built an exquisite 12-bedroom château here, with fireplaces in almost every room. Those who stay at the inn today are treated as house guests in an aristocratic country home: welcoming fruit, cheese, and wine in the bedrooms, which are splendidly appointed with antiques and (in most) whirlpool tubs; afternoon tea in the enormous salon; a formal six-course dinner in the oak-paneled dining room; a light breakfast in bed or in the sunroom. Daytime diversions include a dip in the pool, tennis, croquet, and horseback riding. The **Stonepine Equestrian Center** (where less formal guest accommodations are located) is open to the public for lessons, trail rides, and picnic excursions in a horse-drawn carriage; Tel: (408) 659-2247. If you want to look at Stonepine in style, the inn will send its Rolls Royce limousine (for a minimum party of four) to pick you up at your hotel for a gourmet luncheon at the château and a carriage ride.

Los Padres National Forest

Carmel Valley Road is a gateway to the high country of the Santa Lucia Mountains: Los Padres National Forest and the Ventana Wilderness. Within a small valley in this untamed land is the secluded **Tassajara Hot Springs**, once a watering hole for the Esalen Indians and now a monastery for the **Tassajara Zen Mountain Center**. From May to September, the monks welcome overnight guests for a stay in the sparsely-decorated cabins, a soak in the hot mineral springs, and a taste of their internationally acclaimed vegetarian cooking. The bread alone will send you to nirvana. If you're interested in stopping by just for the day, reservations are still required and are accepted no more than one week in advance; day guests should call (408) 659-2229 for reservations (and be sure to bring a picnic lunch: The dining room is open only to overnight guests). Steep, winding Tassajara Road, which leads to the hot springs from Carmel Valley Road, is an 80-minute, potentially hazardous drive, especially for drivers with automatic transmissions. A four-wheel drive van picks up overnight guests at 11:00 A.M. daily in Jamesburg, 14 miles north of Tassajara.

Another way to explore this backcountry is via two- to five-day horseback excursions conducted by **Ventana Wilderness Expeditions**, a venture of the pioneer Nason family, who count Essalen Indians among their ancestors (Star Route, Box 94, Carmel Valley, CA 93924; Tel: 408-659-0433).

THE CARMEL HIGHLANDS

South of Carmel, Highway 1 heads down the coast past a Spanish Colonial Carmelite monastery of cloistered nuns (stop for a look at the grounds and chapel) and past Monastery Beach to **Point Lobos State Reserve**. Jutting into the Pacific, this craggy finger of land has at various times served as a cattle pasture, a whaling station, and the site of an abalone cannery, but all signs of commerce are now gone and the park's 534 acres of meadows and pine and cypress forests protect black-tailed deer, gray squirrels, brush rabbits, and a variety of birds. Sea otters, sea lions, and harbor seals play in the rocky coves, and the great gray whales swim offshore during their winter migration. A road and hiking and bicycle trails circle the point; guided walking tours are also offered (inquire at the ranger station at the park entrance).

Below Point Lobos in an exclusive residential area, **Highlands Inn** perches on a steep hillside overlooking a spectacular stretch of shore. A historic lodge, built in 1916 of local golden granite, is the hub of the inn; marching up the hillside behind it are rows of contemporary buildings that contain handsome "spa suites" with large living rooms, fully equipped bar-kitchens, wood-burning fireplaces, broad decks, and—sitting out in the room so you can enjoy the view—oversized whirlpool tubs. (Inquire about the heavily discounted midweek rates.) Down in the stone lodge, **Pacific Edge** restaurant (open for breakfast, lunch, and dinner) provides sophisticated new American cooking and dramatic views of the coast; Tel: 624-0471. Highlands is only about a ten-minute drive south of Carmel, worth the trip just for a drink and the view at sunset. Highland's next-door neighbor, **Tickle Pink Country Inn**, shares the same ocean vista but the rooms are slightly less expensive. Most have views and private decks where Continental breakfast is served in sunny weather.

BIG SUR

For most of the 90 miles from Carmel south to San Simeon, the Santa Lucia Mountains thrust almost perpendicularly out of the Pacific to heights of 5,000 feet, the result of a giant cataclysm some ten million years ago. Finding this coast impassable, the northbound Spanish colonists detoured inland to reach Monterey Bay. Homesteaders started settling here in the 1860s, but even then the area was isolated: No passable road existed until the present two-lane highway opened in 1939; telephones and electricity did not reach Big Sur until the 1950s. Today Highway 1 creeps along ledges blasted from the cliffs 1,000 feet above the shore, crosses mighty bridges spanning creeks and canyons of redwood groves, and passes above rocky coves and inlets used by bootleggers during Prohibition.

The Heart of Big Sur

The first 20 miles south of Carmel Highlands contain few traces of civilization until the road reaches **Point Sur Lighthouse**, built in 1899 atop a rock that juts 350 feet out of the sea. On Sunday mornings, tours of the lighthouse are conducted; Tel: 825-4419. Several miles south of Point Sur, **Andrew Molera State Park** occupies part of a land grant where Captain Juan Bautista Cooper once raised cattle and supposedly smuggled in goods to avoid the customs duties at Monterey. The park is also the locale of **Molera Trail Rides**, which conducts guided horseback tours of the nearby beaches, bluffs, and redwood groves; Tel: 625-8664.

From here the road follows the Big Sur River inland for about six miles through the redwood forests of the Big Sur

Valley. Within the valley and then for about four miles south, the restaurants and hostelries that comprise the heart of Big Sur are located on Highway 1; you can't miss them. You'll come first to the historic **River Inn**, where locals gather for food, drink, jazz, and poetry readings. At the inn is a grocery store for picnic provisions and the **Heart Beat of Big Sur Gallery of Gifts**, with an amazing inventory from ethnic musical instruments and tapes to handcrafted jewelry, antique birdhouses, and bronze Hindu statues. Beyond the inn **Glen Oaks Restaurant**, an excellent small dinner house, features pastas, mesquite-grilled seafood, and steaks; Tel: 624-8242.

At the southern end of the valley, the 800 acres of **Pfeiffer–Big Sur State Park** contain hiking trails and rivers stocked with steelhead. The park is named after the Pfeiffer family, early homesteaders who at the century's turn built Pfeiffer's Resort, whose guests from Carmel—a ten-hour stagecoach ride away in those days—included George Sterling and Robinson Jeffers. The resort is now the site of **Big Sur Lodge**, which has moderately priced overnight accommodations, plus a swimming pool and sauna. Just south of the park, adventurous travellers may want to follow an extremely narrow, winding road down Sycamore Canyon to **Pfeiffer Beach**, noted for its beauty but also for its hazardous swimming.

At the end of Big Sur Valley, Highway 1 climbs over the mountains a few miles to the coast. Here, 1,200 feet above the Pacific (and well signposted from the highway), **Ventana Inn** is a serene retreat for rich hippies, nature-loving young professionals, and those who want to absorb the rugged beauty with few distractions—perhaps a walk in the redwoods, a swim in the pool, or a soak in the Japanese baths. The resort's stunning contemporary buildings overlook a mountain meadow where deer often roam. Paneled in knotty cedar, the rooms themselves exude country comfort, with handmade quilts, fireplaces or wood-burning stoves, and broad decks, some with private hot tubs. Ventana further pampers its guests with a splendid breakfast spread and afternoon wine and cheese. Across the meadow, with a terrace overlooking the Pacific, the **Ventana Restaurant** offers light California-style cooking—it's a popular lunch destination for Big Sur visitors; Tel: 667-2331.

Just down the road, the decks of **Nepenthe Restaurant** provide an even more spectacular view of the coast—perhaps the best in this land of superlative vistas. Known for its burgers and steak sandwiches, Nepenthe is built around a log cabin, which Orson Welles bought for Rita Hayworth in the 1940s but never occupied. In the Nepenthe complex, the **Phoenix Gift Shop** stocks a large array of handcrafted items such as jewelry, ceramics, sweaters, and patchwork quilts.

Nearby, **Deetjen's Big Sur Inn** has been putting up travellers since the 1930s. Built by a Norwegian homesteader, this rustic hostelry is now operated by a preservation foundation. The wooden cabins contain modestly priced rooms with a rudimentary Old World charm; baths are often shared, the walls are thin, and in some the only heat comes from a potbellied stove. Nevertheless the inn has a devoted clientele, as does Deetjen's restaurant, a local legend for hearty breakfasts and candlelit dinners accompanied by classical music.

Bohemian Big Sur

In the 1940s a number of San Francisco artists—among them painter Jean Varda and sculptor Beniamino Bufano—discovered that Big Sur was a peaceful and inexpensive place to work. Henry Miller moved here in 1944, and later the Beat poets of the 1950s wandered down the coast to pay homage to him. Miller, known for remaining somewhat aloof, is said to have refused to see Allen Ginsburg, although he did meet with Dylan Thomas and once invited Jack Kerouac for dinner. The latter never arrived; he got lost in the wilds of Big Sur and was discovered at dawn, asleep in a meadow near the cabin of Lawrence Ferlinghetti, poet and founder of North Beach's City Lights Bookstore.

This poetic era is now commemorated with a collection of Miller memorabilia at the **Henry Miller Memorial Library**, located on Highway 1 just south of Nepenthe in the former home of Miller's longtime friend, painter and writer Emil White. Down the road a cluster of huge water tanks houses the **Coast Gallery**, where many of Miller's bright, fanciful watercolors are on display, along with the work of other local artists. Within the next five miles heading south, Highway 1 passes Partington Ridge (where Miller lived until 1962) and continues to to **Julia Pfeiffer Burns State Park**, where trails lead to a picnic area and McWay Canyon, the site of a 50-foot waterfall that cascades into the ocean. Beyond the park a bridge crosses Anderson Canyon, home in the early days of the Big Sur colony to Miller, White, and other artists who lived cheaply in the abandoned buildings that had once housed the convicts who built Highway 1.

A favorite pastime of the locals in those days was soaking

in the waters of the natural hot springs at a cliffside resort down the road. Here—about halfway between Carmel and Hearst Castle—Michael Murphy (whose parents owned the resort) founded the **Esalen Institute**. In addition to its educational conferences and intensive study programs, Esalen holds weekend self-awareness workshops in subjects ranging from Gestalt psychology to massage to lucid dreaming; occasionally, weekends without workshops are also offered. The workshop fees cover room, meals, and use of the hot springs, which are closed to the public (see Accommodations Reference for booking information). If you just want to look, tours of the grounds are conducted every other Sunday afternoon from April through September.

About 14 miles south of Esalen, the largely unpaved Nacimiento–Fergusson Road leaves Highway 1 to switchback east over the mountains to Highway 101, passing Mission San Antonio de Padua (see El Camino Real: The Inland Route, below). This road is recommended only for fearless drivers in perfect weather—never for recreational vehicles. Continuing south, Highway 1 follows the coast for about 38 miles of great ocean views to San Simeon.

SAN SIMEON TO SAN LUIS OBISPO

In the southern part of the Santa Lucia Range—from San Simeon down to San Luis Obispo—the mountains converge with the ocean to form a landscape more gentle than the cataclysmic Big Sur coast. For thousands of years the Chumash Indians hunted on these lands and fished along the beaches; later Mexican *rancheros* raised their cattle here, and finally dairy farms were established along the coast. But the biggest event in this pastoral nook of California was William Randolph Hearst's construction of a hilltop castle 1,600 feet above the former whaling port of San Simeon.

Hearst Castle

W. R. Hearst officially named his estate La Cuesta Encantada (The Enchanted Hill), but humbly called it "the ranch"— never "the castle." In 1919, while living in New York, Hearst commissioned Berkeley architect Julia Morgan to design a vacation house for his family on his San Simeon lands: 240,000 acres he had inherited from his father, U.S. Senator

George Hearst, whose fortune came from Nevada's Comstock Lode. The younger Hearst lavished millions on the project until 1938, when he ran out of money; parts of the castle were never completed. During those years, architect Morgan spent almost every weekend at San Simeon supervising the never-ending construction.

She was probably the least famous of Hearst's weekend visitors. Although his wife and five sons did vacation at San Simeon in the early years, the later hostess-in-residence was his protégée and mistress, actress Marion Davies. Together they entertained the elite of Hollywood and the forerunners of today's jet set. Davies' co-star Clark Gable was a visitor, as were Gary Cooper and Louis B. Mayer; William Powell courted Jean Harlow here; Marie Dressler, Doris Duke, and Adela Rogers St. John were on the guest list; and at times Bob Hope kept them all laughing. On a typical weekend, 30 to 50 guests occupied the ranch's 58 bedrooms. After Hearst's death in 1951 his heirs gave the castle and 120 acres of the grounds to the state of California, and it became a state park.

Daily tours offer four itineraries around the estate. First-time visitors should book Tour One, which focuses on the ground floor of **La Casa Grande**, the main house whose Spanish-Moorish tiled towers dominate the landscape for miles around. Throughout the house the original furnishings and priceless artworks remain intact: in the Assembly Room, Flemish tapestries hang beside a 16th-century French Renaissance fireplace, and in the Refectory festival banners from Siena flutter above Gothic tapestries. Hearst's guests dined here at a polished 300-year-old refectory table incongruously set with paper napkins (he thought they were more sanitary) and catsup bottles alongside massive silver candlesticks. This tour also visits the indoor Roman Pool, where walls are inlaid with Italian mosaic tiles; the open-air Neptune Pool, encircled with an Etruscan colonnade that flanks a Greco-Roman temple; and Casa del Sol, an 18-room Spanish Renaissance villa with gilded ceilings and moldings—one of three guest cottages below the main house. (Tours Two, Three, and Four explore the castle's upstairs bedrooms, guest wing, grounds, and other guest houses.)

Hearst Castle, unfailingly easy to find (you can see it from miles away), is the most popular visitor attraction in Northern California, so purchase your tickets well in advance during peak travel seasons. They can be charged to a major credit card by calling Mistix; Tel: (800) 444-7275 within California, (619) 452-1950 outside California.

San Simeon

Below the castle, in the tiny port of San Simeon, are more Julia Morgan buildings: a mission-style warehouse, which stored Hearst's hordes of treasures, and several Mediterranean-style houses, built for the castle's construction crew (there were 93 workers on the payroll in 1929). Also here is the area's oldest building: the 1852 **Sebastian Store**, which displays whaling implements and vintage photographs; lunch and breakfast are served on the patio. Just south of San Simeon, modern motels cluster around the highway. One of the most attractive is the large **Cavalier Inn**; ask for a balconied oceanfront room.

Cambria

Nine miles south of San Simeon, the picturesque village of Cambria is not only an accommodations and dining center for Hearst Castle visitors, it's a destination in its own right. Nestled in a pine-rimmed valley off Highway 1, the town is home to many artists and craftspeople, who sell their work in the town's numerous shops and galleries. But from the 1860s to the 1890s Cambria was a bustling center for whalers, quicksilver (mercury) miners, and lumberjacks, all lured by the area's abundant resources; a large Chinese colony once farmed for seaweed here, too.

A small hill divides Cambria into two villages, both filled with shops and galleries. Not to be missed in the West Village is **The Soldier Factory**, 789 Main Street, which manufactures, and sells worldwide, hand-painted toy soldiers, miniature forts, and the like; there's a small exhibit of antique toy soldiers, too. Around the corner on Arlington is **Victoriana**, which deals in wooden detailing, wallpaper, dolls, and miniature furniture of the Victorian era.

Go up the hill from the village for a look at **Nit Wit Ridge**, on Hillcrest Drive off Cornwall; this bizarre, multilevel structure assembled from abalone shells, auto parts, glass, beer cans, and other found objects has been the home and life work of Art Beal (known as Captain Nit Wit and Dr. Tinkerpaw) since 1929. Though not open to the public, the house has achieved landmark status as a 20th-century folk-art environment. On Main Street between the villages you'll see the **Schoolhouse Gallery**, an 1881 one-room schoolhouse that exhibits work of the local art association; in its front yard sits Cambria Jail, a tiny, windowless structure typical of the lockups for overindulgers built near saloons in the 19th century.

In the East Village, also known as Cambria Pines, collectors will probably strike pay dirt in a cluster of boutiques on Burton Drive. Among the shops are **The Olde Telephone Co.** (antique phones and early advertising art such as Ferry Seed posters and Coca Cola memorabilia), **Pacific West Art** (contemporary jewelry, sculpture, and graphics, with an emphasis on wildlife), **Quicksilver Gallery** (handcrafted works from contemporary artisans nationwide), and **Suma Sil Gallery** (Native American fine arts, crafts, and artifacts, including some pre-Columbian items). Don't overlook **Heart's Ease**, a small cottage filled with a vast assortment of herb lotions and potions, bulk potpourri, dried herbs and spices, herb vinegars, jams, jellies, and more.

You'll find many of Cambria's 19th-century buildings on Burton, Main, Center, and Bridge streets. Also on Bridge, look for **Banberry Cross**, a country-kitchen boutique featuring English comestibles. A local success story is **Linn's Fruit Bin**, purveyors of preserves made from fruit grown at the Linn family farm near Cambria; there's a shop in town at 2277 Main Street as well as at the farm, a pretty five-mile drive through the hilly countryside along Santa Rosa Creek.

West of the village a row of new motels rims pleasant Moonstone Beach, where you can search for semiprecious moonstones and California jade. One of these hostelries is **Fireside Inn By-the-Sea**, which boasts many unmotel-like amenities: gas-burning fireplaces, wet bars, and fresh flowers in the rooms; some rooms also have ocean views and whirlpool tubs. Down the road is **The Beach House**, a small bed-and-breakfast inn that also offers some fireplaces and ocean views. On a pine-forested hillside above town, **The J. Patrick House**, another bed and breakfast, has cozy rooms—all dressed up in Early American style—with wood-burning fireplaces. A nice spot in town for budget travellers is the newly remodeled 16-room **Creekside Inn**.

The old-timer among Cambria's dozens of restaurants is **The Brambles Dinner House**, located in an antiques-filled 1874 house at 4005 Burton Drive and known for its prime rib with Yorkshire pudding. Reservations are advised; Tel: 927-4716. Across the street, **Robin's** serves breakfast, lunch, and dinner with home-grown produce and multinational ethnic accents from quesadillas to pasta primavera to Thai green curry; Tel: 927-5007. A favorite of locals is **Ian's**, 2150 Center Street, where you can stop for a casual bar snack of burgers or raw oysters or enjoy one of chef Ian McPhee's celebrated California-style dinners; seafood is emphasized: fresh abalone steaks, swordfish with cilantro pesto, planked salmon with mustard butter, and the like. Reserve for dinner; Tel: 927-8649. On the outdoor terrace at **Creekside Gardens Café**, 2114 Main Street, you can buy a hearty breakfast from an extensive menu that includes omelets with heaps of country fries and Danish sausage from Solvang, a Danish enclave about 100 miles south of Cambria on Highway 101.

There's more to do than just eat at **The Hamlet at Moonstone Gardens**, perched on a bluff above Highway 1 north of Moonstone Beach. Whether lunching on a big burger or loitering at dinner over garlicky herb-crusted rack of lamb, you can admire a glorious view of the Pacific. Within the complex a wine bar offers tastings of local wine; the gardens and nursery contain waterfalls, fish pools, and many exotic plants, with a focus on succulents from weird midget cacti to giant yucca trees (Tel: 805-927-3535).

Harmony

Six miles south of Cambria on Highway 1, Harmony (population 18) is barely a speck on the map, but in the early decades of this century the **Harmony Valley Creamery** prospered by producing butter and cheese. One frequent customer was teetotaling William Randolph Hearst, who treated his guests to glasses of buttermilk on their way from the train depot at San Luis Obispo to San Simeon. The folks at Harmony claim that Pola Negri and Rudolph Valentino were among the sippers. Today the old creamery houses a bevy of crafts shops (including one that produces hand-thrown stoneware from kilns behind the shops), and a wine bar. The hamlet also shelters a tiny chapel (a popular place for weddings) and a glass-blowing studio, where you can watch the artisans at work.

The Morro Bay Area

For some 20 miles between Cambria and Morro Bay you'll travel south on Highway 1 as it crosses a pastoral landscape where cattle graze on hills above the ocean. Take a detour into **Cayucos**, a small resort town known for its pier fishing, scuba diving, and surfing. In the 19th century, Cayucos was a thriving little seaport; evidence of those early days remains on the town's main street, where Old West buildings hover over a wooden boardwalk guarded by a cigar-store Indian.

Beyond Cayucos, as the road approaches the fishing town of **Morro Bay**, a miniature Gibraltar looms on the seascape: Morro Rock, a rounded promontory rising 576 feet above the ocean, is home to a few of California's nearly extinct peregrine falcons. In town, Embarcadero Street is a busy marina lined with seafood cafés and restaurants, curio shops, and the berths of excursion and sport-fishing boats. Also here are the small **Morro Bay Aquarium** and the Giant Chess Board, where the pieces are two to three feet high.

South of town a eucalyptus forest covers the 2,000 acres of **Morro Bay State Park**, a wildlife sanctuary, bird-watcher's paradise, and preserve for a large rookery of the great blue heron. Just inside the park gates, surrounded by lush gardens, **The Inn at Morro Bay** overlooks Morro Bay Estuary. Decorated in French country–style, many of the rooms in this deluxe resort have decks and fireplaces. The inn is also a lovely stop for lunch, as you gaze beyond the glass-walled dining room to watch seagulls perform an ongoing aerial ballet, seemingly in time with the taped classical music within.

San Luis Obispo

At Morro Bay Highway 1 turns inland for 12 miles to San Luis Obispo, cradled in a valley between the Santa Lucia Range and a chain of rocky peaks (extinct volcanoes) extending to the sea. Today the town is best known as the home of California State Polytechnic University, but its historic heart is **Mission San Luis Obispo de Tolosa**, founded by Father Junípero Serra in 1772. Although the Mission is only California's sixth oldest, it was the first to be topped with the now-distinctive red-tiled roof—introduced after Indians burned the original wooden structure by shooting flaming arrows through its thatched roof. Stop inside to visit the small museum that focuses on the history of the area, then stroll through the old town around the Mission to see the restored 19th-century adobes and Victorians (a map of historic sites is available at the Chamber of Commerce, 1039 Chorro). Don't miss **Ah Louis Store** (now a Far Eastern gift shop), which in the 1880s served as general store, bank, and post office for 2,000 Chinese who built railroad tunnels through the mountains.

Behind the Mission an imposing stone Romanesque-style structure (built in 1904) now serves as the **San Luis Obispo County Historical Museum**, and across the street the **Art Center** gallery strikes a contemporary note. In front of the Mission a creek meanders through **Mission Plaza**; hovering over the creek's tree-lined banks at the plaza are the outdoor decks and patios of several restaurants, some with live music at lunchtime. Beer buffs should check out **SLO Brewing Co.** here, an upstairs brew pub with a menu of burgers and other pub food at 1119 Garden Street. But for a truly fine meal head across town to **Café Roma**, at 1819 Osos Street near the train depot. You'll find patio seating by day and candlelight at night in this charming family-run restaurant, but the big draw is the superbly prepared Northern Italian cooking; Tel: 541-6800. The route from town to the depot leads by the Kundert Medical Building at Pacific and Santa Rosa, which was designed by Frank Lloyd Wright; around the corner on Pacific is the 1850s Dallidet Adobe and the 1889 Ramona Depot.

San Luis Obispo's many motels and inns range from the humble 1920s Motel Inn (which is the origin of the word "motel") to the outrageously gaudy Madonna Inn. A cut above them all is **Apple Farm Inn**, a 67-room hostelry built in 1987 to look like grandma's house—a rich grandma, that is. Each room is individually decorated in a countryish, yet sophisticated, Victorian style with fireplaces throughout; behind the inn is a swimming pool and a working grist mill that grinds the flour for the breads and pancakes served at the extremely popular **Apple Farm restaurant**. It's easy to forgive some of the commercial aspects of this eatery when you taste the fresh, down-home country cooking; breakfast is truly outstanding.

EL CAMINO REAL: THE INLAND ROUTE BACK NORTH

When the Spaniards' first land expedition up the California coast was diverted by the cliffs of Big Sur, Don Gaspar de Portolá's party headed inland through the gentler mountains around **Paso Robles** and marched some 100 miles north up the Salinas Valley to Monterey Bay. The Franciscans later built their missions along this route, which they called El Camino Real (The King's Highway) to honor the king of Spain. Today Highway 101 more or less follows this road.

From San Luis Obispo, Highway 101 switchbacks up a steep grade to the Paso Robles wine country, the mountainous site of some 20 wineries. The oldest, dating back to 1882, is **York Mountain Winery** on Highway 46 to Cambria. Most of these wineries have tasting rooms; pick up, at any winery, the free brochure "Wine Tasting in Paso Robles" for complete information. Before reaching Paso Robles, Highway 101 bypasses the 19th-century town of Templeton; leave the freeway for a few minutes for a glimpse of the re-created false-fronted buildings on Main Street—reminders of the Old West.

Ten miles north of Paso Robles is **Mission San Miguel Arcángel**, founded in 1797 (after Serra's death), the 16th in the chain. The present Mission, built in the early 19th century, is distinguished by an arched colonnade around its monastery courtyard and by the trompe l'oeil murals in the church. San Miguel is one of only four missions in California still tended by brown-robed Franciscan friars, some of whom are also in residence farther north at lovely **Mission San Antonio de Padua**, Serra's third Mission, founded in 1771. A visit to this latter Mission (located near Jolon in the Santa Lucia foothills west of Highway 101) requires a time-consuming detour on Country Road G-18 for about 40 miles from Camp Roberts to King City, but this totally restored working Mission probably provides the best picture available of mission life in the 19th century. (Turn northwest on to County Road G-18 from Highway 101 one mile north of Bradley.) Another reason for taking this side trip is for a look at **Jolon Lodge**, across the road from Mission San Antonio. An imposing 70-room hacienda that Julia Morgan designed for W. R. Hearst as a hunting retreat in the 1930s, the lodge is now an army officer's club, surrounded by the vast Hunter Liggett Military Reservation.

Salinas Valley

This is John Steinbeck's "Long Valley," where the Salinas River is bordered by flat, fertile farmlands below the eastern slopes of the Santa Lucia Range. It was in this valley that he set *The Grapes of Wrath, East of Eden,* and other works. Agriculturally speaking, Salinas often translates as "lettuce," but the valley—one of the state's newest viticultural areas—is becoming increasingly noted for its Monterey County wines. Two Santa Clara County vintners in search of more acreage—Paul Masson and Mirassou—planted the valley's first post-Prohibition vineyards, in 1962, between Soledad and Greenfield. When they released their first bottlings four years later, the wine world took notice. Today Monterey wines command serious respect, with the most accolades going to the prestigious Chalone Vineyards (not open to the public).

For a scenic look at Monterey wine country, exit Highway 101 in Greenfield (10 miles north of King City) and follow River Road (G-17) either 10 or 20 miles north, returning to 101 at Soledad or Gonzales. Of several tasting rooms en route, the most interesting is **The Monterey Vineyards**, just off 101 at Gonzales; hourly tours are conducted. Even if you don't care to tipple, take a look at "The Story of a Winery," the exhibit here of Ansel Adams photographs.

Back in Soledad, Steinbeck's setting for *Of Mice and Men,* **Mission Nuestra Señora de Soledad**, founded in 1791 as the 13th link of the mission chain, was reduced to ruins by years of floods and neglect, but the chapel and one wing have been reconstructed. East of town the eerie volcanic spires of **Pinnacles National Monument** accent the horizon.

At the northern end of the Salinas Valley, Steinbeck's hometown of **Salinas** is the commercial center for this agricultural area. A fascinating lunch-stop at 132 Central Avenue is the **Steinbeck House**, a Queen Anne Victorian where Steinbeck was born and wrote some of his early works. Now magnificently restored, Steinbeck House is operated by the nonprofit Valley Guild, whose volunteers help prepare and serve lunch on weekdays. The menu is fixed, the food is delicious, and reservations should be made well in advance; Tel: (408) 424-2735. Three blocks away at 110 West San Luis, the **John Steinbeck Library** displays letters, photographs, and rare editions; it also sponsors the Steinbeck Festival in early August, a five-day blitz of films, lectures, and tours of the novelist's haunts; Tel: (408) 758-7314.

San Juan Bautista

Only a few minutes east of Highway 101, this quiet village is virtually a living museum of early Californiana, from the founding of its Mission in 1797 through the 19th century. The core of this town in the hills, about 20 miles north of Salinas, is **San Juan Bautista State Historic Park**, a group of restored buildings facing the town plaza. A self-guided tour includes visits to the Castro House, a balconied 1840s adobe built by the Mexican prefect of northern Alta California; the Plaza Hotel, a major stagecoach stop, now restored to look as it did in the 1860s; the Plaza Stable, where vintage carriages and wagons are displayed; and the Plaza Hall, which was used for public meetings and social gatherings. On the first Saturday of each month living-history events are conducted in the park; Tel: (408) 623-4881.

On the north side of the plaza, **Mission San Juan Bautista**,

15th of the 21 Franciscan missions, was once the home of 1,200 Indians and is one of the few missions where a priest remained in residence after secularization. The Mission's church was severely damaged in the 1906 earthquake (the San Andreas Fault runs just east of town); now restored, this church boasts three naves and is the largest of its kind in the state. It was here that the memorable scene of the classic Hitchcock film *Vertigo* was shot. The wing that contained the kitchen and the padres' living quarters is now a museum.

A block below the plaza, antiques stores, art and crafts galleries, gift shops, and restaurants line Third Street. A landmark eatery for Old California atmosphere, **La Casa Rosa** serves a limited luncheon menu (casseroles and a soufflé) in an 1858 adobe and its gardens. You'll also find outdoor dining in a pretty setting and traditional Mexican food at **Jardines de San Juan**.

GETTING AROUND

The ideal way to explore the Central Coast is by car. In a pinch, a round-trip itinerary from San Francisco to San Luis Obispo (about 500 miles) may be made in three days, with overnight stops on the Monterey Peninsula and in the vicinity of Hearst Castle, but this would allow time only for the major sights. If you want to shorten the route you can cut back to Highway 101 from Highway 1 at Castroville, northeast of the Monterey Peninsula; just south of Cambria, Highway 46 provides a scenic drive on a good road over the mountains to Paso Robles and 101; or Highway 41 leads back to 101 from Morro Bay.

For nondrivers the Monterey Peninsula is serviced by Greyhound Bus Lines (Tel: 415-558-6730), United Airlines, and USAir. (Many hotels and inns offer courtesy pickups at the Monterey Peninsula Airport, which is east of Highway 1 just north of Monterey.) Once there **The Bus** (Monterey-Salinas Transport) operates between the various peninsula towns and south to Nepenthe at Big Sur; for a schedule call (408) 899-2555. Another option is a sightseeing tour: Try **Steinbeck Country Tours** (Box 22848, Carmel, CA 93922; Tel: 408-625-5107) or **Otter-Mobile Tours & Charters** (Box 2743, Carmel, CA 93921; Tel: 408-625-9782). Both have a range of itineraries from short treks around the peninsula to all-day excursions that include Big Sur and Hearst Castle.

From San Francisco, **Gray Line** schedules a daily 11-hour, round-trip tour to the Monterey Peninsula (Tel: 415-558-9400 or 800-556-5660). Two- and three-day bus tours to the peninsula are among the packages available through **California**

Parlor Car Tours in San Francisco (Tel: 415-474-7500); some longer trips take in Hearst Castle. And if you want to try the train, check out **Amtrak**, which has daily service from Oakland (with bus transfer from San Francisco) to Salinas and San Luis Obispo; from the latter, Amtrak operates an overnight motor-coach tour to Hearst Castle (Tel: 800-872-7245).

ACCOMMODATIONS REFERENCE

► **Apple Farm Inn.** 2015 Monterey Street, **San Luis Obispo**, CA 93401. Tel: (805) 544-2040; in California (800) 255-2040.

► **Asilomar Conference Center.** 800 Asilomar Boulevard (P.O. Box 537), **Pacific Grove**, CA 93950. Tel: (408) 372-8016.

► **Babbling Brook Inn.** 1025 Laurel Street, **Santa Cruz**, CA 95060. Tel: (408) 427-2437.

► **The Beach House.** 6530 Moonstone Beach Drive, **Cambria**, CA 93428. Tel: (805) 927-3136.

► **Big Sur Lodge.** Pfeiffer–Big Sur State Park, **Big Sur**, CA 93920. Tel: (408) 667-2171.

► **Carmel Valley Ranch Resort.** 1 Old Ranch Road, **Carmel**, CA 93923. Tel: (408) 625-9500 or (800) 422-7635.

► **Cavalier Inn.** 9415 Hearst Drive, **San Simeon**, CA 93452. Tel: (805) 927-4688 or (800) 528-1234.

► **Chateau Victorian.** 118 First Street, **Santa Cruz**, CA 95060. Tel: (408) 458-9458.

► **Cobblestone Inn.** Junípero between 7th and 8th, P.O. Box 3185, **Carmel**, CA 93921. Tel: (408) 625-5222.

► **Creekside Inn.** 2618 Main Street, **Cambria**, CA 93428. Tel: (805) 927-4021.

► **Cypress Inn.** Lincoln and Seventh, P.O. Box Y, **Carmel**, CA 93921. Tel: (408) 624-3871; in California, (800) 443-7443.

► **Deetjen's Big Sur Inn.** Highway 1, **Big Sur**, CA 93920. Tel: (408) 667-2377.

► **Esalen Institute.** Highway 1, **Big Sur**, CA 93920. Tel: (408) 667-3000.

► **Fireside Inn By-the-Sea.** 6700 Moonstone Beach Drive, **Cambria**, CA 93428. Tel: (805) 927-8661 or (800) 528-1234.

► **The Gosby House Inn.** 643 Lighthouse Avenue, **Pacific Grove**, CA 93950. Tel: (408) 375-1287.

► **The Green Gables Inn.** 104 Fifth Street, **Pacific Grove**, CA 93950. Tel: (408) 375-2095.

► **Highlands Inn.** Highway 1, P.O. Box 1700, **Carmel**, CA 93921. Tel: (408) 624-3801; in California, (800) 682-4811; nationwide, (800) 538-9525.

► **The Inn at Morro Bay.** Morro Bay State Park, **Morro Bay**, CA 93442. Tel: (805) 772-5651; in California, (800) 321-9566.

► **The Inn at Spanish Bay.** 2700 Seventeen Mile Drive,

Pebble Beach, CA 93953. Tel: (408) 647-7500 or (800) 654-9300.

▶ **The Jabberwock.** 598 Laine Street, **Monterey**, CA 93940. Tel: (408) 372-4777.

▶ **The J. Patrick House.** 2990 Burton Drive, **Cambria**, CA 93428. Tel: (805) 927-3812.

▶ **The Lodge at Pebble Beach.** Seventeen Mile Drive, **Pebble Beach**, CA 93953. Tel: (408) 624-3811 or (800) 654-9300.

▶ **Los Laureles Lodge.** Carmel Valley Road, **Carmel Valley**, CA 93924. Tel: (408) 659-2233; in California, (800) 533-4404.

▶ **Mission Ranch.** 26270 Dolores Street, **Carmel**, CA 93923. Tel: (408) 624-6436.

▶ **Old Monterey Inn.** 500 Martin Street, **Monterey**, CA 93940. Tel: (408) 375-8284.

▶ **Pine Inn.** Ocean Avenue and Lincoln, **Carmel**, CA 93921. Tel: (408) 624-3851.

▶ **La Playa Hotel.** Eighth Avenue and Camino Real, P.O. Box 900, **Carmel**, CA 93921. Tel: (408) 624-6476; in California, (800) 582-8900.

▶ **Quail Lodge.** 8205 Valley Greens Drive, **Carmel**, CA 93923. Tel: (408) 624-1581; in California, (800) 682-9303; nationwide, (800) 538-9516.

▶ **Sandpiper Inn At-the-Beach.** 2408 Bay View Avenue at Martin, **Carmel**, CA 93923. Tel: (408) 624-6433; in California, (800) 633-6433.

▶ **Sea View Inn.** Camino Real at Eleventh, P.O. Box 4138, **Carmel**, CA 93921. Tel: (408) 624-8778.

▶ **Spindrift Inn.** 652 Cannery Row, **Monterey**, CA 93940. Tel: (408) 646-8900; in California, (800) 841-1879; nationwide, (800) 225-2901.

▶ **Stonepine.** 150 East Carmel Valley Road, **Carmel Valley**, CA 93924. Tel: (408) 659-2245.

▶ **Tassajara Zen Mountain Center.** Tassajara Reservation Office, 300 Page Street, San Francisco, CA 94102. Tel: (415) 431-3771. No credit cards.

▶ **Tickle Pink Country Inn.** 155 Highlands Drive, **Carmel**, CA 93923. Tel: (408) 624-1244; outside California, (800) 635-4774.

▶ **Vagabond's House.** Fourth and Dolores, P.O. Box 2747, **Carmel**, CA 93921. Tel: (408) 624-7738.

▶ **Ventana Inn.** Highway 1, **Big Sur**, CA 93920. Tel: (408) 667-2331; in California, (800) 628-6500.

CHRONOLOGY
OF THE HISTORY OF
SAN FRANCISCO &
NORTHERN CALIFORNIA

- **circa 10,000 B.C.**: The last Ice Age ends, having shaped the Northern California landscape known today. *Sequoia sempervirens* (Coast Redwoods), once found worldwide, survive in the coastal fog belt.
- **A.D. 1510**: The name California is used for a rich and mystic island described in a Spanish poem, *Las Sergas de Esplandián* by Garcí Ordóñez de Montalvo.
- **1542**: A Spanish ship returning from the Philippines reaches the Northern California coast; a headland is named Cabo Mendocino.
- **1579**: Sir Francis Drake beaches the *Golden Hinde* for repairs at a still undetermined Northern California bay.
- **1602**: Sebastián Vizcaíno lands at Monterey Bay. He calls it a "noble harbor," a comment that confuses later explorers.
- **1768**: New Spain officials make plans to settle California and prevent Russian intrusions there.
- **1769**: Gaspar de Portolá's expedition to find Monterey Bay reaches San Francisco Bay instead.
- **1770 (June 3)**: Father Junípero Serra celebrates the founding Mass for Monterey presidio and mission. Gaspar de Portolá, who led two expeditions north, grumps, "If the Russians want Northern California, they deserve it."
- **1775**: Spanish Lt. Juan Manuel de Ayala takes the first ship into San Francisco Bay.
- **1776**: The Presidio of San Francisco is dedicated on September 17, the Mission San Francisco de Asís on October 4.

- **1777:** San Jose Pueblo is founded at the south end of San Francisco Bay.
- **1786:** Monterey entertains its first foreign visitor, the French explorer François de la Pérouse.
- **1792:** The first Yankee arrives in California, a gunner on a Mexican ship.
- **1808:** Russians establish a sea otter hunting base at Bodega Bay, north of San Francisco.
- **1812:** Russians found Fort Ross, 120 miles north of San Francisco Bay.
- **1820:** U.S. ships begin California trade for hides and tallow. A few Yankees begin to settle in the north.
- **1825:** California becomes a territory of now-independent Mexico.
- **1828:** Fur trapper Jedediah Smith makes the first crossing of the rugged Northern California coastal mountains.
- **1833:** Mexico secularizes the missions in California, having found that conflicts with Native Americans made the institutions too economically burdensome (Mexico would not secularize its own missions until 1857).
- **1836:** Juan Bautista Alvarado marches on Monterey and declares California a "free and sovereign state" within the Mexican Republic. Mexican control begins to grow more and more tenuous.
- **1839:** John Augustus Sutter, a Swiss, founds Sutter's Fort, the first settlement in the interior, near the junction of the Sacramento and American rivers.
- **1840:** Yankee traders who have become Mexican citizens and married locals are by now important figures in California society.
- **1841:** John Bidwell and 36 immigrants from Missouri reach Sutter's Fort after a six-month transcontinental journey. The Russians sell Fort Ross to Sutter.
- **1842:** Commodore A.C. Jones, U.S. Navy, thinking the U.S. and Mexico are at war, occupies Monterey and claims California for the United States. He's wrong, so he apologizes and leaves town.
- **1844:** U.S. Lt. John C. Frémont's expedition arrives at Sutter's Fort. Forty-six easterners make the first wagon crossing of the Sierra Nevada.
- **1845:** Two hundred sixty-nine overland settlers arrive.
- **1846:** Sacramento Valley Yankee settlers begin the

Bear Flag revolt to establish California as a republic. The U.S. declares war on Mexico and claims Monterey and Yerba Buena at San Francisco Bay in early July. Nearly 300 Mormon settlers, led by Samuel Brannan, disembark at Yerba Buena. Winter traps the Donner Party from Illinois in the Sierra Nevada.

- **1847:** Yerba Buena is renamed San Francisco; by year's end it has 200 buildings, 800 residents, and a newspaper.
- **1848:** Carpenter James Marshall finds gold on January 24 at Sutter's Mill, Coloma, near Placerville. By mid-June San Francisco is half empty. Gold-seekers arrive from Oregon, Honolulu, Mexico, Peru, Chile, and elsewhere, and an estimated $6 million worth of gold is mined by December 31. News filters east, and President Polk confirms the strike to Congress on December 5.
- **1849:** The great Rush of '49 begins. A first ship with 365 Argonauts anchors at San Francisco on February 28, and by the end of the year 1,000 ships have arrived. Between spring and winter, 30,000 gold-seekers cross the continent—in all, 90,000 people came to seek their fortunes.
- **1850:** California joins the Union as a nonslave state. Forty-five thousand gold-seekers arrive by overland routes. Levi Strauss reaches San Francisco and starts stitching sturdy britches for miners. The state's Chinese population grows to 789 men and two women. Thirty steamboats ply San Francisco Bay and the valley rivers.
- **1851:** Vigilantes organize to fight crime in San Francisco. Sacramento, the settlement that engulfed Sutter's Fort, has grown to a population of 10,000.
- **1852:** San Francisco culture is launched with the arrival of singer Elisa Biscaccianti; the North Coast lumber town of Mendocino is founded, and the original Almaden and Paul Masson vineyards are planted near San Jose.
- **1853:** The first California-built steamboat takes to the water.
- **1854:** Sacramento becomes the state capital.
- **1855:** Gold production and overland arrivals decline, and California weathers a year of financial woes. The San Francisco *Alta* reports 370 murders in eight months.

- **1856**: California's first train service begins a 22-mile route between Sacramento and Folsom. San Francisco vigilantes hang four men.
- **1857**: Fort Bragg is founded north of Mendocino. The Butterfield Overland Mail travels from Missouri to San Francisco in 24 days.
- **1858**: San Francisco and Los Angeles are linked by telegraph.
- **1860**: The first Pony Express mail reaches Sacramento; an engineer surveys a railroad route over the Sierra Nevada via Emigrant Gap and Donner Pass, and Comstock Lode silver from Nevada enriches San Francisco.
- **1861**: The telegraph links Sacramento and the East Coast.
- **1863 (January 8)**: Ground is broken in Sacramento for the Central Pacific Railroad, which thousands of Chinese will be hired to build.
- **1868**: A charter is issued for the University of California.
- **1869 (May 10)**: Northern California and the East are linked by rail as the Central Pacific Railroad and Union Pacific meet at Promontory, Utah.
- **1870**: Point Arena Lighthouse is built south of Mendocino; it topples in 1906.
- **1873**: Andrew S. Hallidie's cable car makes its first run down and up San Francisco's Clay Street.
- **1874**: California's capitol building in Sacramento is completed at the scandalous cost of $2,600,000.
- **1884**: Sarah L. Winchester, widow of the Winchester rifle fortune heir, settles in San Jose and begins house construction that will continue for 38 years.
- **1887**: Scottish gardener John McLaren is hired to tend San Francisco's Golden Gate Park; he stays 50 years.
- **1890**: Congress creates Yosemite, General Grant, and Sequoia national parks.
- **1891**: Stanford University founded at Palo Alto by Leland Stanford in honor of his dead son. Stanford endows the university with money and land.
- **1892**: Conservationist John Muir organizes the Sierra Club.
- **1898**: The first automobile in California sputters down Oakland's streets.
- **1900**: San Francisco's Fisherman's Wharf is built.
- **1903**: Jack London, California's first native-born writer of note, publishes *The Call of the Wild*.

- **1904:** A. P. Giannini opens the Bank of Italy, "a people's bank." It's now the Bank of America.
- **1906 (April 18, 5:12 A.M.):** An earthquake coming out of the sea at Point Arena and travelling 7,000 miles an hour hits San Francisco with an estimated force of 8.3 on the Richter scale. Water and gas mains burst, and fire follows. It takes 74 hours to stop the flames, which engulf 4.7 square miles. The official death toll is 450.
- **1907:** Muir Woods redwood grove becomes a national monument.
- **1908:** Seventy-seven "skyscrapers" are under construction when Theodore Roosevelt's Great White Fleet visits still-rebuilding San Francisco.
- **1913:** Congress approves the San Francisco water supply dam that floods Hetch Hetchy Valley, northern "twin" to Yosemite Valley. Automobiles are allowed into Yosemite National Park.
- **1914:** On Memorial Day, Mount Lassen begins a series of small eruptions; almost a year later, activity climaxes with a big bang as the peak blows its top.
- **1915:** San Francisco celebrates its rebirth with the Panama-Pacific International Exposition.
- **1916:** Bridge engineer Joseph Strauss says the Golden Gate can be spanned for $25 to $30 million.
- **1921:** Gaetano Merola, an opera company conductor, arrives in San Francisco and stays to organize the city's opera association. Harry Bridges arrives to work on the docks, and later organizes the longshoremen.
- **1931:** Work starts on the San Francisco–Oakland Bay Bridge.
- **1932:** The San Francisco War Memorial Opera House is inaugurated.
- **1933:** Work starts on the Golden Gate Bridge. The Central Valley Project, one of the world's largest irrigation schemes, is approved.
- **1934:** Striking longshoremen, police, and strikebreakers clash at the Embarcadero on July 5. Eleven days later, 150,000 Bay Area workers stage a one-day general strike in sympathy.
- **1935:** Dust Bowl migrants, scornfully called "Oakies" and "Arkies," begin to flow into California.
- **1936 (November 15):** The San Francisco–Oakland Bay Bridge opens.

- **1937 (May 27):** The Golden Gate Bridge opens, and 200,000 people walk across.
- **1939:** *The Grapes of Wrath,* John Steinbeck's novel about migrant farm workers, enrages conservatives. The Golden Gate International Exposition opens on Treasure Island, San Francisco Bay.
- **1942:** Soon after World War II hits the U.S., the West Coast's Japanese-Americans are uprooted and sent to relocation camps. Bay Area shipyards enjoy a war effort boom; Henry Kaiser's Richmond yard will build 23 percent of America's Liberty Ships.
- **1946:** Sardine catches plummet, dooming Monterey's Cannery Row.
- **1949:** University of California employees are required to sign loyalty oaths.
- **1953:** San Francisco's Chinese go public with their New Year's celebration, inaugurating a grand parade.
- **1956:** Lawrence Ferlinghetti's City Lights Books publishes Allen Ginsberg's *Howl,* the anthem of San Francisco's Beat Generation.
- **1960:** Police turn fire hoses on students protesting House Un-American Activities Committee meeting at San Francisco City Hall.
- **1964:** A free-speech movement builds up steam at UC Berkeley. A 9.2 earthquake in Alaska triggers a tidal wave that hits the coast, wiping out Crescent City's waterfront.
- **1966:** Ronald Reagan is elected governor, and wife, Nancy, refuses to live in Sacramento's century-old governor's mansion. Eight thousand UC Berkeley students strike to protest Navy recruiters on campus.
- **1967:** Hippies celebrate the Summer of Love in San Francisco's Haight-Ashbury district. At the same time, city citizens stage what they call a "freeway revolt," refusing to allow construction of a crosstown freeway and halting work on the Embarcadero Freeway.
- **1969:** Peoples' Park riots break out in Berkeley. Ninety Native Americans occupy the deserted federal prison on Alcatraz Island.
- **1971:** Alice Waters opens Chez Panisse restaurant, triggering Berkeley's transformation from Radical Capital to Foodie Empire.
- **1974:** Newly elected Governor Jerry Brown, son of former Governor Edmund G. Brown, refuses to live in the luxurious Sacramento governor's mansion

built by Reagan supporters. The Symbionese Liberation Army kidnaps Patricia Campbell Hearst.

- **1978:** Former City Supervisor Dan White assassinates San Francisco Mayor George Moscone and Supervisor Harvey Milk, a leader of the gay community.
- **1979:** Members of San Francisco's gay community stage "White Night" riot to protest the voluntary manslaughter verdict in the Dan White trial as too lenient.
- **1982:** New Republican Governor George Deukmejian is willing to live in Sacramento's unused governor's mansion, but the Democratic legislature sells it.
- **1984:** San Francisco's cable car system reopens after reconstruction, and the Monterey Bay Aquarium opens on Cannery Row.
- **1987:** San Francisco celebrates the Golden Gate Bridge's 50th birthday by reserving it for walkers for a few hours; an estimated 800,000 take part. Pope John Paul II visits San Francisco and the Carmel Mission on the Monterey Peninsula in light of Father Junípero Serra's candidacy for sainthood.
- **1989 (October 17, 5:04 P.M.):** Minutes before the start of the third World Series Game at Candlestick Park, San Francisco, an earthquake measuring 7.1 on the Richter scale hits. The 58,000 spectators at Candlestick are unscathed, but a mile of double-deck freeway in Oakland and a section of the Bay Bridge's upper roadway collapse, and houses topple and burn in San Francisco's Marina district. Seventy-five miles away, near the epicenter, 60 percent of downtown Santa Cruz is in ruins. The overall toll in Northern California: 100,000 buildings damaged or destroyed; 14,000 people displaced; 67 people killed.
- **1990:** On the 84th anniversary of the 1906 earthquake, Northern California is hit by a swarm of tremors measuring 3.3 to 5.4 on the Richter scale. On the lighter side, hordes of endangered sea lions invade the pleasure boat docks at San Francisco's Pier 39 marina; the beasts enchant tourists and terrify yachtsmen who must pass the quarter-ton animals to reach their boats.

—Shirley Maas Fockler

INDEX